T.J. ROHLEDER'S...
HOW TO MAKE MILLIONS SITTING ON YOUR ASS!

A COLLECTION OF GREAT SECRETS FOR WRITING ADS, SALES LETTERS, AND WEBSITE COPY THAT BRINGS IN MILLIONS OF DOLLARS.

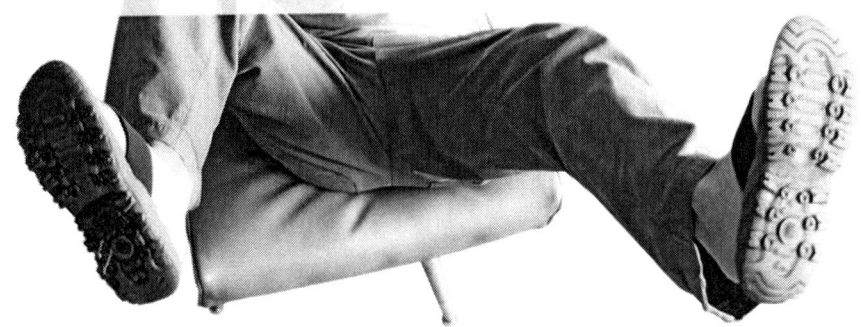

Also by T.J. Rohleder:

The Blue Jeans Millionaire
How to Turn Your Kitchen or Spare Bedroom into a Cash Machine
The Black Book of Marketing Secrets (Series)
The Ruthless Marketing Attack
How to Get Super Rich in the Opportunity Market
Five Secrets That Will Triple Your Profits
Ruthless Copywriting Strategies
25 Direct Mail Success Secrets That Can Make You Rich
Ruthless Marketing
50 in 50
Secrets of the Blue Jeans Millionaire

Copyright © MMX Club-20 International.

All rights reserved. No part of this book may be used or reproduced in any manner whatsoever without the written permission of the Publisher.

Printed in the United States of America.
For information address:
Club-20 International • 305 East Main Street • Goessel, Kansas 67053-0198.

Cover designed by Chris Bergquist
Book interior designed by Mary K. Jones

FIRST EDITION

ISBN 978-1-933356-44-0

TABLE OF CONTENTS

INTRODUCTION: 5

SECTION ONE:
<u>STEPS</u> of the $100-Million Copywriting System 11

SECTION TWO:
<u>SECRETS</u> to the $100-Million Copywriting System 35

SECTION THREE:
The Hidden Sales Pitch 65

SECTION FOUR:
The A-Z Success Formula 99

SECTION FIVE:
Ruthless Copywriting Strategies 187

SECTION SIX:
Ruthless Marketing 365

SECTION SEVEN:
Ruthless Marketing Secrets, Volume One 499

SECTION EIGHT:
Ruthless Marketing Secrets, Volume Two 605

SECTION NINE:
What Ruthless Really Means 663

INTRODUCTION:

Can you really make millions by sitting on your ass?

The answer is "YES!" And "NO!"

After all, there's no way you can make money sitting on your ass if all you're doing is watching some stupid T.V. show and stuffing your face with junk food. But you <u>can</u> make millions when you're sitting on your ass and dreaming up all kinds of newer and better ways to make more money in your business!

And that's what this book is all about: **Working on your business and not in it.**

This requires more thought than action. It requires you to THINK BIGGER. It also means you have to change your thinking and see your business in an entirely different way... For example, it means thinking about your business through the eyes of all of the people who are most important to its ultimate success: Your customers, staff members, business partners, suppliers, and your customers and prospective buyers who have never done business with you. Your goal is to sit around and try to figure out as many ways as you can to give all of these people the things they want the most so they will give you the things that you want the most. It also requires you to think like a marketer and get really good at doing all of the things to attract and retain the largest percentage of the best customers in your target market.

Seems so simple, doesn't it?

Well it is simple. But it's never easy.

In fact in today's overcrowded marketplace, doing all of the things I just mentioned is getting harder all the time. <u>Don't let that fact discourage you</u>. All you have to do is think bigger... think differently... and think even more! Sometimes you're thinking on your feet and other times you're doing it on your ass... But however you do it — the key to achieving your greatest success in business is TO DO MORE OF IT. Do this and…

The more time you spend sitting on your ass — the more money you'll make!

Does that seem funny to you?

If so — good! The theme of this book title was meant to be funny! **You see, so many books on business and marketing are boring as a head of cabbage!** The authors are trying hard to show off and prove they know so much more than you do. They make everything way too complicated and confusing — they throw around big words to prove they're smarter than you are… they talk down to you… and what's more: many of the ideas they give you suck! You must dig through the entire book to get a few good ideas that you can use to make more money in your business.

This book is different.

You won't find too many big words and fancy language in this book. There are no confusing theories or overly complicated concepts… I'm definitely not trying to show off and pretend that I know so much more than you do. Instead, what you will get are simple business and marketing ideas that I use to bring in millions of dollars a year in my own businesses. These ideas work! They have brought in many millions for the companies that I have started or been part of and they can do the same for you. I don't care how much money you want to bring in, you can do it with the simple strategies and methods in this book. As you'll see, everything I have to teach you is simple to understand and easy to put into action.

So, why the crazy title?

This book contains bits and pieces from some of my previous books, plus some other material that I have only published for a very small group of my Clients. I could have called it *"The Best of T.J. Rohleder"* or some dumb title like that, but nobody would care and my sales would be flat. So I needed a catchy title, right? Right! And a few weeks ago, I was sending an email to my friend Ken Pederson and in it — I said:

"The hardest thing I have to do is to force myself to sit on my ass and get my important work done."

I told him that my most profitable work is all made with me on my ass! My email said that IF ONLY I could spent more time on my ass — I could make more money!

Was that funny? I thought so! And since I needed a title for this book that sounded better than some dumb title like *"The Best of T.J. Rohleder"* and because I wanted to stand out among all of the boring business books — I sent this title to one of my graphic artists and presto!

But don't be fooled by this title. You see...

Even though the title of this book started out as a joke in an email — it really is possible for you to sit back and make millions sitting on your ass!

Here's proof: Most small business people are working way too hard for too little money. They are trying to wear all the hats... They're too busy working in their business instead of working on it. And finally, they are terrible marketers because they spend VERY LITTLE TIME AND ENERGY thinking through all of the ways to attract and retain the very best customers. They simply do not understand the basic principles of marketing and because of that they have never developed a well thought out marketing strategy.

But You Won't Make This Mistake.

The ability to become a great marketer and do the activities that are necessary to attract and sell to the largest percentage of the best people who are perfectly suited for whatever you sell is within your reach! This book shows you how. The tips, tricks, and little known marketing techniques you're about to read have been proven to generate many tens of millions of dollars for my small businesses and for many others. In fact, these rare and unusual methods are making a fortune for many other people right now — and they can make a fortune for you, too. Use these methods and gain a genuine unfair advantage over all of your competitors!

One more thing...

Several of my books have the title "RUTHLESS MARKETING" in them, so I thought it was only appropriate to tell you that Ruthless Marketing has nothing to do with ripping people off. In fact, it's just the opposite: It's all about extracting the largest amount of sales and profits from your targeted marketplace... And to do this — you must re-sell to the largest number of customers. However, all ruthless marketers are relentless. You must develop the heart of the lion and the mind of the fox! You must be bold and audacious — and a bit cunning in order to seize the greatest opportunities for sales and profits. It's not about lying to people or cheating them — but it is about mastering the art of getting the largest number of people in your market to give you the largest amount of their disposable income!

And finally...

Working 'on' your business can get complicated at times, but it's also very simple. So whenever you get too confused and frustrated, just remember that there are only 3 ways to build a business. You can do things to:

a. Get more customers.

b. Sell more stuff — for bigger profits to your customers.

c. Sell more stuff more often to your customers!

Just keep going back to those three things any time you are confused or frustrated about any aspect of building your business. Then remember that making millions of dollars can also be very simple. Here's the formula:

1. Just get a large enough number of people...

2. To consistently give you a large enough amount of money...

3. At a large enough profit margin per transaction...

4. And you will get rich!

The market that your business serves is your meal ticket for life!

Strive to understand the people in your market in the most intimate way possible. Know your prospects and customers <u>better</u> than they know themselves. Master the art and science of marketing — so you can make more money than all your other competitors!

Working on your business is a lot like getting in top physical shape... It takes constant activity and great discipline to work yourself into shape and stay fit. You can't just go to the gym when you feel like it. So do spend at least one hour a day in concentrated thought of all the ways to build your business. That's 365 focused hours of <u>nothing</u> but thinking and dreaming creatively! One hour a day of doing <u>nothing</u> but focusing on how to build your business will help you dominate your market and destroy your competition! That's over two extremely productive weeks a year of <u>nothing</u> but planning — plotting — and scheming!

So with all that said, let's start dreaming and scheming together...

SECTION ONE:

STEPS of the $100-MILLION COPYWRITING SYSTEM

The eight steps to becoming a great copywriter and creating powerful ads and sales letters that bring in many millions of dollars.

STEP ONE:

Make a firm decision to become the very <u>best</u> copywriter you can possibly be, in the market you have chosen.

This first step is vital to your success as a Direct Response Marketer copywriter. Why? Because learning how to create ads and sales letters that have the power to bring in many millions of dollars is a skill. And, like all skills, it can take years to become a master. In the meantime, you must put in a lot of time and work.

<u>I REFUSE TO LIE TO YOU ABOUT THIS</u>.

Are there shortcut secrets to learning how to write ads and sales letters that can make you millions of dollars? YES!! But it <u>still</u> takes a lot of time and work to become the <u>best</u> you can possibly be.

However, as Richard Bach once said:

*"The <u>more</u> I want to do something,
the <u>less</u> I call it work."*

He's right! Think about how hard you worked in the past for something you really wanted. If you're like me, you were happy to put in the long hours and hard work, because it was a labor of love! You were working hard, but you were also enjoying yourself. That's what this first step is all about.

Remember: "The 'why' to do something is more important than the 'how' to do it." And here is 'why' you must become the very best copywriter you can possibly be:

Having the ability to write powerful ads and sales letters that persuade a large number of people to continue to

---

SECTION ONE — <u>STEPS</u> of the $100-Million Copywriting System send you huge sums of money is one of the greatest feelings you'll <u>ever</u> experience!

It's a great feeling to come up with an idea that you think people will go crazy over — and then write an ad or sales letter that quickly brings in hundreds of thousands or even millions of dollars. Does this sound exciting to you? Good! **Then decide right now that you <u>will</u> develop the ability to do this!** Get excited about it! Make it your mission to do whatever it takes to develop this valuable skill.

Now for the best news:

You can make tremendous amounts of money while you're learning how to become a great copywriter!

You should focus on writing ads and sales letters to do more business with your <u>best</u> clients and customers. Because these people already have a relationship with you, you will not have to be that great of a copywriter to make a lot of money with all the ads and sales letters you write. **In other words, even a bad copywriter can sell like crazy to his or her warm market.** For example: You can send a very badly written sales letter to a group of people who already like you, trust you, or feel some type of affinity with you and <u>still</u> make a lot of money. This is great news for you! It's exciting to know that you have the ability RIGHT NOW to write ads and sales letters to your existing customers and clients that can immediately make you HUGE sums of money! This is the ultimate way "to earn while you learn!"

And that ties in with the next very important step:

STEP TWO:

You must be passionate about your market and the types of products and services you sell.

Passion is a combination of all of your deepest beliefs, your enthusiasm, and all of your emotions. The more intense these things are, the more passion you have. This power will carry over to every ad, sales letter, and other types of sales presentations you deliver. It will also keep you in the game, keep you from getting burned out, and give you the energy you need to continue to "pay the price" that is necessary to develop all of the other skills you need.

Does this sound like something you'd find in some silly self-help book? Maybe. But when you study the most successful salespeople and copywriters, you'll see that they all have tremendous passion.

The best advice I can give you to get and keep the power of passion is to choose the right market. **Pick a lucrative market that contains the kinds of things you love the most. You can't do it for the money alone. You must choose a lucrative and growing market that excites you!** It must be an area you really enjoy, something you believe in with all your heart. This will be a great asset for you when you're just getting started. It will give your ads and sales letters more power, even though you are inexperienced and still have much to learn. It will also give you the drive and determination to put in the long hours that are required to master the skills of a great copywriter and marketer.

One of my favorite quotes from Dan Kennedy is: *"Do what makes you feel most alive!"* I took this quote and printed it out on a huge banner! This became one of my strongest beliefs. Then a few years later I read a couple of other quotes that helped me complete my philosophy:

"When you are in love,

▼▼▼▼▼▼▼▼▼
MARKETING SECRET

Overview of a successful marketing campaign:

a. Take the best sales points and "schemes" that have worked before...

b. Find new ways to hook them together... new themes, new angles

c. Then smooth it out... So it sounds new and different.

---

you are most alive!"

AND: "The fire never goes out as long as you keep feeding it."

Think about this. You'll see. Passionate people are totally in love with what they're doing and spend a lot of time stroking the fire. **This is the emotional power that you will have when you pick a lucrative market that excites and interests you and <u>not</u> get into something because "there's a lot of money to be made."**

Following this second step will also give you the strength you need to carry out the next step...

STEP THREE:

Strive to become an expert of your chosen market.

Your intimate knowledge of the market you serve is more important than all of the specific copywriting tricks and techniques added together. Remember this. The people who make the most money are also those with the most intimate knowledge of the people they're selling to:

✓ They have spent many hours thinking about their best customers: <u>who</u> they are, <u>why</u> they buy, <u>what</u> to say to make the BIGGEST impact on them, and <u>how</u>

to say it in the most effective way. **They try to understand all of the unconscious emotional reasons that cause these people to buy and re-buy.**

- ✓ They continue to ask themselves, "What are these people <u>really</u> searching for that very few others are giving them?" The answers to this question lead to many new insights.

- ✓ They study the competitors, especially the ones who have been selling to their target market the longest, and ask themselves: *"What are these competitors doing <u>right</u> and <u>wrong</u>?"* Again, those answers are then used to develop products and services that are built around the most important benefits the people in their market are searching for.

In short...

Immersing yourself in your market is the key to becoming an exceptional copywriter.

A genius is someone who looks at the same thing others are looking at — but sees something totally different. This is the type of power that you will develop when you become an expert of your market.

By constantly focusing on your market you will:

1. Gain an intimate knowledge and understanding of the <u>best</u> prospects and customers.

2. Know what motivates these people the most.

3. Discover <u>the</u> <u>biggest</u> <u>benefits</u> that cause them to keep buying.

4. Spot the most important common denominators that cause these people to think and act the same way.

5. Understand the main reasons why the most successful competitors continue to make huge profits year after year.

6. And to develop the ability to also see what the people in your

market are <u>not</u> getting from your most successful competitors.

ALL SIX of these things give you the power to...

Spot the gaps in the market and then make enormous profits by filling them!

There is tremendous power in knowing <u>exactly</u> what the people in your market want the <u>most</u> and then creating products, services, and promotions that are designed to give it to them. **This is a skill that you can develop.** The key to developing this skill is to practice the three steps we have gone over so far. Now you're getting closer to writing ads and sales letters that make you huge sums of money!

But wait. Don't start writing copy yet! *All of this leads to the next very important step...*

STEP FOUR:

Your overall marketing strategy must come first.

You must work on your marketing strategy before you write your first ad or sales letter. This is vital to your success as a copywriter.

This strategy includes such things as:

A: Developing the most powerful and persuasive Unique Selling Position (U.S.P.) that separates <u>you</u> and your company, and what you sell, in the most powerful way.

What are the top-5 things your customers want the most? Get the clearest answer... Then try to build your overall selling position around these things. The more time and work you put into this, the more money you'll make.

B: Creating your own swipe files of the most successful Direct Response Marketing ads and sales letters.

You must carefully study the most successful ads and sales letters that other Direct Response marketers have and are using, <u>before</u> you set out to create your own ads and sales letters. Your goal is to find the most important "common denominators" of all the ads and sales letters that are used by the most successful individuals and companies in your market.

C: Having a solid understanding of all the available media you can use to reach the best prospects in your market and knowing which ones work best and why.

There is no substitution for knowing who the best mailing list brokers are, which magazines work best, and which media is being used <u>RIGHT</u> <u>NOW</u> by your most successful competitors. These individuals must be your most important models and mentors. Developing this type of highly specialized knowledge is essential. As Robert Bly once said: "You must understand the rules <u>before</u> you break them." **Your safest strategy is to make your ads and sales letters look and feel like the most successful ads and sales letters that are generating profits for others, <u>before</u> you test your own ideas.**

And last, but not least...

D: Setting a target goal of sales that you want to get from each marketing campaign you work on.

Set a clear goal for the number of sales you want to make — <u>before</u> you go to work. You must have a clear idea of how many sales you need to break even, what percentage of conversions you want to achieve, and what you're going to do to upsell all of the buyers, <u>before</u> you run your first ads or mail your initial sales letters. This will help you "keep your eye on the prize" and create much more powerful strategies and methods that will lead you to getting the numbers you want.

The bottom line...

▼▼▼▼▼▼▼▼
MARKETING SECRET

Use plain — direct — simple — and FORCEFUL writing that goes straight to the emotions of your reader.

Copy shamelessly.

You must develop your overall marketing strategy behind each campaign <u>before</u> you get started.

Abraham Lincoln said: "If I had three hours to chop down a tree, I'd spend the first two hours sharpening my axe." That's a great visual analogy to think about <u>before</u> you begin to write. You must try to figure out the answers to these questions <u>first</u>:

✓ <u>Who</u> are you trying to reach? What is the most important benefit you can promise to them that will get them super excited?

✓ <u>What</u> do you ultimately want to end up selling them? And how can you do it through a series of carefully planned steps that lead to this sale?

✓ <u>Why</u> should they take action on your initial lead generating ad or make the first time purchase from you?

✓ <u>When</u> and how will you introduce them to your first upsell? <u>What</u> is your plan to get them to buy from you the second or third time? (Try to get a clear answer to these question <u>before</u> you make the first sale.)

✓ <u>Why</u> should they favor you, your product, service, or company over every other choice available to them — including the choice to do nothing?

✓ <u>What</u> is your best strategy to develop solid bonds of trust and rapport with your target market? Remember, you must win a big piece of their hearts <u>first</u> before they give you the largest amount of their money. How are you going to do this?

✓ <u>What</u> reason or reasons will you use to make them want to take action right away? You <u>must</u> create a strong sense of urgency in each campaign. The more 'real' this reason appears to be, the more money you'll make.

Many people fail because they <u>never</u> think past the first sale. They <u>never</u> ask themselves any of these deeper questions. They don't realize that...

"The purpose of the first sale is to get a customer for life."

You must take the long-term view by carefully thinking through your overall strategies <u>before</u> you start running ads and mailing sales letters. **Remember: your mission is to get the <u>largest</u> number of people to re-buy the <u>largest</u> amount of products and services from you, for the <u>longest</u> period of time. THIS WILL NOT HAPPEN BY ACCIDENT!** Having an overall strategy <u>first</u> is vital to your success. This plan will help you extract the largest profits from the largest number of people by providing them with a wider range of benefit oriented products and services you <u>know</u> they want the most.

So think these things through carefully <u>before</u> you start writing... Then and only then are you ready for the next step:

STEP FIVE:

Block out at least a couple of hours each day to write, think, dream, create, and work.

The best copywriters are the ones who have stuck with it, paid the price, learned what they had to learn, "practiced" daily, and ultimately developed their powerful skills and ability to write killer ads and sales letters that compel large numbers of people to gladly part with their hard earned money.

The fact that it takes time, work, and extreme focus to develop your ability to write the most compelling ads and sales letters should <u>not</u> discourage you. In fact, this should excite you! Why? Because most people are unwilling to put in the time and work that is necessary to become a true master in this or any other area. The fact that you are will give you a great advantage. The longer you stay at it, keep striving to get better, and continue learning more and working even harder, the more power you will have.

But before I go on, let me remind you of two things:

1. The <u>more</u> you know about your market and the more passionate you are about the types of things you sell and the people you sell to, the <u>less</u> skills you will need to write ads and sales letters that produce huge profits.

2. Your entire focus should be on selling more stuff to more of the people who have already bought from you, more often, for more profit each time they re-buy. <u>THIS IS THE ULTIMATE WAY TO EARN WHILE YOU LEARN</u>.

Remember, it's so much easier to re-sell to people who already like and trust you. **And since re-selling to your current and past customers is where all your profits are to be made anyway, you might as well put 90% of your time and energy into writing copy to re-sell to them.** Then you can take the <u>best</u> ads and sales letters that produced the largest profits and turn them into some sort of new customer acquisition campaign.

So keep these two points in mind. *Then...*

Go to work each day to think, dream, create, and write!

Great sales letters <u>don't</u> write themselves! It takes time, work, and consistent focus. The key to getting it done is to practice this fifth step: Set aside at least an hour or two each day to dream up new promotions, study, and learn more about all aspects of Direct Response

Marketing. Take this time to think about your customers and what they want the most (and all the other things we have already talked about). Then start writing and testing new ads and sales letters to sell more stuff to them.

The more consistently you do this, the better you will become.

The famous musician, David Byrne, once said: *"Creativity is my job!"* I love this quote because it reinforces another great quote I heard years ago: "Creativity is hard work." Both of these quotes are what this fifth step is all about. In short, if you want to develop the skills of a great copywriter, you gotta work at it... <u>every day</u>.

The Secret

The secret to practicing this fifth step is to find the few hours each day when you are at your best. For some like me, it's the early morning hours... For others like my friend Alan R. Bechtold, it's late at night. Whenever this period is, make sure there is a <u>minimum</u> number of distractions. This lets you put all of your energy into coming up with great ideas, studying, and trying to write your next multi-million dollar sales letter.

Nothing can replace this fifth step. **To achieve maximum productivity and become the best you can be, you must create a disciplined routine and stick with it.** In other words, you can't wait for the spirit to move you. <u>You must move your own spirit</u>.

> Selling is the art of proving that what you have to offer is worth far, far MORE than the money they must give up.

And that brings me to another point...

There is <u>no</u> <u>one</u> <u>way</u> to write killer ads and sales letters.

Writing is very personal work. It's an extension of yourself. Because of this, there is no one-way to put the largest number of the best words on a page. Everyone has their own style. Some sit at a computer, others write

> ▼▼▼▼▼▼▼▼
> **MARKETING SECRET**
>
> The power of the U.S.P. (Unique Selling Position)
>
> How can you separate yourself from every other competitor in the most important way for the customer/prospect?
>
> Answer that question in the clearest and most dramatic way — And Get Rich!

all their copy by hand, and some (including me) write while walking and even talking (dictating on tape). **You must experiment with different ways to write, so you can find the methods that work best for you.** Do this for long enough and you'll develop several different ways to write, some of which work better at different times.

Remember, writing powerful Direct Response Marketing ads and sales letters is a skill. The more you do it, the better you'll be. **Set aside at least two or three hours a day to write, think, dream, study, and create. Force yourself to do this every single day and you will be amazed at how far along you will be in a few short years!**

The disciplined and focused routine of writing copy every day leads you to the next major step.

STEP SIX:

Continue to invest in your own education.

I have spent over one million dollars on my own education. This money has been an "investment in future profits" and not an expense. Have I made some bad choices and bought things I didn't need or had little value? YES! But I've also bought things for thousands of dollars that ended up making me millions. So even the wrong decisions have been good ones...

The money I've spent on my own education

has gone to pay for:

- ✓ Books
- ✓ Newsletters
- ✓ Courses (and now on-line courses)
- ✓ Audio Programs
- ✓ Seminars and workshops, tele-seminars
- ✓ Coaching programs
- ✓ And consulting services.

My library is <u>filled</u> with books and audio programs on all of the various ways to become a better marketer and make more money. I'm proud of all the money I've spent because it has helped me make a fortune.

Here's My Rags-To-Riches Story

I decided to become a millionaire in the mid-1980's. Back then I could barely keep a roof over my head... In fact, when I started my first business in December of 1985, I did not even have a place of my own. I was sleeping on the floors and sofas of apartments that were rented by friends of mine who were only slightly better off than I was. I had everything against me: <u>NO</u> education, <u>NO</u> high I.Q., <u>NO</u> special skills or abilities other than the fact that I knew how to clean carpet and upholstery (which is the service my first company provided) and I had no fear of knocking on doors to pitch my services. All of my friends and family told me that I was foolish to think that I could start and run a business. And when I told a few of my friends that my dream was to become a millionaire, they said I was highly delusional and told me to get professional help.

The only reason I mention my humble beginnings is to convince you that...

If a guy like me can bring in over 100-million dollars in Direct Response Marketing sales in less than 19 years — then <u>you</u> can probably do as good or even better.

I've heard a lot of jokes over the years that *"if a guy like T. J. Rohleder can make millions of dollars, then anyone can!"* That doesn't bother me a bit. In fact, I'm proud of it because I love to inspire people and help them turn things around... The fact that I am the most average guy in the world opens people up to me and makes them very receptive to listening to what I have to say. Now they're ready to find out how I did it... And a big part of how I did it is by continuing to invest in my own education...

This Can Make YOU A Fortune, Too.

The right kind of knowledge is power when you use it correctly. This is especially true when it comes to Direct Response Marketing. **After all, just one great campaign (which includes a complete front-end and back-end marketing system) could bring in many millions of dollars in no time flat!**

Sir Isaac Newton said *"If I have seen further, it is by standing on the shoulders of giants."* This quote is especially true when it comes to learning the secrets of Direct Response Marketing. You see, there are many 'giants' who have and are freely sharing the greatest tips, tricks, and strategies that have brought them many millions of dollars. Using their greatest strategies and methods can be a major shortcut to the wealth you seek.

My greatest teachers have been:

- ✓ Russ von Hoelscher — the marketing expert who helped my wife and I bring in over ten million dollars in our first five years.

- ✓ The legendary marketing guru, Dan Kennedy, who greatly inspired and motivated me to strive to become the very best marketer I could possibly be.

- ✓ Dan's partner, Bill Glazer, who continues to inspire me through his own passion for marketing and through his teachings and training tools such as his online copywriting course which I own and use (and recommend to you).

- ✓ The late great Gary Halbert. I began subscribing to Gary's newsletter in 1990 and quickly paid him thousands of dollars to become a lifetime subscriber. Gary was a true marketing genius who continues to teach me through all of the materials I bought from him.

Every penny I have ever given to people like the experts above has been worth many dollars to me. These and other experts can make YOU a huge fortune, too! Once you realize this and actually experience how the right materials and programs that others provide can put huge sums of money into your own bank accounts, the happier you'll be to pull out your checkbooks and credit cards and start investing more of your own money. You will realize that the more money you spend with the right experts, the more money you <u>will</u> make.

But this is only <u>one</u> of the ways that other people can help you make huge sums of money. *Read on...*

STEP SEVEN:

Develop solid alliances with the right people.

My seventh step is about building solid relationships with other marketers and other people who are moving in the same direction you are moving in. **These relationships can help you become a better marketer and stay committed to moving forward and striving to make your best even better.**

The older I get, the more important the people in my life and business become. It is only through this reflection that I can see how valuable this seventh step is...

In fact, when I look back, it's easy to see that it is <u>only</u> because I had and took the opportunity to get to know and work with great marketers such as Russ von Hoelscher, Dan Kennedy, Bill Glazer, Alan R. Bechtold, Jeff Gardner (and many others) that I have become one of the very best Direct Response Marketing copywriters in my own market. My alliance with these

▼▼▼▼▼▼▼
MARKETING SECRET

Copywriting formula:

- **P**roblem = Make them feel it

- **A**gitate = Bring up the pain

- **S**olution = Sell the solution

THE KEY: People will do more to avoid pain — than to gain pleasure.

---

marketers helped me in so many ways. They helped me to "see the possibilities" and catch a bigger vision for myself. They spurred me on and made me want to be the best I could possibly be. They helped me to realize just how exciting it is to master my marketing skills. They motivated and inspired me by helping me to realize my own potential. Plus, the ideas I have received from these experts have put millions of dollars into my bank accounts that would have <u>never</u> come to me without their help.

The right people really do make all the difference. I am so proud to work with sharp people such as Chris Lakey, Shelly Webster, and Drew Hansen (and the rest of my management team). They understand the dynamics of my business and help me come up with all kinds of ideas that I would have <u>never</u> come up with on my own. **They help me stay focused on the opportunities and not just the obstacles.**

All of us need a little kick in the ass... **Plus, we need inspiration and motivation from people we care about and have our own best interests at heart.** I have been so fortunate to have surrounded myself with good people who are also razor sharp marketers. These people spur me on and keep me motivated and highly productive. They make me want to do my best at all times.

A Billionaire's Secret

I'm not alone in my desire to work with young and ambitious marketers such as Chris Lakey, Drew Hansen, Eric Bechtold, and Jeff Gardner. Recently I saw an interview with the Texas billionaire, T. Boone Pickens. They held the interview in his conference room as he was surrounded by his team of ambitious staff members. All of them were young hotshots with a fire in their eyes. They showed T. Boone during one of his meetings — and you could feel the positive excitement in the room! Later in the interview, the reporter asked him when he would retire. He quickly said: *"I'm having too much fun to even think of slowing down!"* Then he mentioned the joy of working closely with his ambitious young staff...

The bottom line: Forming alliances with other people is about <u>so much more</u> than just the money. It's about the same feeling a basketball or football team has — especially if they're having a winning season!

This seventh step is related to investing in your own success. The only difference is the fact that now we are talking about strong alliances and friendships with other people who can help you greatly. This can be very challenging at times. The fact that most marketers are also entrepreneurs means that there are a wide variety of ego-related problems to deal with. As you know, most entrepreneurs are very independent and can be difficult to work with...

One of my greatest strategies is to try to catch people on their way up. I look for the future superstars and befriend them <u>before</u> they actually become superstars. In fact, most of the value I get by attending seminars is outside of the main ballroom. It's all the people I meet and talk with during the breaks and after the seminar that makes all the difference. I'm constantly on the lookout for people I can work with because of the importance of this seventh step.

Many entrepreneurs will <u>never</u> profit from this step because they are too stubborn, independent, greedy, shortsighted, or egotistical. That's too bad for them, BUT IT'S GREAT FOR YOU! **I encourage you to think carefully about this step and put in the time and do the work that is necessary to build and develop these kinds of business relationships.** Doing this will be an important part in helping you tap into the awesome power of the eighth and final step.

Read on...

STEP EIGHT:

Commit to mastery.

A master is someone who is <u>the</u> <u>absolute</u> <u>BEST</u> at what they do. Or at <u>least</u> they are constantly striving to become the very best they can be.

These people are deeply committed to doing <u>EVERYTHING</u> within their power to fully develop their skills. They are passionate about their area of expertise. **They have a hunger for the subject. The more they learn, the hungrier they become!** You know these people when you meet them. There's a fire in their eyes... An enthusiasm... And a positive energy that draws you to them. Just being around these people makes you want to be better. And if these people are also teachers, they make you want to learn more! They make their subject alive and exciting!

These Are The People Who Have Helped Me Strive For Mastery. They Can Help You, Too.

I consider myself very fortunate to have learned from some very passionate marketing masters. My first teacher was <u>Russ von Hoelscher</u>. Russ is the man with the golden hand! He was the first expert who made me want to write persuasive copy that made people want to buy. In the late 1980's and early 1990's, we began hiring Russ to come to our home for the weekend and help us create and develop new products, services, and promotions to sell to our growing base of customers. We'd sit around our kitchen table, drink a lot of coffee, eat good food, and dream and scheme about all kinds of different ways to make more money. There would <u>always</u> be a stack of legal pads on the table and Russ would sit there with a pen in his hand, scribbling, while we talked. Then all of a sudden an idea would hit him like a bolt of lightning! He would suddenly become very excited and begin writing as fast and furious as he could!

I would sit back and watch spellbound as Russ would burn through one legal pad after another! The words would flow out of him. Once he started writing, he wouldn't stop until he hit a snag. Then we'd eat more food, drink more coffee, and continue talking about the ideas behind our various promotions that he was helping us dream up. Then Russ would have another major inspiration and go back to writing as fast and furious as he could!

It was absolutely amazing to watch this master copywriter at work.

I was only 28 years old the first time Russ came to our home to help us develop new products, services, and promotions. I was brand new to the business, extremely ambitious, and hungry to learn all I could. I'd sit back and watch Russ get all excited because of some great idea, and then write so fast you could hardly read what he wrote. But thank goodness our typist could read it because those words made us a lot of money!

During these weekend sessions, Russ wrote big, bold, and positive words about some new idea we had that not only excited the three of us — but also made our customers super excited! He had an amazing way of capturing his positive enthusiasm on the printed page. All of his sales letters generated huge profits for us... And it was all so simple and easy; Russ would leave after the weekend was over and we'd take his stack of scribbled up legal pads to our typist down the road. She'd type it up. Then we'd edit it and send the letters out. Then within a handful of days the money would start pouring in!

> CREATE IRRESISTABLE OFFERS! "I want to create offers that are like heads of fresh lettuce that are thrown into a pen of starving rabbits!"
> (I wrote this in 1997.)

And to make a long story very short...

These weekend copywriting sessions changed my life!

Watching Russ von Hoelscher take the ideas around our kitchen table and turn them into powerful sales letters that generated HUGE SUMS OF INSTANT MONEY changed my life! **Russ had such a strong passion for the work he did. He is a true MASTER who inspired and motivated me to want to learn all I could!** Being in a position to watch

▼▼▼▼▼▼▼▼▼
MARKETING SECRET

Follow the Leader...

- Who are the biggest and most successful companies in your market?

- What are they doing?

- How can you model after them as closely as possible?

- Match them closely first. Then figure out the subtle differences you can exploit.

a master copywriter like Russ turn our ideas into instant revenue was transformational! I would sit back and watch him become super excited and write so fast, his pen was a blur. Then I'd have the pleasure of seeing those legal pads become sales letters that sold like crazy.

After the second or third time Russ came to our home for one of those weekend copywriting sessions, I was a changed person! Now I wasn't just watching Russ write; I was obsessed with finding out how I could do it, too. I began firing one question after another at Russ. I had to know how I could do what he did! I was obsessed! **And without realizing it at the time, I actually took the first step to becoming a great copywriter:** I became committed to doing everything I had to do to write ads and sales letters that sold like crazy. I started buying every book I could find on writing sales copy and began writing every day.

And to give you the *Readers Digest* version of the story...

Within less than one year I wrote my <u>first</u> sales letter that brought in over one million dollars... and <u>never</u> looked back!

My first "million dollar sales letter" took me three months to write. I wrote it all on legal pads just like Russ did. The whole letter was scotch taped together like a giant toilet paper roll! I would spread the whole thing out on the floor and use a pair of scissors and scotch tape to add new ideas. Every word was re-written many times... I spent way too long on this letter, but then again, a million dollars was a lot of money back in 1990...

Anyway, I was never the same after I wrote my first million dollar sales letter. Without even knowing it at the time, I started practicing this eighth step. **I became very serious about the art and science of Direct Response Marketing copywriting and was obsessed with the idea of becoming the very best I could be. This caused me to begin to follow the other steps I have shared with you.** I began spending a lot of money on all kinds of books, newsletters, tapes, seminars, and workshops. That led me to my <u>next</u> great marketing mentor: Dan Kennedy.

I have been a client of Dan Kennedy's since 1993. That was the year Gary Halbert sent Dan's book, *The Ultimate Sales Letter* out as a FREE gift to all of his subscribers. I went to the mailbox one day and there was this beautiful gold book written by Dan Kennedy. I picked it up, read it from cover to cover, and immediately placed a $700.00 order from Dan's catalog (which was also included in the package). I've been spending money with Dan Kennedy ever since and every penny has been a great investment towards future profits...

Dan Kennedy has made me many millions of dollars that would have <u>never</u> been made without his personal help, support, and guidance. My first great mentor, Russ von Hoelscher, was responsible for creating the initial spark that started my mighty fire. Then Dan came along and dumped a 55-gallon barrel of jet fuel on this fire!

Dan Kennedy, Bill Glazer, and Russ von Hoelscher are my greatest role models for this subject of becoming a true <u>master</u> of copywriting and marketing. Russ is the man with the golden hand, who first taught me the art of copywriting. He is a true master. Dan is the most brilliant marketer I know... and Bill Glazer is right behind him. I first met Bill during our second year of Platinum Membership in Dan's Inner Circle Group. I was instantly excited by his positive creative energy and it has been a great experience to get to know him. His passion is contagious! All three of these experts make people <u>want</u> to know more and become the very best they can possibly be. Because of this — their best keeps getting even better! **And that's what mastery is all about: constant improvement, the desire to continue to keep learning and getting better**. It's all about striving to answer the questions "How high is high for you?" and "Just what are you really capable of?" You see, **once you commit to mastery, you will**

SECTION ONE — STEPS of the $100-Million Copywriting System

develop AN INSATIABLE APPETITE for knowledge that cannot be filled. The more you know, the more you'll want to know. You will find yourself putting in longer hours and working harder; not only to make more money, but because the process of writing new ads and sales letters is a true act of love... I want <u>you</u> to experience this!

SO PLEASE DO THIS... NOW!

Go back and think carefully about all eight of these steps and <u>why</u> each one is vital to your own success. Then take the first step: make the decision to become the very best copywriter you can be. The more you follow these steps, the sooner you will find yourself on this final step that leads to mastery. **This is much more than something you can do to make more money: It will be a great journey that will change your life, just like it did for me and so many others.** I hope to meet you in person at one of my future workshops or at another marketer's seminar. I can't wait to look you in the eye and have you tell me that something in my '$100-MILLION COPYWRITING SYSTEM' made a major difference in your life and business.

SECTION TWO:

SECRETS to the $100-MILLION COPYWRITING SYSTEM

Here Are The TOP-10 Copywriting Secrets That Have Been Worth Many Millions Of Dollars To Me And Can Also Make YOU A Huge Fortune!

SECRET ONE:

A major shortcut secret for writing ads and sales letters that can make you GIANT sums of money!

This is a copywriting formula that is so simple that a 12-year-old could use it to write SUPER PROFITABLE ads and sales letters. But I've made it <u>even</u> <u>easier</u> <u>for</u> <u>you</u>! Yes, my system for using this simple copywriter's formula will make it <u>super easy</u> for you to quickly start turning out powerful and profitable ads and sales letters from day one! This is <u>a</u> <u>major</u> <u>shortcut</u> secret for writing ads and sales letters that can make you GIANT sums of money! Best of all, it's so simple to understand and easy to use — you will be <u>shocked</u> and <u>amazed</u>! Once you get this secret, you will be empowered for life. You will now have the ability to begin easily writing ads and sales letters that make you GIANT sums of money! This one secret alone is a major shortcut that you can use to instantly start writing great ads and sales letters like an old pro from day one.

So what is it?

This 3-step copywriting secret is called the "P.A.S." formula. It's simple to understand and so easy to use — especially when you do it the <u>new</u> way I will teach you. "P.A.S." stands for Problem, Agitate, Solution.

Here's how it works:

Problem — Bring up their BIGGEST problems that are solved by whatever you sell.

Agitate — Make it <u>REAL</u> to them. Personalize it somehow.

Solution — Then introduce whatever you're selling as <u>the</u> <u>ultimate</u> <u>solution</u>!

This is a powerful copywriting formula because <u>people</u> <u>will</u> <u>do</u> <u>more</u> <u>to</u> <u>avoid</u> <u>pain</u> <u>than</u> <u>to</u> <u>gain</u> <u>pleasure</u>. When you are using this simple copywriting formula, you are reminding them of their biggest pains and you're making them feel it! Then you're offering your products or services as the ultimate solution!

This reminds me of one of the greatest analogies I have ever heard:

"Our job is to peel back their scab, throw some salt in the fresh wound, rub it in so it hurts like hell, and then offer them some salve or ointment that will take the pain away."

That's a very graphic, but great analogy!

Think about it! This is <u>EXACTLY</u> what you are doing when you use this simple copywriting formula!

But several of the other shortcut strategies you're about to read make this "P.A.S." copywriting formula even better!

As you may remember, in my sales letter, I promised to show you how to make this simple copywriting secret even easier. Do you remember? Good! Okay, now it's time for me to do this. Are you ready? OKAY, but my shortcut secret is <u>also</u> a major part of the <u>next</u> marketing secret I promised to give you...

SECRET TWO:

<u>I</u> will blow the lid off of what I firmly believe <u>is</u> the <u>single</u> <u>greatest</u> <u>copywriting</u> secret that hardly anyone talks about, yet all of the world's greatest copywriters use. Once you are armed with this secret, <u>you</u> will have the ability to write the same type of powerful ad copy that the world's <u>best</u> copywriters write!

That's a BOLD statement, I know. But I will prove this to you! In fact, as you'll see, once you have this secret you will have the ability to write ads and sales letters that are just as powerful as any ad or sales letter that was written for you by one of the most highly paid copywriters on the planet! Yes, it's amazing but true! This secret lets you <u>instantly</u> turn out powerful ads and sales letters that are as good or even better than the ads and sales letters from some of the highest paid copywriters on the planet!

This one secret alone is worth more than the entire cost of my $100-MILLION COPYWRITING WORKSHOP. Once you know it, you will <u>never</u> think about expensive copywriters the same way — ever again. Why? Because this secret takes the mystery out of what those super-expensive freelancers do to get their clients to stand in line with fistfuls of dollars. Once you understand this secret, you <u>will</u> have the same power they have. This will not only save you tens or even hundreds of thousands of dollars in freelance copywriting fees, but it can also be worth many hundreds of thousands or even millions of dollars to you.

So what is it?

As you'll see, this second secret is closely related to the first one.

Here's what it's all about:

"Most ads and sales letters are written in small 'copy bites' or segments and then pieced together like an old-fashioned quilt."

This is a <u>major</u> copywriting secret that most copywriters use, but few <u>ever</u> talk about. The power behind this secret is very simple, but amazingly powerful. It's the fact that all you have to do is write small amounts of copy that are then hooked together and boiled down.

This is good news to people who want to become great copywriters!

It's so easy to become intimidated when you study the powerful ads and sales letters that are written by the world's highest paid freelancers. I know. There were many times I said, *"I could never do that!"* **But then I got to know some of these highly paid experts and was excited to discover that a major part of their ritual was to write in <u>small</u> <u>chunks</u> and then tie them together and boil it all down.** This took the mystery

SECTION TWO — <u>SECRETS</u> of the $100-Million Copywriting System

MARKETING SECRET

Test new ideas and promotions to your best customers first.

- If it doesn't work to that group — it probably won't work to the other prospects you have no relationship with.

out of what they did to write these great ads and sales letters. It gave me a tremendous shot of confidence and power! Now I was shouting to myself, "Hey, I can do this!" And I was right!

So how do you use this secret and how does it tie in with the P.A.S. formula?

That's very simple, but amazingly powerful!

Here's all you do:

Step One: Make a list of all the problems that your best customers and prospective buyers face on a daily basis. Don't think. Just write as many of these problems down as fast as you can. Speed is very important. The idea is to write as much as you can in the fastest period of time. When you can't write another word, you are ready for the next step.

Step Two: Then start writing down all the ways your product, service, or company can solve each problem. Again, the secret is to write like crazy! Put as much copy down on paper (or on a computer screen) as you can. Don't worry about editing, spelling, or grammar. Just do a massive BRAIN DUMP and get it all out! Then when you can't write another word, go on to the next step.

Step Three: When you can't write another word, it's time to edit it all down, smooth it out, and hook it together. As you'll soon see, this is the most enjoyable part of the copywriting process.

The secret behind this secret is simple:

Writing small BLOCKS of ad copy at a time and then boiling it all down is the simplest and easiest way to write powerful ads and sales letters. This lets you focus on the problems that your prospects and customers face and the solutions that whatever you're selling offers to them. ***HOW TO GET STARTED:*** Start making lists of all these problems, frustrations, and pain that your prospects and customers are going through right now. Then create lists (that you can keep adding to) of all of the major benefits that you can provide to them that solve these problems. **Your most powerful ad copy will evolve out of these lists that you create. The more you focus on these problems/solutions/ and benefits, the stronger your ad copy will be.** And the more you realize that all you have to do is write short bursts of copy that are then added together and then boiled down, the <u>less</u> overwhelming all of this will be.

And that brings us directly to the third powerful secret that I promised to share with you.

SECRET THREE:

This simple secret gives you a tremendous edge over all of the other copywriters, who are just getting started, by avoiding the biggest mistake that almost all new copywriters make. This is another secret that very few people know. Those who do know and use this secret have discovered the fastest and easiest way to write powerful ad copy that sells like crazy! Those who do not know this simple secret will always be handicapped.

Writing powerful Direct-Response ads and sales letters will <u>always</u> be a huge burden and constant struggle <u>until</u> and <u>unless</u> you understand secret number three. With this secret, you will not only be able to quickly and easily write the most powerful ads and sales letters right away, but you'll also get the most enjoyment out of it!

Yes, this secret makes the job of writing ads and sales letters one of the most enjoyable and fulfilling things you'll <u>ever do</u>! You will be super excited when you learn this amazing secret! This will make your job of writing ads and sales letters so much more fun! While other new copywriters are filled with tremendous frustration, you'll be having the time of your life and making a ton of money to boot!

So what is it?

This secret is so simple, and yet it can change your life! But to help you understand this, let me first give you the principle that makes it so powerful.

Here's the secret:

The act of writing and re-writing are two entirely different things and should be done separately.

Many new copywriters try to write and edit at the same time. Big mistake. You see, the best sales copy has a certain "edge" to it. There's a loose feeling to it — much like you would get from a seasoned sales professional if you were being pitched face-to-face in a live presentation. You can put this spirit into your copy by keeping the writing and editing process completely separate. And it's so simple to do...

Here's My Very Simple 3-Step Copywriting Formula In A Nutshell

Step One:

Block out two to three hours a day when you are most productive. What is your most productive time? The two or three hours when you are at your very best? When you have the most energy? When your mind is at its sharpest? The answer to <u>this</u> question will determine <u>when</u> you should be writing most of your sales copy.

Step Two:

Then discipline yourself to use these daily periods to <u>write like crazy</u>! Remember, **a great ad or sales letter is like an old-fashioned quilt with lots of individual pieces of cloth that are stitched together.** So all you have to do is keep lists of all the benefits of your product and service and all the things they will receive when they accept your offer. Then write as fast and furiously as you can about all of these things. Don't think... just write! In fact, one of the most prolific writers I know says, *"When you think, you stink!"* <u>He's</u> <u>right</u>! Just focus on the person you are writing to and all the things you will give them that are far more valuable than the money you are asking for in return, and then write like crazy!

Step Three:

Then during another "quieter" part of the day, you can go back and edit your daily blocks of copy. Remember to keep the act of writing and editing completely separate. Also know this: it takes <u>far less energy</u> to edit than it does to write. Because of this, you can do a lot of your re-writing while you are relaxing. I do much of my editing work on the couch at night while half watching TV with my wife. It's like getting paid to watch TV!

The bottom line: Once you get it in your head that writing an ad or sales letter is as simple and easy as writing <u>small amounts of copy</u> and then combining them together and boiling them down, you <u>will</u> be liberated! Now the entire process of writing copy is far <u>less</u> intimidating. Now you can see yourself actually becoming a great copywriter... and you'll be right! You really can do it. The <u>first</u> time you actually do write an ad or sales letter that brings in huge sums of money — you'll be hooked for life! Best of all, you can do this sooner than you think... <u>if</u> you just write a little at a time <u>and</u> let your <u>sales material evolve</u>.

And that brings us <u>directly</u> to the next secret I promised to share with you...

▼▼▼▼▼▼▼▼
MARKETING SECRET

Spend more time, money, and effort — doing more business with your existing customers.

- 80% marketing to existing customers

- 20% to get new customers.

SECRET FOUR:

Gene Schwartz's <u>hidden</u> secret for writing powerful sales letters that brought in many tens of millions of dollars — and can do the same for you!

As you may know, Gene Schwartz was arguably one of the greatest Direct-Response Marketing copywriters who <u>ever</u> lived. His sales letters brought in many tens of millions of dollars and had a magical quality to them that you seldom see in <u>any</u> other sales letters.

Gene has been gone for a number of years now, but he left some of his greatest secrets behind in a <u>few</u> of the books he wrote and interviews he gave. It was during one such interview he gave that I discovered one of his amazing copywriting secrets that has been worth a fortune to me — and can make <u>you</u> a ton of money, too! This secret was only one small sentence in an interview he gave with Cecil C. Hoge, Sr. in the early 1980's — and yet it is absolute proof that just one idea can be worth millions of dollars. This one idea has and is making me a ton of money. I have <u>never</u> heard any other copywriter talk about it and it was only briefly mentioned in the interview. And yet, once you hear this amazingly simple secret and understand <u>why</u> it is so powerful, you will be as <u>shocked</u> as I was!

So what is it?

Like so many of my "secrets" — this one is simple to understand and easy to use.

Here is: The question that Gene Swartz was asked during the interview was: "How long does it take you to write your average sales letter? Gene's answer was very revealing and can be worth huge sums of money to you. Please read closely. Gene said it took him an average of six hours to write one of his multi-million dollar sales letters. Not bad, huh? No wonder Cecil Hoge called Gene Swartz, "The most prolific copywriter in the world." **But then Gene went on to say that each six-hour Direct Mail package he wrote was spread out over a 3-day period in which he wrote for two hours at a time.** THIS IS, BY FAR, THE MOST REVEALING SECRET DURING HIS ENTIRE INTERVIEW! What Gene was saying to me was that **he wrote in spurts.** He didn't try to nail it all at once. This is a genuine 'secret' because most professional copywriters know this, but don't talk about it...

I read this interview back when I was first getting started and began using it at once. **This one idea has helped me develop my entire philosophy of writing little patches or blocks of copy that are then hooked together and boiled down.** This makes the entire process of writing long form sales letters so much easier. It takes the pressure out of the process because all you have to do is write tiny segments of copy at a time.

But Gene Swartz was not the only brilliant copywriter whose secrets have made me (and can now make you) a great deal of money. There have been many others. In fact, that brings me to the next secret that I promised to give you. Read on...

SECRET FIVE:

How a goofy little guy from Florida gave me the single greatest copywriting secret I have ever discovered. I paid this guy $8,000.00 cash — and only got this one secret — but it has been worth millions to me. Now I can't wait to give it to you!

SECTION TWO — SECRETS of the $100-Million Copywriting System

In 1994 I paid a freelance copywriter to help me with my sales letters and marketing. He stayed in our home for two days and walked way with $8,000.00 of our money. <u>At first I felt cheated</u>. Why? Because all he did was sit at our kitchen table and told us one story after another about his previous life as a marketer. He had lots of great stories, <u>but it wasn't</u> worth $8,000.00 cash to hear them. But he <u>did</u> teach me one very valuable ting about writing sales letters that sell. I couldn't get it out of my mind. It is a powerful copywriting technique <u>that goes AGAINST almost everything</u> that most copywriting experts tell you to do. Anyway, this was the <u>only</u> good idea I got for the $8,000.00 we gave the expert...

<u>BUT IT WAS WORTH 10,000 TIMES MORE THAN EIGHT THOUSAND DOLLARS</u>!!!

I began using this radical copywriting technique on my <u>next</u> sales letter — <u>and got a much higher response rate</u> than any sales letter I had ever written in a <u>fast</u> period of time. That's right — this amazing $8,000.00 secret gives you the power to write ads and sales letters even <u>FASTER</u> than ever before. With it, your sales letters will not only come together quicker, but they will be so much more powerful!

What's more, chances are very good that you will not discover this secret <u>anywhere else</u>. Remember, this secret is a copywriting method that goes directly against what most experts teach — and yet it works like magic! You will be amazed at the way this one secret lets you write faster sales letters that bring you more money and are so much easier to write.

One final note: I have been using this $8,000.00 secret since 1994 and have added many of my own powerful ideas to it. Because of this, this amazing secret is many times STRONGER than the original technique I paid $8,000.00 cash to receive. This one secret alone will put you LIGHT YEARS ahead of most of the copywriters in your market. Armed with this one secret alone, you will leave my workshop and begin writing super FAST sales letters that bring in more money than any other sales letter you have EVER written.

So what is it?

The original copywriting technique I paid $8,000.00 to receive was simply this:

<h1 style="text-align:center">Always write your order form <u>LAST</u> —
not first.</h1>

So what's so revolutionary about that?

Well, to understand the answer, you must know this: Many copywriting experts tell you to write your order form and other enclosures <u>first</u> so you can "crystallize" your offer in as few of words as possible. Then once you have this condensed offer reduced down on your order form, then you can write your ad or sales letter. **But the expert I paid $8,000.00 to in 1994 told me that he completely disagreed with this approach. He felt that writing the order form first was too limiting.** *"It boxes you in,"* he told me. *"Your offer must evolve as you are writing your letter. Then create your order form <u>last</u>, by using the best-of-the-best copy from your sales letter."*

I dropped this expert off at the airport thinking I just wasted $8,000.00. But this one idea kept coming back to me — so I tried it

> **THINK ON PAPER!** The very act of putting your ideas on paper forces you to think!

and it worked! My next sales letter produced a better response rate than any other sales letter I had written in the same amount of time.

Now I Have Made This Copywriting Technique Even More Powerful!

I have greatly expanded the original idea the freelance copywriter in Florida gave me to include many other elements of the Direct-Mail package and follow-up mailings! You see, I did not stop with the idea of "pulling out some of my best copy from the letter and using it in my order form." **Nowadays I use <u>many different</u> <u>excerpts</u> from my sales letters (and the copy that was edited out of the sales letter itself, but is still good) and use them for <u>all</u> of my headlines, subheads, enclosures such as lift pieces and follow-up mailings.** This makes writing Direct Mail letters (and the follow-up mailings that go out as part of an entire campaign) so much faster and easier!

Oh, by the way, the above paragraph is the secret behind my next

▼▼▼▼▼▼▼▼
MARKETING SECRET

FEAR & GREED are the two emotional factors that influence us from the cradle to the grave!

- USE sales messages that hit these two E-Factor

secret that I promised to tell you about!! Read on, and I'll tell you EVEN MORE about this powerful copywriting formula...

SECRET SIX:

A <u>radical</u> new copywriting technique that makes writing sales letters and follow-up sequences faster and easier than ever before! This million-dollar copywriting secret could easily make you more money than all the rest! It will make writing powerful sales letters so much more fun and exciting! It also lets you write faster sales letters that have more pulling power than <u>ever</u> before!

This sixth secret is a living example of the old phrase: "One thing leads to another!" You see, I discovered the first part of this secret back in 1994 when I paid the expert from Florida $8,000.00 cash to come to our home and help us with our marketing. He gave me <u>one</u> idea of real lasting value by coming here — so I will <u>always</u> be very grateful for his help. And as I already told you, I began using his against-the-grain copywriting technique right away and saw a huge jump in my response rate from day one!

But I didn't stop there...

I kept pushing the idea and ended up EXPANDING it into all aspects of my copywriting. The more I did to expand this simple idea, the more money my sales letters made. But not only that, I was also producing more sales letters than ever before and they were much more fun to write! This one secret that I paid eight thousand dollars to receive ended up becoming THE MAJOR FOUNDATION of my entire philosophy of writing super powerful ads and sales letters.

As you'll see, this is also one of the most radically different and somewhat controversial copywriting techniques that I have to teach you. It definitely goes <u>against</u> many things that most copywriters teach and yet it works like magic!

You will use this radical idea to write more ads and sales letters, much faster, and with more ease than ever before! No other copywriter on the planet that I know of teaches this radical approach to writing powerful ads and sales letters.

So what is it?

As you know, this is an extension of the original order form writing technique that the expert from Florida taught me. As he said:

> *"You have to let your sales letter grow and breathe and develop. If you write your order form first, you'll box yourself in and end up limiting yourself."*

I have taken that simple idea of letting your sales letter grow and develop to the extreme! Remember, this doesn't just work with order forms. This works with all of the different elements in your Direct-Mail package and follow up sequence!

So do consider this:

1. Keep the entire process of writing and re-writing <u>completely separate</u>.

2. When you get a new idea for a sales letter, all you should think

about doing is writing as much as you can — as fast as you can. Nothing else matters! This makes getting started super fast and easy! (Which is what Secret #6 is all about!) Just make a list of all the bullets or benefits you can think of. Then ask yourself questions like: What are the main selling points? Then just write your heart out!

3. Then, when you honestly feel you cannot write another word, just BOIL IT ALL DOWN. This is the all-important editing phase. Now you are actively looking for the best copy bites and benefits. There is a great deal of "cutting and pasting" and rearranging of copy. **Only the strongest copy survives!** Plus, a lot of the additional copy that is left over is used in all of the enclosures and follow-up mailings.

The beautiful thing about this entire copywriting process of taking a few days or even a week to write as much as you can — as fast as you can — and then boiling it all down is the fact that...

This completely liberates you!

Now, thanks to this secret, you are not worried about how everything is going to "fit together." All you're doing is writing as much as you can in the fastest time possible. Your best copy is always written when your brain is on fire! These are the paragraphs you will be pulling out and moving up to the top of your sales letters! These are the words that are alive with passion!

Part of the secret is to focus on the main elements of the letter (by using copywriting tools such as Dan Kennedy and Bill Glazer's "Online Copy That Sells" course) and then writing your heart out! **Have fun with the entire process of putting as many words on the page or the computer screen as possible in the fastest time. Then go back and edit.** During the editing phase is where you will find (within your body of writing) the best headlines, subheads, order form copy, enclosures, and the text for all of your follow-up materials.

This copywriting technique is a bit messy, but it's also a lot of fun! You can write your copy with the filters wide open! It's so liberating to write without thinking and not having to worry about how the whole damn thing is going to come together. This is the greatest way to write more great order-pulling sales letters faster and easier and get the most enjoyment from the process.

It's also the technique behind the next million-dollar copywriting secret...

SECRET SEVEN:

The fastest, simplest, and easiest way to start writing the most powerful ads or sales letters.

The BIGGEST PROBLEM for most people is getting started. They are totally confused and filled with frustration. Even experienced copywriters who know how to write ads and sales letters that bring in huge sums of money find it difficult to get started on a new project. They find all kinds of ways to put off writing the ads or Direct Mail packages that they know will bring in more money.

Is this you? Have you tried to write ads and sales letters in the past and been "vapor locked" and totally confused about where or how to start? If so, I know how you feel. I spent many years HATING the process of starting on a new ad or sales letter. During these periods I suffered from a tremendous amount of confusion and frustration.

The bottom line: I just didn't know how it was all going to come together. There were way too many questions and not enough answers. The whole job seemed way too BIG and I became totally immobilized. But then I found the golden solution to getting started in any new project — and now I can't wait to give it to you!

Once you have this golden solution, you will never be confused or frustrated ever again! The entire process of writing a long-form ad or sales letter or entire follow-up sequence will be simple and easy to do. Instead of being confused and frustrated you will be super excited and ready to go! My golden jump-start solution will totally liberate you! With it, you

▼▼▼▼▼▼▼▼
MARKETING SECRET

Your marketing Mantra: What are the 3 BIGGEST THINGS your customers want — and how can you give it to them?

a. Find the answer to that question

b. Tweak it — work with it — refine it — polish it

c. Then shout it as loudly as you can!!!

Let the people in your market hear it in the clearest and most compelling way!

---

will have a major advantage over many seasoned veteran copywriters who <u>still</u> quietly struggle through all kinds of confusion and pain with each <u>new</u> sales letter they write. This amazing solution will make you excited about getting started on all of the new ads and sales letters you write. You will have a lot of fun and end up cranking out one great sales letter after another!

So what is it?

Most copywriters dread the entire process of starting something new. There are many problems that must be solved...

✓ What's the offer going to be?

✓ What are the BIGGEST benefits they'll go crazy over?

✓ What is the strategy that will produce the largest amount of money?

✓ How do I want this ad or Direct Mail package to look?

✓ What am I going to do about the follow-up marketing so we can convert the <u>largest</u> number of leads to sales?

✓ What about the upsell? What will we sell to the buyers?

✓ What is the best price to charge?

✓ How will we take care of the fulfillment on this thing?

✓ And on and on and on...

There are so many different details that

go into <u>every</u> new promotion, so many problems that must be solved and things to think through. It can be so overwhelming and, for many copywriters, this only gets worse over time... not better. Why? Because the more you know, the more you know all the things that can go wrong! Because of this, even experienced veteran copywriters with many years of experience <u>still</u> freeze up when it comes to getting started on some new project.

But the solution to this HUGE problem is actually quite simple. In fact, it's a basic strategy we have <u>already</u> talked a lot about. It's the fact that you <u>must</u> start writing and forget about all the overwhelming details!

Here are two important tips:

1. Allow yourself plenty of time to write as much copy as you can. Spend at least a few days or, in some cases, a few weeks just writing your heart out!

2. Make lists of as many benefits as you can think of and write as much as you can about each one. Use the P.A.S. formula to address all the problems that your prospective buyers are faced with and how whatever you're selling is the ultimate solution.

The more you write, the clearer things will be. Will you waste a lot of words this way? <u>Yes</u>. But you will also come up with all kinds of great ideas that you would have <u>never</u> discovered if you didn't do this.

Listen closely. Brian Tracy says: "The further you go, the further you can see." It's true. **Many times the answers of what you need to do cannot be solved until and unless you are actively engaged. In other words, you must get past the first thing before you can clearly see what the next thing is.** Everything will become crystal clear to you as long as you are moving forward each day. So write like crazy! And even if you end up cutting as much as two-thirds of all the copy you write, in the end the one-third you end up with will be truly brilliant stuff! Why? Because it will have been written when your <u>brain was on fire</u>! **Nobody but you will ever know that the copy that ends up in your ads and sales letters are excerpts of a much larger body of copy.** All they will know is the fact that what you have written is super exciting and now they must order it right away!

SECTION TWO — <u>SECRETS</u> of the $100-Million Copywriting System

And that leads us <u>directly</u> to the next million-dollar copywriting secret that I have to share with you...

SECRET EIGHT:

The little-known secret to cranking out the most powerful ads and sales letters from day one! In fact, you will sit back, re-read your ads and sales letters, and be <u>SHOCKED</u> and <u>amazed</u>! You'll find yourself saying things like, *"I can't believe I wrote this!"* But you <u>did</u> write it and you were able to do it with the simple to understand and easy system that took me years to discover. And now, I will generously share it with you!

Most people who are new to copywriting are intimidated by it. They look at the ads and sales letters that are written by the masters and say, *"There's no way I could ever do that!"* The more they read these ads and sales letters, listen to recordings, and read books on copywriting, the more overwhelmed they are. Is this you? Have you been a bit overwhelmed by the seemingly endless number of new things you have to learn? If so, I have great news for you. I can show you the golden secret that will let you start writing powerful and persuasive ads and sales letters that get people super excited and <u>want</u> <u>to</u> <u>send</u> <u>their</u> <u>money</u> <u>to</u> <u>you</u>!

THAT'S A MIGHTY BOLD PROMISE, BUT IT'S TRUE!

I suffered through many years of frustration and confusion before I learned the secret to writing super persuasive sales copy. But once I <u>did</u> discover this secret, my ads and sales letters began to bring in massive sums of money! The same thing will happen to you once you discover the secret!

I don't blame you for being skeptical about this. <u>I would be, too, if I were you</u>. And yet, what I have to tell you really is a secret. It's something that I suffered for many years <u>before</u> I discovered it. During this period of suffering, I was <u>still</u> writing ads and sales letters that brought in millions of dollars. But I absolutely HATED the entire process of getting started and having to figure out how I was going to create the most persuasive sales presentation that made my prospects super excited about pulling out their checkbooks or credit cards and RUSHING their money to me. There was so much pain and confusion... so many frustrating days where my sales copy sucked... <u>and I knew it</u>! And yet, I didn't know what to do to make my sales pitch come alive with the kind of power and passion I saw in other sales letters that were written by master copywriters. All this changed when I discovered the simple copywriting process I will give you. With my secret, you will be cranking out the most powerful ads and sales letters from day one!

> **LESS IS MORE. It's far better to be a master at 2 or 3 things — than to be average at doing a whole bunch of things.**

So what is it?

Again, this copywriting secret is <u>directly</u> related to many other things I have already shared.

Step One:

Do <u>not</u> start at the beginning! Most people struggle with ads and sales letters because they try to write them from the beginning to the end. Big mistake. Instead, just have fun and brainstorm like crazy!

DO THIS:

✓ Make lists of problems your prospects are faced with that your product or service solves.

✓ And make lists of all the benefits that the people who get your product or service will receive.

SECTION TWO — <u>SECRETS</u> of the $100-Million Copywriting System

▼▼▼▼▼▼▼▼
MARKETING SECRET

Spend more money to reach less, but better qualified prospects.

▼

Focus on re-selling to your best customers!

▼

You must always be looking for the next BIG thing!

Just have fun, get excited, and write as much as you can — as fast as you can...

Step Two:

Allow yourself several days, weeks, or even months to write your long-form sales letters. **This will take the pressure <u>away</u> from you and allow you to put all your focus on the <u>first step</u>, which is writing bullet points and benefits and thinking through <u>EVERYTHING</u> that the people who will send you money will receive.**

- ✓ As you are writing, begin thinking of the offer itself.
- ✓ How will you make people <u>know</u> that they are getting an amazing deal?
- ✓ How will you sum things up in the fastest and clearest way?
- ✓ What are you doing to communicate to their biggest hopes and, even more important, their biggest fears?

Figure these things out. Then go to the final step...

Step Three:

When all you do is focus on writing as much and as <u>fast</u> as you can — for as long as possible — you will end up with a MASSIVE number of words. What's <u>great</u> about this is the fact that there will be <u>golden nuggets of copy</u> that are in your large body of material. The editing phase lets you go through your material and pull out the best of the best of your copy blocks. **The** more copy you start with, the more of these golden nuggets you'll end up with.

- ✓ Then you simply find the best way to string these little copy blocks together, then add a beginning and an ending and... presto! Now you have a sales letter! But that's not all... Your sales letter will be <u>so much</u> <u>better</u> than most of the wimpy letters your competitors are mailing. It will have <u>meat</u> to it! Why? Because now you are taking <u>all</u> of the best of the best of all of your copy blocks (where your total focus was on the prospect's problems and your solutions and your major benefits) and, because of that, it will do a much better job of selling.

- ✓ The editing process is where you will find your best headlines, subheads, lift piece, and order form copy. All of the enclosures, and even the follow-up sales material you ultimately develop to convert the largest number of leads or to upsell them to a related back-end product or service, will come out of this large body of material that you produced in Step One.

This is my revolutionary '3-Step Copywriting Formula' that lets even beginner Copywriters <u>easily</u> write powerful sales letters that are just as good or perhaps even better than the ads and sales letters that expensive freelance copywriters will charge you many thousands of dollars to write for you!

The ability to write sales letters from beginning to end will come <u>later</u> as your skills develop. Don't worry about this now. Instead, use...

My 3-Step Formula

Yes, as unbelievable as I know it sounds, this really is a RADICALLY different approach to writing powerful and persuasive ads and sales letters that will let brand new copywriters produce amazing ads and long-form sales letters that are far better than <u>most</u> of the sales letters you'd get from a freelance copywriter who charged you many thousands of dollars. Best of all, my 3-step formula makes the entire process of writing super powerful ads and sales letters fun and exciting! What's more, even if you have read all the books and other training materials on copywriting and attended or listened to many seminars, <u>YOU HAVE NEVER HEARD ABOUT THIS AMAZING 3-STEP FORMULA</u>! Yes, as far as I know, there is no other copywriting expert who teaches this extremely powerful approach to copywriting. So even if you "think" you've heard it all — <u>YOU HAVEN'T</u>!

This simple to understand and easy to use 3-step copywriting formula was developed after many years of struggle, pain, and confusion that I went through in the early and mid-1990's. I experimented with many different ideas and systems, studied dozens of books (some of which I have two copies of because I literally destroyed the first one with all my notes and dog-eared pages), I attended so many different seminars and workshops, and own over 20,000 cassette tapes (conservative number!) and now CDs, and tried countless numbers of techniques that other copywriters so generously shared. I was able to break it all down and simplify it into this easy 3-step formula. I promise there is no better way to produce powerful ads and sales letters that will fill your bank account!

And now for the last two secrets...

SECRET NINE:

The secret we discovered by accident that took us from $300.00 in 1988 to over $10,000,000.00 in <u>less</u> than five years. I will tell you the full story of this amazing secret — and you will be <u>thrilled</u> to discover how simple and easy it is!

This one secret has enabled us to bring in over $100-million in Direct Mail sales more than anything I have to share with you. In fact, if you came to me and said, "Give me a handful of your greatest secrets that can put millions of dollars in my pocket," <u>this</u> would be at the top of my list. Like so many other methods I teach, this one is very simple and yet <u>nobody</u> that

I know of is teaching it! That's right. I have spent hundreds of thousands of dollars on a wide variety of books, CDs, newsletters, seminars, teleseminars, coaching programs, and one-on-one consulting and coaching services — and nobody has ever revealed this very simple marketing strategy that has been responsible for bringing in an ever-growing flow of money. This is shocking to me — and will be to you, too!

However, because it is such a powerful secret and because nobody else that I know of is teaching it to others or stressing the importance of it, then the fact that you are using it will give you a major advantage over your competitors!

This one secret alone can and will make you huge sums of money that none of your competitors are making. It will spur you on by keeping you focused and making sure that there is always plenty of money that is constantly flowing in to you. This secret may be very simple to understand and easy to use, but it will make you massive sums of money when you put it into action. And speaking of action, that's the best news yet. You see, this secret will only take 90 minutes a week to do. That's it! In just a little over one hour each week, you will be using a very simple secret that hardly anyone knows about or is using correctly. (That's why it's a secret!) And you will have a genuine competitive advantage over them, as well as the power to put so much more money in your bank account! Thanks to this one secret, the money just keeps flowing in forever and can continue getting bigger!

So what is it?

This secret involves these very easy steps:

Step One: Constantly have a front-end and back-end marketing system that automatically attracts a steady stream of new customers to you and then re-sells them more of the same type of products and services.

Step Two: Take a generous percentage of the money that comes in each day and put it back into more of the "things" that made it for you in the first place. Discipline yourself to do this daily.

And then the magic key:

▼▼▼▼▼▼▼▼▼
MARKETING SECRET

Use analogies, metaphors, stories, and comparisons to prove that what you have to offer is worth much more than the money you want them to give in exchange.

Step Three: You must schedule a weekly meeting to analyze your numbers, keep your consistent front-end new customer acquisition campaign going, and plan, plot, brainstorm, and scheme! These weekly meetings are the golden key to keeping your cash-flow generator in motion.

So why don't more people do this or teach this?

I'm not sure about the latter, but here's why I believe most entrepreneurs <u>don't</u> do this: THEY ARE TOO LAZY!

Can it be this simple? Maybe. But here's another reason: Most entrepreneurs (including me) <u>hate</u> meetings with a passion! In fact sitting through a meeting is the last thing we want to do. And yet, **our weekly meetings where we track, analyze, plan, think, and decide what to do next week, month, and year is the one simple strategy that has enabled us to <u>consistently</u> move forward, stay focused, and discipline ourselves to do what we <u>know</u> we must do.** Every successful "bigger" company does things like this. Most small entrepreneurial enterprises don't. When you take the time to do this every week, you will be light years ahead of most of the smaller companies in your market. This will keep you moving forward — especially through the difficult periods when sales are a bit sluggish. Try this... it works!

And now, for the final secret...

SECRET TEN:

The single greatest copywriting secret I learned from the legendary marketing guru, Gary Halbert — that <u>instantly</u> made me a powerful copywriter and let me write my all-time greatest sales letter that brought in many millions of dollars.

I learned so many great things from Gary Halbert. The man was a true genius. I first subscribed to Gary's newsletter in the early 1990's. I didn't just read each newsletter; I devoured it! There were always one or two great ideas that I could add to my marketing and make more money before the next issue arrived. Gary was a great teacher and I am so grateful for the newsletters he published and the seminars he held. He was a passionate man who freely shared his greatest marketing ideas with his clients. And (especially in the early 1990's) there were so many powerful cutting-edge tips, tricks, and strategies that were taught! Some monthly issues were truly mind-blowing! But out of all the amazing secrets Gary shared in his newsletter, one of them has made me <u>more</u> <u>money</u> than all the others combined!

That's right. Just one "<u>secret</u>" that Gary Halbert revealed in just one issue of his newsletter in the early 1990's has been worth far more money than <u>all</u> of the rest of them! THIS ONE SECRET IS TRULY BRILLIANT! It is so simple — and yet it has literally been worth millions of dollars to me. And it can be worth a HUGE FORTUNE to you, too! I can't wait to reveal this to you because I <u>know</u> that this one secret (if you use it like I did) can instantly make you a very powerful copywriter in no time flat!

Gary is the <u>only</u> marketing expert that I know of who <u>EVER</u> taught this amazing secret.

Once you hear it and begin using it, you will be transformed!

Yes, it's that powerful! In fact,

<u>You</u> <u>can</u> <u>start</u> <u>using</u> this secret the very next day after I give it to you — and you'll start to see <u>instant</u> results!

Yes, from the very first day you use this very simple, but explosively powerful copywriting secret, you will <u>instantly</u> begin to notice a difference! Keep doing it for a few months like I did and you <u>will</u> become a very powerful copywriter in no time flat! Best of all, it takes less than 45 minutes a day and it is fun and easy to do!

So what is it?

Gary Halbert taught his students that if you wanted to learn how to become a great copywriter, you should do a simple copywriting exercise each morning.

Here it is:

1. Pick the most powerful full-page Direct-Response ad or sales letter you can find. It must be an ad or sales letter that you <u>know</u> pulled in HUGE SUMS OF MONEY. (I chose Joe Karbo's "Lazy Man's Way To Riches" full-page ad.)

2. Then, each morning, write this ad or sales letter out — word for word. Gary said you must do this by hand so you can get a real "feel" for the language and rhythm of the ad or sales letter. "The more you do this," Gary said, "the more you will absorb all of the greatest ideas behind the ad or sales letter." It's almost like getting into the head and heart of the copywriter who wrote this ad.

Why this works: All great Direct-Response copy is "salesmanship in print." By taking your favorite sales letter and writing it out by hand each day, you are <u>learning</u> <u>by</u> <u>doing</u>. **This is directly related to the way a musician learns how to master a musical instrument. They start out playing <u>other</u> <u>people's</u> <u>music</u> first. They try to copy the rhythm and style of another great musician <u>first</u> and do it over and over again, until finally they have mastered it well enough to ultimately develop their own sound.** This is how I learned to play the drums in the early 1980's. My teacher taught me a very complicated beat (recorded it for me) and then asked me to go home and play it over and over again. I eventually developed my own style. Then, twelve years later — without knowing it at the time — Gary Halbert taught me how to write great ads and sales letters by using this same basic approach! This works! Try it for 30 days and prove it to yourself.

So add it up. You'll see. These 10 secrets really can make you huge sums of money... And, if you read closely, you know: **THEY REALLY ARE SECRETS** because most people do not know them and even fewer people are using them consistently.

I hope you enjoyed reading these ten methods and will use them on a regular basis to become a great copywriter and make all the money you want, need, and truly deserve.

There are only 3 ways to build a business:

1. Get more customers.
2. Sell more high-ticket items — for bigger profits.
3. Sell more often to your customers!

Almost all million-dollar marketing ideas are transferable from one business to another.

SECTION THREE:

The Hidden Sales Pitch

12 Powerful Methods that go <u>below</u> <u>the</u> <u>radar</u> and make people want to give you more money!

PERSUASION METHOD #1:

In the beginning, just get people to make a small promise or take a series of small actions. After that, **they will feel the INTENSE PRESSURE to take even further action.** Their new attitudes and beliefs (that you helped to create) will make it easier for you to get them to do what they previously would have been unwilling to do.

People will always behave in ways that are TOTALLY CONSISTENT with their beliefs, attitudes, and past actions. When they don't, it creates a great deal of <u>internal pressure</u> inside of them. Now they are motivated to do almost anything to feel normal again!

Just get them to take a small action or make some kind of small commitment. This puts them under pressure to <u>readjust their attitudes and beliefs</u> to be consistent with the small action they took. Once this happens, you can get them to take more and BIGGER actions!

Most people will try to follow through when they make you a promise you that they <u>will</u> do something (especially when the promise they made is in writing). Get them to make you the promise and now they will feel compelled to take action and follow through.

Why This Works

When you persuade someone to take a small step or a series of small steps, they <u>must</u> alter their attitudes and beliefs to justify the decisions they made. Their new attitudes and beliefs now make it so much easier for you to ultimately get them to do what you want them to do.

We have a strong urge to remain consistent with our commitments. **People hate the feeling of being inconsistent.** This creates a great deal of inner pain — which can cause them to take some sort of major action to correct. Getting them to take the smaller step first, lets them RE-ADJUST THEIR ATTITUDES AND BELIEFS in an attempt to justify their decision and be totally consistent (so their attitudes and actions are in harmony). Once this happens, it's much easier to move them to the next level.

Here are three easy steps to do this:

Step One: Get them to agree to something that seems rather small, <u>but</u> <u>is</u> <u>directly</u> <u>related</u> to the end action you want them to take.

Step Two: Create the inner conflict, <u>by</u> <u>reminding</u> <u>them</u> that they took the initial action and have <u>not</u> kept up on their end of the bargain.

Step Three: Then show, prove, or explain to them how your product or service can reduce the pressure they feel.

One of the main secrets to using this and all 12 of the persuasion methods we'll go over is to **begin with the end in mind**... Start with the bigger actions you want them to take. Then we WORK BACKWARDS and create the smaller steps that are easier for them to take in the beginning. Each smaller step they take puts them under greater pressure to <u>re-adjust</u> <u>their</u> <u>attitudes</u> <u>and</u> <u>beliefs</u> (to remain consistent) and makes it easier for you to get them to take the bigger steps you ultimately want them to take.

Many great marketing plans fail because they reveal too much too fast or try to move a cold prospect from A-to-Z too quickly. **Marketing is a process**... The real secret is to make people think, feel, and believe that it was THEIR DECISION to buy from you, not yours. The pressure they feel to buy from you must feel that it is coming from them. Okay, with all this in mind, let's move on...

PERSUASION METHOD #2:

Do something nice for someone that is perceived as sincere and you will create a tremendous amount of tension inside of them. This makes them want to do something (often far greater than what you did for them) to relieve this pressure.

The need to return a favor is HARD-WIRED inside of us. It's part of our social conditioning and a very important part of our human nature that has helped us evolve. (One group of people helping another group, which creates the need to reciprocate.) The old adage, *"One good deed deserves another,"* is right! The more indebted we feel towards someone, the more motivated we are to do whatever we can to eliminate the debt.

As with all persuasion techniques, you must be careful about the way you do this... **If the thing you are giving to people is perceived as a manipulative bribe, it will backfire on you!** Now they will not trust you.

The key words behind this and other persuasion methods are sincerity and purpose. You must come across as very sincere, and you must come up with a strong reason why you are doing something nice for them. The more you are able to tie the reason giving them the gift or doing the favor for them into your promotion, the more intense the pressure will be for them to do whatever you want them to do. Pretty sneaky, huh? And yet, if what you're selling is something that can truly benefit them, then you are actually doing a good thing.

The bottom line: PEOPLE HATE TO FEEL OBLIGATED! This feeling threatens our need for independence and control. It makes us very uncomfortable. Now the pressure is on! Once you create this feeling of obligation inside your prospect, they'll do almost anything to eliminate it!

Whatever you give to your prospects or customers must be perceived as altruistic (or a logical-sounding argument must be made as to why you are giving it to them). People must feel that you care about them and sincerely want to help them. You must win their trust first or none of this will work. **Without this feeling of trust, they will run from you.** You must do whatever you can to make them feel and believe that you have their best interests at heart... Then tie the item(s) you're giving them into your promotion in the clearest and most compelling way and they'll be ready to buy!

PERSUASION METHOD #3:

Do all you can to give your prospects and customers the praise, recognition, and acceptance they crave and are not getting anywhere else. They'll love you for it and be much more willing to follow your suggestions.

We all want and need praise, recognition, and acceptance. These are

▼▼▼▼▼▼▼▼
MARKETING SECRET

People want "The MAGIC Bullet":

- The one product/service that is going to make everything okay.

- It's going to solve some major problem.

- Or give them a miracle cure!

- An instant solution!

- And an on-going solution.

If they believe you can give this to them — you will get their money.

some of our deepest cravings… <u>and</u> <u>most</u> <u>people</u> <u>are</u> <u>not</u> <u>getting</u> <u>enough</u>!

People have a deep psychological need to be appreciated, respected, and accepted. All of us need to feel as if we are part of something that we perceive as important… We want praise so we can feel admired. We want recognition to satisfy our need for PERSONAL WORTH. We want someone to believe in us and appreciate and care about us. We all want someone to make us feel special and needed.

The people you sell to want to feel important, loved, needed, respected, and valued. They want to feel <u>understood</u>. They want to feel that you can relate to them and understand their problems… They want to know that you will be there to help them and are grateful for the business they give you. William James said: *"The deepest principle of human nature is the craving to be appreciated."* Burn these words into your memory! Then develop specific actions to fill this need… When you find as many ways as possible to fill these deepest needs, you will be giving them something they may <u>not</u> be getting anywhere else.

Most People Are In Pain

Several credible studies have shown that as many as two out of three Americans suffer from low self-esteem. They lack confidence or are not happy with themselves. Many of these people do have a great deal of pride, but **pride is the <u>opposite</u> of self-esteem.** A prideful person gets no pleasure out of having something, but only out of having more of it, better, or bigger than someone else's, or in having something that nobody else has. It is the comparison with others that makes these people feel proud, they love the feeling that they are above the rest.

Here's The Difference Between Pride And Self-Esteem:

Pride	Self-Esteem
Eternal Security	Internal Security
Scarcity Mentality	Abundance Mentality
Comparisons to others	No need to compare
Value in possessions or positions	Finding value in self
Tears others down	Lifts others up!
Concerned with who is right	Concerned with what is right

People who have a lot of pride or ego have very little self-esteem. They do not feel good enough. This terrible and mostly unconscious feeling drives their behavior. They have an insatiable need TO PROVE THEMSELVES and to believe that they are better than others.

The EGO is the part of all of us that wants and needs to feel important, valued, and loved. When you feed people's hungry egos — they become much more open and receptive to being influenced. The art is to do it without them realizing it. (Of course, this is true of all 12 persuasion techniques.)

People are starving for sincere appreciation

I believe that one of the main reasons that many people die shortly after retirement is because they are not getting their ego needs met. They don't feel important anymore. The phone stops ringing. They're cut off from the flow. They do not feel wanted or needed anymore. They feel useless and unappreciated. And because of all this, they start to withdraw from life and quickly wither away.

The bottom line: Sincere appreciation and recognition is something that most people are not getting enough of. Once you realize this, you can be one of the few — if not one of the only person or company to give this to them! They will love you for it! Now they will be much more open and receptive to anything you want them to do.

Most people are running around with an invisible sign that flashes: *"Make me feel important and special!"* If you can be the one who consistently does this for them, then you will have tremendous power. The key word is: <u>SINCERELY</u>. Once people feel that you're faking it, they will <u>never</u> trust you.

The truth is this: The more secure you are in yourself, the less you will ever need to manipulate other people or play power games. **The love and encouragement you give them will seem real — BECAUSE <u>IT WILL BE</u>!** This is very important. You can only give away what you have to give. People with very low self-esteem do <u>not</u> have anything to give. Any attempt they make to try to encourage others or show TRUE GRATITUDE and appreciation will be perceived as phony <u>because it is</u>! The bottom line: The more you have, the more you have to give and the <u>less</u> susceptible you are to being wrongly manipulated.

Here's A Secret That Most Would Be Ashamed To Admit

According to some experts, what most people really want is to feel superior to you in some way. Because of this, the key to persuading them is to do things that let them feel superior! The more you can do to make them feel comfortably superior to you, the more you will be able to persuade them to do what you want them to do.

Letting people feel they are better than you is a powerful way to get them to drop their guard. Now you are of <u>no</u> threat to them. They relax. Plus, you're helping them to feel <u>better</u> about themselves.

People desperately want to feel important or special. Almost <u>nobody</u> else is making them feel this way. So when <u>you</u> come along and do it in the most sincere way, you will be giving them something they're <u>not</u> getting, but really want.

Many people are filled with self-doubt and negative unconscious thought patterns. They are controlled by their own powerful fears and insecurities. This is especially true of people who have a great deal of pride. <u>These people are starving for genuine praise</u>. They desperately want to feel important once you make them feel this way — and earn their trust — they are now much more willing to do whatever you ask them to do.

PERSUASION METHOD #4:

The more you can do to make people like, trust, and feel connected with you, the easier it will be to get them to keep giving you their money!

You must learn how to create AN INSTANT BOND with your target market. There are three key areas to do this: attraction, similarity, and people skills. The most important thing is to use all three with the right attitude. It takes practice and a genuine interest in other people to really pull it off. As with other laws of persuasion, you must make people feel as if you have their best interests at heart, not yours.

Here are the 3 key areas you must master:

1. **ATTRACTION:** We naturally try to please people that we like and find attractive. If people like you, they will be open to whatever you say or want them to do.

Part of attraction is physical beauty. Looking good, dressing right, appearing to be physically fit, etc. But there's more to it than that... As Ralph Waldo Emerson said in the 1800's, *"EXUBERANCE IS BEAUTY!"* This is a word from the 14th Century that is not used as often today as it was in Mr. Emerson's time. So I looked it up in my dictionary and here's what it means:

- ✓ Abundantly enthusiastic!
- ✓ Full of vitality and health!
- ✓ Generous, open, and wholehearted.
- ✓ High spirited, animated, and full of joy and passion!

You know people who are exuberant. Some of them are <u>not</u> physically attractive, but their overabundant zestfulness for life gives them a magnetic power that attracts people to them. This type of persuasive power is a skill that can be developed.

2. **SIMILARITY:** We tend to like familiar objects more than the unfamiliar. We feel the same way about people. We like people

▼▼▼▼▼▼▼▼▼
MARKETING SECRET

It's so much easier to re-write a successful sales letter or ad than to write one from scratch...

- Whenever possible
  — re-write —
  don't write!

who we feel similar to us. The more you can do to appear similar to your target market in a variety of ways that are most important to them, the easier it will be to get them to keep giving you their money.

The people you sell to will feel connected with you when they perceive that you have important things in common with them. This similarity must be tied in with whatever you're selling, and it must be positive rather than negative. We tend to be very attracted to people who we perceive are just like us or have something very powerful in their story that we can relate strongly to. It's within our nature to build alliances with others that are based on common grounds or goals.

Let me give you an example of how we do this...

We are deeply connected to our target market because our story is very similar to all of the people we sell to. For example, here's our story in a nutshell; "we spent many years searching for a proven way to get rich — <u>before</u> we found the one idea that ended up making us millions of dollars. Our friends and family laughed at us and told us that we were crazy, but we didn't listen. And finally we proved them all wrong! We didn't give up and ultimately discovered the SECRETS TO GETTING RICH! Plus, we found the right people to help us... Now we are <u>dedicated</u> to helping the millions of people who are struggling and searching, just as we did for so many years." This story does a powerful job of connecting us to the people in our market. They love the 'before' and 'after' nature of our story. It inspires them greatly because they want this to be their story! You must find something that's equally as compelling, to create a strong bond with your prospective buyers.

> **3. PEOPLE SKILLS:** Studies have show that most of your success in life depends on your people skills and the ability to get others to like and trust you.

People want to know and like you <u>before</u> they'll be willing to do whatever you ask them to do. There are many proven actions you can take to create this emotional feeling. Just like the other persuasion methods, the ability to do this takes awareness, time, focused study, and practice to fully master. But don't let this stop you from mastering it!

PERSUASION METHOD #5:

Make people feel as if they are part of an exciting and growing group of others <u>who</u> <u>they</u> <u>can</u> <u>strongly</u> <u>relate</u> <u>to</u>. Then begin to introduce the new ideas, attitudes, beliefs, and actions of this group to them. This will create the right situations that compel the largest number of them to be much more willing to do whatever you want.

This persuasion method builds on our powerful desire to be part of a group that we strongly identify with or perceive has something valuable to offer us. It also recognizes that we naturally change our own perceptions, opinions, and beliefs in new ways that are consistent with the way other people in the group think and feel. Their behavior becomes a guide to the decisions we make.

We are social animals. A strong part of our human nature is the desire to belong to a group. Because of this, the more a group of other people find an idea, trend, or position appealing or correct, the more the idea becomes correct in our own minds. When offered two choices, most people will <u>always</u> go along with the one that's favored by the majority of others who they feel an affinity with. **We have learned early on that we make fewer mistakes when we watch and do what others around us are doing.** This is a powerful UNCONSCIOUS WAY that we attempt to save time and energy in figuring out what to do.

Social validation pressures us into changing our behavior, attitudes, and actions — even when what we see others doing goes against our own true feelings or beliefs. People can be easily swayed by the group. Most of us hate to admit it, but we are all conformists to one degree or another... **Even non-conformists are conforming to all of the people who think of themselves as non-conformists!** In every situation, we are unconsciously looking to the actions and approval of others to help us decide what <u>we</u> will do.

Psychologists tell us that most of our actions are unconscious. It's true. **Most people have <u>no</u> idea of the real reasons they do what they do.** So, as marketers, it's up to <u>us</u> to know what makes people buy our stuff... Only then can we <u>create all of the right situations</u> that compel the largest number of people to give us their money.

The pressure that a group can put on an individual is enormous! In fact, people will say and do things while in a group that they would have <u>never</u> said or done if they were by themselves. Here's a great quote from Cavette Robert to sum this up: *"Since 95 percent of the people are imitators and only 5 percent are initiators; people are persuaded more by the actions of others than by any proof we can offer."*

Here are three strategies to tap into this powerful persuasion method:

1. The larger the group, the more people <u>will</u> conform. Because of this, **you <u>must</u> tie your products, services, company, or message into the areas where THE LARGEST PERCENTAGE of people are moving in right now!** Look for the hottest areas! New prospects must be made to feel as if they are part of an exciting and growing group of others who know where they're going! Then begin to introduce them to the ideas, attitudes, beliefs, and actions of this large group.

2. They <u>must</u> be able to strongly identify with the group. The people in the group must seem just like them or be perceived as having something important to offer them that they want.

3. **Then you must connect-all-the-dots-for-them!** You must clearly tell your prospects why your product, service, or company is part

of an exciting trend! Make it seem exciting... and growing! Find all of the proof you can that taking the actions you want them to take is the right thing for them to do. Then tell them exactly what to do and many of them will do it!

▼▼▼▼▼▼▼▼▼▼▼▼

A strong <u>risk-reversal</u> <u>offer</u> takes a lot of courage, but this can make you <u>super rich</u>!

Spend some focused time thinking about all of the ways to use this powerful persuasion technique to make the largest group of people do <u>exactly</u> what you want.

PERSUASION METHOD #6:

Make people feel that they will lose something of great value to them, <u>before</u> they even have a chance to have it. <u>Do it right and you'll drive them crazy</u>! You will create an intense emotional and psychological pain inside of them. <u>The only way</u> to relieve this pain is to give you their money!

SCARCITY SELLS! Whenever choice is limited or threatened, the human need to get a share of the limited quantity makes us crave it even more. In fact, if what you have is truly perceived as scarce and they want it bad enough, they'll do almost anything to get it!

You must do everything possible to make people feel that they will lose something of great value to them <u>unless</u> they take action! The threat of losing something they really want <u>before</u> they even have a chance to have it <u>drives</u> <u>them</u> <u>crazy</u>!

Why This Works

People hate the feeling of being restricted. **The more we feel that something is outside of our reach, the more we want it!** Giving people the feeling that what you have is very scarce works because it makes them feel like they will lose their opportunity to act and choose if they <u>don't do it immediately</u>. The threat of such a loss can create a powerful feeling of

▼▼▼▼▼▼▼▼
MARKETING SECRET

Only 4 reasons why people don't buy:

1. Not interested

2. No money — can't afford

3. Don't believe you.

4. Don't believe in themselves.

URGENCY in their decision-making. When you use the principle of scarcity with the right prospects in the right way, you create this massive pain inside of them.

What we can't have is always more desirable and exciting than what we already have. The old cliché, *"The grass is always greener on the other side of the fence,"* might be even more true today... Every parent knows that when you tell a child they can't have something, they want it even more. And remember, all of us are little children in big bodies!

People assume that if something is rare and scarce, it must be valuable and good. Because of this, anything you can do to give your prospects and customers the feeling that what you have is scarce, the more you will sell and the easier it will be to sell it! So come up with as many ways as possible to create the appearance that the supply for whatever you offer is limited... DO THIS IN THE MOST BELIEVABLE WAY AND YOU WILL CREATE EVEN MORE DEMAND FOR WHATEVER YOU'RE SELLING. The more your customer or prospect can be made to believe that what you have for them is very special and could be gone at any moment, the more they'll want it and the easier it will be to make the sale.

Here are four ways to create a sense of urgency:

> 1. **Give every offer a firm and believable deadline.** You must give your prospects and customers the strongest possible reason to take action... now! The word "deadline" means: If they don't do it, they're dead! It's do or die. They either

take action or lose out forever. When you make the reason for your deadline as believable as possible you will create a great deal of emotional pressure inside of your prospect that makes them want to buy now!

When done correctly, **deadlines create urgency!** The closer your prospect gets to the date, the more motivated they will be to take action. It's up to you to create the most believable reasons why the people you sell to must take the action you want them to take... right now... or lose out forever. In this game, whoever has the most believable and compelling reasons behind their deadlines wins!

2. **Put a realistic limit on the availability of your product or service.** You must make people feel that they are competing for a limited resource. The better job you can do to build this into your promotion, the more they will want what you have. ASK YOURSELF: *"How can you make them feel that they really will miss out on something that you know they want very badly, unless they take action now?"* Think! Plan! Plot! **Try to create the most believable story possible of why the offer you are making to them really will be gone tomorrow unless they take action today.** The more you can do to create the appearance of a supply that truly is limited, the more they will be willing to stand in line, with money in hand, and practically beg you to take it!

3. **Stimulate their fear of loss.** People will do more to avoid pain than to gain pleasure. So whenever you create a feeling of scarcity (or use other persuasion tactics) you create intense feelings of emotional pain. Now they're motivated!

Our two strongest emotions are fear and greed. When used correctly, scarcity hits on both. People get greedy because they must have something that is perceived as limited or restricted. But fear can be even more powerful. **When people really believe that they must take action today or whatever you're offering may be gone tomorrow, they become very afraid.** Now they must have whatever you're offering!

4. **Restrict their freedom.** People want what they can't have. The more you can do to make it seem as if the offer you're making to

them may <u>not</u> be available at a later date, the more they'll be willing to give you their money right now! Create the most believable stories and reasons that your offer may be cancelled at any time.

The most skeptical prospects must be made to believe that what you have for them is very special and may be gone tomorrow <u>unless</u> they take action today — Believability is the key. People all want something that they believe is only available to a small group of lucky others. The more they feel that you have an endless supply of whatever you offer and it will always be available to whoever wants it, the less desirable it will be.

The really cool thing about scarcity and all of the other psychological methods is the fact that they work on the emotions that cause us to do what we do (but are often not aware of). There are many things you can do (without your prospect's awareness) to make people want to do what you want them to do! The only time that using these persuasion techniques is wrong is if you're selling worthless crap! Assuming that you're NOT doing this, then you should use every available form of persuasion possible to get them to give you their money!

PERSUASION METHOD #7:

Use the right words that make people want to buy! Use words that paint strong mental images. Make them see it! Be enthusiastic! Make them feel it! Be dramatic! Do whatever you can to make them see themselves enjoying the benefits of your product or service.

The words you use affect people's perceptions, attitudes, beliefs, and emotions. Your ability to use the right words in the right way has great persuasive power! You must use BIG, POSITIVE, and EXCITING WORDS that motivate people to take action!

The most persuasive people have <u>MASTERED</u> the art of language. They know <u>EXACTLY</u> what to say and how to say it. They know how to fire people up! The words they use give them a tremendous amount of power to influence and persuade others. Jim Rohn said it best: *"Real persuasion comes from putting <u>more</u> of yourself into EVERYTHING you* *say. Words that are <u>LOADED</u> with emotion have a powerful effect."* Jim's right; **ENTHUSIASM SELLS! You must pump your passion into the words you use!** Make them feel it! Show them your intensity... get them excited! Use your voice as a powerful instrument. Don't just talk... <u>sell</u>!!!

BIG, BOLD, and POSITIVE words make people feel great! They get people excited and optimistic. They capture and keep the attention of your prospect or customer. They ease people's fears and make it easy for them to concentrate on what you're saying. This will make them more open and receptive.

To create your most persuasive message, you must consider the emotional impact of the words you use. Choose words that get people <u>excited</u> about the things you're trying to convince them of... **The words you use can draw people to you or repel them. You have the ability to make them want to know more — or chase them away.** One way that many salespeople and marketers chase people away is by telling them too much! They talk on and on forever — and end up filling the prospect's head with all kinds of doubts and fears. Master persuaders do the opposite. First, we learn when to shut up! Second, we use assumptive language. We <u>assume</u> that people will buy from us, or do what we want them to do, <u>and we make sure they know that this is what we expect</u>! We <u>NEVER</u> ask people to do something. That's weak! Instead, our words communicate <u>a much stronger position</u>. We act and talk as if we assume they will do what we tell them to do.

PERSUASION METHOD #8:

When people get involved in something, they become much more connected to it. Their feelings become stronger for whatever you're selling. So get people involved! The more you do to make it attractive and easy for people to take an active role and get involved, the more OPEN TO PERSUASION they will become.

You <u>must</u> get people to take some kind of positive action so they can start moving closer to the desired actions that you ultimately want them to take. That's why you must get people involved. As persuasion expert Kurt Mortensen says: *"The more you can do to engage someone's five senses,*

▼▼▼▼▼▼▼▼
MARKETING SECRET

Being different than everyone else in your market is the #1 thing that will get you noticed and remembered.

- Don't be afraid to upset some people. It doesn't matter who you piss off — it only matters who you sell.

involve them mentally and physically, and create the right atmosphere for persuasion, the more effective and persuasive you will be." Write that down and hang it on your wall! It's all about CLOSING THE GAP as fast as possible from where they are right now and where you want them to be. **The more you can do to physically and mentally move them in the direction you want them to move — the FASTER and EASIER it will be to get them to go all the way!**

This is *"THE KING OF ALL PERSUASION METHODS!"* In fact, if this was the only persuasion method you ever mastered, your sales and profits would SKY-ROCKET!

Here are several very specific ideas and strategies to help you better understand and cash in with this powerful method...

Let's start with...

A Sexual Analogy:

Once there was a famous marketer from Miami who loved to hang out at strip clubs. He had been to all the clubs and noticed that the women in one club were much better looking than in any of the other clubs in the area. In fact, according to him, most of these women were absolutely beautiful! This made him curious. So one day he asked the owner, *"How do you get all of these beautiful women to dance here? Do you pay them three-times more money or what?"* The owner replied, "No, the pay here is only better because we have many more customers and there's more tips... But my secret is the fact that none of these women were hired to be dancers. We hired all of them as cocktail waitresses first

---

How to Make Millions Sitting on Your Ass!

and paid them <u>much</u> <u>more</u> <u>money</u> than all of the other cocktail waitresses get paid. **Then, as much as they hated the idea of working here, they did it anyway.** They began serving drinks, found out that our customers were relatively harmless, and slowly became used to it. Then they started to get to know the dancers and realized that they were only doing it for the money. Then, when they found out about THE ENORMOUS SUM OF MONEY these women were making, it was only a matter of time <u>before</u> they were up on stage!"

Is this a bad story? Maybe. But I'll bet you <u>WON'T</u> forget it! And you <u>SHOULD</u> remember it because it is the perfect illustration of the power of involvement. The bottom line: You must get people to take very small steps which will ultimately lead them to THE MUCH BIGGER STEPS that you want them to willingly take.

So get them to take small and easy steps <u>first</u>. Don't ask them to do too much. The more they do, the deeper their feelings will be...

Here are a few of my favorite techniques for getting people involved:

2-STEP MARKETING

People love to buy, but <u>hate</u> to be sold. What's the difference? One word: <u>choice</u>. The more people "<u>feel</u>" as if it was <u>their</u> <u>decision</u> to come to you, the more power you will have over them. This is one of the strongest reasons why 2-step marketing works. Prospective buyers quickly forget that it was <u>you</u> who approached them. **By making your first step some kind of small (and therefore less intimidating) offer — they "feel" as if they are the one who is seeking you out.** (You can reinforce this message by continually reminding them that they're the one who took the initial step.) The positioning has now been reversed so that now they feel that <u>it</u> <u>was</u> <u>their</u> <u>choice</u>. This is very powerful because people will <u>always</u> favor the ideas that they think or feel are theirs.

The Alternative Closing Technique

Marketing guru, Dan Kennedy, says, ("If you only knew one closing technique that you could always depend on to work, it would be the alternative choice close.") This closing technique can be done many different ways, but the concept behind it is <u>always</u> the same; you <u>never</u> ask your prospective buyers a question that leads to a 'YES' or 'NO' answer. Instead, you offer them a series of "choices" and then ask them to decide which one they want. The fact that they have choices makes them feel empowered. **Plus, it also puts <u>you</u> in control of the situation. (Isn't it ironic that <u>they</u> feel empowered by this closing technique, when it is really <u>you</u> who is in control?)** Now you can lead them to a buying decision and get them involved in <u>your way</u> of thinking. Their way of thinking is "Do I really want or need this? Will I use it, or will it be like all of the other things I've wasted my money on?" Your way of thinking takes the confident stance of <u>assuming they will buy</u>. Then gets them to focus on whether they want option "A," "B," or "C" instead of whether they want or need it to begin with.

Ask The Right Questions

Assuming you have a highly qualified prospect, the best way to sell them is to ask them the right questions and get them talking about the things that will lead you closer to the sale.

Questions are used in the persuasion process to:

> Get them involved...

> Guide the conversation the way <u>you</u> want it to go...

> Determine the objections you must overcome to get the sale...

> Understand the prospect's beliefs, attitudes, and values...

> Force you to slow down, find out what the prospect needs, and show your sincerity...

> Let you take control of the selling process...

People feel tremendous pressure to answer a question that is sincerely asked. **Wanting to please others is an important part of who we are.** We don't want to offend or be considered rude. The purpose of using questions is to lead them to a buying decision. The structure of your questions will determine how the listener will answer them. The key to using questions as an involvement device is to think them through very carefully, before you ask them.

The average prospect does a good job of resisting the sales process. They don't believe a word you say... They don't trust you and have become very good at blowing off salespeople! Because of this, you must use all kinds of POSITIVE MANIPULATION to turn them from cold to hot! You must be the one to get them interested and excited. And above all else, you must do this without them being aware of what you're doing! The first time they feel that you are trying to control them, they will turn ice cold.

> The real business is between our ears and in our hearts — not in the office!

Using Stories To Sell!

Stories and analogies are a powerful way to sell — without people realizing it. People love and remember good stories. Facts presented alone will not persuade as powerfully as they will when you blend them with the right stories. With this method, your sales message goes under the radar of their sales resistance. The right stories create attention and involvement with your audience. The more you can do to tie your story in with the key benefits of what you're selling, the more persuasive you will be.

Stories can be used to...

✓ Get people's attention and interest.

✓ Get them to like, trust and identify with you.

✓ Make them want to know more!

✓ Get them excited!

✓ Sell without them realizing they've been sold!

✓ Get them involved and interested in what you're trying to teach them.

✓ Lower their sales resistance — so you can go in for the kill!

SECTION THREE — The Hidden Sales Pitch

MARKETING SECRET

Direct Mail Principle: Neatness rejects involvement.

- JAGGED — Rough — Raw — and Real is better than neat and polished and professional.

(Just joking!)

✓ Let them get to know you and make them feel that you are a good person who sincerely wants to help them and who has their best interests at heart.

✓ Make complicated ideas seem very simple!

✓ Break their negative and fearful state of mind and get them excited, positive, and receptive to whatever you're selling.

✓ Make them want to take the action that you want them to take!

✓ Put themselves in the before and after picture.

Telling a good story that ties in with whatever you're selling puts you in complete control. People who hear your story can go from cold to hot very quickly! One minute they're bored out of their mind, skeptical, half-asleep, arms folded, lethargic, and now (assuming you tell the right story in the right way) they're alert and ready to buy!

The Power Of Follow-Up Marketing

The most successful salespeople are also the most persistent. Once they know you are a good prospect they think will buy, they won't give up! They will continue to apply the pressure on you in a variety of ways. They won't take "NO" for an answer. These repeated attempts to sell you are a powerful way to get and keep the prospect involved.

The secret to follow up marketing is to:

1.) Start with the most qualified prospect and get them to take a small initial step in the direction you ultimately want to take them.

2.) Have a great offer that is extremely timely.

3.) Have a strong reason why they <u>must</u> take action now!

4.) And keep the pressure on them... until they buy!

Just because someone says *"NO"* nine times doesn't mean they won't say *"YES!"* on your tenth request. Some of our <u>best</u> follow-up mailing sequences contain 20 different pieces of mail that go out to the prospect who initially responded to one of our lead generation offers. We use the simple 4-step process above to get the largest percentage of them to buy our initial product or service.

Most marketers give up on their prospects way too soon. They don't realize how fearful and skeptical people are. They <u>never</u> stop to think about the walls of sales resistance that people have built around themselves and the amount of time and effort it takes to tear down those walls. Because of this, you <u>must</u> keep the pressure on a really good prospect.

And remember, "No" Does <u>Not</u> Mean "No!"

A general rule in the dating world is, *"No does not mean no!"* Most young men are relentless in their pursuit of a beautiful young woman they really want. They <u>won't</u> take "No" for an answer! They keep doing everything and anything to get her to go out on a first date. It's usually something simple: dinner and a movie or even a cup of coffee. Who could say "no" to that, especially after so many repeated requests? And once the young lady <u>finally</u> says *"YES!"* to this small request, the battle is half over! **Think of this analogy when it comes to your marketing. Don't give up! Keep your eye on the prize! Do something <u>BOLD</u> to romanticize your prospects or customers.** Take a series of small repeated and persistent actions to convince them that you care about them and have their best interests in mind. This alone will separate you from all of the other marketers who stop after a few contacts. Each "No" will lead you closer to a *"YES!"* <u>if</u> you don't give up!

SECTION THREE — The Hidden Sales Pitch

PERSUASION METHOD #9:

Always compare whatever you're selling with something that is much more valuable. This contrast between your item and the more valuable item will make people think differently about what you're offering. Now they'll want it even more! And be much happier to give you even more money.

We are heavily influenced whenever we are presented with two vastly different alternatives at once. The contrast between these two things will change the way we think or feel... **If the second item is different enough from the first, we will see the second item differently than it really is.** You can use this contrast to make people think and feel differently about whatever you're selling.

People must be able to see and feel that what you are offering has a much greater value than the price you're charging. Because of this — it's up to you to paint this picture in their mind. Do this right and you can alter your prospect's perceptions of whatever you want to sell to them.

The human mind can't process everything at once so it looks for shortcuts to help make the right decisions. One of these mental shortcuts is the way we judge and compare things. **We do this naturally, with little or no thought.** Without even realizing it, we are constantly trying to make judgments and comparisons. This is especially true when we are faced with difficult or unfamiliar situations. When faced with decisions such as being asked to part with our hard-earned money, we automatically make comparisons with our past experience and knowledge. **When you use this persuasion technique to sell your product or service, you create these comparisons for them.**

Making people believe they're getting an amazing bargain! THIS IS SOMETHING THAT YOU CAN CONTROL. There are many things you can do to increase the perception of value of whatever you are selling. *Remember this:* **People do not want cheap stuff, they want expensive stuff for a dirt-cheap price!** The more you can do to build the perception of value for whatever you're offering, the more money they will be glad to give to you.

So ask yourself:

✓ What can you do to add much more value to what you sell?

✓ What can you do to make people feel they're getting an amazing bargain?

✓ What can you do to prove to them that what you have for them is worth <u>SO</u> <u>MUCH</u> <u>MORE</u> than the price you're charging?

✓ What can you do to make it seem as if the your price is actually very reasonable — even though it may at first seem high?

Think all of this through <u>before</u> you create your sales materials... It's up to you to crawl inside the heads and hearts of your best prospects and customers and figure out the things that are <u>most</u> important to them. Knowing these things in the most intimate way lets you structure your offer so the largest number of prospects are greatly motivated to give you their money!

Here's A Great Way To Use This Persuasion Method:

Many marketers offer a super-high priced package that they <u>know</u> very few, if anyone, will actually take. It's all a ploy to make their other price (which really is their <u>true</u> highest priced package) seem so much smaller. Now people are more than happy to pay the premium price, especially when a few of the things in the most expensive package are thrown in.

This is so easy to do! Just create a special high-level position or type of service that is 50% to 70% <u>higher</u> than your most premium-priced package. When you do this, your originally highest priced package will seem even less expensive! Now more people will be persuaded to give you the larger amount of money.

All this may seem way too manipulative, until you accept the fact that **your prospects and customers <u>must</u> feel like they're getting the best deal possible.** This will reduce their feelings of buyer's remorse — lower your return or refund rate — and set them up for the next sale. Now here's the rub: it's always up to <u>YOU</u> to convince them that they're getting

▼▼▼▼▼▼▼▼▼
MARKETING SECRET

The stronger your "marriage" between the front-end and the back-end — the more money you'll make.

- The secret: Develop your back-end first! Then build your front-end promotion.

---

a great deal.

The bottom line: YOUR PRESENTATION IS EVERYTHING! How you package and present your offer to the prospective buyers will spell the difference between lukewarm results and major success. When you do something BOLD such as starting with an incredibly high-priced offer and then introducing a much lower priced package that offers similar benefits, you make them feel as if they are getting more or less what they would have received if they said *"YES!!"* to your original offer. Now they feel good about giving you their money — while you get exactly what you want!

PERSUASION METHOD #10:

Create the right expectations and you can change people's behavior! Use words and phrases that clearly tell them that you EXPECT or assume they will buy from you or do whatever you want them to do. Make it real. BE FIRM. Be totally confident in your belief that they will take the actions that you want them to take... and many of them will!

Most people tend to make decisions based on how others who are important to them expect them to perform. When someone who has leverage over us expects something from us, we will do whatever we can to satisfy him or her to try to get them to respect and like us.

Here are 3-Steps to put this method into action:

FIRST, do all you can to build A STRONG

BOND with your customers.

SECOND, create the expectation that your prospect or customer will buy from you. Use words and phrases that clearly tell them that you EXPECT or assume they will buy from you.

And **THIRD,** confidently tell them what to do. Don't ask — tell! Be polite, but very firm at the same time.

To a large extent, the way a large percentage of your customers think and feel about you is within your control. By creating the right expectations — you can teach these people how to treat you.

YOU CAN ALSO USE THIS PERSUASION TECHNIQUE ON YOURSELF! Your own expectations of yourself can change the way others treat you and greatly affect the influence you have over them. You may have heard the phrase: *"As within, so without."* It's true; as you change the way you perceive and carry yourself, other people will perceive you differently and treat you accordingly.

Remember these quotes; *"We don't get what we want, we get what we expect!"* And *"Where there is hope for the future, there is strength for today."* This second quote is all about the power of expectation. **It is one of the strongest reasons why optimists tend to achieve so much more.** The more you FIRMLY BELIEVE that you really can do whatever it is you want to do, the more it will greatly influence everything you do.

PERSUASION METHOD #11:

The fastest way to make people feel good about you and what you sell — is to connect your message to the things that already make them feel good. Think of all of the things that you know they already like, trust, and is most important to them. Then blend as many of these themes and elements as possible into your advertising, communication, and image. This makes it so much easier to persuade the largest number of people to buy and re-buy whatever you're selling.

When faced with any new situation or the pressure of having to make a decision, people are <u>always</u> searching for SHORTCUTS to help them do the right thing. They look for <u>anything</u> positive or familiar that they can link this new experience with. This makes them feel more secure. It lessens the pressure and makes their feelings of uncertainty less painful.

Here's One Way That We Use This Persuasion Method

The people my company sells to are extremely skeptical and afraid to give their money to anyone they don't feel that they know and trust. **The fact that our company is headquartered in the small town of Goessel, Kansas, is symbolic of many good things in the minds of many of our customers... and <u>we</u> play up on it — BIG TIME!** We're not "fast-talking city slickers" who are hiding out in some major metropolis. No way, Jose! We're small town people from the heartland of this great nation — and <u>we</u> <u>let</u> <u>them</u> <u>know</u> it!

- ✓ We have re-printed a book about the small town we live in.

- ✓ We show pictures of our headquarters that was originally the local hospital building that was built in 1928.

- ✓ We give away <u>thousands</u> of bags of popcorn that is locally made!

In every way possible, we try to associate our company with the good old-fashioned values of the area we live in which is affectionately known as *"The Bible Belt."* Do these images help to remove our prospects' fears that we will take their money and run? YES, THEY DO! The images of the Midwestern United States takes many people back to a different time and place, where a person's word meant something that you could count on... when a simple handshake was <u>all</u> you needed to do <u>any</u> deal — no matter how large.

These images help our doubtful prospects and customers <u>feel</u> <u>better</u> <u>about</u> <u>us</u>. Now they are much more OPEN and RECEPTIVE to giving us even more of their money! Our image of being small town folks in an area of the country (where things are pretty much the same as they have been for the last 50 years) has been worth millions to us. All of the images of good old-fashioned America — where people do what they say and say what they do — <u>are</u> <u>now</u> <u>passed</u> <u>on</u> <u>to</u> <u>us</u>.

Whatever your best customers or prospects are drawn to, impressed by, or desirous of, try to find as many ways as possible to add it in your sales material or your product or service. This is a powerful tool to influence and persuade the people that you want them to buy and re-buy whatever you're selling. When you do it the right way, you can create the desired feelings, emotions, and behavior in your prospects. This creates THE FOUNDATION to getting the largest number of people to give you more of their money.

You must find the kinds of images that make people feel better about you, your products, services, or company. These things could include:

➤ Any interesting or unusual aspects about the area you're from.

➤ Before and after stories about you, your company, your products or services. Find the best stories that bond you to your prospective buyers.

➤ Interesting facts about the people you do business with.

➤ Any positive associations, analogies, or metaphors that are linked (even in the most general way) to the types of products and services you sell. These are the things that help your prospective buyers COMPARE you or whatever you're selling with others.

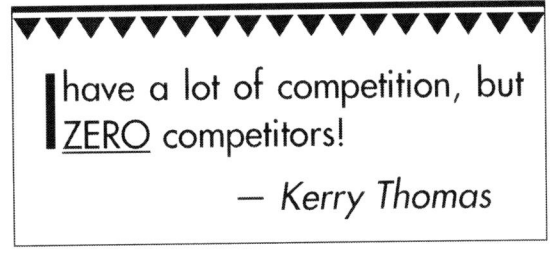

> I have a lot of competition, but ZERO competitors!
>
> — Kerry Thomas

Come up with as many of the most positive and valuable things that could be generally compared with the things you sell. It's up to you to find as many of these positive and valuable things as possible to associate with what you are selling. You must create these links. You must be the one who is in FULL CONTROL of getting them to compare what you are offering with as many other things as you can that have tremendous value... Just ask yourself: What are the most positive and powerful images that you can associate with whatever you're selling? THINK! What are the BEST images that inspire trust and confidence? Then add those things to all of your sales materials and methods.

SECTION THREE — The Hidden Sales Pitch

▼▼▼▼▼▼▼▼
MARKETING SECRET

Copywriting Trick:

Always write more sales copy than you actually need — then start cutting! This way you're able to boil it down — and only use the hardest hitting sales copy.

PERSUASION METHOD #12:

All of your communications must focus on reaching people's emotions first, then backing it up with logic. YOU NEED BOTH! Once you get them emotionally involved, the sale is yours! Their emotions will override their logic. This is the secret to making people want to give their money to you!

People take actions that are based on emotions and then justify those actions with logic and fact. Emotions drive the sale — but you must also appeal to your best prospects logical nature. That way, they can feel good about the fact that they gave you their money after their emotions have cooled off.

Here are two general rules:

RULE #1 — Emotion will always win over logic.

RULE #2 — Imagination will always win over reality.

Proof of these two rules is everywhere. My favorite example is all of the smart people who believe stupid things. I have been fascinated for years by all of the crazy religious and political groups that lean to the extreme sides of certain issues. Some of the things these people believe are absolutely insane! It's easy to imagine that the people who belong to these groups are stupid. But THE SHOCKING TRUTH is that many of these people are very smart!

The fact that some of the smartest people

get sucked into some of the most outrageous beliefs is all the proof you need that emotions and imagination are far more powerful than logic.

Years ago I read a great book called *"Why People Believe Stupid Things."* It was very well written and researched. The most important thing I remember from that book was that the #1 reason why people believe stupid things is because they want to!

People have a strong desire to believe things that sound good or appeal to their self-centered emotions. One of the richest marketers I have ever met told me that the key to creating the most compelling marketing message is: *"As long as it sounds good!"* He's right! Of course, you must back these emotional messages up with logical sounding arguments or comparisons with other things that make perfect sense.

Consider this: When people agree with a certain message, they tend to perceive it as being more logical or rational. However, when they disagree with the message, they perceive it as an emotional appeal. So all you have to do is get someone to agree with your basic message and you can have tremendous power over them.

For a selling message to be perceived as 100% legitimate, it must be backed by some kind of solid facts and figures, even if these things are ONLY GENERALLY RELATED to what you sell! The more you can do to back your sales arguments up with the most substantial and factual evidence that can then be tied-in with your sales pitch, the more people will believe and accept it as true. Once people accept something as true, they are ready to be sold!

Remember, logic is the language of the conscious mind and emotion is the language of the unconscious mind. Tapping into the power of your prospects' emotions is the golden key to selling them. Once you get them emotionally involved, the sale is yours! Their emotions will override their logic. This is the secret to making people want to give you their money!

Great persuaders fire up their prospects' emotions! They think all of this through. Every part of their sales pitch is aimed at reaching their prospects' emotions, such as:

✓ Excitement/Hope

- ✓ Love/ Friendship
- ✓ Fear
- ✓ Anger/ Envy/Jealousy
- ✓ Pride/Ego/Superiority
- ✓ Greed
- ✓ Frustration/Confusion

Master persuaders also control their prospects' negative emotions while <u>building up the positive ones</u>. How? There are many variations, but the basic formula is simple:

<u>**Step One**</u>: **Make the longest and most detailed list possible of your prospects' biggest fears, frustrations, and past failures...** What scares them the most? What are they really worried about? What are their BIGGEST frustrations? What are they most angry about? Who do they envy the most and why? What are their BIGGEST problems and how are they directly tied to their emotions? What are the most common failures they've experienced?

<u>**Step Two**</u>: **Take your very detailed lists of <u>EVERYTHING</u> in Step One and find a way to blend these things into your sales materials and presentations.** Don't be shy about these things... AGITATE THEM! Find as many ways as possible to add these emotionally painful things into your sales presentations. <u>Make</u> them <u>real</u>. The more specific you are about these <u>intensely</u> <u>painful</u> <u>or</u> <u>frustrating</u> problems or experiences that you know your average prospect or customer is going through, the more they will feel that you <u>understand</u> and care about them...

That leads to the final step...

<u>**Step Three**</u>: **Create products and services that offer THE ULTIMATE SOLUTIONS that can solve their biggest problems!**

What people really buy are results! We all want INSTANT SOLUTIONS to our biggest problems. The more time you spend with the first two steps, the more people will want the solutions you are offering to them in this third and final step. So your job is to spend a lot of time thinking about your prospects' biggest hopes, fears, and painful emotions so you can personalize <u>these</u> <u>things</u> <u>and</u> <u>agitate</u> <u>them</u> in the largest and most believable way. This makes them open and receptive to giving you their money in exchange for the solutions you provide.

Do the first two steps the right way and the third step is automatic! Now you have influenced their emotions in the deepest way and they are ready and willing to give you their money.

The bottom line: Our emotions cause us to do many things that we would <u>not</u> otherwise do. To persuade the largest number of people, you must find as many ways as possible to find the hardest-hitting logical arguments that ring true to the people you are trying to sell to — and then <u>BACK</u> <u>THEM</u> <u>UP</u> with the most powerful emotional messages that make people want to buy.

Summing It Up

I hope you enjoyed reading these powerful persuasion methods! I wrote this while carefully studying Kurt W. Mortensen's book: "MAXIMUM INFLUENCE"... If you like what you have just read, then you should buy his book and study it.

Remember, the art of persuasion is in your ability to influence people's actions without them even realizing that you have done it! **Selling is all about your control and your power over the prospect.** However, all of this power must be as subtle as possible or it <u>will</u> backfire. Once people feel that you are trying to pressure them, they will pull back.

In the end, people will always do what they can be made to feel is in their best interest. That's why it's up to <u>you</u> to prove to them in as many different ways as possible **why it is in <u>their</u> best interest to do whatever you want them to do.** Figuring out the best way to do this can take a great deal of time and reflection, but the rewards are great! After all, the ability to persuade and influence the largest number of people is the ultimate skill! It is your unfair advantage over all of your direct and indirect competitors.

In the game of business, there are many millions of dollars just waiting for you. This money is in the pockets, purses, bank accounts, and available lines of credit of all the people in your target market. Someone is going to get this money; it might as well be you!

I hope that you will carefully consider all of these powerful persuasion methods and find and develop as many ways as you can to use them in all of your marketing. Do this and you will have the amazing power to get <u>more</u> people to give you <u>more</u> money <u>more</u> often, for <u>more</u> profit, with <u>more</u> efficiency than ever before!

SECTION FOUR:

The A-Z Success Formula

A list of 26 of the most important things that we've learned over the years, things that could actually grow your business by leaps and bounds.

A-Z SUCCESS FORMULA:
The First Few Steps

Next up, I'd like to share with you what I call my Rags-to-Riches, A-Z Success Formula. This is a list of 26 of the most important things that we've learned over the years, things that have made us the most amount of money. **I honestly believe that just one or two items on this list, if internalized and correctly applied in a passionate way, could actually grow your business by leaps and bounds.** So think of this as a smorgasbord, one of those giant fresh-food buffets. Although it's covered with all different kinds of foods, you just take what you like and leave the rest, making the plate of food that you want. I think that's the best way to approach this formula.

Secret A

Our first secret is becoming familiar with the market, something I've talked a lot about before. **Little did I know it at the time, but the reason Eileen and I were able to go from $300 to over $10 million in just four years was that we were already very familiar with the market.** Of course, we had the right help and there was an element of luck mixed in there, but it was the familiarity with the marketplace that helped us make all the money that we made and it's still helping us. We were customers for so many years that when it came time to produce our own opportunity, we already had an innate feel for the marketplace — even though we weren't consciously able to communicate that clearly at the time. I can see this now only through hindsight. **There's no substitute for developing an intimate knowledge of the people that you want to serve, knowing them like they don't even know themselves.** Their hopes, their dreams, their desires, their fears, what makes them tick, what really keeps them up at night. The more you can know that marketplace, the better off you'll be.

I remember the very first product I ever bought; I even remember where I was, which is a grocery store that no longer exists. I was in the checkout aisle, bored to death, and there was a bunch of tabloids on a rack right next to me. I picked one up, thumbed through it, and I saw an ad by one of our competitors who's no longer in business. The headline was

"$25,000 for a Few Hours' Work Doesn't Seem Fair." Once I got home, I tore the ad out, sent in my ten dollars, and waited by the mailbox.

I re-read the ad maybe 40 times while I was waiting for the product to come. **Just like most good opportunity ads, it was blind as a bat. It told you all the things that it wasn't, but it didn't ever tell you what it really was, so you had to send in your money to get the rest of the story.** That's one of the secrets in the opportunity market, people like to be teased that way. They like that anticipation, so blind ads really work great.

Coincidentally enough, the product turned out to be a book that showed you how to sell moneymaking books to the opportunity market. It was sold by someone out of Virginia who called himself John Christwall (I'm not sure that was really his name). It was a full-page ad, showing a woman standing on the left hand side. At the bottom were the order form and the ad itself. **It was a simple idea; it was a book much like the book I'm writing now, though without all the depth of knowledge that I'm including here, frankly.** But it was a formula, just like my A-Z formula I'm describing here.

Secret B

The second secret of my A-Z formula is something that not everybody has, but it's important: previous business experience. **Years ago, one of the things that used to keep me up at night was the fact that some of our distributers were making tens of thousands of dollars a month with our *Dialing for Dollars* book, while others weren't making a cent.** I've already told you about the man in Provo, Utah, who made $5 million a year before he cut our company out and started going on his own. But on the other hand, we had other people who were swearing that we had ripped them off, that we were selling them stuff that was no good. They'd tried it and it didn't work — so it couldn't be any good, right?

Well, we knew it worked. Not only had it worked for us, we had people who were literally jumping in their car and driving over from several states away just to shake our hands and thank us for this book! And then, we had all kinds of wholesale orders coming in from around the country from people who were making money selling our products — so we knew it was working.

The only common denominator we found was that the successful distributors had previous business experience. **That led me to develop a theory: while those people who were successful were still running into problems, obstacles, and challenges faced by all the people who claimed we were ripping them off, because they had previous business experience, <u>they were able to continue to test new things and they didn't just quit so easily</u>.** They weren't expecting some panacea; they hung with it enough to where they finally started making some serious money.

I don't think there's any substitute for business experience. **A seasoned businessperson is more apt to stay with something and not expect everything to be perfect. They know the value of what they bring to the table; they know the value of their time.** Like the old joke goes, "the best part about being in business for yourself is the fact that you're your own boss... and the worst part about being in business for yourself is the fact that you're your own boss." People with previous business experience know how to flick their own switch. They know how to get themselves out of bed in the morning. They know how to keep themselves motivated so they're not just slacking off all day long and playing around. They don't have to have somebody standing over their shoulder all the time, telling them what to do next.

Secret C

That leads us to Secret C: get yourself a partner, especially if you don't have previous experience. **In our case, the synergy between Eileen and I made a huge difference.** I've already mentioned that I truly believe I would have blown the company up a number of times if it hadn't been for my wife because I was too immature, reckless, and wild — and I had too much learning to do. Eileen is the Queen of Common Sense. She's very well grounded, very conservative. She didn't let me do a lot of the wild and crazy things I wanted to do during the 14 years she ran the company. She constantly held me back — and that was the source of lots of fight between us. But somewhere along the line I did grow up a little bit and I adopted some of her conservative mentality.

Sometimes we need people who are smarter than we are, who have strengths in the areas that we're weak in, to help balance us and keep us

MARKETING SECRET

Wisdom from a marketing master:

"Writing copy for mail-order is a lot like playwriting or writing fiction — it's writing fantasy. It's creating a dream in the minds of the reader... Try to make it a dream life, the kind of life people want to live."
— Lyman Wood

focused on the right path. For me, that was Eileen and some of our key joint venture partners like Russ Von Hoelscher and Alan R. Bechtold and Dan Kennedy. Plain and simply, we need people. **I see too many entrepreneurs who are trying to do it all on their own and that's insane.** They should be leaning hard on people who can help them. Certainly, we would have never made millions of dollars had we not done that.

Secret D

Secret D in my A-Z success formula is timing. We all know that the right idea at the right time is vitally important. **You've got to strike while the iron is hot and you've got to be able to identify things that are culturally, socially, or emotionally important to your audience.** And the neat thing is, there's always something new if you're looking for it, if you keep your mind focused. That's one of the things that people in the opportunity market desperately want — whatever is new, whatever sounds interesting or hot. They love revolutionary, new technology. We were involved with computer bulletin boards in 1993, back when the electronic marketing thing was just getting off the ground, and that was hot for a while. When the Internet came along, we had a 12-year period where everything revolved around the Internet.

People are always looking for something that's hot and there always is something hot out there. I think their mentality is that they're always looking for something that's going to be the next big thing. They don't want to be left out, so they're always jumping on the newest bandwagon, thinking that it's going to be the next big thing. There are new things popping up all the time. Recently we've gotten involved with eBay. It was hot; it was on all the magazines, in all the magazines, it was on all the news programs. **Everywhere you looked, it was eBay! eBay! eBay! So we started developing programs to help people make money on eBay.** It's hot, it's current. You've got to look for things that people are talking about, things that are in the news. You've got to develop your programs, your products, and services around things that sound new, different, revolutionary, cutting-edge.

At the very least, your customers and prospects need to have the perception that it's new. **There's plenty of old stuff out there that you can give a new twist to and offer up to your client.** Right now we've got a program out there based on what we call "chain reaction marketing." But the truth is, it's really something called viral marketing that's been around for about a decade now on the Internet. All we did was put a new, more positive name on it. It'll be new to the people who hear it the first time, so you're not ripping off or misleading them. I think that's the thing that most marketers miss. In the Internet marketing world we're marketing to all these people online, trying to create revenue. We've got our ugly websites selling moneymaking CD series; we're doing all these things specifically to show people how to create money on the Internet. Now that's just one marketing vehicle — but the amazing thing is that there are so many people who are just now venturing onto the Internet. **They have no idea of the availability, of the technology, of the power, or the resources that are here. So when you bring something new to that marketplace, you're actually the benchmark, the launch point for that particular person about this information — even if it's a repackaging of an old idea!**

The same holds true with everything in the opportunity market. There are people that have never been in the opportunity market, they don't know that it even exists until they hear what we're talking about — and it opens up a whole new way of thinking for them. Remember that! **Just because you're sick and tired of a promotion that you've been running for a while, that doesn't mean it's not new to some of the people you're exposing it to.** This is one of the big mistakes that marketers make. They'll have a promotion that's still generating nice profits, but it's been out there for a while, it's old hat, they don't like to talk about it anymore. They're sick and tired of it themselves and so they pull it far earlier than they should. They could just leave it running and let it continue to produce profits for them on a consistent basis — but they scrap it way too fast. They forget that just because they're sick of it, that doesn't mean everybody else is sick of it. <u>There will always be those who are brand new, who are becoming exposed to it for the first time ever.</u> To them it's exciting, fresh, captivating — and that's the only thing that matters.

Secret E

Next, you need to find the right help. In our case, we found a marketing wizard to help us get on the right track. After our first six months, we got a letter in the mail from marketing consultant Russ Von Hoelscher. Russ simply included a brochure on his consulting services and said, "Look, I like what you guys are doing. I've seen your materials and I think I can help you." Then I called the number he provided and Russ started working with us. **At that time he had over 20 years of experience in the opportunity market, so his experience became our experience.** We were just like little Forrest Gumps: whatever Russ said, we did — and lo and behold, within our first nine months of working with him, we went from $16,000 a month to almost a $100,000 a week. He'd already gone where we wanted to go, he'd figured out all of the problems that we had yet to figure out. <u>By simply leaning hard on him, we were able to make a lot more money in a faster period of time than we would have any other way.</u>

Soon after we heard from Russ, he started flying to Kansas and spending the weekends working with us. We would pick him up on a Friday night at the Wichita airport, he'd stay over as a guest in our home, and then we'd take him back to the airport on Sunday morning to fly home. On the way to Goessel that first time, he told me — I'll never forget where I was when he said it, because it just really changed my thinking — **"In this business, all it takes is one good idea to make a million bucks."** That was the first time I'd ever heard that, but I was ready for that message and it stuck in my mind.

Very soon after that, we had one idea, just one idea, that made us well over a million dollars. It was a simple idea and yet it resonated with our customers. **They embraced it, they bought it like crazy, they loved it, and it made us a lot of money.** Here's how it went. Russ was charging us $2,500 every weekend that he came down to work with us. Plus, we paid his airfare, all his other travel expenses, and he also charged us money for every hour we were on the telephone with him and for special copywriting that he did for us and special joint ventures that we did with him — although we never really used that terminology back then. We immediately saw value in what he was doing and what he could bring to the table because we knew that it takes money to make money. Russ has helped us make a lot of money over the years, but he's also been well paid for his time.

Russ became like a 'Dutch uncle' with us, he saw us as a couple of young ambitious kids and he just took us under his wing. It's about more than money because he really tried to help us in every way. **He tried to help us not only from the business side of things with marketing and product development and getting us involved in direct mail, but he also helped us on the personal side because, at that time, we had struggled with poverty for so many years.**

> Blur the lines between your work and play.

We didn't know what it was like to be rich. Once the money really started pouring in, it was such a shock to our systems — and Russ had already experienced that before. He'd made and lost millions of dollars himself earlier on. When the money first comes in, sometimes if you're not careful, you end up like those lottery winners that hit it big and don't know what to do with the money when it comes in. It creates some emotional and personal problems. **Russ helped us deal with all of the aspects of our success.** It's extremely important to have someone like him to help you early on.

Secret F

Often, when people hear our story, they ask, "What is it that Russ helped you do that caused you to make so much money in such a short period of time?" **And the answer to that question is direct mail — Secret F in our A-Z marketing system.** Until we began working with him, we were just running space advertisements. Russ helped us get started with direct mail, he introduced us to our list manager (who's also our list broker) and, within a short period of time, we were mailing out millions of pieces

MARKETING SECRET

Don't bog the prospect down in a bunch of details... Sell the sizzle — not the steak!

- Sell that new car smell!

- Sell the excitement of some future dream!

This works with ordinary plain-Jane products and services too.

---

of mail every year. That let us reach so many more people in a more powerful way than the space advertising we were using. It's because of direct mail that we've made our real fortune. It's an exciting medium. **Once you start getting into direct mail, you'll never go back to any other medium in a serious way.** You might still do other things when it comes to marketing and advertising, but direct mail is such an exciting way to make money. That may be hard to understand, but someday I hope you, the reader, can experience the thrill of sending out millions of pieces of direct mail and then getting tens of thousands of them back, with cash, checks, money orders, and credit card authorizations in them.

Most direct mail experts tell you to go to the reference section of your library and go through the *Standard Rating Data Services* (SRDS) volume to find a good list manager. The SRDS is the big trade reference book that contains all the mailing lists that are for rent; they do a write-up on each of the lists and the list managers and you can do your research there pretty simply. But I've got a simpler way that works better for me. **The problem is that all the big list managers make all their listings look the same. They're all trying to get you to rent those lists, so they say all kinds of great things. You don't know who to believe.** So we've got a couple of good mailing list brokers who go out and find us lists to rent. We trust their opinions, they're working on our behalf.

We know that not all the lists we test are going to work well — as a matter of fact, only a small percentage of the lists that we test actually do work. But since we're constantly testing new lists, we're finding that small percentage that work and then those lists are added to our arsenal. **Over time we've developed enough mailing lists that we're mailing fifty thousand pieces every week.** Some of those fifty thousand names are new, but a lot of them are on mailing lists that we've been using for years.

You work with a couple of brokers who have good reputations, who are honest people with integrity, and you let them go out there and stay on the telephone all day, smiling and dialing and talking to other list managers and other list brokers. That's really how simple it is with us. **They're looking out for us, trying to do everything possible to get us good mailing lists that we'll keep using and re-renting from them because they get a nice little percentage of it — I think it's 15-17%.** We're more than happy to pay that because they're providing a good moneymaking service for us.

Although you're usually required to rent a minimum of 5,000 names from a list, that doesn't mean you have to mail to all 5,000 at once and we never do. We'll rent ten different lists, which represent 50,000 names, but we may only actually test a couple of thousand from each list. If it works, we'll go back and mail the other 3,000 and then we'll go back and get all of the remainder counts. They may have put up 20,000 names during that quarter, and we'll be forced to rent 5,000 as a test. **We'll test 2,000 as a mailing and if that works we'll quickly go back and mail the other 3,000, plus we'll get the other 15,000 they're offering.** The next time they come out with another quarterly list, we may still just take little baby steps until we're real comfortable with them.

Now, sometimes these list owners or managers will give you only the best names on the list. Those names will work like gangbusters for you, then you'll go back and rent the other 45,000 real quick — and the other names won't even be from the same list you tested to begin with. So there are some sharks swimming in the oceans that you have to watch out for. <u>If you work with a good mailing list broker, they'll keep you away from the dishonest people as much as they can.</u>

Since we first got into direct mail, in 1989, we've tested every kind of format and price points. Different things have worked for us at different times. When Eileen ran the company, she had a rule: we always had to break even on the front end. So whatever money we brought in on new customer acquisition had to recover the cost of the mailing.

Now, little did she know that I was sort of doctoring up the books — I was working with the numbers guy and the data that she was seeing wasn't always accurate. Why? Because I knew the companies that make the most money in direct response marketing are companies that always go negative on the front end. What do I mean by that? **It's simple, it just means that you don't always make a profit or even break even on the very first sale you make to a customer.** I never looked at it as losing money, I looked at it as an investment towards future profits, the cost of doing business.

That's the way the companies that are making the most money in this marketplace are doing it. **They're all investing huge amounts of money toward future profits and I knew that.** I also knew that Eileen was playing it way too conservative and so, when Eileen stepped down and I stepped up, I started doing some of the very aggressive things that a lot of the biggest direct response marketers are doing. For instance, on one $50 promotion I was more than happy to pay $500 to acquire the right customer, so we were going negative. **I learned a lot of lessons by doing that. For example, that you can be too aggressive, you can spread it out too fast.** I ended up having some serious cash flow problems — but that was a whole other story.

As it happens, I think most people aren't aggressive enough. Most people should be willing to invest more money in front-end, new customer acquisition, and not worry about breaking even or showing a profit. **All of the money's on the back end, so what you have to do is get as many customers as possible to raise their hands the first time and buy something from you or at least send away for something you offered.** Build your list as big as you can because the real business starts after that first sale. That's when you start kicking in all of your back-end marketing and that's where all your profits come from.

The front end is a tough business. That's the case anytime you're trying to do business with people who have no existing relationship with you. They don't know you and they don't trust you, so it's always going to be difficult to make sales to those people at a profit. **This is a very important lesson to learn because you could be focused on just trying to break even and lose the opportunities for all the future business**

because you've got a program that ultimately is going to make you a lot of money. If you're going to be aggressive with your marketing, then for every sale that you make at a $100 level, you'd better be willing to spend two or three hundred dollars to make that initial sale. Now you've got a deficit for every customer you're bringing in, so you've got to make up that other money as fast as you possibly can so that you break even as quickly as possible. That becomes the game. **Once you break even, then you've got that customer for free; that's how I look at it.** You've got somebody who trusts you and you know what they're interested in because they're voting with their checkbook. When somebody sends you $100 or $1,000, what they're really saying is, "Hey! I want what you have so bad I'm willing to give you my hard-earned money."

When you get to break-even, you've got the customer for free, so you want to get there as fast as you can — but you may not be able to do it on the initial sale. It may take two or three sales, which you'll have to make as quickly as you can. That becomes the game, so that you can break even and get that customer free. **Now, one thing that you have to do with direct mail is to track the lifetime value of each customer.** We have many offers that go out on a consistent basis to all of our best customers, so we're constantly trying to do more and more business with those people. We have a continual front end marketing campaign that brings us new customers and then we have an ongoing campaign that re-sells to them again and again. Some of the people we sell to have been on our list for Lord knows how long — some have probably been there from the very beginning.

The average customer has bought from us maybe four or five times. At the beginning you're sitting there thinking, "Okay, I'm going to go out and I'm put this offer on the table. I know that if I can create a customer with this offer then, based on my previous success, that customer becomes worth ten, twenty, thirty times that amount."

Why does this work as well as it does? Well, with the opportunity market — and I know I've said this before — you're working with rabid buyers. You're dealing with people who will come back again and again and buy more of whatever you're selling. That's one thing that makes this marketplace so exciting. Therefore, whatever it takes to get that customer one time, to develop a relationship with them, to let them know who you are and to give them a taste of what it is that you sell — that's just the first step in a lifelong series of re-purchases they'll make

▼▼▼▼▼▼▼▼
MARKETING SECRET

All customers are not the same! Segment your customer mailing list — so you can develop special offers for the various groups.

Segment by...

- Amount of purchase

- Recency of purchase

- Type of item they bought

from you. <u>And as you educate your customer, the offers can become larger, more extensive, and, obviously, more valuable.</u> In other words, you can keep asking for more and more money.

The main thing you need to do is make sure that the first product or service you sell to the customer is top quality, so it really makes an impression on them. From that point forward they're going to be more apt to buy from you again. **Many marketers out there base their business on this marketing or profit funnel concept, where you sell somebody something small and then you ramp them up.** Maybe you start with a $17 product, then proceed to a $47 product, then on to $97 and $147 products. Later on it may be $1,000, $2,000, or $5,000. Now, you can start a new customer with a big-ticket item without much fallout if you're very careful, but I'd recommend offering a mix of different prices so that people can start where they're comfortable. If I could do nothing but sell products and services for $3,000 or $5,000, of course I'd do it — but that's not entirely reasonable. We do have products and services within our overall mix that sell for prices that high, but there are a lot of people in our customer base who just don't have that kind of money, so it's nice to have a range of different prices of products and services.

Be careful to keep offering a mix of products because, once you get a taste for selling things that are high dollar, you'll never want to go back. One of my weak areas used to be the fact that I was hesitant to try selling information for thousands of dollars. But once I broke through that fear, after 7 or 8 years in business, all I wanted to do was sell things at high prices.

This hurt the company because it really is better to have an overall mix that just about any customer can afford; so I learned that lesson quickly. But don't hesitate to offer high-dollar products because you'll always have some percentage of customers who can afford them and who are willing to pay for them. If you don't offer high-dollar products to these people, you're losing money.

A-Z SUCCESS FORMULA:
Secrets G-K

For ease of discussion, I've broken my set of A-Z Marketing Success Formula secrets into fifths. In the previous chapter, I covered Secrets A-F; in this chapter I'll discuss the next five, which I call Secrets G-K.

Secret G

Secret G is this: you have to keep two different checkbooks for your business, at least in the beginning. At M.O.R.E., Inc. we did this only for the first few years, but it was imperative for us — it helped us establish a certain discipline that we've maintained to this day. When we used this method, we made sure that whatever came in that day — whether it was $50 or $50,000 — we took thirty percent of that money and we put it into a separate account that was used only for advertising. **We disciplined ourselves every single day to make that sure no matter how many bills we had to pay, we always had enough money to cover our advertising.** Some people do that with taxes, too.

With us, there was awareness from Day One that if we didn't constantly make sure that our money was allocated towards advertising, we weren't going to grow the business. **To this day, our Number One priority is to keep our 50,000 front-end pieces going out on a weekly basis.** Every single week, we know we're going to be bringing in so many hundreds of new customers or so many thousands of new leads. That's the first part of our marketing machine — and then we also make sure that we're constantly re-mailing to our existing customers on an ongoing basis. We're raining mail on their heads. We're staying in touch with them. We're selling them more and more stuff. It's a real commitment to continue to funnel more and more money back into the things that made you the money in the first place, but it's also necessary.

A Slight (But Instructive) Diversion

The number of mailings the average customer on our list gets depends on which part they're on, since it's segmented. In some cases, our best customers might hear from us as often as several hundred times during the year. **We do a lot of two-step lead generation campaigns where we're constantly separating the smaller group of our best customers from the bigger herd**. We're still marketing to the bigger group, but the smaller group gets a series of ongoing, systematic repeat mailings. If they keep raising their hands, they're going to get a lot of mail. There may be as many as 14-20 different follow-ups for each of those campaigns. Add in all the voice mail blasting that we do and they could hear from us two or three other times a year.

How do we keep track of it all? Well, we've got people who we've been working with for a long time and we meet every week. We're all in-house except for our mailing house and printer — and representatives from each are there at the meetings. **We also have staff members who really understand what we do because we've been doing it for so long**. All our mailings are numbered and it's all dated; it's a system that we just worked out and have grown into over a period of time. It didn't just happen overnight. **Here's what's behind the system: an awareness that we have to keep new offers going out on a regular basis.** In the past, we used to worry that we were going to be "slamming" our customers too often. That used to be something we argued constantly: are we hitting them too hard? Should we let up on them? We've gotten past all that and what we've found is that there seems to be no end to the number of times you can go after your best customers and make them offers. I think a lot of marketers are too afraid of that, like we were — we were frozen in fear for a good decade, worried that we were going to mail to our customers too often. **But the more we mail, the more money we make.** Of course, you've got to have the people on your list trained not to think that every time you send them a piece of mail, you're trying to sell them something. Think of it as educating them about you. Everything you're sending is part of that education.

I think it's funny how many times I've had customers come up to me at seminars, complaining about all the mail that we send them, and I look at their buying patterns and their histories and I see that they just keep right on buying more and more stuff. I love what Dan Kennedy taught me early on: he said, "Look T.J, it doesn't matter who you piss off; it just matters who you sell. So don't worry about pissing off some of your customers." And I love what Brad Antin said, too: "If your refunds aren't high enough, then you're not selling hard enough." **Too many marketers love to brag about how low their refunds are. Well, that's nothing to be proud of — it just means you're not selling aggressively enough.**

People who care about their customers, who want to keep them for life, are afraid to do this for fear of losing them. But there's no way you're going to keep a lot of them for life anyway — people get obsessed with buying at one time or another and while they're obsessed you have to sell them as hard and as fast as you can. Do not worry so much about whether you're going bother them so much that they're going to leave you.

▼▼▼▼▼▼▼▼▼▼▼▼▼

Test new ideas... but <u>never</u> stray too far away from the winning formulas that have been proven to be the most successful in your marketplace.

As I mentioned earlier, many of our promotions are two-step lead generation — so we're constantly offering free reports, free audio CDs, free DVDs, free tele-seminars, and other items to get people to raise their hands. Many of our offers are designed to separate that small herd out of the larger herd so we can follow up and do a series of sequence campaigns to that small group, market to the bigger group aggressively, and just keep the whole thing in motion so the smaller groups are getting sequenced mailings.

Another big mistake a lot of marketers make is that they just give up on their prospects too soon. So somebody will raise their hand and they'll show an interest, they'll attend a free tele-seminar, they'll buy this and they'll buy that — but if you don't send them enough follow-up materials, if you're not constantly on them, you may lose them. You have to keep asking them over and over again to buy from you.

I think this makes a lot of sense because, if somebody is interested in

SECTION FOUR — The A-Z Success Formula   115

▼▼▼▼▼▼▼▼▼
MARKETING SECRET

"Getting a new customer is like riding a bicycle uphill on a hot summer day. Doing more business with an established customer is like coasting that same bike downhill."
— Jay Abraham

- Re-sell to your existing customers more often.

- Sell more stuff — to more customers more often!

who you are and what you have, then they're going to be more interested in learning more about you and how you can put more money in their pocket or to help them have a better life. What Brad Antin said is so apropos to successful businesspeople. **Everybody has people decide "This is not what I want!" and you have to give them their money back — but you shouldn't complain.** It's a no-hassle, 100%-guarantee world that we live in and you don't want to deal with somebody who doesn't want your stuff. So you can give their money back, get them off your list, and know they're never going to hassle you again.

Realize, though, that in the opportunity market, people are so skeptical that they may test you — sometimes without even being aware of it. So if someone sends something back and you give them a refund, don't necessarily take them off your list right away; they may come back and buy something from you later, knowing that you have integrity. Here's what I mean: about ten years ago we had a seminar that we were selling for about $5,000, and at one point I asked the audience a question, trying to teach them the value of long-term relationships: "How many of you in this room have ever bought something from M.O.R.E., Inc. and wanted your money back?" About a third of the hands went up. **You see, they're constantly testing you; they're constantly trying to decide whether they can believe you and, sometimes, the only way they can tell is by your actions.** <u>When you give them their money back when they're not happy, you're solidifying your relationship with them.</u>

In the same situation, a lot of marketers say to themselves, "That customer doesn't want us;

they'll never want us again." I myself was very immature when we first got started. I had so much learning to do and I took it personally when somebody wanted their money back. It was like an insult to me. I loved my product like every salesman should. I loved what we were doing. I knew it was a good program and, when somebody wanted their money back, it was like a slam on me — so I had an immature attitude and I used to get ticked off when people asked for a refund. The same thing is true for a lot of us who are on the Internet and have someone jump off our lists. **I don't think you should give up on people that soon, especially in the opportunity market where you're dealing with the heavy emotional issues that cause people to buy from you to begin with.** You have to realize, there's a general sense of unhappiness that flows through this marketplace; if people were truly happy, truly satisfied with their lives, they wouldn't have such an insatiable desire to get rich in the first place.

There's a great book by Nobel Prize winner Eric Hoffer called *The True Believer.* **In the first sentence of the first chapter, it says that it all starts with a frustrated person — and there could be nothing truer when it comes to the opportunity market.** These are people who are frustrated to begin with; they're not happy. They all want to get rich quick; they all want to make a lot of money overnight; they have delusions of grandeur. They believe in secrets; they believe that there's an easy way and it's all going to come raining out of the sky. If that sounds negative, I'm sorry; it's not a judgment, it's an observation. **That kind of emotion causes people to Federal Express their orders and, in some cases, to wire them through Western Union because they're in such a hurry to get whatever you have.** That same emotion also causes them, sometimes, to pick up the phone and call you every name in the book, to abuse you and your staff verbally, to demand their money back, and threaten to take you to the Attorney General's office and the FTC. It's all part of life.

Secret H

This is one of the most important elements of success: back-end marketing. To me, this is the real business. I see too many people putting all their emphasis on front-end marketing, which is illogical. First of all, it's really hard to make any kind of profit on the front end. We've done it — we're doing it right now — but it's not the norm. **Normally, the real money comes from doing more business with the customers that you**

already have; that's going to make you rich. So we put all the focus on back-end marketing, unlike many of our competitors

So let's simplify the back end, especially for people just starting to understand what this whole marketing realm is all about. A "back end" is something additional that you sell to a customer you've already converted. Actually, it's a whole bunch of somethings additional because the goal is to attract the best people as new customers and then continue to sell to them again and again. **Every time you resell to an established customer, the profits can be higher and higher.** The expense lies in getting that new customer initially, so the goal is to bring in as many new customers as you can and resell them all the products and services you can.

It sounds like a daunting task, but it's fun — and that's the thing that people don't realize. When you have an existing group of customers who already know you — who trust you, whom you understand intimately — then trying to decide what products and services to sell to them becomes much easier. **Because you're focused on them and now, instead of being confused about what to sell, your only real challenge is this: what are the few things I can sell that will produce the largest amount of profit?** Your decision-making becomes easier and it's easier to develop products and services for people you really care about. And you should care about them because they're the people who are paying your bills. They're continuing to give you money, financing your dreams, and helping pay for your financial goals. So you're really reaching out as one friend reaches out to another and you're trying to give it all you've got.

Once you create a customer, it's easier to go back and sell to them because you and they have a relationship. **You can take the same promotions you have going out to new customers and, without changing a thing, you'll get double the response, at least, from your best customers.** Sometimes you'll get as much as 10-20 times the response, because when people trust you, they're more open and receptive to giving you money. The biggest challenge of new customer acquisition is the fact that they don't trust you, so they're less apt to do business with you. The good news is that once you do have customers who have already done business with you once, they're likely to do business with you again.

That's where the passion lies in doing business, for me, because that's where the real business is. **The front end is a necessary evil; I call it an** "evil" because it's difficult to make money with it. Oftentimes you're not making money at all — you're actually going negative on the front end. You can spend a lot of money on the front end, hoping to get a customer, and it simply may not develop the way you want it to. I became a reverse millionaire a while back because I got too aggressive — and that was a lesson I had to learn just once. I wasn't watching my numbers carefully enough; I was actually spending far too much money on every new customer I was bringing in and it got to the point where I couldn't pay my suppliers, I was having trouble meeting payroll, and I was having to go talk to bankruptcy attorneys just to explore my options. I was drinking milk and eating crackers because that's all I could handle. But most people are pushing at the other end. **For every crazy and wild entrepreneur like I was back then, there are probably hundreds or thousands of other people who could be doing more.** They should be marketing more aggressively both on the front end, to acquire new customers, and on the back end, to resell to their old customers.

There's no real formula regarding how much you should apply to the front end vs. the back end to maximize the amount of money you're trying to extract from a customer. I think it depends on the individual marketplace and your actual promotion. You can be as aggressive as you want to be, as long as you're just testing small groups of prospects. I think the real answer to that question is. Do you have a back-end product or service that's directly tied to what they brought from you on the front end? **If the answer is yes, then if you can tie your back-end promotion with your front-end so that it's a natural, logical up-sale that's directly related to what you sold them the first time, then you should be fine.** If there's enough money and profit in that back-end sale, then what you want to do is test small, so if you lose everything on that test you're not losing it all.

That's the smart way to approach it. **Always develop back-end offers; always have a good idea of what you're going to sell them next after they buy that initial product or service from you.** The closer that you can marry the two together, the better. One of the ways we do that is with two-tier distributorships, where we bring people in as distributors for a product or service. Now they're all excited and, suddenly we have a master distributorship opportunity. It lets them come in at a higher level, where they're able to get more money on every transaction. It's closely related to what they bought the first time, so it's a natural logical step for

▼▼▼▼▼▼▼▼
MARKETING SECRET

A famous writer was asked: "What is the most important quality to becoming a successful writer?" And he quickly replied: "AUDACITY!"

- I agree! You must be bold! You must honestly believe that what you have to share is extremely important — even vital to the people you are communicating to.

them to take. It makes sense and, therefore our conversion levels are higher. We're able to convert as many as 50% of all of those initial buyers who come in at a lower price point.

Generally, with brand new customers, you can't ask for a lot. They don't have any trust developed with you. It would be foolish to try to sell them something big and expensive, in most cases — and of course we've done it. We've tested it and, in some applications it works; but in general, it's foolish to ask a brand new customer to spend thousands of dollars with you. **The smart thing is to take them through a series of very logical, closely-related steps that lead to that additional money.** Once they've bought something from you and you've treated then right, they trust you. They're more willing and able to go ahead and make the commitment, to give you the larger sum of money.

I'd like to re-emphasize the need to make sure that you're always testing small groups with your back-end marketing, so you're not really spending a huge amount of money on a product or service that might end up failing if sold to your initial front-end customers. Now, a lot of us hate to test, but like front-end marketing, it's a necessary evil. Of course, the more successful somebody is, the more they tend to feel that they don't have to test things — and I've fallen for that myself, when I actually knew better. I've lost tens of thousands of dollars by not practicing what I'm preaching right here because I just said, "Oh, hell! We don't have to test; it'll work!" Sometimes you have a gut reaction to something based on past experiences, or based on ego, or based on somebody else's input — but that doesn't necessarily have anything to do with that product's relationship to the customer because you don't know what the customer is going to do, or how they'll react. Sometimes your gut feeling is wrong, so you test.

Here's what you do. You start out testing every new idea you have, to your very best customers first. First of all, by doing that you'll never lose money — your best customers will buy anything from you, as long as they know that if they're not happy, they'll get their money back. You could sell them a box of rocks, if they knew they could get their money back if they wanted. **So you test your idea to your best customers first and then slowly start rolling it out to the rest of your customer list; and then, if it's still profitable, you use it for new customer acquisition.** You turn it into a lead generating campaign, a two-step new-customer-acquisition front-end marketing plan. There's a Zig Ziglar quote my wife and I like, it's really our mantra, and we actually put it on the back cover of the first product we ever developed. Since then it's sort of become an overall theme for our company: **"You can have anything in life you want, if you'll simply help enough other people get what they want."**

Secret I

This one involves forming a habit of constant front-end promotion. Your pool of customers is always going to shrink through attrition; people will die, lose interest, or move away, so you have to replenish the pond constantly. **You have to have at least one front-end promotion going all the time and, ideally more; though more than a few is hard to hard to manage.** Back when I was teetering on the edge of bankruptcy, I was trying to manage two front end promotions at the same time; that was part of my downfall.

What works best is to have one front-end promotion that consistently brings in a steady flow of brand new first time customers and then have a series of back-end promotions that are out there bringing in more business from existing customers. <u>A lot of people fail on this very important principle</u>. They don't have a consistent way to bring in brand new customers or they do it haphazardly, sporadically. Business gets a little bad and all of a sudden they start running a bunch of promotions to bring in new customers. Then they stop and work those customers for a while, until business gets bad again. Then they go back out there and repeat that same crazy insane marketing.

What's better is that every single week, every single month, you run your promotion, space ad, or whatever it may be. It should be your most profitable promotion and you should constantly be testing new things. Your front end's always evolving. With us, we make sure we always send out those 50,000 pieces of direct mail — week in, week out.

Even in the retail market, people are too focused on the front end. **They run all that advertising to get new customers and then forget about selling to existing customers again.** This is one of the reasons it's so exciting to be in the opportunity market — because it's filled with competitors who don't understand the value of selling to people on the back end. They're trying to make all their money on those first sales and they're just not treating their customers well. They're not building relationships with them and they're not developing specific back-end related products and services to sell to those people. That's insane, but it's also one of the great things for those few people that want to step up to bat and do it right. **There are millions and millions of dollars on the table, just waiting to be made and I'm living proof that it can be done.**

Secret J

Secret J is essentially making sure that you have great resources and the right suppliers. I see too many people who are what I call pennywise and dollar foolish. They're looking for the cheapest prices for everything and they're constantly shopping around and tapping a variety of different suppliers for all of their needs. Say, for instance, they'll have 4-5 different printers and, every time they need some printing done, they'll try to get bids from all of them. They may do the same with audio and video duplication companies or any of their other suppliers. They're not loyal to any of them; they're just price shopping. **Well, one of the secrets of our success is that the suppliers we work with are more like employees or staff members.** We continue to do business with the same suppliers over and over again. We don't always get the best price, but while price is important to us — we're not trying to be foolish or make stupid decisions here — what we're looking for are suppliers that will give us all three of the things we want. **We need great price, great service, and great turnaround time, too.** We bring these people into our office once a week; they're in our management meetings because they're an integral part of our business. We try to look

> **The question all marketers must constantly ask: WHAT'S NEXT?**

out for them because we look at them as an extension of our companies — and they go out of their way to help us.

They're trying to keep their costs down because they know that's important to us, but they're also trying to give us the best services and the best quality and helping us think things through. Our mailing house comes to our meetings every week; our representative's bringing us different mailings she sees and different technologies we're not aware of. They're constantly looking for ways of increasing the value of the services they provide to us. My printer is the same way and my duplication company is always looking for ways to give us more value.

One of the greatest relationships you can have is with people who have knowledge of other resources, people who are successful in business, who are using other vendors, and are willing to share those relationships with you. The more you befriend these people, the more they're going to do things to look out for you. Now, suppliers are just one aspect of that. **You can also develop joint venture relationships with other people who have the knowledge, experience, and skills that you lack.** They've gone where you want to go, they've made their mistakes, and now they can help you to avoid those mistakes. We've surrounded ourselves with people who are smarter than we are, who are more talented than we are, and they fill all the gaps we have within our own company. I'll talk more about joint ventures in a later section.

Secret K

Become a marketing junkie. There's a book that's sold millions of copies because it's got a jazzy title that people like: it's called *Do What You Love, and the Money Will Follow*. I think it sells well because it appeals to a certain laziness people have, despite the fact that the title doesn't make much sense. After all, what people really love is to screw off; they love to just take it easy, to relax, eat at nice restaurants, and sleep in nice hotels. **I think it's better to find out what brings you the largest amount of**

MARKETING SECRET

Inspiration comes in the midnight hour. When the deadlines are creeping in — and your back is against the wall. When the gun is pointed at your head and you're forced to solve the problem.

- The key: You must consciously put yourself in these do or die situations!

money and then to fall in love with that. By and large, what brings us the largest amount of money is marketing. All the things you do to acquire new customers and re-sell to them as long as you can, as often as you can, for as much profit as you can — that's the thing to fall in love with. Like chess, marketing takes a day to learn and a lifetime to master.

The biggest element I try to focus on is relationship building because, if you can build a relationship with somebody, they're easier to manipulate (and I use that term in a positive way). **It's a lot easier to get those people to do what it is you want them to do. As long as it really helps them, then they need to be manipulated.** Hell, I've needed to be manipulated. A friend once said to me, "T.J., if somebody would have told me 25 years ago what I was going to have to go through to get to where I am today, I would have hung myself." And I understand because I feel the same way. People lied to me in the beginning or they misled me or they told me what I wanted to hear. I wanted to become a multimillionaire — and thank God there were people who came along telling me I could do it, that it wasn't going to be that difficult, it was going to be a piece of cake, no problem, go for it, go for it. Later, I found out that there's a tremendous price to pay and, the more money you want to make, the larger the price you've got to pay.

When I see a word like "manipulate," I view it in a lot of positive ways. I think that all selling is somewhat manipulative to begin with, but I also think some of us can't handle the truth and we need people to mislead us just a little bit so that we can stay on the right path. I don't mean to be sarcastic about this — and I don't mean to sound like a weirdo about it, either — **but some of the greatest things have happened to me because somebody manipulated me and I got in over my head before I knew all the problems and challenges I would ultimately have to overcome.** I was led to believe that it was a lot simpler than it really was, so that I could move forward on the path.

But back to becoming a marketing junkie. The very first thing you have to do is make a very strong commitment. First comes the hunger, the desire to set the goal that you're going to learn everything you can about marketing. It's worth it; this is one thing that can make you rich and it's your meal ticket for life. **It can make you all the money that you ever want, need, and deserve — if you'll just learn the right skills.**

Once somebody is deeply committed, once they decide that come hell or high water they're going to learn everything they can about marketing, they're going to be willing to invest in various programs and seminars. **There are so many marketing experts out there sharing their greatest tips, tricks, and strategies for making more money.** It's something that we want to share and there are so many wonderful programs on the market right now. Check into them, send off for marketing materials, and set up swipe files. See how other people are selling their products and services; one thing always leads to another once you set that goal to become a marketing junkie.

What are some of the telltale signs you've become a marketing junkie? If you're spending thousands and thousands of dollars on all kinds of books, programs, and tapes, you might be a marketing junkie. If your whole life becomes marketing and you can't get it out of your head, you might be a marketing junkie. If it's 3:00 AM and you're still thinking and dreaming up new ways to make more money — well, you might be a marketing junkie.

A-Z SUCCESS FORMULA:
Secrets L-P

We're now ready for Secret L, which is learning how to write copy that sells. **There's no more important skill in our business than the**

ability to write a sales letter that will get people so excited that they'll send you their money. There's no greater feeling when you can do it right, either. It's a feeling of being in control of your destiny since, after all, as entrepreneurs we're stepping out there with the courage that we're going to do this without the security and safety blanket of a regular job and a paycheck. It took me a long time to learn to do this well and I think the same is true for most entrepreneurs.

Even during those ten years when I was cutting my teeth, while I was learning everything that I had to learn, I realized something very important: **that when you're writing copy to people who already trust you and have a good relationship with you, you don't have to be the best copywriter in the world to make nice profits selling to them.**

For years I was forced to use expensive outside copywriters to do all of our front-end material. It bothered me that I wasn't a good enough copywriter to do my own new customer acquisition, but I wasn't — and if you're like I was, remember that there are plenty of copywriters who can help you with that end. **But I would encourage you to remember this: once you gather a group of customers who have bought from you once, start writing to them yourself.** Craft offers they like, keep working on different sales letters, and, not only will your copywriting skills improve, the more money you'll make.

Now, keep this in mind: while I do believe you should hire outside copywriters if you really need help, I think too many people become dependent on those copywriters. **I don't care how skilled these top guns are: they're never going to put as much effort and energy into it as you are**. It does take a while to learn how to master this skill, but you can always make more money writing your own copy than you would by hiring copywriters to do it all for you. I think not learning this skill is a big mistake that a lot of people make. It's such a great tool in your marketing arsenal.

In the beginning you have to emulate other people. **This was a tip that was given to me by the great Gary Halbert; he suggested that you take the best ad or sales letter you can find and re-write it in your own handwriting as many times as you can in order to get the feel and the language of copywriting down.** It's as though you're channeling the copywriter who wrote that particular copy. You're not thinking creatively, you're just going through the process of writing copy and you're basically training your brain to do that. Personally, I used Joe Karbo's Lazy Man's Way to Riches ad to train myself. I probably wrote that thing close to a hundred times over a period of 3-4 months — to the point where I had it all memorized. This single one-page ad, 2,000-3,000 words long, made Joe Karbo millions of dollars. Rewriting it so many times really did help implant the language of good direct response, the flow of it, into my brain.

What made that sales letter perform for Joe Karbo? Well, first of all, Joe had a lot of experience already in the business before he wrote the first word of that ad. It had been an idea that had been percolating in his head for a while. In my experience, an idea sometimes does have to percolate for a long time but, as the story goes, he got to the point where all of a sudden he was ready to do it and he basically did just write it all from the top down. He actually woke up in the middle of the night, went to his kitchen table, and hand-wrote that ad. There's a certain power to writing sales letters when you're fired up. **There's an energy you get when you're firing on all cylinders, when an idea is fresh and new to you; that's why you should always write the sales letter first, before you develop the product because, by the time you get the product developed, there goes all your energy and now the last thing you want to do is write a sales letter about it.** But the sales letter obviously is the most important element of the whole process. If you build your product around the sales letter and you write the sales letter when the idea is fresh and new and exciting, it'll make you a lot more money.

While you're in the moment, inspired by your idea, don't go work on the product: go work on the sales letter and tell the person that you want to buy this product every single thing the product's going to do for them. **Tell them all the features and benefits, all the elements — because then you've not only got an outline for the product, you've also got a level of excitement going.** That's what the Lazy Mans Way to Riches is all about. That ad makes you want to buy the product when you're done reading it. You get excited.

Now, Joe made all of his millions on the front end. The market has changed since then, so you can't do that today, but it worked like gangbusters for him. I just love that ad; <u>I would encourage anyone reading this book to go find that ad, read it, and study it</u>.

SECTION FOUR — The A-Z Success Formula   **127**

▼▼▼▼▼▼▼▼
MARKETING SECRET

People buy for emotional reasons and justify their purchase logically. People often buy for strong unconscious emotional reasons. We can never know the real reason people decide to give us their money. America's first billionaire, J. P. Morgan, said it wisely: "A man has two reasons for what he does — a good one — and the real one."

Secret M

The next secret in my Rags to Riches success formula involves developing skills in product development. It's something that you should work on every single day. So many people come to me and say, "I want to write a book. I've been dreaming about it for years!" **I tell them all you have to do is write a page a day and every year you can have half-a-dozen small books done — or one big one**.

Product development is so very important because customers always want something new. If your job is to re-sell to your old customers again and again (which it is), you'd better be creating new items — or at least, items that have the appearance of being new. One of the things we've done at M.O.R.E., Inc. is to constantly recycle the same materials over and over again. **So it looks like we're cranking out tons of new stuff, but all we're doing is pulling up the same old files and putting facelifts on them**. Now, it's always different, at least to some extent — but many times it's basically the same message. Every time you get it with a different slant or a different twist, you learn more; you get more.

I'll be specific: every one of the products and programs we sell contains the same basic start-up manual. Why? **Because when people spend hundreds or even thousands of dollars for the program, they expect a nice, big, thick start-up manual.** However, most people never read the damn thing. If they do read it, it's only the chapter that shows them how to get started, which is just 30 pages out of a 500-page manual. The rest of those 500 pages are the same pages we put in every one of our projects. Even if the customers realized that, they still wouldn't care; when they spend a few hundred dollars, they want to see you kill some trees. They want some bulk; they want something that's heavy in the mail. Even if you're just selling them web products, they still want something they can stick on their bookshelf to show they received something for their money. So we just keep selling people the same things over and over again, with new twists. It makes product development quick and easy; it might take just a few days to produce that manual. **People want things that are different or sound new, but they want some solidity to them also — so you keep finding things that are proven, that really work, and you just keep giving them facelifts.**

Even if you have customers that know they're buying the same stuff over and over, essentially if they're buying basic, solid information that has a different twist or a different spin each time — well, maybe the next one they buy is the one they actually sit down with, listen to or read, and comprehend. What people in the opportunity market want is not information — they really don't, and I know this is going to sound like I'm cynical, but it's the truth. **There are exceptions, but what most people in the opportunity market want is simply a turnkey distributorship of some type, an opportunity where you've already put everything together for them.** They don't want to learn anything; they don't give a damn about that, so if you're going to teach them anything, you've got to sneak it in on them. **They want a product that promises them they can pull it right out of the box, do a few very simple steps that aren't going to take much time, and have something extremely simple that's been proven to make a lot of money.** The more you can do for them, the higher your sales are going to be.

Let me re-emphasize that there are exceptions to this, thank goodness. There are people in the opportunity market who are willing to work their tails off and learn what it really takes to make millions of dollars. But most people in the opportunity market are lazy. They'll admit it if you ask them. **They want you to do everything for them; they just want to collect the check every month.** I have people admit this to me at seminars all the time. I mean, they'll laugh about it — it's a joke to them. If you can't handle that, then you can't handle the opportunity market. When I get together privately with my best customers, they'll make jokes about the fact that they want us to do everything for them, while they sit back and do as little as possible and collect the most money possible. Don't believe me? You'll eventually find out if you get really involved in this market.

You must develop opportunities that are as turnkey as possible, as simple as possible. So when I talk about product development, I'm talking about turnkey opportunities that give people a product to sell things, the sales material to sell those things, and some kind of a system for selling that allows them to do as little as possible and still get the largest amount of return for the smallest amount of investment in time, money, and effort.

When it comes to product development in the opportunity market, there are two basic categories. **There's what we call the soft product and the hard product.** The radio program this section is based on is a soft product. It's information-based; it's designed to teach people something. Some soft products are motivational, some are educational, and some are a little of both. A hard product, on the other hand, is a turnkey product. It's a distributorship or a master distributorship start-up manual that contains sample copies of the sales material and information about the product to be sold (which in many cases is an information-based soft product), as well as suggestions on how to market it.

When it comes to soft products, keep in mind that you can still sell them to the opportunity market all day long, even though they don't want to learn anything. You sneak it in to them, eventually maybe a switch will flick, and they'll get a little serious. **Usually, what they want is a hard product like I've described earlier. It needs to include a marketing scheme to sell that product or service <u>and the more revolutionary you can make that marketing scheme, the hotter your sales are going to be</u>**. They're always looking for some edge to help them make a fortune — so give it to them.

Here's an example that's worked well for my friend Mike Lamb. What he's done is create a radio book, an audio book that plays on Internet radio, to further promote and help build his brand. He calls it his *Listening Partner Book* and people pay him to be allowed to go out and promote and give away the proprietary player that people download to their computer desktop. Then they can download and open up the book for free. Every time somebody gives away the player and finds a new listener, if that listener buys anything, they actually get a commission on whatever's sold.

This is very illustrative of the types of products and services that sell the best in this market. All Mike's listening partners have to do is give out this desktop icon that Mike created and then the listening partner gets half the money they bring in, forever.

All these people have to do is take one basic step and, from that point forward, they have the potential to make lots of money. **Now, you can't make them a promise or guarantee that they'll profit because you'll go to jail if you do that.** But Mike's listening partners have the potential to make huge sums of money on an ongoing basis and all they have to do is take that one little step. People in the opportunity market go crazy over that general theme of residual income. They love anything that promises residual income, they love anything that promises passive income, they love things that offer huge profit margins. They buy licensing rights packages, they buy websites, and they buy Internet services. **They'll buy all kinds of services related to every opportunity you sell**. Anything that's associated with the product that's being sold, the marketing scheme that you've created to sell it with, and all the tools that go along it, they'll buy like crazy.

Another thing that they buy is what we call a two-tiered distributorship. This is where we bring people in as distributors. Sometimes we give the distributorships away for free; sometimes we make the customers attend a tele-seminar we'll charge a couple of hundred dollars for and then we'll appoint them as distributors — sometimes for a low fee, sometimes for free.

As distributors, they get so much money on the sale of whatever product or service is part of that turnkey program. It's usually a very small percentage; that's the bad news for them. The good news is that our requested entry fee is very small. Then,

> All this talk about retirement is nonsense! <u>Work</u> gives <u>our</u> <u>lives</u> <u>purpose</u>, <u>meaning</u>, <u>and</u> <u>structure</u>. Stop telling me to take it easy... *I'll have eternity to take it easy!*

we send them their distributor kit. **Once we appoint them at that bottom level, we've got them.** Now they're serious, they're distributors, they're representatives — and then we come along and we tell them, "Thank you for being a representative or a distributor. Now, you're going to get 20-25% of

▼▼▼▼▼▼▼▼
MARKETING SECRET

Our job is to buy as many sales as we can at a nice profit!

- Every sale must be bought.

- You decide how much money you want to spend to get the sale. Then you decide what strategies to test.

- This allows you to be aggressive and confident with your marketing.

the money you make per sale of this product or service. If you would like to keep more money on every transaction, here's your opportunity to become a master distributor."

The conversion level is high because they're already distributors or representatives — so now it's easy to ask them to shell out hundreds or, in some cases, thousands more dollars for those higher-end opportunities. You've appointed them as distributors, so now they take it more seriously; so what starts out being something you sell for a few hundred dollars becomes a very easy up-sell.

Now, I know I'm spending a lot of time on product development, but this is a very important element in your success as an opportunity marketer. Having told you what you should do to be profitable, I'm now going to tell you what you shouldn't do. **The most vital thing is this: don't spend that much time on product development. It's not that important to the customer.** Again, at the risk of sounding cynical or disrespectful, they're very lazy people. But that's okay. They know it, you know it, and we're all in it together.

At a seminar I'll say, "Who here in this crowd wants us to do all the work for you, while you sit back and do nothing and get a huge check?" and they all start jumping up and down and cheering. That's the opportunity market for you, like it or not. **If they weren't lazy, they wouldn't buy all this stuff. If they were true entrepreneurs, they'd be out there doing their own thing. They wouldn't be buying these turnkey programs that promise to put everything together for them; they'd be out there creating their own stuff.** That's what my most successful distributors all do. They break away from our company after they use us as a stepping stone to help them get started. As soon as they gain the confidence and knowledge and experience they need, they start developing their own products and services and they're gone. The rest of my customers aren't true entrepreneurs. They just want to get rich by doing the minimum amount of work possible.

So what do people need to spend time on to be profitable in the opportunity market? The sales material, the start-up manual, and the actual products that are sold as part of the turnkey program. Every single turnkey program has to have those three elements. The more bells and whistles you can put in the message contained in the start-up manual, the better. It needs to sound exciting. This approach is significantly different than the way traditional marketers approach their customers. **If our customers really cared about the materials that we send them, we would spend a lot more time preparing them — but they don't.** Back 10-15 years ago, I thought it all had to be perfect. But then I found out the customers don't care.

We're all in business to serve customers, so you have to give them exactly what they want — and I'm telling you, your customers in the opportunity market just couldn't give a damn about most of the instructive material you send them. **It's going to end up on the shelf because they want you to do all the work and they don't care about your tips and tricks on how to maximize your profit.** If they actually have to do any work, it may as well be written in Greek because, frankly, they're going to blow it off. To think that this is a marketplace that's made up of business people is ridiculous; they're consumers and, in most cases, they're not entrepreneurs in any way, shape, or form.

A lot of the marketers I know don't understand this. Some of the sharpest marketers I've met — some of whom have made me millions — are broke now because they don't understand it. They think they're going to help make people money and that's a nice, high-level concept — but they think they can help anyone make money. I believe it's foolish to think so because you don't have that kind of power. **You can help them do it and show them all the tips and tricks if they're willing to work hard, but if they'd rather sit in front of the TV and let you do all the work, they're not going to get wealthy.** You can't give them everything. You do what you can, but there are many things you can't do. A lot of people are going to screw it up no matter what you do. You can give them a map

SECTION FOUR — The A-Z Success Formula   133

and tell them where the gold mine is and all they're going to do is sit around saying things like, "Well, how do I get the shovels? How do I get there? I don't have a way." It doesn't occur to them that they have to put in a little effort to find a way.

I hope you, the reader, aren't this way. I'll be honest with you: while I may sound cynical, I don't mean to be. Yet it ticks me off that more of these people don't do anything. I'm very upset about that at times, but the reality is that I don't worry about it like I used to. There's no point. **Some of my customers will make good money with our programs, but some aren't going to make a cent and they're going to blame us for it.** They'll say that we cheated them. That used to just drive me crazy, but nowadays I'm just more calloused about the whole thing. I've come to the conclusion that some people misplace the map I give them, or the map gets destroyed inadvertently, and they don't know what to do after that. What they really want instead of a map is for you to just pull up in front of their house in a limousine and unload the cash.

I used to be one of those people that wanted everything without doing a lot of the work. I just wanted to be a millionaire 25 years ago, that's all I wanted. **I didn't realize I was going to have to kill myself for it, to work my tail off and learn a whole bunch of new skills that were going to be frustrating and time-consuming and emotionally painful.** I just wanted the millions of dollars myself, so I understand exactly how they feel. But you know what? <u>As far as I know, nobody makes millions without paying a tremendous price for it</u>. There's a lot of delusion in the opportunity market and I'd tell my customers to wake up and be willing to work a lot harder than they are. The basic business is pretty simple, but that doesn't mean it's easy; learning some of the skills necessary to make a lot of money will cause some real pain, especially during the initial learning curve.

When you look at all the little things you have to do to put a direct mail piece together, you'll see that it's not necessarily a huge undertaking — but you have to pay attention to what you're doing and it's very time consuming. It's a skill that takes years to develop. My friend Mike Lamb has a keychain his wife got him 15 years ago and it says "Whatever it takes." That's what real entrepreneurs do — within the limits of the law, of course! **The people who don't make any money just aren't willing to do whatever it takes.** That may be the essence of what I'm teaching you here: Whatever it takes. Don't think about this as a short-term situation; don't think of this as something else you have to do; don't think of this as something like a job. Think of this as an integral part of who you are, of your basic makeup.

If you want to have a better lifestyle, if you want to be able to put food on the table for your kids, if you want to have a legacy to leave behind, if you want to create something, if you want to have employees and be responsible for other people, or just be responsible for yourself, then you have to be the driving force. I don't look at this as a job. I wake up in the morning, I go to bed at night, and everything that I'm doing is all part of my business. It's more like a lifestyle than a job. It's a part of who I am. **I've come to realize that being a business owner is like being a farmer. It's a lifestyle; there's no time clock to punch any more.** <u>The business tends to be all encompassing</u>. When you look at it that way, you tend to do more and commit more of your time and energy and more of you to the business.

Secret N

This secret involves testing many, many things. You're always asking what's next. One of the heartbreaking things about this market is that it's a lot smaller than you might think. If you want to make millions of dollars in this market, you're going to go through opportunities more quickly. For instance, I've got a friend of mine in Birmingham, Alabama, who's been running the same ad virtually unchanged for 25 years. Every few years he'll give it a little facelift, but it's the same damn promotion it ever was. Because he's running a small little ad, it doesn't cost a lot of money and it's a little promotion that's what I call evergreen. **He can run that little ad forever — his kids can be running that ad 25-30 years from now — and it'll still make money because it's a small ad**. You don't need a lot of sales to make a nice little profit on it, especially if it runs in enough publications. Over the last 25 years he's become a multi-millionaire, so he's happy.

But if you really want to go for the gold, you can't just run small ads. You have to run big, giant, full-page ads. **You have to mail millions of pieces of direct mail — and the one thing you're going to find out real quick is that the market is limited.** The promotions fizzle out after a while.

MARKETING SECRET

The 4 laws of self teaching:

1. You are your greatest teacher.

2. You can learn anything you want to learn.

3. You must take total responsibility for everything that happens to you.

4. Experience + Reflection = Wisdom!

The first time this happened to me, it broke my heart; I was depressed for 6-8 months. The market does replenish itself a little, but not fast enough to keep up with you when you're trying to do something in a major way. So you've got to keep coming up with new stuff, especially if you want to re-sell to your old customers again and again to maximize your profitability.

At M.O.R.E., Inc., we're constantly testing, we're constantly tweaking, and we're constantly looking for new angles. We model what other people do. We take the things that work for them, and that might work for us, and we test them.

You develop confidence and experience along the way and with that confidence comes the ability to test even more things because now it becomes more enjoyable. <u>The longer you play the game, the more you'll realize that some of the things that scare the hell out of some people will excite others.</u> So now you want to find out what you can do and how many different ways you can re-package things. It becomes a game to see how many different ways you can create new stuff out of the old. **You're constantly looking for ways to give it the appearance of new material, to put new twists on it, but it's really just the same old stuff over and over again.** You're just finding ways to make it look new and fresh and exciting and different.

My best example goes back to the world of rock 'n roll music. One of my favorite bands is Rush, the three-piece band out of Canada. All their songs — or at least all their songs for the last 20 years — are pretty much the same. **They follow a theme and there's a range that they stay within; some rock 'n roll bands stay within an even smaller range than that,** where the same chords used in every one of their songs sound the same. <u>Your customers want that, too</u>. Sure, they want new, new, new. You'll always need something new to offer them because that's the way you get the most profit. It's just like the way a band will come out with a new album or new concert: there's always something new in the mix — and yet it's really just the same thing with the same recurring themes stamped out so they look a little different each time.

You need a certain amount of familiarity to make it comfortable for people to re-buy, but there's got to be a certain amount of buzz that makes it a bit more enticing for them to pay more attention to these new things that you come up with. As long as it sounds new, as long as it sounds exciting, you'll do well.

We've seen what the future is and it's the computer. All the things that we want someone to do, they're going to funnel through the desktop of their computer. That's the theme for this year — but next year there may be some new theme. **It's always got to be something and it's got to sound revolutionary.** I'm not saying that the computer angle is overhyped, but ironically, the programs that sold best have been the ones with the most hype. They've even outsold the programs that were more solid and based on proven methods; in fact, those solid programs often sell the least.

To me, there's no greater irony than to see a program out there that's earning people millions of dollars, when I know it's pure crap. But it sounds exciting and interesting, so their sales are sky high. Then I see other people selling stuff that's really based on something solid and proven, that has some real value, and those people struggle along. It's nice to come up with a little bit of both — to have something that's proven, but make sure there's enough hype in there so that the cash registers keep on ringing. **I think you need that excitement to drive someone to pay attention to what you're doing.** You need that sizzle to get them in the door, so they'll take some time to take a look at what it is you've put time and effort into, what your plan is.

It's all a part of your scheme — and let's take a little diversion to explain that word a bit. "Scheme" is a word like "manipulation"; whether it's negative or positive depends on how it's used. The first time we got called to the Kansas Attorney General's office so that they could meet with us and find out who we were, we were sitting in the Office of Consumer

Affairs and they were saying something about our scheme and my little wife popped up and she said, "We don't sell schemes!" They said, "Look, we didn't mean scam." They started backing down from her — I mean, here's this little bitty gal, a hundred pounds soaking wet, and they were saying quickly, "Sorry, ma'am, we didn't mean scam!" **Sure, there are regulatory issues in this market you have to pay attention to, but they're nothing to be scared of, nothing to keep you out of the market.**

You need to have your earnings disclaimer — that's vital. You need to have your terms of service and you need to have your privacy policy. All this needs to be stated explicitly, so when anyone comes to your website or really reads your materials they know what's going on. **It's all in the fine print that nobody reads; it's there for the lawyers and the regulatory police, but it is there. It has to be because in this day and age everybody has to know what's what.** If you're walking up to a line, you have to know where the line is.

Some of the best legal disclaimer language can be stated in ways that are friendly and folksy and sincere. It's funny to me how, the more we practice this, the more we find ways to disclaim all our stuff without using a whole lot of legalistic mumbo-jumbo. **We just tell people straight out what they're getting.** We use language like, "Look, we're not promising that you're going to become a millionaire or make any specific sum of money — or any money at all. You do understand that, right? Now, let me tell you why this has the potential to make a lot of money." There are ways you can do this that will be less scary than normal.

But back to the subject of testing! You've constantly got to try as many different things as you can, watching the numbers closely and letting the customers vote with their checkbooks and credit cards to tell you what they like the most. **Then you take your bestselling items and pump more money back into the areas that customers want the most.** <u>That's where the sales are</u>. Now, what works best varies with the promotion, but what I mostly look for are the themes that I know, from past experience, the customers get the most excited about.

One of the things we're doing right now is simply taking something we started on seven years ago and giving it a facelift. **We're heavily involved now in the world of viral marketing — what we call chain reaction marketing — where customers can give stuff away for free.**

Other people can pass it along and keep passing it along, just like a snowball rolling down a mountain. A thousand people can give it to a thousand more who can give it to a thousand more and then our customers have these links that are embedded into free eBook so the business can just keep coming back forever. It's those themes that we look for.

More than anything else, though, doing well with testing involves having something that offers the promise and the potential of easy money that can keep rolling in forever, that residual income that gives the customer the chance to make the most money for the least amount of effort and expense. Those things probably affect the overall health of the company more than any other single factor, period. We try to find as many ways as possible to incorporate and re-incorporate as many of those elements into every new promotion that we have.

> Salespeople get paid to hear the word "no!" A "no" does not mean "no" to the aggressive person who wants the sale!

How you test can be very important. We used to test every week, as part of our weekly new customer acquisition mailing, but that got frustrating and unprofitable, so we stopped that. Our marketing plan is very simple and effective, so now we just test things to our best customers. Then we take the hottest items that get the best response and we test them to the outside list, for new customer acquisition. **That's how we find the promotions that work the best for us: by using established customers as guinea pigs.** If our established customers — who love us, trust us, feel bonded and connected to us — won't buy something, if we can't make tons of money from them, then we know we're never going to attract new customers with that promotion.

Don't worry about overwhelming your existing customers, they want to hear from you. I spent years worrying that I was going to try to sell too much stuff to our customers, that they were going get ticked off because they heard from us too much. It doesn't really work that way. Now I worry that I'm not selling to them enough.

Today, I have a mindset that I need to create more products and make

▼▼▼▼▼▼▼▼
MARKETING SECRET

A new twist on the 80/20 rule:

- Focus your attention on the activities that rank in the top 20% in terms of importance — and you'll get an 80% return on your investment!

- Are you all spread out — or are you focused on the few key areas that can bring you the maximum sum of money?

more offers for these people or at least do more joint ventures with people. These customers have an insatiable demand for new stuff. That's the thing I didn't realize at first, even as recently as 5 years ago. **The customers are insatiable.** Our best customers are like drug addicts; no matter how much they pump into their veins or sniff up their noses or drink, they just can't get enough. **Dan Kennedy says that consumption expands with usage; the more people get, the more they want. The more they buy, the more they want to buy.**

I think part of the reason I'm successful is that other people aren't making enough offers to my customers. At the same time, I'm a big believer in abundance. In one way I'm grateful that more opportunity people out there don't do this — but it's a great situation that you, the reader, should take advantage of if you want to make plenty of money. I honestly don't believe that the extra competition will hurt us. **Our methods have served us well in a market well-populated by fly-by-nighters, constantly chasing new customers, because they're not doing nearly enough to develop relationships with the customers they have.** If you do that, you can sell them a huge amount of stuff on the back end.

<u>**Consumption expands with usage**</u>. If that's the case, then the more companies that come into the market, the bigger the market becomes. It really does work like that, in my experience, although the opportunity market is smaller now than it used to be, back when I entered it in the late 1980s. It can be that way again.

Secret O

Our next secret is, simply enough, passion. **You've got to fall in love with the business.** Once I got started, I became 100% obsessed with the business in every way. It dominated every waking moment of my life, year after year — and along the way, it's made us millions of dollars. It's an easy business to fall in love with because it's just so exciting. **That's one thing I want to convey to you here: it's amazing to get involved in a marketplace that's as lucrative as the opportunity market, where people habitually spend thousands and tens of thousands of dollars just to get the right opportunity.** It's a business you can easily fall in love with. That's large part of the secret of our success.

For years I just wanted to be a millionaire; that's all I thought about. Yet when we finally did start making millions of dollars, I got depressed. I guess I had some crazy idea that once the money started coming in, it was going to change certain things — but it didn't, really. Since then I've fallen in love with the acquisition of the money: the hunt, the chase, the idea of making a game out of it. In this mindset, you use money as a way of keeping score. **It's a great game; you get an idea and you throw it at your best customers. If they love it, they send you hundreds of thousands or even millions of dollars in a relatively short period of time — and it's such an awesome feeling.** Now, it's nice to have a good home and a good car and go on long vacations. But nothing compares to the thrill of waking up one morning, having an idea, and finding a way to make money with it. As long as you're testing it to your very best customers first, you're never going to lose. We're doubly efficient that way because we use direct mail to reach out to our customers. We're able to take an idea that we get on the 1st of the month and turn it into hundreds of thousands of dollars by the end of the month.

Every morning I get up and drink a couple of pots of coffee and brainstorm. I'm always taking notes, I'm always thinking of new ideas. Then we have a meeting every single week where we get together with senior staff, along with representatives from our printer and mailing house. All these people have a deep understanding of our business and those meetings are where we actually plan all the mailings and develop the strategies we're working on to go out there with.

We have a strong system within the business and the weekly meetings force us, on a regular and consistent basis, to deal with the important questions: "What are we doing next month? Where's the income we want this month and next month going to come from?" We're constantly planning new mailings all the time and using that as a springboard to take care of all of the implementation.

Now, we have our mailing house and printer there because we schedule our mailings carefully. The mailing house has to work with our staff to get the right list we're mailing that piece to and just having them there, rather than taking care of it on the telephone, lets us solidify our relationships. **It's fine to do business with people you never meet, but it's also nice to have people that are part of your regular team, that you're eyeball-to-eyeball, belly-to belly with on a regular basis.** <u>Relationships get developed, communication is solid, systems get put in place that strengthen over time</u>. What we're all trying to do is turn our businesses into moneymaking machines. The way we do that is by developing good, capable, competent people who can implement all of these wild ideas we come up with.

At our weekly meetings the manager who's in charge of customer service is there because he's got to be able to communicate all these ideas throughout our company — so when customers call up to ask questions, we've got answers for them. It helps to keep the machine running; it's just like taking a car in and having the oil changed and your tires rotated on a regular basis.

The people in our meetings are also offering ideas; as we brainstorm, they have input. And they've got incentive, too, because we've got a bonus that pays them a percentage of the gross sales that come in. It was one of the smartest things my wife did before she stepped down; now the employees are all "incentivized." When the business is doing well, they're doing well; when the business is doing bad, they do bad. They're the ones helping us shape our ideas. They're the ones constantly saying, "Hey! Wait a minute, T.J., what about this, what about that?" They play an intricate role in helping take these wild and crazy ideas that mostly originate from me and my marketing director, Chris Lakey, and turning them into reality. There's no substitute for falling in love with the business and being passionate about it, seeing it as more than just the money. **It's not just about some way to get rich or to suck**

money out of customers; it's a game, it's a lifestyle, it's something to put your whole heart and soul into.

It's such a creative, fun way to make money: art, science, war, sports, with a little bit of politics thrown in there now and then. Passion obviously is a heavy driver.

Secret P

This leads us into the next big secret, which is seminars, tele-seminars, audio programs — all ways you can bond with the audience. Now, I see so many people who are attracted to direct response marketing who are in love with the idea of getting cash, checks, money orders, and credit card authorizations from around the country. They love the idea that they can stay home and do business nationwide or worldwide. **I see a lot of Internet marketers, especially, who are in love with the idea that they can sit around and play with their computer all day and get all this e-commerce coming in — <u>but the dark side is that too many of the same people just want to put a wall up between them and the customer.</u>** They want to do business with people they never have to talk to; they want to handle everything with email; they want to hide out.

I understand this. The people attracted to this business are those who like spending a lot of time by themselves. **But the best advice I can give people like that is to get to know their customers intimately; that's the way you're going to make the real money.** You have to understand your customers better than they even understand themselves; to know them in such a deep way that you can develop the precise products or services they want. There's no better way to do that on a regular basis than getting in front of the customers, meeting them, looking at them eyeball-to-eyeball. **There's no substitute for interaction with people, even if it's something you hate doing.** It's an absolute necessity when it comes to understanding the customers in the most intimate way, so that you can sell them the most amount of stuff for the most profit.

These entrepreneurs who want to avoid people are really missing the boat when it comes to audio programs. They don't really accept that audio is a great medium for people to get a feeling for who you are, but it is — because you can be there in front of them without actually being there.

▼▼▼▼▼▼▼▼
MARKETING SECRET

Test small — but aggressively. You can lose money on 9 out of 10 of your tests — and still make millions by rolling out your 1 winner!

- You'll never find your greatest winners — without aggressive testing.

You can be there in front of them at their convenience, even in their cars. **They always want to be listening to something new**. So if **you send a lot of audio stuff out to your customers, chances are good they'll listen to you while they're driving or while they're doing other things that are relaxing and enjoyable to them.** You'll develop a relationship with them through audio programs that you just can't do through print.

While there are writers who can connect with people in powerful ways, those writers tend to be extremely talented — and that takes a lot of time and years to learn. What doesn't take time to learn, what can be mastered quite easily, is the ability to communicate to people through audio products, where you're expressing an essence of who you are. **All you're really trying to do is keep your heart in the right place. You're trying to help people, trying to reach out, so they'll forgive you for not being professional.** You don't have to be a polished, professional speaker. What you have to do is be totally focused on really trying to help them, reaching out to them, trying to give them more of what they want. Your customers will bond with you in the most incredible ways when you send out audio programs to them on a very regular basis.

My friend Mike Lamb, who's a professional broadcaster, knows more than most that radio is theatre of the mind. **It's a one-on-one communication with somebody, whether he's a truck driver driving down the street listening to the radio and hearing the DJ play his favorite songs, an office worker listening to a talk show host who's trying to raise their** ire, or just someone listening to another person sharing their opinion. Many of us listen at work because it helps make the day go by faster and more pleasantly. Bonding happens and radio stations can turn into multi-billion dollar businesses over the years.

But now anybody can take the same concept and build an audio program into their business. **I think people know when you're talking from the heart, when you're talking sincerely, and when you have a genuine approach to the message you're promoting.** By the time you meet them in person, they already feel that they know you. They've already spent hours listening to you; the ice is broken, the trust is developed. They know you're trying to reach out and help them and they get a sense of who you are.

I believe you should share your personal stories with those customers. Don't be afraid to tell them who you are, to talk about your struggles and your adversities, to discuss some of the painful lessons that you've gone through. In some cases you may shock people by telling them things about yourself that other people would never dare tell them. <u>You shock them by being so honest; they never forget that</u>. I see so many people who are holding back; they're trying to be professional, trying to be so very polished and perfect, and they think that's the way you have to communicate with people. They don't realize that it's not what people want. **What they want is a relationship with somebody who's just like them, somebody who understands them and their problems and pain, somebody who's trying to help them get what they really want.** That's more important than being perfect and polished.

Those people are too cautious about every word that comes out of their mouths because they're afraid of offending people. So they become lukewarm. Nobody really pays that much attention to them, they never stand out in the minds and hearts of customers, and they never develop strong bonds with them. **The way to do that is to simply take off all the filters, express yourself in the fullest possible way, and show the customers in as many ways as possible that you really do care about them, that you're committed to them.** And be honest with your customers: tell them, "Look, I do want to make money here, but I want to make my money by serving you in the highest way." People will respect that. Those are the things we've done that have allowed us to keep doing business with the same people year after year. They keep coming back and spending more money because they trust us, and there's a genuine relationship there.

Anyone who's been to any of our recent seminars has seen this. Some people talk about how they've been involved with us for years and how they've spent thousands of dollars with us. It's amazing to me how powerful these relationships are that we have with our customers. **It has a lot to do with the fact that we've always told our story honestly.** The customers know we've struggled with the same problems and confusions and frustrations that they've had; they see themselves in us, as they should. I was out there flat broke for a number of years — just dirt poor. I could barely put a roof over my head and yet I was sending away for all these crazy get-rich plans and programs. That's the way a lot of my customers are, too. They're struggling so much financially and yet they have an obsession, just like I did back in the 1980s.

Now I'm trying to help them along and they know it. They know I'm trying to help them get rich. But the key word in that statement, of course, is "help." We can't do it all for them, no matter how hard we try. Whether they do anything with what I give them — well, that's another story. We still have lots of customers who have never made any money, who continue to buy from us on a regular basis for whatever reason they have. Maybe they just stick our stuff on the bookcase and never do anything with it at all; maybe they half-heartedly try something, and give up way too soon. **A story we keep hearing over and over again is that someday they're going to get to it, when they finally do quit their day job.** That's a common theme. I think some people actually do this for entertainment purposes, too. Instead of going to the movies, gambling, or taking vacations, they spend their money on information products that they can turn around and read for entertainment. The act of buying satisfies a deep desire they have.

My wife, Eileen, has a similar obsession, God love her. She's got multiple sclerosis and it's a terrible thing, something I wouldn't wish on my worst enemy if I had one. She can't exercise — and yet she continues to buy all this exercise equipment. We've got a whole houseful of exercise equipment that she's bought because it promises to be simple and easy and painless. It just sits around; she can't really use it because of her condition. But the very act of buying the equipment soothes her — that, plus all the books that she buys on weight loss and diets. **Again, the act of buying fulfills a deep, emotional need that some people have.** It doesn't matter whether they use what they buy or not; just the fact that they buy it that makes them feel that they're on the right path.

A-Z SUCCESS FORMULA:
Secrets Q-V

In this chapter, I'll discuss Secrets Q-V in my A-Z Success Formula.

Secret Q is maintaining a stable staff. They say it takes money to make money and, in my experience that's very true. At M.O.R.E., Inc, we've invested significantly in the infrastructure of our business. All my friends call me a kingdom builder and, if any of them read this book, they're all going to snicker to themselves because for years I've taken a lot of criticism for that — as if I had to do this because of my ego! Oh, maybe there is some truth to that, but there's also truth to this: **if you want to make millions of dollars, you better have a certain number of staff members for every thousand customers you bring in because it's a waste of time bringing them in if you can't support and service them.** The whole idea is to attract and retain customers and the ability to retain customers requires infrastructure.

When you're in a market that's as heavily regulated as ours is, you'd better have staff just to try to take care of every little customer service problem and make sure that your customers get treated right because you don't want those little customer service problems to snowball into something big, which could happen if you don't have the staff to follow up, call people back, and do everything right. So maybe my friends are right to accuse me of being a kingdom builder all these years. I also know it's an absolute necessity to our ability to give good customer support and take good care of all of the people we're bringing in.

> Take good care of the people who take good care of you!

SECTION FOUR — The A-Z Success Formula   147

▼▼▼▼▼▼▼▼
MARKETING SECRET

The ideas you think will work best often fail. The dumb and crazy ideas you threw out there without much thought often produce the biggest results!

- That's why you gotta test! Don't be afraid to test all kinds of wild and crazy ideas.

- Make a game out of testing and have fun with it!

Early on, we bought a hospital in our town that was up for demolition — but the town couldn't even come up with the money to do that much. When Eileen and I bought it, we were two young and dumb kids, just 30 and 28. We thought we were getting a great deal because this building offered something like 30,000 square feet — and we bought that thing for a dollar a square foot. The day we bought it, we thought that was all we'd ever spend on it. Ha! Since then we've put about a million and a half into it — so the joke was on us because the whole thing was caving in.

It's a beautiful old building, but it was built in 1928 and needed a lot of work. We're very proud of it and we've filled it with a staff of people that have been with us since the early 1990s. **Every year they keep hanging in there: they love our business and they actually love working for us because we're constantly doing new things.** Direct response marketing in general is a fun business. I see it as a very challenging, very creative, very rewarding way to make money.

We've always had a very loose management style; it lends itself to people who don't want to be micro-managed. I've got a general manager now, though. **The important thing is that the employees are still hanging with us.** I don't know why they stay; but we try to treat them right and we pay them well. There's no question that we pay more money than most companies in the area, so if they do think about quitting, all it takes is a little research to realize we're taking good care of them financially. Add to that the fact that we've got an interesting business and we've all learned how to do it together. The core group of us who have been there the longest have worked together for years, creating systems and developing a lot of the ideas that we use daily. When it's all running smooth, which it usually is, it's just a massive profit machine.

I think it's very exciting to watch my staff work. **They're a creative, energetic group of people and they have the discipline to carry out what they need to — but they also have a lot of fun doing it.** And it's more like a family thing; I actually love most of these people as family and we've got four different married couples who work with us. We've got a mother and daughter who've been with us for six years; their offices are right next to each other. My son works for the company, my son-in-law works for the company, and there are some employees who are related but aren't married. Usually things like that just don't work, yet we've found a way to pull it off.

Secret R

Secret R in our A-to-Z rags-to-riches formula is planning sessions; I touched on this when I talked about meetings. **Having regular ongoing discussions to find out where the next dollar is coming from is a pivotal point of the growth of any business**. We've been doing regular weekly planning meetings now for over 10 years. We get together on a regular basis, number every single mailing, and check it sequentially. We started with Mailing Number 1, and at one recent meeting, we scheduled Mailing Number 7854.

Every week we get together specifically to schedule new mailings. My printer's there; he wants more printing business. The mailing house is there; they need more business, too. And so I'm committed to them, just as they're committed to us. We know that the more we mail, the more money we make. Naturally, we just want to mail more and more stuff because that's the bottom line. I've mentioned several times that I used to worry that I was going to mail too much stuff to the customers, that I was going to tick them all off, and they were all going to stop doing business with us. That used to just keep me up at night: I don't want to make my best customers think they were walking wallets. Well, I don't feel that way anymore. I'm more worried that I'm not doing enough with them because there's an insatiability in the marketplace. **My customers are going to go** buy from other people if I don't market to them. **We might as well be the ones getting the money, rather than our competitors!** <u>If for no other reason than that, you should be making offers to them as often as you can</u>. We mail to our very best customers at least 50 or 52 times a year. Sometimes it's even more than that; if a customer sends away for a free audio CD or a free report, they might get an additional 20 pieces of mail coming in to try to convert them to buy that particular program.

Again, in our weekly meetings, we spend most of our time scheduling and planning our mailings. As far as looking at the numbers goes, we do that probably once a month because it takes time for the mail to get out there and back, especially if you're using bulk mail. We used to look at it a lot more often, but there wasn't any real reason to. If business starts to go downhill, we'll study the numbers more closely.

We spend most of our time in our meetings looking at the mailings we scheduled the week before, so we can find out where they're at, when they're going out, if we're meeting our deadlines. We also constantly keep a new front-end promotion out there at all times. We've been doing 50,000 pieces a week for a long time, just to bring us new customers. We also have at least 52 different campaigns per year going out to our established customers. As I mentioned a few paragraphs back, many of these are two-step campaigns that are followed up with multiple back-end mailings that go out once people raise their hands. So, at any given time, we'll have a lot of different campaigns in action. This does get complicated, which is why we have our mailing house representative there. All the follow-ups are taken care of for us by the mailing house; it's all systematized.

It's a pretty simple business or at least that's how I see it. Admittedly, we've grown into it — so maybe some of my confidence is just because we've been doing it for a long time. And business is good right now. We've had times when it hasn't been, so it hasn't all been a bed of roses; there have been some real struggles over the years. **We've paid a stiff price to learn what we're doing, but the longer we do this the more aggressive we are; the less we think about making big decisions, the less we test when we come up with a new idea for a plan or promotion.** We just automatically send it out to our 30,000 best customers all in one bang, without dividing it up to smaller bites. In the past we were more conservative about that, but you let the numbers tell you what you can and you can't do. If you've got all these great customers who are always going to buy from you, then why not just try to get as much mail out to them as possible?

That's how confidence gets developed — over a period of time. You see all of these entrepreneurs doing wildly aggressive things and you say, "Man, they're nuts!" But most aren't — they've just been doing it for so long that they know what they can and can't get away with, so they naturally tend to grab attention for bigger and bigger things. It's not that they're being reckless gamblers or anything like that. **On the contrary, they have a track record. They know what makes them money, so they know they can always be more aggressive and turn up the volume.** I see so many entrepreneurs who think they're going to cross that line and blow their companies up. But for every wild and reckless entrepreneur that takes their company into bankruptcy, there are tens of thousands of others who just aren't pushing it hard enough.

An entrepreneur named Brad Antin used to appear at many of our seminars as a speaker — and he'd just bowl people over. He'd jump up on tables where customers were sitting and yell at the group, **"If you're refunds aren't high enough, you're not selling hard enough!"** And he's right, too. Here's what I mean: when people brag about how low their refunds are, that just means that they're not getting the money that could be theirs if they were just a little more aggressive, offering more outrageous guarantees that would cause more people to buy. Sure, some of those people will end up asking for their money back, but the amount of money you'll get to keep will be far greater if you're more aggressive.

Secret S

Secret S is our $100,000,000 Roundtable. This innovation started with the times that Eileen, Russ, and I would get together to develop products. We didn't call it joint venturing back then; that name didn't enter our consciousness until 6-7 years ago. We'd just get together to develop products, with Russ at first, and then we started inviting other people to join us: Alan Bechtold, Jeff Gardener, and a few others. **It's the simplest kind of joint venture you can do, where you get together with like-minded businesspeople involved in the same marketplace you're in.** We developed products together where we'd meet on the telephone, do some recording, and maybe add some print material — certainly the

▼▼▼▼▼▼▼▼
MARKETING SECRET

Always write in 2 steps. First, get it down as fast as you can... Let it come from your heart. Don't think too hard... Just let your words flow freely. Then comes the second step: The re-writing. Now is the time to keep going over your material to sharpen it and make it more powerful and compelling.

- Writing is hard for many people because they try to do it in 1 step instead of 2.

transcripts of the recorded text at least. Then we each sold these products to our own customer bases and kept all of the money, so we didn't have to worry about this or that person paying us. That's how it all started.

Now why aren't more people doing this kind of brainstorming, recording the calls, joint venturing, grouping the way we are? That's a good question and it may have to do with a dark side to joint venturing that nobody talks about — though anybody who joint ventures on a regular basis knows all about it. It has to do with egos. **Sometimes the most talented, successful people, the ones that who can contribute the most, are the most difficult to work with.** There's a level of ego there that makes it hard for people to work together, especially over long periods of time. Sometimes there's a disagreement, here and there, and sometimes those disagreements develop into feuds. That's human nature; it's going to happen, but I think that's the reason why more people don't joint venture.

People in direct response marketing generally want to be left alone, especially the Internet marketers I've met. **They want to hide out from the rest of the world.** I can relate to that. I enjoy long hours of solitude working by myself, too. One of the reasons I fell in love with this business is because it's a way of selling to millions of people without ever having much contact with them.

A lot of independent entrepreneurs are also freaked out over competitive issues — which is a joke. You're not competing with your joint venture partners. That partnership is one of the easiest ways I can think of to make money. **You**

did your part, other people did their parts, then the product is sold, there's a split, and you get a piece of it. Quite frankly, that's the easiest way to make money on the planet. You work with somebody, sharing the work, then you both go out and promote it and you make money.

Our $100,000,000 Roundtable group is currently 14 members strong. For years we operated with 5 or 6 members and there were advantages and disadvantages to that, just as there are advantages and disadvantages to having 14 members. I'd have to say that bigger is better when it comes to money, simply because you have more choices available to you.

On the other hand, you're always going to make more money with one joint venture partner than with several others combined; not only is it easier to work with some people than others, simply because of how your temperaments and business plans fit together, but different people get "hot" at different times. **I have one joint venture partner who's making me more money than all of the rest of my partners combined right now, but next year he may be off doing something completely different.** So I think having more joint venture partners is definitely a strength when it comes to making money, although it becomes a weakness in the sense that the more you have, the harder the group is to manage.

In some ways, JV partners are like employees. **The relationships you have, what you expect from them, their strengths and weaknesses, and how much work they actually do affects how much money you make.** My best joint venture partners are the ones who put everything together for me, then come to me and say, "T.J., let's mail this out to thirty or forty thousand of your best customers." Those partners are the ones I love to work with because it takes time, effort, and energy to put these things together. With these guys, all I have to do is show up for a tele-seminar or produce a pitch tape or schedule a mailing or make sure the graphic artists touch the print product up and make it a look a little bit better. And then I have other joint venture partners who come to me with ideas that are unfinished and they want me to put it all together for them — which takes a lot more time and work. All of us only have so many hours in a day and, the older we get, the less energy we have.

People are people. As I've mentioned, the best people, sometimes, are also the worst people. **The ones who are most talented, who have the most to offer you in terms of actually putting money in your pocket, who can**

consistently bring you huge sums of money — many times those people also have massive egos. You have to treat them a certain way and it takes a lot of work just to do that. But even though they may be pushing the envelope a little too much, they often make you the most money, too.

There's more to it than that, of course. Last summer, I was having a heated debate with somebody and this person was saying, "Look, what do you want, money or friendship?" And I told him, "I want both. Why can't I've both?" A lot of times people don't understand this lifestyle. They accuse you of only caring about the money; it's almost like they want to make you feel guilty about it. Well, why can't you want money and all the other good things, too? Why does it have to be either/or? **I think you can have it all or, at least, a decent quantity of both.** Some people just want you to feel guilty about the fact that your business, your money, is very important to you. But you don't have to give up money to get other things you want.

Our $100,000,000 Roundtable group has produced hundreds of hours of audio programs. We've also reworked a lot of the audio to create print materials, in the same way that the chapter you're now reading came about. For years, all we did was give up a couple of hours of our time every week and, simply by doing that, we were able to produce hundreds of hours of audio programs that we found many ways to use to make money. Now we're moving into other markets. We started with eBay — and since none of us really knew much about making money on eBay, we started interviewing all kinds of experts, learning their secrets. Now we're doing it with real estate experts. **There are so many different experts out there, who want to share their expertise, and many have books and products and workshops and seminars they're trying to sell; and so now the group is working together effectively on that topic.** The beautiful thing about working with a group is the fact that it really does let you use that acronym of TEAM, where Together Everyone Achieves More. Better ideas come from people working together and, while it hasn't been perfect, the business rewards can be great.

When you do a joint venture with one person, it's usually a 50-50 split: you both put in the necessary amount of effort and time to develop the product and then you go sell it. Either you make a split on each sale or each person gets the product to sell individually. With our $100,000,000 Roundtable, M.O.R.E., Inc. generally puts the materials together after the recordings, so we're doing most of the work, spending a lot of our money on mailings, production, and postage — so our split is weighed somewhat more toward us.

All of our joint ventures have been based on three different models. The first one is the best because it's the easiest and simplest; this is where we all get together just to develop information products that discuss some aspect of moneymaking. Most of our products are based on Internet and direct response marketing; we get together to share our best ideas, producing the product as part of these weekly phone calls we've had for years; then each of us has the ownership to that product. **The only rule we have is that we can't undercut each other when it comes to price**. Usually we get together and help each other develop the sales material to sell the products, too. We all just share it, we all own it, we can do whatever the hell we want to do with it, as long as we don't try to undercut our JV partners' price. Otherwise, there are no rules. It's great; it's simple.

Our other joint ventures fall into two other categories. As of this writing, Russ Von Hoelscher is getting ready to do a seminar. In this kind of situation, 50% of everything sold at that seminar goes to the seminar promoter; so if we all go to Dallas to do Jeff Gardner's seminar, we give him 50% of what we make.

> All growth comes from consciously living outside of your comfort zone. If you're not doing things on a regular basis that scare you just a little (or a lot!) — *you're not growing.*

If, on the other hand, it's based on direct mail, the rate is 50% after expenses and the expenses are simple: the printing, postage, and production cost for any audio product, that's it. The only thing that complicates it is jealousy amongst certain members. Some people have this crazy idea about competition that I think is so limiting. I scratch my head and try to figure it out because I'm genuinely confused.

I don't really think about competition at all and yet, some people are obsessed with it. They just can't get over the idea that one person's going to take their slice of the pie... but our market doesn't usually work that way. The pie just isn't limited in size. **There's enough money out there for everybody and, if you can learn from somebody else, it's going to**

MARKETING SECRET

Are you a professional or an amateur?

- The difference: Amateurs only work hard when they feel like it. Professionals work just as hard, whether they feel like it or not.

help you do something great or make more money in the future — so why wouldn't you want to have an association with that person? People who are overly conscious of the competition, who are very egotistical, tend to be people who have other issues hiding behind all that ego. It's just a cover-up for low feelings of self esteem, so those people tend to cause the most unhappiness in life in general. It's those people who feel good about themselves in a well-rounded way who are the easiest people to work with.

I've met a lot of talented people who are just pains in the ass to deal with. They blame other people for their lot in life. If you're like that (and if you can actually see it), you need to go pick up a copy of Jack Canfield's book *The Success Principles*. If you do nothing else, read the first chapter. It tells you to take 100% responsibility for everything that you do and everything you are because, at any time, no matter where you are, no matter who you are, no matter what you've done, no matter what you're doing — you can make a change. **If nothing else, change your reaction to what's happening to you.**

I know how this works. I've gotten so irritated at people in the past because of something that would happen on a Friday afternoon that the entire weekend would be ruined because I was stewing in my anger. Monday morning, I'd be even more ticked off than I was Friday night — and I'd lost a whole damn weekend.

Here's an example. About eighteen months ago, I got so angry at one of my employees because they embezzled $30,000 that I slammed my hand down on the counter at work. My hand still hurts — but it's good. Maybe I should go to the doctor, sure, but the pain reminds me that this is what anger does to a person. It can just destroy you. I've hurt myself because of my anger and I have to take responsibility for that. It wasn't the embezzler's fault that I did that, at least not directly. Yet I see a lot of egotistical people who are blaming other people for all their problems and they're not happy at all.

Secret T

We're down to Secret T on my A-to-Z Rags to Riches list. This is Dan Kennedy's Platinum Group, an organization Eileen and I were part of for about 6 years. It was a wonderful experience. Dan Kennedy is a marketing genius and he's helped us as very few people have ever been able to do. So let's talk about the concept of this particular roundtable and a little bit more about Dan. You may have heard his name, but may not be aware of the extent of his reach. He's been in marketing for years and he's been involved in practically every infomercial that's come down the pipe.

I first became exposed to Dan Kennedy when I was a subscriber to Gary Halbert's newsletter. Dan worked out a joint venture with Gary where he sent us a copy of one of his books, *The Ultimate Sales Letter*. I'd never heard of Dan, but I discovered after I got to know him that we both ran in somewhat the same circles. **I read his book, ended up buying some stuff from him, and ended up on his mailing list**. Of course he knew about what we were doing because our ads were plastered all over the opportunity magazines before 1992, when we stopped advertising in magazines. Until then, every time you picked up any kind of an opportunity magazine, we had a full page ad running in it.

Later, we started doing a bunch of business with him, and then we started consulting with him, driving out to Phoenix, spending good quality time with him, and going to his seminars. When he formed his Platinum Group, he invited us to become members. It was such a rewarding experience. It helped me sharpen my skills and develop my knowledge as a marketer and it helped me move in new directions that I would have never moved in had I not been a part of that group. **Everyone in the group was as committed to success as we are and it helped us in so many ways just to be around them.** We learned new marketing strategies; all of the members of our group freely traded information since that was part of our commitment to the group. You couldn't be a member unless you were willing to reveal all of your secrets and to discuss all of the things that were working for you, so the other members could profit. The support and guidance from these likeminded people was a tremendous boost.

This is a prime example of how people can form relationships and then take those relationships to new levels. It's more than just the camaraderie of getting together every once in a while and talking on the phone; it's about actually putting your heads together, doing joint ventures, and having long-term relationships that put money in everybody's pocket.

There's a synergy that comes from people freely sharing their best ideas with other entrepreneurs. I think Dan was a genius to put the group together — but many times we were the ones who were doing the work and he was just mediating it and keeping the whole thing moving in a certain direction. **It became a giant brainstorming session where you would get up and present your best ideas, just like show-and-tell when you were a kid.** We met four times a year and, in every meeting, we were required to bring the best ideas we were working on at that time and do some type of a presentation to the group. **The rest of the members then attacked our ideas, showing us the weak areas we weren't thinking about, but they also gave us support and showed us new ways of thinking about what we were doing.** Then we helped them do the same thing. It was fun; it was creative. It was sometime during that period that my skills as a marketer truly became sharpened and it made me millions of dollars. Sure, it may have cost us $10,000 a year, counting travel expenses and such, but it was a good investment because we made millions of dollars just from our involvement and contribution to the group.

When we got involved in the Platinum Group, the fee was about $5,000 per year. **Of course, the more value Dan proved the group had, the more people wanted in, so the higher the fee got.** I believe it's about $10,000 now, if you can even get in; there's a waiting list. Dan is in a great place: he's got a group of people just begging him to get into his Platinum Group, standing in line with their thousands of dollars in hand, and he just can't let them all in because there's no room — even though he's raised the number of people he includes. It's still under 20 people, but more people wanted in — and Dan is in this business to serve his customers and doesn't want to turn anybody down, so he let in a few more members.

When you get together with that many likeminded marketing experts, the excitement level gets to be huge. **The thing that was most exciting and useful was the fact that everybody was there to be brutally honest about all of the aspects of their business, <u>both good and bad</u>.** Since the meetings were closed-door sessions, people were able to reveal certain aspects of their business at a very intimate level — in terms of how much money they were grossing, how much profit they were making, what their exact expenses were, the biggest struggles and challenges they were facing. <u>It was a chance for entrepreneurs who had already gone where I wanted to go to show me how to get there</u>. There were people in those meetings who had been in business for three or four times longer than I had; they'd already made the kind of money that I wanted to make, had solved the problems that I still had to solve. There were times when I would go to one of those meetings and share my problems with my friends — and I would leave that meeting a couple of days later knowing the solutions to those problems because my friends were able to give me shortcut tips, tricks, strategies, and moneymaking ideas that I would have never thought up on my own.

Your brain can't help but come up with new ideas when you're sitting there and somebody gives you an inkling about something, somebody else helps it blossom a little, and then you work on it and go home and you're thinking, "My God, if I hadn't gone, I would have never created this product!" That product might ultimately put hundreds of thousands of dollars in your pocket — or more. **I got some of my greatest ideas while I was sitting in those meetings and, to be 100% truthful here, several of the ideas I got were because I was committed and obligated as a member to sit in that seat for two days or two and a half days.** If I hadn't been obligated, I might not have gone. I can't sit still for two and a half days. I've got to be moving constantly — but I was forced to sit there in that chair, going crazy. The rest of the members thought I was taking notes on what they were talking about, but what I was really doing was working on all kinds of product ideas. I walked away from some of those meetings with ideas that made us millions, just because I had to sit in a chair for two days. I don't mean to be disrespectful if any of my old Group members ever read this book, but you know, it's impossible for me sit still for two hours, let alone two days. <u>Keep in mind, though, that the Group did for me exactly what it was intended to do: it helped me make a lot of money</u>.

MARKETING SECRET

READ THE SUPERMARKET TABLOIDS!!!

- The heart and soul of direct response marketing is inside the supermarket tabloids... These publications are aimed at the perfect direct response customer... The writers have mastered the art of reaching out through print and touching the readers' emotions...

Even if you can't get into Dan's Platinum Group, you can probably still join or create a mastermind group to help you move forward. What you're doing when you put a group of likeminded people together is, you're feeding off of each other; you're sharing ideas and receiving constructive criticism, which is always very helpful. That's why we put together our $100,000,000 Roundtable group. Now, I realize there are some members who don't get anything out of our group. I know that because they'll be in for a year or two and then they drop out, they really don't contribute much, so they don't get much in return. **Those who are the most active get the most out of it, period.** It was the same way with Dan's group. I was one of the ones who got a lot out of that group, I think, because I also tried to contribute heavily. I tried to bring things to the group that would really help people and I tried to help all the members shape their businesses and learn some of the things that we'd learned. You get more out of something when you put more into it. Naturally, some ego is involved here; you want to show-off a little bit to your friends.

By the way, Dan Kennedy has made more people more money than any other person on the planet. **He's worked with more of what he calls "first-generation millionaires," people like me who started with nothing, than anyone in the business.** He's one of the top three mentors who helped Eileen and me make the most money. I'd be doing all of our listeners a disservice if I didn't tell them to go to http://www.dankennedy.com and start buying everything that Dan offers. At least become a member of his inner circle and start subscribing to his newsletter.

Speaking of mentors: I've already mentioned that Russ von Hoelscher was the first person who became a mentor; the second is Dan Kennedy. The third isn't really a single person — it's a combination of everybody who's been involved with us in our $100,000,000 Roundtable. I look at the $100,000,000 Roundtable as a whole rather than as individual members. **There's something remarkable about interacting regularly with likeminded people who are moving in the same direction that you're moving in, who are going where you want to go; you can learn things from those relationships that can help you make huge sums of money, especially when they've already been where you are.** When you have a relationship with somebody who's already had the problems and figured out the solutions and has made money using certain strategies that you're just starting to use, it's almost like you get to live vicariously through them.

You do all kinds of joint ventures with them, first of all; so that's taking it out of the abstract realm and putting money in your pocket immediately. **When most people think of joint venture they think of one-shot deals, but when you're working with a group of people long-term, after you get done making money on that one deal, you'll like them, they're your friends, you trust them, you respect them, and they feel the same about you.** So naturally it's, "Hey, what can we do next?" So, you do something else and you keep asking "What's next, what's next?" The ideas that come from these kinds of relationships can be amazing.

These people are equally as committed and knowledgeable as you are, they have the experience, and you trust them. There are so many things you can do with joint venture partners that you trust. It opens you up, just like all good relationships. You look at an old married couple; they can finish each other's sentences and they even start to look alike after a while. That's the way it is with all our closest business partners. **They become a part of us and we become a part of them.** Whoever said that business and friendship don't mix doesn't understand that as long as the friendship is centered around the business, then those will be the best friendships you'll ever have in your life.

You have to make sure, too, that any friendship that turns into a business relationship, or vice versa, has a strong degree of sincerity. Honesty is crucial in joint ventures because, if you work with somebody

SECTION FOUR — The A-Z Success Formula 161

in a such a situation and you get screwed, if something is supposed to be done and it doesn't get done, or you didn't get what you thought you should have gotten, then you're not going to want to do joint ventures with that person again. The word's going to get out and nobody will want to do joint ventures with that person.

Entrepreneurs tend to be people who are very independent and stubborn; they also tend to be egotistical. Some of that egotism is essential, if you're going to go out there and face some of the adversities you have to in order build your business from the ground up. **You've got to have pretty strong feelings about who you are and about your place in the world.** But some entrepreneurs are too egotistical; they're too difficult to work with, they're afraid of competition, they want to keep all of their best secrets to themselves. They don't mind if you share your best secrets with them, but boy, they don't want to give up any of theirs! How can you work long-term with people like that?

There are other reasons people don't take more advantage of joint venturing. I think part of it's fear; they're worried that somebody's going to get one over on them. **People like that have a constant barrier up. Sometimes you can peek over it or crawl over it, <u>but it's always going to be there</u>.** They're fearful that you're going to steal all their ideas, go make all the money, and they're not going to get what they deserve. These people have self esteem problems. They put up the face, if you will, of somebody who's confident and energetic and they're out there making noise and doing business — but the truth is that they're very sheltered. They're not open to a true long-term, honest, genuine relationship. Now, I've dealt with some self esteem issues myself and I know that part of the benefit of working with a group is that you'll tend to take on things that you might never take on alone. We're moving in some new directions right now where, if it weren't for a few other people who were deeply committed, I would have never moved. I would have been too intimidated; I would have stayed where I was comfortable because, whenever you try something new, you always have to deal with a lot comfort zone issues. **I just can't stress enough how important it is to work with a group of people moving in the same direction that you are.** You'll move forward faster, you'll constantly search for bigger things, and you'll end up helping each other reach your dreams.

The friendships that come out of joint venturing are very important because being an entrepreneur can be a lonely experience — even if nobody talks about it. We work a lot of hours, and nobody understands us. People around us pity us; they call us workaholics and think we need professional help. **But when you're working with other entrepreneurs, you're working with people who understand you and your problems.** They know how important your business is to you. You're able help them build their business and they're able to do the same for you. The more you do to help them, the more you help yourself.

> ▼▼▼▼▼▼▼▼▼▼▼▼▼
> Better to strengthen your back than to lighten your load!

I think we all have self-esteem issues at certain times in our growth as business people, even if you're the strongest, most socially active, open, energetic person on the planet. You're going to face hesitation and frustration and you have to move through them. I used to have a quote from Dan Kennedy hanging in my office: "Distractions abound; we must fight for focus." I see so many business people, including myself, fighting the distractions. **During my twenty years in business, there have been so many times when I've been anything but focused and I see that as a continual problem with entrepreneurs.** It's a struggle; don't let anybody try to tell you otherwise. No matter how successful people are, I believe that there are always times when they have to fight for focus. You have your good days, you have bad days, you have some days of **struggle. A lot of people think that they're eventually going to get to a place where that ends — and I just don't believe that happens for most people**. It does get better, though, when the money gets better. Heck, everything does. That's the name of the game.

One of my biggest pet peeves is this book that sold bazillions of copies called *Do What You Love and the Money Will Follow;* I've mentioned it before. I think it's a joke. Let's get real here: how many butterfly collectors are millionaires because they collected butterflies? None, I'll bet. No, what have to do is fall in love with those few things that bring you the most money. Spend all of your time doing those few things and let everybody else do all the rest. **This concept that you can make money with what you love to do is a great idea, but in the real world you usually can't make money doing those things <u>because the market doesn't allow you to</u>.** I've said it before and I'll repeat it because

SECTION FOUR — The A-Z Success Formula   163

▼▼▼▼▼▼▼▼▼
MARKETING SECRET

Stories sell like magic!

- People perk up when we tell stories.

- People like stories...

- Stories use metaphors... People put themselves in the story... They visualize as they listen to it.

- Use stories to drive home your biggest sales points.

---

it's important: what most people love to do is screw off and eat at nice restaurants, stay at nice hotels, get pampered a lot, go drink coffee all day at Starbucks, and go to movies and concerts and cruises. Good luck with that. If you can figure a way to make a lot of money and do all that stuff, great, but it's not likely.

Really making money as an entrepreneur is all about multiple income streams. I heard an acronym several years ago that sums it up, from a book by Michael LeBoeuf called *The Perfect Business*. **He talked a lot about PIGs, Passive Income Generators. Well, I want to have a whole farm of nothing but PIGs — and not the kind that slop around in the mud.** To set some of these things in motion, you have to learn from people doing it and then you have to go out and do some trial-and-error yourself. If you have your own ideas and your own ego driving you, you're going to make some mistakes, but an effective entrepreneur learns from those mistakes. Then you come back and decide how much time you're going to put into it. **I know some people who work 20% of the normal work week and make huge amounts of money, while playing the other 80% of the time.** If that's what you want to do, fine; if you feel you've earned that and that's the lifestyle you want, more power to you. With me, it's been a total obsession; I wish I could work a few more hours sometimes, but I can't. There are only so many hours in a week. I'm very, very wrapped up in the business, but I know other people aren't and they're able to make a lot of money and have plenty of leisure time.

A million different people will run their businesses in a million different ways; there's no one way to do it, but there are guidelines, there are directions you can follow, and lots of food for thought in the way other people are making their money.

Secret U

We're up to constant product development, which is crucial. In my company, there's a constant evolution of ideas and always has been; that's part of our strategy for dominating the market as best we can. So let's talk about how people develop ideas and why it's important to constantly produce new products.

The reasoning is pretty basic: your customers want and demand new things constantly. <u>If you're not giving them new things to fill their needs, they'll go somewhere else</u>. Our customers are insatiable. They want to buy more stuff and they're going to buy more stuff, whether you're selling it to them or your competition is. It might as well be you, right? If there were no other reasons to constantly develop products, that reason alone would be enough. The money's on the table; it's up to you to develop the new products that will put it in your hands. **The ability to do so comes from an intimate knowledge of who those people are and what they want the most, combined with your ability to use that knowledge and turn it around on them.** You're able to develop products that match the mold of what the customers want. The more you do it, the better you get.

Some of our early products are a joke to me now. I only keep them to remind myself of how far we've come and because I want to get a little laugh every now and then. But hey, we were doing our best back then — and hopefully ten years from now I'll be laughing at some of the stuff we're doing today.

How do you create these products? Work on them a little every single day. There's just no other way, really; every day you need to be spending an hour or two on nothing but product development. If you'll do that, you'll be amazed at how much you can get done every year. **If you're looking for effective ways to re-package the same stuff, to give things facelifts, you'll always have something new to offer.** It may look brand-spanking new, even if it's just a variation on everything else you've been doing. It's not cheating; a lot of time you just approach the topic from a different angle. You can create multiple themes, using the same basic materials again and again, so you keep coming out with variations that take you very little time to produce. Update old packages. Create deluxe editions that sell for a little more than the original.

Here's an example of something we often do. We've got something called a Joint Ownership Package; it's a special licensing package we sell people that allows them to sell one of our products and services. It's all in the way that we package things. **We have the manual all put together and, while I worked my ass off to produce it, <u>I did it just once</u>.** Now, whenever we want to come out with a Joint Ownership Package, all I've got to do is spend two hours of my time telling my typesetter to change this, change that, change these numbers to this, change this title to that. I call my graphic artist and say, "Change the cover," and that's it. Basically, I built a template that takes very little time to modify. Now, every time I want to sell a Joint Ownership Package, I just make cosmetic changes to the text. These things typically sell for $2,000-$4,000, so it's a nice bit of income that I don't need to work too hard at.

Secret V

Secret V is closely aligned to Secret U: you need to rework your past sales material and promotions continuously. Our customers don't care if a new product is set up using a template, even if they've bought another package and can compare the two side-by-side. After all, despite the similarities, they've got something new, a Joint Ownership in another product or service. They're not really paying for the material anyway; they're paying for the opportunity to represent that particular package. Why re-invent the wheel? **When you've got a system that works, all you're doing is tinkering with internal mechanics.** Remember: customers like things that are new, but they also like it if those new things have a familiar element. They don't want things to be totally new. Nobody wants to be the first one out on the dance floor; nobody wants to be the guinea pig. Your customers want things that are based on proven principles, that have been part of something that's older and more established, because that gives them the feeling of security that they like to have when they buy this stuff.

Let me re-emphasize: you only have to do a little of this every day. It's amazing how this adds up; you can easily have several products in development at the same time. This is especially true when you're doing audio products. **The customers really don't care if it's all professional and polished, what they want is for you to be real with them, to share secrets that really can help them get where they want to go.** They want usable information. I've produced hundreds of hours worth of audio products that are just me ranting and raving and screaming and howling, but I'm sharing ideas that really do work and I'm giving my customers what I know that they want. So who cares if I stutter and stammer and say things that are politically incorrect or whether I repeat myself constantly? They don't. *What they care about is that I know my stuff, that I care about them, and that I'm honestly trying to give them more than what I promised I would in exchange for the money that they gave me.*

Now, regarding this area of constant product developments: are there any pitfalls? Sure there are. Earlier I told you that you shouldn't spend too much time developing your product because it was unnecessary and the customers really don't care that much about that. **What I really meant was that you should spend the majority of your time on the promotional materials that sell your product.**

I have a good friend (whose name I'm not going to mention here) who just spent over one year of his life working on this great product. It really is a dynamite product, quality through and through; it's perfect, a product that he can be proud of for the rest of his life. It was an enormous effort on his part; he sacrificed long hours to put this it together and then I asked him the other day, when he was just finished with it, when he was still exhausted from the effort, "So... did you have a sales letter for it?" And basically he told me he didn't. He had a little bit of copy written for it, but that was it. In my opinion, that's a huge mistake. <u>The majority of your time should be spent developing the sales material</u>.

Quite often, in order to sell the product, you don't want to teach them anything in your sales material**,** you just want to share the benefits, not the actual features. Or, you want to cover the emotional advantages of the ideas you're sharing rather than the ideas themselves because you want them to spend their money to find out what all the ideas are. Thus, you want to keep it somewhat blind. **By the way, blind advertising really works well in the opportunity market.** A lot of the ads we've written over the years have been blind ads.

▼▼▼▼▼▼▼▼
MARKETING SECRET

Front-end marketing to acquire new customers is a necessary evil...

It's something you must do — but the real joy (and all the profits) is the back-end marketing.

For instance, we've got a promotion we're doing right now for this company out of Paramount City. We're promoting their multi-level company called Emerald Passport, but we don't tell people the name of the company in the ad. I've got a six-page sales letter that goes on and on about all these people making $20,000, $30,000, $50,000, $100,000 a month in this totally new kind of company — but I never tell them what the hell it is. They're not going to find out, either, until they shell out $500. Part of the reason they're going to be glad to do that is to get the rest of the story.

A-Z SUCCESS FORMULA:
Secrets W-Z

Secret W in my A-Z Success Formula is joint ventures. I realize I've already talked a lot about JVs, but these points are worth repeating. For anyone just starting out, I think it's vitally important to look for joint venture partners, especially those willing to be long-term rather than short-term partners.

In other words, look for people like Russ von Hoelscher was for us. Look for people doing big things; try to find people who are already where you want to be. Create what I call a "hit list" or "target list." Find fifty or hundred people you want to do business with, who have something to offer you — and then go after those people. Write them a letter and send them some stuff that you're doing. If you write a new report or produce a new audio CD, send it to them, and don't ask them for anything. **Don't try to solicit** business; just try to ask them how you can help them, how you can serve them, and what can you do for them and it's going to set you apart from every other person they hear from. Don't think that you can't do business with some of these big-name people, because you can. Just realize that you need to proceed slowly and build that sense of trust before trying anything colossal.

What I mean is, don't just come at them and say, "Hey I want to do this, I want to do that, can you do this for me, can you do that for me?" You've got to make them fall in love with you a little bit at a time; you've got to wine them and dine them and tell them you love what they're doing and ask them if there's anything you can do to help. **Show them some of the materials you're creating and offer to let them use your stuff as free bonuses.** <u>That's the way you win people over and I can't give any better advice when it comes to joint venturing</u>. Too many people are looking for one-shot deals; too many of these Internet marketers are trying to hide behind their computers and they never want to talk to anybody. They want to handle everything through electronic mail. I understand that, but I really wonder if they're not missing the boat.

Actually, I know a lot of them are. I appreciate their need to be independent, but the benefits that you get from a joint venture have nothing to do with being dependent on anyone. **It has to do with contributing to the group, trying to do things that really reach out and help their business.** <u>It's not just take, take, take, it's give and take</u>.

Even if you're the independent type who doesn't want to be a part of a group, I think you should try a joint venture at least once. When you actually get a check, then you're turned on to the fact that there are other people that you can duplicate this scenario with. My God, wouldn't it be great if you could have fifty joint ventures a year and make $25,000-30,000 on each one? Well, that's not impossible! We know people who do nothing but joint ventures now; that is, they create products for the sole purpose of doing JVs with others.

There are a lot of people that could be benefiting from joint venturing who aren't. I would just encourage you not to be afraid of the competition; if you're willing to be open and helpful, you can easily work with people who are involved in the same marketplace you're in. We've found a way to make it work. It hasn't been a bed of roses; there have been some struggles and we've had members of our group who ended up hating each other and going to war with each other. **I don't mean to paint an unrealistic picture here; like everything in life, sometimes the best things are also the worst things.** <u>But the advantages far exceed the disadvantages in this case</u>.

And I think it's safe to say that everybody is going to have a bad joint venture here and there. But the good ones are going to far outweigh the bad ones. People ask us all the time, **"Why do you just continue to do business with the same people over and over again?" Well, one of the reasons is that we've had some really bad relationships.** We had a situation like that recently — a joint venture relationship with a guy out of Atlanta who ended up screwing some of our clients. That's a terrible thing that makes you appreciate your good JV partners a whole lot more; it makes you want to do more business with them instead of going out and finding new partners. It's easy to remain in a comfort zone, especially when there's such a huge payoff. Some comfort zones are good.

Look at my situation with Russ von Hoelscher; I can't think of a better situation. Am I comfortable working with Russ? Hell, yes. I trust the guy, I love him, he's a good friend of mine, he's somebody who's extremely knowledgeable, he's easy to work with, there's a mutual respect and admiration for each other there. It's the most comfortable thing in the world to do business with somebody like that. **So, do I feel that in some ways it's a bad thing to stay with what you're comfortable with? No. It's like a fine wine; it gets better with age.** That's how a good friendship is and it's nice to do business with people you really care about on a personal level.

Those same feelings that make you so connected to those people also make doing business with them a lot more fun. You want to do more business with them because it's part of your social life. When you're working with people, making money with them, then you're able to have a good time with them. I think these are the best social lives for people who are absorbed in their business the way I am. You don't have time for anything but your business, so if you're working with other JV partners who are helping you, and you're helping them, then it really is a win-win situation; and, to me, it offers the best of all things. **More people should look at joint venturing as a friendship deal; you don't need to deal with all the complicated legal crap that a lot of people recommend.**

I've done millions of dollars worth of joint venture deals with no contracts, no lawyers, none of the technical BS. It's just done on a handshake — two friends doing business with each other. If you're friendly, honest, and genuine, you're going to come back and do it again. Joint venture deals can be structured simply and easily and, as long as both parties are keeping it simple and doing what they both say they will, you don't have to worry about getting screwed. And, naturally, when you get past one deal, you start looking for the next.

Secret X

I call this one Operation Money Suck, a term invented by the master copywriter and marketer John Carlton. You might be surprised to learn that this is all about delegation, which I've discussed previously. **Carlton teaches that the whole concept of "money suck" is to focus all your energy and time on those few areas that make you the most money or could, potentially, make you the most money.** Let everything else go; either delegate it or just don't do it.

> Your business is like a bicycle. Either you keep it moving or you fall down!
> - Keep searching for your next big winner!
> - Keep finding better ways to give your customers and prospects what you know they want the most!

There are so many things we can do to make money; that's the problem. We have an endless number of choices. You have to fight for focus and it's a never-ending battle, given all the distractions we face every day.

But you need to leverage the maximum number of available hours and energy you have into those few things that could make you the most money. This includes anything that you can do to become a better marketer. Self study, attend seminars and tele-seminars, purchase products, and study advertisements — anything that will help sharpen your marketing, copywriting, or communications skills is a good thing. Your time should be focused on product development, so you're

MARKETING SECRET

The jigsaw puzzle:

- The secret to writing a powerful sales letters is to write it in small pieces — and then hook the best pieces together like a jigsaw puzzle.

- This makes a BIG job very simple and easy. All you have to do is write small bites — then join them — and boil it all down.

constantly creating new products for your existing customers and for the people you're trying to attract as part of your new customer acquisition programs. Sure, you'll have some ideas that are more exciting than others and some that are going to make you more money — but you never know which ideas those are. **Sometimes the things you think are going to be the biggest winners aren't, so you should constantly do everything you can to keep coming up with more new stuff, so that every once in a while you'll hit a grand slam.**

Let me re-emphasize that you need to let other people do all the other work. There are too many distractions in any business and I think the worst thing anybody can do is try to wear all the hats in their business. **The best thing you can do, if you're a marketer, is hire a good manager.** As you grow, you might need a couple of them; but in any case, you need to stay away from the company itself and the day-to-day operations, which are boring anyway, so you can create products and market. Let somebody else do the customer service. Find good, capable, competent people and then spend all your time working on the specific things that can bring you the most customers and keep those existing customers coming back: product development, working on new promotions, working on new ideas, developing copywriting skills.

While I have a pretty sizable staff, I realize there are a lot of people out there who don't — who work for themselves out of a home office. **Well, you can still delegate much of your work by outsourcing.** For example, with Elance.com, you can find thousands of people willing to do a wide variety of work for you. For example, my good friend Eric Bechtold has been handling everything himself, but he just can't handle the phone calls any more. Well, there's a client of ours who's been coming to our seminars for years and he's looking for opportunities and he's just about there. He just needs a little bit of a leg-up, so Eric's going to start filtering all of his calls through this client, who is very capable.

There are good people everywhere — you can find them if you look for them. You don't have to hire them as employees although I would suggest at least one good full-time staff person who can handle all of the little things — the things that take five minutes here, ten minutes there, fifteen minutes here, that when you add them all up together represent a large block of your time, energy, and your focus that could be channeled into something a lot more productive.

Let your staff take care of those little things that distract you from the big picture, even if it's just little stuff like putting letters in the mail, paying bills, or shipping stuff to people. Find somebody who doesn't mind doing all that, someone who's easy to work with, capable, and competent. Let them schedule your phone calls for you, so that when you do get on the phone with people, it's done at pre-arranged times when you're able to block out a bunch of calls together. Look — most people are constantly putting out brush fires every day because they've been led to believe that you've got to be the first one in the office in the morning and the last one to leave at night. They're working their asses off, putting in tons of hours, and they come home every day exhausted. They're getting old before their time. I used to do that when I was trying to run my company. I would come home tired at night and my wife would say, "What did you do today, T.J?" and it was hard for me to tell her what I'd done. I knew I'd done something — I'd spent five minutes on this problem, ten minutes on that problem, then somebody else had a problem here that took fifteen minutes... **I was putting out brushfires all day and the company suffered greatly because of it. I wasn't focused on all the things necessary to bring in the largest amount of sales and profits.** That's what Operation Money Suck is all about.

Here's another point to consider: the loss of creativity when you're not focused on the big picture, when you're always dealing with small things and always taking care of the day-to-day mechanics. It's easy to do and entrepreneurs love to stay busy. **They love constant movement —**

but you have to school yourself to remember that the things that you should stay busiest with are those few things that can potentially bring you the most money on a long-term basis.

Are there certain skills that someone needs to have to be one of the people you delegate to? Of course there are. But it's not about competency nearly as much as it's about willingness. There are some people who are willing to do whatever you ask them to. If you say, "Hey, go down to the store and get me a gallon of orange juice, will ya?" they'll just go. They're not going to say, "Well, do you have a couple of dollars? How much is it?" or "What? You want me to go to the grocery store?" The best people just do it. **There are some people who, although they're very smart and capable and competent, also think that a lot of things are beneath them.** They think they're overqualified to do most of the stuff you need them to. They're just not easy to work with — and they're not going to be around very long, either.

Even those people can have a place in your company as it grows. But the person you choose to be your assistant needs to be somebody where you can give them a list of a hundred things and walk away, knowing they'll handle all of them — that nothing is beneath them and that they'll do a good, capable, competent job for everything you've asked them to so. You'll be amazed to discover all the little things you have to do — and when you get them done, they're not weighing on your brain and taking space in your mind. You just hand them off.

Now, there's a difference between delegation and abdication. Abdication is when you just hand something to somebody and say, "Look, I don't want to deal with it. You deal with it." Delegation is where you hand it off, but you're constantly overseeing the whole process. **Of course, there are some people who are so competent that they're going to do what you tell them ably and without fault, so with them you can abdicate something, to an extent, knowing it's going to be done and it's going to be done right.** But there are also people who tend to be less reliable — and again, it's more about attitude than mental capacity. If you were to give me a choice of either a person who has a low I.Q. with a heart of gold who's willing to do anything or some super-smart Mensa genius who thinks he's better than everybody else and is a pain in the ass to work with, then I would much rather choose the former than the latter.

Most entrepreneurs have trouble with delegation because they want to control everything; that's part of the reason we become entrepreneurs. But one of the biggest mistakes we make is that we expect other people to be like we are; we really do. But other people aren't like we are. They're not that driven; they're not that motivated. In order to work with other people, consistently, you can't hold them to the same standards you hold yourself to. And you have to praise them, tell them they're good people and they're doing a great job. **Everybody loves a pat on the back, so you always have to make sure you reinforce those great feelings. If you do, they'll pay more attention to you and they'll do the things you need to have done on a more consistent basis**. Catch them when they're doing things right, give them lots of praise and lots of encouragement, and pay them well.

Some entrepreneurs look at their relationships with employees, joint venture partners, and suppliers as costing them something. What they fail to realize is that if you find the right people to put in those slots, it's almost like an investment towards future profits. Those people will make you money you wouldn't have made without their help. It's very important to be able to hand something to somebody and know that it's going to get done.

Secret Y

You shouldn't be in this business just for yourself; that's my next secret, the second-to-last on this list. You're in it for the company, family, friends, and staff; you should regard people as the most important element of your business because they are.

There's something that never shows up on the profit-and-loss statement; I call it the emotional side of the business. I've surrounded myself with people that, by and large, I really, truly care about; the best examples are my son and my son-in-law. Both work with me on a daily basis and I love both these guys — and I know that they love me. There are other staff members with whom I also feel very deep emotional connections, especially the ones I've been working with for years. **They're more than just people I work with; they're people I really feel connected to and I enjoy them.** Then there's the emotional connection I feel with joint venture partners I've been working with for years. It's about

▼▼▼▼▼▼▼▼▼
MARKETING SECRET

One reason why you must repeat your offer throughout your sales copy is because even the best prospects read it in such a lazy, passive, and apathetic way.

- You gotta beat your offer into them!

---

a whole lot more than just making money — but here's where the money comes into play.

When you're looking out for people you really care about, and you're trying to serve them and contribute to their lives because they're contributing to yours, you'll come up with ideas for making more money that you would never have come up with had you not had those relationships. Dollars and cents are important, but it's about a hell lot more than just that; it's about people who will spur you on. You'll find yourself doing more because you're committed to these people. This is one of those things that's hard to talk about; I know for sure it doesn't show up in traditional business classes and you won't find it in most books about business, but I also know it's true. **Working with people whom I truly care about and who care about me has made me a lot of money that I would have never made if I'd tried to isolate myself and do everything on my own.**

It's a good idea to look at your best customers in much the same way. I enjoy mine; I enjoy spending time with them and I feel the connection with them. **I get very upset sometimes because I'm really trying to help them and I wish I was able to help them more than I do.** That's one of my biggest frustrations. Sometimes I get frustrated because, although I'm trying my best to help them, either they don't get what I'm doing, they don't understand the value of it, or for some reason I haven't connected with them.

Let's go back to something we talked about earlier. It's not a very attractive idea, but it's reality. Most customers in the opportunity market want to get rich without doing a single thing and they'll even joke and laugh with you about it. I'll go to seminars and hear them whining and complaining and all of a sudden I'll have enough of a connection with them that I'll pat them on the back and say something like, "Hey, John, you just want to get rich without doing a damn thing, don't you?" and then they'll chuckle and say, "Well, yeah." This is part of the insanity of the opportunity market. I was like that myself, once. I had delusions of grandeur and I thought the money was going to come right out of the sky. **But I always had a work ethic; that's the one difference between me and a lot of the customers that I work with.** They're really just looking for something for nothing and I don't mean that as a judgment call. I really care about these people, but by their own admission a lot of them are too lazy to accomplish anything. They want somebody else to do everything for them. In many cases, those are the promotions that worked best for us — the ones where we promise to do everything for the customers. But they would benefit much, much more by learning some of the things I've been talking about in this book.

Secret Z

This is it! The last secret in my A-Z Rags-to-Riches Success Formula: knowledge and experience equals confidence and wealth. This goes back to that whole myth of the entrepreneurial hero. When Eileen and I did our first seminar, if it hadn't been for Russ von Hoelscher, we never would have made it through. We were like those scared little bunnies that you see in the pet store: they shiver and just want to hide out in the corner. **We were attracted to direct response marketing because we loved the idea that you could do business with people you would never meet and, in most cases, never talk to; as I've mentioned, that's the way most direct response marketers are.** They want to live in their own private, little world and be shut off from everybody and still make great money. Russ is the one who talked us into having seminars. He convinced us that this would be a good move... but we were like scared rabbits and wouldn't even get up on the podium and say 'Hi' to the people because we were too frightened and insecure.

Nowadays, we do three-day seminars without thinking about it. You can't pull me off the stage now. Looking at me, you'd think I was born with the confidence to get up there and perform, but nothing could be farther from the truth. A lot of entrepreneurs are confident, but people don't realize that their confidence was developed over a period of time, with them learning new skills and facing lots of adversity and uncertainty along the way. You get confidence by slaying those dragons. From a physical standpoint, let's say you were to go to the gym and work out for an hour every single day. I guarantee you that, after a while, your body is going to start toughening up. You can't help it — if you go to the gym and work your tail off every day for an hour, it's only a matter of time before you have a better body. **It's the same way with building a business: you get better, stronger, more capable, more competent, more knowledgeable over time. It all comes, but it comes through a process <u>and that's what the newcomer doesn't realize</u>.** They see these established entrepreneurs and they're intimidated by the level of confidence these people have, without even realizing for one single second that that was all developed over a period of time. I wish somebody had told me that back when I was first getting started.

It's a genuine confidence. You start feeling that you have a lot more power and that means you can use that power in ways you never thought possible. With me it started out with egotism. Now, on the outside, egotistical people can fool you sometimes; if you get around them enough and know the symptoms to look for, you'll see that there's a difference between egotism and true confidence. **Real confidence is something that's developed by getting very, very good at just a few things that produce the largest amounts of revenue for your company.** So, did my confidence move my egotism out of the way? Eventually, yes. And here's what else moved my egotism out of the way: facing a lot of adversity and, to put it bluntly, getting my ass kicked.

Currently, we're starting to getting involved in real estate marketing. We're interviewing a number of real estate experts and recently I was talking to a new speaker who's been helping people make money in real estate for 15 years now. He said to me, "T.J., do people really think they can go to a three-day seminar and learn everything it takes to get rich in real estate?" Well, yes. They do. It's ridiculous to believe that because, in most cases, it takes years to get really good at anything. **But that shouldn't discourage you; as long as you have customers, you don't have to be a perfect marketer to re-sell to your same customers again and again.** These are people who trust you; once the ice is broken, it's easier to resell to them than to hook a new customer. This may seem difficult to pull off, but your abilities and your confidence will grow over a period of time.

There are people who believe they know more than they do. There are people out there who see certain things and think that's all they need. But you've got to have a little bit of humbleness going into a business, knowing that you're not going to learn everything overnight, that you're certainly going to make mistakes, that you're going to lose money. The ultimate thing is to make sure you feel in your heart that if you put good time and effort into something, if you're on the right track, then eventually whatever it is you're doing is going to be a success.

> Get your best offer in front of more people and follow-up like crazy!

Sometimes you've got to find out a few things you don't want before you find out what you do want. **Sometimes you have to test a lot of different things before you finally figure out where your niche is — and in the opportunity market you will find a certain niche.** The most successful companies in this marketplace have found certain areas they're very comfortable in, so with their programs they just keep re-stamping out the same themes over and over again. You've got to test the water a little — maybe a lot — before you find out which direction is best for you.

The moral of this A-to-Z wealth formula is simply this: nobody gets rich by accident or by themselves. **A lot of what I've been trying to share in this book has come from reflection. The ability to reflect takes time and experience, so you can look back and see everything through different eyes.** Sure, obviously some people get lucky right away and achieve great success early on, which can distort their perceptions of how good they are. We made over $10,000,000 in our first four years — but we also struggled for a number of years before that. It's almost a bad thing for somebody to hit it by accident right out of the gate. That's probably more of a curse than a blessing. I think this is an aspect of the same concept that holds true in the music industry or Hollywood. **When you're a young performer and you get really big really fast, not only can it go to your head, but it can mess up your whole life.**

The money is like a drug, in some ways, because it can be addicting. It can lead to as many bad things as good things. It gives you more choices, so sometimes you make wrong decisions. But hey, the real joy is in the

MARKETING SECRET

Everything you want to know about marketing can be understood by observing an attractive and ambitious single woman who is on the prowl for the best husband possible.

- Observe her... Then use her seductive and manipulative secrets to sell your products and services!

work that you do; it's in the business that you built; it's in the people you work with on a regular basis; it's in all the creativity that comes from developing ideas and turning them into reality. The money is nice, but it's the other things that make it all worthwhile. **I would especially encourage you to go back and reread the sections where I talked about joint venturing and falling in love with the business. All these things do affect the money — there's no question about it.** Don't fall in love with just the money alone; it's not worth it. You hear about so many people who have all the money in the world, yet they're living miserable lives. They're killing themselves in a thousand different ways.

I honestly believe that the business itself is the most important thing. Business is a game. Finding the right players, the right resources, the right vendor partners, the right elements that will make your business the success you want it to be — it's all part of the game. The majority of the companies in the opportunity market are, unfortunately, what I call fly-by-night companies. They have no concept of building long-term relationships with customers and getting those customers to come back again and again. **But this is a marketplace where anybody willing to work hard can get rich by following the ideas I share in this book, if only because so few of our competitors are doing it.** There are so many seminar companies that literally blow into a city, generate a seminar, and then blow out of the market and have lousy customer support. They're totally hit-and-run and they give a lot of other companies — the ones that are genuine, the ones that are sincere, the ones that are out there are doing a good job

— a really bad name.

You find that in every industry, by the way. Look at my friend Ray Prieba, who's in the massage business. He's a serious, dedicated massage therapist; and yet because the name of his company is TLC, he gets every kind of pervert calling him on a weekly basis. They're all looking for an erotic massage. There's sleaziness in every marketplace, companies that are dragging it down, but the opportunity market is especially bad. It's filled with people who don't understand the value of a long-term relationship, so they're trying to make all their money on these initial sales. **In my opinion, the purpose of a sale is to get long-term business. That's where it begins, not where it ends; that's what's made us millions of dollars.** Just practicing that good old-fashioned business, like the kind your great-grandfather used to do, where you're trying to look out for your customers.

I realize that we have customers who don't love us; they're not happy with doing business with us; we're not able to satisfy them. But why do they keep coming back? Well, a lot of them don't. I don't want to try to paint an unrealistic picture here. We've got customers that we've never been able to satisfy and that's fine; we send them on their way and wish them the best. You can't satisfy everybody in any industry. **The point is, we have enough customers who continued to do business with us — though a lot of those people aren't satisfied entirely either, to be quite honest with you.** <u>Part of what drives the opportunity market is this dissatisfaction, period.</u> A lot of the people in the opportunity market — I've said this before and it's worth repeating — are not really entrepreneurs. My friend Mike Lamb calls them "hope hunters"; they're looking for hope. That's not a put down. As the great copywriter Gene Schwartz put it, "What people want is a miracle." And we're trying to find those miracles for them, by constantly learning and constantly reapplying the very ideas that I've talked about in this book.

Information-selling is the most interesting and exciting business there is. You're creating a wide variety of different products and services that are 100% proprietary and are totally unique. **There are competitors out there, but there's no real competition because, again, this is an extremely rabid market.** These people keep buying and re-buying like crazy and they'll spend huge sums of money doing so. I hope you, the reader, get involved in this marketplace; we need more people willing to do it big and to do it right. Those two things are synonymous in my opinion because doing it big means that you can't just go for those one-shot deals.

New customer acquisition is the hardest thing in this business and people who aren't deeply committed to building relationships with their existing customers are hurting themselves and the field. They're focusing their efforts on trying to do business with people who don't know them, who don't trust them. **They'll get some sales, sure, and maybe turn a little profit, but they're never going to get rich.** To do that, you've got to focus on your back end and relegate your front-end marketing to the status of a necessary evil. Fly-by-night companies put their whole focus on going out there and trying to get new customers to buy their little gizmos; but to a real marketer, that's just a means to an end.

I recently had lunch with a gentleman who's in the business of buying and selling businesses. I found out more about it at lunch than I already knew, but I also shared with him what we're doing. **It was an entirely new world to him; his eyes opened up as we were talking about various elements of it and what can be done — the eBook and the eZines and the whole suite of web marketing-related items that we currently use.** It was literally an eye-opener for him to discover that this market actually existed to the extent that it does — and that it can earn you a huge amount of money. If you can develop a good understanding of the insatiability of this marketplace, and learn how to keep giving the customers what they want, well, there's your meal ticket for life.

I just love the opportunity market. It's filled with some unique challenges, there's no question about it, and you have to get over and though them or you might just get bogged down. **There are regulatory issues, first of all, that you need to be concerned with. You have to be very careful about what you say in your advertisements, particularly when you're promising certain things.** Earning disclaimers, profit, and privacy — it's all important for you to include it in the fine print. Or the not-so-fine print, as the case may be. There are many people out there who have gotten into serious trouble because they pushed it too far.

There's also this element out there that wants to know "The Secret" right away, when the fact is that, despite what Oprah and her favorite authors would have you believe, there is no secret. They want a miracle and they'll get mad and blame you if your product doesn't deliver it. **They want to believe that there's an instant formula to get them where they** want to go, so you have to include disclaimers that tell them, very plainly, that these shortcuts won't work if they aren't willing to work hard and use them properly.** These products may help people make the largest possible amount of money in the fastest period of time in the easiest possible way, but they're only business opportunities — not get-rich guarantees.

In this marketplace, the people who want to make the most money are the ones least likely to ever do it; that's one of the ironies of this business. God love all these people — they keep us in business and, hopefully they get something positive by doing business with us. As I've mentioned repeatedly (because it is, after all, a very important point) these people are looking for miracles and they want somebody else to do everything for them. **They're not willing to do the kinds of things that I've talked about here: becoming a great marketer, working with customers, developing relationships with them, learning product development skills.** Are they more lazy than most? Are they more frustrated or do they just not understand the value of all these things? Well... a lot of them are delusional.

This event occurred at the second truly expensive seminar we ever held; Russ von Hoelscher worked with us as a partner on it. We were upstairs in the hotel trying to get our game plan established when Russ said, "Look, we've been pushing this whole get-rich thing way too much. Let's really go out there to help these people — let's just try to get them to that first $50,000 a year and show them how slowly, over a period of time, they can build that to something larger and larger until they finally they get to where they need to go." We decided that made sense, so we went downstairs and asked our attendees, "Who here wants to make $50,000 a year their very first year in business?" **Absolutely no hands went up.**

Though I accept this now as part of the reality of our business, it was like a slap in the face for me at the time. I was thinking to myself, "What's wrong with these people? Most of them have never made $50,000 a year in their whole lives — they're like I was back in the 1980s, when I barely had a pot to piss in." But it goes back to this whole emotional thing; it's just one of the brutal realities of this business. Now, at every seminar, I ask the attendees what Russ asked them next at that seminar years ago: "Who here wants to make millions of dollars right away?" Now, as then, they all just start jumping up and down and celebrating. But they don't

▼▼▼▼▼▼▼▼▼
MARKETING SECRET

Testing a lot of different ideas is the only way you will ever discover the things in your business that make you the most money.

1. You test a lot of different things.

2. Find the ideas that work the very best.

3. Then discover new ways to combine these "winning" ideas — while testing new ones.

realize that it takes baby steps to make those millions, that there are things to learn along the way, that there's struggle and adversity to go through, that new skills have to be developed, that new knowledge has to be learned. **They're simply unwilling to go through all the things it takes to slowly get there — or even a small fraction of those things.** Now, there are plenty of exceptions, thank God. We meet people at these seminars who are willing to work their tails off, who have realistic ideas that most of the people in the opportunity market do not.

Most people want instant cures, easy answers, quick and easy solutions. I used to think this was something limited to the opportunity market, but the truth is most markets are this way. If I had to come up with three reasons why the Dan Kennedy Platinum Group was such a wonderful life-changing experience for me, one of those three reasons would be the fact that it gave me an opportunity to meet other marketers who were selling to other markets. **It just blew me away to find out that their customers were a lot like mine, at least in this sense. Their companies were selling niche programs and books to people who weren't these delusional opportunity buyers — <u>and yet those people would still just put these items on the shelf and wouldn't do a damn thing with any of them</u>.** It's as if the very act of buying something satisfies a lot of their hunger. It makes people feel like they're on the right path. They'll get into the heat of the moment and they'll go out there and spend a whole lot of money. Even if they never end up doing anything with any of the stuff they buy (which is usually the case) the very act of buying it satiates them at an emotional level.

Another challenging thing about this marketplace is the fact that it's filled with hype and BS — there's no question about that. **But one of the reasons it's like that is because, unfortunately, that's what people respond best to.** Back in 1994 Dan Kennedy taught me that the secret is to sell people what they want and then give them what they need. That's what we strive to do. Sure, sometimes our sales material gets pretty hyped up with all sorts of things that get our customers all excited. But for those who want to do the work, in the fulfillment products we're honest with them and straightforward about the things you have to do to make the most money. We really do try to educate people with good, solid information that will help those few who are willing to put in the time it takes to study what we offer and really put it into effect.

One thing that I've noticed recently, although I didn't before, is that a lot of people buying our products are looking to the future. When I ask customers what they've done with the stuff they've bought in the past, I often learn they're just a few years away from retirement. <u>They all honestly intend to use our materials someday</u>. These materials are sort of like an the insurance policy they mean to put effort into later, when they have the time and energy. There's no question that they're sincere.

Still, it's the programs and books that are most filled with the hype that end up selling the most and not just in the opportunity market. Lately, we've been dealing with real estate speakers quite a bit. What they sell is technically not a business opportunity — I wouldn't look at it as such, anyhow — but they're telling me the same thing. The things that really jazz people up the most are the hype-filled promises.

Having read through the 26 tips in the A-to-Z, Rags-to-Riches Success Formula that my wife and I used to get where we are today, I hope you'll go back and read them again, more than once. I've tried to be candid with you in every way here. I don't want to paint a false picture of our business; I'd rather be honest with you, so you can go into the whole thing with your eyes wide open and help us make this market even better than it already is.

SECTION FIVE:

Ruthless Copywriting Strategies

The ability to put words on paper that make people take action, that inspire people, that influence people, that cause them to give you money.

Study the Lively Art of Copywriting

I love to talk about copywriting, because it's something I absolutely love to do. While it's just one part of the direct marketing strategy that we teach to our clients, **it's supremely important, because it's what brings in the money directly.** Now, all the other things that go along with marketing are important, too; I can and I have spent whole books, not to mention countless seminars, discussing those subjects. But copywriting is extra special to me.

I'm glad that you're reading this, and I hope you'll get a lot out of it. I hope you'll read it more than once, in fact, and take a lot of notes, too. Write in the margins, scribble in the end pages, highlight specific passages, **do whatever it takes to help you internalize this material.** All modesty aside, there's a lot of great stuff here, advice that can literally make you millions. (I know I say that a lot, but only because it's true.) And the truth is, I've had to pare down all the knowledge I could potentially share with you, in order to present it in an easily accessible format. I could always produce the marketing version of *War and Peace* here, but how many folks have ever read *War and Peace* itself? Damn few, and for good reason — it's huge! In order to give you something you can read in a reasonable amount of time, I've whittled down the complete library of things I could discuss to the most valuable items, things you should be able to start putting into use immediately.

I'm going to give you a broad overview of some very specific things, which I'll go into in detail as I go along. There's a lot to learn, but you can learn the basics fairly quickly. **As with chess, good copywriting basics can take a day or two to learn, but a lifetime to master. Along the way, you'll learn how to leverage your knowledge into undeniable success — if you just keep at it, and keep learning.** I've been at it a good 20 years, and I can tell you that I haven't mastered it all yet. But don't let that get you down; as I've said, I've made a lot of money at it along the way.

My Director of Marketing, Chris Lakey, recently reminded me of something called the 10,000-hour rule. According to business author Malcolm Gladwell, while talent and intelligence have their place in any endeavor, it takes you about 10,000 hours to really become good at anything. **Mastering something doesn't necessarily have anything to do with your skills or your education level, it has to do with how many hours you put into practicing it.** Gladwell uses the example of athletes who start at age 3 or 4, like Tiger Woods. By the time they're teenagers, they excel at their sport, because they've spent about 10,000 hours practicing it. Musicians are the same way. A kid who sits down at the piano at age 2 and starts learning to play ought to be able to play the piano as well as any adult, after putting in their 10,000 hours. That's about five years at 40 hours a week — ten years if you look at it more as a hobby and just spend a few hours a day at it.

Chris and I have passed our 10,000-hour marks for marketing already, so we can safely say that, yes, we're experts — but we're still learning. Reaching our level of experience at copywriting just takes getting out there and doing it. But guess what — and this is really exciting — **you can still make money as you learn!** I'm here to give you the foundation to help you get started, even if you've never written a sales letter before. You've got to start at some point, no matter how amateurish you think that first effort might be. **You've *got* to do it.** I won't lie to you here: **if you want to make any significant money as a marketer, you're going to have to get started and really work at it.** If you already have, I congratulate you — you're on the right track, and I hope this book helps! If you haven't, start practicing what I preach immediately.

I'll be blunt here: I know from experience that some of you will see that word "work" up there in the previous paragraph, and that'll be it — this book will go back on the shelf. Others will read the book all the way through with the best of intentions... but won't try anything I've said here. That's fine. This book is for the rest of you: the ones who aren't afraid of rolling up your sleeves and jumping right in. **I encourage you to take what I share with you here, and let that be your foundation.** Use the resources we give you, learn more about writing sales copy, and put all that into practice — because it's in the doing that you'll get better at it. You'll discover things when you get down in the trenches, so to speak, and start actually putting copywriting principles into practice.

You don't even need to start with full-blown sales letters. **A classified ad is a good way to start learning how to write sales copy,** simply because it's short. It doesn't require many words. Once you feel you have a good grasp of writing a decent classified ad, from there you can go on to writing a small display ad, or maybe a postcard — just several hundred words — and make that work. And then you can start working on long-form sales letters. We've occasionally written sales letters that were as long as 60 pages.

You might think, "Wow, how could I write a 60-page sales letter? It's hard for me to write just one page of copy!" Well, the way you get to the point of writing a 60-page sales letter is to understand all the concepts that go into writing a *one*-page sales letter — and just expand them to the new length. **The strategies I'm going to teach you will work whether you're writing a Yellow Page ad, a postcard, or a 60-page sales letter.** Just start small, and build from there.

So just take some notes; **write down the main ideas that excite you.** Do more research on the Internet. Ask other marketers questions. I want to help you be the best copywriter you can be. I guarantee you that I can use the competition, and there's plenty of room in the field. You don't have to be the best copywriter ever; you don't even have to be good. **You just have to be *good enough*.** You just have to understand a few basic things to write sales letters... and those sales letters can make you good money.

So I'll be sharing some basic strategies with you as a foundation that you can start with. It's up to you to take that and run with it.

Let me emphasize, again, that this is not rocket science. **Just about anyone can learn to be a decent copywriter, if they're willing to work at it.** The strategies I'll show you here are the most important things you need to know. When you decide to become a good copywriter, you start out with several things in your favor. For example: the writing part of it is something you all know how to do. You're already a writer, every time you take notes, write a letter, or put together a grocery list. Trust me on this. You *know* how to write! **It's the *strategies* that make you the most money. It's the things that you do with the words that you write that matter,** and I'll be focusing heavily on those things.

Here's something else I want to say again: Copywriting is exciting! When you put words together that cause people to give you money, when you get an idea and get excited about it, and you write sales copy during that moment of excitement — *that's* where most of your money comes

MARKETING SECRET

Bob Costas asked Bruce Willis how he beat out thousands of other struggling actors when he auditioned for the role in Moonlighting that made him famous. His response is important to all marketers who are trying to "win" our customers' money. "I just went in there and pretended I didn't want it!"

- This is the heart and soul of take-away selling!

from. Even if you're not a Pulitzer Prize-winning writer, **when you convey that excitement in your writing, it's contagious.** I try to write only when I'm excited, and I try to make sure I'm excited every morning at 5:37 AM. I drink a gallon or two of coffee and I get all animated, and I have a big stack of legal pads that I attack, and I just write like crazy. Later, I review it and have it typed up. When that copy goes out to people, they get excited about it too — and they give me money!

Copywriting is one of the most enjoyable things that I do in my business. My colleague and friend Ted Ciuba likes to say that writing copy is better than sex. I'm not sure I agree, but I do know that it's exciting and profitable. It's also something I do well, so it's one of the few things I do in my business — which is another thing you absolutely have to take to heart if you really want to succeed. **You need to farm out the extra jobs that you're either not good at, or that are unprofitable for you to do personally.** Hire people to do some things on a part-time or full-time basis, so you can concentrate on the things that make your business the most money — like copywriting.

The strategies that I'm sharing in this book are directly applicable to any business you may be involved in. We've all been taught that business is a highly competitive environment, right? You've got to have your ducks in a row, and mind your P's and Q's, and you've got to know what you're doing; and if you *do* know what you're doing and you build a better mousetrap and you have integrity, then people are going beat a path to your door. That's true to a certain degree. **However, copywriting**

gives you an added edge, which is something you *must* have. Why? Well, let's look at it with a ruthless analogy: Does the wolf shed a tear when the caribou it's been eying goes down? Of course not. As Americans, we're all taught that we live in a competitive world. We provide for our families by going out and being in business.

Most businesses say they're competitive — and yet the majority of people in these businesses are running around like caribou in a herd. They're all doing the same thing, whereas a direct-response marketer using good copywriting strategies is the wolf amongst the caribou. You're not following the herd; you're directing it, taking down your competition at your leisure, at will. You're using these strategies because you're in touch with your inner wolf as a marketer, as a businessperson. I'm using the wolf analogy because a wolf can be ruthless. It can be very aggressive — but the wolf is very selective in what it targets. It doesn't want to waste its energy, time, and money spinning its wheels while trying to earn a living for its pack. In a similar way, that's what we, as ruthless marketers, are doing. **We're using copywriting to focus in on the specific prospects who are most likely to do business with us;** to hell with the rest. **We use our copywriting skills to convince those prospects that the money they're giving us isn't *anything* compared to what they're getting — and then we prove it.** We have to use our words to get them to do that. These strategies are powerful and exciting, and they're *fun*.

When I started my business, this was a whole new world to me. I could write, of course; I could construct sentences with proper subject/verb agreement. I knew where punctuation went, for the most part. But copywriting is different. **It has less to do with proper grammar and punctuation than with grabbing people by the emotions, getting their attention, and using human nature to get them to act.** But so many businesses out there don't do that! They just say: "I've been in business for 25 years. I'm the best there is." And to some extent, that's worked for them. But a ruthless marketer, using ruthless copywriting strategies, will out-perform those bland ads every single time. The guy who understands ruthless marketing — because he's sharpened his ax carefully by learning these strategies — is going to raise fat kids because he's going to have lots of money.

I urge you to immediately start using these strategies. Start writing small ads — little classified ads, small space ads — and start learning how

SECTION FIVE — Ruthless Copywriting Strategies

to get someone's attention, to keep their attention, to make it exciting. **It's all about learning how to make an effective call to action,** to get your prospects to take that step toward rewarding you with their money. I guarantee you'll find that you get better and better at it. Practice, practice, and practice some more, and you'll become familiar with how to weave these strategies into a sales letter, a classified ad, or whatever it is you're working on.

Why is this important? Quite simply because *copywriting is the engine that makes the whole marketing process work.* It's those words, and the ideas they manifest, that get people to do what we want them to do. **As a business person, what you want them to do is become your customer, and keep coming back.**

Again, it's all about emotion, and how much of it you can inject into your work. **Get pumped up before you start writing.** If I'm a little sleepy, if I'm tired, or if I've had a hard day, my writing reflects it; it's not so good. But when I'm fresh or I put on some music and drink my coffee, I'm all pumped up, and then that emotion — that super-charged feeling — comes across in the words I use. I lose track of time when I'm really "in the zone," as the athletes put it. Hours can literally go by and I'm like, "Oh, crap! I had all this other stuff I needed to get done, but I got caught up in writing this sales letter!"

Have you ever had a time in your life when you found that you were pretty good at something, or at least you had a lot of fun doing it — and then time would just fly by? Let's take algebra. My colleague Chris Hollinger, who used to be a teacher, has told me that he remembers well the day he finally realized he was good at math. It was his freshman year in high school. Up until then, he says, he was average at best. He always struggled with math. And then, in his freshman year, he was inspired by his algebra teacher, a mathematician who had once worked for NASA. The way she taught algebra that year caused Chris to pick it up and learn it, bam, bam, bam. It came so easily for him that he got straight A's in math from then on. It felt good to do math; it was exciting.

That's how copywriting can be. For me, copywriting — putting words down on paper that can lead to heaping piles of mailbox money (as Chris Hollinger calls it) — is fun and energetic. All the truly successful marketers I know feel the same way. If you take one thing away from this section, **it** should be the enthusiasm to sit down and write something, even classified ad you can put in a local newspaper, to get someone action and call a phone number or go to a website. Take something here, and apply it. When you see it turn to money, you're going to say, "That's so cool!"

I want you to be in touch with your inner wolf, as a marketer and as a copywriter. If you keep that in mind, you're going to go far.

Practice These Basic Strategies

In the next few chapters, I'm going to share a wide variety of basic strategies that you can use to become a profitable copywriter. I'm going to start by unfolding just a few very crucial ideas, four or five strategies that I think are the most important I have.

Let me get the first one out into the open immediately. It's something I already promised you: that you don't have to be all that good to make good money. This is a strategy that's so easy that most people just miss it altogether, though **I have to admit that it does presuppose one factor on your part: that you know your marketplace, the people that you're communicating to, very well.** The better you know those people — the more intimately you know who they are, what they're excited about, what turns them on, what they're spending their money on — the more money you will make, period. You need to understand exactly what they like about the products and services they're buying right now, and what *don't* they like. What problems are inherent in their lives?

▼▼▼▼▼▼▼▼▼▼▼▼▼▼

JUMP — and the net will appear!
√ Make the commitment first.
√ Set the deadline!
√ Run the ad — then scramble to put the fulfillment together!
√ Make <u>BIG PROMISES</u> to groups of customers — and then scramble to make them real!
√ Do whatever you can to force yourself to do more!

SECTION FIVE — Ruthless Copywriting Strategies

▼▼▼▼▼▼▼▼▼
MARKETING SECRET

The ideas that will make you the most money are evolutionary.

- You keep testing — tweaking — improving — adding — subtracting — and discovering newer and better ways of increasing your revenue.

- It's stupid to think you're going to make huge sums of money without a lot of testing and tweaking.

What gets them excited? What drives them crazy? What angers them? What frustrates them? **All marketing is, basically, is selling to people the first time, and then re-selling to them. Every successful business does that.** The more you know about the common denominators of the people you sell to, the more money you'll make.

From the very beginning, this was the biggest strength Eileen and I had. When we met Russ von Hoelscher in 1989, we'd been in the business for six months, so we were babies in the business. We didn't know anything back then, except for this one thing — **we knew the people we were selling to, so we were making about $16,000 a month. Not bad, right? We knew who we were marketing to because they were just like us.** They were people who habitually bought one moneymaking program after another, and that was my story, too. I understood how they felt; I was frustrated. I was angry. I was confused. I was disappointed by all these programs, and I was getting all kinds of criticism from my friends and family. My friends mostly just laughed at me. Most of my family laughed at me, too, but some of my family members, those who really cared about me, begged me to stop. In fact, my Dad, who was not a violent man, got so angry with me one day that he threw me up against the wall and shouted, "Look, give up these crazy ideas that you're going to get rich someday!" I was in my early 20s when he did it, and I was living at home — so obviously, I was broke. After being on my own for about eight years, I had to go live with him for a while, that's how broke I was. I was eating his food. I was under his roof. I wasn't paying any bills. I was running up his long-distance phone bill, and I was sending away for one get-rich-quick program after another. All I was doing was dreaming about making millions of dollars — when according to the normal scheme of things I should have been out looking for a job like the average person does. According to my dad, I should have resigned myself to the fact that I was never going to make any significant amount of money, and that I had all these things against me.

So he shoved me against the wall one day and said, "Get rid of these crazy ideas that you're going to make millions of dollars, because you're not going to do it. You're *never* going to do it." That's the same general mindset millions of other people are dealing with right now — though maybe not as extreme as what I went through. Maybe they don't have somebody who actually throws them against the wall. He was trying to get my attention, you know? And he did! But I was determined more than ever after that.

I didn't know it then, but there are millions of people out there who fit that demographic profile I just expressed to you. They're habitually buying one moneymaking program after another. They're addicted to buying these programs. **They've got a strong ambition and they want to do** *something***, so they keep buying programs — and they're frustrated and confused when those programs fail to deliver.**

When we finally put together a moneymaking system, it was called *Dialing for Dollars*. **This was our first little publication, based on a couple of programs that really worked for us.** We weren't getting rich, but we were steadily making hundreds of dollars a week, and it was the first time ever that we'd actually done that. So we wrote a little booklet about it. I was on all these mailing lists and I was getting all this stuff in the mail and I thought, "You know what? I betcha there are other people out there just like me." What I didn't realize was that there were *millions* of people just like me! So we decided to try to sell this little pamphlet, which cost us maybe 40 cents to print up, for $12.95. It was worth at least that, we figured, because it worked — it was a proven plan.

Before long, we were actually making about $16,000 a month from selling this plan — because we understood the market. We *knew* that, even though some of my family members looked at this thing and said, "Man, this is crap. This is total crap. You're selling this thing for $12.95? Look, you can't even write. It's filled with the worst sort of writing. It's terrible." It was a proven program, but they thought we were ripping people off. My dad's wife even threw it across the room one day when I showed it to her. She said, "That's crap. You're ripping people off."

But we *weren't* ripping people off; we were helping them. **We understood the marketplace; and because of that, we didn't have to be that good to make good money.** So I want you to realize this; if you forget everything else you read in this section, just remember this one thing, and let it be your foundation. Let it be your source of inspiration. **Just know that as long as you're writing to people that you already know about, people you understand at a basic level, you'll succeed.** You have to know what they like and dislike, who they are and what they're excited about. That was our strength, and it can be yours. Do this, and you can make a lot of money without having well-developed skills at all. **You just have to *really understand* the people to whom you sell.**

Your first few tries don't have to be great — just honest, enthusiastic, and good enough. *Dialing for Dollars* is a good example. I'm embarrassed by that little booklet today. I mean, it was written 20 years ago. I'm still not that good a writer today, but back then I was really bad! Yet it was good enough to launch a company and get some serious money coming in, if only because it was the right product for the right market.

You may be reading this and thinking, "Heck, I don't have the time, energy, or the skills to become a great copywriter." Well, come on — it doesn't have to be *great*. My friend Chris Hollinger tells me that when he was a teacher, one of the things he tried to do early on was to put an example out there for his students regarding what he was looking for in a particular assignment. And the students would close down, because they'd say, "I can't write that well. I'm not as good a writer as you are yet." His examples were intimidating to them. A lot of people are like that; when they see a piece of copywriting they just close down, saying, "Well, I'm never going to be good at it," so they just stop. But you don't have to be a prize-winning writer the first time around!

One of the best things you can do with copywriting is to copy the ideas and structure of the best copywriters you can find. Don't plagiarize, but use their work as a model. Pretty soon, you'll find that what you produce is passable. Keep writing, and you'll get better — though I'll be the first to admit that there's a never-ending learning process when it comes to copywriting. But good enough is good enough.

Knowing your market is absolutely crucial. If you're going to fire a missile at something, you'd better have an idea that it's at this longitude and latitude and this range, and that it's the second adobe building on the left; you want your missile to be guided. Any guided, targeted marketing campaign using ruthless copywriting strategies starts with knowing your market. Whether your market is the home-based opportunity market, or if you're a plumber wanting to take away your competitors' shares, **you've got to know what's going to motivate your customers to act.**

How do you do that? How do you get to know your market? In my case, I *was* the market. **That's the best advice I can give to anybody who's just getting started: go with what you know.** The time to experiment — the time to go into other markets that you think are cool but don't know anything about — is when you have a few million in the bank. **Become a customer of the kinds of businesses you want to emulate.** Collect their ad copy and study it closely. Always go with what you know.

And don't be satisfied with that, either. **Be aggressive.** Here's an example, again from Chris Hollinger. One of the things he did when analyzing the market was to call customers up and interview them — basically, he asked them directly what they wanted. For a while he ran space ads, doing a lot of advertising and marketing; he was generating a lot of leads and prospects, and he qualified those prospects and made some sales. But, quite frankly, he wasn't satisfied with his conversion rate. So he picked up the phone to ask people, "What are you looking for?" That gave him a very good feeling for what the prospects he was going after really wanted. It wasn't easy, but it was worthwhile.

Spending that time putting yourself in the prospect's shoes, understanding and thinking critically about their needs, is like Abe Lincoln sharpening his ax before cutting down the tree. It's critical to really understanding that what you're doing needs to be laser-guided toward the specific prospects you want to convert into sales.

Our *Dialing for Dollars* booklet speaks volumes about what I'm talking about here. It's a thin booklet; there aren't even page numbers. It *wishes* it could be a book. It's a little thing that hopes someday, maybe, it will grow up and be a book. And it did! But in its original form, it was a

▼▼▼▼▼▼▼▼▼
MARKETING SECRET

Quote as many reputable sources as you can to confirm your statements. This instantly increases your credibility. Now people are much more inclined to believe what you say.

- Use examples they trust — to make your claims.

tiny booklet — and it still did the trick. It got us started. It made us money. And more importantly, the system described in our booklet made money for the people who used it. **Its value came from the information it offered, not its size, not the materials it was made from.** Sure, I'm still a little embarrassed by it, even though there's no reason to be. Just like with my early sales letters, when I read it I think, "What was I thinking? What was I *not* thinking? Why did I write that?"

We do that sometimes. We're allowed to have those moments. The point is, that book got us started, and we were on our way at that point. **The important thing is to make that start.** If you never write a sales letter, if you never get started — well, there's nothing to analyze later. There's nothing to critique. There's probably also no money to be had, so you've got to do *some*thing. **It's a journey,** just like being a star athlete is a journey. Even if that person makes it to their sport's Hall of Fame, they didn't *always* play like a Hall of Famer. Most likely, when they first got started, they made some rookie mistakes. Everyone has a journey to success, and nobody looks back and says, "Okay, I did everything right along the way." In fact, those who succeed are usually the ones who simply manage to outlive their failures until they achieve success. Today, *Dialing for Dollars* is a representation of what it took for Eileen and me to get started. Even though it embarrasses us now, it's a part of our journey to success — just as what you do to get started today will be a part of *your* journey to success. Everybody looks back and critiques their early work, whatever it is. Artists, musicians, copywriters... everybody does it. **But it's a starting point and a** foundation, and you've got to have those in order to succeed later, to get to those works that you're proudest of.

We have sales letters we look at and say, "Wow! This one was right on target." It was the perfect message to the perfect audience at the perfect time, and everything about that offer was right on the money. **We know that because it worked like a charm and made lots of money.** But we also have the ones we look at and say, "Hmm, I don't really understand why I did it this way or why I did that," and **hopefully, as you're learning, you continue to have fewer of the kind that you shake your head at and wonder what you were thinking,** and more of the ones where you say, "Yes, I did it right," because you're using these strategies I'm showing you here. You're learning from them as you go.

There are writers I adore, people whom I know in my heart that I'll never be able to write like. I don't care if I live to be a hundred and if I work at it for hours a day, there is no way on God's green earth that I'm ever going to be able to write like some of my favorite writers. Let's face it: they just have more writing talent than I do. **But what they do is inspire me to want to be better, so that's a positive thing.** I read their work and I say, "Man, I've got a long way to go," so it helps move me forward.

But again, the point I want to make is that you don't have to be that good to make good money. **You just have to really, *really* know your market well.** So find a market that you know very well and get to work!

One of the people who attended the real-life seminar that this section is based on is a man from Maryland named Paul Daniels — and he's deaf. He brought a couple of interpreters from Wichita to translate what I said into sign language. I'm trying to sell him on the idea that he needs to go out and work with other deaf people, because if there's one group who will read those sales letters, it's deaf people. If you write a 60-page sales letter, they're a lot more apt to read the whole thing than most people are. Reading is the main way they get their information, and Paul could be an excellent spokesman for that marketplace. It's a niche market, and it's one he understands well — as you only can if you grow up deaf. When he goes out to speak to that market, if he does what I'm asking him to do, he's going to be able to communicate with those people in a much stronger way than anyone else ever could. They're going to pay attention to him. He knows what to say to them that will help him connect with them at an emotional, heartfelt level. So do like I'm suggesting Paul should do. Find a market full of people you understand at a visceral level; if you can do that, you don't have to be very good at copywriting. **You just have to focus on them. Marketing begins and ends with the prospect.**

Let's move on to another strategy, one that took me a while to realize. It's related to a big mistake that a lot of new copywriters make. In a sense, they're trying to drive their car down the road with one foot on the gas pedal and the other on the brake; in other words, they're trying to write and re-write at the same time. **I do my best copywriting as a two-part process.** The first part is when I just write and don't really think about what I'm writing about. **Instead, I try to think about the person I'm writing to, and what's most important to them;** I try to present the benefits of the product or service that I'm selling, in such a way that they'll get enthusiastic about them, will appreciate them and find them valuable. That's all I'm thinking about, the person I'm writing to — just like when I write a letter to my mom. I don't necessarily think about what I'm writing. I love my mom, I'm thinking about her, I know what's important to her, and I just sit there and write her a letter. I don't think much about it; I just do it.

Writing and rewriting are two entirely different processes that require two entirely different frames of mind. When you're re-writing you're critical. You're looking for all the misspellings, the poor word usages. **You have a critical analytical mind that's focused on details, and focused on looking for things that are wrong and things that could be improved.** When you're writing, you're just writing. You're focused on the overall goal, and you just put it all out there. **You can edit it later.** Some of our best sales letters, the ones that have made us more money than any other sales letters, started out being 30 pages long before they were edited down to size.

The mood to write can strike at any time, but **it's best to make sure you can write at a specific time every day.** I've already told you how I do most of my writing: I get juiced up on coffee early in the morning. That's my only real vice: I love good coffee. Now, I'll get a buzz if I drink too much. My wife tells me to quit drinking — she says, "T.J., you've had enough coffee!" It's almost the way you'd you tell an alcoholic they've had enough booze. I usually have to drink coffee for about 90 minutes before I ever write my first real word. Oh, I'm writing little things during that time, but mostly I'm just doing other stuff. I'm reading and getting myself in the proper mental framework, preparing myself. When I do start to write, I just let it all out. I'm not critical of myself at all. I'm focused on what I'm trying to do, which is selling. **It's all about selling.** You're trying to convince people to buy by giving them the benefits of your product or service.

I do my rewriting mostly at night, because I'm tired and I'm sitting next to my wife while she watches all these dumb TV programs that I pretty much hate. But I do want to spend time with her, because I'm trying to have a happy marriage and they tell me you have to spend time with your spouse to do that. And so,

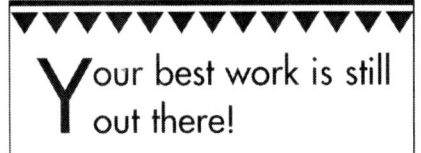

> Your best work is still out there!

she'll be sitting there on the couch and I'll be sitting right next to her pretending I'm watching the show, but I'm really just doing my editing work on my laptop. It's a relaxing thing. When I'm writing, I'm not really relaxed — I'm putting a lot of energy out there. So, one of my best suggestions is, **don't try to write and re-write at the same time.** It's using two different sides of your mind; it's using two different mental frameworks, and all you're going to do is make it frustrating. Not that writing isn't a little frustrating anyway, but **if you try to keep these steps separate, it'll be much more enjoyable for you.**

Also, you have to set regular routines. There are exceptions, but for the most part I only write at a certain time every day, and that's it. I do all my writing in the early morning. That works for me. My friend Jim Brewer writes all his stuff at one or two o'clock in the morning. You may have another time of day when it's easiest for you to write. The point is, there's that one time that's *your* time, whether it's in the morning, night, or afternoon. **It's a time when your energy is highest; it's when your mind is working the best.** I try to make sure I write every day during that time, because if I don't, I'm just not as effective. It's something that I like to do seven days a week, too.

Here's another tip that took me years to figure out, and I touched on it earlier. I used to look at other copywriters' work and tell myself, "Man, those guys are a hell of a lot better than I'm ever going to be," and I'd get very discouraged. What I didn't realize at the time — and what I want you to consider deeply right now — is this: they may want you to think that they just sat down and wrote those things, but the truth is, they do what I

MARKETING SECRET

There must always be some kind of good reason you are making someone a terrific offer.

- Build this reason or reasons into every promotion.

do all the time now. **They keep writing and rewriting until they just absolutely have to put the copy out to meet a deadline.**

Consider a sales letter that we were working on while hosting the seminar this section is based on: it's for a $5,000 package. We want to sell a lot of them, of course; and to get somebody to give you $5,000, you have to do a lot more selling than you would to get them to give you $500. So with the letter I'm talking about, we kept trying to make it perfect. Every time we went through that sales letter, we made significant changes — though eventually, we had to stop, because we had a deadline to meet. The point I want to make to you is that somebody who doesn't know better is going to look at that letter when it comes out and they're going to say, "Man, that guy can write his butt off." And maybe they'll be intimidated, because it's a really good letter. It's powerful. **But they're not going to realize that it went back and forth and back and forth and just drove me, Chris Lakey, and my assistant Keli crazy. It's grueling work.**

One night recently, I worked on an order form for close to four hours, and when I went to bed, I was almost ready to send it to the graphic artist — but there was something inside me that said, "No, wait. Take one more look at it tomorrow," even though I'd just worked on it for four hours. It was a little over a page long. It started out being three pages, but then I narrowed it down and re-wrote it and re-wrote it and re-wrote it. Well, the next morning I woke up thinking, "Oh, maybe I'll find a couple things wrong with it." But you know what? I found quite a lot wrong with it, and I made even more changes to it that morning — for probably a total of five and a half hours worth of work. Five and a half hours to write a little over one page on an order form!

Most people don't understand this secret. They think that somehow the copywriters who produce all the ad copy they see are just gifted somehow, and they write it all perfectly from the start. Well, there might be some of those people out there, but I ain't one of them... and I'm thinking most people aren't either. There are a lot of people out there doing just what I do all the time, every day. **They write it, then they rewrite it, and then they re-write it again** and they keep going over every sentence until, finally, they either run out of time or view it as perfect. They've done everything they can possibly do.

This idea of writing sales letters is funny to me, because if you're just looking at a sales letter, you might think it was written from front to back — that the writer sat down to stare at a blank screen, before all of a sudden coming up with a pre-header (that's the smaller print at the very top of the letter that goes right before the headline). And then you've got an idea for a headline, and you write that. And then there are a few words below that, and then you've got the "Dear Friend," and then you start writing the sales letter and several hours later you sign it and you write a P.S. and send it to the printer.

But that's not how most sales letters are written. **Most letters are just bits and pieces thrown together in a way that makes some organizational and reading sense,** and they might be written backward for all you know. **The money is made in the editing, not in the writing.** The first time you write, you're just dumping ideas on paper — and that's the best way to describe it. **You're taking everything and anything that comes to your mind, and you're dumping it all out onto paper.** I write it up on stacks of yellow legal pads, and poor Keli gets to type them up. I only get a few words down per page, because I write really big and fast, and that's really what it's all about. I freeform it, dumping it all on paper, writing anything that comes to mind. I'm thinking about the clients that I'm writing to, knowing in the back of my mind what I want the offer to look like (in general, anyhow), and I'm just writing longhand on legal pads. Maybe something else works for you — Chris Lakey is a typer. He grew up typing, so he's always done everything on a computer. Whichever way you do it, **the first process is getting those ideas down; a paragraph**

paragraph there. Maybe all of a sudden as you're writing you'll lea that might work for a headline, so you write that, and you make a note that it might be a good headline or a sub-head. Maybe you sit down and you write a string of bullets. **You think about the prospect who'll receive your letter, you think about your product, and you think about the main benefits you want to convey to them** — so maybe you spend an entire day just writing bullets down, documenting all the benefits you're offering.

When you're done with all that, you go back and try to piece it all together. You might say, "All right, this block of copy *here* would be better towards the front of the letter," and so you cut it and paste it where you want it to go. Then you look at something else and think, "Man, that would make a great P.S.," so you drop that piece down to the end of the letter. **You just mix and match, cut and paste, and write new copy as you need it — because of course it's choppy at that point, so you have to bridge things together.** You might say, "Hmm, these two paragraphs don't really flow that well. How can I write a new sentence between them to make them flow together?" and so you do that. It's a process of constantly patching and patching.

When I say "the money is made in the editing," what I mean is that, again, your first time through just involves dumping your ideas onto paper. It never comes out smoothly — unless you're doing it wrong. There may be some people out there who write sales letters front to back, but I don't know of any. In my opinion, the best way to do it is get those ideas out, and then edit. **When you're editing you're looking for the clarity; you're looking for multiple reader paths; you're looking for all the things that make your sales letter something that makes you money.** Sometimes the rewriting can take a week or two; sometimes it take a month or longer.

And let me be honest — there are times when we would never finish a sales letter were it not for deadlines. **There's *always* something to change.** Every time we look at a sales letter, we find something to change. Every single time. So at some point you just have to say, "I'm done. That's it. It's going to the printer." And even then, if you find out that it works, there's time to go back and edit it again for the second run. But there would be an *endless* number of things you could change. Sometimes we'll spend hours going over a letter word-by-word, sentence-by-sentence, looking for

How to Make Millions Sitting on Your Ass!

better adjectives, better ways to describe the product, more flowery language that simply sounds better. **We do that line-by-line, and it's tedious work. But in the end, when someone reads your sales letter, to them it doesn't read like you did that.**

I've never written a novel, but I imagine a novelist writes much the same way. They have their main story line, and they piece it together — and all of a sudden they've got it in chapters and it's all formatted and then it goes out the door. But there's always something to change. How can they make that character come alive a little bit better? How can they describe what's happening in that character's mind, and make it a little more flowery to the reader so that it's more exciting to read? We want that in our sales letters. **We want them to hang on every word.** We want to make each word have a maximum impact as it relates to the entire sales letter. Whether it's a four-page lead-generation sales letter or a 32-page back-end sales letter that asks for big money, we want to make sure every word counts. If you're editing sales copy and you find useless words in there, take them out. If there are words that aren't descriptive enough, change them. And if you need to add more words, just do it. You look at every phrase, every sentence, every word along the way — front to back — and that's all done in the editing process, which is what makes your letter make you money.

Here's one more tip I'd like to share in this chapter: **the swipe file. That's a collection of all the so-called "junk mail" you've received. This mail is not junk to you.** All that unsolicited bulk sales copy is like a textbook; **it provides models for writing, certain ideas that you can use over and over. Now, I'm not talking about plagiarism;** I'm talking about recycling ideas. I'll be writing something and I'll think, "Oh, hey, I remember this one guy, he wrote *this*," and I'll run over and check my swipe file, where I've kept a copy of that particular ad, sales letter, brochure, or whatever. I try to keep those as organized as I can, because there's a good chance I'm going to use it someday.

I might look at how he worded his guarantee, for example, or try to determine what made his headline powerful. Maybe it was just word choice, or the way he strung these emotionally charged words together that struck me as something that I really wanted to use. So I'll say, "Okay, I'm going to now take my swipe file, and I'm going to look at this headline. I'm not going to copy it verbatim; **I'm not going to plagiarize it, but I'm**

> ▼▼▼▼▼▼▼▼
> **MARKETING SECRET**
>
> They say you should do what you love and the money will follow... But I find it very productive to continually have one or two projects on the back burner that I hate!!! Why? Because I get some of my most creative ideas when I am avoiding the pain of working on these projects I hate!

going to try and generate the same effect." Having that swipe file full of things that you've identified as pretty good writing, going through and getting that idea, working that idea into your own... that's a powerful creative process that helps you synthesize the power, the emotion, the passion, the effect of a headline or a sub-head or even a guarantee into a great new offer.

Realize the Importance of Relationships

When writing copy, it's important to create the best, most grammatically correct copy you can — **but you must never, ever forget that the overall effect is more important than anything else.** Does it sell? Does it convert? Does it get people to take action? Does it strike a chord with someone so that they'll connect with you, so that a relationship can be built between you, as a marketer, and your prospect? That's paramount above anything else. **Successful marketing requires constant and consistent relationship building.**

The idea that you can have a relationship with your customers is just a concept until you actually live it; in fact, all of this stuff I'll teach you here is, really. You have to actually experience it to understand it. But one of marketing's strengths is that if you do it right, you can enjoy wonderful relationships with your customers, relationships where people feel they know you and you know them, because you *do* know a lot about them in advance. Remember, that was the first thing I told you: you don't have to be all that good, you just have to really understand your audience. **As long as you're writing directly to your prospects about things that interest *them* the most, and as long as you're doing things to let them get a sense of who you are, then you're going to grab their attention.** That's the basis of what I call "relationship building."

Some people take it to extremes. I'm trying to, when I tell my customers my personal story. Many of my customers know my story — and that's part of the way you develop a relationship, by just telling your story first off. **You use things in your story that are common denominators with your customer's stories. You try to let them get to know you; you try to be personable.** Every business should be in the business of developing relationships with their customers — whether you have a little restaurant and you want people to come back again and again, or you have a huge company that grosses a billion dollars a year. You're trying to establish bonds of trust and rapport with people. **Those are strategies that you incorporate when you write copy, so you're never writing "down" to people.** I know you've read stuff where the writer was writing down to you; and we've all spoken with people who spoke down to us, who weren't really trying to make a connection. These are people who are always keeping themselves at a distance, always keeping something from you. They're usually too polished, too professional.

I'm a jeans-and-T-shirt guy. That's just how I am. Sure, I could go out and buy a $5,000 suit, or get a haircut from somebody who charges hundreds of dollars an hour to snip every little hair just right. We've all been around people like that — people who are too perfect, too slick. I don't want to name him, but I have a person in mind that everyone in the marketing field knows. He always dresses in expensive suits, and every hair on his head is always perfect. He watches his words very carefully, so that when he talks to you, you get the feeling that every word was well-chosen before it ever came out of his mouth. He says all the right things. **And yet, the way he delivers it, the way he presents himself... well, I don't trust the guy at all.** I know that some of my colleagues feel the same way, because there's just something that's too polished about him, too perfect.

I feel that as a good copywriter, **what you're trying to do is make connections with people.** You can't do that if they can't relate to you. **You have to win their trust. All copywriting is really selling.** That's something I've said before in these pages, and yes, you're going to keep hearing that over and over. And what is salesmanship? **First, it's winning people's trust before you win their money.** People who don't trust you are going to be much less inclined to give you money — and most of the time they won't give you money at all. Even if they do, it'll just be token amounts; they're never going to commit to anything large. **You have to first let them know that you're somebody they can trust, somebody looking out for their best interests.** So you do things to build a true relationship with your customers. You're personable with people, you tell them your story, you tell them the things that you have in common with them — because common denominators are part of rapport building. After all, all friendships are built on either two things: a mutual enemy, or commonalities — things you share with someone else.

A lot of people are afraid to write in a warm, personable way. They're trying to be too careful, too perfect, too polished. In real life, those are folks we often run from or never fully trust. The same thing is true for all forms of communication with your customers. **Just be yourself.** Don't be afraid to tell your story; don't be afraid to show your picture. **You're a real person.** Don't make your copy too perfect. Oh, we talk about writing and re-writing to *try* to make it perfect, but you also need to have a likeable, humanistic element to your writing. **If your copy's too polished, that part of your writing dies.**

Chris Hollinger often kicks his copy up to his wife, who happens to own her own company, to proofread. Well, she's a stickler, so she changes certain words to make them more grammatical. **Unfortunately, that sometimes makes them less effective.** We direct-response marketers drive English teachers crazy! We violate the rules of the English language on a daily basis, because we write the way we talk. We're trying to sell, so we try to do things to build relationships. **If people don't feel they can trust you, they're not going to re-buy, so you have to write in a way that makes things feel personal to them.**

Here's an example. As of this writing, I've got almost two weeks invested in a 20-page sales letter. The problem with this letter is that it's been rewritten so many times that it's almost *too* careful. So what I've done is had the graphic artist put all these handwritten comments — hand marks, I call them — throughout the letter using a big, black magic marker to make it look more like it was just done off the cuff, and less like it was written carefully over a two-week period. And we're trying to make it more personal, so we're personalizing every page. The letter has the person's name at the top of every page, and on the P.S. it mentions their name specifically. We're paying extra money to have it done that way — thank goodness for modern technology! When the customer gets this letter — a 20-page letter with their name on every page, with hand marks all throughout it, with their name on the order form — they're going to feel like it was written *just for them*.

That's just one example of relationship building. There are many, many more. **Here's the gist of it: don't be afraid to tell your story.** Don't be afraid to get personable with people. Don't worry about being perfect. **People will forgive you for a lot of things, as long as they feel you're looking out for their best interests, and as long as they feel they can trust you.** We forgive our friends all the time — and what you want to do is create friendships with your customers. I know that that's just a concept for you right now, but it's a reality for the marketers who make the most money. Think about the relationships that you've had in your lives: what made them good, what made them great, what made them crumble, or what kept them from growing — whether those relationships were romantic, friendships, or family. The same principles apply to all. **The easiest way to connect with someone is to be open and honest, to be yourself.** Be willing to go ahead and open up to your prospects, to your customers — because it does turn to dollars.

> More business problems are created by <u>indecision</u> than bad decision.
>
> Go ahead and take massive action! Try many different things and fail and learn from all your mistakes while daring big and failing again and again!

Look at network marketing in particular: it's a multi-billion dollar industry built on one simple concept — relationships. How many companies say, "Okay, all you have to do is go get three of your friends or family in on this?" They're building their fortunes on the backs of other people's relationships. Well, **if you're using the right copywriting techniques, what you're doing instead of exploiting personal**

SECTION FIVE — Ruthless Copywriting Strategies

▼▼▼▼▼▼▼▼▼
MARKETING SECRET

Testing is like fishing — you use the BIGGEST hook and the BEST BAIT — and only fish in the areas where others have caught the biggest fish!

- Keep lots of lines out there, you never know what you're going to catch!

- "If you want to catch a whale, do not use a minnow for bait."
— P. T. Barnum

relationships is going out there and building new professional relationships with people, getting to know them through your copywriting. They're getting to know us, too. There's got to be a give and take — and that happens within a framework that we, as marketers, can control through the copy we produce for our prospects. Of course, it could involve more — it could be popcorn, or cookies. Food's a great relationship builder!

However you do it, you need to find ways to make your business relationships "sticky," so your customers never want to leave. **Serve them well, help them be more successful, so they keep coming back for more and more.** Chris Hollinger reminded me recently of a seminar we did up in Hillsboro, Kansas, at Tabor College, where two marketers did a very good job of making their sales stick — because they had an ongoing continuity program where people were paying a considerable amount of money every month for their services. They would take a nice chunk of that money and put it back into food, into gifts, into good quality information that they were feeding back to their customers, because they wanted to keep those customers paying that big chunk of change every single month. That all goes to building relationships and being creative. And here's the neat thing about it: most marketers don't even think about making their sales sticky!

Why is that so neat? Because it leaves you an opening to steal their customers away! That may sound ruthless, sure, but that's what good marketing is all about: capturing a significant part of the existing market share. **Most people don't even think about doing creative things**

to make their sales stick. So if you just go out and spend $200 on a bunch of popcorn and sent it to your customers, then a month later maybe your customers are sitting there and they're thinking, "Okay, I could go to XYZ for this item... or I could go there. Well, this guy sent me popcorn; I'm going to go there!" It's just human nature, and it's things like that that will get you ahead, because so many of these other businessmen and entrepreneurs are out there acting as part of that caribou herd, just doing what everybody else does. All you did was send someone some popcorn!

Now, I want to talk a little bit more about making sure you're not too perfect. None of us is perfect — though we feel bad when we're not. **If we could just all be real, the world would probably be a lot better place, and that's true in marketing, too. Just be yourself.** If you look too perfect, people will think something's not right.

Chris Lakey recently bought a car on eBay from a dealership in another city. It just so happened that he had a friend who lived in that city, so he asked this friend to go look at it for him. Chris got a report back that said, "Well, it's a nice- looking car." It's a little older and has a lot of miles on it, so Chris was concerned about it. If it was brand new he wouldn't think twice, but it's a well-used 2002 Suburban, so he wanted to make sure that the pictures he saw online matched what he saw when he was actually there looking at it. So his friend emails him and says, "It looks nice. It looks real clean. There are some scratches on it," which you'd expect. Nothing major, but this guy also said, "When I looked at the engine, it looked really clean." He was concerned that this meant maybe something was wrong. Was the engine new? Had it been replaced recently? The engine was too clean, and in his mind, that was a concern — because it looked too perfect.

I think people in general have that perception. **If something looks too good, if it looks too perfect, they question it. Whereas if there are some flaws, if things look rough around the edges, it looks real.** People believe it because it seems more authentic. It's just like if you have a relationship with someone, and they seem like a goody-goody perfect person... well, something's wrong with that picture, because no one is perfect. If someone seems too glossy, too slick, you're less likely to trust them. People think that way of your sales letters, too. **If your copy looks too perfect, then they don't trust it.**

Now, you can do things to make your sales letter look what we call "dirty." Earlier, I told you about a letter we're creating that has handwriting throughout. By putting handwriting on it, it looks dirty — that is, it just doesn't look as polished. You can also use different sizes and types of fonts. You can have some stuff in smaller print, and some in giant print. Some writers have even gone so far as to make their copy actually look a little dirty... like the paper doesn't look clean and sharp. I happen to think that's going too far, but the point is, people do it. Some people even put typos in there on purpose, because a typo makes it seem like it was written by a real person — by someone who pounded it out on the computer in a state of excitement and sent it out immediately. Having a typo in your letter makes it look more recent. It looks like you wrote the letter, put it on the press, and sent it right out.

Using improper English is a big way to make your sales copy look more real, more immediate. Now, English teachers and others who are super-critical about writing are going to look at your sales letter, and they'll either do what my stepmom did to my original *Dialing for Dollars* book or they'll *edit it for you*. We've had people actually send back sales letters with red ink all over them, like they were proofreading for us! But most people won't do that. **You want your letter to read like people think, and like they speak.** They speak differently than they write, if they're writing proper English. So forget all the English rules and "dirty it up" a little, so when people are sitting there with your letter in their hand and reading through it, it sounds like they're hearing you speak to them.

You don't want it to sound like you wrote a proper English paper. **It should sound like they're reading it as if they would *speak* it.** One of the ways you can help with that is to actually read your sales letter out loud, and have someone else sit there and listen to it. Or have someone else read it, and listen to it yourself. Does it sound like something you'd hear yourself say? If it doesn't, change it. **If it *does* sound like you would say it aloud, then you know you're on the right track.** Some people actually dictate their sales letters onto tape or a CD and then transcribe them, because the way you talk is simply different from the way you write. You want people to read your sales letter and hear it in their minds as if it were something you were saying, because it comes across better in their mind. So don't be too perfect, because perfection is never real. **People are more likely to trust something that seems authentic, even if it's not**

perfect. That's one of the reasons I fell in love with my wife 21 years ago: She's just an extremely real person. She doesn't B.S. in any way, shape, or form. She tells the truth, no matter how much it hurts.

And that's a good thing to do with your copywriting, because you need to keep in mind how skeptical people are these days. A big mistake many copywriters make is that they fall so much in love with whatever it is they're writing about that they have the delusion that other people are naturally going to fall in love with it, too. Nothing could be further from the truth. **People are very skeptical, even if they don't express it.** It's an unconscious thing for most, but we're all holding back. All of us are. Every time you see a claim, you're wondering in the back of your mind, "Can I really trust that person?"

Because people are always skeptical, you need to write to that skepticism. Assume that when you're writing copy, you're writing to the most skeptical person on the planet. You can't just accept they're going to believe anything that you say. You have to try to remember that.

I'll wrap up this one with an old quote, well worth repeating: "In the land of the blind, the one-eyed man is king." **You don't have to be perfect; you just have to be a little better than everybody else.**

Hone Your Salesmanship

Copywriting is nothing more than salesmanship, as I've already mentioned several times. And what is salesmanship, if you really think about it? **It's the ability to present your products and services well, and to get people to exchange their money for them. The best copywriters are the best salespeople.** They're people who know how to present their products, who know how to convince their prospects that what they have to offer is worth more than the money they're asking for in exchange. That's salesmanship in general — you're asking people to give you their money. Well, they worked hard for that money, and they're not going to just give it up that readily, especially in trying economic times. People always tighten up on their spending during hard times.

So you're always looking for effective ways to make offers to people.

▼▼▼▼▼▼▼▼
MARKETING SECRET

Don't ask for the order — DEMAND that they give you their money! Make them feel bad if they don't send you their money! This is what separates the BIG DOGS from the whimpering puppies!

That's what we sell, really — we don't necessarily sell products and services. **What we sell are *offers*.** And what is an offer? **It's all the things that you do to package up whatever you sell in an attractive way, to help get people to make that buying decision.** Here's an example: there's a man named Mike who attended the workshop this chapter was adapted from. One of the things he does is make wonderful soy candles, made from agricultural products grown right here on American soil. I bought a hundred dollars' worth a few months before the workshop, and just before he came down, he emailed me and said, "Hey, T.J., do you want some more candles?" Well, I still hadn't used the ones I had yet, so I said, "No, I'm good. Thank you."

But Mike's a salesman, and as a salesman, he wasn't going to take no for an answer. So a couple days later he came back at me with this other idea. He said, "Hey, T.J., I know how you always give out free popcorn to your customers in order to make them feel appreciated and to let them know how important they are." He said, "I'm coming down here to this seminar. Why don't I just make up a little candle that you can give to each and every person, to let them know just how much you appreciate them. You're already doing it with popcorn; why not do it with one of these healthy soy candles that I personally will make for each and everybody at the seminar?"

It was an offer! He made me an offer! I already liked him, and I was already sold on the soy candles. And then he made me an offer, and he wasn't going to take no for an answer. So I said yes. Something tells me that if I would have said, "Oh, Mike, that's a good idea... but no, thank you," a couple days later he would have found a new way to come at me with something a little bit different, and he would have kept bugging me and bugging me until finally I said, "Oh, why not. Let's give everybody a good healthy all-American soy candle." **I think Mike's case is great example, a perfect illustration of the things that salesmanship is all about.**

Remember, the copy you write isn't nearly as important as the strategies that you use. **And one of those strategies is that you've got to stay on top of people until they buy.** You've got to keep going after them again and again. New marketers often make the mistake of thinking that just because somebody doesn't buy the first time they send them the stuff, or the second time, or the third time, or the fourth time, then that somehow means they're not interested and they're never going to buy. Nothing could be further from the truth. It all starts with a qualified prospect, of course — nothing can replace that. You have to find somebody who really wants what it is that you sell. **As long as you have a prospective buyer you know is serious and they really do want what you offer, you've got a good chance to sell to them eventually — even if it takes a while.** As long as they're very qualified, you can keep trying. Sometimes it takes as many as 15 tries — so you keep coming at them again and again.

But let me caution you here: Don't come at them in such a way that you're bothering them too much. The best approach is to be altruistic in your approach. **Try to express the benefits; try to show them a self-serving advantage.** That's what Mike did for me. He tried to show me the advantage, using an argument I found hard to say no to. And he gave me a good price, because price is important.

Salesmanship is a subject that a lot of people know about, but few have ever given much thought. That is, they've never tried to actively apply it to their lives and businesses, though they know it's there. Worse, some salespeople aren't really salespeople at all; they're really criminals, con men. A few bad apples have poisoned the whole batch for us. For this reason, a lot of people have the wrong idea about what salesmanship is, because they've fallen afoul of cons who claim they're salespeople, but don't care one bit about their product or the people they're selling it to. They couldn't care less about trying to deliver things that are of real value. All they're trying to do is get your money.

Consequently, the whole art of salesmanship has largely been ignored. People haven't focused on it. Nobody wants to be a salesman! Why be a salesman, when the whole concept is that you've got to be some cold-hearted, manipulative, greedy jerk? And just because the title of this section is *Ruthless Copywriting Strategies*, don't think that I'm advocating treating your customers badly. **Being a ruthless marketer is more about just being aggressive — "ruthless" just sounds better.** We chose that word because it paints a different word picture than "aggressive." **If you're being truly ruthless to anyone, it's to your competitors, not your customers.**

As long as you've got a product or service that people can benefit from, as long as what you're selling really *does* have value that delivers on the promises that you make, and as long as you're targeting a qualified prospect who really wants what it is you're offering, then in some ways, **you're doing them a disservice by *not* doing everything possible to make that sale.** You really have to put yourself in that mindset. You have to convince yourself first that what I just said is true, and then you develop the strategies necessary to aggressively go out there and make as many sales as you can. **And you use strategies that let you multiply salesmanship.**

Previously, I discussed a letter that I've been reworking for a month; and as of this writing, I'm probably going to work on it for another month. It's a powerful sales letter. Once it's done, we're going to blast it out there to as many people as we can, using as many different media as we can. In this case we're going to use it in print form, and we're going to post it on a website that Chris Lakey's building. So it's salesmanship multiplied to reach as many people as possible, to make as many sales as possible. But here's a question you may be asking yourself: "With something like this, how do you know when to stop before you alienate your prospects?" That's a great question, one I've asked myself and my teachers plenty of times. The thing is, *everybody* is worried about going too far. Everybody! How far is too far? **The short answer is that you have to let the numbers tell you what to do. As long as you're still getting sales, then you haven't alienated your prospects; you haven't gone too far.** You may not have gone far enough!

It all starts with two-step marketing, which is a very simple, fast way to qualify prospects and *know* that they're qualified. In the first step, you get them to raise their hands and express an interest in what you're offering. They prove to you through that action that they're serious, that they really do want what it is that

> Create as many "businesses within your business" as you possibly can.

you sell. This first step can involve a small sale, so they're not just raising their hand saying "Send me your free stuff" — because sometimes people who send away for free stuff aren't qualified at all.

From that point forward, you have to watch your numbers and let them tell you what to do. Let's say, for instance, that I mail out 10,000 postcards to get people to take that first step to prove they're qualified. Suppose I get 400 prospects who say, "Yes, send it to me." They're showing me they're serious, that they want the offer I put out there in those 10,000 postcards. **Now I'll go after them on a sequential mailing system, where I continue to follow up on that initial offer.** If I get people calling me up and saying, "Hey, quit sending me all that stuff," then I've got to take a look at the numbers and see what they tell me. It may be that no matter how angry these people are, I find that every time I mail to that group of 400 people, I'm getting more and more sales. If that's the case, you ignore the angry people. Part of being a ruthless marketer is that you listen to the people who are giving you money — and you don't necessarily listen to those who aren't.

You have to be willing to take a little criticism and you have to be willing, as long as you're making good money, to keep going out there and keep applying the pressure. You don't have to apply that pressure in a negative way, though. **You don't have to be pushy.** You can be altruistic in nature; and when I say "altruistic," what I'm talking about is a situation where you're really trying to serve people. That's one of my definitions for selling, by the way. **Selling is serving.** You're trying to help people; you're trying to give them something that will benefit them.

Mike might have seemed a little pushy if, every time I said, "No, Mike. No thank you," he came at me two or three days later with a different offer. But he would have kept coming at me with a way of showing me why it was in my best interests to go ahead and write him a check and have him make these candles. He would have kept coming at me knowing what's

SECTION FIVE — Ruthless Copywriting Strategies

▼▼▼▼▼▼▼▼▼
MARKETING SECRET

Do everything possible to make your customers feel that you truly understand them.

- Make the connection.

- Let them know you are just like them.

- Tell a dramatic story that gets them to identify with you.

important to me, which is keeping my clients happy. He would have kept coming at me saying, "Hey, I'm not trying to sell you anything, T.J. I'm just trying to help you get something that's important to you." **You have to keep coming at people with that angle — and you have to be willing to have some people get angry with you.** If you're going to maximize your profit, you have to be a little thick-skinned. As long as the numbers are still good and holding out, just take the complainers off your mailing list and keep mailing to the rest of those people.

I've mentioned many times in my other publications and workshops that **the people you chase off this way are probably the people who aren't going to buy your item in the first place.** That's a good point that I believe I should re-emphasize here. From the standpoint of marketing and business, there are just two types of people: those who count and those who don't, and you've got to be able to separate the two. If someone's not giving you money, if they're complaining and giving you nothing but trouble, then they don't count. Now, if you've got a bunch of good customers who are complaining, then you've better wise up!

One thing that took me a little time to learn early on was the whole follow-up thing. I'd write a sales letter and launch it out there and maybe get some sales. But I hadn't learned the whole art of the follow-up and the sequential mailing. **Following up on interested prospects and on completed sales is vitally important.**

When we're talking about copywriting, we're talking about space ads, we're talking about classified ads, and we're talking about sales letters. **But a good part of the copy-**

writing you need to do in your business involves following up with prospects who have identified themselves as serious by raising their hands and saying, "Okay, send me the packet" — especially if that packet cost money. That's how you know you've got a real, seriously qualified prospect in this business. When you get a whole list of people who've sent you money, that's a pretty serious list. **You need to spend some money to focus in on those people, and try to generate as many sales as possible.** You do that with a follow-up campaign. I usually do it with direct mail; my colleague Chris Hollinger uses email. If he has a list of email addresses, or a phone blast to drive them to, maybe, he uses a conference call that he's got planned — anything he can do to get people to raise their hands and respond to his offer.

Chris tells me that one thing he did early on in his business — something he learned the hard way about — was blasting out more mail pieces than was prudent all at once. We've all done that. **What you should do is test that mail piece first before spending a whole bunch of money on printing and postage.** I've been guilty of this myself; I've sent something out there and the sales weren't where I wanted them to be, and I was like, "Crap, that was a bad list!" Actually, it very well could have been my poor copy! Or it could have been a lot of different variables. The point is that I gave up and moved on to something else, where maybe what I should have done was tested more carefully, and tailored my primary offer to results of that test. All that matters is results. **If you don't get the results you want, then take a really close look at your copywriting and at the systems you had in place.** What can you change to produce more sales? That's what testing is all about. Not only does it save you a lot of money, but it also helps you refine your approach to converting those sales, because in the end it doesn't matter how big a prospect you have. **The only thing that matters is conversion: How much money you make versus how much you spend.**

If you're smart, you'll test. I've lost a lot of money by not testing. Sometimes I get an idea and I'm all excited about it and I'm so confident it'll work that I think I don't have to test — I just throw it out there. And it sinks, despite my false sense of confidence. Remember, just because you're crazy about it doesn't mean that the people you're presenting it to are going to be crazy about it. It's easy to get caught up in your own hype.

Earlier, I mentioned two-step marketing as a way to really qualify folks. **With direct mail, you can do that with mailing lists.** There are hundreds of lists out there that you can rent. When you're researching those, you can usually find a little synopsis that will tell you about a particular list you're interested to try. Are those the prospects you think would respond well to your offer? If you think so, then you design that sales piece and you test it and get people to raise their hand and say, "Okay, yeah, I want to know more." **You're basically sifting and sorting, paring that big list down to the people who have identified themselves as those who want to hear what you have to offer.** Once you've done that, you're able to spend more money on that smaller group to convert sales.

There's no better way to make money than two-step marketing, where the first step is *always* to get people to take a smaller, simple action. People have sales resistance. Remember, everybody is skeptical; I talked about earlier. We're all careful; we're all cautious, and we should be. We know that if we're not, we're going to get taken advantage of. You never really know people. No matter how hard you try, there will always be some people that you just can't read. **So skepticism is necessary, and you should always expect it.** In a perfect world, if it weren't for skepticism, you could just go to a cold prospect — somebody who's never done business with you — and sell them something for thousands of dollars right out of the gate. But because few people are that trusting, we have to use two-step marketing as one of our strategies to separate the smaller group of the people who are qualified and interested in what we have to offer from the larger group that isn't. It costs money to do that. You've got to advertise, and you've got to do something to get people to take that first step. **There's always going to be some expense there; but once you get that smaller group defined, you're able to tailor your offers to them in ways that make you money.**

Now your whole strategy is to spend even more money per person, though less overall, of course, because the list now is so much smaller. **That smaller group of people has proven worthy of your attention.** They've proven that they're serious. **Now you can afford to go after them in a more assertive way, and you can try to do everything possible to make the largest number of sales to that group.** It's a great strategy; not only is it the most proven way to make money, it's also the safest way. As long as you never try to make people do too much too fast, you're guaranteed a profit.

Consider one of our current offers (current as I write this, anyway). We start with a $39 sale as our first step; we're not just giving away free information. Then, on the back-end, we offer them a $495 package. So we take the people who give us the $39, and we immediately up-sell them on a $495 package that's very closely related to the $39 package. It's a natural up-sell; it's a perfect fit, because it was designed that way. Then, from that $495 sale we've got a multitude of other items that we offer to that smaller group. **Once someone has given us $495, we know that they're very serious.** The question of whether they're qualified or not goes right out the door. You still have to wonder at $39, of course, because $39 isn't a lot of money. But $495... that's a lot of money to most people. When they give you hundreds of dollars, what they're really telling you is, "I'm serious about what it is that you offer." So you have to have more things to offer to those people. You may not be able to go from $39 to $3,900 in one step (though sometimes you can), but **you can stair-step your prospects from one price up the ladder to more profitable products and packages.**

Two-step marketing really is the best way to make sure you're spending your money in the right place. It's tough to try to make a cold sale to people who have never met you before or don't trust you, even if you're using a list that you're already familiar with. **If you'll first get them to raise their hand and say they're interested, you've got a much better opportunity to turn that lead into a sale.** Send them a short letter and tell them that you've got something exciting to show them and you want them to request it; maybe for free, maybe for $5, maybe for $39. By making them do something, they've expressed an interest. Once they respond, they can find out the whole story.

Not only does this qualify them, it gives you a chance to talk to them as someone who has requested information. You can be more firm with them. You can say, "Hey, I'm sending you this because you requested it." **When you do follow-ups with them, you can remind them that you're only communicating with them because they *asked* that you communicate with them.** This gives you a stronger position to approach them from, to try to get them to convert from a lead to a sale. It puts you at an advantage over them.

Now, I want to point out that you don't need to get hung up on the idea of two-step, because it really could be five-step marketing, or six-step

▼▼▼▼▼▼▼▼
MARKETING SECRET

Continuing to make BIG MONEY over a period of years never happens by accident. It is always the result of high intention, sincere effort, intelligent direction, and skillful execution. It represents the wise choices of many alternatives and the cumulative experience you gain from all the years of disciplined and focused work.

marketing, or ten-step! **Again, that's the whole secret.** Consider the restaurant business; that's my best example. Now, if you're one of my frequent customers or have ever heard me talk in public, I'm sure you're sick of me talking about the restaurant business, because I always do it; but it's a damn good example. If you've got a little restaurant — a business all of us can understand, because we all have our favorite restaurant — your goal is to get people to come back again and again, to keep sitting in the same seat they sat in last time. In some bars, they have one bar stool that's reserved for just that one person. A good restaurant's the same way. The idea is to get you to keep coming back. You understand how that works in a restaurant business.

What you also have to understand is, that's exactly how things should work in *every single business*. If you want to make the most money, that's how it *has* to work in your business! So, it's not just two-step marketing; it could be 222-step marketing. The idea is to get people to come to you to show that they're serious, and then your job is to do everything possible to develop relationships with those people and to provide additional products and services that give them more of the things you know that they're interested in. **Get them to keep coming back again and again, helping them to get more of what they want — so that you, in turn, get more of what *you* want.**

You can take these copywriting and marketing skills and directly translate them into any business that you want to be successful with. Maybe it's the restaurant business; maybe it's the plumbing business. A plumber could start by applying a strategy to target a specific area of a town, simply because the gas prices are so high that he doesn't want his vans and service people having to travel all over the city. Maybe it's an affluent area of town that he specifically wants to go after. He wants to concentrate his marketing in this one area, and he wants to get as many of the people as possible in this one area of town to be his customers. He's applying a specific strategy he's devised to do that, whether it's through mailers, or his ad in the Yellow Pages, or emails, or little refrigerator magnets — or whatever else he can think of. Now, once he gets that established and he's got that area locked up, he's forced his competitors to be the ones who have to spend the money and gas to drive all over town to do their business, whereas he's right there.

The point is, you can apply the strategies and direct-response marketing to any business. But it's something that, as I mentioned earlier, many businesspeople and entrepreneurs *aren't* doing. They're not using the kinds of headline writing and copywriting and marketing that I'm teaching you here to develop a selling system — because ultimately, that's what we're talking about. **We're talking about a *selling* system.** Whether it's a lead-generation sales letter, a follow-up offer, a Yellow Pages ad, or a space ad in the local newspaper — it's all part of your system for selling. **Once you have a system for selling, it takes a lot of the guesswork out of making money.** If you don't have that system for selling, then you're at the mercy of your customers' system for buying — if they have one. Even if they do, they'll buy things haphazardly, sporadically, only when they're really in the need for whatever they're looking for.

If any business is having sales problems, the answers to those problems can be found in their selling system. **How effective their selling system is has a lot to do with overcoming sales resistance, as I've mentioned, because people are skeptical and don't want to be sold.** Some companies use very manipulative, aggressive ways to sell you their products. For example, consider vacuum-cleaner salesmen — or better yet, people who sell water-purification treatments. These are some pretty savvy marketers, and I've had the pleasure of having them in my front room of my house, where I'm sitting there and actually taking notes on their system of selling, and what pressures they're putting on me. One of the pressures they use is fear. They have this little chemistry set they carry with them, and they'll take your water right out of the tap and add these chemicals to it. You see all that stuff start popping out of your water, and you're like,

"Oh, I don't want to drink that!" That's their system; they want to scare you into buying this high-dollar water purification system... and it works for them! If they get in your house, they know they have a system that closes sales. The numbers tell them if they can do enough prospecting to get in front of enough people, they're going to make sales, because their selling system works.

So a good, solid marketing system solves your sales problems. **Even better, a good, solid marketing system can be systemized to the point where it can be actually automatic.** It contains, first of all, something that got them to raise their hand the first time. With our current promotion, we ask for $39 in exchange for a package that we promise to deliver to them on a particular subject matter, which has to do with the recession and the nature of our economy, and all the associated things they're worried about. Once they buy, we have an automatic back-end up-sell that goes out to them immediately, trying to make that $495 sale. This is all brand new; we're just developing it right now. But based on other models we've developed in the past, the people who don't give us that $495 and take that up-sell right away will receive a series of postcards and phone blasts trying to make the sale. Maybe we'll do another tele-seminar for them. Those people who give us the $495 will receive a series of sales letters and postcards and other attempts to get them to move to a higher level with us and buy our additional higher-dollar products and services. We'll just keep doing anything and everything we can possibly think of until the numbers tell us that people just aren't buying, that we've already taken as much of the profitable business out of that list as we possibly can.

This is how marketers think. I'm not trying to reduce this to absolutes, but at some level it's all about the numbers. It's also about the people, of course, but you keep have to following up and following up and following up. **We create this marketing system once, and from that point forward it becomes automatic and systematic.** Felicia Crosby, our shipping manager, keeps all this organized. She knows that if it's Follow-up Letter #7, it's got to go out to *this* group on *this* day. All Chris Lakey and I had to do was design it once, and it becomes salesmanship multiplied. It works for us automatically.

This promotion could last a year or two, so that for a couple years we might have thousands of people sending us the $39. And then hundreds of those people might send us the $495, followed by five or ten follow-up offers until it stops being profitable. This organized, systematized marketing system is designed to do one thing, which is to sell. It's all about salesmanship, and the best salespeople are the ones who are the most aggressive. There was a book written by Zig Ziglar's brother called *Timid Salespeople Raise Skinny Kids*. You don't want your kids to be skinny, do you? Of course not. **Salesmanship is all about the person who's the most aggressive, the most assertive, the one who won't let you go** — the one who keeps bugging you until finally you say, "Okay, Mike, I'm sold. Bring the candles, and we'll give one out to everybody."

Develop Your Own Writing Routine and Style

To be an effective copywriter, **you have to develop a writing routine — and then you have to stick to it,** just like you'd stick to an exercise program or any other form of discipline if you wanted it to be effective.

> The best product does not always win, *but the best marketing always does!*

Make your writing routine a part of your lifestyle, because it's the one common denominator that all the best copywriters have. The thing is, no one can determine what routine works best for you except you.

Writing is a personal thing. Nobody writes the same way; everybody has different habits, large and small. **Your writing is an extension of who you are, so you should experiment with many different ways until you find what's comfortable for you.** Once you do find what works best, my best advice is to set it in stone. Every day, at that particular time, you *must* write new copy. At M.O.R.E., Inc., we try to have about four or five sales letters going at one time. Part of the reason is because we get bored of working on the same things all the time, so we try to have different projects available to work on. This helps fight the boredom a little. But boredom or not, the **copywriting has to be a part of your schedule every day.** You have to find a "best time of the day" that serves you best; not just the writing part of it, but also the editing part of it. I treat it almost as a religious ritual that I perform every single day.

SECTION FIVE — Ruthless Copywriting Strategies

MARKETING SECRET

Formula for Millions:

- Write your sales letters first.

- Then promise them the sun, the moon, the stars, and the sky.

- Then scramble like hell to figure out how you're going to actually give them all this stuff!

Discipline yourself to do this. None of this will come easily to you if you're not already a writer who does it on a daily basis. **It's a skill-set, and by its very nature a skill-set is something that has to be developed. But it's also something that's fun, creative, challenging, stimulating.** It's a beautiful thing... but it also can be a lot of work sometimes. I don't want to paint an unrealistic picture for you. It's challenging, which means that it's frustrating occasionally, and can be difficult at times, too. So anybody who tells you it's not any of those things isn't telling you the whole story — and I don't want to be like that. Yes, there *are* times when you're going to be frustrated. It's going to be somewhat challenging. When you run into those times, there are models that you can work from to get you through, particularly the copy of people whose work you admire. Remember what I said earlier about swipe files? **This is where they come in handy.**

Chris Lakey was talking to his son the other day after school, about why he needs to learn cursive handwriting. And Chris thought to himself, "You know, I don't think I've ever used cursive." Chris hates writing in cursive; as he puts it, his handwriting is a mishmash of all the ways he learned to write, and it's barely readable even to him. And let's get real — is there any practical purpose for writing in cursive anymore? Yet it's important to learn it, because it teaches discipline. If you're disciplined enough to learn to write in cursive, then that helps you in other areas of life, simply because you're learning discipline. You don't really *need* to learn how to write in cursive these days — it just teaches discipline. **I think that's what having your own copywriting style and sticking to it is about.**

Earlier, I talked about making sure you write at the same time every day. **A lot of these strategies I'll discuss in this section really come down to being disciplined.** I get up every morning and drink a pot of coffee before I start writing; that's part of my style, part of my discipline. I write everything out on legal pads first — longhand — and then I have it typed for me, and I edit it from there. It's the system that I've developed. It means that I have a system in place that helps me be disciplined enough to keep writing every day. Maybe a discipline for you would be to write so many words or pages per day, or write for so many hours. Maybe, for starters, it's just 30 minutes. If you don't have a lot of time you could say, "Well, I'll devote 30 minutes every day — from *this* time to *this* time — to writing. I'll learn to write sales copy by spending 30 minutes a day writing sales letters or writing ads." It doesn't matter exactly what that discipline is. Does it matter whether you get up every morning and write at 5:00 AM, while someone else does it better at 10:00 PM? No. Both of you could be excellent copywriters. **It's not the actual time you write, or even necessarily how much time you spend at it. What's important is being disciplined, and what that gets you.**

Let's take a look at personal style. Style is something I liken to a movie producer, or maybe a fiction writer. Each has a style. When you see a movie made by a certain producer, you can peg it. You say, "Oh, I can tell that's a Spielberg movie," or whatever, because you know their style and that their movies tend to have the same flow; the feel is similar from one movie to another. A fiction writer sometimes can have the same thing; for example, John Grisham writes legal thrillers, and there's a certain style there. You, as a copywriter, can also have a certain style.

Many marketers produce newsletters that have a certain feel to them. They've got a noticeable writing style, and people get used to that. **Having a discernable style is important, because it helps people get comfortable with you.** They get to where they know and like your style, and that's one reason why they do business with you. So continuing to write in that style becomes important; it can be a benefit to you from the relationship-building perspective.

Having said that, one thing that you can do to start on your road to becoming a better copywriter is to find some really good sales letters and copy them out in your own hand. **As you go through this exercise, as you're actually physically writing out each word, you start to think**

about the elements that made this particular piece of copy good. This gives both your muscle memory and your brain time to absorb the strategies and concepts that went into developing a particular sales piece.

For example, you may see a huge headline in 38- or 42-point type and ask yourself, "What emotions is that headline stirring in me personally? Why is it such a big headline? What's it saying? How is it saying it?" Do that enough times, and things are going to come together for you. **Connections are going to be made in your mind as to how you can then go back and write your own copy and innately incorporate the elements that you've learned from somebody else's writing.** Because you took the time and were disciplined enough to do that, the exercise in and of itself is the reward — because there will be things your mind absorbs that you don't even know you're learning as you're copying. It's an exercise in discipline, because who really wants to copy something in their own hand, over and over? It takes some work to do that. But this is work that eventually puts money in your pocket — heaping piles of mailbox money.

Is it worth it to spend that time? Of course it is. Do you want to do it? Is it hard? Yeah, it's hard. Chris Hollinger used to be a basketball player and coach. But every time the season would start, season after season, from Bitty Ball all the way through grade school and college, he was always out of shape at the start of the season. He didn't want to do what it took to be in shape at the start of the season, without the coach there, pushing him and his teammates to get in shape for that first game. None of it was fun, but they were better for it.

I've read a couple of books on Oliver Stone's filmmaking. In one of the books, they interviewed Michael Douglas about the movie *Wall Street*. Douglas said that Oliver Stone made his life a living nightmare for almost four months, because he kept making him re-shoot shots over and over. He would give his best performance and Oliver would say, "That's terrible. That sucks. Re-shoot that." He made Michael Douglas' life a nightmare for four months, re-shooting shot after shot after shot. He was so glad when that four-month period was over; he said, "I hate this guy. I hate him!" Then he won an Academy Award for his role in that movie. And as he got up to collect his Academy Award, he told the story about how Oliver Stone just drove him crazy for four months and made his life a living hell by making him re-shoot all these scenes over and over again... but they got it *right.* That's the good thing about discipline.

As an entrepreneur, when it's your business and your butt on the line, can you get motivated to be disciplined enough to do the kinds of things that you *need* to do, to improve yourself so that your bottom line improves? **The answer had better be yes.**

This is how I feel about discipline: It never feels good as you're doing it. **But it always feels good afterwards, once you've paid the price and profited from it.** There's some discipline involved in writing; all the writing teachers will tell you that. It does require routine. That strategy I told you earlier, where you repeatedly write the same good ad over and over again until you internalize it? The famous Gary Halbert wrote about that in his newsletter 15 years ago. When I did it I chose Joe Karbo's "Lazy Man's Way to Riches" ad, which is a full-page ad that made Joe millions and millions of dollars. I knew it was a proven ad, so every morning for 45 days in a row, I spent a little less than an hour just re-writing that whole ad, word for word. I did that every single morning until I could almost do the whole thing by memory. And what I found was, there's a language to it all. **There's a rhythm to good advertising.** I see similar metaphors in the music world. If you study the lives of some musicians, you'll find that no matter how famous they got, no matter when they ultimately achieved their fame and fortune, they all started out by playing other people's songs first. First they learned how to play the Beatles songs, or the Rolling Stones songs, or the other popular songs of the day on the radio. They learned the chords, they learned how to play other people's songs, and then slowly, over a period of time, they developed their own style.

When I took drum lessons 27 years ago, the very first day the drum teacher showed me this drum pattern to play and recorded it for me. He showed me exactly what to do and then he said, "Look, I want you back here one week from today. Every day I want you to practice for at least an hour, just playing this little drum pattern. Every single day, try to match what I just did, what I showed you how to do. You can call me if you have problems during the week." So I called him every day! I could never do what he tried to show me, but he just kept encouraging me, saying, "Just keep going... keep going... keep going."

Eventually, months later, I told him, "You know, Keith, I never *have* been able to play that pattern." And he replied, "Well, I knew you never

SECTION FIVE — Ruthless Copywriting Strategies

▼▼▼▼▼▼▼▼
MARKETING SECRET

Your customer list should be thought of as the ultimate testing ground to develop an endless number of successful new customer acquisition campaigns.

1. You develop these new promotions for your best customers.

2. You take the things that work the very best...

3. Then you use the most successful ideas and methods to attract new customers who have never done business with you.

---

would be able to play it, because it was a little too advanced." As it turned out, it took him years to learn how to play that pattern himself! He said, **"But through the process of *trying* to play it, I knew you'd develop something that was your own, that was based on something sort of like that."** And sure enough, that's still the only drum pattern I can really play 27 years later. It never did sound like it sounded with him — but it's my own style.

Good writers have their own style. We used to have a freelancer who did a bunch of work for us before I was good enough to do my own new-customer acquisition, which is the hard part of our business. This freelancer copywriter out of Denton, Texas wrote the same sales letter over and over again. That's all he did his entire career (he's retired now). You could take a hundred sales letters, where just 10 were his, and put them up on the wall — and if you knew him at all, you could walk along and say, "That's Luther's. That's Luther's letter. That's his letter. That's his letter." He just kept re-writing the same sales letter over and over again. Now, his sales letters all worked. They all produced profits, and that's really the only thing that counts in the end. But he had his own style; he had his own way of writing. **It's something that anyone can achieve, but it does take time, work, effort, energy** — and that's the bad news. You get it through daily routine.

That's one reason I want you to get rid of the words "junk mail." It's true that some of the stuff you'll get really is junk mail; some of it's not well-written, and it doesn't look good. But a lot of what some people call junk mail is treasured by us copywriters, and we save it in our collections. One of the best compliments anybody ever gave me was when I met this famous marketer in Jacksonville, Florida, in 2002. I'd never met him before. He came up to me, shook my hand, and he said, "I've got a whole box at home with just your stuff in it." That's the ultimate, supreme compliment a copywriter can get. **We save back the well-written sales copy because we look at it, we study it, and we get ideas from it.** If you look at enough of it, you'll get an eye for what's good and bad. It's just like my printer, Steve, is with stuff in his field. He can look at any piece of printing and he can say, "Oh, this is terrible. This is just terrible." Whereas we might look at it and we say, "Hey, it's not terrible. It looks pretty good to me." And he says, "No, no... look at this, and look at this, and look at the fuzzy lines over here. Man, that's not right. And look what they did there." He has a trained eye, and that enables him to see things that a person who's not in the business can't see. It's the same thing with good copywriting. **If you read enough sales letters, you'll see the same ideas over and over, the same themes, the same language — and that's a good thing, because you realize that it really *is* simple.**

I drink a lot of coffee in the morning when I'm writing. I have one brand that I really like. I've tried others, but this is the one that really works for me. I know just how to make it, and just how much of it to drink, and I get that good caffeine buzz. After about 90 minutes of drinking coffee, I'm ready to start writing. I grab the legal pads and start writing as fast as I can. I know what I'm going to write about and I know the general ideas, but I don't think about it too hard in advance. That's where I take a page from Neil Young, one of my favorite musicians. He's written five or six hundred songs, and he says, "When you think, you stink." What he means is what I said earlier, when I told you that **you needed to view writing as two separate processes.**

Process one is where you just write and don't edit. You just don't even think; you just let it all out. That's what I do. I drink my favorite coffee, I grab my favorite legal pad and my favorite pen, and I start writing as much as I can as fast as I can. The reason I do that is because that's how I used to see Russ von Hoelscher do it. Back in 1989, Russ used to come to our home for the weekend to work. He always told us, "Whenever I come to your house, make sure you have a big stack of legal pads for me, and plenty of pens!" And Russ drank a lot of coffee! I sat and watched him, and we would talk about these different ideas for promotions and things we were going to sell and things we were going to do, and different product ideas. And then all of a sudden, Russ would get all excited and start writing real fast and I'd shut up (which is hard for me to do!). Russ would write like crazy until he finally ran out of steam, and then we'd just talk. We'd eat and we'd drink some more coffee and we'd talk a little bit more — then Russ would get excited again and he'd start writing again! Then, when he left on Sunday, we'd take that big stack of legal pads over to our typist, who would then type them all up into sales letters. We'd put them out there, and people would send in their money.

It's simple! You write the copy, you put the letters out, and people send in the money. I learned it by watching Russ. I developed my own style of writing by copying him, and I didn't even know that until about 15 years later. We talk a lot in this business about the importance of models, and not only in this sense, where I picked up my style from Russ — as a child will model after their parent in so many ways. There are other models. There are sales letters that are already written by other people that you can model yourself after. **Now, you can copy the structure; you can't plagiarize, because that's illegal and immoral, and shows no creativity on your part.** You're taking little bits and pieces from a lot of different people, and you're finding your own unique way to combine them. There are lots of models out there.

The way to do that is to get on the other side of the cash register. **Stop thinking like a consumer who only buys stuff.** A consumer buys mostly in an unconscious way, and they just keep buying. **There's a certain mentality to being a consumer, but there's another mentality of being the marketer, where you're thinking about how to go out there and reach consumers.** So start looking at ads and sales letters for themes and ideas and structures, and start trying to see them as a businessperson sees them. Then model accordingly, and start developing your own styles. Past that, you're simply doing what Luther did. Once you develop your own style — once you've got some experience under your belt, and you have a bunch of sales letters that you've already written — now you're just copying yourself over and over again. A lot of our sales letters look the same for this reason, because at some level, they are. We're copying from ourselves now — and you can't steal from yourself, really. **As long as it makes money, why reinvent the wheel?**

Models can be anywhere. Anytime you see something that looks interesting, put it into your swipe file. Of course, you need to make sure your swipe file contains good models only; there are bad models, and you don't want to get caught using one of those. **Be sure, when you're swiping something, that you know it worked.** You can find models for your swipe file in all kinds of places; just keep studying the media that reaches the same marketplace you reach, or that you're trying to reach. If you're in the business-opportunity market, for example, look at ads running in the business-opportunity magazines. See which ads are repeating month after month, and use those as models.

You may have a different opportunity than they do, but you can use their models. **If you see a lot of ads that have the same kinds of headlines, then obviously they're working, still bringing in money.** Just as an example, if the headlines that keep working over and over again use the same font, then you can make your headline match that font. In a similar vein, you can do other things to make your ads look like the others. It can be completely different copy, but it can have a similar look and feel if you know that look and feel has produced results. If you see someone mailing a sales letter in a certain type of envelope and making money at it, then put your sales letter out in a similar envelope. That way, you're using a model that mimics what's already proven to work.

> Most marketers are weak.
> - They quit way too soon.
> - They are too worried about offending their prospects or customers.
> - Or, they simply don't know that there is a great deal more money laying on the table that could and should be theirs — if they simply went after it more aggressively and then stayed after it until they got it!

Of course, if you've run a successful ad yourself, you can use your own model: you can make your new ads look like your old ads, or your new sales letters look like your old sales letters. **It's all about finding something that you know worked, and then modeling your new offer after it.** Maybe it's something in the offer. Maybe it's just the way the sales letter looked, the size of the letter, the font, maybe the color of paper, or

▼▼▼▼▼▼▼▼
MARKETING SECRET

My very best marketing ideas always come after I have spent well over 1,000 hours working on each project!

- By that time — my brain is sizzling hot! And the ideas start flowing like lava from an exploding volcano!

maybe you're matching an envelope. You can model all kinds of things. There's so much out there that's already been done that creativity is overrated in direct-response marketing. There's so much good stuff out there to sample that to sit down with a blank paper or screen, with no idea of what you're going to write, is a big waste of time. It's a hassle, and it slows you down. **Use models to your advantage, and it can be really profitable.**

There are so many things out there to borrow ideas from. Take a look at the advertising and marketing that's going on around you, almost on a 24/7 basis. Wherever you're at, there's someone out there with a sign, with a headline, with a teaser, with something to grab your attention, something that's designed to get you to do business with their company or pay attention or invoke some curiosity. Before I got into the field, I didn't pay much attention to most advertising, as most people don't. Most of us are so inundated with advertising that we tune out the vast majority of it. **As a marketer, though, my antennae are always up to catch an idea or a headline or something that I can use —** and I really like what some newscasts and media outlets do.

Tonight, while you're watching the news, note how the anchors do it. At the start of their program, they'll give you a little teaser to keep you hanging around till the end, won't they? They'll say, "Stay tuned for details on..." and they won't give it to you till the end. But what did they do? They just used one little blurb to pique your curiosity. I've even sat there for the whole hour, getting mad because I know that they've totally manipulated me to sit and watch the entire newscast just because they've piqued my interest — and they're not going to give me that payoff until the end.

The trick is that when you see a teaser, you can turn the TV off for about 50 minutes. You know that if they "tease" it, they're not going to show it until later. Sometimes they'll tease at the top of the hour for the bottom of the hour. Generally, it's either at the very bottom of the hour or the very end of the program. If you see a teaser, you're going to wait.

Now, how can that be applied to your copy? Can you start developing your skills to generate people's curiosity? Can you use a headline where the only intention is to get your reader to go, "Hmm, that makes me curious"? **When someone is curious, they'll have an innate desire that compels them to satisfy their curiosity.** That's an element of human nature that you can start weaving into your copy, whether in a headline, a sub-head, a pre-head, or in the body itself... to the point where you get them curious, you heighten their curiosity even more, and then they're absolutely compelled to read the rest of your copy so they can satisfy their curiosity. It's just another element you can use to sweeten your copy. So look for how other marketers have used curiosity, fear, greed, love, and any other human emotion to get their reader or viewer to pay attention and take that desired step. **With a teaser, you're telling them to "stay tuned" for this life-shattering information that you're only going to receive here.**

This is a strategy that's used over and over again by good writers. Once you become aware of it, you'll see it repeatedly. The writer will say something like, "And in a minute, I'm going to show you..." and then they make you some wild promise and get you all excited and they say, "More on that in a moment. But first..." So you have it in the back of your head — and then they keep doing things like that to keep you getting involved, taking you by the hand so that you don't lose your interest. In face-to-face sales training, they tell you that the idea is that you're supposed to try to get people to nod their head and agree with you on all kinds of simple, easy things — so when it comes time for them to ask you for the order, you're continuing to nod your head. You see it all the time.

Once you become aware of this, when you consciously start trying to see how other people are trying to sell to you all the time, you think to yourself, "Why do I do what I do?" You know, most people buy in an unconscious way. The factors that cause them to spend their money are emotionally based. **So the idea is that the more you can understand yourself and why you buy what you buy, the better you'll be at understanding why other people buy things.** What is the motive here? Why are you so excited about all this stuff? Understand that, and you'll understand other people, too.

One of Chris Hollinger's favorite movies is about Beethoven — *Immortal Beloved*. There's a part in the movie where Beethoven is describing to the guy who will become his secretary and life companion about what music can do. He asks the guy, "Now, what's this piece of music all about?" And this guy starts to describe very superficial things about the music itself. But Beethoven comes back with, "No, music is about taking the listener into the mind of the musician." That's where Beethoven starts talking about how he wrote this particular piece because his carriage was bogged in the mud when he was on his way to a rendezvous with his love, and he couldn't get to her because of the mud, and he tried to express the angst and frustration that he felt.

It's our job as copywriters to enter the conversation that's already going on in the minds of our prospects. That's the art I'm talking about. **Once we've entered that conversation, it's up to us to take them where we want them to go — which, ultimately, is to get them to buy what we have to sell.** So you've got to consciously be aware of the fact that the habits and routines that are involved in developing your art form are critical. I don't consider myself an artist by any means, but I'm involved in an ongoing process of discovery, of learning, and of discipline. Like any creative person, there are days where it's hard to write anything that I think is even remotely good; and then there are other days where it just pours out of me.

So be mindful of all the things that you can draw from — whether it's a teaser on a letter or an example from big business. Hell, you can learn a lot from big business. Microsoft, for example, is very good at letting mavericks go out there and do the testing for all their new technology. And then they come in after the market has already been somewhat created and tested, and do the originators one better. They've seen what's working out there, and then they take it to the next level. You can do the same with your models. **See what's working, and borrow some aspect of it** — whether it's an envelope or a headline or a particular genre. Don't just come in there and try and capitalize on it just because someone else is doing well with it.

Sure, if you see a bunch of marketers doing something and making money with it, that means there's money to be made in that market; **but you can do even better.** Come in and capture more of that market than they have, by using more of the same but better. Infuse what they're doing with better ideas and new elaborations they haven't thought of. Be mindful of all the marketing and advertising that you can use to capitalize on and reach that entire market.

Chris Hollinger told me about a church near his house that's really packed every Sunday. They have a big marquee out by their parking lot, and the pastor posts the best headlines up there. He does a really good job with headlines, and I want to share some of those that he's used — because obviously, the church is successful. It's been there a long time, and Chris has noticed that they have a good mix of older and younger congregation members. One week the headline was, "If God is your co-pilot, swap seats." It's always something catchy like that! Chris says he giggles every time he drives by it, even though he doesn't agree with this particular denomination. Once the headline was, "Stop, drop, and roll doesn't work in Hell." It's not like I'm going to use that particular one in a sales letter or anything, but it was a great headline! See, my antennae are always up, looking at billboards, looking at signs, and all the advertising that I hear, see, and feel. What's going on around me hopefully translates into making me a better marketer. **I think that that's a good point to remember: to always be looking for ideas you can use.** That's not just true of copywriting, it's true of marketing in general. Just being in tune and having your radar up and watching for what other people are doing, just being receptive to other advertising messages and noticing them and seeing how you can incorporate them into your business, can make you a lot of money.

I got something in the mail recently that I was completely surprised by. It was a political letter. It was a guy running for a local office... except that, in the end, he decided *not* to. When he wrote the letter, he was expressing concerns that he thought he could fix if he won the office. At the end he had an attachment that said, "You know, after thinking about it and verbalizing all of my concerns, I've decided that the best person to do this is me. So I want you to write me in. It's too late to be on the ballot officially, but I want you to write my name in." What was really weird was what I found on the back of the envelope, a sticker that he put there after it was sealed. The sticker said, "I changed my mind. I don't want to

▼▼▼▼▼▼▼
MARKETING SECRET

Your sales letters must be so clear, simple, and easy to read that the dullest, laziest, and stupidest person quickly understand them.

- Dumb-it-down and keep dumbing-it-down!

- You are writing to apathetic people who don't care about you!

run for office, but I think all my points in here are still valid, and I'd like you to just look them over — so I thought I'd go ahead and mail this to you."

First of all, I thought that was funny. It was interesting. Here he is, running for this small township office, and there's this sticker on the back where he says, basically, "Ignore what I said about running for office at the end of this letter." But all the rest of this stuff in the letter was valid, and he wanted people to consider it. He listed 10 grievances he has with the current administration, and how they're blowing our money. He decided he was the best man to fix it, and asked us to write him in on the ballot. But then, on the sticker, he says, "On second thought, I don't want to run for office. But still, these are concerns I had, so I thought I'd share them with everybody before the upcoming election." **The sticker became the tease!**

And I thought, "Man, I don't know how exactly to use that, but I've got to find a way to use it. Here you've got a letter that's sealed up, and then on the envelope is a sticker that offers a last-minute thought or something like, "Here's something I couldn't get this inside the envelope," or "Ignore what I said on page 18," or something like that. **That's a great tease. It struck me that something like that will make you open the envelope.** Otherwise, if I would have recognized it as political letter, I might not have even bothered opening it up. He put *personality* into it. That made me open it and find out what he was talking about inside.

You just have to be in tune for unique, useful things. Normally, you might not think such a thing would have any application for business. **But I saw it as a way to get people to open the envelope.** Just stick something on it that points to something inside. It makes people curious; it makes them want to open your envelope and read your letter to find out what it is that you want them to ignore. It's going to get people's attention. **The point is, if you're just being watchful and mindful of what's going on around you, ideas for copywriting will come from all over the place.** So keep something with you where you can note them down — a legal pad, or little notebook, or even a cheap voice recorder. When an idea strikes, record it so you can use it later. You never know when one of those ideas will hit you, or when you'll remember it as you're working on a new idea or a new letter. You may suddenly, unexpectedly, find the perfect place to implement that strategy.

Embrace News-Style Advertising

Let me hit you with a nice little headline: **News-style advertising gets up to *500%* greater response than image advertising.** That's a fact. If you've got a business of any kind and you're thinking about doing some marketing, **don't skimp on the news-style advertising, because it gets up to five times the response of plain image advertising.** And these are industry- specific statistics — there have been plenty of studies on what works and what doesn't. Obviously there are a lot of big companies out there that spend millions of dollars on image advertising, basically protecting their brand. They're not asking for anything specific, they're not selling anything specific, and they're not asking the prospect to do anything specific; they're just saying "This is my brand," so no one else will lay claim to it. Unless you're a multinational, you probably don't need to do that.

News-style advertising gets up to 500% greater response than color brochures, business cards, and all other forms of product or image advertising. Why? Simple — news-style advertising doesn't look like advertising. **It looks like news.** Very few people read advertising, but a lot of people read news. If it looks like advertising, most people won't read it. The reason's simple. We're all inundated with advertising, so we have to tune it out. **News-style advertising gets by this filter.** When you see a news story, you see a pre-head, a headline, a sub-head, a story. A good news-style ad will have all the same elements — just like all the sales letters I've been talking about throughout here.

Let's take a look at a popular form of advertisement: the Yellow Pages. You can go to any Yellow Pages in the country today, rip out a page, and you're going to see a bunch of ads that look exactly the same. You could literally go in there and swap out the names and the telephone numbers in a particular category, move them from ad to ad, and those people wouldn't notice a difference in their business.

But after hearing the statistic that news-style advertising gets up to 500% greater response, don't you think that maybe if you paid attention to some of your copywriting and made your ad stand out dramatically from your competition, then you might come out on top? This is where people compete with their ads. But all the Yellow Pages guys want to do is sell ad space; they don't care about the real ad. And they want it to be homogenized, too. That's the whole thing about traditional Yellow Page advertising: they don't want to upset any of their other advertisers. They want to make all those ads look exactly alike, and they're ineffective because of that.

So take the next Yellow Pages ad you're planning to run and start applying some of the copywriting strategies I've explained. **Try using a news-style headline that's benefit-laden for the customer** — or maybe a unique selling position, built into your headline, that's automatically going to out-perform all the other guys on the same page, because it's proven to work. We know that we are, by and large, employing proven strategies. Recently, Chris Hollinger sat down and wrote a headline right off the top of his head, based on some of the things I've been talking about. More than likely it's going to change during the editing process, but I think it's great, and it's easy to imagine and prepare in a news-style format.

Here's the headline: "This May Be Your Only Opportunity *Ever* To Lock In Your Spot At The Top Before The Big Boys Blast Their Way To A Fortune." Notice how all the words are capitalized. You can juggle some of the elements of the headline to make them stand out; for example, in Chris's original headline, the word "Your" was a lot bigger than the other words. He's saying "This may be YOUR only opportunity ever...". Now, why would you want to use a word like that? **Because you want to make it benefit-laden to the person reading it.** You want to get their attention — so you make it bigger, or maybe you underline it. **You're trying to** make the person reading it see the benefit of locking in their position before the big boys do. It's YOUR turn to be on top, right? Below is a subhead and a piece of the copy that says, "With this economy, wouldn't it be great for you to make heaping piles of mailbox cash automatically, by being at the right place, at the right time, ahead of some of the biggest and best marketers in the world?"

This is based on the news-style advertising that I'm talking about in this chapter. Chris has no idea, at the moment, whether he'll use this headline. It'll probably change — and doubtless will have by the time you read this. But it's still a great example of news-style headline writing and copywriting, of the kind that's proven to be more effective than image advertising. **It's considered news-style because it talks about something that's brand new.** It uses a new angle on a brand new upgrade that they're going to be able to lock in before it really gets up and going. It's a beta-tester deal. But by calling it news-style, we're talking predominantly about how we use news-like headlines, sub-heads, body of information, and more. **This is the news-style print that gets people's attention and then, ultimately, asks for action of some kind.**

Our job as salespeople — or as copywriters — is to get people to trade their money for what we're offering. That's what it's all about. **Our job is to give people what they want.** There are few things people really want, and one of them is whatever's new.

Strive to be <u>more</u> "human" in all of your communications.

√ Be real!
√ Be raw!
√ Be imperfect!

Let them feel what you feel and see the REAL person behind the words they are reading.

If you look at the word "news" and you take off the "s" at the end, **you have what people really want: something that's *new*.** They don't call it "the news" for nothing. My wife is addicted to the news, so she's got it on all the time — and they always have "Breaking News." Once I said to her, "What happens when there *is* no breaking news? What happens when there's nothing to report?" Well, you need to ask yourself the same thing; and if this occurs, realize that you still have to come up

▼▼▼▼▼▼▼▼▼
MARKETING SECRET

Failure is the best education.

- Test a lot of different things.

- Set out to try bold things (on a small basis).

- And then never repeat what didn't work!

- The more you test — and fail — the better! Why? Because you will ultimately discover what works best.

with something. That's what they do on CNN and the networks. They've got their market to serve, and their market *always* wants something new. So there's got to be breaking news, even if there *is* no news! That's what you have to do as copywriters, too. **The process of getting rich is based on reselling to your customers again and again, so you've got to keep giving them something new, something that's different... or at least something that *sounds* different.**

So, I like the idea of editorial-style ads. But I like the general theme behind them even more — and that general theme is that if everybody is zagging, then you've got to zig. **If everybody's zigging, you've got to zag. You've got to be different from other marketers.** You have to separate yourself somehow from the crowd. If your ad looks exactly like theirs, if everything you're doing looks exactly like what they're doing, then you're going to get the same poor results that everybody else gets. So when you start looking at ways to separate yourself from the herd, ask yourself first what people want. The best answer I can think of, besides "something new," is this: **they want what I call an irresistible offer. They also want that offer made to them by somebody they feel is honest and trustworthy** — somebody who feels real in a phony world. Because after all, we're living in a world that's pretty phony. As a copywriter, I think you should write to that. **You should write to peoples' skepticism.** They want something that's real, something that's new and interesting, in a world where all copy is homogenized. It's too similar. It's too bland. Since it's your job to separate yourself from everybody else, **don't be afraid to be real, to be raw, to be honest, to be truthful with people.** Don't be afraid to *upset* some people. Go out there and try to do it in some unique way.

For a good example of what not to do, let's look again at the Yellow Pages. Most Yellow Pages ads are watered down, dumbed down; they all look the same, and they're all pretty boring and bland. Most don't use direct-response-style copywriting at all. It's kind of funny; you'll notice that almost all of them lead with the name of their business, as if that's going to make me pick up the phone and call them. I don't care who they are; I want to know that they'll do for me what I want them to do for me! If I need a plumber, I want a headline that specifically tells me why that plumber is a good one to choose. If I need someone to do some electrical work, I want to know other things besides that they're called XYZ Electric Company. **I always ask myself the infamous WIIFM: What's In It For Me? Because that's what people want to know when they read your ad.** Having a plain ad with the name of your business as the headline isn't going to produce any kind of results. Having an ad that looks like everybody else's isn't going to produce results. **You have to be *different*.**

Again: if everybody else is zigging, you want to zag. And if everybody else is zagging, you want to zig. It's not necessarily what you're doing or specifically the style you use that's important — it's that you want to be different. You want to stand out. **You want to do things that are unique and creatively unlike what everybody else is doing.** If you look like everybody else, why should someone choose to do business with you? They'll probably just close their eyes and point to the page and say, "Okay, *that's* who I'm calling!" Or, otherwise, you'll be in the fight to name your company AAA Whatever. If you look in the Yellow Pages under certain industries, you see them: there'll be A Company, AA Company, and then AAA Company, and maybe someone comes along and they're AAAA. They do this to try to get to the very top of the listing alphabetically, thinking that by doing so they'll be called first. And that is such delusional thinking! If that's the best they can do to make themselves different from everyone else, they're in way over their heads.

I started this chapter by telling you that news-style advertising gets you up to 500% more response than traditional advertising. Here's another good point to remember: **news-style advertising looks editorial. It looks like it's information, and not just an ad.** Therefore, it stands out among all of the other "me too" ads. That's what makes it so valuable as a model. And, yes, it can also be newsworthy! Look at what we're doing right now our Recession-Proof Wealth promotion. This nasty recession is in the right now; it's on the top of people's minds. The media is blasting away at it, with one bad story after another. They're having a field day with this whole thing — and they're scaring the crap out of people. We're aware that people are already in that mindset. We didn't create it; we're just cashing in on it. **We're hitching our wagon to something that they created — and in the process of making money, we're helping other people.** There's not a thing wrong with that.

Follow These Five Steps to Copywriting Success

In this chapter, I'll outline a five-step process that you can start using right now to improve your copywriting. **These steps form a sort of formula, a blueprint for writing better copy.** Taken together, they're something like a recipe that you'd use in the kitchen to cook something. If you follow a recipe exactly as it's laid out, you'll come up with something that tastes very good. The same's true here.

I suggest that you give yourself at least one day for each of these steps. So if you've got a sales letter that you want to write, give yourself a minimum of five days to write that sales letter — and then, **every day, focus on one of these steps and write as much copy as you can that's focused on achieving that step.** In five days, you'll have a whole bunch of interesting copy, and then you can spend another five days editing it down and rewriting it. This is a formula that works!

Step One

Samuel Johnson, the 18th-century British writer, once said that a big promise is the soul of an advertisement. That's as true today as it was 250 years ago. You've got to start with a big promise, and it has to be a promise that's custom-tailored to the type of person you want to reach. It has to offer a big benefit. **Take the one thing that's most compelling in your offer, focus in on it, and try to make it as big and as bold and as audacious a promise as you possibly can.** That becomes your lead. If you write copy the way I write copy, you're going to spend one whole day on that. Whatever you write, however much time you spend on it, all you're doing is focusing on your big promise.

Now, this process can take a while to really get moving, which is why I prefer to take a week, or even longer, on my sales letters. During that week, if I'm just focused on writing that one sales letter, my mind becomes obsessed with the whole idea. I start getting ideas on the second and third day, and by the fifth or seventh day my mind is on fire! It's all flowing by that day, whereas the first day it may have been slow; and then, the second day, I did a little bit more; the third day I was writing a little bit more; and by the fifth, sixth, and seventh day, I'm jamming that copy out! By that time the copy is flowing like hot lava, it's a hell of a lot better than the copy I started with on Day One. That's because by late in the week, I was obsessed! I'd been working on it for a whole week — and I get my best ideas when my brain is alive and on fire.

However it works for you, you're starting with the big promise. **One of the things you absolutely, positively have to do when copywriting is to grab your reader's attention from the very beginning.** You've got to put a stranglehold on it and not let go. As soon as you let go of that attention, they're gone, like a fish that breaks your line. A big promise helps you to grab their attention and pique their curiosity — or scare them, or invoke some other emotion that's going to keep them charged up enough to make it through to the next headline that grabs their attention and moves them forward through the copy.

Begin by writing down some of the biggest features, benefits, and values that your product, service, or opportunity offers to the consumer. **Of those, pick the biggest and create a solid headline that really synthesizes a big promise.** That big promise launches the rest of your sales material or sales letter; **it grabs their attention and forces them to keep going with your copy.** That big promise is really the big picture, and the whole big offer is synthesized in that big promise. From a nuts-and-bolts perspective, it's the big promise that first grabs their attention and won't let go. That being the case, you need to determine what it is in your offer that's the most exciting. Which benefit is the most compelling, the most interesting, the most stimulating? **What one thing is going to grab people and take them away from everything they're doing so they'll focus in on what *you're* trying to do?** I've mentioned several times one problem that can make this difficult. It's simply the immunity that people

▼▼▼▼▼▼▼▼▼
MARKETING SECRET

Whoever said: "Do what you love and the money will flow" was wrong! It should be: "Learn to love the activities that are capable of producing the largest sum of money — and the money will follow!"

build up for advertising messages. As prospective buyers, we've got all these marketers trying to get our attention all day long, screaming and shouting in almost every medium we're exposed to. We've learned to filter it out; it becomes white noise. Like at home, where my wife has the TV running all the time. From the minute she gets up in the morning till the minute she goes to bed at night, that television is on. The only peace I have from that TV is three hours in the morning!

But really, I don't listen to the TV. It just becomes white noise. That's how a lot of the marketing messages are for the customer: white noise. **Nobody's paying any attention, because they've built up an immunity towards it.** People are so inundated with their own problems, their own challenges, their own situations, that nobody's paying attention. **That's why you start your sales letter with the biggest, boldest, most audacious, most compelling promise you can possibly make: because you want to cut through the clutter.**

In order to find that big promise, you need to spend that whole first day of writing carefully examining your offer. **Once you've got that promise, keep writing it down in as many different ways as you can, because eventually you'll find a set of words that sound better than any of the others.** Keep trying again and again. Focus on the features. Focus on the benefits. Keep looking for the things that are the most exciting, the most unusual, and the most interesting.

It's very, very difficult to go over-the-top with a big promise, no matter how hard you try. People in this field are always worried about that, but it's not really possible. The truth is, despite the fact that you have this recipe, this five-step blueprint to writing sales letters that quickly make you millions of dollars, it's very rare that you'll write a big enough promise or headline on that very first day. You can't be big enough, no matter how over-the-top it may seem. **Never be afraid to blow it up and make it as big as you possibly can, because if you don't grab their attention, then your sales letter is done.**

It's hard to go over-the-top because people buy with their emotions. One of my best stories illustrating this took place in 1997, when we had our second big, expensive seminar. We charged $6,700 for that seminar. That first day, right before the seminar, Eileen, Russ von Hoelscher, and I were upstairs at the Broadview Hotel, mapping out some strategies on how we could open this thing in the best possible way. Russ said, "Look, let's not go out there and talk about making millions of dollars. Let's first tell people the simple truth — which is that you don't make millions of dollars overnight. First, you start with $50,000, and the next year you try to make $150,000, and the next year you try to make $400,000 — and then eventually, by your fourth or fifth year, you're into the millions. So let's go out there and tell them how it really is."

We thought, hey, well, he's got more experience than us. We had a hundred people in the room, and they'd all paid big bucks to be there, and we wanted to start it off on the right tone. Well, we went out there and I said, "Who here is interested in making $50,000 this year?" It fell flat. You could've heard a pin drop — and things were very uncomfortable and kind of scary. And then all of a sudden, after a couple of very awkward minutes, I quickly said, "Now, who here wants to make millions of dollars?" and everybody jumped up and started yelling and screaming and hollering and whooping... and *then* we got the seminar started right!

From a logical standpoint, Russ was correct — and everybody knows that logically. People know they can't go from zero to millions right away, that there are some intermediate steps. They've pretty much got to crawl before they walk, and they've got to walk before they run, and they've got to run before they learn how to slam-dunk basketballs. But they don't care. *We're selling to people's emotions.* **You can't try to think logically when you're working in matters of the emotions.** Emotion knows no logic, and you can see that in the most extreme examples of marketing. And certainly, when you're trying to sell in a market that's overcrowded, and you're trying to get people's attention, you do have to go over-the-top sometimes with your promises — as much as you can. You have to watch things from a legal standpoint; **you can't make promises you can't deliver on.** But you do have to go over the top. **The person who makes the biggest, boldest promise usually is the person who wins out.**

Step Two

The second step is painting the picture. This is a metaphor, of course, because we're really talking about words here. **But it's the images that we create with our words that matter.** We want people to visualize our offer and its benefits. **We want them to see themselves using our product or service.** In the business opportunity market, which is where I've worked for 20 years, one of the number one rules of selling is that if people can't see themselves doing it, they're not going to get involved. So you need to do things that make it real. You're using examples; you're telling stories.

Take, for instance, this new Recession-Proof Wealth program that we're promoting. Some experts say this recession we're entering could become a full-fledged depression. So we try to paint the picture. We make it real. We remind them of all the news they've been subjected to. We give them quotes from famous talking heads, credible experts that they've seen on the three major networks and CNN and FOX News. This is how we're painting the picture; and while it works better with some products than others, it's something you should always try to do. **You should always try to put yourself in the shoes of the prospect, to see how they visualize the picture you're trying to paint.**

There are several different ways you can do that. Obviously, getting them to imagine themselves being successful with your product, your service, or your opportunity is vital. **Getting them to see the benefits that they'll enjoy is important.** Also, they'll respond to concrete examples of how your project will do that. Infomercials are pretty good at providing that imagery, showing what your life is going to be like with that new product, or once the money comes rolling in.

Also, the process of explaining in detail how you make money with your product or opportunity is very effective. In the process of the hows and the whys and wherefores of showing them how it works, you're

People are looking for and willing to spend a ton of money for: <u>The Magic Pill</u>!

This is the product or service that they perceive can instantly and automatically give them something they badly want.

giving them the opportunity to place themselves into the equation so that they can visualize their own success at whatever it is you're offering. So you have to use the type of language that helps paint that picture. Maybe you can do that in a page, or half a page; or maybe it requires a 20-page hand-marked letter with big quotes and large type.

Here's an example from my Recession-Proof Wealth sales letter, which we're already generating leads for. This line of copy illustrates what I was saying above: "Imagine waking up every Monday morning to a mailbox that is stuffed full of cash, checks, and money orders for this powerful Recession-Proof Wealth System, which is desperately wanted and needed by millions of people who are very worried about their financial futures. All you have to do is let our simple marketing system make money for you — automatically. This takes as little as 10 minutes a day, and your day is over. Now you're free to go anywhere. You're free to do anything you like. This is the kind of life that's possible when you're using this Master Distributorship, and I will help you cash in with it." And then it goes on to give them some income projections down at the bottom, based on certain numbers of sales.

What we're trying to do is make it real for them. We're trying to paint them a picture. We're trying to get them to see themselves actually using this product and benefiting from it, so they'll say, "Yeah, that's great! That's the opportunity for me!" That's part of that process of painting the picture. **Those income projections I mentioned can be very powerful, especially when they're backed up with proof.** I show them what happens if they make this many sales, or what happens with that many sales. Then I show them copies of actual commissions or sales checks, and/or testimonials that backup the idea that "if you do this, this happens." By using income projections, you're painting that picture very vividly, making a direct causal connection in their minds.

SECTION FIVE — Ruthless Copywriting Strategies

▼▼▼▼▼▼▼▼▼
MARKETING SECRET

What millions of people really want is someone to do it all for them!

- "We will do it all for you and send you a check every month!" is a popular message!

- People all want to be led.

- They want someone to do all the thinking and doing for them!

- They want the reward without the risk.

Be absolutely sure to give them proof of your claims. This is very important because, again, I feel that people are more skeptical now than ever before in history. I firmly believe that. They're constantly bombarded with advertising and news, and so they're forced to filter it out, to grow so skeptical that they don't believe anything. That's why you've got to do something to show them proof. You can't expect people to be sold on something just because you are. Why should they believe you? **Show them proof: copies of real checks, or better, testimonials.** Testimonials are very powerful. However you do it, **prove to them you're telling them the truth, the whole truth, and nothing but the truth.** In the past, we've spent page after page trying to do just that.

As part of that proof, **we also tell them that we back our product up with a guarantee.** And we tell them that we don't blame them for being skeptical... that it's *good* to be skeptical. We acknowledge the fact that they already have that in their minds; we don't try to run or hide from it. We just tell them, "Of course you're skeptical. Of course you don't believe me. But here's why you should... And in case you don't at the end of the day, **if you're still not happy, you can get all your money back.**"

I was watching TV recently, and I saw an infomercial for an Internet guy. He had, literally, ten minutes straight of nothing but testimonial after testimonial, videos of people saying, "I'm using this and I'm making this," and "I went from zero to $15,000 a week," and it just went on and on and on. It was very persuasive. Although I thought the whole infomercial was cheesy, the testimonials did a very good job of offering social proof and getting people's attention. This works with written media as well as TV. People read testimonials, and it helps take it to their exact level. **They think, "Well, if he can do it, I can do it!"** That's what social proof does for your product, service, or opportunity.

Step Three

Next, tell them why your product is unique. What we're doing with our Recession-Proof Wealth System that makes it unique, that really gets people stimulated and makes them curious to want to know more, is that we're telling them a simple story that happens to be true. We point out that during the Great Depression, when unemployment was 25 percent or higher in some cities, there was still a small group of people who did extremely well — even when everybody else was struggling and barely making it. That's true of any great social change, by the way, whether it's good or bad. **There's always a group of people who do well.** Some are exploiting the problem; some are just trying to do something positive.

Anyway: we tell people that during the Great Depression, there was this group of people who, because they had a secret, were able to make excellent money when everyone around them was suffering. Now, 80 years later, we're faced with a similar situation that may end up being worse that what we suffered through then. But we've discovered a new way to capitalize on something that enabled that group of people back in the Great Depression to become very, very wealthy, and we've got a whole new way of doing it now. **That's our hook.** That's our angle. That's what makes it unique.

There has to be something that sets you or your offer apart, and that's just an example of how we're doing it. Everybody likes something that seems different, whether a little or a lot. And in reality, it may be that what you have isn't *that* much different. Most things aren't. Take my example from earlier: plumbers. How much different could one plumber really be from another, honestly? I don't know that much about plumbing, but I'm pretty sure that the work isn't much different from one plumber to another. Yet can your marketing be different? You bet! **Your marketing can be the part about your business and your company that makes you stand out.** You may be in a bland, homogenized industry, but that doesn't mean that your marketing has to be that way. So for purposes of this five-step blueprint, **spend some time on identifying things that you**

can put in front of people that makes your offer look unique and special and different.** You might have to get pretty creative. You have to ask yourself constantly, "What is it about this that makes it unique?" Or, "What can I *do* to make this offer unique?

There's this great Jackson Brown song that goes, "You take Sally, I'll take Sue. There's really no difference between the two." I love that line, because that's just the way the market is! There's no real difference from Company A to Company B; you might as well flip a coin. There's nothing that's unique. If you're in that kind of business, you have to be the one to *create* that uniqueness. **You have to be the one to find that angle,** like my friend Mike did with the soy candle. You can go to Wal-Mart and pick up a candle for a dollar that's made in Vietnam or Indonesia — but you can't find a soy candle at Wal-Mart. I know because I checked; it's unique.

In order to know what's unique, you have to know what's out there in the marketplace — especially what's being done on a regular basis by other companies. **You can't really have something that's totally unique until and unless you know what's out there, what's the norm, what people are buying. Then you look for points of differentiation, things that mean the most to your customers or your market.** That goes back to the very first thing I told you: that you can be the world's worst copywriter, and *still* make really good money if you just know your market. If you intuitively and intimately understand who it is that you're selling to and what excites them, what interests them, where their passions are, what frustrates them the most — then you don't have to be a good copywriter, because you're locked in on the exact type of person you're after. At that point, coming up with something unique is easy, because you really understand them.

Step Four

The next step is to close your argument by telling your customer why they must act now. Not doing so is a big mistake that a lot of marketers make; in fact, it's a big mistake that I make sometimes, too. I've made every mistake there is to make when it comes to marketing, so don't ever think I'm coming at you from an angle like I've got it all figured out. I constantly make mistakes, and this is a mistake I've made many times.

I've talked about people building up an immunity towards advertising and marketing, to the point where they just tune it out. Well, one of the things that people tune out all the time is those ads that say, "You must respond in the next 10 days!" *Click.* Nobody believes that. They're thinking, "Yeah, right. I could respond *10 months* from now and get the same deal." **If you don't give people a compelling reason why they should take action right now, then the chances are good that a lot of people *aren't* going to, and you're going to lose money that could and should be yours.** They're qualified prospects, they truly want what it is that you have to offer — but they're holding onto their money. So you have to find a reason; if necessary, you've got to create one. After all, there's no reason why they have to give you money — they don't care about your bills!

So close your argument by telling them why they must act now. **One thing that comes to mind is scarcity or limited resources.** It's one thing to say "You must act now!" and another to prove why they should. People get inundated with a lot of those offers, and they know that this is, in fact, a marketing tactic. It is a strategy to get people to act. They know that 99 times out of 100, marketers who tell them this are pulling the wool over their eyes. You need to give them a good reason why it's true in this case, or they're not going to believe you, and you're going to lose credibility.

So if you tell them to act fast before it fills up, **tell them *why* it's going to fill up quickly.** Give them a good reason to want to be in there before it does. You'll turn them off or lose credibility by not giving them a compelling reason to act. Just to go back to this promotion that we're finishing up now: it's limited to only 250 distributors. If our prospects want to respond to our offer, it's for them and for 249 other distributors *only*. Period. We tell them that after that we may terminate the program forever, and that's the truth. On the order form, it says the offer expires on November 1, 2008, or when all 250 positions are filled. **And then we give them the incentive: if they order now,** "Plus, I'll get all the private secrets behind this amazing new wealth-making opportunity, at least 100 days *before* all of the other distributors. This gives me a huge head start to make even more money." We tell them in the sales letter that it's all brand new; and because it's brand new, that's the good news. But because it's brand new that's also the *bad* news, because we're still developing things — that's how new it is.

▼▼▼▼▼▼▼▼
MARKETING SECRET

"I've seen companies so obsessed with competition that they keep looking in their rearview mirror and crash into a tree."
Sergey Brin — 31-year-old billionaire co-founder of Google.com

Then we're telling people that as distributors, they need to watch their mailboxes, because over the next hundred days we're going to give all this to them. And because we gave them that distributorship at such a low price, they can either tolerate waiting another 90 days, *or* they can become a Master Distributor immediately. We're going to give them all the secrets right now, right away; they're going to be the first to get them! That's a reason for them to step up to the plate, to go ahead and upgrade their position. **There's a Money Back Guarantee.** They can upgrade their position and then, **if they want to back out later, no problem. No questions asked. It's a reason for them to take action.**

Make them that special offer to get them to respond now. You've seen it time and again: **"But wait! That's not all. If you act now, we're going to throw in this XYZ special gift."** It does get people to go ahead and respond. Obviously, with our copywriting and our Direct-Response, we're writing and pushing for a response. In this case, we're pushing for that sale. We're stacking all these benefits and bonus gifts and everything up until they're saying, "All right! I get all this? Okay, I'm done. Where's the order form?"

You also need to offer an upsell — something associated with your product or service but better, something that interested clients can purchase for a higher price. Remember the Master Distributorship I mentioned earlier? That's the upsell with our new program, and it's got some unique aspects that really draw people's attention. We're taking people who are already distributors, and now we want to upsell them to a Master Distributorship. Since we've appointed them as distributors already, it's easy to take them to that next step. It's a logical upsell; **it's directly tied to the first offer that they bought.** They get a wonderful, unique bonus when they trade up: right here on the front page it says, "Plus, you'll also receive the world's greatest free bonus gift, guaranteed to have an honest value of $33,248.20." Now, if that's not over the top, if that's not unique, I don't know what is. You're selling something for $495 — and that's a half-price sale, by the way. The regular price is $987, but we're letting people come in early at half price. For $495, we're going to give them something that's worth $33,000. When they get to the last five pages that explain the world's greatest bonus gift, there is a headline that says: "How Can We Give You A Free Bonus Gift That Is Guaranteed To Be Worth A Total Of $33,248.20?" And then it says, "Listen, I don't blame you for being skeptical. After all, getting 50 powerful recession-proof websites..."

See how we tied the websites in with the whole offer? They're not just websites; they're *recession-proof* websites. We did that for a reason. We wanted to maintain cohesiveness with the whole thing, to keep it all locked in to the original offer. And then we explain to them that the websites are also brand new, they're still being developed, and that they need to go through extensive testing — which they do. It's all true. Nobody is lying. There's no dishonesty here. We tell them that these websites, if they went out there and tried to build them all on their own, would cost them every bit of $33,000 to put them all together... but we're doing it all on our dime. What we don't tell them is that we then collectively give the whole group the same basic replicated websites. That's the secret we don't tell people, but it's true that the sites do have that type of value.

Next, we show people how it's possible for us to give them such a valuable bonus gift for just $495. What we're trying to do is create that irresistible offer, such that the $495 we're asking them to give us pales in comparison to everything they're going to receive in exchange for it. **It's all part of stacking and building that offer.** It's a fact that those websites have an honest value of $33,248.20. We could have just said $33,000, but making it $33,248.20 makes it more believable.

What we're going to do in the follow-up marketing is what we call "taking the cream off the top." So we put this upsell offer out there to the people who already are distributors; that is, people who gave us the $39 for the distributorship. We're going to take all the immediate revenue that comes in from the people who say, "Man, this is a great deal! Here's my $495. Take it!" **Then, we're going to go to the people who didn't send in their $495 right away with a series of sequential mailings that proves the value of our offer.** It breaks it all down, it shows them where we came up with that figure of $33,248.20, and it speaks to their skepticism. A lot of people will still think it's a number we just pulled out of our heads, that there's no logical reason why that number is even real. **They still don't believe it... so we're going to show them.** We're going to break it down. Each one of these websites has a value of $649. Plus, we're going to give the distributor three years of hosting on top of that. Here's our normal price for hosting. When you add it all up, it's $33,248.20.

These days, people don't just trust you; **you have to win that trust.** Part of the way you do that is by making your case for your product or service: by showing people why you're not just leading them on, why it's real, and why you can do what you said that you were going to do. This backs up your claim: it's an honest value of $33,248.20. When you add it up, people say, "Okay, yeah, it really *is* worth that."

Here's a true story. In August of 2002, we had a huge seminar with four or five hundred people. On the third day of that event — a Sunday morning — we made our customers a special offer, and then went through a two-hour presentation that proved to them that we were going to give them $484,000 worth of free websites. The offer was simple; they just had to pay the hosting. We were going to build these websites for them, and then they had to help us by letting us run a series of these tests to get them ready for the marketplace. Software companies do this all the time — it's called beta testing. Those were the only two conditions: they paid the hosting, and let us use their sites for beta testing. We spent two hours showing them exactly what they were going to receive. We made a great presentation, and when the presentation was over, people literally stampeded the stage. We made them a compelling offer, and they stampeded us trying to get it. One guy was injured in the process — he either broke his thumb, or thought he had.

I was frightened! I was thinking, "Crap! Get them away from me!" Now, I've heard stories before about how the crowd can sometimes respond in a way that's just overwhelming, but this was the first time I'd witnessed it. People went crazy! We made them an irresistible offer; we did our best to prove to them that it was real, that it was true, and that it was something that, in the end, they just could not say no to — and they responded! **I think this is a wonderful illustration of the power of Direct-Response Marketing, and of stacking an irresistible offer.** We did a couple of million dollars worth of business right then and there, because we gave them a great offer. And that's really what I'm talking about. **You absolutely have to give people good value in exchange for their money.** In order to compete out there in the marketplace with all these very aggressive marketers, you've got to make your offer stand out above theirs.

> Strive to make your offer so attractive, compelling, and irresistible that only a lunatic would say "No!"

Here's a good example. I have a colleague named Dr. Gallant who provides an amazing value to his clients. The items he sells them are, taken altogether, worth about $100,000. But he offers it all to them as 105 courses for $97 — a total of $10,185, assuming they buy all those courses. For ten grand, they can get a $100,000 worth of stuff! That's an irresistible offer — because he proves that it really *is* worth $100,000. That's the challenge you've got to meet and overcome.

Step Five

Finally, you need to end with a reminder of the promise, a summary of your offer, and a strong call for action. You've got to summarize it — especially if you're doing long-form sales letters, which are the ones you use if you're really trying to sell high-ticket items. Take the letter for our recession-proof system that I've been talking so much about. It only asks for $495, but it's a 20-page letter. We're taking 20 pages to prove our claims, to make it real, to show them proof, to establish its uniqueness, to go through this whole thing. Twenty full pages! Now some people would say, "My God, do you need 20 pages to sell something for $500?" I believe that in our market, to our customers, more is better — and you *do* need that kind of thing. **You need to make all your claims, however many pages it takes.** You need to do a thorough job of selling, and then to summarize it all in the end.

▼▼▼▼▼▼▼▼▼
MARKETING SECRET

The more I want to do something — the less I call it work!

- Now it's fun and challenging! Now you can pour your heart and soul into it!

- The secret is to make yourself want to do the hard stuff that brings in all the money!

When I think about this need for a strong call for action, I'm reminded of the HBO series "Hard Knocks." This year it's about pro football. In a documentary on the Dallas Cowboys, Jerry Jones — the colorful, very charismatic owner of the Cowboys — was addressing the team and he said, "People have said I've been a very successful salesman, and there are three things that I've learned about sales in all my years in business. Number one is, you ask for the money. Number two is, you ask for the money. And number three is, you ask for the money." He's hit the nail on the head with that statement. **When it comes down to your call to action, that's exactly what you're doing. You're asking your prospects for the money.** You've built a good, solid case, sure — but if you don't take that last step and ask for the money, you're sunk. **Sadly, a lot of people are afraid to ask for the money.**

I've already mentioned Zig Ziglar's brother, Judd Ziglar, who wrote a book called *Timid Salespeople Raise Skinny Kids*. As he points out, even if you're a good salesperson, if you can't ask for the money at the end of your pitch, then you're going to lose a lot of sales — maybe even most of the sales that could be yours. **So you've got to be aggressive with it.** If you're offering products and services that truly do offer value, don't hesitate to ask for the money. **Make that call to action.** Those hundred reports that you have — what is their worth? A couple of thousand dollars apiece? Is that the value you've established for them? Are they *worth* a couple thousand dollars apiece? Sure they are, if people can use and benefit from what you're offering. **So as long as you're providing real value that does exactly what you say it's going to do if they use it, then you have every right to ask for the money. It's your responsibility, in fact.

That's the mindset you have to get into. You need to be aggressive when asking for the money. Otherwise, you're always going to be losing sales, all the while wondering, "Man, am I too pushy here? Am I really too pushy? Should I be less aggressive? Should I back off a little bit?" No way! Because if you really believe in what you're doing and you really believe it can help people, and that they need it and can benefit from it, then just get out there and do everything short of physical violence to sell your product. **Do whatever you have to do to try to make the sale. If it's really going to benefit people, if they can really be empowered by it, then you** *owe* **it to them to do that.**

Speaking of Summaries...

That's the basis of the five-step formula. What I would recommend here is that you do what I was suggesting earlier: **Get on the other side of the cash register, and start studying other Direct-Response marketers immediately.** Don't just look at general marketing stuff; study the copy of direct-response marketers who are doing a really good job with it, and you'll see the same formulas repeated over and over again. That's the key to your developing the skills and ability to do them yourself — by first understanding, in as many ways as possible, how other people are using these strategies on a daily basis.

Learn the Ten Commandments of Marketing, PART I

In the next two chapters, I'll outline what I call the Ten Commandments of Marketing. Internalize these, use them every day in conjunction with I've already told you, and once again you'll find that you don't have to be the world's best copywriter to make money. **You just have to continually use good strategies.** That's what these Ten Commandments of Marketing are, and almost all of your competitors are breaking each one every day. **This is to your favor, if you're the one following the rules!** Some of this is going to sound like common sense — and yet, as Mark

Twain said in the 1800s, "Common sense is a very uncommon thing." I'd say it's even more uncommon today.

The First Commandment

Give people what they want. It's just that simple. Again, this seems like common sense, and yet so many marketers forget it. They fall in love with whatever it is that they're promoting, and they think the whole world is going to naturally be in love with it, too. Instead, they should be asking, "What are people buying right now? What are the things that excite them right now? **What are the things that cause them to spend the maximum amount of money on related products and services?** What are those common denominators? What are the benefits that people want the most? Who are the competitors in this marketplace that are doing the best jobs?"

Let's look at M.O.R.E., Inc. I'm proud to say that we're probably one of the top 10 companies in the opportunity market, by almost anybody's standard. We've earned our position in the marketplace. If asked, I think most people in the field would say, "M.O.R.E., Inc.? Definitely, you guys are Top 10." We think we're even better, but that's our sense of pride showing.

Why worry about who's the best in your market? Because you need to copy the very best things that they're doing. Not literally, of course — that would be plagiarism, and it's illegal — but you should use them as models for your own initiatives. **If you're in the opportunity market, look at what we're doing and get some ideas from us.** If you're going to be serving this market, you should definitely do what we're doing, because we've been doing it a long time and we work very, very hard at trying to be the best in the business. Within any market, there are leading competitors — people who are out there really trying to do the best job. Year after year, they're performing well in the market. It's good to copy what they're doing. Really focus on what is it about the products and services they sell that causes them to be one of the leading companies in the market year after year. Then ask yourself, **"What are they doing to give their customers what they want?"** That's the big question. Answer that, and then determine how you can create your own products and services that are similar to theirs, while building in some distinctions.

Often, the market itself will tell you what's hot. Occasionally you might hear someone say, "Hey, we've got this product, and we have absolutely no competition!" **That sounds nice, until you consider why they have no competition. It's because there's no *money* there.** You want the money to dictate where you're going with your offerings. Chris Hollinger recently went through a process of trying to determine what his prospects really wanted. He started by looking at what was selling in this economy, and then got on the phone and started interviewing some of the people who had responded to his ad but hadn't purchased. He asked them, "What is it that you want? What kind of home-based business do you want? What kind of product do you want to offer? What kind of money do you have to spend?" Then he took his notes from all those interviews and told himself, "Okay: to the best of my ability, I'm going to create exactly what they told me they wanted." **So one way that you can find out what your prospects want is to *just ask*.** Too often, marketers try to come up with all these clever, unique ideas on how to determine what the market wants, when the easiest thing to do is just to ask them. In Chris's case, the jury's still out. He's got some test pieces out there that are working; but his whole goal was to give his prospects exactly what they told him they wanted. We'll see if it works.

I see too many businesses that are very rigid in their thinking. Their idea of marketing is to say, "This is what we have. This is the way we do it. If the customers don't want it that way... well, then, we'll find the ones who do!" This isn't very smart, because it could lead to problems with sales. **When a company is inflexible, they miss out on what the prospects really want — which changes constantly.** The public might want something quite a bit right now; it might be superhot right this minute, but six months or a year from now they don't want it anymore. The market can be fickle that way.

This principle is important because it's all about the prospect, all about the marketplace you're serving. In business, too many people approach the subject completely backwards: they come up with a product, then try to figure out who wants to buy it. **The better way to do it is to find a marketplace, and then figure out what that marketplace wants the most... and *then* develop products and services that give them that.**

The opportunity market, the one I've been working in for the past 20 years, is made up of millions of people who want to find a way to make

▼▼▼▼▼▼▼▼▼
MARKETING SECRET

Hype sells!

- Take whatever you are selling — add a heavy dose of hype — and instantly make more money!

- This is what people really want!

- Why? Cause it's more dramatic and appeals to their emotional side (which is the side of people we sell to!).

money from home. Everything we do at M.O.R.E., Inc. is oriented around serving that marketplace, by providing them with products and services that help them make money from home. **Nothing we do goes the other way;** we *never* start by developing a product and then try to figure out who to sell it to. Everything we do is built around knowing the marketplace, and then developing products and services for that marketplace.

It's all a matter of giving people what they want. A century ago, Henry Ford said about his market, "They can have any color Model T they want, as long as it's black." He was trying to give them what *he* wanted — and that's the wrong way to do it. **You want to give people what *they* want, and the way you do that is by knowing your marketplace intimately.** That's why I always talk about selling to a marketplace that you're a member of. You have firsthand expertise of how the people in that marketplace think, what their hot buttons are, what they respond to, what they care most about. **You can develop products and services based on your own understanding of the marketplace.**

That marketplace might be one that serves a hobby you're interested in. Look at golfing: the golfing marketplace is huge, and it generates a lot of profit for some marketers. Golfers buy like crazy; they're never satisfied with their game. I know that because Chris Lakey's a golfer, and I know how he thinks. He tells me that he sees all the people he golfs with get frustrated with the same things over and over again. There's a multi-million dollar marketplace that consists of people buying golf-related products and services. So if you're an avid golfer, you could get into in the golfing business — say, by selling information products or real golf tools to help people become better golfers. Based on your own knowledge of the marketplace, you'd have a good idea of what those people were looking for, wouldn't you?

It all starts with giving people what they want... so it all starts with the customer, not the product. That ties in well with the Second Commandment — but before we go there, let me just say this: **a "want" is an emotional desire.** And emotions know no logic. You can especially see that in the most extreme examples, so I would encourage you to think about the most extreme examples of why people do things, both good and bad, and **realize that we're dealing with matters of the heart, not the head.** We sell to people's emotions, not to their brains.

In a general sense, what most people want is to make more money, lose more weight, have more sex appeal. However, they don't want to pay the price to get the result. That's an emotional thing. **We all know logically that the only way to get a specific result is by paying the price — monetarily, physically, emotionally.** We know that *logically*. Emotionally, we all want the result for the smallest price possible. **Again, emotions know no logic, and we sell to the heart of the emotions.** You've got to remember that. Pay attention to the kinds of things that people are spending the most money on, and you'll see that there's an emotional element behind those things; and try to understand what that is. The best way to do that is to understand yourself. Look at your own life, pick some crazy thing you've done, and ask yourself, "Why in the world did I do that?" You did it because you were following your emotions rather than your logic.

The Second Commandment

The Second Commandment of Marketing is simply this: **It all starts with the market, not the product or service.** So many marketers worry because they're lacking a product or service to sell; but really, what they should be doing is focusing on their chosen marketplace first. The marketplace is just a group of people who buy certain types of products or services, and they're reachable through specific media — specialty magazines, TV ads, email lists, or whatever.

The marketplace will tell you what it wants. Getting back to the golf example: What do golfers want? Well, basically, they all want to shave points off their score in the fastest, simplest, easiest way possible... and so they buy all kinds of goofy, outrageous gadgets so that they can show off to all their buddies and they can be the heroes out there on the links. There's a debate over whether you shave points off best by using a better driver or a better pitching wedge or a better putter; there are different schools of thought about which particular tool of the game is the most important. Some of them will say, "Hey, you've got to drive; and if you have this perfect driver you'll shave points, because you'll be driving farther," while some people say, "Drive for show, putt for go." If you want to make the most money on the tour, it's all about putting, they say; so if you want to shave strokes off your game, you do it at the putter — and so they sell people these fancy putters. Whatever your specific school of thought, in the end, it's all about lowering your score and impressing your friends — and finding a faster, simpler, easier, less painful way to get that result even quicker.

Those are matters of the heart; those are matters of emotions. With the Second Commandment, you're starting with the marketplace first, and really paying attention to the items that are most appealing. Think about that. One of the themes of this section is that you don't have to be that good at copywriting to make good money. **If you're focused on the things that people really want, then you can be a mediocre copywriter and still get wealthy — because you're focused on those key areas that you know are red-hot.**

I was looking at *Opportunity* magazine the morning I wrote this, and I discovered that there are a whole lot of people copying something that Chris Lakey and I started doing about five years ago. As far as I know, we were among the first to take this idea and really expand it, to try to do something with it on a major scale. What I'm talking about is the way we started building marketing systems around multi-level marketing companies. **Nowadays, we see a lot of people copying those ideas, and this is a great example of what I've been telling you here.** These people are putting into play the ideas we originated, ideas that are the most appealing to our marketplace.

You need to look for the most appealing items that other people are selling. If you focus only on trying to sell those items, you won't waste your time beating your head against the wall, trying to sell things that only excite or interest *you*. **You'll be focused on what excites your marketplace, and how you can create something even better than what's out there right now.** This really will help you understand your specific niche market and get you even deeper into that niche, because as I like to say, there's riches in niches.

So as a marketer, when you're looking to do anything, start with the market. **Look at who that market comprises, and exactly what they're buying.** Let the market tell you what direction you're going to go. Do that, and you're not going to be spinning your wheels with something nobody wants to buy. **You're going into a market you know is full of eager, rabid buyers.** You're just going to recreate the wheel a little better than your competitors are doing, and grab some of that market in the process.

This ties right in with what I was saying earlier about the First Commandment. **First of all, it's all about understanding what people want, and then developing products and services that appeal to that specific marketplace.** You start with their biggest desires; what does that marketplace want the most? Then you develop products and services that give it to them. That's one of the reasons I like information marketing. If you sell widgets or anything else you have to manufacture, whether it's a bottle of water or a dining room table, there are certain limitations to how you can market that and how you can go about creating products. **But when you're an information marketer, there are all kinds of ways to create information.** It could be as audio CDs, it could be as DVDs, it could be books, it could be reports, it could be digital, or any number of other delivery mechanisms and shapes that information takes.

> The great Olympic runner, Steve Prefontaine said:
>
> "There may be men who can beat me — *but they'll* have *to bleed to do it!*"

Let's go back to the golf market. If I'm selling to the golf market, I could write a book that contains tips and tricks for shaving strokes off your game. I could produce a CD containing the same information. I could decide today that I want a new product and that I could sell it, and then I could go about creating that product. I could have an information product where I interviewed golfing pros. I could go all over interviewing the pros

SECTION FIVE — Ruthless Copywriting Strategies

▼▼▼▼▼▼▼▼
MARKETING SECRET

Spend more money — to close more sales!

1. You can't go wrong if you are spending this money on super qualified prospects.

2. You are selling big ticket items with good margins.

- In some cases, (as long as your percentage of conversion is going up!) you can't spend too much money!

---

at all the different golf clubs around my area for half an hour each, and then I could create an information product where they shared their best tricks and strategies. That would let me quickly and easily put together a product I could sell.

Let's say I've developed a special putter that helps you putt better. Well, I could sell that putter. But if I want to branch out and sell other related products, I've got to create them. Do I come up with a different kind of putter and sell that? If I do, then I've got two competing putters. Or do I say, "Well, if I've got a putter, maybe I need to also manufacture a driver," and approach that side of the game? If I do, I've got to put all that work into creating that new driver.

As an information marketer, you can quickly and easily create products that target your marketplace. **It gives you more freedom to be in tune to what the marketplace wants, and to adapt to it on the fly.** We've created products that show you how to create products in 48 hours or less. Information products are fast and easy to create, and you can actually be out there selling them as you're creating them. If I wanted to write a book today on a subject, I could compile it pretty quickly. Granted, it wouldn't necessarily be a really thick book, but I could write a 100 to 150 page book if I had the material. I could start selling that book immediately. If I wanted to create an audio program, I could interview the right people and create the program within a matter of days. Being in the information business gives you some freedom to be able to do this.

What I'm talking about here is developing products and services that give people specifically what they want. **With information** marketing, you can quickly and easily do that — regardless of the industry you're selling to.

The Third Commandment

The Third Commandment of Marketing is to make sure the products and services you offer for sale have the largest profit margins possible. Nothing that we know of has a larger profit margin than information products. That's part of their very nature. And the amount of money that you charge for information products has little to do with the amount of money it costs you to produce them. **The real value is in what you're delivering to people.** A good example of this would be painters who sell their works for hundreds of thousands of dollars. My wife Eileen is a painter; I think her paintings are very good. Sure, I'm very biased, but people have bought them for a few hundred dollars. The point is, the canvas she paints on is the same as the canvas that those top painters paint on. Her paintings may sell for a few hundred dollars, while a Thomas Kinkade painting, for example, might sell for hundreds of thousands. But here's the thing: The basic resources used to create those paintings, the canvases and paints, are more or less identical.

Information products are the same way. The papers or CDs they're presented on are inexpensive, and the costs don't change significantly from one product to another. **It's the results they deliver that enable you to charge huge sums of money for them, in spite of the fact that, technically, it didn't cost you that much to create them.** Software is the same way. There are so many high-profit products out there that cost very little to produce. You should focus on this fact, if only for one reason: *everything* **costs you more than you think it's going to.** That is the God-honest truth. And if you don't watch it, you could break yourself. In order to be an aggressive marketer, you have to spend a lot of money. Well, that money you spend has to come from somewhere, **so you need to be focused on products that have high profit margins in order to acquire the extra money that you need to out-market your competitors.** Do that, and you're going to be able to be more aggressive with your advertising.

One of the secrets to making the largest amount of profit possible is by "stair-stepping" your customers. I've mentioned this before. Look at the Recession-Proof Wealth promotion we're working on now. First, we're selling them something for $39. As soon as they get the $39 item, we send the letter that sells the $495 item. So we go from $39 to $495, and then we focus on selling products and services for thousands of dollars to that smaller group of people that first gave us $39, then $495. Now we're focused on spending the money to try to move them even further. We could always try to sell the $495 product first — but that wouldn't really work, would it? **You can't just take somebody from cold to hot that fast.** That would be like a young man who meets a beautiful, attractive woman and instantly asks her to marry him. If she's a good woman she's going to say no, even if she might want to or might consider it. Similarly, in our field you can't ask people to do too much too fast — so you have to stair-step people.

Here's an example from my friend Chris Hollinger. When he first started his business, he was preparing to sell websites to entrepreneurs around the country, and was giving a lot of thought to where his price point needed to be. Obviously, a website has a lot of design time invested in it, but there's not a lot of physical product, is there? At the beginning, coming from the Midwest and having just been a teacher and launching this new business, Chris couldn't fathom charging $1,297 for a website — mostly because there was no way he, personally, would spend that much on a website. And yet, when he discussed this with me, I told him, "Oh, hey, absolutely! You should charge $1,297 or maybe even more for your higher-end websites. And you could consider offering a middle-level website, and then an entry-level website." **Chris was convinced that people would buy that entry-level $490 website before they'd buy the more expensive one — but the reality couldn't have been further from the truth.** The vast majority of the sales that he made with that initial product offer were at the $1,297 level. People ate them up. They wanted the very best. And, of course, at $1,297 Chris knew how much time was involved in creating such a website — and it was surprisingly low. The profit margin in the majority of websites out there is just ridiculous because, especially now, there are so many different websites that can be used as templates. You just replicate them to a certain degree, and then add to and change them as necessary.

So let's say a local businessman in Wichita wants to buy a website, because he doesn't have the skills to build his own — even though there are a lot of good programs out there that would allow him to do that. He wants Chris to do it, and Chris is going to charge him for his time, his design fee, his overhead, whatever. Most of the time, the customer is willing to pay that. What really was an eye-opener for Chris were those higher-level sales. About 75 to 80 percent of his sales were the $1,297 level. It's really fun when you start getting orders for $1,297, $1,297, $1,297... and they keep coming in.

Six years later, it's still hard for Chris to determine a price for his products. That's a conversation he and I have had many times: will people really spend $999, $3,500, $5,000 for products? Well, yes, they will. As I mentioned earlier, **people buy in an emotional vacuum.** If you can build the value and the benefits in your sales copy to the point to where you can say, "This is why it's worth $5,000," and offer proof, then yes, they'll buy, if that's what they're looking for.

Of course, if you're going to charge $5,000 for something, you've really got to build that case up! **You've got to have some serious, believable proof there: features, benefits, and value.** And oftentimes, it might involve a stair-step type scenario. But if it's there, and it's convincing, people will buy it. Some people might claim that they don't have the money, but if they really want it, they'll *find* the money. It's almost a law of the universe: **People will find the money for something they really want.** If your copy's strong enough, they'll feel they really want what you're offering, and they'll find the money.

That's one reason it's always a good idea to have a bigger option or bigger package available. If at all possible, and generally it *is* possible, you should have A and B packages, or maybe A, B, and C packages — a good, a better, and a best. A silver and a gold. A basic and a premium; something like that. If you have just one package of products, split them into two. **All you have to do is take some of them and make them available for the base price, and take the rest of them and make them only available with the upgrade.** You can divide your content out to deliver it over a couple of different package options. So maybe Option A, your basic package, costs $397; and your premium package, Option B, includes all these additional products and services, features, and benefits and costs $997. If you have the ability, split it into three and offer an Option C that goes for $1,497 or $1,997. You'll find that just by having the more expensive option available, it does a couple of things.

Some people will always go for the most expensive option; they just

MARKETING SECRET

Steal the best ideas from other people as often as you can!

- Work at stealing these best ideas!

- Keep your swipe files near you at all times! — And use it as you're creating your own stuff.

- "Many ideas grow better when transplanted into another mind than the one they sprang up in."
— Oliver Wendell Holmes

do it. **It's psychological. They want the best.** Think about cars: when you buy a new car, you want all the options! So even though the base price is only $23,000, it's loaded up at about $35,000 — and almost everybody goes for the $35,000 option, because they want all the goodies on their new car. It's that way with most things. Sure, some people are cheapskates and always go for the cheap option, but some people always go for the most expensive. Having that package available increases your average ticket size.

Here's another thing it does. For the people who still opt for the lowest price, it makes that package more valuable in their minds, because they see that there are other things available out there that are even more expensive; **this makes that lower price seem more affordable to them.** If you have $397 on your order form and that's it, then they've got nothing to compare it to. But if you've got Package A, B, and C, and Package A is $397 while the others are even more expensive, it makes people feel a little better about that lower price. It can help get more people to go ahead and take it. So if you've got multiple products or services, divide them up into different packages. **That can really help you make more sales *and* have a higher average ticket sale.**

The great thing about information products is that their value is based on what's inside them, *not* **what the product is made of.** A single CD costs maybe a penny or two to manufacture. All a CD is is a piece of plastic that holds data. And yet, you could put content worth thousands of dollars on that single CD-Rom. If it's the right information, sold to the right person, they'll be happy to pay thousands of dollars for it. It all depends on what's on the CD. It's the same way with a book. Several years ago, a gentleman was selling a book no more than 50 pages long for a $1,000, and he sold it with a notice clearly stating that there were no refunds. It was just a little book about the size of a legal pad, not very thick at all. At M.O.R.E., Inc., we printed some up for a few of our friends and gave them away. I think that was the reason he said, "No refunds" — because he knew it would be easy to make a photocopy and return the original to him for a refund.

The point is, it's the information that's presented that's important, not what it's presented on or what format it's given to you in. Books sell all the time for $15, $20, $25. There's no reason that a book 100-200 pages long couldn't also sell for $1,000 if it contained the right information.

That's the great thing about information marketing. It's not the same as selling most products. There are certain abilities you need to sell what I call "mainstream" or physical products. If you have a product sitting on your desk, there are limitations on how much you can sell that product for. And it gets even harder to make bigger profits on a product that's available through other people. If your prospects can get your product at Wal-Mart, you're probably not going to be able to make much money on it, because Wal-Mart is selling them by the millions for a very small margin that you can't beat. In the Internet age, you have very little ability to sell your product for much more than what Wal-Mart is selling it for. If someone sees that you have it available for "X" dollars and they can go to Wal-Mart and get it for half that, then hey, they're probably going to buy it at Wal-Mart. That's reality.

With information products — especially proprietary ones, where you're the one developing them — you control the entire situation and all the content. You control the inventory, the supply, how many of them are available, and you can set the price. **The price is based on whatever value the prospect perceives it as having.** So you could sell information products for any price you want, as long as you can justify the price to a customer, they're willing to pay it, and they can see value in giving you the money you're asking in return for it. There's no limitation to that. People regularly sell information products for thousands of dollars, and sometimes even more — whereas very few physical products demand that kind of money, except vehicles and electronics like high definition televisions. **The largest profit margins are usually made with information products.**

There's an economic theory that says, "There's what's something is worth, and then there's what the market will bear." Add the ruthless copywriter to the mix, and it becomes, "There's what's something is worth, and then there's *what the copywriter can sell it for.*" A lot of business people out there are operating on the economic principles that there's what it's worth, there's supply, there's demand, and there's what the market will bear. **But a copywriter can get the market to bear a much higher amount.** I think our old *Dialing for Dollars* booklet is a fair example. The paper, the staples, the ink that went into that booklet cost, oh, forty cents; and in mass production, that cost went down even further. And yet, the First Edition sold for $12.95 — and later, we created other editions that were bigger and beefier that sold for up to $39. That's a pretty good markup. **We parlayed the ideas in that booklet into millions of dollars.**

And how did we manage that? By giving people what they wanted. *Dialing for Dollars* did that so well that we had thousands of people sending us checks and cash by FedEx (we didn't accept credit cards for the first eight years we were in business). They also wired their money to us by Western Union. In more than one case, they just jumped in their cars and drove from four or five states away just because the mail was too slow, and they had to get our product right away. *That's* how much it captured their imaginations. *That's* how well we hit on the giving people exactly what they wanted. **We created the right product for the right market.** That goes back to the First Commandment.

Remember, it's the market that determines the price, not us. So many people just don't feel a particular product is worth a certain amount, so they don't try to sell it for more money. They don't understand that the market is willing to pay more money, so they lose out! The richest man that I've ever spent good, quality time with was George Douglas. At one point, he was making $1,000,000 a week in our market. We feel great when we have a million-dollar *month*, and he was generating a million dollars a week! He told us in a very commonsense, laid-back kind of way, because that's how he is, "Look, my average ticket price was $13,000. I always felt that the more money I charged, the more people wanted it — because everybody wants the best." And when they want the best, they're more than happy to pay for it.

Here's a phrase I want to share with you. It not my phrase, and it's a bit insulting, but it's worth thinking about: **"Buyers are liars."** You won't forget that, right? "Buyers are liars." The thing is, buyers always say they don't have the money for something. But what they're really saying is, "Get rid of the guilt... get away! Get out of here!" What we teach our sales reps is that every time a client says they don't have enough money, **what they're really saying is, "You just haven't told me enough yet. I don't know enough yet. I'm not sold enough yet."** It's a poor salesman who, as soon as he hears those words, "I can't afford it," says, "Oh, thank you sir." *Click.* They hang up. They're done; that's the end of the sales call right there! But remember this title, which was from a book by Zig Ziglar's brother Judd: *Timid Salespeople Raise Skinny Kids.* A timid salesperson gives up the first time someone says, "Oh, I don't have the money." But an aggressive salesperson will just stay after them, over and over again; so they won't just take no for an answer right away.

In order to maximize profitability, it's great to have all kinds of options for your customers, especially choices for those few willing to spend more money right away. **There's always a small percentage of your customer base that's willing to spend big, big bucks with you.** And if you don't have something to sell to them for big bucks, then you're losing out on money that could and should be yours. They're willing to spend that money; they want to spend it. They've got it. They trust you, they like what you're doing, they want more of the benefits you provide. **If you have nothing to offer them, you're leaving money on the table.** All you have to do is find or develop the products or services that sell for more money, and you'll have a small percentage of your customers that are willing to pay it. **Even better, it'll raise the perceived value of the rest of the products you offer, even for the majority who won't pay the big bucks right away.**

Our Platinum Plus Membership, a coaching program, sells for

▼▼▼▼▼▼▼▼▼▼▼▼

The 4 laws of self teaching:

1. You are your greatest teacher.
2. You can learn <u>anything</u> you want to learn.
3. You <u>must</u> take total responsibility for everything that happens to you.
4. Experience + Reflection = Wisdom!

MARKETING SECRET

The ultimate power is to figure out a way to make a nice profit — even if your actual response rates suck!

- This is the secret to getting rich in Direct-Response Marketing!

- Spend your time playing around with "worst case scenarios" — and figure out a way to turn a good profit with bad numbers. Then prove (through testing!) that you can do it! And if so — you're on your way to making a ton of money!

$17,885 a year. We've only got one Platinum Plus member right now; we've turned a few down, though, because if we feel we can't help a person or if we feel it's going to be too much of a strain on them financially, we don't take them on. So we've got one Platinum Plus member; and although normally the cost is going to be $17,885 a year, until we get 12 members we're grandfathering in our first members and letting them just stay aboard with us, year after year, for free after they pay that first fee. So we're doing something special for them. But the point I want to make is this: we started out two years ago with just two coaching programs; I believe it was Silver and Gold. But now we've got four coaching programs. The most expensive is the one I just told you about, at $17,885 a year. The cheapest one costs $495, plus $50 a month. So there's quite a bit of diversity between those two prices. Though just one person is taking advantage of that large $17,885 package right now, it does tend to elevate the value of our other packages. For example, it makes our $5,000 program seem a little less expensive. **That's just perception, of course, but perception is reality in the marketing world.** I'll just admit it straight out: one of the reasons we came up with the Platinum Plus package is because we wanted to make our $5,000 package seem cheaper. When you have the big package to compare to $5,000, you think, "Oh, come on, it's only $5,000." It really does alter people's perceptions — and that's not a bad reason to have the Platinum Plus, if for no other reason.

You don't want to just make something up, of course! If we had a Platinum Plus position but we never allowed anybody to be a Platinum Plus member, that would be wrong. That's not what

I'm talking about. When we came up with Platinum Plus, we invented a new membership package that gave the buyer even more. It's a real package, even though we created it knowing that we'd have a hard time getting people to pay for it. After all, it's almost $18,000 a year! It's for a small, small group of people — and we've turned down more people than we've allowed in. But we do have one member, and we're working on getting a second one as I write this.

The point is, having that higher-priced package — that ultimate option — makes our other options look more affordable. Our main "sweet spot" package is our middle one — the Platinum $5,000 package. But it's only our sweet spot because we now have the bigger package to compare it with. If we didn't have the big one, then people would probably opt for the next one down — because for psychological reasons, people often opt for a middle-of-the-road package. Chris Lakey bought tires for his minivan a month ago or so, and I remember him telling me that when he asked, "What are all the tire options?" the guy at the tire counter said, "Well, there are five you can choose from. We've got the cheap options here. These have this warranty, and they cost this much. And the most expensive ones are over here on this end." And what did Chris do? He said, "I'm not a tire expert. Let's go with the one right in the middle!" and so he picked the middle-priced one. All the tire options probably would have served his van fine. They probably all would have been driven about the same number of miles.

Well, a lot of people do what Chris did: **they go for the middle package.** And so if we only had $500, $1,250, and $5,000 coaching packages, our average ticket would probably be in that middle range. By having an $18,000 package, it makes our $5,000 package look more affordable. More people opt for it, and that brings our average price up. **So the higher you can get that high-end package, the higher your average ticket will usually be.** Arrange things so you have several package options available, if you can. If your products and services lend themselves to it, divide them up. Split them into Packages A, B, and C. It will increase your average ticket.

Even if you don't have A, B, and C packages, what you can do is this. Let's say your sales letter has an offer in it, and your main price is $495. **What you do is, you offer an upsell** and say, "Right now you can get this..." and you just give it a little bit of mention in the sales copy, maybe

SECTION FIVE — Ruthless Copywriting Strategies

on the last page of your sales letter: call it a "Last Minute Opportunity" or something like that. "For a limited time only, we also have this extra package. Normally it sells for $1,000, but you can have it TODAY with your $495 package for just $495 more. That's half price!" So then you have product for the regular price of $495, and then you have a check box that says, "Thank you for making me this extra-special offer. I'd also like to add this other product. Here is my total of $990." **You get people to take that add-on sale, just like that.** It's not really an A, B, C package; it's just another thing that you've added on as an option — and some people will take that option. **It helps with your bottom line;** your main sale is $495, but a certain percentage of your customers will go ahead and check that box. They'll send you $990, so it brings your average ticket price up.

The idea is that when people are hot for what you have, you should try to make the upsell to them as fast as you can. That's when you should offer them more choices. Even if only 10% of the people check the box and spend that extra money, it raises your average ticket price, which increases your overall profitability. It's simple. It's easy. If you hadn't added the option to your order form, you would have lost money that could and should have been yours. **All you have to do is add one or two little lines, and BOOM! All of a sudden you make 10-20% more money.**

If I remember right, the first time we tried this, the upsell was about $1,500 — and the main product was just a few hundred dollars. It was a significant bump up, yet some people still opted for it — and so we increased our average ticket. At the very least, this process helps with your mailing costs. **Direct mail is expensive; the more you can do things to bump your average ticket price up, the more you can help offset your mailing costs and get yourself into the black faster.**

Let's look at our coaching programs again. We started a couple of years ago with just two of them; now we have four, which is probably where we'll stay. However, we're constantly taking the sales material for those four coaching programs and improving it. We're making it better. We're reworking it over and over again. As I've said before, people who aren't insiders don't realize that these sales letters they see others using were refined over a long period of time. Our Platinum package is undergoing revision right now, as I write this. I'll make more changes next week, and the week after that. In the case of our Platinum coaching program, I expect Chris Lakey will just put his foot down about three weeks from this writing, and he'll say, "Okay, T. J., we're done. This is it. We're finished."

When you're a copywriter, nothing's every really finished — but sometimes, you just have to abandon it. Most people don't realize this. They think copywriters have some innate ability that lets them put together this magnificent, heavy-hitting sales material the right way the first time. What they fail to realize is that a lot of times, they're working it and re-working it and re-working it — and that's what gives it its strength and its power, and causes more people to send more money when they read it.

Here's another strategy. If you're personalizing a sales letter, **try personalizing the order form, too. If you do that, it makes it easier for someone to order, because all they have to do is enter their payment information** — their name and address is already on the order form. The easier you make it for people, the more likely they are to not put it off. If they have to fill out a form... well, sometimes people are busy. Even if they like your product, if they have to stop and do something to order it, what will happen is this: they'll say, "I'll get to that later." So they set it aside — and never get back to it. Putting their name on the order form for them, personalizing it, is an excellent idea. **If all they have to do is fill out their payment, it makes it easier for them to order.** Similarly, if they're already excited about your offer and there's a check box that says, "Give me even more..." and it describes what it is and has a price, then a percentage of them are going to check the box because they want more of it.

It's easiest to get that upsell if it's related to the original product. We have an offer right now that we've been mailing for a short period of time that includes, for the base price, a manual — basically a three-ring binder. But if you check the upgrade box, you also get audio CDs and some other stuff. It's related; it's easy to make that jump, because you already got them excited about the first thing. It's more of the same, just in a different medium. **The fact that the upsell is closely related to the original offer is a way to remove any barrier that people have to the order.** If it's easy for people to check a box, if it's easy for people to send their order, they're more likely to do it.

And people do things out of habit. When we held the original event

▼▼▼▼▼▼▼▼▼
MARKETING SECRET

Keep searching for products and services with the largest gap between perceived value and actual cost.

- These are the items that can make you rich!

- Look for items where the prospect doesn't know or care about your actual cost.

this section is based on, we had about a hundred people who said that they were going to attend. Well, we didn't get that many. So why would a hundred people say that they wanted to attend, and then not show up? One of my employees, Jeff McMannis, told me, "Because you gave them an order form, so they filled it out and sent it in!"

There was a time, years ago, when I would have said to Jeff, "Man, that's such an overgeneralization! That's overly simplistic!" But those days are over; now, I'm inclined to believe *exactly* what Jeff said. People just do things out of habit; there's an order form there, so they send it in! **We're all creatures of habit, and we buy for mostly unconscious reasons.** The best example of that is where people are faced with a decision of good, better, and best, like I discussed earlier. They've got three choices, and out of habit alone, they'll often gravitate to the middle one. Maybe they look at the price and know they can't afford the highest-priced one, so they go for the next one down. **If you didn't have that higher priced package, there's no way they're going to move in for that middle spot.**

Recently, Chris Hollinger had a gentleman call him up and say, "Hey, I just faxed you my order form. Did you get it? Huh? Did you get it?" Chris says, "Hold on, let me go check." So he went to the fax machine and yeah, there it was. Then the guy says, "You know what you need? You need an investor's position for, say, $12,000." When your customers get to that point, the sky's the limit!

That's another reason why you want to have additional products and services to offer someone who buys something from you once.

This gentleman wanted to do more business with Chris, because he provided good value. If you can get out there with another related offer to them and say, "Hey, I know you bought this, so I think you also might enjoy this..." then you can make additional sales.

I buy a lot of stuff online these days from Amazon, and I use an electronics website called TigerDirect.com. Both are really good about sending an email that basically says, "People who bought this..." and "this" is whatever I just bought, "also have enjoyed this... and you might be interested, too." Amazon will do things like say "58% of the people who bought this also bought *this* item." What they're saying is, **"Hey, do you want to be in the minority, or do you want to be part of the majority?** Because most of the people who bought this also bought that, and you should probably add that to your shopping list too." Amazon makes it really easy — you can just click a button, they charge your credit card, and the product is on its way.

What you've sold your customers the first time should show you what they're interested in, so that should prove to you that you can sell them related things as well. **So don't neglect getting back out there with a related offer to the people who bought something from you once, because oftentimes they'll buy other products and services that are similar.** That should be the basis of your system for getting your customers to buy more. If you don't have a system for selling to your customers, you're at the mercy of their system of buying — and they don't have one. At best, most customers just say, "Do you have anything else?" and that's about the extent of it. The type of person Chris Hollinger encountered, the one who told him he should offer a specific new product, is truly rare.

We have a few customers at M.O.R.E., Inc. who have been with us for 20 years. We have even more customers who've been buying from us for 15 years, and an even larger group of customers who have been buying from us on a consistent basis for the last 10 years. The group of customers we've been selling to for five years is larger still. We have these customers identified as such in our system; we know exactly who they are, and we're constantly offering them more of the types of items we know they've bought from us before. People who aren't familiar with our market might say, "My goodness, why would somebody just keep buying such things?" Well, think about your own life; think about the products you like, and the types of things you've bought again and again. **There's always that group**

of customers that's insatiable. They want what you have, and they just can't seem to get enough. **The more they buy, the more they want to buy!** It's as if the hunger increases. It's like feeding a fire. You just keep feeding it and it grows bigger and bigger. Their consumption leads to a desire for even more consumption, and they just can't be satiated.

As long as you're selling products and services that offer real value to these people, then you're going to keep bringing in the money. That's the key here. **As long as you're providing good, solid value and delivering on your promises, then you'll sell people more and more.** If you're not, and you don't have those offers, you're going to lose money that could and should be yours. It's on the table; people are willing to spend it. If you're not offering them something in exchange, you're just going to lose that money.

Anybody can go through a company and, in an attempt to increase profits, say, "Hey, let's cut here. Let's shave this. Let's fire him. Let's get rid of her. Let's X-out that department. Let's cut here. Let's cut there," and, yes, those are all things that can increase profits. But it takes a certain mindset to do that. Another mindset for increasing profits, one that may be easier to handle, is, "Hey, let's sell our customers more of this. Let's sell them more of that. Hey, we can sell them more and more and more of this other stuff!" **What's really required when it comes to increasing profitability is a little bit of both of those mindsets: a bit of the frugal thing, and a lot of finding ways to do more business with people you already know.** They like you, they trust you, and you already know they're buying from all your competitors — so they might give you more money!

Remember that phrase, "Buyers are liars"? God knows I love my customers, and I'm not trying to put them down here; I'm just trying to prove a point, that's all. We've had people tell us, "Hey, I want a refund. I can't afford this. I'm hurting for money." So we give them the refund — and then we find out they took that money and gave it to one of our competitors right away! People will never cease to amaze you. As marketers, you find out the good things about people, but you also find out the not-so-good things. You see, we're dealing in a world of emotions here. Think about that. **Logic plays a very small part in any of this,** and it's all kind of crazy — but kind of interesting, too. It's fun. That's where the romance of business life comes from.

The Fourth Commandment

The Fourth Commandment of Marketing is to develop marketing systems that identify the right prospect, and then communicate the right message to them.

What is marketing? If you ask a hundred experts, they'll give you a hundred slightly different answers. But here's something I think they could all agree on: **It's those things that you do to attract the right customers to begin with, and it's the things you do to re-sell them again and again.** The first step is a necessary part to get to the second step, which is where all the profits lie. It's simple, if you use that definition; then you can develop your marketing plans accordingly.

So if that's what marketing is — attracting and then re-selling to customers again and again for the largest profit possible — **then a marketing system is simply something that allows you to do that in a systemized way, so you don't even have to think.** You set it up once. It does take work to set it up that one time; but from that point forward, you arrange for other people to manage it for you. You don't have to do anything. You can be busy working on other things.

> ▼▼▼▼▼▼▼▼▼
>
> P.T. Barnum-ize every offer!
>
> - Big!
> - Blow it up!
> - Bold!
> - Explosive!
> - Wow them!
> - History making!
> - Whiz-bang!
> - Hype it!
> - Jazz it up!
> - Make it rock!

People often ask me, "How do you prioritize your customers?" We do it two basic ways, but the first way is the most important. **Our customer list is divided by the amount of money that people spend.** Let's look at it as a triangle; up at the very top is the smallest group of customers, those who spend the most money. At the bottom are the customers who spend the least money. That's the easiest way to do it. People who spend the largest amount of money are on the smallest list; we call those "Primo A" customers. And then we have B, C, and D. You have to spend, I believe, $49 bucks to get on our D list.

When you're talking about promoting the right products to the right group of customers,

SECTION FIVE — Ruthless Copywriting Strategies

▼▼▼▼▼▼▼▼
MARKETING SECRET

Customers are insatiable!

- "The more they buy — the more they buy!"
  — Dan Kennedy

- "A buyer who buys twice is twice as likely to buy again."
  — Dick Bensen

this kind of segmentation is crucial. But it's also important for other reasons. Here's an example. **Whenever we have a new idea we're uncertain about, we test it to that small "Primo A" group of our very best customers first.** That's pretty much an acid test for us. If the Primo customers don't respond like crazy, then we'd better abandon the idea and move on. **If people who like you and trust you, people who've already spent a lot of money with you, don't want your product — then other people probably won't either.**

So you develop your systems to help you handle things. **The systems can be very easy to build, so don't let any perceived difficulties stop you.** Let me explain an easy system; it's the one that we're working on right now. We've got a $39 initial offer. It's a one-ounce package, First Class, so it contains just the basic two-page sales letter, a large order form, a return envelope, and maybe a lift piece. All it does is ask for $39 — and if they'll send that to us, they get a free gift, a gift voucher for $495. It comes in a window envelope, so the first thing people see is the FREE $495 gift voucher that they get if they give us the $39. That's Step #1 of the system. **Although this is an offer that's going out to our established clients first, we expect that it's also going to be used for new customer acquisition.** So once we get past the testing phase and prove it's successful, then we'll use it to acquire new customers — people who have never done business with us.

That's how it becomes systematized. Once we know the promotion works and all the back-end related marketing upsell materials are in place, then every single week we'll mail out as many as 50,000 of those letters. I wrote it once. We're committed to it. And if it works week after week, we're going to send out as many as 50,000 of those Direct Mail packages every week. The printer will just print them up, the mailing house will mail them out, and we don't do anything except open up the envelopes with the checks, money orders, and credit card authorizations, and process the orders.

Then, we have the **back-end sales letter,** the second part of the system. **This is a letter that asks for an upsell.** It can be of any length, but let's say it's five pages long. If it's successful, if we convert enough people to that next sale for $495, then it becomes part of our system, too. On Day #1 we get the checks, money orders, and credit card authorizations for $39; on Day #2, or Day #1 if we're really operating fast, those who bought will immediately be sent this package for the $495 upsell. Then, over the next month, we'll create as many different follow-up letters as we can for all those people who gave us $39 but didn't give us the $495 right away. Then we're going to have a sequence of maybe 10 to 12 different follow-up offers that, again, we'll create just once. That's the point I want to make: that's the part of it that makes it a system! **We'll work hard to do it this one time. We'll put together as many as 10 or 12 different follow-up offers** that keep saying, "Hey look, why didn't you upgrade? Why didn't you upgrade?" and we'll continue to give them more reasons why they *should* upgrade, and we won't let go of them. Again, that's what salesmanship is all about. **Stay on top of them!** Keep telling them they need to upgrade. Keep making more convincing arguments.

Then, from that point forward, we'll start developing other upsells for the people that gave us the $495. We already know the things that we want to sell to them; it's important to know that from the beginning. This is part of our overall strategy; in this case, we have at least two things that we want to offer people. One is a $3,500 product we want to create with one of our joint venture partners called Global Resorts Network, and it's a great opportunity. We also have our Platinum Membership in the Direct-Response Network; that's a $5,000 sale. Those are the two ultimate sales that we *know* that we want to make to the largest number of people. But first we're starting by asking for the $39, for which they'll get a great opportunity. Part of the secret of upselling is this (and it *is* a secret, because most people have never figured it out): **We're giving them so much value for their $39 that they're going to say, "Holy crap!",** like Frank Barone used to in *Everybody Loves Raymond*. They'll go, "Holy crap! This is great!" and they'll be happy and excited. That's part of our goal. **When they spend 39 bucks, we give them a *really* nice package, and they feel good about what they've just gotten — and now they're ready to move on. We've won their trust.**

Only a fool starts out automatically trusting someone. Smart people are always holding back; you have to earn their trust. So, we're earning people's trust by first giving them a great package for $39. Then we go for an upsell that's directly related to what we sold them first. Now we've got a Master Distributorship opportunity that's so connected with what they bought that it's a natural upsell. It's a perfect extension. The goal is to convert the largest number of $39 buyers to the $495 sale. The idea is that we stair-step people. **You can't just go from $39 to $3,900; there needs to be a more realistic progression.** Each point along the way, you're earning more of their trust, showing them more and more that you're the kind of person they can depend on, and that they don't have to worry about losing their money or being taken advantage of.

If we do our jobs right, they'll spend $10,000 or more with us, because they'll get involved in all three of those big upsells that we have for them. They've got the money to spend. They're willing to spend it, and they *will* spend it with us if we do our jobs right. Sure, it may take us six weeks or eight weeks to put together all those steps and lay them out, but once it's done, it will work just like clockwork. It's like all those websites that have those auto-responders that marketers are familiar with, where they can set them up so that on Day 3 people are going to get this email, and on Day 10 they're going to get that email, and on Day 20 they're going to get this other email. Well, you can do the same thing with Direct Mail, too. It just takes a few people to work it and make sure that it happens right, somebody who's paying attention to the details. **Once you get it going, once you prove that it's profitable, you can just sit back and create the next deal while the first deal keeps the money coming in.** The system is really what you're building, and the copywriting is just all part of making that system work. **Once the system is in place, it keeps cycling.**

Some people, like my friend Chris Hollinger, might just use an outline on a dry erase board to document their system. It doesn't have to be terribly elaborate. Your system can be a list or flow chart that guides you through the process so you're not flying by the seat of your pants. It starts with just building an outline of the necessary marketing and sales steps, and it can look something like this: let's say it starts with a small space ad you could run in a publication that meets your criteria for the people you're going after. Interested people can call a 24-hour recorded hotline. So that's Step #1. The copywriting you've done has got them to the point to where they've picked up the phone and listened to that recorded message. If they're interested, then at the beep they leave you their information. What happens then? Boom... the mail package goes out, and it's a sales letter, an order form, and maybe a lift piece about you, to help them connect with you. Once you have a few sales, your outline takes it to the next step.

Some of the people who receive this first piece will order the product or service you're trying to sell them. Most won't. By not ordering, you assume those people said no. Of course, anything could have happened; your piece could have gotten chewed up by the dog, it could have got piled on, it could have gotten thrown into a desk drawer, or someone else's letter might have worked better. **That's why you want your piece to be compelling — so when they get it, they act right away.**

The sky is the limit on what you can do with your follow-up. Will it be a postcard? Will it be another letter? A CD? I might send a letter saying, "Hey, you didn't respond to my first offer, so I wanted to let you know about all this other stuff that wasn't in it." Or, it can be a simple email. Some of us, for example Chris Hollinger, like to use emails because they can be very inexpensive. There can be problems with email delivery, but at least it's another point of contact that you can put on your outline. Again, these are going out to that list of people who said no. They haven't responded yet, so now you want to try and drag them in so you can outline the features, the benefits, and the value of this particular offer, and have a specific call to action at the end of the offer.

Now, at M.O.R.E., Inc., I have an infrastructure. **I have to make sure that they have an order form in their hands, or they can easily call in and order.** That's all part of building the system. But bear in mind, as I'm putting this offer together, **I'm building this system just once** — and then it's a matter of the mailing house or our printer actually handling a lot of the day to day stuff. You need to concentrate on those things that make you the most money, and that's making sales with your copywriting.

I like to think that ours is a top-of-the line Direct-Response mailing

MARKETING SECRET

A powerful secret from one of America's foremost Direct Response copywriters:

- "Most of the items I sell can be easily explained in one or two pages. But they cannot be sold in one or two pages!"

- I can clearly explain them in 1 or 2 pages — but to sell them it takes an extra 20 to 30 pages!"

system. It's systematized. It's just boom... boom... boom; and once we've proved the numbers are there, we can roll it out pretty big. **You can, too. But you can also start rather small, and test carefully; and once you get some results and the margins are there — the *money* is there — then you can roll it out bigger and really start raking it in.**

There are three things that stand out in this particular commandment. **The first part is developing marketing systems. A system allows you to, well, systemize.** You can boil things down to a step-by-step process, so you don't have to figure things out as you go. Earlier, I talked about the systems we have in place for when orders come in, for when packages are shipped out. We've got an Administrative Department that handles all of the incoming orders and everything associated with them. We've got systems in place so that every order gets processed in the fastest time possible. From there, we have systems in place with our Shipping Department to get things shipped out.

So orders flow in and out of our offices in a systematic way, using the systems we've put in place. We have systems in place for making sales, and we have a system in place for communicating with our printer so that he knows exactly what we need printed and exactly what it's supposed to look like. The system also includes working with a mailing house to make sure our mailings get out the door quickly and for the lowest price. That system works on the marketing side, to efficiently communicate our sales message to our clients. **All of that is part of having systems in place, so that we get orders coming in the door and we get products going out the door.** We have systems in place for customer service, for when people call and they need help; we have Internet support options, and people can email. We have systems in place for coaching, so people who purchase our coaching programs can get support and help from us.

We have systems in place for just about everything we do. There are even marketing systems in place for how we write sales letters. **All of that is systematized to maximize productivity and get the biggest results.** Those are the systems that we've put in place to help us run an efficient operation. We need to have rigorous systems in place because we have a large overhead: we have a building and a staff to pay for. If you're working by yourself, your systems can be slightly different, because they'll probably involve a lot of outsourcing.

The next part of the process is identifying the right prospect, so you have to develop marketing systems that do that. How? Well, obviously, I've talked at length about giving people what they want. You start by knowing who your prospect is, at least in a general sense. The opportunity market may consist of millions and millions of people, but not all those millions are going to be interested in what you have to offer at any given moment. You could have a particular offer that appeals only to a small percentage of them, so how do you identify the right prospect for each offer you have? **You do that through lead generation. That's why we recommend two-step marketing — so you can identify the prospects.** You would never do a mailing to every opportunity seeker out there, but if you did, you could safely bet that only a percentage of them would be interested in what you have to offer. That's part of your two-step marketing effort. Maybe you mail out a four-page teaser letter first; maybe you mail out a postcard. Maybe you're doing it online; in any case, you've identified them somehow, and you're emailing them. **Whatever the delivery method, you attract them, get them to request more information from you. That's how you identify the right prospect.**

The final thing is to communicate the right message to them. That means you've identified them, and you're talking to them about the things that they're interested in. You're writing to show them that you can give them just what they want. **You're telling them that you can solve their biggest wants and needs. And you do that through your system, so it's really a three-part equation here.** First of all, start with the system, then identify the right prospect for your product or service, and then

SECTION FIVE — Ruthless Copywriting Strategies

communicate that message to them in the right way. Those three things work hand-in-hand.

We're only marketing to the buyers — those people who have already bought the kinds of products and services we sell. We communicate to those people as part of our new customer acquisition program. You can have a mailing house that does all of this for you, by the way; you don't have to have a large Shipping Department. You can have your mailing house take care of everything for you. You can put together 12 different direct mail packages that go out after a certain customer spends money with you, and then they can manage the entire process. For example, on Day #3 they can send out the first follow-up, and on Day #5 they can get the second follow-up out. You tell them which customers actually bought from you, and they mark them off the list so those people don't get the rest of the sequence. A good mailing house takes care of it all for you. They're spending their money on their equipment, they're spending their money on their infrastructure, they've got their representative who's in charge of knowing where every step needs to go in the process, and they can take care of it all. You can also find companies that do all the shipping for you, too. **So don't think you have to have a large infrastructure to run these heavy sequences.**

The point is that if you're not following up enough with people, you're losing money. **You can *never* assume that just because people don't respond, that they're saying no to you.** You just keep asking them and keep asking them, until the numbers tell you to stop; that is, until the overall profitability for that list of prospects becomes so low that it just doesn't make any sense anymore, because you're not converting any more sales.

There's one more point I want to make. Let's say you have a local company that sells only to businesses, and you're looking for long-term customers. You're selling a product or service where the customers just stay with you year after year. You would easily lock in all of the prospective buyers in your area. Let's say you're located in an area of a million people, but there are only a couple of hundred primary prospective buyers. As a matter of course, you'd know where those couple of hundred companies were. You would have them on a list, clearly identified: here are the prospective buyers in our area. Then you would hire a sales rep or two. Their job would just be to work the territory. They'd go around on a regular basis and knock on the same few hundred doors until the people at those companies said, "Get out of here! We never want to see you again!" And even if that happened, you, the company owner, would probably send another sales rep there. They'd just keep it up again and again, until finally the sales rep would say something like, "Look, we've been coming here for two years. You haven't bought anything; so either you place an order with us today, or this is the last you're going to see of me for a while." You can see that this is how it's done in a traditional model. That's how Fortune 500 and Fortune 1000 companies are built. They've got sales forces that go out there and cover those territories; they just keep showing up on a regular basis, and they keep asking people over and over again, "Are you ready to do something this time? Are you ready to buy something this time?" Ultimately, they try to weed out those people who are never going to buy.

> Do everything possible to shift the power and get them to chase you — rather than you chasing them!

It works the same way with all direct-response businesses. **The follow-up is where all the money is.** Staying after them again and again is where you profit. You can do that in a systematized way just by putting those pieces together once, and keeping it running on automatic after that. Every direct mail package you produce or create, every follow-up email, every tele-seminar that you record once can work as a system for all those new prospects. **It's like a funnel:** You're taking in the new prospects at the top of the funnel, and then as they go through the system it's all laid out, organized and designed to take that large group of people and whittle them down to a smaller group. **Your goal is then to get the largest number of those people possible to invest the most money in the other products and services that you offer.**

Here's an analogy that illustrates the process. Recently, Chris Hollinger took his daughter to a place called the Kaufman Museum in Newton, Kansas, where they have an old-time corn de-cobber. You put the corn cob in there and crank the handle, and it starts spitting out all these dried corn kernels. That's what a system really is. You have the hopper there, the funnel, and a good solid marketing system that helps you keep the prospects pouring in at the top. The cranking of the handle is all those follow-up pieces and mechanisms that you send to your prospects. **When**

▼▼▼▼▼▼▼▼
MARKETING SECRET

Quantity leads to quality.

- The secret to coming up with the greatest ideas is to come up with lots of ideas! Go wild! Don't hold back! Just get into the habit of letting it flow! Set a time every morning for brainstorming as many ideas as you can come up with, make it fun and enjoyable to crank out huge quantities of ideas — and you'll be amazed at the little gems that come out of this process!

you crank the handle, dollar bills start shooting out the end.

The Fifth Commandment

The Fifth Commandment of Marketing is reaching and selling to your customers as fast as possible, for the largest possible profit. Now, a lot of what I'm going to talk about now is repetitive. You've seen it mentioned before — but as they say, repetition is the mother of all skill. So whenever you see these things again and again, you should know that they're the common denominators that you should focus on.

Again, the basic idea is that you're looking for a primary, targeted prospective buyer — somebody who has already purchased the same types of products and services that you provide. You want to upsell them as fast as possible, for the largest profit possible. **But you still have to realize that you can't take somebody from A to Z without going through the intermediate steps.** You can't just start off by asking them for many thousands of dollars; that usually doesn't happen until and unless you've established just how qualified they are, and until you've done a few things to earn their trust. Then you're looking for the most natural, logical upsell, one that's closely related to what you sold them initially. Let's take a look at our current promotion again. The first packages are going out today with a distributorship for $39. Later, we'll follow up with the Master Distributorship for $495, which is closely tied to what they got from us the first time; it's a natural, logical fit, and that's part of the secret to maximizing your profitability. It's easy for somebody to grasp the idea of upgrading a distributorship to a Master

Distributorship.

If you're doing two-step marketing, that means you want to get to the sale as fast as possible. So you need to get that lead to request your information, and then you need to get your sales material into their hands as quick as you can, so that you can convert that person from a lead to a sale.

I've already talked about large profits and selling information, and being able to have a high-ticket sale with a large profit margin. But you also need to keep this in mind: **You shouldn't try to do it on the cheap. Too many people try to cut corners on their marketing.** I'm not saying that you shouldn't pay attention to the bottom line, because it's important. **It's a factor in profitability** — that is, how much money you spend in relation to how much money you make — so there's certainly something to be said about watching for that. **But it shouldn't be your main focus.** If you focus on doing it as cheap as possible, you probably won't be as effective as you could be. **It's much more important to focus on bringing in the largest number of sales and doing everything it takes to do that.** Generally, you're never going to out-spend yourself. You can spend more money than you have, of course, but in most cases you can't spend too much money to make a sale. Too many people try to shortcut that part of the process. As you try to sell your products and services as fast as possible, to as many people as possible, for the largest profit, keep in mind that we're not talking about spending as little money as possible.

What's truly important is being ready to reach and sell to those people as fast as possible. I've talked about people being heated up and ready to buy. You want to reach them right then, because there's a time frame involved. Systems help you do that. As soon as that prospect has identified himself as being interested in what you have, boom — you want to be right on them with your sales message to get them while they're hot. To do that, you have to spend money to make a sale. Back when Eileen ran the day-to-day operations of our business, this was something that we went around and around about, to the point where it caused friction in our business. Chris Hollinger tells me his wife is the same way. She's always got her finger on the budget button saying, "I don't know…", while he's saying, "No, no, no… we'll spend this much to make these sales. It'll be worth it because we'll gain these customers, and we'll re-sell them." That one point takes a lot of us quite some time to realize, but it's reality.

As a business person, you're going to have to address that at some point — how much money you're willing to spend to break that first sale or that next sale. **Here's the key: knowing the lifetime value of a customer.** How much are you willing to spend to make that first initial $39 sale, in this example? You've got a whole system in place to upgrade them from the $39, to the $495, to the $5,000 sale. If the numbers are working, and you're getting those closings and conversions at the higher levels, you can spend a lot of money on the front-end. **I was in the business about eight years before I realized that every sale must be bought.** By that time, we'd already generated millions of dollars in sales, but I'd just never puzzled it out.

A sale has to be bought. **In other words, it's going to cost you "X" amount of money to make that sale, and you have to calculate that cost against the potential lifetime value of your customer.** A lot of people have difficulty understanding this concept, especially when they're getting started. They don't *know* what the lifetime value of a customer is yet. But look at the situation closely. What's the total value by the end of the sequence you're planning to build? Let's just go back to the example I've been using. We start out with a $39 sale. We're mailing thousands of pieces on the front-end for new customer acquisitions, so we get enough people who give us that $39 initially. Then we've got the $495 upsell. We're going to spend some money on the sequence to try to convert the largest percentage of those people who've already bought to that $495 sale. Then we've got the third sale, which consists of one of three additional, more expensive items — or all three, if possible. **So if you can't figure out the lifetime value of a customer, just figure out the value as that whole sequence plays out, and let the numbers tell you what to do.** It's all about return on investment. It's about dollars spent versus dollars made, and not being afraid to spend some money in order to make some money.

Yet most marketers are trying to catch a whale by using a little, tiny minnow as bait, as the great marketer P.T. Barnum used to say. In this analogy, the whale would be those customers who spend thousands of dollars. Everybody's looking for those customers, because that's how we make all our profits. But they're using minnows for bait; and by that, I just mean they're trying to spend as little as possible to acquire those big customers. It's foolish thinking. Sure, every once in a while, you might get lucky. **You should, instead, be willing to invest as much money as** you can, at least initially.

Let me just give you an example of that to make the concept clear. If we ultimately prove this model that we're just getting started with, we'll end up with many thousands of dollars for the final back-end items we have. On that $495 intermediate upsell, we might be willing to give up every penny of that. Why not? If we do, it will let us spend more money in order to make that initial upsell. We'll be spending up to $495, maybe more, knowing that we're going to get the largest percentage of those people to convert to the $495 offer, **so that now we can make them that additional offer, which is where *all* the profits are.** That's an example of spending money to make money.

Learn the Ten Commandments of Marketing, PART II

In the last chapter, I discussed the first five of what I call the Ten Commandments of Marketing, which I believe every copywriter has to study and internalize if they want to make any real money. In this chapter, I'll finish up the list.

The Sixth Commandment of Marketing

Our next Commandment is simply to re-sell to your clients as often as possible, in order to squeeze the largest amount of money out of them. That may sound ruthless, but that's what you're here for, isn't it? This is one basis of any ruthless, aggressive marketing or copywriting strategy. As long as you're delivering products and services that have real value, then you're doing people a service by doing more business with them.

There are only three ways to build a business: just THREE. First, you can bring in more new customers constantly. As a matter of course, a percentage of those people are going to do more business with you. By the way, that's how a lot of businesses handle things: They just keep trying to find new customers all the time. **But the other two ways to build a business are where all the profits are. The second way is to increase the number of times you re-sell to those customers.** So if you've got a

▼▼▼▼▼▼▼▼
MARKETING SECRET

People buy to satisfy their wants.

- Buying our products or services temporarily fills their urge.

- The very act of buying makes them feel as if they are doing something.

thousand customers, and the average company you're competing with is only trying to re-sell to those people three times a year, while you're trying to re-sell them six times a year — then potentially you're doing twice the amount of business your competitors are, because you're going to the customers more often. **Finally, the third way to build a business is to increase the size and profit margins of your transactions.** In other words, you're trying to sell people more expensive items with bigger price points.

The real secret to overall profitability is to do all three of these things. First, you'll need a system in place for bringing in new customers — that's #1. Number 2: you're trying to re-sell to those customers more often, which is Step #6 on the 10 Commandments list here. That's what I'm talking about. But #3, you're also trying to increase the average transaction size, every single time you do more business with your customers.

This is where most business people blow it, because they ask themselves, "When is it too much?" **The fact is, it's almost impossible to overdo it.** For every marketer who's too aggressive and ends up going bankrupt (and we all know they're out there), there are God knows how many thousands of *other* marketers who are holding back too much, too often. They could and should be doing more to make additional sales. People *will* buy more. **People in most markets are insatiable, though in some markets they're more insatiable than others.** And for the most part, most companies are just not re-selling to their customers nearly as much as they could and should be.

I was talking to a fellow marketer recently,

and one of the points he made is that he never sends a prospect anything unless it's got a call to action of some kind on it. Even if he's fulfilling something they've already bought, there's another offer in there. **You need to consistently make those re-sells; consistently give them the opportunity to buy more.** It took me eight years to learn that — which is why I'll keep trying to pound it into your head! I want to cut your learning curve down. That's one reason why it's good to keep reading books like this, to go to seminars and just generally spend time studying and learning this material: It cuts your learning curve down dramatically.

The easiest sale you'll ever make is the one that you make to an existing customer, because they're already pre-sold on you and what you're doing. *That's* **where all of the profitability is in your business: re-selling to the same people again and again.** There are a lot of marketers who never learn this. All they ever do is try to acquire new customers. All they want to do is keep slamming in new people, new people, new people — and then they just move on. They don't service their existing customers. That's not even part of their system. All they're doing is bringing new people in, making that initial sale, and moving on, happy with the money they're making. And that's a mistake!

You should *never* pass on an opportunity to attempt to sell something to your customer. **They've proven a few things by buying from you in the first place.** For example, they've proven that they like you and trust you. They've decided that you were worthy of giving their money to, at least once. And they've proven that they're interested in the types of products and services you sell. Armed with that information, you can be confident in making them additional offers, because you know they're interested. **You've already built some kind of a relationship with them.**

One of the things to keep in mind with this principle is that you don't want to let too much time lapse between communicating with your customers. **A mailing list is extremely valuable when it's used properly. But that list can also go stale; if you don't mail to it, then there's no bond with it, no relationship with it, and it *will* go bad.** One of the ways that people get around this is by offering a newsletter. This ensures they're mailing to the list on a regular basis. If it's an email list, you can have an email newsletter that costs you nothing to send out. Even if it's not, this is a systematic way to stay in touch with your customers on a regular basis. A lot of people who have newsletters sell products in their newsletter.

Maybe they have a spotlight on a particular product; sometimes they offer affiliate products they didn't even create. Sometimes they're just pointing you to a website where you can get information about someone else's product. Maybe they offer a product of the month. It all depends on the business model.

In any case, staying in touch with your customers is important, because if you don't communicate with them regularly, you'll lose them. They won't have a relationship with you, and so they'll become no different than a person you haven't sold to already. **The value in your list is in the communication; your ability to re-sell to that list is often predicated on you having an ongoing relationship with the people on it.** That bond can grow stronger with time, just like a friendship. The more you hang out with a friend, the stronger your friendship can become. **The more you communicate with your customers, the more they do business with you.** And the more that relationship is nourished, the stronger those business bonds can become. So it's important that you cultivate that relationship, and through that, start re-selling those customers over and over again — squeezing as much money out of them as possible.

Again, it sounds like a ruthless marketing strategy, which is really the point here. When I speak of squeezing the largest possible amount of money out of your customers, **I'm talking about discretionary income, of course.** Just about everybody has a certain amount of income they spend on things they don't need to sustain them. There's all the money they're spending at McDonald's twice a week, or going bowling on a Friday evening, or deciding to go play a round of golf or buy the latest electronic toy. All that extra money is going to be spent somewhere; we Americans put less than 2% of our income into savings. So you know we're blowing it somewhere, right?

The trick is to find the best ways to squeeze as much discretionary money out of your marketplace as possible, because you know they *are* going to be spending that money somewhere. If they don't spend it on you, they're probably going to spend it on your competitors, on other non-related products and services. As a marketer, you want to get them to choose to give the biggest percentage of that discretionary income to you, by offering good value and by keeping the lines of communication open. Again, most business people just aren't doing this nearly enough. That's why it's a real, competitive advantage for you to determine that you *are* going to do it

— and certainly, I've strived to do that myself. There have been times when I probably haven't done it enough, either.

If you have a large, well-developed mailing list, all it takes to make a profit is for a small percentage of the customers on that list to buy from you. Let's say you're doing a mailing to your customer base every month. **Depending on the price point, you could make that an excellent profit even if 95% of the customers *didn't* buy from you that month.** That explains why we're able to "rain mail on your head," as Chris Lakey likes to put it. That's why people who have been with us a long time get a lot of mail from us. Sure, they can throw it away every time — and if a customer doesn't purchase something from us, we'll eventually take them off the list. But it'll take three or four years before we'll decide that we have to do that, for whatever reason. Meanwhile, we'll continue to send mailing after mailing to our entire group of customers — and if only a small percentage of them buy from us every month, we've made excellent money. **I want you to think about that in terms of your business, because it's exciting.**

> Failure is the best education.
> - Test a lot of different things.
> - Set out to try bold things (on a small basis).
> - And then never repeat what didn't work!
> - The more you test — and fail — the better! Why? Because you will ultimately discover what works best.

Let me repeat again that when you're writing to existing customers, you don't have to be as good a copywriter as you have to be to get them on your side in the first place. Now you're writing to people who trust you and like you, and they've shown that through their purchases. They've voted with their checkbooks. What they're really telling you every time that they spend money from you is, "I like what you guys are doing. I want more of what you sell." That's the language of spending money.

The Seventh Commandment

The Seventh Commandment of Marketing is to create sales

▼▼▼▼▼▼▼▼
MARKETING SECRET

Fortunes are made by combining ideas in new ways that nobody else has ever thought of!

- Creativity comes from the labor of a driven person...

- You become a genius by focusing all of your energy on a few key areas — for a period of years...

▲▲▲▲▲▲▲▲

messages that build strong bonds with your customers. I'll tell you how we've done it — and again, I didn't figure this out all on my own. Now, I've got a friend who's just getting into this business, and he keeps grilling me over and over again. He wants to know, "When did you start figuring *this* out? When did you start figuring *that* out?" Well, we really didn't do it all on our own! **For the first five years, we just copied some of the best companies that we had seen and done business with, and who we knew were good marketers.** And we didn't reflect a lot on what we were doing; we were just out there doing it!

But hindsight being 20/20, our story has made us millions and millions of dollars. The quick version is that for years, I was struggling; I was on every single opportunity mailing list out there, and I kept sending away for program after program. I was buying one program after another, spending all the money that should have gone to pay bills — electric, rent, and water. I hated my job, and I knew there was a chance to make real money. All my friends and family said I was an idiot; they told me I was wasting my time, that I was a fool. My wife was the only one who believed in me.

We didn't give up. We finally found a couple of programs that worked, and started making $16,000 a month. That wasn't bad at all, but then Russ von Hoelscher started working with us. We went from $16,000 a month to almost $100,000 a week within nine months. **The best part of the story is that because we didn't give up** — like all of our friends and family told us we should — we ended up making millions. That's why *you* shouldn't give up either. **You have to keep believing in your dreams!**

That rags-to-riches story has made us a fortune for the simple reason that people identify with it. **Everybody identifies with the fact that we're just average Midwestern folks.** We have no special knowledge, skills, or abilities; they just look at me and say, "My God, if that guy can make millions of dollars, what's my excuse? Why can't I do it? I ought to be able to make a hell of a lot more money than he's making!" And they're right! This inspires people, and it motivates them. Sometimes I wonder, at three in the morning, "God, am I going to be 70 years old and still telling that story?" Well, I imagine so, if I'm still in this market, selling to the same type of people. I imagine I'll be telling that story if I live to be a hundred. I'll be telling it a little differently then, I'm sure, but the story remains. It's absolutely true, and it's a story the market has identified with. It's a story that bonds us with our customers, because in large part, they've also been sending away for one program after another. **They've experienced the same frustrations I've experienced, and so they connect with us at a deep emotional level.**

In almost every sales letter that ever goes out now, we tell some version of that story, because it's our signature story. You need one, too. **This is the thing that connects us with our market.** If you'd told me 20 years ago that you could have relationships with tens of thousands of people, that would have sounded like the shallowest of concepts to me. My mind couldn't have grasped that idea. How in the *world* can you have a relationship with thousands of people? Well, if you think about it, these rock stars, actors, and other celebrities feel much the same. They have people that they feel they have a relationship with. Admittedly, some of those people are a little fanatical, but they *do* have those relationships with thousands of people. That's real. The same principles apply to business. You actually can have a relationship with thousands, tens of thousands, hundreds of thousands of people; real relationships where they feel connected to you, they feel like they know you, and they like you and identify with your story.

I've got all kinds of stories that I tell about me, my family, and my past. They're unique to me, and help to build a relationship with my customers — and that does lead to more money, because people are drawn in by stories. **Once you've found those stories, you need to be practiced at the best way to tell them, the best way to draw people in** — or they can come off as hokey, or stale, or unbelievable. The more you tell your story, the better you'll get at that. And that's one of the keys, actually, to building sales copy that gets attention and arouses interest, because it helps to draw your prospect in, to get them paying attention to your sales message and to start building that bond.

Ultimately, direct-response marketing is a form of relationship marketing. We build relationships with people through our marketing efforts — through the ads, the sales letters, and lift pieces — that we send out in the mail, post on websites, or mention in conference calls. It's all about building relationships. The entire industry of network marketing, for example, exploits existing relationships. **Our industry usually builds those relationships completely from scratch.** It starts with the initial sales generation piece, whether it's a mail piece or an ad in *USA Today* or some other publication. You get responses from people who don't know you at all. So while I've told my story for 20 years now, I know I'm likely to keep telling it for another 20 years. Why? Well, let's say that ten years from now, we get a brand new customer who's never done business with us. Well, guess what? That story is brand new to them. So even though we may get tired of telling our own story, to that new person, it's the first time they've heard it. **We tell it because it's proven to work and to build relationships. And still it's inspiring because, again, it matches the market.** It's just human nature to be drawn in to those stories. The unfortunate side of this particular strategy, of course, is the fact that some people just make up stories. They make them up so they can pull you in, and they're good at it.

Think about some of the catalogs and magazines you get in the mail, and the sales copy they use to sell the products in those catalogs; think of the storytelling methods that they use. They talk about how they found this product in the jungles of South America, and how when you rub it on your wound it instantly heals — things like that. True or not, it's a good story. **Writing good stories is an effective way to get a sales message across, assuming you're telling the truth.** Everybody can identify with a good story, and people feel *good* about hearing stories. Some stories have humor in them, and that's a good way to build relationships with customers. **Put simply, one of the quickest ways to bond with someone is by telling them stories and finding common bonds with them.**

This building of strong bonds with your customers happens over

time, just as it does with friends. The longer the relationship has been cultivated, the stronger the connection is — the stronger the friendship. It's a lot easier to tear a friendship down in an instant than it is to build one up in an instant. So you have to build strong bonds by constantly communicating with customers, by doing things that relate to them, by telling stories. The nice thing about personal stories is that they change a little over time. Now, the historical aspect of a story stays the same; mine will almost always include the first time that Russ von Hoelscher contacted us and said that he could help us. It will always include talking about how Russ took us from $16,000 a month to as much as $100,000 a week in sales. That will always be there; that's the historical nature of the story.

But the *ongoing* nature is that my story's being written every day; so there will always be something new to add. When I tell my story five years from now, it may include things that happened to me this week, this month, this year. **So your story evolves over time; and the more you tell it, the more you find ways to improve upon it.** My business experience goes back over 20 years, so I have many aspects of my story that I could expound upon — but most would be pretty boring for most people, even though they might contain valuable truths. **So I hand-select the stories that best illustrate the points I'm trying to make, the ones that best build the bonds I'm trying to build.** Over time, you can perfect your story so that you're illustrating the highlights and downplaying the lowlights. You're telling the story to present the case you're trying to make to your customers, and that story evolves over time as you grow as a person, as your life unfolds, and as you gain experience in life.

One way to do this is with a newsletter. Your existing customers are along for the ride, and communicating with them through a newsletter is a great way to continue to build those bonds with them. You spend a few pages talking about whatever the newsletter is about, sure; but maybe the first page or two of every newsletter covers something interesting or funny that happened to you that month — something that will help build a connection with your customers, something they can identify with. You can continue the relationship with your existing customers, and they'll build on that story in their minds. They know your past. They know the story you already told them, and you continue to build on that story through the ongoing relationship. Someone who's new hears the story for the first time, and it contains all your life experiences that you want to share with

MARKETING SECRET

The #1 thing that many people in the opportunity market buy is: anticipation!

- This is the secret of a blind offer! They can't wait to see what they're going to get.

- Anticipation is often better than the real thing!

them up to that point.

Building strong bonds with customers is vitally important, because people aren't going to buy something from you unless they trust you. So you have to build that bond in some way; you need to try to build a connection to your customer as fast as possible, and get that relationship going. From there, continue to develop it so you can have the relationship that's required for ongoing sales.

We have a lawyer named Shelly whom we've only used a half-dozen times. He has a law firm in New York City at the Empire State Building, and he charges about $500 an hour — which is one of the reasons we've only used him a few times! But the other reason is because he specializes in just one area of the law, involving certain regulatory agencies. He's got a solid reputation. Frankly, if you have problems and you need that type of lawyer, you'd be a fool to hire anybody else. Now, he came out to our house once and spent a couple of days with us, and I asked him, "Okay, Shelly, what's your secret?"

Shelly told me, "If I have to go to a certain city to meet with one of the regulatory agents I work with on behalf of my clients, I'll have my secretary dig up all the newspapers for that metropolitan area first. Let's say, just for example, that it's Atlanta, Georgia. Well, first I'll study every sport teams in Atlanta. I'll memorize the top players, I'll look at their schedules and how they're doing this year; and of course, I'll take note of other things going on around Atlanta. Then, when I get into the agent's office, I just kind of feel him out. We make some small talk until I find that one thing that interests him. I might see something in his office regarding one of those sports teams — the Atlanta Braves, maybe — so I'll say something like, "Hey, the Braves are having a pretty good season this year."

So the guy gets excited about the team, and then he and Shelly start chatting. Shelly knows everything about the Atlanta Braves, because he just spent the last five or six days studying all the local teams. He knows the names of the superstars, the kinds of scores they've been achieving. They have a great, animated conversation about the Atlanta Braves — how does this season rate with last season? What are some of the biggest issues they're dealing with? And then, suddenly, their hour is almost up and Shelly says, "Oh, well, hey... we've got to take care of some of this business here. What about that case?" And the guy says, "Well, just give me the short version of it." And then they work out a favorable deal, they shake hands, and Shelly's out of there with what he wanted. During the hour-long meeting with that regulatory agent, they spent maybe 45 or 50 minutes talking about everything else that interested the regulatory agent!

When I heard that, I was dumbfounded. Shelly charges $500 an hour, so you'd think the secret of his success wouldn't be anything like that at all. Right? It ought to be something like the fact that he knows more about that one area of the law than anybody else. You'd think that since he's the established expert in that one area, he'd go in there and use all that knowledge, skill, and experience to overwhelm the regulatory guy. But it's not that at all — Shelly just makes friendly conversation about what the agent really wants to talk about! I just thought that was great — it's a perfect illustration that salesmanship is salesmanship is salesmanship! I don't care what it's about: If we're dealing with people, we're dealing with human emotions. **So we need to look for common ground, things that build rapport.** The fact that you can do that on a one-to-one basis is fairly easy for people to understand. But to think that you can also do that with thousands, tens of thousands, even hundreds of thousands of people... it's amazing. But it *does* work, and knowing that could make you millions of dollars.

Shelly's story just proves the power of building relationships — even if it happens within the confines of a structured meeting between a regulatory agent and an attorney. What really came to mind when I asked Shelly his secret was that old TV image where attorneys sit down on either side of a table and go at it. But in reality, one of the most successful guys in this legal niche goes in with an entirely different agenda. He spends a while chatting with the agent, then the next thing you know, boom — time's up, the agency guy is happy because they have a workable deal, and nobody's ticked off! **There's a new, profitable relationship there, just because Shelly spent a few hours boning up on the city the agent calls home.** If this doesn't illustrate the power of relationship-building in your business, then nothing will. **It's just salesmanship; that's all it is.**

The Eighth Commandment

The Eighth Commandment of Marketing is to position yourself and your business so that you seem unique. That's a tough one for some people. At some level, we're *all* unique — we just don't always see it. Sometimes it takes other people to see it for us, and to help us see it. Early on, for example, Russ von Hoelscher got us to do seminars for our customers; in fact, this section is based on a seminar we did in October 2008. Now, I love doing seminars; one of the smartest things my wife ever did when she was CEO was to encourage me to expand that part of our business. It's really been a great thing — but, unlike most business professionals, I refuse to dress up. I don't enjoy it. And so Russ came up with this idea: "T. J., why don't you just start calling yourself the 'Blue Jeans Millionaire?' That'll set the stage right then and there that this is who you are. You're the Blue Jeans Millionaire. When people come to your seminars, instead of being upset because of the way you're dressed, you're just the Blue Jeans Millionaire; that's why you're wearing blue jeans and tennis shoes." What a great idea! It's unique, and it's part of my story. **I think you should also find something that's unique about you, something that helps people understand who you are and helps dramatize certain things about you.**

Whether it's right or wrong, good or bad, all great marketers are shameless self-promoters. You have to get comfortable with that — but it's a tough thing for a lot of us, since we're trained from childhood to blend in, not to stand out. Personally, I never learned that lesson well; but it's still been hard for me do some of the self-promotion I do. But I do it because I know I have to. **As a marketer, you have to get to the point where you're not afraid to tell your story, where you're not afraid to tell people who you are.** You're expressing yourself. You're finding those things that you feel make you unique.

I've watched Russ von Hoelscher do it. I've had a relationship with Russ for about 20 years, but every year I see Russ doing this more and more, and I think it's kind of cool and interesting. He gets more outspoken each year; he's not afraid to express his political ideas in his newsletter, and he's very forceful. He's no Democrat, and he's proud to tell you that! And if you really want to know how Russ feels about this liberal government thing, he'll tell you that, too. Does he upset some people? I'm sure he does. And I'm sure he wouldn't do it if most of his customers were Democrats — but they're not. I've seen him take a heavier stand in expressing his opinions about excessive government, and every year I see him just turn up the volume more and more.

I think that's a great thing. All marketers should do it. That's part of relationship building; **you can't have a relationship with somebody unless you let them know who you are.** So don't be afraid. Don't hold back. Always tell people more and more about who you are, but try to make it as interesting as possible. Let's take my colleague Chris Hollinger as an example. He's a former teacher turned entrepreneur; that's his unique position. He's the Professor of Profits — that's how he bills himself. You need to do things like that, because by and large no one else is going to toot your horn for you. **You have to sell yourself!** Oh, sure, you can get some good testimonials, but you still have to be that shameless self-promoter. **It might run contrary to your personality, but it's something that adds to the bottom line of your business and helps you build your business.**

> Happiness is... a never-ending stream of positive cash-flow!

Look at certain industries out there: pizza, for example. Yes, maybe some pizzas are better than others, and of course you have your own preferences. But pizza is basically pizza, isn't it? If you're a pizzeria owner, you have to find a unique selling position (USP) that you can work into the headlines of your advertisements to make you seem dramatically different from your competitors. Maybe it's how you provide the delivery of your pizza. Domino's Pizza used to have a guarantee: "Hot, Fresh Pizza Delivered in 30 Minutes or Less or It's FREE!" That was a very good USP. It built the whole company. You were getting hot, fresh pizza faster than all the other competitors, guaranteed! It's a way to make the brand seem

MARKETING SECRET

The jigsaw puzzle:

- The secret to writing a powerful sales letters is to write it in small pieces — and then hook the best pieces together like a jigsaw puzzle.

- This makes a BIG job very simple and easy. All you have to do is write small bites — then join them — and boil it all down.

different from the next one — even though both are basically crust, cheese, toppings and sauce. C'mon, there's not a big difference from one freshly made pizza to another.

But there's another marketing colleague of ours who has a client who sells pizzas for $50! And that lady's little pizza franchises are taking off since he took over her marketing. But a $50 pizza! When I first heard about it, I couldn't imagine anyone who'd pay that much for a pizza. But then I got to thinking about it and I asked myself, "I wonder what a $50 pizza tastes like?" I was curious! And now I'm trying to find a place where I can buy a $50 pizza just so I can satisfy my curiosity. Now, I imagine I can find someone to sell me one — but the thing is, I'd better not be let down. It had better be one damned good pizza, or they're not getting a re-sell out of me!

But this lady's still got a great idea going. She's positioned herself uniquely with her company. She's the high-end pizza provider, and she's going to find some people who are willing to spend fifty bucks for a pizza. Maybe they just want to impress their friends at their next party. Maybe they just have to have the very best of everything, or they're not happy. Whatever their motivations, some people will be willing to spend that money. That's just one way that this lady's pizza franchise is unique: Her pizzas cost $50. She just has to find enough people willing to pay that price, and she can thrive.

There are a lot of extreme food items like that — thousand-dollar hamburgers with all kinds of exotic ingredients, for example. One restaurant in New York City sells a chocolate sundae for $1,000, and for really special occasions they have one that sells for $25,000.

You eat it out of a crystal goblet with a gem-encrusted gold spoon. There's a burger chain in the Dallas area that will sell you two burger-and-fry combos and a bottle of Dom Perignon champagne for $300. Quite a few restaurants are famous for a certain thing that's really expensive compared with what it would cost everywhere else. **They do that to make themselves unique.**

It's noteworthy that this commandment tells you to position yourself so that you *seem* unique. It doesn't say you have to *be* unique. **So you don't have to be that creative, or that unique a person, to have a USP that makes you *seem* unique.** You have to come across that way, do things that make you stand out. You've got to find some way to position yourself so that customers don't see you as a "me too" product. If they can get your product from everybody else, what's going to make them want to buy it from you? You can always try to be the cheapest, but that's usually not a good strategy. Almost everyone says they're the cheapest, and there's *always* somebody willing to undercut your price — no matter how badly it hurts them in the long run. So instead, are you going to be the most expensive? Well, that might not be a bad strategy, as long as you can justify it somehow. **But in most cases, price isn't where you're going to be unique.** Prices are all over the place. You've got to do something different, something that draws people to you, something that makes them want to seek *you* out instead of your competition. If you're advertising in the Yellow Pages, it's what makes them see your listing and say, "Yep, that's the one I'm going to call." If you're into Direct Mail and your offers are arriving at the same time as all this other mail from your competitors, what makes them open *your* envelope instead of your competitors'? What makes them choose to fill out your form and send it to you? **That's what you're looking for: something that separates you out in the marketplace and makes people want to do business with you instead of your competition.**

Sometimes you have to create that distinction, which all goes back to self-promotion. Take our good friend, Ted Ciuba, the world's foremost Internet Marketing Specialist. How do you know he is? **Because he *says* so.** There's no Foremost Internet Marketing Specialist Institute that anointed him! But, obviously, he's got a tremendous track record to back up that claim. That's his USP right there, his claim to fame.

The Ninth Commandment

The Ninth Commandment of Marketing: **Create offensive marketing strategies that allow you to control the selling process.** If you don't have a system for selling and re-selling to your customers, you're going to be at the mercy of their system for buying — which is sporadic and haphazard at best. **So you always have to be looking for different strategies so you can control the sales process.** I like the idea of controlling the sales process. Of course, there's some illusion with that; you can't control everything, but you *can* develop specific strategies that go out on a regular basis to try to re-sell to people. **Offensive marketing simply means you're not waiting for people to come back and do business with you.** Some people will, sure — but usually, you have to go to them.

We've got many customers who have been doing business with us for five, ten, or 15 years, or sometimes more, but here's the shocking part about our business: Any time we decide we want to fold the tent and be out of business, we can just stop mailing to our list — and the orders will stop coming in. Maybe I'd keep a couple of employees on to answer the phone and reply to the stragglers who might keep trying to buy from us, but otherwise I can let my employees go. I'm sure there might be a little bit of business coming in for a while; I'd hope so, after 20 years of doing business with the same people. I would hope that for a while, we would continue to get a lot of phone calls. I could probably keep about half of my employees for six months; then I'd have to let half of those people go. And within a year, it could just be one person and a telephone, and maybe one other person coming in part-time to ship stuff. The business would be gone.

In some ways it's sad, but that's just reality. There would be a certain amount of what we call "drag business" that would naturally come in over a period of time. But eventually, it's one person and a phone. It would probably be profitable for me to pay that person, because there'd be enough business coming in that it would justify the expense. But otherwise the whole business would just be gone. It's different in other businesses, of course, but **I think this illustrates the point that if you're not out there and mailing to people on a regular basis, the orders won't come.** We mail constantly, and sometimes it takes one or two people, or even three, just to open all the envelopes containing the cash, checks, money orders, and credit card authorizations that come in the mail every day.

But all of that would be gone if we stopped promoting.

Offensive marketing of this type is a direct opposite of the kind of passive marketing most traditional businesses do. With passive marketing, you're just sort of there. You've got a Main Street business and your doors are open, your sign kind of indicates what you sell, people know where you're located, and they can stop in if they choose. There's not any aggressive marketing at all. If they were using an offensive marketing strategy, those businesses would say: "It doesn't matter that people know where I am. I need to do something aggressive to go after their business. I need to run ads. I need to sponsor local events so that my name's out there. I need to be aggressively promoting my name and my business's name so that people know who I am, what I sell, and where to find me. I'm going to aggressively go after this marketplace and get as much money out of it as I possibly can." **That's the difference between an offensive attack versus a passive one, where you're hoping that people will find you.** I suppose it's a lot like a football team's offense and defense: both are important, but the offense is the part of the team that scores the points. **In business, the offense is the part of your strategy that scores the cash.**

Our friend and fellow marketer, Russ von Hoelscher, tells a really good story about an ex-printer in his area who was a friend of his. The guy's business was kind of slow and he was looking for advice, so Russ gave him some very tangible, quick advice about putting together some flyers and mailers and distributing them, along with some discount coupons. And the printer shot back something to the effect of, "People know what I do. If they want it, they'll come get it." That's a good example of passive marketing. He just said, "Here's my business. I do really good printing. People should come to *me* when they want their printing, because I'm the best." He wasn't being offensive at all, and now he's an *ex*-printer. He couldn't get enough business, even though I'm sure the guy did great work. But so what? Even if you do great work, if you can't get out there and toot your own horn and tell people that, they're not going to just come to you naturally by osmosis, just because you put your shingle out there on the door. **You've got to give them a reason to come in and do business with you.** That's what creating an offensive marketing strategy does. It goes out there and drags people to you.

MARKETING SECRET

When getting ready to write a sales letter — ask yourself the toughest questions in the mind of the most skeptical prospect and make sure your best answers are woven into the copy.

The Tenth Commandment

The Ninth and Tenth Commandments of Marketing could be considered the same basic principle, because the Tenth just clarifies the Ninth somewhat. **What the Tenth Commandment says is this: When you're making specific offers to your customers on an ongoing basis, you're taking them by the hand and compelling them to come to you instead of waiting for them to somehow gravitate to you on their own.**

The key point in this last Commandment is that you're making them offers. Whatever business you're in, **what you really sell is offers — not products and services.** Think about that. This is something that took me years to figure out. An offer is more than just a product or service. It's all of the other stuff that goes with it — the free bonus gifts, the special price, the extra secrets and tips. **It's everything you're offering to give to someone in exchange for the money you're asking for in return.**

Those infomercials you see on TV do a great job with this. They tell you, "You're going to get this, this, and this. But wait... there's more! If you order now, you're going to also receive this and this and this as a bonus, absolutely free! But wait... there's still more!" and they just keep building it up. The idea is to finally make you just say, "Holy crap! What am I waiting for?" So you run to the phone or get on the Internet and order. That's why you've got to think in terms of offers — and the more you study great direct-response marketers, the more you'll see that's what they're selling. They build their products and services around all kinds of free bonuses and premium gifts, special pricing, and special limited situations, reasons for people to take action NOW. They give it the greatest appeal possible, so that people are excited and they're compelled to do business.

It's all about the offer — not necessarily the product or service. You see, anybody can sell a product or service, and that's kind of flat. It's just not enough anymore. We've got a client who's always saying, "Is that all you can do? Can you do any better than that? Is that all you're going to do?" He's always coming up with those questions whenever someone makes a presentation at our seminars. He says it as a joke, but I like the way he says it — because that's how people think these days. **They want more and more and more.** People want great prices, there's no question about that. **But what they really want is a great offer.** Give this some serious thought, because, again, it took me years to figure it out. **What people really want are items that are very expensive and very valuable for dirt-cheap prices.** When you're creating an offer, that's the perception you're trying to clearly communicate: that what you have is worth a tremendous amount of money or, if it isn't, it can potentially provide tremendous benefits that are important to your prospective group.

If it's not money, then give them something else that's really important to them. **Give them so much that when they're weighing out what you've got on the table, they're just overwhelmed and feel that they'd be a fool not to take you up on the offer.** That's something that Chris Lakey and I did recently. We hosted a teleconference for some of our clients and we made them a special offer, but here was the deal: Today Only. After that, they had to pay full price. We laid it all out, we showed them all the benefits, we showed them everything we were going to give them, we added all these great incentives and proved the value, and then we said, "Now, here's the deal: today, you can get it for half price. Tomorrow, full price." And sure enough, 80 of the 130 people on the call ordered right away. We made them an offer that most of them just couldn't refuse.

Again, you're going to them and doing all this for them, instead of waiting for them to somehow gravitate to you on their own. You go on the offensive and get them to do business with you, instead of waiting for them to find you. Sometimes it's costly. Let's go back to those infomercials I mentioned earlier, the ones that just keep building and building the offer. It's always "But wait — there's more!" and you have to wonder how the heck they can possibly give all that stuff for only $19.95.

The answer is simple: They can't. What they're doing is making you such a compelling offer that it would be hard for you to say no. They pile benefits on top of benefits; they throw in so much stuff that it makes it hard to turn them down, so you pick up the phone and call. At that point, they've bought you as a customer.

You're right to think that there's no way they could sell all that stuff for just $19.95: They might have spent $50 to make that sale. But when you call them, they instantly make you another offer while you're on the phone. Then, even if you say no that one time, when your product arrives, guess what? There's another offer with it. **They try to recoup the money they just spent "buying" you as a customer as fast as possible by making you additional offers.** They have to! Even if they got all those items they just sold you from Malaysia or China, their cost is going to add up to more than what you're going to pay them. And think about all the ads they run — the infomercials themselves cost a lot of money. But they have a system in place where they're immediately going to try to upsell you on something else as soon as you contact them. **All their profits come on those back-end sales that happen when make that first order.** It's a gateway product. It gets you in the door and captures you as a customer, even at a loss, so they can convert you on the back-end. They know that's where they're going to make money... and usually a lot of it.

You get that profitable repeat business by continuing to make more offers. You can't ever simply assume that someone will find you and do business with you. Sure, if you're a retail business on Main Street, some of the people who live in your town will stumble upon you, decide to stop in, and maybe buy something. But if you're selling on the Internet or by direct mail, there's no way someone's going to just stumble upon you easily. **It's up to *you* to let people know you're there, to let them know exactly what you sell, and to present compelling offers that make them want to give you their money.**

Use the PAS System

In this chapter, I'm going to reveal a copywriting formula that can make you more money than any other I personally know of. And best of all, it's amazingly simple and easy. **It's called the PAS Formula, because** there are only three steps involved: **Problem, Agitate, and Solution.**

When you read sales letters as a marketer, you'll see this formula used again and again. **First they bring up the biggest problem that's solved by whatever it is they sell, then they get you agitated about it, and then they offer the solution.** Let's use my friend Mike's marketing as an example; he's the guy who sells the soy candles. His marketing does a really good job of illustrating the PAS Formula, because it first brings up the problems with traditional candles. They're made of paraffin, and paraffin is this sludgy stuff that's left over from the oil refinery process. It's poisonous goo that they couldn't figure out what to do with, until somebody said, "Hey, let's bleach it and sell it to candle makers!" Well, it's bad for your health, and it's hurting your children, and it's just a *terrible* thing. You have to tell people that; that's the "P" part of the PAS Formula, the problem. In making that problem clear and telling them what it can do to their children, you're agitating them; that's the "A" in the PAS formula. You're personalizing the situation; you're making it real to them. And then, of course, you offer the solution — the "S" part of the formula. In this case, it's All-American soy candles. Forget those candles made in Vietnam and Indonesia and Malaysia, the ones they pay people 20 cents a day to make. These candles are made in America from healthy agricultural products that benefit the farmers, and they're good for you — so just burn them like crazy! **The PAS formula is very effective, which is why you'll see it used again and again.**

> If the desks are too neat and clean... and the people all look relaxed... the company is in BIG TROUBLE!!!

All you have to do when you decide to use the PAS Formula is to try to identify 10 or 15 of the biggest problems that your product or service solves. Then you just write these little bits of copy, where first you talk about the problem, then you agitate it and make it real to that person, and then you introduce the solution. **Instead of writing this huge sales letter, all you're writing is just a little bit of copy each on these 10, 15, or even 20 different points. Then you just link them all together, and you've got a sales letter!** Your very best copy becomes part of your headline, and you build the whole thing around those problems, which you're making

SECTION FIVE — Ruthless Copywriting Strategies

▼▼▼▼▼▼▼▼▼
MARKETING SECRET

"You can't steal in slow motion!" — Larry Goins

- When you find something hot that others are using — grab it as fast as you can!

- Speed is everything!

- Find as many ways to steal and use the best ideas others are using! Find a way to add them to your arsenal!

---

real to people. You're personalizing it, making them agitated, and then you're introducing the solution — which is the thing that we all really sell. We sell solutions and results. Well, people can't appreciate solutions and results until they know what the problem is — and that problem has to be real for them.

Marketers use the PAS formula to do everything they can to scare their prospects. It can happen in a TV commercial in 30 seconds. A big industry that uses this method extensively is the maternity industry. They use fear to sell their products. They insinuate or even outright tell you, "Your baby could be harmed if you're not using these certain kind of wipes that eliminate all the germs." And they'll even show you the little microbes growing on all these surfaces if you're not using their product. They grab your attention and captivate you with fear, or a problem that you have — even if you didn't know you had it until then. It goes back to understanding your market. What are the wants, needs, desires, and *fears* of your market? This particular strategy — Problem, Agitate, and Solution — is such a powerful strategy because, again, it captivates. **It grabs your attention.** You're using something that's very personal to them — the fear of not being able to lose weight, the fear of a bad candle, the fear of not having enough money, the fear of their children suffering — to agitate then. This is a ruthless strategy, obviously, because you're capitalizing on the human emotion of fear. **Metaphorically, you pull back that scab and pour salt on the wound, and then you rub it in. You agitate that pain.**

And *then* you get them to the point where

the only way they're going to relieve the pain is through the solution that you can provide. You offer them the most compelling, concise solution to the pain that *you*, as a marketer, helped to aggravate. So many different industries use that. You can't go to the grocery store without seeing a form of this strategy in play somewhere. It works very well with information products, too — especially with a bad economy.

Again, this is one of the truly great and simple strategies for making money with advertising. There are just three steps: Problem, Agitate, Solution. **It's easy to build an ad or sales letter around this concept — or you can build an entire campaign around it.** If you'll write the three words down and then spend a few paragraphs talking about each one as it relates to your offer, that's a good foundation for a postcard or classified ad — or it could be the start of a sales letter. You start with the Problem. You're making people aware of a problem you know they have, because you've followed the other formulas I've been talking about. You know your prospects inside and out, and you start with them in mind. Until and unless you can convince people that those cheap candles are ruining their home by getting all this black soot all over the place, and they're stinking up their houses and ruining their children's health and killing all the house plants, you're not going to be able to Agitate them enough to make them want the Solution you're offering.

I've had water-purification system salesmen who've sat down in my living room and made their presentations, using the PAS formula. Those expensive vacuum cleaner guys do the same thing. They tell you, "We not only clean your carpets phenomenally well, but we clean the air your children are breathing — and that air is just filthy." They'll happily show you how filthy it is. There's a commercial on TV as I'm writing this that's very similar. They say, "If you had a mouse, you'd trap it." Then they show you this baby sitting on the floor, watching a mouse walk by. That's ruthless! "If you had bugs, you'd trap them," and they show roaches run by the baby. Well, they're selling a filter for your furnace that catches 98.9% of the germs in the system. And then they show these creepy-looking microscopic bugs that you normally can't see all around this beautiful baby. The baby has this look on his face like, "Oh crap, Mom, you've got to go buy this right now!"

The flipside of that is, how long have we, as a species, survived without this filtration system? I don't want to ruin the sales for these guys, but lots of people have been born and lived their entire lives on regular water and air. But this is marketing, selling a product. Okay, you get nice soft water, and you get nice clean air. Who doesn't want that? **But they use that fear to sell their expensive water and air purification systems.** And they *do* sell them. They know that if they can get in your house and make this presentation, they're going to close enough sales to keep that money rolling in.

And it works! Problem — Agitate — Solve. **For the most part, people won't even realize that you're using this formula.** The average prospective buyer who buys unconsciously in an emotional vacuum is never going to be able to see that you're using *any* formula, assuming you're doing your job right.

Keep Your Eyes on the Prize

By now, you've probably realized that being an effective marketer takes work, dedication, and a willingness to learn a lot of new things. It's not easy, but don't let that get you down. **Along the way, you need to keep your eye focused on the prize — the exciting things about the business, like the potential to make millions of dollars, and having the time and freedom to do what you want.** The more you're able to do that, the more you'll be willing to pay the price necessary to develop and practice these skills I'm teaching you about, and to learn whatever it takes to get where you want to go.

The Two-Step (Not the Texas One)

I've told you repeatedly that you don't have to be the best copywriter ever to make good money, you just need to use the right strategies. But let me make this abundantly clear: It *does* take work. I realize that work is a four-letter word for a lot of people. Let's face it: Many of us are looking to get rich with no work at all on our parts. In fact, we had a program that was quite successful for a number of years called "The No-Work Wealth Maker." I know that sounds cynical, but it's what people want! We sold a lot of copies of that one, because we offered to do the work for them. **But in order to achieve the biggest results consistently, you have to be the** one to carry the ball. I hope I've made that clear so far. This is a creative, fun kind of thing. It's challenging and stimulating. To me, that's part of the joy of life. In fact, that's one of the *biggest* joys of life — doing things that are creative and fun. **This is the kind of business where there's a million ways you can win.**

One of those ways to win, and one you really need to focus on, is two-step marketing. I've mentioned two-step marketing a number of times already, but I haven't stopped to really explore the topic. In this chapter, I'm going to remedy that. **Two-step marketing is one of the foundations of any successful marketing campaign,** especially ad-based and direct-mail campaigns, so you need to know why it's important and how to put it into play in your own campaigns.

How you handle two-step marketing depends on where you're planning to use it, and for how long. If your approach is a published ad, for example, how you angle it depends on the publication. A lot of opportunity magazines are monthlies, whereas something like the opportunity section in the Friday edition of *USA Today* is weekly. *USA Today* is a pretty good place to run a classified ad. The neat thing is, it's going to hit Friday and it'll be out there on the stands on Saturday and Sunday — so you'll immediately generate prospects.

I like 24-hour recorded messages, because they let you hit those prospects with a good, solid sales piece and follow-up. In 99% of the ads, there's an 800 number listed — for good reason. They no longer say, "Write to us," because so many people now carry their cell phones with them, and it's so much easier to get people to make a call. The challenge there is that it's also easier to get all the deadbeats to call. And by "deadbeats," I'm talking about people not in the market for what you're trying to sell — so they end up wasting your time and money. **You have to look for ways to qualify people, and to ensure they're qualified; that's the true value of two-step marketing.**

I was in Jacksonville, Florida, in 2002 for a marketing seminar, and I sat next to this guy who had kind of been my hero. His name is Rick Neiswonger, and at that time he was out of Las Vegas. He's a famous marketer, and I got to spend a couple of hours of good quality time with him. This one idea that Rick gave me made me a lot of money — and I probably haven't used it nearly as much as I should. Rick had a program

▼▼▼▼▼▼▼▼▼
MARKETING SECRET

A strong desire can never be fully satisfied.

- Remember this! Why? Because all of the rabid buyers in your market have insatiable desires! They will keep buying an almost endless supply of your products and services — if you offer it to them!

- Most marketers lose a ton of money by not offering their best customers more stuff.

that sold for $12,000. He told me that his whole strategy was that he ran his commercials on major networks. His most successful commercial ran during Larry King Live, and it got people to call a recorded message. That's all it did: it gave them a little teaser and got them to call the 800 number. He didn't want to waste his money on people who either didn't have $12,000 or who are going to be very difficult, so three different times during that brief message, he told people flat out, "The opportunity costs $12,000 — and if you don't have that kind of money, then this isn't for you." And I thought, what a great idea!

Immediately after that, I sent out a simple postcard offer, of a type that usually doesn't work for me. Now, postcard offers can work great in follow-up, but for the most part I can't use postcards in my business, because I have too much infrastructure. Yet this time I used Rick's idea, and I was able, for probably the first time in the history of our company, to use postcards effectively. In this case, I was selling a $4,000 package, and I used the postcard to have people call my 800 number and listen to a recorded message. Three or four different times during that recorded message I told people, "Look: I want you to know, right up front, that *this* is the kind of investment that's necessary. And if you don't have that, then I'm sorry, but this is just not for you. But if you *do* have that kind of money, you need to know that you can get all these secrets for $4,000. Don't worry, nobody is going to high-pressure you." And sure enough, we made it work.

The point is, there are many ways to keep your eyes on the prize. **What you can accomplish is limited by your creativity and** your knowledge, and by the strategies that you know that are theoretically possible. Luckily, marketers love sharing ideas. Over the years, you can subject yourself to more and more strategies, which give you more potential power. **Remember, power is the ability to act.** The more strategies you have at your disposal, the more knowledge you have, the more ability you'll have to do that.

When using the strategy of laying it on the line like I did with my $4,000 product, you don't have to be blunt about it; you can say it in a nice way. Use it as an advantage and say, "Look, if you're looking for a less expensive offer, that's fine. They're out there. But if you're looking for the *best* and you've got this amount of money, then here you are." Sometimes we don't even tell them the exact price; sometimes we just say, "The start-up costs are about the price you'd pay for a weekend in Vegas." We say things like that to people so that they know it's going to be kind of expensive. For example, "This opportunity costs about the same as a used car." Of course, we've had people who said, "Great, I can get a used car for $500!" Well, yeah — but not a very good one!

Look Around Occasionally

I'm the first to tell you that you have to be careful with any opportunity — and while you should always keep your eyes on the prize, **you also have to look around occasionally so you don't stumble.** Here's an example of such a stumble, one that plays a riff off that two-step marketing idea I already discussed. Once upon a time, Eileen and I bought a company from Russ von Hoelscher and a fellow named George Stern called "Profit Ideas." George wanted out of the business, so he told Russ to find a buyer — and we were right there. As part of the company, we got this full-page ad that they'd run for a number of years. We acquired "Profit Ideas" after we'd been in business for three or four years; we'd already experienced a little success, and I'll admit it, I was cocky and arrogant. I thought I knew more than I really did.

In that full-page ad, Russ and George asked for one dollar for information, and one dollar for shipping and handling. And I thought, "Let's get rid of that dollar thing, because then more people will respond!" And I was right! On the short-term it looked like I knew more than Russ did. I was patting myself on the back, all inflated with my own stupid sense of self-importance. **Sure enough, we got double the amount of leads — but we just couldn't get the conversions.** It didn't work. And had I listened to Russ, he would have told me (as he did later), "You know, that asking for one dollar... that's nothing. Everybody has a dollar. Everybody." A dollar's not that big a deal; you really can't buy much with it. And yet, just asking for that dollar was enough to make people feel a bit more qualified. They remembered us, then. I think that's a lot of the success of two-step marketing: People remember that they've qualified themselves. They remembered sending the dollar in, whereas if they'd just picked up the phone and called that 800 number, they might have forgotten. The dollar made the difference. Yeah, they raised their hand... but they remembered it, too; whereas the ones who just called and left their names and information blew us off. There has to be a mechanism there so that the dollar is exchanged. **It's another step, another hoop they jump through in the process of qualifying themselves, of raising their hands higher and letting you know they're serious.**

Different Strategies Work for Different People

There are all kinds of ways to do things in this business, all with their weaknesses and strengths. Some might work for you even when they don't work for me. **We learn what does and doesn't work by testing, and the numbers tell you if you should continue or not.** In the aforementioned case, not asking for a dollar for the information failed to work for us. Here's another good example, associated with our *Dialing for Dollars* program. Now, this is a marketing system based on voicemail that still works today; people are still using the basic system 20 years later. But just as a way of showing you that there's many different ways to work even an effective system like this, let's take a look at Jay Peterson, our distributer out of Provo, Utah.

When Jay was still working with us, we were bringing in about $2,000,000 a year using the system — and he was making about $5,000,000. I knew that for certain, because until he cut us out, all his wholesale orders were coming through us. He was doing almost three times more business than we were by using the "COD Method." You called an answering machine and listened to a message, and you were told to leave your name and address, and Jay would ship you the product by COD — Cash On Delivery.

Well, the bad thing about COD is that people would call the number, they would listen to the COD message, and then they would say, "Yes, ship that $39 package to me by COD," and leave their name and address. But when the package came and the postman asked for the money, most of them would say, "No, thank you. Changed my mind." In some cases, the postman just couldn't contact them. In any case, when push came to shove, as many as 60% of the recipients wouldn't write the check — and the package came back "Postage Due."

Those are the major problems inherent with the COD model. And yet, Jay was making it all work. He factored it all into his business plan. The 40-50% of the money that he was able to collect on was more than enough, for him. It's kind of like if you have a liquor store in a really bad neighborhood of Los Angeles or Miami, where every year you're probably going to get robbed an average of three or four times — and you're also going to lose money through shoplifting. You have to factor all that into your business; you charge three times more than the other liquor stores charge, so you build it into your business plan, and you still make money year after year.

Different marketing methods work for different people, because there's no single, perfect marketing model — and believe me, I'm still looking. I still fantasize about the perfect marketing model, where it's all upside, just good, good, good with no downside.

> **FORMAL GENERALIZED EDUCATION SUCKS!**
>
> The only thing that's important is specialized knowledge and experience that is directed in a very specific direction.

That's all just a great big fantasy, because I know in my heart that reality will never live up to it. **But you still need to keep trying out those different methods until something clicks with you — and you have to remember that good copywriting, words written while your eyes are firmly on the prize, is crucial.**

Words Really Can Make a Difference

Here's something I've been putting off telling you, because it's a bit

MARKETING SECRET

The secret of selling "blind" offers:

- It's always easier and better to sell blind offers that tell the prospect about all the advantages — but force them to give up their money to get all the facts. The reason is simple: It's better to sell the fantasy because the realty is often so boring!

- The reality never lives up to the fantasy! The benefits are all part of that emotional power that drives the sale and makes people want to give you their money!

off-color — but it does serve to illustrate something important. You see, I've never really cared that much for doctors. So when my friend, Steve (who's a great salesman), went and got a colonoscopy, I told him, "I'll never do that. I will never *ever* allow somebody to shove a camera up inside of me." And Steve said, "T.J., you've got to do it! Colon health is very important." I said, "I don't even want to think about my colon, and I don't want to think about the *health* of my colon." Then Steve told me, "T.J., you've got to do this. If you've got a problem and they catch it early enough, they can fix it; no problem at all. But if you've got a problem and you don't catch it fast enough, here's what's going to happen. They're going to put you on an operating table — and they're going to gut you like a fish! They're going to cut you open, and all your insides are going to be spread out on that operating table. They're going to have to cut into those insides and take out huge portions of your colon. And from that point forward, you're going to have to carry one of those little poop bags with you everywhere you go. For the rest of your life you're going to have your poop bag, and it's just going to be a terrible, terrible thing."

Well, sign me up! From that point forward, I started caring about my health of my colon. I never cared about it before, but when Steve started talking about how they were going to gut me like a fish, well... I got this certain visual image. I used to fish when I was a kid, and I've cleaned them, so I know *exactly* what that means. Nowadays I eat so much roughage it's not even funny. I buy Benefiber in those giant containers that you can only buy on the Internet because they're so big. I still haven't let them shove the camera up me yet, but I now care very deeply about the health of my colon.

The reason I tell you that story is because the words somebody uses can make all the difference in the world. Now, I could die tomorrow; none of us really knows how much time we have. But because my friend used such descriptive words to get me to reconsider the health of my colon, he may have saved my life. I won't know for sure until I have that colonoscopy, **but I do know that words really can make a difference.** As Mark Twain famously said, "The difference between the right word and the wrong word is the difference between lightning and lightning bug." **So I want to encourage you to think about the power of words, and think about how certain visual images that you can express to the people you care about can change their lives.** Steve cared about me, so he helped me think about something that I never wanted to think about.

As marketers, we can do that in our sales material. **We can say certain things in a certain way to get people to take the right action.** Consider the Recession-Proof Wealth System I've talked about With this program, we're really helping people. We're showing them secrets that they've never been exposed to before. As I write this copy, I'll have the help of five other experts; they're going to help me rewrite that copy and sharpen it like a razor's edge. We're going to try to make people think about things they don't normally think about — things like, what would happen if the world economy went to hell? What would happen if the worst possible situation developed? What would they do if they had to live through another Great Depression? You've seen pictures from the Depression. It was a sad, miserable time. And yet, there were people who did quite well for themselves, because they knew some of the things we're sharing with people on this Recession-Proof Wealth Program. We have the proven methods, and we're teaching people things that normally aren't taught in business school. **We're showing them how to take their financial lives into their own hands and start making them better, instead of depending on the government to somehow provide for them.**

So we really can change people's lives. We can! Back when we were selling our *Dialing for Dollars* program, we had customers who were making thousands of dollars a month for the first times in their lives, because they bought this program and made it work. Some people went on to make millions of dollars with the ideas we shared with them. **I didn't know anything about writing copy back then, but the sales letter I** wrote was so passionate and enthusiastic that the excitement came through to our readers.

There are a million copywriting techniques that you can master, and you can spend your whole life learning them if you like. **But when you get down to it, marketing, and the copywriting that defines it, is as simple as good salesmanship.** What my friend Steve was doing was trying to sell me on the idea of living a better life, without some of the health problems that less vigilant people have had to go through. With our salesmanship, we're trying to make a difference. **We're trying to deliver value.** As long as you're committed to delivering good value that really does help people, then all the ideas I've shared about squeezing the largest amount of money possible out of the mailing list, of going out and "attacking" people in an aggressive way — these ideas are valid.

Think of it like this: What's the last really good movie that you saw? And when was the last time that you heard someone else talking about it — maybe a friend or a family member, saying, "Well, I wonder what that's like?" Remember how your eyes got a little bigger and you were like, "Oh, it's a great movie!" Do you remember how you tried to explain it to them — but didn't want to give it away? So you said enthusiastically, "You've got to go see it!" That enthusiasm is what happens when you've been working on an offer for a while and you're all excited about it. **That's the kind of enthusiasm that you want to come across in your writing.** You want to grab people and say, "You've got to take a look at this opportunity here; it's absolutely fantastic!" That's what you're really trying to get across in your writing. If you really focus on that one thing, you can create a very powerful sales letter, because people respond to that kind of enthusiasm. It grabs people, and it's what you're really shooting for. Sure, there are all kinds of strategies that can guide you and help you with your copywriting, but they're useless if they're dry and boring and monotonous. **Practice getting that enthusiasm in place.** That comes from that first strategy I shared — write when you're fired up. I get that way early in the morning, when I've got some coffee in me. That's the best time of the day for me; I haven't been worn down by meetings and business and life. The morning is nice and fresh, and I'm all pumped up and ready to go... and that comes across in my writing.

I tend to be naturally enthusiastic, but it's something we all can develop more. **And people *do* respond to enthusiasm.** Case in point: my sister Ellen. Over at M.O.R.E., Inc., I have an extension that I never answer; but I've got a message that says, "Hi, this is T.J.! Thank you very much for calling," and I'm all enthusiastic and I'm saying, "Man, I'm sorry I missed your call. I hope you have a great day." So whenever Ellen gets depressed, she calls and listens to my extension — and it picks her up just **a bit. See? Enthusiasm is a great thing. You can be a poor copywriter, but still hit the jackpot if you're enthusiastic and sincerely believe your offer helps people.** I'm a perfect example. I didn't know what I was doing 20 years ago, when I did that first *Dialing for Dollars* sales letter — I was just excited about the idea, and I wrote about it, and it took off! One of my pet peeves is the fact that some freelancer copywriters charge way too much money, and don't deliver enough value for what they charge. They know all the secrets, tricks, and advanced strategies, but they lack the enthusiasm that a person who's in love with what they're doing can share with another person.

So I would encourage you to start paying attention to good writing versus bad writing. What makes good writing good? Usually, the writer's extremely opinionated about what he believes — this makes him enthusiastic, and forceful in the way that he clearly communicates exactly what he believes. **A good writer doesn't try to go for the middle of the road to satisfy everybody. He has firm ideas about what he believes is right and is wrong, good and bad. A good writer is extremely clear about those ideas.** When you read a good writer's copy, you can tell what he believes.

Writing is just a form of communication; that's all it is. But let's face it: English teachers ruin it for most people. The joy of writing is one of the greatest joys there is — and they ruin it because they make it so technical and difficult. They split it into its component parts, and make you memorize all these stupid little rules. Today, if you asked me what an adjective or an adverb is, if I thought about it long enough, I could tell you. But when I'm writing, I don't worry about all the bits and pieces, the structure of the sentences and paragraphs. I don't even know what a dangling participle is, and I couldn't care less. I know the English language only in relationship to copywriting, and that's what's important here. **It's all about one person getting excited about something and then sharing their passion with somebody else.** That'll sell better than a knowledge of all the dry details of the language.

▼▼▼▼▼▼▼▼▼
MARKETING SECRET

Set goals for every promotion.

- The more clear you are about what you want, the more power you will have!

I've mentioned that Russ von Hoelscher has become more opinionated in his writing lately. Maybe he did that consciously, maybe not; but it's something that helps him connect with more people, and so he profits from it. **People don't identify with the gray areas of personalities; they're attracted to extremities.** Those at the extremes are cut-and-dried, black or white. Wishy-washy people who don't know which way they're going don't sell very well. I realize that some of the best people in this world are the ones in the middle; but nobody will ever find out about it, because they're always so nice, polite, and quiet, and they get overlooked. They're not putting their ideas out there in a bold way.

When you see an ad or read a sales letter that excites you, you should study it, look at what they've done. But don't be intimidated. For years I was intimidated whenever I saw good copy; first it inspired me, but then it made me depressed because I was thinking, "Oh my God, I'll never be able to write like that!" But I didn't realize that oftentimes, those letters were written in patches and edited down severely. Maybe the original was 30 pages long — but what I saw was 12 pages, the best of the best. **While you're writing, you have to think about the benefits for the person you're writing to,** just as if you were going to sell them on a particular movie. You'd try to get them excited about certain things without revealing the plot, because curiosity is such a big factor in what we do. In order to get the rest of the story, we want our prospects to send us money. **That's the only way that they can satisfy their curiosity, and it's always done with a money-back guarantee** — so if they get the answers and they're not happy, they can always get their money back.

We're not here to cheat or hurt people.

Look for copy that's alive. Look for copy that moves. Look for copy that makes you excited, and then try to figure out what it is about it that influenced you in those ways. **Realize that we're all more alike than we are different, especially emotionally.** Emotions, human nature — those are the things that never really change. In a world where everything is constantly in motion, where markets do change, certain things that get people excited one year may not quite get people excited the next year. Regardless of whether it's changing in good ways or bad, your market is always changing a little, based on numerous factors. **But the one thing that never changes is that good ol' human nature.** People are exactly like they always were: they're creatures of emotion, and those emotions run the gamut of good to bad, happy to sad.

To me, the secret of dealing with emotions is pretty simple: **the right motions create the right emotions.** I don't start out being all enthusiastic every morning, believe me. But by going through the right motions, the emotions do catch up with you. **To put it another way — fake it till you make it!**

Put These Nineteen Secrets into Play

Much of what I'm going to share with you in this chapter you've already heard in one form or another, but I want to repeat it all for emphasis. **These are the 19 marketing secrets that have brought us more than $117,000,000 over the years.** I'll go through each one and cover them as fast as I can, but this will still be a long chapter!

I don't want you to think that these are just off-the-cuff items I came up with out of the blue. This is a list I boiled down from something much larger. Many of you may be familiar with my five-CD set of 3,529 Ruthless Marketing secrets I did a few years ago. It's a work in progress — I'm trying to do a new volume every single year. Well, I do my best thinking toward the end of a project, as I'm wrapping up a new volume. That's where these 19 secrets came from. While I was wrapping up Volume 4, I did a lot of heavy thinking, trying to analyze all the things we've learned over the years. I asked myself, "What are the top strategies that did it for us?" These 19 were the answer.

FIRST UP is premium pricing. Charge more for your products, because you're after better customers who will buy additional stuff and cause fewer problems. **Plus, it gives you the ability to make good money in spite of bad numbers.** Now, like any business, we have our bad customers. But when I've looked closely at the worst customers we have, it never ceases to amaze me that these people are almost invariably new customers who buy very little from us — and yet they cause us the most grief. And then we have all kinds of established customers who have been buying from us for years who are a joy and a pleasure to work with. If for no other reason, *that's* why you should have premium prices. **People who spend more money with you are just better-quality people, at least from a marketing perspective, since they usually cause fewer problems.** It's just a fact of business. Your biggest troublemakers are usually the people who spent the least. In fact, we occasionally get people who will complain about something, and then we find out they haven't even bought anything from us! Or maybe all they did was request some information from us, so we sent them something for free — and they're still complaining. Think about how ridiculous that is!

On the flipside of that are people you've established a relationship with, who are good clients; that is, they've spent more money. Maybe it's not even that you have a long-term relationship, it's just that one time they paid a lot of money for a premium-priced product. Those people tend to cause fewer customer-service nightmares. **They're the ones who are happy you're doing business with them; the relationship is strong and solid, and there are no problems.** Again, I wish I knew psychologically what causes that to happen, but it's a reality whether I can explain it or not. **The people who spend the least typically cause the most problems.** Of course, a lot of people who spend no money with you, or very little, *don't* cause problems. Not everybody is a problem waiting to happen. But if you look at your problems, you'll see a good portion of them come from people who spent the least money.

And then there's the concept of slack adjustors, which is an extreme form of premium pricing. That's the whole basis of this first strategy — even if your numbers are bad, because you're selling things for premium dollars, you don't have to worry about going out of business. You're making enough profit on those fewer transactions. **So you absolutely, positively have to have that slack adjustor built in to your business, because it will mean higher profits in the end.** And then you need to have the system in place to upgrade your customers to those higher-priced items. Don't think for a second, like Chris Hollinger did when he first started with that $1,297 website that he thought was way too expensive, that no one is going to go for it. They will. **People will end up finding the money for the things they really want in life.** If you have that premium-priced item that you can convince them it's in their best interest to buy, they'll find the money for it.

If you don't try this, you're leaving money on the table. If you're not offering customers premium priced items, you're losing money that could and should be yours, because they trust you and they want more of what they bought from you the first time — and they're willing to spend that money. All you have to do is make them the offer.

And remember, **buyers are liars.** It's true. They'll claim they can't afford something when they actually can. I actually caught myself doing this recently, when somebody was trying to sell me something for $25,000. This was somebody I have some respect for, but the first thing that came out of my mouth was, "I don't have the money." Well, I probably could have come up with the money... but I just didn't think it was worth it. And he wasn't selling hard enough anyway. Everybody has that reflex. It's that initial thing we come up with — and for most people, I believe it's wrong.

NUMBER TWO: sequential follow-up mailing campaigns. You've got to keep the pressure on. You have to be like the persistent man who asked the beautiful

> ▼▼▼▼▼▼▼▼▼▼▼▼▼▼▼
>
> Love will find a way — indifference will find an excuse.
>
> √ Learn to love the things you do that bring you the largest number of sales and profits!
>
> √ Love makes all burdens light. This is the key to doing your <u>best</u> work!

woman to marry him a hundred times, in a hundred slightly different ways, until she said, "Yes!" Speaking of marriage: When my stepson got married,

SECTION FIVE — Ruthless Copywriting Strategies

MARKETING SECRET

A good marketing system is the solution!

- Pour your heart and soul into the process of building it.

- Then sit back and let it generate leads and close sales for you automatically.

he told me that he wanted me to wear a tuxedo to his wedding. And I said, "Chris, I'll never do such a thing. When I die, you can put me in a tuxedo and then you can have an open casket and come see me in my tuxedo then." Well, that was about a year before his actual wedding. He just bugged me about it. Every single time we spoke, he came at me at least a hundred different ways, until finally, to make a long story short, I went and got a tuxedo. I have the pictures to prove it. And I'm glad I did, because I would have been the only one dressed down. He just kept at me. He wouldn't take "No!" for an answer. **When I think of aggressive salespeople, I think of people that just keep coming at you.** They want your business. They want you to do what they want you to do, and they just keep applying that pressure.

So keep the pressure on, and get creative about it. If I see that it's a good deal and they could use it for their business, I give my prospect examples of exactly how this particular advertising or marketing is going to work in or will promote their business, and **I give them concrete, meaningful specifics about how to take it and use it in their business.** Too many times it's easy to get lazy and not give people what they need; and we do it, too. We'll just mail the same letter over and over again as part of a follow-up campaign. And while that may be effective, perhaps a more effective approach is to change it up, be creative, approach them in different ways. I talked about this a bit earlier. Mail them a sales letter, mail them a postcard, call them, email them, fax them, do this, do that. Hit them with one kind of offer and then hit them with another kind of offer. **Change it up.** Make the envelope look different. We use shiny envelopes sometimes. We even have a mailing that goes in a wallet. It's paper, but it looks like a wallet; and when you open it, it has a flap in it like a wallet would and out pops something. You can put, for example, a hundred dollar bill in the wallet that's got a sales message on it.

Try being creative, while sticking to proven direct-response principles. Creativity, in that process, means you're not sending the same thing over and over again. **You're doing sequenced follow-up mailings, but they're unique.** Each one is different than the previous, and you never know which mailing will strike a nerve or catch someone in the right way. Maybe you mail them a letter and it hits them at a time where they're busy, and then the next time you send them a postcard. Well, a postcard is easy to read, so they just see the postcard, they pull it out of the mail, and think, "Oh yeah, I *do* need to contact them or visit their website." Or maybe you call them on the phone and they're busy. But then they get your letter in the mail and they sit down and read it. **The key is to put constant pressure on them by continuously reminding them to do business with you.**

The only time you stop following up is when it becomes unprofitable to continue mailing. You have to figure out when that is, but you continuously mail and re-mail to people over and over again until it stops being profitable. That's when you know it's time to stop. So follow-up, follow-up, and follow-up some more. Continuously keep your message in front of your clients, until they buy or until it becomes unprofitable to keep telling them they should. Remember, I talked earlier before about the fact that most people just give up way too soon. By continuing to follow-up, you *don't* give up. And every time that they don't buy, well, you're following up; **it's wrong to assume that they don't want what you have.** Because they could just have a million things going on that day, or their whole lives could be traumatic. You never know. Just to assume that they don't want it to begin with would be a wrong assumption, as long as they're qualified.

NUMBER THREE: The concepts we sell are these: fast, simple, and easy. Here's a quote from the late, great Gene Swartz, one of the best copywriters in history —he died about 20 years ago, and made God knows how many tens or hundreds of millions of dollars. His famous quote was, **"What people really want is a miracle!"** I used to have that hanging up on my wall so I could just see it all the time. That's an emotional thing, and we sell to emotions. **People are looking for easy answers. They want**

things that are very simple, so you've got to dumb things down.

Now, I'm not trying to insult people or say that they're dumb. Quite the contrary: people have built up an elaborate immunity to advertising and marketing, and **so what you have to do is make it simple and easy to digest.** People don't pay much attention to marketing messages. They read them in an apathetic, passive kind of way. They know you're trying to sell something. They know you're trying to get their money — and they've got a resistance for that. They're trying to hang onto their money! They don't want to pull out that credit card. So it's a fight, a tug of war over their money. They're fighting to keep it; you're fighting to get it. **So you do things to make your offer as simple as possible, with the most appeal. The benefits are all out there up front.**

Chris Hollinger has a phrase on his wall that he says reminds him of this particular factor whatever he's doing about anything: KISS — Keep It Simple, Stupid. **If you get it too complicated, you'll lose them.** And here's another little thing on his wall that's always there: "A confused mind says no." And we're "yes" men, in the sense that what we do is get people to say "Yes! Yes! Yes!" **But if the mind is confused, if your marketing or your offer includes things that are just too complicated... the mind says no.** It doesn't matter how good a deal it is for them. If their mind is confused, you get a no. You don't get the yes; you don't get the money.

Fast, simple, and easy is really the motto of society these days. **We want everything fast, simple, and easy.** Think about how many fast-food restaurants there are on every corner. Now they've got credit cards where you don't actually have to give it to the clerk. You just stick it up to the reader, and the RFID chip in it reads your card and charges you. We have drive-thrus so we don't have to go in and get our food anymore. Banks have drive-up windows. There are ATMs so you can withdraw your money fast, simple, and easy. There are fundraisers where the money is automatically deducted from your checking account. These days, a lot of churches have automatic giving, where you just give them your credit card number or your bank account and they'll draft your tithe. Everything in life is set up now for fast, simple, and easy. **We don't want to wait.** We have microwave dinners — and even microwaves are too slow. We want everything that way. And so, as a marketer, it's your job to find out how you can give people things in a fast, simple, and easy way.

We have one product where we offer to do everything for the customer. That's another example of fast, simple, and easy. Our society has turned toward more of the "done-for-you" type services, as well. That's a part of what we do for our clients, and more and more industries have options now where they'll do things for you that you used to do for yourself. A lot of home improvement has gone that way. You don't even have to go to the hardware store and buy the materials yourself; you just have to tell them you want them to do it for you. Places like Home Depot and Lowe's have installation services, whereas you used to have to go find your own installer. Now you just go pick the stuff out, and they have their staff install it for you. So society, as a whole, is moving more and more toward fast, simple, and easy. **If you can find a way to incorporate that into your marketing, that's great; you're giving people exactly what they want.**

NUMBER FOUR is to drive the sales. I've already mentioned our 20-page sales letter, where the premium is $33,248.20. Now, I know that sounds unbelievable, and I take five pages to show people why we can actually do it, so we're not expecting anybody to actually believe it without proof. We want to get their attention, and we do — but then we've got five pages of copy that explains how we can give them a bonus that big. **Bonuses and premiums help drive sales.** We're calling this one "the world's greatest free bonus gift," so we've got a big, huge bold title. "The World's Greatest? You want the best, we've got it!" **The right premium won't cost you money, if you choose it right. It will *make* you money.**

This is one of the greatest sins of marketing. Everybody's constantly looking for ways to save money and pull back and do things in a more economical way, when really **the only thing that they should care about is ROI: Return On Investment. That's it.** What you spend versus what you make. Things like choosing the right premiums will cost you more money, but you'll make more money because more people will end up buying.

Those premiums force people who wouldn't ordinarily buy to go ahead and take action. Our big premium that I just mentioned is a good example of that. Obviously, it just sounds outrageous! Imagine $33,248.20 worth of bonuses. But then, it takes five pages to go ahead and explain exactly where that came from, and why we're able to do it. And so it's believable; it builds up that value. They're like, "Oh wow, I'm going to be

MARKETING SECRET

The art of selling is do everything possible to make it "seem" as if you are not trying to sell!

- When done properly, they practically stand in line and beg you to take their money!

able to get so much!" It's all a part of stacking that offer, stacking it so high and deep with the benefits, values, premiums, and free bonus gifts that they're thinking, "This is unbelievable! It's fantastic. I'm going to do it!" And then they get a "thud" factor. **They get so much stuff that it helps to drive later sales.**

Looking back at some of my earlier stuff, where I had no concept of offering premium gifts, I can see that my sales suffered because of it. **Remember, all that matters, ultimately, is results.** If you concentrate on your marketing systems, your sales problems will disappear. When I go back and look at some of those sales letters and why they didn't perform well, I might say, "Okay, there was no free bonus gift there. There wasn't a good enough explanation of the free bonus gift itself." There's so many more things that I could have done with some of those sales letters to make them better. And that's one of the meaningful specifics there — did you offer a premium at all?

Doing so helps drive sales and gets you the yes. **Big, bold premiums are the key.** If a premium is weak, it's not going to drive sales like you intend it to, so you've got to use premiums that stand up and make people pay attention to them. It's been proven that some people will buy a product just because of the premium. And premiums are everywhere. People know they're buying a package deal; it's not like they really think they're getting something for free when they buy your product. People know that they have to make a purchase to get the premium. **But still, there's something psychological about getting a free gift with your purchase that makes them buy.**

A lot of stuff is sold this way. You're in the mall and someone's trying to get you to sign up for a credit card. When you sign up for a credit card, you get a free T-shirt. Premiums are everywhere. Cell phone carriers use premiums to drive sales. "Come in today and pick up this great new phone. We'll not only give you the phone, but we'll also throw in a car charger, a home charger, or a Bluetooth headset. It's free when you come in and sign up for a new service."

The thing that you've got to do is to make sure your premium is a strong, bold one. If you're selling something for $100, don't be afraid to give away something that has a perceived value of $1,000. **The bigger the perceived value, the more people will want what you're selling them.** The thing you have to watch out for is to make sure your premium is believable. You can't just say, "This premium has a $1,000 value!" If people don't believe it, they're not going to take what you're offering. **It has to have the three B's — Big, Bold, and Believable. If you've got those three things, then any premium will increase your sales. It doesn't cost you money.** Don't think about having to give it away; think about how many increased sales you'll get if you use that premium. If you're uncertain about it, the smart thing to do is test. Add the premium to half your list, and keep the premium out for the other half. Do that, and you'll be able to see and measure how much difference the premium makes. Ideally, you would run with or without a premium and you'd be able to see, "Well, without the premium this is the response I got; with the premium, I got this much of an increased response." You'd know exactly what level of increased business you received as a result of using that premium. That's the way to answer the question, "Am I spending too much?" **Most people never do spend too much; they're more likely to suffer from the opposite, which is spending too little.**

For too many marketers, the premium is an afterthought. Okay, they're going to do a sales letter. They're working on it; now they know they have to come up with a premium, so they just pick anything. Well, **what they should do is find something that ties in with the promotion as much possible.** With the Master Distributorship for our Recession-Proof Wealth System, the websites we give people are called Recession-Proof Websites. That's how we tied it in, and then we had to make it believable. Even on a whopping premium like this one, we had to take five pages just to explain to people why we could actually do something like this, because people are skeptical.

NUMBER FIVE: Total risk reversal. The average prospect would never admit it, but they're scared. They're afraid you're scamming them. They're afraid you're going to rip them off. They're afraid they won't do a thing with your product or service. We talk about how skeptical people are, but we don't talk about that fact. Most marketers don't even take that into account.

With total risk reversal, we try to stack all the benefits on the client's side of the table, so that all of the chips are on their side of the table, metaphorically speaking. **All of the risk is on our shoulders, not theirs. We want to ease their fears, we want to take care of them, we want them to know that if they're not happy, we're not happy.** Sometimes we even give them a free gift — and they can get their money back and still keep the free gift. We do all kinds of things to make them happy. It empowers them rather than us, but ultimately we're the ones who are empowered, because our sales increase when we use these tactics. Stacking all those chips on their side of the table and **then throwing a big fat guarantee on top of it just speaks volumes.** The idea is to get them to say yes. A lot of these sales letters are just stack, stack, stack and guarantee... and off you go and make a sale. They're formulaic, but they work.

Risk reversal is important. People are afraid you're scamming them, they don't believe you, they think that they won't be able to do it, they know how lazy and apathetic they are... All these things enter someone's mind when they're deciding whether to respond to an offer you have. It all goes back to Point #3: we sell fast, simple, and easy. The faster, the simpler, the easier you can make something, the more likely they are to see themselves doing it. If they can't see themselves doing whatever it is or benefiting from the product or service you have, then they won't buy. So you want to stack everything in their favor. **Explain to them how easy it is for them to use or how easy it is to do. Be descriptive in your sales copy.** Write a paragraph or two describing how they will easily use your product or how easy it will be for them to benefit from it, how fast it works, whatever. That helps convince them that it's going to be simple and that they won't have a learning curve, that everything will be figured out for them.

One way to eliminate the risk is by giving them a ton of free stuff that they get to keep even if they back out. It's the ultimate risk reversal

> Whoever owns the BIGGEST and MOST RESPONSIVE mailing list is king!

to say, "Hey, you're going to get this gift that's worth $1,000 even if you send our product back. So the worst that happens is you end up ahead, because you got our free gift just for checking us out." Or you might say, "Take a 30-day risk-free trial of our coaching program and we'll give you all these products absolutely free. If after 30 days you decide you don't want to become a member, that's fine. We won't bill you, and you'll get to keep all the free gifts we gave you." You're making it so they win even if they decide they don't want to participate. *Everything is stacked in their favor.*

Using risk reversal in that way puts all the pressure on *you* and none on *them.* **If they feel pressure, they're not going to respond.** They'll hold back. If they feel like there's some reason why they maybe shouldn't make a decision, well, they won't. So put it all on you and not on them, by saying, **"Hey, the risk is all on me. If I don't perform, you're going to get to keep this free gift and I'm out the money.** So it's all on me to perform to your expectations. If I don't, then you're out nothing." That puts all the risk on you and takes all the risk away from them, which makes it more likely that they'll respond. Tell them, "You have everything to gain; nothing to lose. All the risk is on our shoulders, not yours. All the chips are stacked on your side of the table, not ours."

NUMBER SIX: Two-Step Marketing. It's the safest and most profitable way to build your business. STEP ONE: Separate the smaller group of the best buyers from the rest by getting those people to take some initial action. STEP TWO: you focus on doing everything you can to sell to those people that initially responded to your first step. The strategy involves spending more money per person on the smaller group of people who were more qualified, who initially took that first step. **All marketing is about selling and re-selling to customers, and two-step marketing is the safest, most profitable way to do that.**

I'm involved in a business with two other guys, and we just did a mailing. Well, we didn't get the results we wanted from it. It was a small promotion; nothing big. We made all of our money back. We made a little profit, but nothing to get excited about. But I was talking to one of my partners some time ago, and I told him, "If we would have used two-step

SECTION FIVE — Ruthless Copywriting Strategies

MARKETING SECRET

When customers say "No!" they're really not saying "No!" — they're saying "Give me a reason to say "YES!" — *From the movie "Diamond Men."*

marketing, we would have definitely done better on that promotion." On the first step, we would have asked them to raise their hand and send for the information, and maybe offered them a nice little free gift to incentivize them for doing so. And then we would have had a smaller group to work with, and would have put them on a sequence and stayed after them and reminded them that *they* were the ones who initiated the whole thing by taking the first step. We would have made more money; and we'll probably still do that. **Two-step marketing is always the best; it lets you go after the smaller group of better qualified prospects in a more aggressive way.**

I'm convinced that if you could employ just one marketing strategy, two-step marketing would be your best bet. Really concentrate on generating qualified prospects and then making them good, solid offers. **Then follow up.** That one concept alone is really the heart and soul — the core — of the type of marketing that I do on a regular basis. Produce qualified leads, make quality offers to those leads, and apply these strategies as they fit into that process. Stay after them. Hammer, hammer, hammer!

Occasionally we do one-step marketing, but not very often. If you rent a mailing list and do a mailing to a large group of people without two-step marketing, all you end up with is a small group of buyers. Maybe you even made a small profit at it, but you can't mail to the rest of them again unless you re-rent the list. **You did a one-time mailing to a list, and you got some sales, and that's it.** You have whatever buyers you got from that mailing. **But if you do two-step marketing, you can mail to that entire list with an invitation to get more information.**

And then you have a list of leads — people who requested information from you. **You can then mail to those people all you want without renting the list over and over again. They're your customers now.** Even though they just asked for information from you, they "belong" to you. They're your names. Then you mail to those people over and over, and you get a percentage of them to buy. You're probably going to end up with more sales in the end anyway, but you get those sales from a smaller group of people that you followed up to over and over again.

So you end up with two lists: a lead list and a buyers list. And while that leads list isn't as valuable as your buyer list, over time it can grow. Maybe it's a list that you can email periodic offers to. You can joint venture with other people and say, "Hey, I know these people are interested in making money," or, "I know they're interested in x, y, z products. They might be interested in your product," and together you can mail to that list. **Also, you can rent that list.**

NUMBER SEVEN is tele-seminars. We've been having tele-seminars since the early 1990s, and we've experimented with many different formats. We even had some live tele-seminars that lasted five and six hours! **Tele-seminars give your customers the same basic advantages that they'd get from coming to a seminar, except that they can stay at home.** They don't have to travel, which is especially appealing to people since 9/11. Here's another good thing about tele-seminars: **you can record them and turn them into audio products later.** In fact, last Thursday (as of this writing) we had a tele-seminar, and we had about 130 people on it when we were recording. Now, all we were initially going to do was record a "pitch" CD; but we knew that by inviting customers to listen in, we would do a better job. Because if it was just Chris and I, and there was no audience to present to, we wouldn't have the same energy; we wouldn't have the same passion, we wouldn't put it out there as much, and we wouldn't work as hard.

So we decided to let some of our customers attend this event. We had 130 on the call. We were promoting a $495 product, and after the call 70 or 80 of those people called in. So it was extremely profitable, and we did a much better job knowing that there were people on the line. We were performing more. We were putting that energy out there, so we produced a better "pitch" CD than we might have. **This just goes to show that tele-seminars can be great tools for communicating with your customers.**

They're excellent for relationship-building.

When we talk about copywriting, we're primarily talking about print or on the Web. But one point I want to make clear to you is that the more you write in a physical way, where you're expressing again and again the benefits that you sell, when it comes time for you to verbally communicate with the customers, it's going to be so much more powerful, so much more effective, so much easier — because **the writing process also helps with other forms of communication.**

My colleague Chris Hollinger does a lot of tele-seminars with events for follow-up, or even to launch something brand new. **It's very inexpensive to, say, do a voice blast and drive people to a tele-seminar. It's also a good way to test things.** And the neat thing is, there are a lot of companies out there that offer inexpensive tele-seminar services that are easy to set up, easy to use, and easy to run. You can literally have a tele-seminar set up in a couple of minutes and scheduled to run. Then you have to promote it. Maybe you need to send out a postcard or two; but Chris has done this a lot lately with email lists, where people that have opted in or given him their email address. He'll go ahead and send them a quick email out and invite them to a seminar, for no other reason than that it gives them a little opportunity to get to know him and start building that relationship a little.

And he'll spend a lot of time on the tele-seminar itself, even if it's just him presenting. Now, we've all done that a lot, but I do recommend using somebody else, because two or more people can play well off each other. In any case, spend a great deal of time on tele-seminars just building a relationship, getting that warm-and-fuzzy feeling going with people who up until now have only seen your ad and received something in the mail from you. They don't know you from Adam, really. **But you can invite them to a very low-cost tele-seminar, get them on there and spend some time talking about who you are, what you do, what you're all about.** That improves profits, and goes a long way when it comes time to ask for the money.

There's a service called freeconferencecall.com that lets you host free conference calls. **A conference call is just another term for a tele-seminar.** Whatever you call it, it's a service where you can have people on the call with you. When you're done, it actually gives you a link so you can download the recording it just made of your call. **It's absolutely free.** They have other services they hope you'll buy, but you can use their conferencing services for free.

Tele-seminars are good for many things, and can serve several different purposes, depending on what your goal is. **You can use them for product creation,** where you're actually on the call with customers, recording product. We've done that many times. The customers are in "listen only" mode, usually. They don't talk, but they're listening as we record live. Having live people listening provides a little added energy, because you know that you can't mess up. You can't just hit the "stop" button and start over! **We also use seminars as sales tools,** where we have people listening in with the intent of making a sale. **Or we use them for information purposes.** Sometimes we've had tele-seminars for members only, where we'll share information and news with them as members.

The great thing about a tele-seminar is that you can put one together fast, any time you want to, with email blasting, with faxes, with phone calls, through voice blasting. You can let someone know that you have a conference call coming up, and have that call happen in as little as a few hours, and certainly within days. Chris Lakey sometimes gets emails from a gentleman who throws together conference calls in one day. He'll get an email in the morning that says, "Hey, I'm going to have a conference call tonight. Here's what we're going to talk about. Join us if you want to." Chris never has, because he's too busy and rarely does things like that in the evening, because that's his time with his family. But I'm sure the man has people on the call, or he wouldn't keep inviting him.

Conference call lines are easy to get these days; you could have a conference call line available to you virtually any time you want it. Some of them have toll-free numbers; some are toll numbers. You should find a way to incorporate tele-seminars into your business model for all the reasons I've already talked about: for information, to create products, to sell things to your customers. Plus, you can pre-record them so that they play as if they're live. You do them once, and then just like a radio show that keeps playing over and over again, you can repeat them. **You set it up and just let it go.** We've had the same tele-seminar run for a year or more on a weekly basis — every week, sometimes twice a week, and sometimes three times a week. People are coming to it as if it's live. We never tell them it's recorded, but we're not trying to hide the fact that it is.

MARKETING SECRET

Hope is not a marketing strategy!

- Keep your emotions out of it!

- Let the numbers tell you what to do.

If somebody asked us, "Hey, is that a recording?" we'd say yes. But they assume it's live; and in fact it was recorded live to begin with. **So it's a good way, again, to do that thing where you do something once and get paid for it again and again.**

NUMBER EIGHT: The power of personalization. We use it in two ways. The first way is more subjective, where we use our rags-to-riches story. That story is an important part of our relationship with our customers. We tell that story over and over. It's a very personal thing. We tell other parts about who we are, and just like our friend, Russ von Hoelscher, as we go along we continue to tell more and more. For example: For years I wouldn't tell my clients that I'm a recovering alcoholic/drug addict, because I felt they just wouldn't understand if I shared those parts of my life. But I started experimenting, very slowly, first just mentioning the alcohol, no drugs at all. They were okay with all that. By the way, I've been clean and sober now for 28 years, since 1981.

The more my clients reacted to that, the more I met other people who had the same story. But also, I started to see that it wasn't a problem. People were saying, "Well, okay." So then I started mentioning alcohol *and* drugs. When I was a kid I had a problem with both. I got help, I straightened my life out, and then I met my wife, and *then* we started the business. It was that sharing of my story, the sharing of who I am and certain aspects about my life, that I was always so terrified to do; but once I did it, I found that people were pretty positive about something that's normally pretty negative. **The more you tell your personal story, the more it bonds**

people to you. So that's one aspect of personalization.

The other aspect where we spend a lot of extra money is on people. We've got a room over at M.O.R.E., Inc., that contains a huge machine that does all our personal letters. It's like a giant laser printer, and it will put out a sales letter that's up to a hundred pages long — and on every page it will put the customer's name up at the top. The machine can even put a colored cover on it, so eventually we're going to do custom manuals with the customer's name on every page.

People are more inclined to look at a letter with their name on it. That's why we spend extra money doing things to personalize those letters, to make them more special. Our system does a nice job, but you can do the same on a small scale from a home office. That's what Chris Hollinger's wife does in their operation; she uses software to customize the front page or the cover letter that goes with their mailings. There are things you can do on the outside of the envelopes, too. I've done some of it myself.

The more of this kind of personalization you do, the better the odds are that you'll get a better response. Why? Because people like to see their own names. That grabs their attention, and that's what it's all about. It's part of relationship building. Most people like their name, and they like when people call them by their name. When you're having a conversation with somebody, they say that's a sure way to build a relationship faster with them: to say their name. People like to hear their names said. Well, there's a similar effect when you're writing sales copy. **Use their first name (or sometimes their last name) in the sales letter.** Say "Dear John" instead of "Dear Friend," and then throw the name in throughout the copy. "By the way, John, did you also know this?" And, "One last thing, John. I wanted to remind you of this…" It makes people feel good, because they like being talked to by their given name. Now, you can overdo this. Some people get going and drop the name in every paragraph: John, John, John. And then they mention the name of their town… "For people just like you in Goessel, Kansas," and just overdo it totally, ruining a good idea.

NUMBER NINE: We're totally real with our customers and prospects, and more so all the time. We show pictures of ourselves, our community, our families; we've got thousands of pictures that we send out to people. **We're in a market that's full of skepticism — as all markets are these days — and so we have to do things to combat that skepticism.** That's how we get past some of the skepticism. Plus, we do a lot of audio products. This is based on an audio product we recorded at a three-day event back in October 2008. It's going out to different groups of customers who weren't part of that event, and they'll hear us goofing up and saying stupid things; they'll hear our jokes and some of the crazy things we do sometimes. We won't edit any of that stuff out (as we've done in this book!). Again, it may turn some people off — but hopefully it will turn off the people who are wrong for us anyway. And even some of the people who aren't turned off will still say to themselves, "You know, I hate that guy. I can't stand him. He's a blowhard. He's an egotistical jerk. Those two Chrises aren't so bad, but that T.J. is just a jerk." But at least they'll know that I'm a *real* jerk! I'm just trying to be myself, and I think there needs to be more of that in marketing.

Don't be afraid to tell your story. Let people know who you are and what you're about and what you stand for, and how you're different from everybody else. **You need to express your honesty and integrity from the get-go. You need to just be yourself.** Don't try to put up some façade that's not real, because you'll just end up lying and lying and lying, and it'll turn to nothing. There'll be no substance there. You'll just be an empty vessel, and who wants that? Just be you, and don't be afraid to be you. I went through that with some of the things that I struggled with and didn't want to share, and found out that I'm better off sharing. You're better off just being human instead of the perfect marketer guy with the slick hair and the white teeth and the million-dollar diamond smile. It's better to be yourself and be totally real with folks. **That way you don't have to worry about anything. It's a liberating experience; it really is.**

Back when I was first running ads, I thought about running the type that showed me and Eileen standing in front of the fancy cars and fancy homes we didn't actually own. Hey, that's how everybody else did it! But Russ suggested that we just be ourselves. That approach would have been fake. But you do see that in a lot of business opportunity ads. Maybe some of them are real, but I think most of them want you to feel like they're successful because they're trying to show you *how* to be successful. So in their pictures, they've got this fancy sports car in their driveway, and they're in front of a big mansion wearing a really fancy suit — and everything looks like they have extreme wealth.

But when Eileen and I were getting started, we went the opposite direction and said, "Hey, we're just like you." I'm the Blue Jeans Millionaire! **There's no difference between me and you, except that I've discovered a secret formula that's proven to make money with direct-response marketing. And now I want to teach that to you!** So that's the angle that we took — and it's a real, sincere angle that people can identify with. That's what I mean by saying that just being real, being yourself, is important. **It's unauthentic to try to put a façade up and pretend you're someone you're not.** We're all kind of goofy. Nobody's perfect; we all have flaws, and we're all in this human race together. We all struggle with various things, so why try to pretend to be perfect when we know no one else is perfect? If you can just be real, be yourself, tell your story, then people can identify with that. And yes, you may turn some people off.

> Database marketing in 3 words:
> 1. Segment
> 2. Concentrate
> 3. Dominate!

I've mentioned that Russ von Hoelscher has started to talk more about his political beliefs as he gets older — and I expect that there are some people — especially die-hard Democrats! — who said, "I'm not going to buy from that guy ever again because I don't agree with his politics." But other people have said, "Hey, I like what you're saying. Maybe I don't necessarily agree with you 100%, but I like that you're bold. I like that you're putting yourself out there, and I like that you're talking about it." Again, it goes back to what we talked about earlier, about offending some people and having other people drawn to you. You're going to offend some people if you speak; there's no way around that. If something comes out of your mouth, someone's probably not going to agree with it, and they're going to be upset. That happens, because we're a polarized society. There are enough people on both sides of the political fence that when you say anything political, you're going to make about half the people in the room upset. **But by being sincere, people who you want to do business with you will be drawn to you.** And, hopefully, the people that you don't want to do business with you will be repelled.

The right people will accept you for how you are. I spent a number of years being a people-pleaser. I'm still struggling with it. The bad thing

> ### ▼▼▼▼▼▼▼▼
> ### MARKETING SECRET
>
> Keep going back to your best customers again and again... Just because some of them may say "no" today doesn't mean they won't say "YES!" tomorrow.

about being a people-pleaser is that you're always worried about what other people are going to think about you. **When you're a people-pleaser, the stress is outrageous.** I don't have that anymore, for the most part, and thank God! It's so damned liberating to just be myself. I used to only want to tell people what I thought that they wanted to hear. I don't do it nearly as much as I used to.

NUMBER TEN: This is an aspect of our rags-to-riches story. Earlier, I talked about the PAS Formula: Problem, Agitate, Solution. Well, here's another great copywriting formula. **It's called "Before & After."** You see it all the time. **"Here's the way I was before. Here's what happened to me. Here's the way I am now... and now I'm going to show you how to do it, too."** It's like the plot you see in most movies. Here's the character, and then something happens. He works through whatever happens, and there he is, a different man at the end. It's a formula that's used over and over again. **Our rags-to-riches story bonds us with the customers.** It's inspirational for them. You know, I got sick and tired of telling it about ten years ago, but I realized that I have to keep telling it to people, because it's part of the story that they connect with, and that's what we're trying to do — build relationships with people. So we keep telling our story over and over... even when we don't want to.

NUMBER ELEVEN: Audio recordings. Remember, the more you write, the more you can communicate in other ways and speak with real authority and force. **The writing helps with the audio.** The audio has been so good for us, because people can actually listen to us, rather than just read our words. That has helped us enormously. We've mailed out God knows how many hundreds of thousands of audio recordings; it started with cassette tapes, and now it's audio CDs. **It lets our customers feel like they know us a whole lot better, in a more emotional way than they would ever feel if they just read our stuff.** You know, the act of someone actually taking something that you've written, and sitting down with it for a period of time to read your words — it's kind of flattering. Reading is a very intimate thing. Audio takes that to next level: they're sitting there and listening to your voice. **It's very intimate, because you're putting your ideas, your thoughts, your call to action between their ears, in their brain, and hopefully it's going to help you make a sale.** These audio recordings also help you to connect and build that relationship with new customers, or maintain that relationship with current customers. The technology is such that it's easy to make and reproduce these things, and get them out there like you need to. **Audio recordings help you to get that "yes" you're looking for.**

Chris Lakey likes to compare audio recordings, and building relationships with your customers and getting them to know you and feel like they have a connection with you, with stalkers. Now, before you decide Chris is just one weird dude, let me explain! People who stalk Hollywood movie stars or musicians feel like they have some bond with them — even though they've never met them, and have no real connection to them. It's not real. It's based on the fact that the stalker *hears* them, that their audio gets inside the stalker's head. Take a musician, someone who's been in the music business for 10 or 15 years. They've produced a dozen CDs, and they've got a fan base in the millions. Well, a certain percentage of those people feel connected to them. Some people just like their music, but others get connected on a deep, emotional level.

I think it's the same thing with movies. You build a relationship with an actor or actress because you see them in movies and you like their work. And so you buy other films that have that actor in them, and you feel an emotional connection with them. It's a subconscious thing that you don't really think about. It just happens.

You can use audio recordings, as an entrepreneur, to do some of that same kind of thing. **People will get to know you better.** They'll feel a connection with you. They'll feel like they know you more than if you never use audio, if the only way you ever communicate with your customers is in print. By adding the audio dynamic, you build the connection, taking that relationship to a completely different level — a much deeper level — and that makes it easier to get through to people with your sales messages. **They feel a connection to you, they're more inclined to read your copy, and they're more inclined to respond to your offers, because of that deep psychological connection.** Using audio gets you a closer connection with your customers, and makes it easier to do more business with them. And again, don't be afraid to just be yourself. **It takes a lot less energy and in the end, people will appreciate you more because they'll sense that you're real.**

NUMBER TWELVE: Seminars. Seminars are tough for me, personally, but every time we have one, I thank my wife Eileen for getting us involved in them to begin with. She ran the company for the first 14 years, and she was always very supportive of doing seminars. Now, it's a lot of work to do these events. We make it look easy because we've got a staff of people who just get them done like clockwork. And certainly the smaller ones are easier, compared to the bigger ones where we have hundreds of people.

We had our first seminar on September 22, 1990 — and Eileen and I were so scared to face our customers that we wouldn't even get up to the podium just to say hello! We sat in back the whole time, while Russ ran the seminar for us. And all throughout the day, people kept coming back there anyway, if only because that's where the bathrooms were. And we were out in the hallway, so we met everybody; and then at lunch time we sat and ate lunch with everybody. All afternoon Russ had a hard time keeping people in the room because they were out in the hall talking to Eileen and me! By the end of the day, we went from being scared and insecure to really loving it!

We held 13 different seminars here in Goessel in 1992. From that point on, we've done hundreds of different seminars — which is kind of odd, if you really know me. The truth is, I'm kind of an introvert, even though I can express myself well in public. If you didn't know me better, you might think I'm a real extrovert. In reality, I'm a loner. That's just who I am. I'm not lonely; I'm a loner. **I actually enjoy spending alone time with myself and with my wife, and having a small, quiet life.** Recently, one of my seminar attendees said to me, "You've got 500 people in Goessel. How long have you been here?" And I said, "Well, we've been in the area for 20 years." He said, "You must know all 500 of them." I replied, "I know five people in Goessel. That's it. Five, not 500." I'm a loner. They all know of our company; they all know who we are. But I only know a handful of people here, and that's it.

So seminars haven't come natural to us. Loners like me tend to want to stay that way, and so I've had to put myself out there. But it's been a great experience to meet with our clients, to get to know them, to spend time with them. It's been one of the best things that's happened to our company, and I thank Eileen for every single seminar. There are so many people in the direct-response marketing business who never want to go face-to-face with their customers. They never want to meet them. They never want to spend time with them. They're attracted to this business initially because they want to do everything by mail or over the Internet; they want to hide behind a computer and hide in a P.O. box. **But having seminars has been one of our greatest experiences, because it puts us right there, eyeball to eyeball, with our customers.** And although it's a little scary, it's not as scary as it used to be. I used to throw up in the bathroom before the events. But it's been a positive thing. In fact, it's been a great thing! So I would encourage you to meet with your customers, talk with them, spend time with them, get to know them. **There are some phenomenal things that can happen at seminars, sales-wise.**

Chris Hollinger and his wife had their first seminar about a year and a half into their business. They were actually doing some training on a specific opportunity, on some of the materials that they had created, and they had probably about 30 to 40 people at that event down in Wichita. He tells me that it was a little scary! Well, your first time with anything *is* a little scary. It was a lot of work — just the logistics, and getting it all put together, and the anticipation, and then the actual seminar. It took three straight days of being out there talking, presenting, and teaching, and by the time Friday rolled around, Kim and Chris were relieved it was over.

But they've had people who attended that event five years ago who purchased something from them *last month*. Now Chris looks forward to his seminars. Like all of us who take this step, he's learned things, and it's helped him get out of his normal weekly and daily routine. Now he comes and presents at my workshops! And he's learned by doing so; as he told me at this workshop, he got new ideas for one of his products and made some changes to his copy while he was here.

▼▼▼▼▼▼▼▼
MARKETING SECRET

In all you do — strive to place yourself in the greatest possible position of power.

- After all, "Players depend on luck. Casinos depend on math. That's why casinos always win!" Wherever possible, be that casino! Find many ways to make money — even if the whole thing fails or everyone else loses money.

I also like the way seminars build the trust relationship with your customers. Even if they don't attend, the fact that you have a seminar means that they're able to have access to you. Even if you have an event that only a handful of people attend, by letting all of your customers know about it, they feel like they can trust you more because you have an event that they can go to. You're not hiding; you're making yourself accessible.

Seminars also offer a good revenue stream. Not only can you make money getting people into the room, but you can make money while they're there by offering them other products and services. **So there's a chance for additional revenue there, as well. You can also launch new products and promotions when you have a live event.** Consider the event this chapter, is based on. We were recording audio the entire time, so it became an audio product that we could sell. Now it's a book, too. So while we were standing there teaching our customers in the workshop, we were also building our product library, so we could make this available to other people in the future.

It's hard to put on a three-day event. It wears you out. It makes you physically and emotionally exhausted. But it's also fun at the same time. We love doing it. **And so, you can have an event that totally drains you and wipes you out, but is simultaneously fun and profitable.** We used to have two-day events instead of three. We changed it to three partially because of selfish, self-centered reasons. It's that I get a natural high. The first day is a lot of work for me; but even so, by the end of it, I'm feeling good. I'm feeling a natural high. It's a drug-free, pressure release kind of buzz that I love, because it's a great experience! **You're really trying to help people at the seminar, and you end up helping yourself in the process, too.**

NUMBER THIRTEEN: Use food to warm the hearts of cold prospects and customers. I have to credit this one to Dan Kennedy. I once asked Dan, "What's the fastest, easiest, simplest way to take a cold prospect and turn them into a warm prospect?" And Dan said, simply, "Food." I realized he was right. I started remembering that in a lot of these direct sales organizations, food is involved. Maybe you've experienced this before, where they invite you to some hotel or a nice restaurant. They buy you a steak dinner, and after you eat the steak dinner they try to make a sale to you. In every city, every week, there's some direct-sales company that's doing that for small groups of people, where they feed them first and then ask for a purchase. After a meal, people are usually pretty happy. And now, of course, **the whole concept of reciprocity kicks in; they just gave you a free meal, so you have to listen to them now. And then they pitch you.** A lot of businesspeople do that: they take somebody out for a meal, and during the course of that meal they'll try to get you to do something or buy something or whatever.

So we started giving people all these popcorn bags. We went to a company in Wichita, and had them put our label on their popcorn — and then we started sending out God knows how many tens of thousands at a time. It's added up to a couple of hundred thousand bags of popcorn, just in the last six or seven years. It's lightweight, so it mails cheap. We don't have extra postage costs, customers like it, and it serves us overall for building relationships. It separates us from everybody else. That's one of the big things that marketing is supposed to do.

NUMBER FOURTEEN: consistent front-end marketing. This is critical — and it's one of those things that I scratch my head about, because I know marketers who should be doing this and they're not. **We have a consistent plan for bringing in new customers every week of the year — no exceptions.** Each week we invest a specific sum of money to attract new prospects and customers. We mail year-round, 52 weeks every year, and we're constantly bringing in new customers. **We've got another plan for constantly re-selling to those people. You** *have* **to do it.** It confuses me when I run into marketers who don't have a consistent, steady way to bring in new customers on a regular basis.

SECTION FIVE — Ruthless Copywriting Strategies

Our lead generation method is to consistently do mailings, but there are other lead generation techniques you can do online and offline. Other marketers I know do space ads, and have gotten good at finding ways they can do that. We gave them up long ago in favor of direct mail, but space ads served us well in the beginning. Learning to do this well is an ongoing process. For us, it's absolutely never-ending. **It's a consistent system of mailing, mailing, mailing.** If you're not bringing new folks in, pretty soon the flow dries up; there's no one going into the top of the funnel. A lot of people don't reinvest into that part of it; once they have a nice pool of customers, they decide not to go ahead and keep prospecting, keep bringing those people in and generating qualified leads. But it's something you have to do. **Find something that works for *you* and then keep tweaking it.**

There are two parts of your business, in general: the relationships you have and the business you do with your current customers, and then all the things you do to attract new customers. **If you're not constantly attracting new customers, your existing customers will dry up.** You can only keep doing business with your existing customers so many times before you lose some of them, for one reason or another. People get out of your marketplace, they change, they move, they die. If you're not continuously working to bring in more customers, you'll lose the customers you have and you won't be bringing in any new ones to replenish your customer base. So you've got to constantly be doing new customer acquisition, as well as doing things to re-sell to your current customers.

The key here is consistency. If you're sporadic with your front-end marketing, yeah, you might bring in some new customers here and there, but you don't have any consistency. **You want to be systematic about it. You want to do it *constantly*.** We have weekly mailings. If you don't do direct mail — if you advertise in magazines or newspapers — then you should make it a goal to do it on a monthly basis, so that every single month you've got new ads running. If you're running classified ads in a newspaper, maybe it's weekly or monthly. Whatever you do, it needs to be systematic so that you have some kind of accountable plan where you know that on a regular basis you've got new mail going out, new ads running, whatever the case may be, to bring in new customers. **You need to have a consistent front-end marketing plan so you're attracting new customers while continuing to build relationships with your existing customers.**

There are some marketers out there that do it sporadically. They'll do it, make some money, and then they'll just kind of glide for a while. And then they do it some more; and that's fine, too. They've found a system that works for them and their lifestyle.

Another thing I'll say here is that **you need to make sure it's trackable.** If you've got multiple ads out there, make sure that you can track how many prospects came in from each ad, and how many you closed. **If not, then you're not going to be able to identify exactly where the success came from, and you won't be easily able to duplicate it.** You're never going to know how much money you're making or losing.

I've got a friend who markets things sporadically. He'll put something together, the money will come rolling in for a while, then he'll quit until he starts getting broke again, and then he'll work really hard and he'll put something together and the money will flow in like crazy. He just keeps repeating that process. He's always complaining about it, and yet he's the one who's doing this to himself. **Inconsistent marketing produces inconsistent revenue. Consistent marketing produces consistent revenue. Period.**

▼▼▼▼▼▼▼▼▼▼▼▼▼

> Getting rich <u>and</u> staying rich are two entirely different things. They require a different set of skills.

NUMBER FIFTEEN: I think I did a good job earlier of talking about how we build very expensive follow-up mailing sequences to convert the largest possible percentage of leads. All you care about is how much money you spent versus how much money you made. And here's a copywriting secret that I don't think I've given you yet: **all of your sequential follow-up mailings should be what I call "chips off the block."** Consider the 20-page sales letter I've mentioned many times, the one that promotes our Recession-Proof Wealth System. From that sales letter, we'll derive a number of follow-up letters. We'll just cut and paste parts of those letters. We'll write some new headlines. We'll add some new things to the beginning. We'll add some new stuff to the end. **All these follow-ups that you send out to your customers — well, you just write the sales letter once, and then you're able to take little bits and pieces of it and re-do it.** This is one of the areas where you can be very competitive — just by doing a better job of following up, staying with them, not quitting.

SECTION FIVE — Ruthless Copywriting Strategies

▼▼▼▼▼▼▼▼▼
MARKETING SECRET

My grandfather's favorite sales pitch can still work today...

- "The bitterness of poor quality remains long after the sweetness of low price is forgotten." Peter Rohleder (A great salesman who knew how to get the money!)

Let me re-emphasize this: you definitely don't have to re-invent the wheel for your follow-ups. You just take a chip off the old block. After you've done a lot of work creating that sales letter in the first place, it should all just pop together pretty quickly anyway with all the ideas that you've put into it. I don't think your sequences necessarily have to be very expensive, though they can be; but you do want to keep an eye on costs. You don't want to frivolously blow money. The idea here is that most people don't do nearly enough. We have very expensive follow-up sequences because we want to put a lot of money into converting sales. We know what our profit margins need to be, and we know, more or less, what we can spend to convert each sale. **You have to spend money to bring money in; you can't have a cheap follow-up campaign. You can't skimp on your marketing.** You need to spend money on your marketing campaigns, especially when you're doing follow-ups to new customer acquisition. You want to spend some money with an effective follow-up campaign to convert those leads to sales. It's very important to do that. If you go cheap, if you try to cut corners, you're probably not spending enough money. It's not necessarily that you have to go all out and try to break your budget, but it's that you need to be aware that you need to spend some money in order to make money and convert those leads to sales.

NUMBER SIXTEEN: We're constantly re-packaging all our old offers. We do a lot of recycling in our business, where we re-write sales letters that worked for us once. **We find ways to give them a new facelift, give them a new headline, re-position things a bit.** Sure, plagiarism is illegal, immoral, and unethical...

but you can't plagiarize yourself. It's interesting that you can just keep finding ways to re-do things that worked for you before. You want to give people something new, but keep an eye on the market. It doesn't change that much. People still respond to the same kinds of things they responded to before.

Six or seven months ago, as of this writing, one of our good friends asked, "Man, how in the world do you guys keep coming up with so much stuff?" And I said, "We just keep re-writing the same sales letters over and over again." It was meant as a joke, but when I thought about it later, I realized it wasn't. That's how we do it!

The same things that make you money once can make you money again and again. You have to keep finding creative, new ways to re-package them. For example, **a secret strategy that we use in our marketplace is that we sell a lot of blind offers** — where we're writing about the benefits that we know our customers want without telling them precisely what we're offering. A lot of the language we use in our sales copy is blind. We're not talking about specific products; **we're talking about benefits our customers are going to receive when they use our products.** We talk about how our products will help you make more money. In this case, it doesn't matter what the specific offer is. All our offers are built to help our customers make money! So we can take a typical sales letter and change it up a little — give it a facelift — and that same letter (or big parts of it) can work for a different offer. Again, we're not necessarily talking about a specific product, but about the benefits we provide to our marketplace.

I suppose if you were in a retail business where you had a specific product you were trying to sell, it would require a little more creativity. **But in our marketplace we're selling business opportunities and information products, all of which deliver the same types of promises and benefits to our clients.** That allows you to interchange the parts and mix it up without having to do a lot of rewriting. And speaking of interchangeable parts, a lot of my sales letters — including, by the way, my 20-page Recession-Proof Wealth letter — uses them. I've never heard anybody confess this before, but I will. I strongly suspect other copywriters are doing the same exact thing. Sometimes I'll write a 24-page sales letter and, the truth is, I may have gone back and used parts of four or five or six or seven different letters. I cut a couple paragraphs out of this one, and a few out of that one, and mix them together. **Why create something when you can just re-create? Recreating is so much easier.** It's fast, it's easy, it's simple, and as long as it works, that's the only thing that really matters. It's a benefit that you can all have, although first you have to have the letters written to begin with.

NUMBER SEVENTEEN: blind offers, or semi-blind offers. That's one type of offer that works in our market. People love to be teased and taunted. **They love the idea that there are secrets, and if they can only find them, it will turn everything around for them.** They love the idea that all the super-rich got their wealth because they had some secret short-cut method, and that once attained it will become their magic key to the wealth and power that they crave. **A blind offer, if done right, can make people almost thank you to take their money.** They go ape crazy. They can't wait to get the secrets. Many people FedEx their orders; some even wire the money to you just so they can have what you're offering now. You'll always know something is hot when you start getting FedEx orders. You'll know that you tapped a group chord. It's the curiosity factor that makes blind offers so effective. People are so curious that they just can't wait to find out what the secrets are going to be — so we try not to tell them too much. **We try to tease them a little, and it does increase our sales dramatically.**

I think that a lot of marketers in more traditional businesses could and should be using more curiosity. I was part of Dan Kennedy's Platinum Group for more than five years, and there were all these other marketers who were part of the group who weren't involved in the same opportunity market. They all sold things in a very straightforward way. And yes, that might be okay after you've gotten the customers to raise their hands. **But in order to get more people to raise their hand and initially respond, there is *nothing* that works like curiosity.** They could have all been finding ways to use it in their business, but they just couldn't see it. We saw it in our market early on, simply because that's the way everybody does it in the opportunity market. It's not like we were some kind of geniuses or something; we were just copying the way everybody else was doing it. Curiosity in the opportunity market is very, very common... but it could and should be used in other markets, too.

Here's an example: An infomercial where two women with the microphones kept hinting and hinting about those secrets they were offering. They didn't show a shred of proof; it was all about the secrets, the secrets, the secrets. They were using the curiosity factor I'm talking about here in combination with a blind offer. They never would tell you what the secrets were, but they kept telling you how much money you could make by using them. They kept showing all these testimonials. The idea is that you'd get to the point where you were so curious about what those secrets were that you were compelled to buy the product, regardless of who was pitching it and how.

Blind offers are interesting because they allow you to focus more on the prospect. If you're selling a widget, you do everything you can to describe it; you try to make sure that the customer knows everything about it; you do everything you can to make sure that they have a full idea in their mind of what this product is. **But if you're selling blind, you don't reveal what the product is.** This allows you to focus more on the prospect, because all you're doing is talking about the benefits that the customer will get when they buy your product. You don't ever tell them what the product is. **You just talk about the benefits.** You offer bullet points that describe how they're going to feel when they use your product, some of the results they're going to get, what it's going to do for them. **So it's more prospect-driven rather than product-driven, and that's what makes a blind offer so powerful** — because it's all about the prospect, not the product.

The prospect likes to be curious. People are like that. That's one of the best things when you're a kid: At Christmas time you couldn't wait to open your packages. You couldn't wait to see what was in there. That's part of the specialness that we look back on fondly when we're adults. And even though we *are* adults, emotionally, at some level, we're still like children. **People like to be curious, so you're making it fun for them by harnessing that power of anticipation.** Remember the ketchup commercial with that song?

Another thing: **if you offer a refund guarantee, it takes the pressure away.** After all, they really don't know what they're getting; they just know that you've promised them some pretty amazing benefits and they want those benefits. So you take all the pressure away by saying, "Hey, I know I haven't given you all the details — but remember, there's a money-back guarantee. Take 30 days to look it over. If you don't like it, send it back. We'll give you your money back *and* you'll keep this free gift just for checking it all out." **Taking that risk away from them makes**

SECTION FIVE — Ruthless Copywriting Strategies

MARKETING SECRET

A good marketing system automatically filters and screens out the deadbeat prospects who will only waste your precious time and money.

a blind offer even more appealing.

NUMBER EIGHTEEN: the "ten-fold readership path." Basically, you take your main benefits and express them again and again, in as many different ways as possible. I got this idea from Dan Kennedy. He calls it "the double readership path," where you take all the main benefits and express them at least twice. But we took that and cranked up the volume full blast. **We keep hammering those benefits home again and again.** Are my sales letters redundant? Yes, they are. But people read in a very passive, apathetic sort of way. Most people aren't staying up till three in the morning reading that 20-page letter; they'll barely read it at all. They skim through it, and that's all they do. So that's where the repetition really comes in. **If you have the same benefit expressed ten different ways, hopefully even the apathetic reader will read it at least once.** For some readers, it really does take that repetition just to get it into their head. **Saying things over and over again helps to get your message across, and it helps convert sales in the long run.**

As I write this, I'm looking at a 44-page sales booklet we used as an example during the original seminar this section of this chapter is based on. It's pretty lengthy. Most people aren't going to read it all the way through. They'll read the front page, maybe they'll thumb through it, they'll kind of scan it a little... maybe a sub-head catches their eye, and they'll read for a couple of paragraphs and then they'll flip through it some more. Oops, that catches their attention, and they'll read a little bit. And then they'll flip back; they'll look at the back cover, and maybe they'll read the P.S. and try to figure out how much it costs. Maybe they'll look at the lift piece you added. Maybe they'll go straight to the order form. **People read all over the place.** Very few will read your 44-page sales letter from the opening word all the way to the end. People don't read that way. **They skim and they scan. And so, if you use this ten-fold strategy and employ ten different readership paths, you're more likely to snag their attention.** Some people are going to scan and they'll read the sub-heads all the way throughout it, **so you want your sub-heads to kind of tell a story.** You want to say things enough, in different ways, so that as people are skimming they pick up on the main points, even though they're not reading the whole letter.

To summarize: Different people take different readership paths through your sales copy, and you want to try to present your message in enough ways, enough times, to catch them regardless of which readership path they're on. If they're scanning, skimming, reading different pages, just flipping through it, **you want them to be able to get the main points without having to read the entire sales letter from front to back.**

And last, but not least, **NUMBER NINETEEN: segment your list and be aggressive with it. You *have* to segment your list, because not all customers are the same.** People who spend more money are showing you they're more serious, and that's how you have to interpret that spending. **So always separate people by the amount of money that they spend, and also by how recently they've bought.** Make them offers while they're still what I call "in heat." I don't know how else to say it. That's when they're the most passionate, the most enthusiastic about what it is that you offer. You've got to strike while the iron is hot! **You have to realize that timing is essential here.** Nothing drives me crazier than when we've got leads that are just sitting there.

I was in the grocery store at lunchtime recently getting some snacks when Keith Banman, the man who owns that store, asked, "Well, T.J., you going to take the weekend off?" I just looked at him and he goes, "No, you're not, are ya?" We'd just gotten our first lead in two days for a new promotion we were doing, and I knew it would drive me crazy if I didn't have that thing ready to go by Tuesday. Here's the metaphor I use: "When it comes to leads and getting things to people fast, today's salad is tomorrow's garbage." You've got to get them while they're hot! **Every day you sit on those leads, every day you're not sending stuff out to the people who requested it, you're shooting yourself in the foot.** You have to realize that right after someone buys, they're willing to buy more. So they're putting the pressure on you to have something to send them, which is the pickle I was in on the weekend I was just telling you about. I had leads coming in, so I had to get that sales piece ready to go so I could get it to the printer and then to shipping so it could be mailed out.

So segment by the type of product that they bought from you, by the dollar amount, and by how recently they purchased. Another good way to segment is by the frequency of their purchases, because people who buy more often are telling you things about themselves that, if you're a smart marketer, you're paying attention to. Segment that list! And you *must* have a list. I know people who've been in business for several years now, and they don't have a very good list. Some don't even know how to keep a good list. Well, it's easy. Most computers come with a database program that's adequate for someone starting out in direct-response marketing. As your business grows, you're going to need a stronger database that can do a few more things in the query and sort department, and spit out the kind of information that you want. But with most of the programs, like Microsoft Excel, you'll be able to keep track of customers and generate the types of lists you need.

The main thing about segmenting your list is to make sure you're keeping one. If someone's responded to you, they need to be on a list that says what they responded to. If they bought something, they need to be on the list that tells you what they purchased. **Before you can segment, you have to *have* a list, so start building it! And then attack it. Be aggressive.** Stop worrying about mailing to your customers too much. Yeah, you'll probably make some of them upset; but if that's the case, get rid of them and keep the pressure on. If a customer's upset, it means they don't want what you have to offer anyway — and if they aren't attracted by your offers, they've got no pressure. The pressure comes from the desire to buy what you have to sell, and the conflict in their minds that they don't want to spend money, or they don't believe it's real, or they don't believe you're really going to give them the benefits you're offering. So the pressure is on them when they feel like you really do have something that they want, but they're conflicted for a number of reasons. If someone's just upset with you and they want off your mailing list, they're probably not going to be a customer anyways.

So segment your list. Purge it of the people that decide to not do business with you. Continue putting pressure on the ones who do through more offers, more mailings. **You can't mail to your customers too much, as long as you continue to provide them with valuable products and services and as long as you do it in the right way, using the right methods.** I haven't heard of anybody who over-mails their customers; most people don't do it often enough.

> Your <u>best</u> will continue to get better!
>
> √ Stay committed to mastery! Stay hungry. Continue to learn all you can. Give each project everything you've got — and your best will continue getting better!
>
> √ The real joy of mastery is when you finally have the ability to do amazing things... in the most natural way. To get to the place where great things seem to flow out of you in the most natural way... where all of the things that were once difficult are now easy, and even fun!

SECTION SIX:

RUTHLESS MARKETING

5 Proven Secrets to Gain an Almost Unfair Advantage Over Your Competitors

SECRET ONE:

Direct-Response Marketing

In this chapter, I'll introduce you to Direct-Response Marketing, and show you how you can use this powerful tool to dramatically increase your profits. The tips, tricks, and strategies I'll reveal to you here can make you huge sums of money, but you're going to have to read this chapter several times to really understand it. **Direct-Response Marketing is a complicated subject that deserves in-depth study.**

At its most basic, **Direct-Response Marketing is whatever you do to get your customers to respond to you directly.** It's not the kind of brand awareness you see when Pepsi or AT&T run a commercial on TV. That's not really asking you to do anything; it's just them getting their name out there. Direct-Response Marketing, on the other hand, is meant to get people to respond to you directly: to pick up the phone and call you, or to fill out an order form and fax it or mail it to you. **It's anything you do in business to get people to order from you, or to request more information, or to take a specific action.**

In some ways, I consider Direct-Response Marketing an art form. It's the process of identifying the audience most likely to purchase your product or service, and then approaching them directly at the right time to solicit their business, using a direct-to-consumer advertising medium. This can be postcards or other mailings, sales calls, special emails, handing out discount cards — **any form of advertising that directly targets potential and existing customers,** rather than something just thrown out there in hopes that someone will remember you when it comes time to fix the muffler or buy roses for Mother's Day. I call it an art form because it takes a while to understand and perfect the strategies you *must* use to truly match the right people with the right message at the right time.

But Direct-Response Marketing is also very much a science. It's an organized, multi-step system for selling, which starts off by targeting and contacting the people who might be interested in what you're selling, in such a way that you get them to respond and make their interest clear. Then the system kicks in, working to elicit their response again and get

▼▼▼▼▼▼▼▼
MARKETING SECRET

"We are more easily persuaded by the reasons we ourselves discover than by those which are given to us by others."
— Blaise Pascal

- How can you help your customers sell themselves on whatever you are pitching?

- How can you get them actively involved in the selling process?

- The answers to those questions can lead to more sales and profits for you!

them more involved in what it is you're offering. This works whether you do it through direct-mail, on the Internet, in seminars, or even one-on-one. **The science is also in the mechanics that make it all work: the ability to put together a database, to build a list, and to market to various elements of that list.** Regardless of the advertising media or strategies you choose, you have to immerse yourself in the science if you want to even get close to achieving art.

You have to employ the mechanics of Direct-Response Marketing in a way that makes sense to **the people with whom you want to build relationships.** You have to get their attention, you have to grab their interest, you have to create desire, and then you have to get them to take action. If you do that right, eventually you'll be able to create your masterpiece — the kind of life you want to live, lubricated by copious amounts of money.

The Name of the Game

Your goal with Direct-Response Marketing is to get an immediate action from your prospect, whether it's a visit to your business, a call, an order, a purchase, a request for more information, or a promise. To accomplish any of these things, you need to create **salesmanship in print**. Not only does your Direct-Response Marketing strategy need to evoke an immediate action, but it also has to do everything a real salesman would do, in terms of generating that response. **Just like a living, breathing salesman, here's what that a good Direct-Response Marketing campaign does:**

- It tells the prospect about the benefits of

the product;
- It overcomes objection;
- It answers questions;
- It provides a guarantee; and
- It makes promises.

A good Direct-Response Marketing campaign does all these things and more; it has to, in order to succeed. I think the biggest benefit of Direct-Response Marketing over face-to-face salesmanship or even telemarketing is that you have the power to let Yellow Page ads, sales letters, classified ads, or display ads in the newspaper, magazines or on the Internet generate the response you want. Direct-Response Marketing allows you to multiply your effort, to reach a lot more people, and generate a lot more responses without wasting your time — and that makes it a very powerful strategy indeed.

In order to work effectively, **Direct-Response Marketing has to be a very targeted form of marketing.** Think of a rifle, versus a shotgun. With Direct-Response Marketing, you don't just blast out a message to everyone at random: **your message is delivered in the clearest and most compelling way possible, to the specific people who are most likely to buy and then continue to buy from you.** Those people could be highly qualified prospects that you've identify through various methods, or they can be established customers, people with whom you already have an ongoing relationship.

Marketers use lots of metaphors to describe Direct-Response Marketing. In addition to being a combination of art and science, to many of us it's also a combination of sport and war. This is a fun way of making money. You can be very strategic using this marketing method, just as a couple of generals would be when planning how to stage an attack on their enemy. Because make no mistake: no matter how much you'd like to believe otherwise, **your direct competitors are your enemies**. They're out there trying to get the same dollars you're trying to get, and you can't let that happen.

Laying a Firm Foundation

Direct-Marketing is a system for selling, and if **you don't have a system for selling, then you're at the mercy of your customer's system for buying — and they don't have one.** What most businesses do — sadly for them, but fortunately for you — is the direct opposite of Direct-Response Marketing. They set up shop, put up some signs, and maybe run the occasional radio ad or newspaper spot, but they do it in such a way that it's mildly effective at best. They're not using Direct-Response Marketing to get people into their selling system.

Now, in order to do Direct-Response Marketing right, you need to start with a firm foundation. One excellent way to do this is to achieve an intimate understanding of what I call the *Three Keys to Effective Direct-Response Marketing*. These keys will help you preform Direct-Response Marketing right; I've seen a lot of people make a lot of mistakes that could easily have been avoided if they'd just done the simple things I'm going to tell you to do here. The Three Keys are relatively straightforward, and they strip Direct-Response Marketing down to its basic elements. Without further ado, here's what's required for effective Direct-Response Marketing:

- The right message
- The right audience
- The right time

Or to put it all together into one sentence, you've got to **carry the right message to the right audience at the right time.** I consider this the Golden Rule of Direct-Response Marketing.

Many marketers boil this concept down to what they call the KISS Principle, where KISS stands for "Keep It Simple, Stupid." I think that's a little offensive, so I'll use my own term, thank you. Now, if you don't get the right message to the right audience at the right time, you're going to hear "no" a lot more than you'll hear "yes." **Instead of using a shotgun, pull up that high-powered rifle**, identify exactly who the prospect is who's most likely to buy your product, and go directly to that consumer using a direct-to-consumer advertising medium. In the following sections, I'm going to discuss all these things in greater detail, and in the order I think is most important.

Key One: The Audience

If you don't play to the right audience, you're never going to have a very good response to anything you do. You've failed right from the beginning: game over, time to go home. Identifying the right people is the most important key to successful Direct-Response Marketing, and I suggest you use three methods to accomplish this.

First is what I call "customer hijacking" — or **letting your competition do your work for you.** This is simply where you go out and rent a list of your competition's customers and then try to make them your own. It's not possible for every industry, but it's the number one tactic I suggest *if* it's possible. So if you're Sears, and J. C. Penney is selling appliances, you try to get a list of those people to whom they've recently sold appliances. Then you can send them a Direct-Mail piece that gives them the option of buying their next appliance from you.

Second is demographic profiling: analyzing your target audience and **coming up with the profile of your ultimate customer or target audience.** In using demographics like age, gender, income level, and location, you're basically looking for anything that helps you identify who's most likely to buy your products and services. Once you've figured that out, you can go out and acquire a list of clients who meet those criteria. You're going to use list brokers for both customer hijacking and demographic profiling.

Third is customer corralling. This is where you capture information on your past or current customers, and add them to a list so you can continue to solicit business. Keep in mind that **the easiest sale you're ever going to make is to a customer to whom you've already sold.** A good example of this is Harrah Casinos' Loyalty Programs. You go in there to gamble one time, they get you on a little card, and pretty soon you're getting more mail than you've ever known — and you're going back to Harrah's a lot more often.

Key Two: Your Message

Now, let's talk about the right message. You need to **study your products or services from your customer's perspective.** Remember, it's all about them; you have to keep in mind their view, which can be

MARKETING SECRET

Don't let a single day go by where you do not do something substantial to bring in more sales and profits.

- I don't care where you are or what your particular situation is... You must make this a rule.

summarized as WIIFM — *What's In It For Me?* That's what your prospects want to know. So build your message around the strongest benefits to your customer, and keep in mind that there are only five real reasons people buy anything: greed, guilt, fear, pride, or love. We marketers call this the *psychographic* of your audience, as opposed to the demographic; and **the two most important of those psychographic motives are greed and fear.** That's why you see so many commercials that play on people's greed, or that make them afraid that they're doing something wrong: raising their children wrong, not brushing their teeth enough, or not wearing the right deodorant.

You need to **understand the emotional reasons that people buy products and services. Make sure you build your benefits toward one or more of those reasons.** Identify your customer's strongest motives to buy, and you're going to do very well identifying the right message.

Key Three: the Right Time

Once you've identified the right audience and the right message, **you need to identify the time your prospects are most likely to purchase your product or service.** For example, if you run a mortgage company, aim your message at people who are selling their houses. If a person's selling a house, they'll most likely need to buy a new house shortly thereafter — so if you hit them with a mortgage opportunity right then and there, there's a good chance they'll take it. If you wait three weeks or a month after your prospect puts his property on the market, chances are that he's already found another mortgage if he was planning to buy another piece of property. Therefore, you need to respond within a few days, no more. If you plan this properly and do it correctly, the time *will* be right.

Effective Direct-Response Marketing is all about the right audience, the right message, and the right timing. And while I've discussed Direct-Response Marketing as an art form, don't worry about going out there and trying to paint the *Mona Lisa* right off the bat. **It's kind of like playing chess. You might start out a bit slow, but you're going to get better at it the more you do it.** Like chess, Direct-Response Marketing takes a day to learn and a lifetime to master; but use these guidelines, and you'll have a solid foundation on which to build your business.

What Kind of Bait's on Your Hook?

One thing you should be aware of from the get-go is that **Direct-Response Marketing isn't cheap.** If you use it right you can make millions, but as the old saying goes, it takes money to make money. Continuing with the mortgage example, here's an interesting way that some people have attracted new customers. They combine the right message with the right audience at the right time, they send their message by Federal Express — already an expensive proposition — and then they sweeten the proposition by throwing a $100 bill in that Federal Express package. That's right — a $100 bill. You see, they know it's a numbers game, but it's also a game of finding the right people to deliver your message to, and knowing that **you can spend a lot more money to reach that right person** (assuming that other things — your price points and your profit margins — are high).

So these marketers are throwing a $100 bill in a Federal Express envelope, and then sending a personalized letter along with it. There's none of that "Dear Friend" crap — that's counterproductive. Instead, they're saying, "Dear John: Why have I sent you a $100 bill by Federal Express? Two reasons: **1)** Your time is very valuable, so I'm paying you well to spend a good, solid hour looking over everything in this package; and **2)** I believe you're the type of person I'm looking for, and I'm willing to back up my beliefs with a solid investment." That's an excellent example of getting the right message to the right prospect at the right time, and not being afraid to spend a lot of money in the process.

So many people fail with Direct-Response Marketing, and they don't have to. This is a $300 billion a year industry; so why doesn't it work for them? When you dig a little deeper, it turns out that **they didn't have their hearts in it**. They sent out some postcards, they didn't get the results they expected, and they gave up. They thought they were doing Direct-Response Marketing — but they're really weren't. *You have to spend money with Direct-Response Marketing to make money*. It could be worth it to send out $100 bills once you know what your customers are worth. You want to get their attention, and their time is valuable, and paying them for it is a great way to grab them by the throat and make them give you a fair hearing.

P. T. Barnum, who is one of my heroes — a great, great marketer — once said, "Don't try to catch a whale by using a minnow as bait. **"If there's one general mistake I see a lot, one that people who are brand new to Direct-Response Marketing are making over and over, it's that they want huge results from the very beginning**. They're expecting enormous things from this form of marketing, which it can and does deliver to the people who understand how to use it. But they're starting out trying to capture a whale by using a minnow as bait, and in doing so they're being *far* too conservative. **As long as you've found the right customer and the right message, and the rest of your mechanics are in place, you can afford to spend a ton of money to reach that person."**

If I said this approach always works, I'd be lying. You don't know for sure what's going to happen. Even if it's the right thing to do, you're going to reach a certain percentage of people who can't follow through because other things are going on in their lives. Maybe, for example, they've just broken their leg, or they're getting a divorce, or they've lost their job. So you won't catch every prospect, but remember: you won't catch any if you use the wrong bait. Don't be afraid to gamble a little, because if you're trying to catch a whale by using a minnow as bait, you'll never have any real success.

Knowing What You're Doing

Here's another thing I'd like to add about the person who says, "Well, I sent out a postcard one time and I didn't get any responses." When I hear that, I say, "Let me see your sales material." Usually, I find that they've done a terrible job of getting their message across. Sometimes people believe they're great writers, and they're not; or they're not focusing on right kind of communication. They may write copy that sounds really good and has a lot of big words in it, and what those big words do to a lot of people is turn them off. Many of their readers might not understand them, and **a confused mind says "no" automatically.** Also, if a prospect doesn't understand a word, they may subconsciously feel like they're stupid. They shut off at that point.

> **Delegate your weaknesses. Focus on your strengths.**

There are all kinds of factors that go into Direct-Response Marketing that a novice isn't even aware of. They may have written a postcard, and had their buddy with an English degree edit it so it's grammatically correct and looks nice, but it just doesn't elicit the response they wanted — because they didn't really know what they wanted it to do, or they didn't know how to compel people to say "yes." **In order to solicit business, you need to get into those psychographic factors I mentioned before (fear, greed, guilt, love, and pride), as well as the nuts-and-bolts science of what makes people say yes.**

If you don't know how to do this, don't try to wing it: either hire people who do, or go find people who've done it and emulate them. Don't steal from them, but model your copy after what they've done. **Do the things you know have already been successful for others, then fine-tune those strategies so they can work for you.** There are a lot of strategies floating around out there, and lots of little ways to tweak your performance. Even the colors of your postcards can make a difference in response. As a Direct-Response Marketer, you're going to have to do a lot of things you've never done before. Think of all these things as broadening your education.

You'll want to continue to market to your prospects in a systemized manner, using follow-up campaign sequences — one following the other. This will cost you some money, but it's justified. Once you implement the three keys I talked about earlier —getting the right message to the right people at the right time — you're not done. That's really where you start. Do those things right, and you're going to grab a nice percentage of your target audience; they'll go through your selling process, and you'll make some money. But you need to continue to market to them! Once you've

SECTION SIX — Ruthless Marketing

> ▼▼▼▼▼▼▼▼
> **MARKETING SECRET**
>
> If you're going to screw up…you might as well screw up BIG!
>
> - Success is the result of good judgment.
>
> - Good judgment is the result of experience.
>
> - Experience is usually the result of bad judgment!

gotten the responses from a mailing, do a second mailing, and then another. **The great thing about Direct-Response Marketing is that you know the results very quickly** — with direct-mail, for example, it may take a couple of weeks, at most. Online it's even faster.

Once again, remember this: your offer does need to be tweaked and made more efficient, but it doesn't have to be a masterpiece from the word go; it just has to be good enough. Once you've got everything together and you've followed all the steps, go for it. Send it out, and learn from what happens. You don't have to flood the market right away, either — you can test and improve on your message quickly if you **start out slowly**. Start mailing, testing, sending out little bits and pieces, and see what happens.

AIDA Ain't Just an Opera

Here's an interesting acronym that some of my fellow marketers find useful: AIDA. It stands for:

- **A**ttention
- **I**nterest
- **D**esire
- **A**ction

AIDA dovetails nicely with the three keys we've already discussed here. But these four elements have more to do with the overall process once you've already targeted your prospects and figured out what you want to say, and you know you have the timing down.

Once you've done all these things, look at

the actual Direct-Marketing media available: the piece, the letter, the ad, the email message, or whatever it is. **First of all, you need to grab your prospect's Attention**, and typically you're going to do that with your headline. That's what it'll be in print or on a website; if it's an email, it's your subject. If you're addressing people in a conference, it's the first thing you say. If it's a postcard, it's in bold print. The headline has to grab their attention and make them want to read further. That's its only purpose — to grab their attention, and get them interested in continuing to read.

One of the greatest headlines ever was Dale Carnegie's "How To Win Friends and Influence People." "How to" headlines are not only often the easiest to come up with — because you already have the first two words down — but quite often they're also the most effective. What should that "how to" promise? **It needs to be benefit-laden**. I've mentioned "What's In It For Me?" already. WIIFM is the essence of writing your headline.

Once you get their attention, **you need to grab their Interest. Quite often, this is done with a sub-headline that states your Unique Selling Proposition.** A USP is what sets you apart from everyone else. It answers the question in the prospect's mind: "Why should I deal with this person or company, or buy this service, or get involved in this, or even accept this free report over all the others out there?"

Your next goal is to stimulate a Desire as they get into your offer. Most people think in words, but they take those words and put them into pictures. A picture is a stronger, more effective way of thinking. Most people, being visual, require the painting of these word pictures in their minds, and that's what you want to do as you tell your story. You want them to be in this story; they're the star of the show you're creating here. **That's how you really create desire in people: by the way you place them in the copy, and the way you overcome their initial apprehension.** Testimonials from people who have benefited from what you offer can work wonders here.

Now we come to the second "A," which is Action. You have to **make sure that it's easy and convenient for prospects to become customers.** This is where you ask for their response, whether it's an order, or for them to call an 800 number, or to send an email — whatever it is you want them to do. This is where you make it convenient for them to respond. Give your prospects several ways to get in touch with you. You don't want to give them too many choices, ever, on anything, but you want to give them basic choices. This is where understanding your customer is really important. Some people may have misgivings about certain ways of responding to you, so you want to give them options that are comfortable for them. Maybe the psychodemographics of your customer base makes them more likely to pick up the phone and call a number; or maybe they'd prefer to FAX their order in. You should also give them the option to mail their order in, even if you're strictly doing an online transaction. That's a big mistake I often see online: not even offering that option. The way a lot of websites work — you put your credit card in or you don't buy, and that's a mistake. Some people just don't feel safe putting their credit card number out there in cyberspace.

Calls to Action

Let's go back to something I touched on earlier: the way that **many businesses try Direct-Response Marketing, then dump it quickly because it doesn't work for them.** That's because they're not using it right. I've discussed using the right bait, and this next point plays into that concept: you have to give your customers a great offer. Some businesses try Val-Pak, where you get all these little full-color inserts about various businesses; you've probably gotten these packets yourself. But that's not Direct-Response Marketing. That's just coupon marketing. Most of the coupons are horrible because they're either designed by the advertiser, who doesn't know how to market properly, or they're designed by a person who wants to get the work done and move on to the next customer. Yes, you're sending that coupon out to a list of human beings, but it's not targeted, and the ads are uninspired. If you look at them, basically what they're saying is, "Hey, we're your plumber! We've been in business for 80 years. We're the best in the business!" That's not Direct-Response Marketing, because that doesn't evoke an action. Someone who gets that will say, "Wow, they've been in business 80 years. I'd go crazy if I had to do plumbing for 80 years! Poor suckers!" And then they throw it away.

You have to give people an offer that will evoke an action. Maybe you've done some image advertising, where you just try to get your name out in front of people, say through postcards or in the Yellow Pages, and hope that somebody will contact you because your ad just happened to appear when they had a plumbing problem, or they needed an attorney, or whatever your business is — but that's not going to happen very often. You absolutely have to target your market, you have to get the right message to them, and you have to use the right timing. **You need to capture their attention by making them an offer that will actually get them to take an action — whether that's calling your business, coming by, or purchasing something from you.**

One great example is a gentleman by the name of Bob Stupak, the founder of the Stratosphere Casino in Las Vegas. As you know, most Las Vegas casinos do image advertising. They don't say, "Come on in, we've got this special deal for you," and things like that; instead, they've got these beautiful billboards and beautiful ads, and they show the fountains out in front and the people gambling and having fun inside. That's supposed to be enough to evoke an action in you, to have you come to their casino. Well, Bob Stupak was a great marketer as well as a great gambler. **When he started out, the Stratosphere was a tiny casino, and he needed to pull people in, so he created an offer: for $198 you got a three-day, two-night stay at his casino. You paid this in advance, before you ever showed up, and you had an entire year to use it.** He ran his ads in *Parade* magazine and did Direct-Mail and got his ads out everywhere. It wasn't an image ad; it was an actual *offer*. For $198 you got a three-day, two-night stay at the casino, but you also got two tickets to their headliner show, several meal coupons, as much as $500 in slot tokens, and $200 in casino chips.

People bought into Stupak's offer like crazy. He was selling literally tens of thousands of these packages, and that's how **he built the Stratosphere into a multi-billion dollar business.** It was a hot offer, and he continued to make it better and throw in more bonuses over time. Here's the kicker: plenty of people bought the offer, but only a relatively small percentage ever actually showed up at his casino. So all those people who didn't show up, didn't take up space in the room, didn't come to get their chips — they'd still paid all that money, and he got to pocket that.

Now you're thinking, "Okay, that's a casino. How am I going to make a hot offer like that to my customers?" **Use your imagination. There are people in every business niche — plumbers, attorneys, restaurateurs — who are making hot offers people can't turn down.** There aren't very many of them, but they're out there. Here's another example: there's a certain restaurateur who realized early on that the lifetime value of each

▼▼▼▼▼▼▼▼▼
MARKETING SECRET

Your goal for each day is to come up with at least one new idea that you didn't have yesterday for increasing your sales and profits!

of his customers was very high. He knew that if he could get people into his restaurant to sit down and eat a meal, they'd come back not one or two times, but five times, 20 times, 100 times. They'd be coming back for many years, which made the lifetime value of the typical customer literally thousands of dollars.

So, what was his offer? He mailed out sales letters to people in his area, and offered them a free meal. That's right. I'm not talking about a "buy one, get one free" deal, or a child's meal free if you bought an adult meal. There were no strings attached: he offered an actual free meal. You got the entrée, you got an appetizer, you got your drink. Every single thing was free! In his sales letter, he told the truth about why he wanted you to come in and enjoy this free meal: it was because he knew you would come back again and again, since the food was so great. **His business practically exploded, because people thought that was an incredible deal.** They'd come in, enjoy the meal, and then come back again and again.

This takes us back to the concept of how much money you're willing to spend to get people into your business. A lot of business people are scared to go too far out on a limb; they don't want to spend too much of their limited advertising budget. Maybe a few cents for postage on a postcard is all they think they can afford. **But if you're delivering the services people want, and you're giving great value, and you have customers with a very high lifetime value, you can afford to make great offers in order to get prospects in the door.** You can go negative on that initial offer and still make money.

Your offer doesn't even have to be a price deal. Let's say you're stuck on your price: maybe you can't give your customers the lowest price out there, or maybe you don't even want to try. Instead, give more for what you're selling. For example, let's say you're a dentist. You can offer a lot more things than just a regular cleaning. You might say, "Come in, and we're going to give you a regular cleaning and a personalized toothbrush. Then we're going to have a customer appreciation party, and every six months you can get a free ticket for yourself and your family. We've got free drinks and free food." You can throw anything in there! **There's all sorts of crazy stuff you can do to create a great offer that catches prospects and brings them in.** If you make good on your promises, you're going to keep them.

So get over your fear of trying something wild to draw your customers in. The response can be phenomenal. Make a tremendous offer; do things that shock people; do things that would scare most business owners to death. Now, you don't have to be a fool about it. **One of the greatest things about Direct-Response Marketing is that you can test all kinds of wild and crazy and outrageous ideas to a small group of customers, so you're not really risking a lot of money if it doesn't work.** You can make sure you take what we call a stratified sample of your list and market to that — assuming you've built up a list.

You can stratify or segment your list by the products and services your customers buy, or by the dollar amount they spend, or by the last time they did business with you. The reason you do this is because, first of all, you can tell everything about a person from their actions. When somebody's buying a certain type of product or service from you, that speaks volumes. Or, if you have a few customers who are spending ten times more money than the rest of your customers, those people are showing, by the money they spend, a certain level of seriousness that the rest of your customers aren't showing. **You've got to be able to segment those smaller groups of better customers or to segment for other reasons so that you can speak directly to those groups of people in a different way than you speak to the rest of your customer list.**

So don't drop a Direct-Mail campaign to your entire customer list with some crazy new idea that you're not sure is going to work. You want to see how a stratified sample is going to respond before you stretch your neck out too far. **Take little pockets of customers from your customer** base and use them to test your wild and crazy stuff, so you don't end up with a fiasco where everybody wants what you're offering, and you can't supply it to them all.

This brings up another point. When you're building your offer, you can also add a line like this one: **"While supplies last."** This will invoke urgency in your prospects, because now they know they'll need to hurry to get all the extra things you're throwing into your offer. In addition, this covers your bases in case you get an overzealous response. Your prospects won't mind being part of a small, select group, because when you market to a stratified sample, you're actually treating those customers special. Go ahead and tell them what you're doing; they'll appreciate being treated special. And to you, they *should* be special, because by marketing to them first, you're lowering your overall risk.

Common Sense — It's So Uncommon

It's easy to wonder why more people don't try test-marketing offers the way I've outlined above. I think one of the big reasons they don't do it is that they don't know *how* to do it. **Most people learn marketing by looking at other marketers in their field.** So if their major competitor is running a half-page Yellow Pages ad, they think they'd better do that — instead of thinking, "Okay, maybe this isn't the right way to do it." Well, sometimes in marketing **you have to go against the flow, and do something that makes you stand head and shoulders above the crowd**. Then, once you know that, you have to get past the fear. If you own a restaurant, you may be thinking: "Good Lord, I can't even imagine giving away a free meal. I've got staff, I've got food costs, and I've got overhead. I can't even imagine making that type of a deal." You've got to break through that fear barrier.

So once you've got your offer, **test it to a small portion of your list, and see what happens.** You don't have to mail it out to 20,000 people in your area; you can mail it out to a couple of hundred people and see what the response is. If it does well, roll it out to more people. **If it doesn't do well, try something else.** It's important to at least make that offer. Because if you don't, you're going to continue to market like everybody else and continue to get the same type of response as everybody else — and in most cases, that's a pretty poor response.

If you don't already have a list, you need to build one. A lot of businesses are of the opinion that they don't need one: "I don't have a list. People come in, they buy, they leave." But not creating a list that they can use for Direct-Response Marketing is where a lot of people stumble. **There's gold in your customer list, because you're able to go back to those people, make more offers, and get them back into your business — as opposed to always going out and trying to bring brand new people in, hoping that the people who did business with you one time will remember you the second time.** If you're hoping, instead of actually mailing to a list that you've created, you're not going to be making as much money as if you were smart enough to get some simple database software, ask people for their names and contact information, and actually mail to the resulting list.

> ▼▼▼▼▼▼▼▼▼▼▼▼▼▼▼
> You have to *roll* with the punches! Keep getting up — every time you get knocked down.

Most merchants aren't even gathering up their customers' names to begin with — and frankly, that's just ridiculous. **If you ask most business owners how much money they spend on communicating and building relationships with their existing customers, most would say, "Huh?"** They may spend money to *attract* new customers, and they think that's what advertising and marketing is. Real marketing, however, is customer relationship marketing — and that's now an accepted way of running a business, thanks to a lot of us Direct-Response Marketers who've proven that it's successful to build and maintain those relationships. It makes sense, but so many businesses out there just don't grasp it, and they don't spend a dime to develop and maintain relationships with their customers.

Then again, **you could just do like just about everyone else, and sit around and wait for customers to come to you.** Let me share with you a story I heard from my good friend Russ von Hoelscher. He knows a guy who has a print shop in a little strip mall, and the guy's always whining and complaining about how bad business is. Russ likes the guy, but he gets sick and tired of hearing him moan. So one day Russ said, "Look, John, there's got to be 400 businesses within a five-mile radius of here. Since you've got those printing presses, why don't you just print up some sales

MARKETING SECRET

The whole world is looking for an easier and softer way!

- They all want easy answers and really quick solutions that will take all the pain away and let them go back to sleep!

- Those who give it to them in the biggest way are the ones who make the most money.

material and I'll help you, and we can target all those businesses, and you can get them to start coming to you." And here's what the guy said to Russ: "People want printing, they can come to me." That was his whole attitude! It's ignorant, it's horrible, and it's unbelievable. Apparently, **it's easier to whine and cry and complain about how bad things are than to do a thing to change it.** Unfortunately, that mindset is more common that you might think.

It's Two, Two, *Two* Mints in One!

In the introduction to this chapter, I pointed out that Direct-Response Marketing is often considered both an art and as science, and I want to focus on that perception in this section. I want to clarify the fact that there's absolutely no way to achieve art, or even get close to it, without understanding the science involved in Direct-Response Marketing — and it's immense. So how are you going to master such a big topic, with all the variables it includes? You can start by breaking it down: learn the technology that's used to reach your market, for starters. If you're using a specific medium, you've got to understand how the process works, how to get the best rates, and what resources you have at your disposal to let you best use this medium, whether it's TV, radio, the Internet, or print. **Knowing the technology used to reach your market is one key to your success, and it's all part of the science.**

Another part is database management. Building or finding a list of highly qualified prospects is key. **Knowing and tracking your market is also crucial.** You need to know what they've purchased in the past and why they bought what they bought, because this will help you to sell them in the future.

Something I've mentioned several **times is understanding the psychological aspects of marketing — the emotional factors that prompt people to buy or to act.** Those are, again, pride, love, fear, greed, and guilt. **Practice weaving those psychological factors into your copy, into your message, into your headlines, and into your sub-headlines, because that will ultimately produce the actions you're wanting.** Now, you just can't say to yourself, "Okay, I'm going to really concentrate on pride," and whip out something that sucks in the customers. **It takes practice. It takes time to understand your style, and how you're going to invoke these factors in your audience.**

Another important factor here is communication: learning to use plain, direct, and simple words and ideas, because a confused mind says "no." If you're writing something and you think, "Man, that's really clever, the way I did that," then you might be overthinking things. There's no need to be cute with this type of writing. You want to grab them by the heart or grab them by the gonads or grab them by the mind, and the best way to do that is to do it with plain, direct speech.

Here's another big factor: **testing.** Yes, I'm repeating this too, because I want to make you see how important it is. **You don't want to commit tons of money to something you're not even the least bit sure is going to work.** Our example is the guy who tried a bunch of postcards and failed; we've talked a lot about him. He went out there, spent a lot of money on getting them printed up and on the postage to send them out — and it flopped dead. Well, that money is just gone, because he didn't test his postcard before he sent it out. He wasted his advertising dollars.

As I mentioned at the start of this section, **there's no way to achieve art without understanding the science.** It's like when you first learned to ride a bike and you had training wheels, and it was fun. You learned that you pedaled and it made you go, and you learned how the brakes worked. But then you took those training wheels off, and pretty soon you were building ramps so you could jump your bike and do crazy stunts. The same thing goes with immersing yourself in the science of Direct-Response Marketing. You learn how it works, you learn the ins and outs and how to do it cost-effectively, and next thing you know you're jumping from ramp to ramp and you're building success on success. The art simply won't come unless you understand the science. **The science allows you to know your audience, know where to find them, know what to say, and know how to say it.**

You may never get to where Direct-Response Marketing is an art form for you, but that's a goal you can set for yourself — and maybe, someday, you'll end up painting the ceiling of the Sistine Chapel. You're always striving for that masterpiece. I've already told you that **marketing is something that takes a day to learn and a lifetime to master.** The real art comes only after a lot of work. It's no accident that the best freelance Direct-Response Marketers are charging thousands of dollars for every piece they write, plus a nice chunk of the residual royalty income from the gross sales. These people have one thing in common: they've been doing it for a couple decades. There are some exceptions, but they're rare. The people in this world who are the best at this form of marketing, who really know how to do this, have been doing it for a long time.

Good Enough for Government Work

You're not going to create a perfect Direct-Response Marketing campaign from the start, but that shouldn't discourage you from trying. Remember, good enough is good enough, especially when you're starting out. You don't necessarily have to become an expert marketer before you take the plunge. The truth is, **some of the best marketing I've ever seen wasn't written by professionals — it was written by sincere business people who really love what they're doing, who really want to connect with the prospect, and who don't know all the fancy tricks and marketing secrets that somebody who's been in the business 20 years might know.** What they do have is *heart*. They have an understanding of a few of the basic principles, an understanding that you have to make an offer and you have to go to the right market with the right message at the right time. Knowing that, they're able to go out with a message that really hits home and drives business in.

Most people are convinced that advertising is best done by experts. The advertising agencies of the world want to convince you that all this is so damn complicated that you've got to be educated to do all this stuff. One of the definitions of Direct-Response Marketing I mentioned earlier is that Direct-Response Marketing is salesmanship in print. I promise you, **the best salespeople aren't the ones who went to college and got a degree (with some very notable exceptions, of course). The best salespeople are the ones out there in the trenches, face-to-face, belly-to-belly, eyeball-to-eyeball with their best customers.** They've got relationships with those people. They know what those people want. They know how to give them what they want. They're out there serving them like crazy. Oftentimes the best Direct-Response Marketing doesn't look pretty; some of it really looks like crap! But it does a powerful job of getting the right message to the right customer at the right time. **It's just salesmanship: one person wanting to do business with another person.** Those are the people you want to emulate — the ones who are getting the job done, actually seeing results and generating a profit.

You're going to get better over time. Even better, once you've got it down, it's a skill you'll have forever. You're not relying on another company to create turnkey materials for you, take your money, and disappear. **You're able to create and make offers whenever you want, and that's a real power — a power to generate cash whenever you need it.** In that way, Direct-Response Marketing is the power to create money on demand. It's the opposite of just sitting around waiting for customers to come to you, which is what most people do. Good marketers are proactive: they're out there attracting people. They're not pushing; they're *pulling* people in with their messages. You can become one of those effective marketers. Once again, you don't really have to be perfect at it when you start out — it's actually quite a forgiving business. **You can make a ton of mistakes and still make a ton of money.**

Don't Overthink It

As human beings, we tend to overcomplicate things — and here's a good example. When NASA decided to send astronauts into space, on the first mission they discovered that the common ballpoint pen wouldn't work in zero gravity. So they spent millions of dollars developing a pen that would write in outer space. Now they've got one that writes underwater, upside-down, in temperatures over 100 degrees, on ice-capped mountains — in just about any condition that anyone could possibly imagine. But the Russians did something else that was pretty elegant: they used pencils instead.

There's a tendency, when you're coming up with all these ideas and

MARKETING SECRET

"We are what we repeatedly do."
— *Aristotle*

- What are you doing to dramatically increase your sales and profits right now?

- What are the main problems that are keeping you from making all the money you could and should be making?

- What's holding you back? Forget the excuses. Get honest. Focus. Nobody gets and stays rich by accident. You can always do more than you think you can.

strategies, to get a little overwhelmed. But **there's no need to make your marketing more complicated than it has to be. Don't try to do everything at once. You can learn one strategy and implement that strategy, then learn something else.** Look at what other people do, then tweak and fine-tune your strategy at the level you're currently at. You don't have to do everything with every promotion. There are so many different, elegant, and simple ways to make money in Direct-Response Marketing.

Why Don't More People Do Direct-Response Marketing?

Most business owners don't do more Direct-Response Marketing because they don't understand it, and they don't realize it's one of the most cost-effective ways of advertising. They've been duped into thinking that other types of ads work better. Radio and television is what a lot of local businesses specifically focus their dollars on, at least in the very beginning — because it's a new business, the medium is glamorous, and they need new customers. Those media are actually training those advertisers to buy in that manner, and so advertisers often don't have the time to even consider Direct-Response Marketing.

And, of course, **there's hardly anybody showing up at their door to sell them good Direct-Response Marketing.** You've got the Yellow Pages guy, who keeps bugging you to get a bigger ad. You've got the advertising specialty people, who want you to print up everything with your name on it. The newspapers and some radio and TV stations — those guys bug the hell out of you. But you don't have anybody coming along saying, "Look, I specialize in good Direct-Response Marketing that's relationship-building and long-term, using strategies that will let you quadruple your profits — or, in some cases, make more than ten of your competitors combined." There's nobody out there who's doing that as a profession.

A Dearth of Decent Offers

Here's one reason a lot of people don't do Direct-Response Marketing: they don't know how to define and create decent offers. They're simply buying the advertising they can afford, when they can afford it. Most advertisers think that Direct-Response Marketing has to be very expensive. Sure, you've got to cut through all the radio, TV, newspaper, and magazines ads, and all the crap your prospects are getting in their mail and on the Internet. Does that mean it has to cost a lot of money? No. You can give something away that has a large perceived value, but may not cost that much. It depends on exactly what your prospect wants.

Sadly, many advertisers don't even know what a decent offer *is*. I'll give you a good definition: **an offer is a reason to buy. It can be anything: a low price, unusual products, a special sale, special bonuses and extras — all the things you're offering to the customer in exchange for the money you want them to give to you.** Too much of the advertising out there doesn't have any real offer attached. People are spending their good, hard-earned dollars running this advertising — and they're not really trying to *sell* anything. They're not giving their prospects a clear and compelling reason to come do business with them right now.

In creating an offer, you should ask yourself what the prospect wants. If you're a restaurant owner, what do they want when they come into your restaurant? Let's say, for example, that you want to make a special offer for Valentine's Day, and normally you'd do "two-for-one," or you'd offer a free dessert, or something like that. Those aren't really eye-popping offers. Instead, think deeply about what your customers *really* want on Valentine's Day. They want the whole romantic feel, right? So how about this: you offer a "Valentine's Day Lovers Package." If they come in as a couple, the female of the party is going to get a bunch of roses, and there's going to be free champagne and there's going to be chocolate-dipped strawberries. There's going to be a person going around playing romantic music on the violin. By creating that type of special offer, you're going to set yourself apart from all the other restaurants out there who want that Valentine's Day business. And as I mentioned before, make it a limited offer. Say something like, "There's a limited number of spaces so you'd better act fast, because these Valentine's Day packages will go quickly."

Here's a good idea about which my colleague Randy Charach told me. He was going to the same hairstylist quite often, and one day he noticed that she had a little sign hidden behind her box of scissors and some business cards that said, "Please refer me." She asked him, "You're the marketing expert. How can I get more business?" He said, "It's really simple. You can make yourself as busy as you want by doing what I'm going to tell you right now. I hope you do this, because I know it will work. Give out a card to every one of your customers that gives a free haircut, on the first visit, to anybody they give that card to. All you're doing is giving a free haircut once to one person."

Now, that's going to attract a lot of people to come for a free haircut. She does a good job, her price is reasonable, she's nice to talk to, and there's no reason for them not to come back. The only reason they may not even take her up this offer is that they're afraid to leave whomever they currently go to. That isn't the case with most people.

See? You don't have to spend much money to get good results from Direct-Response Marketing. If you can spend money, that's fine — maybe it's more profitable for you to do that. **You can afford to sell something for $50 that cost you $70, if you know the lifetime value of your customer is $1,000.** You've just got to do the numbers. Direct-Marketing is psychology and math, that's all it is: figuring out what the people want and then calculating the metric. Most advertisers don't bother, just as they don't bother to build a decent customer list.

Summing It Up

There's a lot of money out there that's just lying on the table — and it's waiting for you to pick it up. This chapter shows you the tip of the iceberg regarding what Direct-Response Marketing can do for you. So let this be something that whets your appetite, and gets you hungry for more. By all means, go on to the next chapter, but be sure you come back to this chapter and read it again. **Do everything possible to learn everything** you can about Direct-Response Marketing, because it's something that can increase your profits dramatically and give you an unfair advantage in your marketplace.

SECRET TWO:

Front-End and Back-End Marketing Systems

In this chapter, I'm going to discuss front-end and back-end marketing systems, and why it's imperative that you develop your own. These systems are extremely important to any business, and if you'll practice the things I'm going to teach you here, you'll benefit dramatically.

Put simply, **front-end and back-end systems are the methods you use to attract customers, and then to sell to them again later.** I look at front-end sales as low-cost hand-raisers that you use as an introduction to new prospects, so they can express an interest in what you have to sell. But every front-end system is created and offered with the intention of making a back-end sale of a much higher-priced item. Your front-end breaks the ice; it's the secret to breaking through your inability to sell high-ticket items to people who don't know you. It lets you make that initial introduction, and identify those who are interested in what you've got to offer.

> ▼▼▼▼▼▼▼▼▼▼▼▼▼▼▼
>
> NEVER FEAR OBJECTIONS. Don't hide! Be upfront about the skepticism you know they feel... Bring up the biggest objections yourself. Then overcome them one by one. You'll win their trust and respect —and you'll get their money.
>
> *The best prospects have major objections that must be faced head-on and not skated around.*

SECTION SIX — Ruthless Marketing　　　　391

▼▼▼▼▼▼▼▼
MARKETING SECRET

Wisdom from one of the greatest copywriters who ever lived:

- "What people want is a miracle."
  — Gene Schwartz

You should **look at your sales system as a funnel.** You're trying to bring in a large number of would-be buyers and get them into that huge opening at the top. You use a low-cost (or even a *no*-cost) offer to do this, but only to get them acquainted with you and what you have to offer. **The back-end is where you really make your money.** Once you've broken the ice, most of your would-be customers will fall by the wayside; and that's okay, because you're looking for the wheat, not the chaff. You simply have to take in a huge amount of people to get that small percentage of customers who will buy in the back-end, and then continue to buy from you in the future.

What it all boils down to is this: the front-end sale — **that first sale at the top of the funnel — is meant to get a prospect on your buyers list.** That's all it's for; it's not about profit, although it's nice if you can make a little. This is where a lot of people make their biggest mistake: they think that the front-end sale is the thing they're going for. Perish the thought! That's just to get the prospect to the point of being a customer, and to get their name on your house list. The back-end is the next sale and the next, and that's where you make your money.

That said, your front-end and back-end systems are actually interlocking components of a complex whole — the overarching Ruthless Marketing System that forms the basis of this book section. Once again: **with the front-end system you're bringing people into your marketing funnel. On the back-end, you're nurturing the relationship with those people, and helping those people who give you more and more money.** It's a lot like running an automobile. The front-end is the key that starts the engine; it's small, and doesn't cost much by itself. The back-end system is the fuel that drives the vehicle. It costs a little more, but it's what really drives your business.

In the largest perspective, all this is just marketing — part of the package of things you use to attract and re-attract the best customers. **An effective marketing system is one that does it all for you automatically: the front-end automatically attracts the right people, and a back-end system automatically re-sells them.** I see the front-end/back-end interaction as something like the plate-spinning people you used to see on the Ed Sullivan Show, and that you can still see in some carnivals and circuses. They start spinning those plates, and eventually they get 14 or 15 plates spinning simultaneously. Once they're spinning, all the performer has to do is casually walk back and flip the first one, and then the second, and the third, and so forth. They can keep 15 plates spinning with a minimum of effort — but it does take effort, or they all come crashing down. That's how it can be for your marketing, too. **You can put systems in place that attract and then re-attract all the best customers, with a minimum of effort on your part.** Think of it as a kind of self-perpetuating money machine.

In its simplest manifestation, **your front-end is your lead generation system.** It's the process of taking all the prospects out there and determining which of them you can convert to actual clients. **The back-end becomes the continual marketing to those clients already on your customer list.** The marketing is different for those two aspects of business, since the marketing you'll use to get people to try your service is going to be different from the marketing you'll use to keep selling to the same customers repeatedly. Ultimately, front-end and back-end marketing systems are the best way to build business and create cash on demand.

Gaming the System

Like so many of the components of the Ruthless Marketing System, **front-end/back-end marketing is a systemized way to make on-going, automatic sales.** You should always develop your products and services with this approach in mind, because it's so valuable and proven. My good friend, Alan R. Bechtold, is in the process of developing a new marketing course, for example, and that's exactly how he's going about it. His new course is based on a series of recorded tele-seminars and a live workshop that he recently conducted. He led a whole group of people through this process in real time, and they each paid a princely sum to be a part of the group; but it goes without saying that it was all recorded, so it could be turned into a course for later use.

First, he recorded five preliminary calls. These calls served two purposes. The first was that they helped those people who paid for the original coaching, and kept them happy until the project officially got started. Second, Alan knew, in the back of his mind, that he was creating a front-end product that he could sell for $17 or $27 — maybe more, maybe less, based on the test marketing — to find prospects who most want to buy the complete course, which he'll sell for a lot more. Now, Alan knows that he'd have very little luck going out to strangers on the street and trying to sell them a course for $997 or $1,499. **But if he sells them the $27 introductory course and follows up with the right pieces, and maybe even a few phone calls, then the sale is very easy** — because he's giving them a chance to get started very inexpensively. Those first five calls and the tons of information on that one CD-ROM make up almost one-third of the course.

Here's a similar example: Video Professor. They have all these information products that teach you how to use your computer, and what do they do? They offer you the basics on a free disk; all you pay is $6.95 for postage and handling. It's a fantastic method that's used everywhere in the business. Similarly, almost every infomercial you see is a front-end offer of one type or another. **Start paying close attention to those offers.** Call up some of them, and express your interest in buying. Listen to what they have on the back-end, because every offer you see for a low-cost product is a front-end offer, a set-up for the higher-priced back-end offer from which the marketer derives his profit.

The idea is to **introduce yourself to the prospect by over-delivering on a low-cost hand-raiser that's worth many times more than what the prospect paid.** At the risk of sounding sexist, **it's a bit like courting a woman.** You may get her attention initially, but you're not going to propose on the first date. Of course, by nurturing that relationship and getting her interested, at some point you can pop the question and expect a reasonable chance of making your "sale." That's what Alan is doing by leading with his $27 offer, and then introducing the bigger course later.

His customers are going to be amazed and excited about paying him $1,000 when they think, *Imagine what I can get for $1,000 if I got all this for just $27!* And here's a point to keep in mind: when making a front-end offer of this sort, be sure to charge something to **qualify the prospects.** Otherwise you'll get a lot of people who aren't serious, and some who are will avoid your offer, because they'll think you can't be serious if you're giving it away for free.

Here's something that a lot of people overlook; I've already mentioned it here, but it's worth re-emphasizing. **You have to understand that a front-end sale is simply a customer's entry point onto your house list; it's the subsequent sales that are the source of your real profit.** I can't tell you how many items I've purchased through the mail, over the Internet, or whatever — and never heard from that vendor again. Obviously, they had no idea what they were doing; they were going for that first sale, and that was it. They got my money, they sent me the product, and it was over; they were on to the next sale. They're spending more money chasing new prospects to get that one front-end sale. It's like the two guys with the potato cart, where at the end of the day they lose money, and they figure, "Well, tomorrow we'll just have to sell more potatoes." But you can get by on fewer new potato sales, as you'll just implement a back-end system so you can rake in the profits by selling to previous satisfied customers. Do that, and you're going to have a huge, unfair advantage over 80-90% of the advertisers out there.

Catching a Clue

It's a sad fact of life that most businesses — especially mom-and-pop operations — have no front-end offer to get people in the door. Their philosophy seems to be, "OK, I'm located at 608 Main Street here and I have a sign in the window that says OPEN FOR BUSINESS. That should be enough." Well, that's the wrong approach. You need a front-end offer to get people into your store — or if you're a service provider, a reason to get them to call your business. It should be something that costs you very little, but has a high perceived value. Don't make the mistake of either having no front-end, or of having a shoddy front-end that nobody wants. On the other hand, it shouldn't cost you too much to sell it at a big discount or give it away for free.

If you're a business owner, you have to keep asking yourself, over

▼▼▼▼▼▼▼▼▼
MARKETING SECRET

Here's a great idea from our founding father:

- *"It's wonderful how much we can do if we are always doing."*
  — *George Washington*

and over again, **"What's next?"** I think you should even put it on your wall in 200-point type, where you can look at it all the time: "What's next?" When you've got somebody who's interested and passionate about whatever it is you're selling — whether it's knitting supplies or Army boots — those people are insatiable. They'll keep buying and rebuying. It's up to you, though: **the responsibility is on your shoulders to keep dreaming up new things to sell them.**

Most business owners are either out there chasing the next sale, and wearing themselves out in the process, or they're not doing anything. **Remember Russ von Hoelscher told a story about the printer who worked in the strip center close to his office?** He was always complaining about how there was never enough business. Russ finally told him, "Look, you've got to get some people in — there are hundreds of businesses within a mile of here. Paper them with flyers, go after the business, and be aggressive." But the printer said something amazingly stupid: "Look, pal. I'm open for business. I've got a printing press. If they want printing, they can come to me."

Now, he's on the backside of a strip mall, and he's unwilling to make that effort to sell his product. That's an absolute recipe for disaster, and it's hard to feel sorry for him! But **he verbalized the way that most people think, as rotten as that attitude is.** That kind of attitude will only work if you've got a printing press back there and you intend to *print* the money you need to survive. Or, hey, you could print your own "GOING OUT OF BUSINESS" sign. Why not?

In my experience, the people who have that attitude are, for the most part, the people who've opened a business because that's what they've always dreamed of doing. They're already going into it with an attitude that they're the king on the throne, ruling over their new kingdom — their business — and the great unwashed masses are just going to come through the door and be thankful that they've thrown the "OPEN" sign in the window. Sorry, that's not the way it works. It's true that there are some people who do that and actually make a profit, but that only works under certain circumstances; if you have a dynamite location and you give good service, you might be able to survive, a least temporarily. But even if you do, you're losing so much more. **If you're not serving the customers properly, you're leaving room for someone to come and take them all away.**

If, on the other hand, you'll do the things I'm talking about here, **you won't just survive — you'll thrive.** It's easy: offer a great, cheap offer to get them to come in the first time, let them get comfortable with you and understand a little about your business, then hit them with your back-end offer. Try handing out samples, if your business is amenable to that kind of thing. If you've got a hairdressing salon, offer a $5 perm. Once they're in, make sure you over-deliver, and they're going to be back.

Servicing the Client

Even if you have a great front-end offer on which you over-deliver, **you can't count on every customer to come back on his own.** A good front-end system is useless unless you couple it with an effective back-end system, so you can take advantage of that goodwill and sense of reciprocity you've generated with your front-end offer. What comes next is a regular, systematic communication that goes out to those customers and gives them a specific reason to keep coming back and buying from you. **Even the people who know how valuable a customer list is are losing a whole lot of money that should be theirs, simply because they're not aggressively re-inviting their customers to come back and buy from them on a regular basis.**

You see, your customers are (silently) begging to be acknowledged. They want to be nurtured; they want to be responded to. If you take that first order and do nothing with it, then you're doing a great disservice to the customer. So the obligation you have as a marketer is to massage the egos of your customers, and help them give you more reasons to serve them. **So many times we worry about making that first sale, when in** reality what's important is our ability to **help our customers improve their lives, fulfill their desires, and solve their problems.** We do that by continually offering them new products, related products, and related services. They may not even know what direction to go in after they've bought that initial product; so if you just pitch them something at that point, they'll probably come back and buy from you again. So what if it costs you a cent for a postcard and a few cents for postage? That's just a dollar or so per customer per year, and those who respond will spend at least a hundred times that on repeat business with you. What business owner wouldn't exchange a dollar for a hundred dollars every day, and as many times during that day as they possibly could?

Now, this goes right back to what I said earlier about what you, as a marketer, should always be asking yourself: "What's next?" The customer is *already* asking that question, even before you ask it yourself. Sometimes they're asking it even as they purchase that first product. In other words, **they're looking for reasons to do more business with you,** and you've got to be able to answer that question instantly.

An Offer They Can't Refuse

The combination of aggressive front-end and back-end marketing works well with just about any advertising medium, from the Internet and direct-mail to infomercials. Just combine this method with the other techniques in this book, especially Direct-Response Marketing, and you've got yourself a well-oiled moneymaking machine.

In order for this strategy to work most effectively, however, **you've got to start out with an excellent, high-value offer that your prospect will think they'd have to be a fool to refuse.** A lot of us in the business accomplish this by offering a free report or even a free book as a lead generator. If you want to charge a dollar or two for the book, go ahead; most people appreciate things for which they have to pay. But in the case of a report, which is really a glorified sales letter, just give it away free. That'll bring a whole bunch of people into your funnel (you remember the funnel, don't you?).

Let's say I'm selling a book distributorship; I'd offer them the distributorship for several hundreds of dollars on the back-end. But like most people who market information products, I use a 1-2-3 approach with most items. That is, **1)** to get the people into the funnel, **2)** to make a medium-sized sale on the back-end, and then — the third spoke on the wheel is the most important — **3)** offer them an even bigger package: maybe reprint or resell rights for a bunch of tapes and books, at a price that could be $1,000 or more.

My friend Russ von Hoelscher has owned a number of retail bookstores. An effective offer he once used was to have people sign up for a $250 free book-shopping spree every month. All three of the stores he operated at the time used the promotion in their ads, and that enticed people in. There was no obligation, and no purchase necessary. They just signed a card and dropped it into a big bowl. But Russ found that with book customers, even browsers — well, they couldn't just come in and drop the card. They'd start looking at the books, and Russ would often get a sale. Another thing he did, when faced with heavy competition from some of the huge conglomerate bookstores, was to give away, at cost, his top ten bestsellers. It was an effective strategy; he never made much profit with them anyhow. **But by giving a discount of 40% off — literally giving them away at cost — people would come in to get the hot books, but then they'd go deeper in the store.** They'd look at some of the other books and audio programs, and often they'd leave not just with a couple of bestsellers, but two or three other items that made Russ a nice profit.

That brings to mind an especially effective front-end/back-end offer that a lot of different businesses can and do use: a low-cost yearly membership that includes a free report or a free product. You see this kind of thing at Barnes & Noble and at large record stores all the time, but it could be used with just about any business. You start out with a good front-end that leads to bigger and bigger back-end purchases, plus customer loyalty. When people are members of something, they feel better about themselves and what they're buying. Remember, **people want to feel important.** It's almost like they're running around with these invisible signs flashing, "MAKE ME FEEL IMPORTANT, PLEASE!"

▼▼▼▼▼▼▼▼▼▼▼▼▼
The front-end builds your list, but the back-end makes you rich!

We all want to feel special. **When you make your customers**

MARKETING SECRET

Advertising as an art form...

- "Advertising isn't a science. It's persuasion. And persuasion is an art." — William Bernbach

members of something, or give them some association they can join, the real purpose is to develop them as customers and to sell them more stuff. If they're a part of some membership, it makes them feel like they have that inside angle or that inside scoop on everyone else. And to a certain extent, they should. You should segment your client list so that your "Gold" or "Platinum" customers get an especially nice deal — for example, a sharp discount, or maybe you open the store only for them on particular days. That can really get some excitement going.

Now, maybe at its root the whole membership thing is phony, since you're more interested in them spending their money than in developing a club — but the more real you make it, the better. Then you're able to educate the customers. If you're selling knitting supplies or beads or books, you can have all kinds of workshops and seminars and bring in book authors to speak. **You can do all kinds of things to get people more addicted to whatever it is that you're selling.**

If you don't have a club for them to join, then have people come in and sign up for a drawing to win a grand prize, the way Russ did. Of course, only one person will win that; but by the end of the promotion, you'll have captured the names of everybody who participated. Remarkably, everyone can be a second-place winner, and get a discount on whatever you're selling! Just send them a little letter that says, "Unfortunately, you're not a first-place winner, but..." and then play up the fact that they *did* win second place. Little do they know that everybody else did too — but that's not important. **Coming** in second makes them feel important; it makes them feel appreciated; and again, it gives them a reason to come back in.

Here's another thing that a contest does, as it relates to the front-end. **The only people who sign up for any kind of contest are those who are already interested in whatever the prize is that you're giving away.** In my first business, I tried everything to get customers. You name it, I tried it — as long as it didn't cost very much; after all, I was on a limited budget. I used to knock on doors till my knuckles bled. The one method that worked best for me was a giveaway. This was when I had a carpet cleaning business, by the way — several years before I got into mail order and information products. I had a contest that ran continually, to give away three rooms of carpet cleaning, absolutely free. I put these little boxes up in different places around town, and I'd go collect my leads every day. I'd call them up and I'd give them the bad news, which was that they didn't get the three free rooms worth of cleaning. The *good* news was that they'd won the consolation prize, which was conditional. I'd do some free work for them if they would take a minimum amount of other work. Then, once I got in their house, I'd try to run the bill up as high as I could. I was closing between 30% and 50% of all of the people who were signing up for the contest, and the reason **I was closing those people is because they were pre-qualified to begin with.** Only a fool would enter a contest to get three rooms of free carpet cleaning, if they weren't interested in getting that done.

You can always make your consolation prize a lead generation tool, where they get so much off the goods and services you're selling. If you're working with a women's clothing store, like my friend Kris Solie-Johnson, you can run a contest where the winner gets a free outfit, while all the second-place prizewinners get 20% off all their purchases. But you can sweeten the pot a little, too; so why not offer 25%-30 off their purchases if the second-place prizewinner brings in a friend who hasn't been to the store before? **Set it up that way, and you'll have customers bringing in customers who are like them,** people you *know* will like what you have to offer — because why would you bring one of your girlfriends to a store if you knew she'd hate the clothes? This can work not only to bring in more customers, but to get everybody back into the store a second time.

You Can't Have a Front Without a Back

Here's something I wish I'd known when I got started: make sure, **once you've got that front-end attractor in place, that you've got something with which to back it up.** Once that system's in place to attract new customers, you've got to have your "What's next?" ready to offer to that new customer as the back-end sale. Let me say this again: you need to have that decided and worked out before you even think about making that first offer to the customer, or your front-end can backfire on you!

The last thing you want to do is to get all excited and worked up about your front-end and then go scrambling to find a back-end to offer your customers. Oh, you can certainly do it that way, but it's a pain. Instead of scrambling when you get that first order, instead of running around trying to figure out what you're going to do, you need to have that already mapped out in your marketing model. You want to put that offer in the fulfillment package for the front-end product. In other words, **whatever it is you're using for your front-end sale** — whether it's a book or a report or free yarn — **when they open that package up, there needs to be that back-end offer staring them right in the face.** Because, remember, people are going to be asking themselves right away, "What's next?" And you want to be there with the answer.

That's one of the reasons that **I love information products: because you can always use a piece of that information product as your front-end, and you know already what your back-end is.** But if yours is a physical product, consider the possibility of planning your front-end offer from the back-end offer. You need your goal — *What am I going to do?* — on the front-end to get them in. What will raise that hand? Now, the worst thing you can do is let that hand-raiser get cold. They're eager to buy *now*. They've just met you, and they're excited about you. They're more excited about you when you deliver that front-end product than they will be for the rest of your relationship, probably. Why on Earth would you wait and let them cool off for three weeks while you think of what else you're going to offer them? You want another offer to go in there — preferably with the front-end package, but if nothing else, immediately following.

Here's another tip: **never have a front-end offer that isn't related to the back-end.** I don't just think that's important, I think it's *essential*.

Your front-end offer must dovetail with your back-end approach; otherwise, the person raising their hand isn't necessarily interested in what you're going to sell on the back-end. In fact, in many cases, your back-end can be the same product as your front-end; for example vitamins or supplements. The front-end sale is the product, and **the back-end sale is more of the same.** Sometimes you can get the back-end sale at the same time you make the front-end sale, but that's a whole other strategy.

Think it all through so that **your front-end gives them a small sampling of what they're going to get, so they get to like it.** Be like the Chick-Fil-A or Mrs. Fields cookie people; they're out there passing out free samples. The people who take those samples say, "Thank you" and walk about 20 steps, and all of a sudden they turn around and come back and buy a dozen cookies.

What the Heck *is* a System, Anyway?

Now, *there's* a question that's been begging to be asked: what is a system? By definition, it's a group of interacting or interrelated parts that make up a whole. When you're developing a front- or back-end system, at first glance the whole thing may seem overwhelming; it may seem too complex for you. **The best thing to do is to look at this system as a set of pieces that all fit together to create, first, that front-end system, and then the associated back-end system.**

Your front-end system is designed to promote new products, or generate leads, or sell an order to a first-time customer. But within that front-end system, you may have a series of mini-systems that compose the system itself. Maybe you've got a mini-system that generates leads for your business; then you might have a system in place that you use to create a new offer or new products for customers. Then, of course, you may as well have a system that sells the prospect. Maybe it's your Direct-Mail System, where you regularly and systematically contact those leads on a week-to-week or month-to-month or semi-annual basis.

The back-end, of course, is the system where the real money really is. It's designed to ethically extract money from the pockets of clients and customers and prospects, and put that money into your bank account — into your own pocket. (Notice, again, that it's important you

MARKETING SECRET

"When you advertise fire extinguishers, open with the fire."
— David Ogilvy, Advertising Legend.

▼

Your mission: Sell more stuff — to more people — for more money per transaction!

do this ethically — if not because you want a clear conscience, then at least because you don't want your misdeeds to jump up and bite you on the rear someday.) You might have a mini-system within your back-end system that progressively and aggressively follows up with your clients every 15 or 30 days. If you do that systematically, you're going to see your sales and your profits grow substantially.

The secret is to bridge the gap between that front-end system and the associated back-end system. The front-end system lets you leverage off your knowledge of your industry, your experience, your background, what you do best; **the back-end system lets you leverage off what you know about your clients.** It's important that you have a system in place that lets the clients tell you what they want. As the old saying goes, "The only votes that count are the ones that are paid for," and your customers vote by paying for products that you offer on the front-end. You know that on the back-end, you're going to offer them more and more products related to that first purchase.

Most business people are too focused on the front-end, though, to ever make any money on the back-end. They get so excited about making that first sale that it's just like almost being on a narcotics high. But what happens when the sale is over? They've got to immediately go get another high by making another sale. In doing that, they're just leaving money on the table. If they would just work the back-end properly, they could create five or ten times more income and business for their company. You see, **your largest marketing expense is always new-customer acquisition. The easiest business is**

selling to people who already trust you, who've already bought from you. Knowing that, you want to create products on the back-end that appeal to those people.

A good example of a back-end system is what happens at Amazon.com. If you go there and buy a book, that's the front-end. But when you go through the process of purchasing that book, you're going to see a page that says, "People who bought this book also bought…" Well, that's a back-end offer. Or you may go to a concert, and spend $70 for a ticket. When you get there, they're going to try to sell you a T-shirt, a cap, a CD, or something else. That's the back end. You may end up spending $150 or even more, all told.

The question is, how do you develop a good back-end system? First if all, take a good look at your business. What do you sell to your customers? In what are they interested? Can you upsell them — that is, can you get them to buy something bigger and better? Can you cross-sell to them — can you get them to buy something that's related to that product that you sold them on the front-end? **The ideas you come up with will help you create a back-end system for your business.**

I look at as being it like riding a bike up a tall hill. That's the vision I have of getting new customers. Man, it's difficult! I'm riding that bike up on a hot summer day, and I'm pedaling and I'm breathing hard, and I can't even ride all the way. I actually have to get off and walk the bike up the rest of the way. But then, when it comes to reselling those customers again and again, it's like coasting that bike right down the same hill. I've got my arms up like I'm on a roller coaster ride, and I'm not even putting in any effort: I'm zipping right on down the hill. **The fun part of the business is *not* getting the first sale.** The fun part of the business is developing relationships with customers who love you and trust you, who let you get inside their heads and inside their hearts. You get to know them better than they know themselves; and then, whatever you want to sell them, **you create the money at will.**

You've got to realize in business that you're going to spend a certain amount of money to acquire any customer; I discussed this fact in some detail earlier. All your customers come with a price, whether it's what you spend in ads, or what you spend in time and energy to attract them. **But it's worth it if you can figure out the average lifetime revenue of every**

new customer you acquire. You can literally lose money in the short-term while attracting your customers, if you determine that their value, down the road, is many times more than what you're spending now.

Let me reiterate: *you can afford to lose money on your front-end sale.* You can sell something at less than your cost, if you must. A good 90% of your competition won't do this, because they won't do anything that affects their bottom line. But if you lose a few bucks on the front-end to entice people to come to you, and *then* have great, related items on which you can make a huge profit — then so what if you lose money on the front-end? There's tons of money to be had on the back-end. The most important part of this is knowing what the lifetime value of the average customer is. If you know that, you can go negative on the front-end, because you know that you're going to recover any losses.

Some people call these kinds of offers "loss-leaders." I prefer to think of them as investments towards future profits. If you do everything possible to know your best customers intimately, and make them the kinds of repeat offers to which you know they'll be attracted, you'll make money hand over fist.

But Why Doesn't Everyone Use This Method?

Some people are just too softhearted for their own good to make a system like this work. This all sounds somewhat ruthless — because you're trying to extract every last dollar of disposable income from your customers. But if you're providing products and services that represent true value to your marketplace, then there's nothing ruthless about it. It's more *aggressive* than anything. **I wish more business people would realize the tremendous amount of money they're losing by failing to vigorously resell to their customers.** As a business owner, you should always try to do more business with people who've already shown a certain level of trust in you.

Then again, many business people feel that the high point in their business is getting that first customer. They've never developed the art and science of attracting customers, and they never will. But if you know your system and your customers well enough that you can lose money on the front-end — if you know the lifetime value of your customers, and really nurture relationships with them and help them become not just customers but an integral part of your own life — then there's value there for everyone. The problem with most marketers today is that they only see the quick money, the upfront money, the easy money. They want the get-rich-quick money — when in reality, getting rich is in the *back-end*. It's in the long-term. And hey, let's be honest about it: **a lot of marketers are just flat-out lazy.** They don't want to go through all the necessary steps, and they don't want to take the initiative to do those things that need to be done to make it a business instead of just a hobby.

> The <u>true</u> <u>art</u> of selling is to make people feel that they are the ones chasing you!
>
> To be very aggressive with your marketing <u>without</u> appearing like you need or even care whether they do business with you.

Another part of the problem may simply be that things have changed in the business world in the last few decades, and people haven't gotten used to thinking about, much less using, this new way of doing business. Twenty years ago, if you were the only grocery store on the corner, people went there. Think of it as the Field of Dreams business model: "If you build it, they will come." **But there are so many choices today that we've gotten a bit jaded and cynical about the different marketing messages we see. So the smaller business owner, especially the home-based business, needs to stand out from everybody else out there.** The Field of Dreams business model is mostly dead in America. You have to compete vigorously, and provide additional services that the Big Box companies aren't going to provide.

The key is establishing reciprocal relationships with your customers so your business can survive in the long-term. Let's say you're a novice knitter, and you don't know how to cast off the needles. You're not going to go to Wal-Mart and have someone show you how to do that — because, frankly, they're not going to. You have to go to a smaller neighborhood store that's going to have some of the personal service that the Big Boxes lack, a place that's willing to build a relationship with you. But if they don't pitch to you and don't market to you, you may not know what to ask them. Whereas, if a little knitting store regularly sends you a postcard to tell you they have beginner classes or new types of yarns, **they're educating you,** and you'll probably spend more money with them. Therefore you'll enjoy your hobby more, and they'll get more sales — it's win-win all around.

Hubba Hubba!

Sometimes **it's the worst things in life that provide the best examples,** if only so we can draw parallels to the good things. **So I'm going to discuss pornography** for a while. I realize it's a controversial subject, and I'm going to keep this PG-rated all the way. But there's this story I heard a long time ago; I've never forgotten it, and I think it illustrates something very important when it comes to understanding the power of front-end and back-end marketing. It's the story of Hugh Hefner.

As most people know, Hugh Hefner was the man who started *Playboy* magazine in the early 1950's. At that time, it was a revolutionary idea — though maybe "revolutionary" is the wrong word, because some people are so anti-porn that they may think it was a *terrible* idea. But in any case, it was new; let's just put it that way. Hefner was the first to go this route, and he was very insecure about the fate of his little publication — which, by the way, is rather innocent by today's standards. My wife gets the Victoria's Secrets catalog in the mail, and it's a lot racier... not that I ever look at it or anything!

Anyhow, the first *Playboy* was very innocent compared to today, but at that time it was new and unprecedented. Hefner was so unsure about it that he didn't even print a date on his first publication, since he figured it might just sit on the newsstands

---

▼▼▼▼▼▼▼▼
MARKETING SECRET

Everyone is looking for the same basic thing.

- We want as much of it as we can possibly get — for the least amount of money!

for a year or two before it sold out. He printed 5,000 copies, hoping that he wasn't going to lose all his money. But all 5,000 copies sold out in just a few days, and the rest is history.

Some people saw his success and started saying, "Hey, here's a guy who's found a new market!" One of the very first magazines to take him on was *Penthouse*. The story I heard was that when *Penthouse* went into business to compete against *Playboy*, all the experts in the publishing world said, "Look, there's no way this marketplace is big enough for two of these magazines. There's just absolutely no way!" And they did everything possible to advise the people behind *Penthouse* not to do it. "Don't spend your money! The marketplace just isn't big enough for two!" Now, of course, we can see what a ridiculous statement *that* was. Nowadays there isn't just *Playboy* and *Penthouse*; there are about a hundred other publications out there, and some are really quite pornographic.

Here's my point. It has nothing, really, to do with pornography, except as a means of illustration. The point is that **people are insatiable. They can't get enough!** The person who collects one gun is going to have a dozen before long. If there was just one fishing book on the market, that would be ridiculous, because readers would have an insatiable appetite for more — and so there's hundreds of them. The same's true for poker books, and hunting, and stamp collecting. **We're a nation of people who get involved with something and want more, more, more.**

Certain products and services lend themselves more to this emotional intensity than others. Look at casinos. When the government made it so that any Indian tribe in the country could start a casino, everybody said, "Well, there's the end of Vegas. There's the end of Atlantic City." When VCRs first came out in the 1980s, all kinds of people were saying, "There goes the movie industry." When it became possible to download free music on the Internet, all the experts said, "There goes the whole music industry right there. People can get it for free." Well, as you know, none of that has happened. **The marketplace is absolutely, positively *insatiable*, and the people buying this stuff from you right now will buy from you again and again, *if* you make them the right offers and make it easy for them.**

The problem is that **you have to be creative enough to come up with all kinds of different products and services that somehow relate to what you're selling** — and it really does take some creativity. You can do exactly what Hugh Hefner and all those other guys have done, only you don't have to do it with something like pornography. You can build an empire! You can resell, and you can copy someone who's doing something right. This is especially useful for the small business owner. Find out what your competitor is doing. If he's making a lot of money doing something, you want to do the same thing — only try to do it better than he does. **Don't steal from them, but borrow their best principles.** Even what some people would consider old, crowded markets can be revitalized if you work them right.

The bottom line is that the market is absolutely insatiable. If you grow a garden, next year you'll want to know how to grow a better garden. If you raise a rabbit, you'll like to know how to breed rabbits and sell them to other people. In other words, you — the customer — want to know more. One key to success is *not* looking for the place where there's no competition, but focusing on the place **where there *is* competition that's making money in spite of the fact that they don't understand front-end/back-end marketing** — places where they aren't even using those techniques but are still raking in the cash. Now you can step in and dominate that category and they'll be left in the dust, shaking their heads, going, "Wow! What happened here?"

So if you're looking to start a new business, **look for the places where there are plenty of competitors, because that shows just how rabid the market is.** You want to find a market that's not only hungry, but spending money too. Look for people already making money in spite of the fact that they don't know what you know. Let's go back to the pornography example for a minute. My wife once asked me, "What's wrong with men? Don't they realize that when you've seen one picture of a naked woman, you've seen it all?" And she's right — what else is there to see? But this illustrates the fact that people buy for emotional reasons. If everybody thought logically, then you'd see a picture of a naked person and you'd say, "Oh, well, that's interesting," and that would be it. But people can never get enough. While there are certain markets that are more prone to this insatiability, everybody buys for emotional, not logical, reasons. **It's up to you as the business owner to determine what those emotional reasons are, so you can use that as your ammunition and go out and try to get every disposable dollar you can from your customer base.**

There are a few businesses that, at first glance, you might think are *not* emotional — and I've run one. That would be carpet cleaning. But believe it or not, carpet cleaning can be a very emotional thing, because most of my customers were women. Generally, men couldn't care less about whether or not their carpets are dirty; my female customers, on the other hand, were all extremely emotionally attached to their homes. Their homes were important to them, and the more involved they were with social life, the more deeply they cared about what all their friends, family, and neighbors thought. Anybody walking through their home was judging them by the appearance of their home, after all. Once I really got into the heads and hearts of these people, it was so easy to go in there for a $50 job and walk out with a couple of hundred dollars; all I would have to do was point out a few little things here and there. It's all about learning where you can squeeze those emotional triggers.

People buy stuff that excites them more than they buy stuff that they just need. But it's important to point out that they select among the competitors even for those items that they need, and those selections are *still* made for emotional reasons. That's why your message — your offer of a free or inexpensive trial — is important. Now they're getting something for nothing.

Setting Up the Systems

Let's talk a little bit about setting up your own front-end and back-end systems. What I'd like you to do is take out a piece of paper and make three different columns on it. Make one column for low-cost items — typically something that's free or up to about $20-25. The middle column is for items in the $100 range. Make the last column for big-ticket stuff — $500-1000. For every business, you should be able to come up with different ideas about what you can offer in each of these categories, and as I go on, I'll give you examples of brick-and-mortar businesses and how this relates to them.

Next, **start brainstorming ideas for different types of products** that you put in each one of those columns — because if you set up the system with the back-end *before* you set up the front-end, you'll end up with a continuous flow of products. Once you've got new customers in, you don't have to scramble around trying to figure out something for the back-end.

▼▼▼▼▼▼▼▼
MARKETING SECRET

*"Most people are jumping over the dollars to get to the dimes! Stay focused on the BIG picture and don't get blindsided by the details." —
Ron LeGrand,
Master Marketer*

In the beginning, focus on free or low-cost items. The Video Professor example I mentioned earlier is a great one; it's a free CD with information on it — though it does cost $6.95 for shipping and handling. But even though they have to pay shipping and handling, the customer still sees that as a free product. So your front-end offering, at least in the beginning, should be a free or low-cost item that's very easy for you to deliver. You don't want to get into something that's complicated to deliver, because that will just eat away at your profit margin.

The second thing you want to **focus on is something that's of very high value to your prospect or customer.** Look at information — maybe insider information. I discussed the usefulness of memberships earlier: about how valuable it is to make people feel important that they're insiders, that they're really part of something, maybe even a part of history. Give them information that can change their business.

I want to make it clear that this isn't the place to give away junk — say, something that wasn't selling very well, or that you couldn't even give away. If new customers start receiving junk, they'll assume that the rest what you have to offer is junk, and that they shouldn't pay any more for whatever else you have. **Your front-end could be some part of a high-end product that you're going to give away,** like the first chapter of a book, or the first few tele-seminars in the beginning of a course. Offers like these really lead people to buy the higher-end product.

After you brainstorm all of these categories, you can start crafting different offers. How can these items work together? What would the flow of one to the other to the next be like? The last step, of course, is finding other businesses that offer your type of product, and studying them for pointers.

Let me give you just a couple of examples of good front-end/back-end systems I've heard of recently. A local library offered a summer reading program for kids, and if the kids read so many books they got a free cookie at a place called the Great Harvest Bread Company. Since the librarian tells kids that they get this free cookie if they read books, they not only read the books, but they become a pain in the butt to their parents to go get that free cookie. When the parents take their kids to go to get this free cookie, they can't just walk into the Great Harvest Bread Company and ask for a free cookie. They have to buy a loaf of bread, too. The bread is $3.50, so suddenly that "free" cookie has cost them $3.50. And if the Great Harvest Bread Company took their names and addresses at that point, they could continue to offer the parents different products by mailings — and the parents might listen. After all, they know where the store is; they've been there before. The people there were nice to their kids — they gave them free cookies — so the parents will probably continue to go back.

Here's how the front-end/back-end worked in this example. First they got the customer in with free cookies, then they upsold to the $3.50 bread. Now it's time to move up to the mid-category, the $100 range. That may be something like a year's supply of bread that the customer pays for at the beginning of a 12-month period. Maybe it's a membership — a "Bread of the Month" Club. There may also be other things they can try to get that customer to give them more and more money, as a result of their initial "free cookies for kids" program.

As you can see, **there are many different things out there that businesses can do to generate business.** If you start mapping out, in the beginning, some of the low-cost, mid-cost, and high-end things that you as a business owner can offer people, you can quickly create a good, step-by-step path from beginning to end, so you're not trying to come up with something all of a sudden later.

Here's a handy tip: **be sure to get it all down on paper.** So many times we try to internalize these things and juggle them in our minds, when really the best thing is to document it all. Create a flow chart of how the different elements of the system are interconnected. What makes one

SECTION SIX — Ruthless Marketing   413

work? What makes it work better? Then you can see the flow of money. If you're constantly creating value, you're constantly going to be getting maximum income from each of your customers.

Here's another thing. Unless we put something on paper, it may be that everything I'm saying here just sounds like a great idea. You're going to read this chapter, it's all going to be somewhat entertaining to you, and then you're just going to forget about it. For this to work, you have to document your strategies and implement them. My best advice for implementation is to do what I've been trying to do for a number of years: get up every morning and try to focus on your business before all the workaday interruptions get started, before all the distractions get in the way. **Try to think these things through, to develop a plan. Use these very clear, step-by-step strategies to do it, and for goodness sake, write it all down!** That's the best piece of advice I can give you.

A Backup Back-End

One of the most useful things about mapping things out in detail and documenting them is the fact that you can include a plan for those people who won't take you up on that first offer — a backup back-end offer, if you will. Maybe it's a lower price; maybe it's got more bonuses or more value than your other offer; maybe it's something related, but in a sub-category in a different direction. In a week or two, after you've seen whether your customers have responded or not, **you can take those same people who raised their hands in the first place and give them another shot at doing business with you. You know they're going to want to do business with you, because they're pleased with what you over-delivered for the $10 or $20 they gave you to start out with.** You don't want to let them sit too long and forget who you are. I think it's a good idea to make sure your plan branches out. Make contingencies. If they *do* buy your backup back-end offer, do you then send them a higher-end offer, and when? If they don't buy that, do you send them another offer that's going to move them into the funnel better? More to the point, if you have multiple items in your low-cost and mid-cost categories and one isn't working, you can try another.

In any case, **it's important to keep going after them.** You might think it's a pain to keep getting postcards from the same realtor, over and over, month after month — but when you're ready to sell the house you're living in, who are you going to call? Probably the agent who sent you 25 or 30 postcards over the years. So don't give up. Keep sending; stay in touch with your customers, because the more you stay in touch with them, the more likely they are going to respond to you if you have something they want. And make them specific offers every time. You're not just staying in touch with them, asking them to call you for no reason; **you're telling them *exactly* what you want them to do. You're telling them *exactly* what's in it for them. When they do respond to you, they're doing it for a very clear and compelling reason.**

The best part about all this is that once you've got them with your front-end offer, it doesn't matter if you're not the best copywriter in the world. At that point **your copy doesn't have to be perfect,** because you already know they're interested in what you have. Chances are, they're going to want more of it — they're going to be asking, "What's next?" So don't worry about being a world-class copywriter; just whip out a sales letter talking about your next product and send it to them, because you've already broken the ice with that front-end offer. I've said it before and I'll probably say it again: good enough is good enough.

> If you think the way you've always thought — you'll get everything you've always got!

The Sum of Its Parts

There's an old marketing question every business owner should ask himself: "Am I in the business of making sales?" And the answer is: No, **you're in the business of building relationships with customers.** When you develop that relationship, you'll have a pool of customers ready and eager to buy whatever it is you have to sell. Isn't that worth developing a front-end system?

The answer is yes. Earlier, I mentioned the fact that a lot of business people are lazy. Well, if you're lazy — and we all have that streak in us — then you should be excited about what I've gone over in this chapter, because doing well in this business is really about developing relationships. The front-end — the things you do to attract the best prospects, those who are most likely to end up doing business with you in the future — is just the beginning. It's a necessary evil, and it's a lot of hard work. But then

▼▼▼▼▼▼▼▼▼
MARKETING SECRET

All your best answers come while working hard on your current project.

- Keep moving forward.

- Cross bridges as you get to them.

- Focus on making more sales and profits to your current customers.

- And figure it out as you go!

Many times having a "target" to aim for is far more powerful than a specific goal.

comes the real business of making money: the back-end business, where you're building relationships. **For those of us who are lazy, this is the easiest money you'll ever make** because all you're doing is being a friend. People will do things for their friends that they won't do for anybody else; when somebody has a relationship with you, there's a trust built up there. They'll do whatever you ask them to do, as long as they trust you enough and as long as they believe in you enough. Really, that's all this is about. It's the easiest money you'll ever make in your life.

SECRET THREE:

Harnessing the Power of Direct-Mail Marketing

It's time, now, to let you in on the secrets of Direct-Mail Marketing — and there are a lot of them. If you think you already know all about Direct-Mail, you're probably wrong! You'll need to pay close attention to what I'm going to share with you in this chapter, because **Direct-Mail is something that can make your business obscene amounts of profit — and most people don't understand it at all.** If they're using it, they're using it in the wrong ways. Therefore, by practicing the methods and strategies I'm going to reveal in this chapter, you can quickly rise to the top to the heap, because you're going to know things of which none of your competitors have ever heard. Among other things, this chapter is going to teach you how to formulate a good Direct-Mail piece and how to come up with good, moneymaking ideas for this format.

First of all, what *is* Direct-Mail Marketing? As the name suggests, it's a form of Direct-Response Marketing, that super-effective marketing tool I discussed in detail earlier. It's very important for any business, especially since you can't communicate on a personal level, with every client or prospect with which you're doing business. One thing about Direct-Mail that you should really take to heart is the fact that if you send a letter to somebody, it cuts through all the advertising clutter with which they're faced. **It puts your message directly in front of the right prospect at the right time, unlike any other medium out there.** Direct-Mail then, is a personal medium that really gives you the ability to go out there and communicate one-on-one with your client.

One of the biggest advantages of Direct-Mail is that it's targeted. You use it to communicate directly with people who have an interest in your product, many of whom have been your customers in the past. When you're doing the latter, **you're talking to people without dealing with the waste you have to face when you use most forms of advertising.** What you've done is filter out all the extraneous advertising that people are hit with; if they're reading your ad, they're not seeing the undirected ads sent out by all your competitors. It's not in a publication, surrounded by similar offers that could beat you in terms of price or some other aspect. Direct-Mail puts your message directly in the hands of someone who has the capability and the interest to buy your product.

Here's another thing that makes Direct-Mail so useful: **the amount of control you have.** In most businesses, the advertising you do is really broad: you put an ad in a local newspaper or the Yellow Pages, so anyone can see it — *if* they're looking. That's not targeted at all. With Direct-Mail, you have the ability to control exactly who sees your offer and when they see it; what time of the year they see it and, in some cases, what day of the week they see it. I think **that level of control makes Direct-Mail one of the most useful tools in the serious marketer's arsenal.** Plus, most TV, radio, and even newspaper advertising is superficial. You can only use a certain number of words to get your message across. But with Direct-Mail, you can use several pages, you can go into detail, and you can present all the benefits of your services and products. Largely for that reason, **it's low-rejection marketing.**

Nobody likes rejection. When you're doing face-to-face selling or working with someone on the phone, you take the chance that they're not going to accept your offer, whatever it is. Even if it's the best offer for them, it may not be the right time for them to purchase that product or service. Even so, it's a very personal rejection. Whereas with Direct-Mail, you can stamp a few thousand envelopes, send them out in the mail, and only the ones who want to do business with you respond. So it's really a positive feeling; instead of suffering through 99 rejections for every time you get a person to buy, **you hear only from the people who want what you've got.**

Direct-Mail also gives you the ability to multiply your effort, in terms of selling. You don't want to base your marketing initiatives entirely on face-to-face or one-on-one selling, if only because you can reach just a small percentage of your potential customers in person or by phone. With Direct-Mail, you have the ability to sell to 1,000 people at a time, or 10,000, or even 100,000. And you always let that sales piece — your Direct-Mail letter — do the selling for you. The best thing about that is your sales piece never has a bad day, unlike a real, live person: it's your best employee every single time someone reads it, and it can go out to the perfect people and give the perfect sales pitch thousands of times in a very short period. **A good Direct-Mail offer is nothing more than a salesman in an envelope.**

Think about that last statement for a moment: a good Direct-Mail offer is nothing more than a salesman in an envelope. With Direct-Mail, you can have thousands of little salesmen working for you every single day — and it's the rare company that can afford thousands of flesh-and-blood salesmen. Your sales piece never needs to eat, sleep, take off sick, or get a pay raise. That typifies the power of Direct-Mail, because they're like little genies in a bottle out there, popping up and grabbing the customer's attention and provoking them to do what you want them to do, which is buy from you.

Direct-Mail is a proven and time-tested method of marketing; it's been used for decades, if not longer. Recently, my colleague Chris Lakey was doing some research for one of his projects, and he came across a book on Direct-Mail that was written in 1952. Amazingly, that book discusses many of the same marketing theories we use today — particularly the psychological and emotional reasons that people buy. The book is 55 years old, but it tells you all the same stuff you hear today! Obviously, Direct-Mail worked well then, and it still works well now. Oh, and did I mention the money potential of Direct-Mail? With this medium, **you can get your sales letter in the mail and have money coming in in as little as 48 hours.** Most other methods of advertising are slow, or they're for brand awareness only — that is, you're just running ads to get people to recognize your name or stop into your store next time they happen to need whatever you offer.

Here's how effective a good Direct-Mail piece is. If you'll take a few minutes to think of the top three salespeople you know — the best ones you've personally met and spent time with — and make a list of all the qualities those three salespeople have, you'll get a good indication of what a good Direct-Mail sales package is all about. Just looking at all the qualities you listed will teach you more about Direct-Mail than most people know. Most business people think they can throw anything in the mail and get results, but then most business people don't understand that it really *is* all about salesmanship.

Getting Your Feet Wet in the Direct-Mail Ocean

It's fairly easy to understand what Direct-Mail is. We all get it in our mailboxes (physical and electronic) just about every day, so we understand the forms it takes. But understanding how to get started, how to put together a good Direct-Mail piece — well, that's a trade secret, and I'm going to reveal it to you here.

Developing a decent Direct-Mail sales piece is all about preparing and planning — something that many business people don't bother with. Too many people start developing their sales pieces before they ever know what they should be writing, and that lack of preparation is the reason that most of them fail in their Direct-Mail efforts. Therefore, let's start with what you do before you even put pen to paper.

First off is problem hunting, an exercise you can perform for any business, regardless of what business you're in. **In order to be a good problem hunter, you've got to become an expert on your customers, so you can get inside of their minds and hearts. Just immerse yourself in your knowledge of your customer base, and think about everything**

MARKETING SECRET

Human nature is very predictable.

- "Men are all the same. They always think that something they are going to get is better than what they have got."
— John Oliver Hobbes

that your target audience wants and desires — all the biggest problems in their lives. What you're going to do is identify their irritations and their frustrations and, more to the point, their *pain*. What's really the thorn in their side that makes it hard for them to do business? What can you help them do that will make them more successful, and make them really want to do business with you?

Not only do you have to know how you're going to solve that problem, but you have to know how you're going to package what you're offering so that it's attractive. **You're essentially going to be asking people to give you their money in return for your solution, so you want to make certain that you create a solution that's much more attractive to them than what they get by holding onto their money.** They've got to be willing to give up what they buy in order to have what you're offering. Sure, that's really simplistic, on the face of it — but the truth is, most of us don't think that way when we're constructing an offer. We think of "offer" as, "Gee, what kind of price? If I sold it for $100 before, and I'm offering it for $50 now; that's a hell of an offer!" But that may not, necessarily, be the offer. The degree of pain that you're going to solve for your customers and the benefits they're going to get may be more important than the price.

Often there are multiple problems available for you to tackle, but you want to handle one at a time. Therefore, it's a good idea to focus your attention on one big problem per offer, though sometimes you can do a combination if you handle it carefully. One of the things about which I need to caution you — and this is big! — is that you have to make certain that it's not just a problem in your mind; that is, be sure your customers actually see the problem as a problem. A good way to do that would be to contact a few of your customers and ask them if the problem you perceive is something that's really a concern to them, because you don't want to spend time writing copy that's not going to make you any money. Once you've confirmed the problem these customers are all having, you can go through a relatively straightforward process when you're developing and constructing your Direct-Mail piece.

Develop Your Empathy

First off, you need to **take the time to understand your customer — to understand what they're going through, what they're feeling, what they want, need, and desire.** Once you've done that, take all that you've gathered, and *then* start to put the offer together. Many people who go out there and try to make money in Direct-Mail, and in their heads, hearts, and souls, they're thinking, "This is a great deal!" when actually they didn't spend the time to look at the market and understand their potential customer base.

The trick to really succeeding with Direct-Mail — and, really, with most aspects of your marketing — is to **know your customers and prospects more intimately than they know themselves,** because often they're buying things at a deep emotional level. This is the problem with focus groups: in real life, **people buy for all kinds of weird emotional reasons that defy logic, and those aren't things you can capture in a focus group.** Some marketplaces tend to be much more emotionally driven than others, so it's up to you to try to get a handle on who your best customers are, and what they're all about. For years I kept a running list of all of the qualities of my customers in a three-ring binder, until I filled up the whole thing. It's all color-coded and pretty thick, and I still have it.

This type of customer understanding is vitally important, because most business owners believe that people are coming in to buy a certain product; so whenever they create any type of marketing, they sell the product itself. They say, "This product looks like this and it's got this many pages, or it kills this many bugs, or it makes your lawn this much greener." But **if you have a real understanding of your target market, you'll understand that customers aren't really buying the product; they could care less about the product itself. What they really want are** *results.* People have a problem, and the result they want is the eradication of that problem. They want that problem gone.

You're going to be ahead of all your competitors if you can really understand their pain at an emotional level, and understand that your product has to hit the hot button of dissolving that pain in their lives. In the text of your copy, **you're actually going to spend most of the time talking not about your product, but about how it gives the user the result they want — how it eradicates their pain, or maybe even gives them pleasure in the fastest, quickest, easiest way possible.** Sometimes that's difficult for business owners to do, because they're so bonded to their product. But you have to move past that and understand that you're not just in business to make yourself happy; you're not in business to shine your product and stock your shelves. No, you're in business to make money. If making money means that **you're delivering what your customers want,** then that needs to be your focus — **not falling in love with your product.**

An important step in developing this kind of understanding is asking some of your customers and prospects about their problems. Many business owners take their customers for granted; they don't ask people walking through their store for their feedback. If you do, you may be able to get ahead of your customers, at least in regard to what they really want. They may even help you tailor your offer even better than what you'd originally anticipated.

Feeling Their Pain

The first thing to do with your sales letter is to state the problem, and make sure your customers or prospects feel it. You need to bring the pain to the surface — so really rub it in, but in a nice way. You don't want to get out there and go, "Ha ha ha! This is your big problem!" You want to make sure you do it using language with which your customers are familiar, presented in a nice, conservative fashion... **but make them feel the pain, because then you're going to sell them the solution.** Keep in mind that people will typically do more to avoid pain than they will to gain pleasure. So if you can bring that pain to the surface — make them feel it in your presentation to them — you're going to grab the attention of a lot of people. This is where the *ruthless* part comes in. You twist the knife and make it hurt, make them really feel it, and make them focus on their problem so you can offer them a solution.

Every time you come up with a new piece, just make sure you go back and **focus on the big problem.** Before you get started with anything, look at what your product is and think about all of the problems it solves. If you're still searching for a product, understand your audience and develop your product to overcome or provide a solution for them. In either case, focus your Direct-Mail message around the problem you've found, and make sure your prospects are really experiencing that problem.

> All business is show business!

Sharpening your Salesmanship

Another thing you need to do is **make sure you understand how to sell your product before you sit down and write the piece.** If you've got people on the phones selling and interacting with your customer, find your best salesperson, the one who's really good at addressing these problems. Chances are, if they're really good at what they do, they're really good at identifying the customer's problems. Record their presentation to a customer, and take that presentation and use it as a basis for starting your sales letter. If you don't have anybody selling your products, you could always call some customers on your list or in your target audience and try preselling to them first, and find out how they respond. Then go with whatever worked best on the phone as your starting point for your sales material.

It's all about salesmanship. That's what the heart and soul of Direct-Mail is all about: **persuading people to give up their money in exchange for something that they perceive is worth more than that money.** If you're one of those people who can't sell things, you need help. You need to find the best salesman in your company or hire someone who knows what they're doing, or else you won't succeed in Direct-Mail — or in marketing in general.

Choosing Your Target

Before you actually create your Direct-Mail piece, you have to know exactly to whom it's going, because that knowledge will be informative on how you put your offer together. The primary question you'll need to ask yourself is this: "What mailing list should I use?" If you're going to

▼▼▼▼▼▼▼▼▼
MARKETING SECRET

Always write in 2 steps. First, get it down as fast as you can... Let it come from your heart. Don't think too hard... Just let your words flow freely. Then comes the second step: The re-writing. Now is the time to keep going over your material to sharpen it and make it more powerful and compelling.

- Writing is hard for many people because they try to do it in 1 step instead of 2.

rent an outside list, it had better be of people that you *know* are interested in your services or products. If it's your own list — **which is the best mailing list you can use, of course** — then you know they're interested in what you're selling (at least to some degree). Now, in conjunction with that big question of "What mailing list should I use?" **you've got to ask yourself several associated questions**:

- "Who are my prospects?"
- "Is this list going to go right to them?"
- "Does this list include the people that we have to reach for this offer?"

Once you've set up your target, you have to start thinking conceptually. Ask yourself, "What motivates these people to want what I'm selling?" As I've said before, **you've got to go beyond the obvious.** They're not simply looking for your products and services; they're looking for the solutions to their problems, or they're looking for the anticipation of getting something of value that they want. So consider that, and then start thinking about the most important benefits of your services and products.

Jumping in Head First

Your Direct-Mail piece is a letter to your prospect, and it needs to begin with a headline. I believe in **writing the headline before you even do the sales letter, because it will guide you as you write the sales piece.** A good way to look for the right headline, if you're not an accomplished copywriter, is to consider the "how to" approach. Here's a good one: "How to eat more and weigh less." I honestly don't know how or if that works, but it's a good headline. Here are some others:

- "How to win friends and influence people" (the old Dale Carnegie approach).
- "How to make yourself judgment-proof."
- "How to fire your boss."

All these are great headlines that you can emulate. You don't want to use them verbatim, of course, but follow their lead. You'll be able to take the "how to" approach and then put in your details that pertain to your own products or services.

When you finish doing that, you can go into your letter and start listing the benefits, because it's the benefits that make people buy. **Exactly what action do you want the reader to take? Make it very specific.** Then it's a good idea, too, to look at your competition and see what they're doing. If you have a really good competitor who's using sales letters, get ahold of one of their sales letters. **Don't copy them word-for-word, but *do* look that piece over and see how you can create a letter that's every bit as good or better than what they have.** This is an approach that will get you started right.

Okay, so you're thinking about the headline, which will have a big benefit in it. You're mailing to the right people, and you're testing. Even if you plan to mail it to 5,000 people, it would be smart to mail 500 first to see the response. **Most of us don't do enough testing, and I can't emphasize its importance enough. Testing is what separates the winners from the losers.** You can make subtle changes if something isn't working, or you can increase the volume of outgoing mail when it *is* working. These are just some of the things you need to think about when creating your sales letter.

Some people will say, "I could never write a sales letter." But the truth is, if **you can write a good, emotional letter to a friend or to a loved one, you can write a sales letter.** Put your love in the letter. Don't get gushy with your customers, but convey the message that, "I have something here very important that can help you, and here's why it can help you." Then list all the different reasons why it can, and make both the sincerity and empathy you feel obvious. That's a very important part of the whole process. They'll use the information you give them to decide if it's important to them, or if it can really help them.

Here's another fact about sales letters, and I think it's one that a lot of people don't realize. Maybe there are some copywriters out there who can do it differently, **but most sales letters are written in pieces over a period of time.** My first sales letter took me three months to write. It's not at all uncommon to spend three solid days or even a week writing a letter; you just do them a piece at a time, though you're never trying to give people the impression you're doing that. You try to make it look like you did it all from start to finish, even if it actually took a lot of time and was done patchwork quilt style. Of course, it probably doesn't take a week to get the words on paper; but you get them on paper once, and then the next day you look at them and you say, "Well, maybe this belongs here, and maybe this word would be better than that word," and you play with the text until you're happy with what you've got.

When you're done you think, "How could I have ever put in a week on this?" Sometimes, when you look at a letter after it's been re-written several times, to the naked eye it may not look a whole lot different than it was three or four days ago, when you looked at it before. But the devil's in the details, as they say. **It's all in the minutia: the little things that you do and tweak differently that have the biggest impact.** It's not necessarily that it looks a whole lot different than it did before. The real difference is in the fine art of tweaking, and going back over it again and again, **looking for little details that need to be changed. This comes with experience.** Even if you can't tell a big difference in a quick scan of the letter, those changes can make a huge difference in sales.

Another key is **reading your letter aloud.** I've found that if you read your letter out loud, **you'll find gaps where the text doesn't quite fit together, it doesn't flow,** or it doesn't really progress the way you want them to — and you can easily make changes. Sometimes, you'll come to a point in a letter where the words just don't roll off your lips, or the rhythm changes, or there's some indefinable awkwardness there. You may not know why necessarily, **but simply changing one word here or adding a word there can help.** It may be that it needs three adjectives instead of two, or vice versa. You'll feel a rhythm when you say it out loud that you'll never detect if you're reading it silently. This is important, because you have to remember that your customers and prospects aren't going to see your letter the same way you are. Most of time, when you're reading a book or reading an offer yourself, it's like you're saying it out loud in your head while you're reading. If a customer is reading your offer, they're going to stumble on those same points that you stumbled on when you read it aloud. Anytime you have a spot that you stumble on that doesn't seem real clear — one that makes you stop and say it again, because it was confusing — that's a point you need to work on polishing out, because when your customer is reading your offer they're likely to have the same problem.

The bottom line is, a sales letter is a piece of art. It's a challenge, and that's the fun of it. That said, don't let the challenge of producing a work of art keep you from sitting down and actually putting pen to paper. One of the things you've got to remember is that while you're crafting the ultimate salesman by making this sales letter, **you're probably not going to get it perfect the first time.** If you do, you're a genius, and that's great — but you should always at least have a shoddy salesman out there. Get something down on paper and send it out. Test it. If it doesn't sell as well as you'd like, sit down and rewrite it. Don't be scared. Just because you've created a sales letter and it's out there in the world doesn't mean that it's written in stone. You can always change it, reapply yourself to it, and tweak it until you get it to the point where it's performing optimally. Then go back out there and do more mailings with it. Here's a truism you should take to heart: *You're never going to make sales with a sales letter if you don't have it in the mail.*

Facing Your Fear

I'll be the first to tell you that I understand there's a certain amount of fear involved in creating any sales product. You want to get things right, you want to make money, and most of all you don't want to look like an idiot. I've got a newsflash for you: this nervousness, this fear, never goes away entirely. I've been doing this now since 1988, and in the process I've created sales letters that have earned more than $100 million. I've done hundreds of promotions, but still, on a big promotion, **I always go through a period of total confusion.** Now, of course, it's become so common that it doesn't bother me anymore. It's not nearly as painful, because I expect it and I realize that I'll get beyond it. But **there's always a period of frustration and uncertainty** I experience when I'm developing something new, and that part is not so easy to deal with. Those are the times when

▼▼▼▼▼▼▼▼▼
MARKETING SECRET

Sell them what they want — and give them what they need.
— Dan Kennedy

▼

"Any fool can make soap — but it takes a genius to sell it."
— Thomas J. (T.J.) Borratt, Pears Soap 1888.]

I'm trying to figure out all the answers, and things aren't coming together very well. But that's a hump that you get over, and it gets easier after that. Many times, if I spend three days working on a sales letter, I'll get more done in the last day than I did the previous two days together. The last day is like coasting downhill; it all just starts to flow.

It takes work and effort to make things come together the way you want them to. According to my friend Jeff Gardner, he usually finds that when it gets to be very difficult, he's over-thinking it. He's so focused on getting it right that he's paralyzed, and I've felt that myself. But **you can't let indecision, uncertainty, or the need to get everything just right keep you from doing anything.** Let that feeling go; tell yourself, "Okay, look, I know what the product is. That's not a problem. I know what the results are. I know my target market. What I need to do is just sit down and connect with the customer."

Even though you may know all that intellectually, there's still that point where it's all frustrating; it's difficult, and it's a real challenge. But if you work through that, believe me, it does get easier. It probably won't be easy right out of the gate, but if you stick with it, you're going to be successful. This attitude gives you the ability to ease up on yourself. Sure, you should understand that it's going to be a difficult situation each time; but you should also understand that **if you go past that and get through all those things that keep other people from writing great copy, you're going to be able to make a lot of money.** You're not alone; a lot of copywriters at all levels go through those same type of struggles, and if they can make gobs of money, why can't you?

Naturally, there are some people for whom this all comes easy, and you might find that you're one of them. I admire and I'm envious of people who can whip out sales copy in no time, because it can be extremely difficult — and writer's block is no laughing matter. But once you get in the flow, you can make tremendous amounts of profits, profits that your competitors will never even *begin* to make, just by mastering this skill. This is because **a thousand sales letters, if they're done correctly, are like a thousand salespeople going around knocking on doors.** Just like any great salesperson, they're enthusiastic; there's a tremendous belief in the product or service being sold, so they can do a powerful job of selling. That being the case, it's worth all the extra effort you put into it!

The Personal Touch

Here's something that I always keep in mind while writing a sales letter, and I know that many of my colleagues do too. **Try to make the letter as personal as you can.** If you're writing to 1,000 people or 10,000 people, **the key to success is to make it look like you're writing to *one* person.** Always think of one customer, not 500 or 5,000: that's the key to success when writing Direct-Mail copy. You want to address this person with passion; you want to convince this person that they need whatever it is you're selling them, and ideally you should explain why. **The passion in a good salesman's voice has to come through on paper** just as if you were saying it to someone — one of your best friends, or your parents, or one of your children. You don't necessarily have to follow perfect grammar rules; you just have to **talk to the prospect as if you're talking to them in person, and you'll get through to them.**

Avoiding the Blank Page

For some of us who struggle with writing, the problem's not so much being unable to communicate, it's dealing with that blank page. **Some people are born writers, but others are born talkers** — and I'm one of them. I can communicate something in speech much better than I can in print, and if you're like me, you might find it hard to get started when you're faced with that blank page (or these days, that blinking cursor). It can be overwhelming to think of writing a long-form sales letter when you have to start with that blank page.

Technology can come to your rescue here. If you struggle with actually getting something written down, then why not **grab a tape recorder and record your sales letter on audio?** Once that's done, you can let someone else transcribe it and get it into print, and then all you have to do is some judicious editing. Recording your sales letter is one way to hit that tone where it seems that you're speaking directly to your customer, communicating one-on-one. You don't even have to record the whole letter; maybe it's just the headlines, or good benefit-driven bits and pieces of a letter, that you get out of your mind and onto tape. Maybe you record your headline and then rattle off a bunch of benefits off the top of your head, **as if you're telling a customer, face-to-face, about what makes your product so special. Then you talk about the offer and the price.** Once it's transcribed and on paper, you'll end up with pages worth of good copy that you can shape into a sales letter — and you never have to worry about staring at that blank page.

Here's another good option, and I suspect it's one that most copywriters employ: **use another sales letter as a template for your new one. Basically, you just keep writing the same sales letter again and again.** So if you had a seminar for your customers last year and you're getting ready for this year's seminar, just pull up last year's copy and change the titles, dates, and some of the offers to come up with *this* year's copy. That way, you're not dealing with a blank screen or page, ever. Just keep files of those previous promotions that you did, and you can easily pull them up, change the name of the file, and rewrite a new offer.

Elements of Style

One of the reasons that copywriting can be so difficult is that you have to grab your prospect's interest from the word go. The first page is crucial, because it's where you hook them. If the first page doesn't work, all the good stuff later is useless. Some writers rewrite and polish that first page as much as possible before moving on, and they find that the rest of the letter flows more smoothly as a result. Once you have your beginning and you know your ending, the letter can flow between those two points.

Here's something to avoid on that first page. Amateur copywriters writing their first sales letters often start out by talking a lot about themselves, about their business, how old Grandfather Jed started it all back in 1901. Don't overindulge in that kind of writing, because the prospect really doesn't care. You can touch on some of that stuff, but what you really need to do is **get as many benefits as you can on the first page.** If you're sending a six-page letter, some people will make a decision within a matter of seconds about whether they're going to continue to read it. You'd better be talking about benefits for *them*, not the fact that Grandfather Jed had this vision and started the company in 1901.

> What are you willing to do?
>
> The answer to these six words will determine how much money you will ultimately make.

Beyond Page One

By now, some of you are probably horrified, if only because you came into this chapter thinking that a sales letter was a one-page document. Remember though, we're speaking in terms of a Direct-Mail letter, and that's often much more than a single page. There are long-form sales letters and short-form letters, and **long-form letters can be surprisingly effective.** Obviously, if you can tell your entire story on a single page, that's fine. But in most cases, if you're trying to make a sale, it's going to take a lot more information than that.

People considering Direct-Mail for the first time are often flabbergasted to learn that serious marketers regularly send out 15- or 16-page letters. They think that no one is going to take the time to read a 16-page letter; **but if you're trying to make a large sale and it takes 16 pages for you to tell your story, then a 16-page letter is what you need to write.** If you've targeted your prospect right, he'll probably read that 16-page letter. In fact, if it's written well and tells him the benefits of a product or service that will fill his needs and fix whatever problems he's facing, he'll probably read a 30-page letter. That may seem a little extreme, but it works if you set it up right.

The Sincerest Form of Flattery

If you're new at the game and don't have any old copy of your own to use as a template, one way to learn what works is to study the masters.

> ## ▼▼▼▼▼▼▼▼
> ## MARKETING SECRET
>
> Wisdom from a true master: "Without joy of work there can be no creativity."
> — *Frank Lloyd Wright* from the book, "Rebel In Concrete."

Find yourself some really good sales letters, then sit down and write those sales letters down, in longhand, word-for-word. Rewrite them too, if you can. **This can get you into the mind of the copywriter,** so that you can see how they went about identifying and bringing out the benefits of whatever it was they were selling. **It's a very powerful method, because it can help you see the different elements that are flowing through a letter.** If this sounds a lot like homework — well, it is. Writing a sales letter word-for-word can help you understand how the whole letter is set up. You could never use that letter to sell to clients — that would be plagiarism — but the practice will help you understand how the copywriter who wrote it was truly thinking.

This is one way you can pick **up the language of good salesmanship in print,** and you have to be careful when you do it; you can take it too far, and lose what makes your own copy special. You can even take special classes to learn how to write the perfect sales letter; I know a famous marketer who teaches copywriting seminars, and he has a loyal following of people that he's instructed. He gives his students all kinds of formulas for writing copy, and yes, I've seen a lot of the work done by his students. If there's one big criticism I have, it's the fact that **everybody follows the formula to the point where their copy is too homogenized.** Not only does it lack any scintilla of their personality, it's too perfect overall. It looks too pretty; it looks too clean; it looks too neat. In other words, **it's not human enough!** There's no life to their copy; it's too bland.

When you look at a good Direct-Mail

package, one that really inspires and motivates you, **there's a humanness to it. It's raw. It's real. It's just like a salesperson.** The best salespeople I know aren't necessarily attractive people physically, but they do have overbearing personalities. They will not be denied, and they believe in their product or service very strongly. They may be hairy and ugly looking, but who cares? They're passionate, and they're real. They inspire trust. They inspire confidence. They have total believability in what they're doing. You cannot help but be moved by these people. They're hitting your buttons; **you're getting pumped up, so excited by their pitch that you can't wait to send back an order or get to that store.** And that's *exactly* what you, as a marketer, want to accomplish.

The Value of a Deadline

Copywriting deadlines can help you in two ways. First of all, you should set one for yourself. Rewriting is important in copywriting, since the right changes can increase your profits tremendously; the only problem is, you've got to stop at some point. I'm convinced that you can overwork your copy if you go too far. There comes a time when you can actually screw it up if you don't step back and accept that what you've got is good enough. You need a deadline to keep you from doing that. If you set a date that the letter has to be finished by, you can rework it all you want — but when you get to that deadline, it's done and you're ready to mail.

Don't forget to **add a deadline for the prospect or customer as well.** *Always* give them a deadline when they should act; **never send out a sales piece that just lets them decide, at their own leisure, when they're going to take advantage of your service or product.** Make your deadline ten or twenty days from the time you mail it; make it clear that they have to take action *right now* to get what you're offering at this special price.

The Seven Steps to Super-Profitable Direct-Mail Copywriting

By now, you've probably gotten the point that with Direct-Mail, it's all about salesmanship: getting to know your customer, explaining the offer in a clear, beneficial way, and carefully crafting what you're going to send out and do. **This all takes a lot of learning and experience to get just right, but I've boiled it down to seven steps that anyone can handle.** Most of them I've mentioned before, but I want to take this opportunity to re-emphasize them by summarizing them in easy-to-swallow morsels (this is the teaching method also known in some circles as Pounding It Into Your Head). Without further ado then, the Seven Steps to Super-Profitable Direct-Mail Copywriting are:

- Research
- Prewriting
- Writing
- Rewriting
- Mailing the Offer
- Studying the Results
- Testing

In the following sections, I'll talk about each of the Seven Steps in more detail.

Research

The first step is research, and researching your copy involves several different elements, all of which have to happen before you take any further action. First of all, you have to know your prospect: you have to know who they are, how they think, and what their hot buttons are psychologically. You also have to know your offer inside and out, before you even sit down to write. **Be clear on your offer's biggest benefits. Then take some time to study your swipe file.**

That last suggestion may have you a little confused, since you might not even know what a swipe file is. Remember how I suggested earlier that you should emulate successful copywriters, at least at the beginning? One way you can start doing that is by building a swipe file. At its most basic, **a swipe file is just a collection of winning ads, sales letters and offers that have been proven to work.** Of course, you'll want copy that sells products and services similar to your own to similar prospects. Send off for offers, collect the Direct-Mail that comes to you, clip out well-done ads in magazines and papers, and put those together in a swipe file so you can research what's been working in the marketplace.

Prewriting

Before you sit down and actually write a sales letter, you should list, on paper, all the benefits, selling points, bullets, and other items that you're going to need to include in your offer. Also list all the other "must have" elements — how to order, the action you want your prospects to take, and any questions and answers that you feel you need to include. Basically, **you're creating an outline of how you want the sales copy to flow.**

Writing the Offer

Once you have your outline together, it's time to actually start writing the offer. This is arguably the hardest part, though some copywriters will say that it's easier than the research phase. In any case, start with the headline. If you don't have a good headline, you're not going to be able to draw people into your offer and get them to read anything else in your sales letter. Use words that sell. I could go on for chapters and chapters about how the words that sell, like *you* and *free* and *new* and all the others, are so important, but that'll have to wait for another book! At the very least, be sure to use the word *you* a lot, so you can make it personal: remember, you need to **write this as if you're talking to your prospect one-on-one.** Talk about *them*; don't talk about all your customers in general, and don't make broad statements about whom you're trying to sell to. *Speak to your prospect specifically.*

While you're at it, **make strong, even outrageous guarantees.** If you can't guarantee your product, then you shouldn't be selling it. You've got to have some kind of guarantee; that's a given. Be sure to **carry the main theme from the sales copy to the order form.** Order forms — where you tell people to order and let people order from you — are a great place to restate your offer and your guarantee. Some copywriters actually do the order form first. Now, that's a big pet peeve of mine: I think those people are boxing themselves in. A better formula I've adapted is to write the sales letter first and then work on the order form, because you never quite know where you're going to go with your letter when you're in the thick of it.

In addition to using the personal touch and offering solid guarantees, use testimonials if possible. Scientists like to make a big deal about how anecdotal evidence isn't worth squat, and maybe that's true in scientific

▼▼▼▼▼▼▼▼
MARKETING SECRET

A major part of the power of 2-step marketing is the fact that it makes the prospect or customer feel that "they" are chasing YOU rather than the real fact — which is the exact opposite!

- The prospect feels they are choosing you.

- They feel that they are in control and have the power.

- They feel less threatened.

- And this is the gateway to the sale.

research — but it's gold in marketing copy. **People want to hear from other people like them about how your product made their lives better.** Some of your current customers will be willing to give you testimonials about your products, and if you can include their names and a little bit of a description about who they are, that's good. If you can include their picture, it's ten times better.

Nobody likes to make a decision all on their own. If the customer knows that people have made these decisions before, or that people are actually using the product and seeing these results, that's something they can use to help them make their own decision. The best part is, the power of testimonials works no matter if you're selling to an individual consumer or to a corporation. You see, **people don't do business with companies; they do business with people, and Direct-Mail is all about one-to-one communication.** It's the next best thing to going up to somebody, looking them straight in the eye, giving them one of those great big Bill Clinton handshakes where you use two hands instead of one, even slapping them on the back a little like every good salesperson does. **It's all about that human element.** Make the customer feel important — learn the names of their kids, and their birthdays if you can.

You need to realize that people all want to feel special. They want to feel like they're loved, appreciated, respected and admired — and they're usually surrounded by a whole bunch of people who are sick and tired of them. They go to their mailbox, and if we do a good job — and this works especially well in niche markets — **we can build bonds with customers in which**

we give them all the things they're lacking in their regular life. You see this a lot in women's business groups, where they get together for just those social events. Mary Kay Cosmetics has done this for years with their conferences. The average consultant doesn't make a whole lot with Mary Kay, but they have this incredible social environment. They're made to feel important, they get medals, and they get to wear different colored blazers if they get to a certain level. They can even get a pink Cadillac if they work hard enough. It's a social network that makes a group of women happy; it's their way to feel important. With a little skillful copywriting, you can do the same for your customers.

Rewriting

Ask just about any writer, and he'll tell you that **writing is mostly *re*writing.** Very rarely are you going to get something just right the first time through. Take a little time between your first draft and the rewrite; put the copy in a drawer for a few days, and go on to something else. Fresh eyes always give you a new angle; often, something strikes you that you didn't catch the first time. **You may discover that half of what you've written during your writing phase may be total crap, while the other half may be brilliant. You don't try to decide what's right and what's wrong when you're in the thick of it; you just throw it all out there, and then you start the rewriting.** The rewrite phase is where you weed out all the bad stuff and save all the good stuff — just like you boil down a good gravy.

As you're going over the text, make sure all your benefits and selling points from the research and prewriting phases are included, that you didn't leave something out. Pay close attention to the headline and closing. Just like in golf, you drive for show and putt for dough. **Your money in sales copy is generally made on the headline and the first page — where you draw them in — and on the last page, where you make your closing arguments.** As you're rewriting, revise any areas that focus too much on you and your company, because, like I've already said more than once, your prospects really don't care about that. They prefer that you focus more on them, and the benefits of your product or service that relate to them.

As you're looking for any of those areas to polish over, be sure to read the copy aloud so you can catch any snags that aren't obvious in print.

Here's an especially important point: be sure you **mention the offer** *at least* **three times.** Most people aren't going to read your entire sales letter from first to last word; they're going to skim and scan it, and you may miss giving them a good reason to buy if you don't mention your offer over and over again, and in various formats throughout your letter.

Mailing the Offer

There are many routes you can take when you're mailing out a Direct-Mail piece. You can go totally commercial, where the piece is plastered all over with benefits and sales copy, or totally personal, where you send it in a generic, bland envelope, and make it look like it was written by their cousin or their nephew or their brother. **There are all kinds of tricks and strategies you can use when putting that offer in the mail, in order to make it rise about all the background noise.**

The list of people to whom you're sending is one of the most important things in this entire series of Seven Steps, and this takes us back to the research stage. Knowing your prospect is crucial; if you don't know to whom you're mailing, then what you mail doesn't really matter. **You could have the greatest offer in the world for basket weaving, but if you're sending it to people who could care less about basket weaving, you'll never make a dime. That's the reason you should capture the names and addresses of every single person with whom you do business. Most businesses don't bother to do this,** and as a result they have no real idea who their customers are. People come in the door, they buy something, and they go out the door. Even if they write a check, which has their name, address, and phone number printed on it, most businesses won't bother to record that. Well, you'd better start!

The most important point — and I can't emphasize this enough — is that **you've got to get that offer in the mail!** You can't make any money at all if your salesmen aren't selling. As I've said before, your copy doesn't have to be the best in the world, though it should certainly be the best you can do. But you can even learn this skill poorly and have a competitive advantage, because most businesses just don't mail out copy. So even if you put something out there that you might not think is the best of the best, but it still hits all the customer's hot buttons and you're talking to them on a personal level, and you really pour it on right from your heart — you're going to have a huge competitive advantage, even if your copy's not perfect.

Studying the Results

One part of becoming a good marketer is learning from your mistakes. It's crucially important, after you mail an offer, to take a close look at the results of the mailing. You may make money hand-over-fist, and by that you'll know you've done it right. On the other hand, you may make just a little money or you may not make any money at all, and that tells you that you have to retool, look at a new market, and even look at new products altogether.

Testing

The seventh and final step is testing. **Once you know what works, your next goal is to try to find something else that beats it and works better. You do that by testing.** From that moment forward, every time you mail an offer, you can split the mailing equally in half and run the one you already mailed versus something new. However, you should never test more than one thing at a time. If you try to test more than one thing, you'll have no way to easily quantify the results.

> The <u>why</u> to do something always comes before the <u>how</u> to do it! *This is the secret behind all great achievers.*
>
> Great achievers set the goal — and then figure it out as they go along. You can't let a little thing like not knowing how you're going to do something stop you!

Keep testing new things: the headline, the price, the offer, the letter length — even the color of the outside envelope of your package can be tested. Sometimes the changes that work best can be as subtle as the way you sign off the letter. That alone could be the one little change that makes a difference between a mediocre letter and one that makes millions. So, yes, the **testing is a continuous, ongoing process, but it's worth the effort when the money comes flooding in.**

▼▼▼▼▼

And there you have it: the Seven Steps to Super-Profitable Direct-Mail Copy-writing. Of course, I have to admit that my colleagues and I

SECTION SIX — Ruthless Marketing   **439**

▼▼▼▼▼▼▼▼▼
MARKETING SECRET

A good swipe file can make you a ton of money!

- Use it to jump-start your thinking.

- Get new creative ideas that you would have never discovered without it.

- It's a brainstorming tool — if you realize that all great selling ideas can be transferred from one product, service, or business to another.

- In other words, the ideas that are or have brought in a ton of money for one person or company can be worth a fortune to you!

don't necessarily follow all the steps every time. Often, we just sit down and write our letters and don't follow a particular formula point-by-point. But I'm not being a hypocrite here by telling you to do these things while I don't; because I can guarantee that by the time I'm done, the copy I've produced *does* fit these guidelines. You see, it all comes with experience. When you're just getting started in the business and you're just beginning to write sales copy, it's best and easiest to follow these steps.

It all sounds like a lot of work, doesn't it? I can assure you, it is — but it's probably the most valuable thing you'll ever do in your business. You may sit down and work like a demon for a week or two, but in the end, mail that sales letter out for five or ten years or more, and in the process, generate millions of dollars in income. That's a pretty good return on your investment: one week of strenuous mental work for millions of dollars. Works for me!

Getting in the Groove

One thing that I want to point out is that for me, and for most of my colleagues, copywriting is as much a labor of love as it is hard work. You have to remember this: 99% of your competition won't bother to do this at all. They'll just put a sign in the window that says they're open for business. This is one way to get a competitive advantage over your competitors, and very quickly, too — and why is that? Because as my favorite quote has it, "In the land of the blind, the one-eyed man is king!" Read this book, and you'll be the one-eyed man in a marketplace full of blind businessmen, who have little or no understanding about anything I'm telling you here.

You may not think that you have the time to work on your copywriting, but in most businesses — especially the information business — you can't afford *not* to write consistently, day after day. Like I've said, **your copywriting will eventually become your most profitable activity.** Even if you're cruising along with a workable offer, talking on the phone or working with current clients, you're not growing; your income level probably won't change much. So if you just **make it part of your daily routine** to sit down and write, say, one paragraph of a sales letter, or look over something that you've already written, and edit a little section or something, you can start to make progress. You don't have to do it for two hours at a time; start with 20 minutes, and see how that works for you. You're going to find out your business is going to grow exponentially because you're talking to many more people, a lot of whom will become new clients. Here's a bit of incentive: according to one Direct-Marketing guru, every word that he writes generates another $20,000 for him. Imagine that! So if instead of spending an hour watching TV one night, he writes a paragraph or so — or even a couple of good sentences — he stands to make hundreds of thousands of dollars.

This might not happen to you right away, but if you'll just write a paragraph or two every day, eventually you'll have a whole sales letter with which to work. **Over time, as you gain experience, you'll find that every word you write is going to generate dollars for you — and you'll get to the point to where you'll feel guilty if you don't write.** After all, the money you want to come in next month has got to come from somewhere, and Direct-Mail is a good way to get it. It's an addicting kind of marketing, too, once you get in the groove. Once you have some successful promotions that pull in big bucks, you'll be addicted for the rest of your life, and **it won't be work anymore.**

In Summation

In this chapter, I've talked about selling to people using the Direct-Mail method of Direct-Response Marketing. Selling of any kind is an emotional, human undertaking, and it works best whenever you're able to connect with the people to whom you're selling. I have a favorite Mexican restaurant that I take all my out-of-town friends to whenever they come and visit. My wife and I have been going there since they opened. They have hundreds of loyal customers, and they know all their best customers by name. They come out and cook special things for you; they make you special desserts; and they do things that make you feel guilty as hell if you don't go there on a regular basis!

Ultimately, it's all about treating people well. Every salesperson knows that instinctively. **What we're talking about is a powerful marketing method where you're able to translate the best of the best of what physical, one-on-one salesmanship is all about into print, so you can stick it in an envelope.** That way, you end up with a whole bunch of the best salespeople out there. They never call in sick; they never go smoke dope at lunchtime; they never quit to go to work for your competitor down the street, or quit to start another company. **They're salespeople that you control in every way,** and it's worth learning to be an expert copywriter in order to get them.

SECRET FOUR:
Take-Away Selling Made Easy

In this chapter, I'm going to share another powerful marketing principle that can lead to tremendous profits for your business, *if* you're willing to master the techniques involved. This one's called "take-away selling," and I'm not talking about fast food here. I'll be frank: **you may find take-away selling a little disagreeable at first, because it's not just one of the most powerful marketing techniques you can use, it's also one of the most ruthless.** That said, take-away selling is a legitimate part of marketing, though naturally you'll always want to err on the side of the ethical — and you'll always want to avoid using it cruelly.

The thing is, even if you're being perfectly ethical, take-away selling *feels* cruel — and it should, if you do it right. That's why it's such a ruthless technique. Basically, it involves putting an offer before your prospect that's so desirable that they desperately want it. You get them to the point where they feel the desire, the *need*, to absolutely have it, and then you put a roadblock or a barrier in their way — some caveat that removes the satisfaction of obtaining what you've just built that desire for, at least until they reach another goal or meet another step. Consequently, although it seems to go against the grain of logic, you can actually double or triple the desire for what you're offering, making them ready to buy even faster. **That sounds a little perverse, but human nature being what it is, that's how things are.**

Here's a quick idea of how take-away works. Say you walk into a department store and check out some new shoes you're interested in. Because you don't see any in your size, you ask the sales representative if some are available. They go into the back room and emerge a few moments later saying, "I found a pair in your size, and it's the only one we have left in stock." Now, how much more do you want those shoes?

Faced with a choice like this, some prospects will just get irritated and walk away. But that's okay; you can use this reaction to your advantage. One of the good things about take-away selling is that once you're in a position where you can pick and choose customers, you can use the method to get rid of those customers who are more trouble than they're worth. Now, that may sound like a horrible thing for any businessman to say, but while **80% of your profits are going to come from about 20% of your customers,** the same's true of your problems — though ideally, it's a different 20% who bug you. Take-away selling allows you to get rid of that bottom tier of customers who are giving you the most problems and ultimately, raise your profits by not having to spend so much money on that group. We'll talk more about that later.

What it comes down to is this: **take-away selling is a lot like taking a starving man to a restaurant, closing the door before he's fed, and telling him he's got to wait until morning to get the food. It creates urgency and scarcity, and it makes people want your product that much more.**

Take-Away Selling in Action

To show you how take-away selling works in practice, I'm going to use an example provided by my friend and colleague, marketing genius Alan Bechtold. In early 2006, Alan launched an E-Publishing Marketing Mastermind, a small group of people he gathered together who were

▼▼▼▼▼▼▼▼
MARKETING SECRET

The best time to use your swipe file is when you are actively involved in writing your own ads or sales letters.

willing to pay a substantial sum of money to work with him personally, and with the rest of the group, utilizing the Mastermind Principle. Each member was guaranteed that by the time he or she finished the group, they'd create an original eBook, launch an original eZine, and tie the two together into a marketing system that works every time.

Now, that's a pretty sweet offer. Alan was asking $4,000 per seat for this Mastermind Group, and he limited it to 120 participants, maximum, by the launch date. Do a little arithmetic, and you can see the profit potential. He took it a step further, though; **instead of selling those $4,000 seats right off the bat,** he announced that he was also shooting for the highest success rate for this kind of Mastermind in the history of Internet marketing — **so every potential participant had to _apply_ for a position.**

In other words, when prospects visited the sales website, read the material, and clicked the "APPLY NOW" button, they found that this didn't mean that they could order. What they could do was fill out a fairly extensive application so that they would be considered for joining Alan's group. The application was his Take-Away #1. It set the prospects up for the fact that even though they might have $4,000, even though they might be willing and able to spend it to join Alan's Mastermind, they _still_ might not be accepted in the group, and so might not get all the benefits as a result. What's really cool is, the information he gathered about each applicant in **that application form allowed him to cherry-pick the best applicants — to actually stack the deck to increase his success rate.** But even with those he rejected, he got some useful, detailed information about what they wanted in the future, and what they were willing to spend to get it.

But he went one *more* step further. He also recorded the entire six-month process that he went through with this Mastermind. Every weekly call, and every minute of the hands-on live workshop he held for the members, went into a course he's putting together. He recently test-marketed the course with a special pre-publication sale, and he used take-away marketing extensively for this sale.

First, he sent a series of five emails to his mailing lists. The emails, which went out over an entire month leading up to the sale date, first pointed people to the original sales website that his Mastermind prospects had read. **Only now, when they clicked "APPLY," all they got was, "Sorry, this Mastermind is closed." He stressed in the emails that you couldn't join because the Mastermind was already underway; enrollment was closed; you missed it.** But, for a very limited time (one day, actually), you could order the entire recorded Mastermind, notebooks and course in advance. On that day, on the last day possible, he sent those people to a site where they could order it all.

This ended up being a great example of a successful failure. Alan set a goal that he didn't hit with that one-day sale: he wanted to make a million bucks. He didn't, but he still generated over $50,000 in sales *in one day* with this technique. Now, that's a good month by anyone's standards! The point is, despite not making the money he wanted off this offer, he did what he said he'd do, and pulled it after one day. He'll still be able to roll this course out later, but it'll cost a lot more, and everybody who came around the first time and didn't take advantage of that special offer will know that he meant what he said. That's classic take-away selling.

Take-away is, in general, scarcity marketing. Alan calls it "scarcity marketing with a knife," because it's really scarcity on steroids. **You offer something, make people want it, make then actually ready to order it, put it within their grasp — and then you yank it away.** Putting up a roadblock to their satisfaction only makes them want it all the more.

Here's another example. Recently Randy Charach, another savvy marketer with whom I work, was telling me a story of a client who had just bought one of his courses. The client had received the course three days earlier — and he was calling to complain that he hadn't made any money yet! Randy's employee put him on hold and said, "Boss, what do I do with someone like this?" And Randy told him: "Insist that we give him a refund. Tell him to send it back, and we'll refund him right away." No surprise there, because none of us wants to deal with an irrational client like that. Of course, as soon as was told that, the light bulb went on in the client's head, and it was impossible to convince this person to return the course. Immediately, the customer came to realize that he was being ridiculous, and all but begged Randy to let him keep it.

What Randy did is something that most business people are scared to death to do. We're trained that it's the worst kind of sin to give up money that could be and should be ours — but thinking like that can hurt you. In the business world, you have all kinds of competitors who are willing to do anything and everything to get business. I call them **business whores.** They carry their cell phones with them constantly; while they're in the bathroom, they're talking on the phone to their clients. They even give their clients their home phone numbers! They're too accessible, and you know what? **People tend to value what they have to work hard to get.** Sometimes, in order to make the real money, you've got to make people jump through some hoops.

First of all, you've got to qualify them, in order to make sure they're the right kind of person. You do things to get them to raise their hands, to show their interest by taking some action. **The bigger the action they have to take, the more they reveal how interested and serious they are; and the more you can take control over the entire selling process.** You get them to start chasing *you* instead of you chasing *them*. In Alan's case, he started getting all kinds of calls after he let those applications sit there for a few days. "Well, did I get accepted? Am I in yet? Man, I'm really sitting on pins and needles here." They were hoping Alan would accept their $4,000, and that made him appreciate them all the more. He treated them special from the beginning, and after he'd converted them from applicants to prospects to surefire customers, he kept treating them that way. **He wasn't treating them like every other client that comes in the door: he made them do things. He made them participate. He made them** *interact*.

In so doing, he also controlled the relationship. The process of qualifying them made them feel privileged to be a part of the group, and privileged to give Alan their money. At the same time, it created greater value in their minds, and took them to a higher level. I like the fact that when Alan's organization called to accept them into the Mastermind, they weren't calling to sell them anything; they were calling to give them the good news that they could write Alan a check for $4,000.

You see, **most people don't like to be "sold"; but often they really want to buy, especially if they feel there's a scarcity of what they're after.** With take-away selling, your goal is to let your customers feel like they made the buying decision themselves. It's really just psychological manipulation; or, to put it more bluntly, it's a kind of head game you play with the customer. You get inside their minds and take them step-by-step to the point where they're actually asking you to let them buy.

It has to be done correctly, of course. **In the hands of a beginner, the savvy consumer will see right through this tactic.** You have to mean it, too. If you tell your customers that you're not going to take everyone, or that the offer will go away if they don't act soon enough, that really does have to happen. In Alan's case, he followed through with his threat and didn't accept more than half the applicants. Of the 150 or 180 who applied, he only ended up taking 75 of them. Of course, when you do this, you have to tell your customers you've done it, because most won't know until you make it a part of your marketing message.

If you get a reputation for making it difficult to do business with you, all of a sudden the word gets out amongst the best prospects that there really must *be* something here! The building isn't just one of those movie props with 2 x 4s behind it; it's a genuine offer, genuinely limited. The word spreads. That kind of message — that kind of seriousness — just blows some people away, because

---

▼▼▼▼▼▼▼▼▼▼▼▼▼

Spend <u>more</u> money — to close more sales!

1. You can't go wrong if you are spending this money on super qualified prospects.

2. You are selling big ticket items with good margins.

In some cases (as long as your percentage of conversion is going up) you can't spend too much money!

MARKETING SECRET

Stay very busy on the projects that stand the greatest chance of making you the most money.

- Massive action generates inspiration!

they're used to hearing, "You must respond in ten days or the promotion is going to be over!" When they hear that, they just roll their eyes and say, "Bull! You're lying to me! That's not true!" and most of the time, they're right. **When you actually do things like this, you shock these people. Now you've gotten their attention, and they're sitting up and taking you seriously.**

You have to be a real hard-ass to perform take-away selling well. But a reputation for being hard to do business with — a reputation for meaning what you say, for being unwilling to prostitute yourself for a quick buck — can help you in this business. There's this guy most of us in the business know; I won't mention his name here, but he's famous for doing all kinds of Joint Venture deals. But he's also famous for suing people! He's sued enough people who were former Joint Venture partners that nobody would ever cross him — he's got a huge reputation for that. But everyone wants to do business with him, because first of all, he's got a huge customer base, and you can make a ton of money by partnering with him — as long as you don't get crosswise with him. **He demands respect.** From the very first moment you start seriously considering a Joint Venture with him, you're doing it on his terms, not yours. He's got your respect right from the start, because you know he's sued a dozen different past partners. I see that as a good analogy with take-away selling, because **what you're really doing is separating yourself from all your competitors by letting your best prospects know that you really are completely different than the rest.**

Sure, I'll Buy It... Tomorrow

Take-away selling is all about overcoming procrastination. Even if the product or service you're offering someone is exactly what they need or want, they may not buy unless they're given a gentle, friendly ultimatum: "Hey, you can do this now or never. Buy now, or forever hold your peace."

Take-away selling, in the simplest terms, is a way to limit the supply of a product or service in order to increase its scarcity. It's a proven fact that scarcity sells, based on that age-old law of supply and demand: the less the supply, the greater the demand. People don't know how much they want something until it's about to be taken away from them. It's just human nature.

The great marketer Jim Rohn once said, "Without a sense of urgency, desire loses its value." Why? Because procrastination is the biggest killer of sales. This is particularly the case online, where the chances of a prospect staying on or returning to your website in today's click-happy world are minimal. **You really need to grab that person's attention and cut through those natural tendencies to procrastinate — to get them to take action now, right away. You do this by shaping your offer, not just your product and services, but your whole offer.** Many of its elements should be time-sensitive or quantity-bound, and you shouldn't hesitate to turn people away when the time's up or the quantity's exceeded. Of course, you have to provide a reasonably logical explanation to justify your qualification. And you've got to follow through. That's critical.

But Take-Away Selling Won't Work for My Business... Will It?

If you take the attitude that take-away selling won't work for your kind of business, then you're sunk before you've even gotten started. The fact is, take-away selling can work for absolutely any business. Here's an extreme example: Randy Charach, who started out as a professional magician. That's right: hocus-pocus and abracadabra. He was very, very good at it, and he started it at a very early age; we're talking younger than ten years old here. At one point, when he was doing his magic shows as a youngster, he started getting double-booked. This happened by accident. Say, he'd have a booking for Saturday, March 5th at 2:00 p.m.

for some kid's birthday party, then he'd get another call from someone who wanted him at the same time. All of a sudden, they weren't asking him how much he charged; instead they were saying things like, "Oh, gee... can we book you for next year, then? Because we can't change the time of our party."

So now Randy's getting booked up a year in advance, and he's thinking, "Well, maybe I should charge a little bit more," which was another form of take-away selling. Other people were charging $5, so he started charging $6. And then, when they started charging $10, he went to $25. And then they came up to $25, so he raised his own price to $50. Soon he was far more desirable, because now he was the most premium-priced magician out there. He continued performing right up until a few years ago; by then he was demanding a cool $10,000 per booking, and getting it. He's not doing it anymore because his marketing business is more interesting and more lucrative, and hey, he just doesn't feel like it. He has a family now that he doesn't want to leave to go off and do these shows.

Basically, Randy charged $6 for his first show, and it quickly went up from there when he realized that other guys were getting more. By then end of his magic career, he was a top non-celebrity performer; not a household name like David Copperfield or David Blaine, but well known within the corporate market in which he was performing. He was getting top dollar, where other people were charging $1,500 or $2,500. Did his clients get good value? Absolutely! His show was as good as, or better than, anybody else's. In fact, there were other people in that price range who weren't as good as Randy, so Randy's clients were definitely getting good value. They knew he'd show up, he'd do a great job, and that he was 100% consistent.

Now, I'm not suggesting that you should overcharge, but **by having this premium, it's clear that you're in demand. When your product or service is in demand, people want you more.** It comes back to my earlier example about Randy, when he first started to get rolling. When he wasn't available, price was no longer an issue — and all of a sudden he was booked a year in advance! That was something that Randy learned fairly quickly, and that's one of the reasons he was able to become a millionaire as a magician, and do over 5,000 shows during his twenty years as a professional entertainer. That's the essence of take-away selling.

About ten years ago, Randy spent a year as a business broker, just because he wanted to learn more about business in general. All the other business brokers he worked with were going out and begging for listings, and taking them on and paying for advertising themselves, and going after small businesses at the beginning. Well, Randy knew a little more about take-away selling than they did, so he started off with Direct-Marketing in the business magazines. This way he attracted people to *him*, rather than cold-calling them. He also didn't list any businesses under a million, which is really unusual. So is the fact that he charged a fee for advertising upfront, which none of the other agents did. He ended up being in great demand as a business broker, and turned out to be very successful — but he didn't really enjoy it, so he moved on to other things. Now he's become successful again as a marketer. The point here is that he was able to take the take-away selling principles he learned as a magician, apply them to vastly different fields, and *still* make a lot of money. If he can, then you can too. I firmly believe that.

Take-Away Options

There **are three basic specific types of take-aways you can use for your products and services, whatever they may be.** You can mix and match all three in various combinations, of course, but I'll go over each individually. Here they are:

- Limiting the time.
- Limiting the quantity.
- Limiting the offer.

The first option is *limiting the time*. That's done by adding a deadline to the offer; I talked about the value of deadlines previously. You've also read a few real-life examples about how to apply time limits here in this chapter, too, so you can take the principals that Alan and Randy used and apply them to your own situation.

We've all seen the websites and ads that have date stamps on them, saying you're going to miss out if you don't ACT NOW. Then you go back the next day, or see the ad in the next issue, and it hasn't changed. It still says you've got to ACT NOW. Well, we've all fallen for that; it's an acceptable strategy, but **its value gets diluted if you overuse it.** The words

MARKETING SECRET

Negative motivation often works much better than anything positive!

- The stick is always better than the carrot!

▼

The tighter your deadlines and the less flexibility you have in your daily schedule — the greater your productivity will be!

"LIMITED OFFER" and those date stamps stop meaning anything if you don't mean it. What you really want to do is employ true time sensitivity, and stick to your guns.

Time sensitivity may simply be a result of the way you prefer to do business. Every marketer in the information business knows people who sell a limited quantity of their product, and then move on to the next product, because they don't want to do that product anymore. In their mind, they're moving at light-speed, and they've got all these other products they want to create and bring to the marketplace. Even though a product might still be selling, their emphasis — the time and effort that they put into it — is limited. Therefore, there's an urgency in marketing that particular product. Yes, they might have created the urgency; but it's there.

Next: *limiting the quantity*. You can limit the number of units available, assuming it's stock or inventory, or openings if it's a service offer. Again, consider Alan's Mastermind offer, and Randy's schedule as an entertainer. Here's another case, offered by my friend Mike Lamb. He limited the quantity of his product, his coaching services, the same way Randy did: by raising his rates. Last year, he started charging $2,500 for ten hours of his time. Before that, he was charging $95 an hour and was only doing it one hour at a time — and it was costing him a lot of time and effort. He was putting a lot of time into the marketing without a lot of great results, and he spent a limited amount of time with his clients, so they didn't see the kind of results that they would have if they'd spent a longer period of time together. So one day he decided that there are only so many hours in the day, and he only wanted to work with so many clients at a time. To really make this work, he had to raise his rates. That was it, and he let people know the specifics right up front. For the customers who really mattered, money was not an issue.

Later on, he raised his rates again: from $2,500 for ten hours to $5,000 for fifteen hours. He actually gets more people coming to him now, and he has to turn away business. He gets a better quality of client, too, because if somebody is willing to spend $5,000 up front, then he knows that they're serious enough to spend the time they need to with him, and do the assignments and all the other things he wants them to do.

The last — and arguably the most useful — way to create scarcity is by *limiting the offer*. **You do this by limiting elements that are part of the offer, such as the guarantee, the bonuses, the premiums, or the price.** I'm not suggesting you should offer a discount, but you can use something like an imminent price increase after a certain time, perhaps to cover the extra cost in dealing with more customers, or for something logical like the packaging. Maybe, since the product is bundled with other products or components, it won't be available after "X" number is sold. You can limit the extras, too, as in free support, free installation, or free shipping, and so on. I've noticed that Dell Computers is really good at this, offering limited-time extras like an extra two years of support, or free shipping, or discounted shipping. **There are so many different variables that you can play with in limiting the offer.**

Strategic Pricing

One of the things I want to drive home to you about take-away selling is something I mentioned earlier — because it's the key advantage to practicing this principle. That's the fact that **you can raise your prices, and** *still* **get a whole bunch of people who want your goods or services!** Remember my story about Randy Charach? He ended up charging $10,000 per show, and people were willing to pay that because he was so good at it. Similarly, Mike Lamb went from charging $95 per hour to $5,000 for fifteen hours for his coaching services, over the course of a couple of years. I can't think of a better advantage than being able to raise, and raise, and raise your prices, because that means more profitability in the end. It means **you can have fewer customers, so you can do a better job of taking** good care of your best customers — and since birds of a feather flock together, that can help you attract more of the best types of customers. You can charge more money, have more enjoyment, get rid of all those deadbeats I was alluding to earlier, the "price whores" who just want the lowest price, no matter the quality. You can clean out all that sludge, work with the best people, and charge premium prices.

Remember: one of the most important things about **take-away selling is that it's based on a proven economic principle of supply and demand.** I've got a story here that's probably going to make you a little mad, but there's no better example of supply and demand in action. My friend and colleague Chris Hollinger was recently speaking with a client who plays golf with a major oil company executive. Now, I think we can see the effects of supply and demand every time we go to the gas pumps nowadays. The conversation Chris' client relayed to him was this: the oil executive told him, "Over the last two years I've been instructed to close three of the refineries I oversee." The client was surprised. He said, "What? Why are you guys closing refineries? We have a shortage of refined gasoline here, and it's driving the price up!" And the executive said, "Exactly."

There might be thousands of reasons why the oil company would want to close those particular refineries, but if you think about supply and demand, I believe you'll see the real reason right away. Now, that seems sinister, and I don't want to be conspiratorial here — but if they dry up the supply, what happens to the price? It's supply and demand in action. We've all seen prices going up, and it's always blamed on various things — but all it comes down to is a lack of refined fuel.

Randy Charach tells me that when he was in the magic business, other magicians used to ask him all the time: "Should I raise my prices? I'm afraid to raise my prices because if I raise my prices, I might be out of work." His own experience was that **every time he raised his prices, people wanted him more.** But don't be too eager with this tactic: the thing to do is to gradually increase that price. Let everyone know, for example, that after 30 days, you're going to increase it a certain amount. Then in 30 more days you can always say, "I've got to raise my price again. But before I do, you'd better get in now — because on this date, it goes up again. I've got to do it." And do so.

I know of one marketer who raises his price with every offer he sends

> ▼▼▼▼▼▼▼▼▼▼▼▼
>
> Your best customers are like fires. They go out if unattended.
>
> - The key word is "relationship."
> - The better they "feel" about you — the more money they will give you!
> - Remember, the fire never dies as long as you keep feeding it!

out the door. He once had an eBook for sale, and it started out at something like a dollar — but then it went up a dollar every sale. All it took was a nice, automated script on his website, and the 500th guy who bought the book was paying $500 for the same book that the guy who acted first got for a dollar. Not a bad deal, eh? There comes a point where you have to level it off, of course, but it was a way to sell a whole bunch of his eBooks right away. You can get some testimonials, it's fun, it's interesting, and it's just plain good marketing.

I think this indicates that **raising your prices on a regular basis can be very effective in not only gaining you more money, but also in drawing in better qualified prospects.** Now, there's a limit to this. You need to make sure that in your heart, you have a genuine feeling that you're worth it: that you're offering great value with what you're presenting. Because ultimately, if you just raise your prices over and over, and you don't feel like you're offering good value, it'll come back to haunt you. If you don't have the goods, that's a great recipe for putting yourself out of business very quickly. You always have to have the goods, and you have to be able to deliver and over-deliver the value, no matter what. Frankly, I think a lot of goods and products and services are undervalued out there, so it's not hard to raise the bar.

Here's an example of how to do that. **One of the best ways I know of to increase the value of what you're offering is to make yourself a celebrity in your marketplace.** Celebrities — at least the most famous ones — represent what take-away selling is all about, because there's such a tremendous demand for them. These people can't even go to the bathroom without being followed by reporters and people wanting their autograph. They sometimes need a tremendous herd of bodyguards and entourage to go before them, just so they can live something approximating a normal life.

▼▼▼▼▼▼▼▼▼
MARKETING SECRET

Stop waiting for inspiration! Instead, you must get up every morning with the determination to press on — and do creative work — eve if you don't feel like it. Your motion will create the emotion.

- "Most of life is routine — dull and grubby — but routine is the momentum that keeps a man going. If you wait for inspiration you'll be standing on the corner after the parade is a mile down the street."
— Ben Nicholas

You can become a celebrity in your marketplace. Some businesses lend themselves more to this than others, but **there are definite things you can do to break out of whatever crowd in which you find yourself** — whether it's having your own local radio show, or a local-access TV program, or doing seminars or workshops, or writing books, or creating information products. There's something that you *can* do to rise above everyone else and make yourself an expert in your marketplace, where people just naturally see you as somebody who really knows their stuff. And then, all of a sudden, everybody just goes crazy over you! You position yourself in a way that your competitors don't even think they *can* position themselves. By positioning yourself in that way, you're offering yourself so that your clients automatically believe that there's far more value there than they can ever afford. It does more for your credibility than you can imagine. It also gives you a tremendous power, in the sense that **it suddenly makes clients start coming to you, rather than you having to go out and constantly attract them.**

Marketing as Sexuality

There's an old marketing joke that goes like this: "What's the difference between a $25 street prostitute and a $1,000-an-hour call girl?" The answer? Marketing. That may seem crude, but in reality, it's the only difference. They're selling (ahem) the same product, but they do different things. You're never going to see a $1000 call girl out on the street trying to flag down traffic, like a street prostitute would. Same product, different presentation.

The same thing is true in business. We're all trying to find ways to differentiate ourselves from our competitors, but **sometimes there's really not a lot you can do.** That's why you have to be a smart marketer and do things to make yourself an expert in your marketplace, to gain celebrity status, and to do things like limiting the supply of the product — or at least to limit the *perception* of supply — and to **increase the demand by being as different as you can from everybody else who does this.**

I think take-away selling lends itself more to sexual metaphors than most marketing principals, because, again, it's all about supply and demand. I did a program years ago on Internet dating. It was called "The Secret of Internet Dating." We produced something like six audio cassette tapes, and we brought in experts to reveal the secrets. There was one principle that's written in stone when it comes to online dating, and it also applies to business. And that is: Never, never, *never* answer another person's ad. Never be the guy who goes out and answers all the girls' ads on the Internet, or a girl who answers all the guys' ads. You run your own ads, and you let the lonely-hearts come to you, because **there's a difference in the whole relationship when it's them chasing you.**

Something changes when the prospects feel they're coming to you, rather than having you seek them out. That's part of the perception you're trying to get with take-away selling. You see, it's the old strategy of "playing hard to get." That's why it's so natural and easy to fall into this. Just remember that old rule of playing hard to get — the way every girl was raised by their Mom, where they were taught that you don't go after the guy. You play hard to get. You bat your eyes, and then you disappear into the crowd. You don't give them your phone number; you make them beg for it!

That's another reason that marketing-as-sexuality is such a natural analogy for take-away selling. It fits so well. In marketing you do the same thing as when you're playing the field, and you do it **by the way you build your persona.** That's the whole idea of **making yourself less available, making yourself more scarce.** You can do it with each of your product offerings: limiting the quantity, limiting the time frame, limiting the pricing. Combine those, and you've got a power-punch that just won't fail.

SECTION SIX — Ruthless Marketing

The Guru Principle; or Nothing Succeeds Like Success

If you don't like the idea of marketing as sexuality, think of it as being like the guru at the top of the mountain. One way or the other, you'll do best when you make your prospects chase you. There's no question that you can dominate your market, have a competitive edge, and have an unfair advantage over all your competition if you understand how to properly execute take-away selling. But to do that, you've got to understand the principle that **no one goes to the bottom of the mountain looking for the guru;** they want to find the guy who's sitting on top of the mountain, the guy who's successful, who's making money, who's doing something with his life.

Keep that in mind. Psychologists have proven, over the years, that **people often want what they can't have.** Using take-away selling in offers makes people want to get that service or own that product even more. It creates a sense of urgency. You've got to understand people: how they think, how they reason, how they *feel*. If you do that effectively, you'll be able to use take-away selling to produce bigger profits and more sales.

As I noted in the previous section, take-away selling helps eliminate problems and increase profits. It gives you, as a business owner, a proven and profitable way to a) get rid of your problem customers, b) leverage off those customers who are bringing you the most profits. One way to do both is simply to contact your customers using Direct-Mail, email, or even the telephone. Tell them, "Hey, thanks. I appreciate your business, but here's a situation that's developed. In the last few weeks we've found the demand for this product has increased so dramatically that we're going to have to cut back on supplying it, except to a very select group of our customers." **If you do that, you'll create a sense of urgency, a demand for the product that might not have existed originally. Now, understand that when you do that, you're really benefiting your client, as well as yourself, because the value of what you sell only increases more and more when your clients think they can't get it easily. It's all about accessibility.**

It's just like the guru on the top of the mountain: everybody wants access to him. People want access to you and your product, if they feel it's being withheld from them. This gets people to take action immediately.

The thing we all hate as marketers are those folks who, when they're reading our sales copy, are saying, "Well, let me think about this." Take-away selling gets them to stop thinking about it and do something. In their own minds, they've raised the demand for your product, just because you've told them the supply is limited. Why is it limited? Because it's selling like hotcakes! You're a hit, and people want to do business with successful businesses. They want the guru at the top of the mountain. **If you seem like you're desperate for business, or desperate to make that sale, then you probably *won't* make the sale** — because your prospects will think, "Well, maybe nobody really likes this guy, or he doesn't have a product that's really worth owning."

If you're not quite there yet, then you just have to **"fake it til you make it."** Believe it or not, you can buy tapes that make it sound like you're in the middle of a busy office. If you're a solo operator working at home, you can play the tape in the background when you're on the phone with someone, and it's got all kinds of office noises in the background, with people slamming file cabinets and all that sort of thing. It makes you sound like you're part of some busy organization, instead of at home in your underwear. You see, it's not that different from the salesman who dons a new, really fine designer suit and hops in his nice new Lincoln to go close sales — even if it's the first sales call he's made at his new job, and he's flat broke. You don't want to look flat broke, because success breeds success. That's the one thing to remember. People equate you being at the top of the mountain, or you being a success, with your accessibility.

Limited accessibility indicates a scarcity of time. If that scarcity is there — if they've increased the demand for that product, at least in their own mind — then they want to do business with you. When you take away the accessibility to that product, they'll find a hundred different reasons why they've simply got to have it. Limiting an offer creates urgency because it creates scarcity in your prospect's mind.

My colleague Michael Penland has a tale about what he calls "another lifetime" — back when he was selling franchises for a travel company in New York. One of the things they did was have people fill out an application prior to an interview, to see if they qualified to own that franchise. There were 32 questions on the application, but the most important one was Question 15: "Do you have the money to invest?" As far as Michael and the people selling the franchises were concerned, that's

> ### ▼▼▼▼▼▼▼▼▼
> ### MARKETING SECRET
>
> Confusion, pain, and ongoing frustration are all part of the creative process.
>
> - You'll do your best work when your back is up against the wall!

really what qualified them; but in the prospect's own mind, there were 32 points on which they had to qualify, so the questionnaire created a sense of scarcity, and it created a sense of an elite group of individuals who could possess this franchise.

You've got to make the customer want you. You've got to make them become afraid that they're going to lose out on something. You've got to create that sense of urgency, because urgency helps people to buy *now*. Customers respect you more, you have more value in their own eyes, and you provide more value to them. They feel privileged, and that allows them to buy. It gives them a good feeling, and it keeps you and your product at the top of the mountain — because remember, with take-away selling nobody's going to the bottom of the mountain looking for gurus down there. They all want what's on top of the mountain. They want to buy from successful people, and successful people are often short on the product or service they're offering simply because they're so good at selling it, and it's so useful to those who receive it. So make that product non-accessible unless they qualify. Get them to jump through the hoops, and take-away selling will work for your business well.

A Sense of Belonging

Looking for a new way to connect with your customers? Try sharing some of your success with them. It's easy, because we all want to feel special. These days, a lot of marketers don't call their customers *customers*. Some call them *clients*, but the smart ones call them *members*, and **they create membership-type** opportunities within their company. **Then they have a way of identifying each level.** For instance, a lot of marketers now have Silver, Gold, and Platinum levels among their memberships. Some marketers find even more ways to break it out: so you'll have Silver-plus, Gold-plus, Platinum-plus. Each level costs the member more money, but it also represents more value: there are very specific kinds of products, services and benefits that are attached to each level.

With each level the purpose is to turn all your Silvers into Golds, to turn all of your Golds into Platinums; and marketers who use these schemes do things to increase the scarcity of what they're offering, particularly at the highest levels of their membership. The very topmost slots may be limited to only 18 or 19 members — and that's it. **So what happens is, you get a waiting list of people who are ready to fill one of those 18 or 19 slots, just as soon as one becomes available.** The price points for those slots are right there in the sales material, so they know how much you're charging. It's no secret, no surprise. You may have thousands of members down at the lowest level, and they know all about the structure that moves them on up the ladder. Scarcity is up at the top, in terms of limited quantity and increased price, so you're helping to educate them. If you do it right, some of the customers just can't wait to get to that next level, so they keep moving right up the ladder. This brings to mind a quote I once heard**: "A satisfied customer is apathetic. But a loyal customer — one that you've really developed a relationship with — is your advocate."** If this member has a connection with you and your product or your service, they're willing to go that extra mile and become a Platinum or Platinum-plus member.

Membership has its privileges; that's been the slogan for American Express for years. Your customers want to feel special; they want to belong to a special community, and they all want something that no one else has, or at least something that most people don't have. Our ability to manipulate this desire to belong cuts at the heart of take-away selling. It really pokes into their psyche, if you will, and pulls out that behavior that you want them to exhibit, at a time when you want them to be part of what you're doing.

Making Your Offer Very, Very Clear

You've probably gotten the point, by now, that when you're the guru on the mountaintop, you can set your prices higher. But you have to be very clear, from the outset, that you're doing this. I know a guy in Las Vegas who sells $10,000 biz-ops; he's very famous within our industry. I got a chance to spend some good, quality time with him a few years ago in Jacksonville, and I learned that his whole marketing strategy was very simple. He was using lead-generation TV commercials that got people to call a toll-free number that gave them a recorded message. Three times within that recorded message — three different times — he told the caller that this was a $10,000 investment. Does this sound familiar? Previously, I told you that when you're writing sales copy, you should always mention your offer several times within the text. That's exactly what this guy was doing with his sales pitch. By the time the listener left their name and address so they could get more information, they already knew that he was going to hit them up for ten grand.

I think that's so smart! **It's a form of take-away selling, because it's a form of qualification. That's what we're really talking about here: ways to separate out the best prospects from the worst, and then making the best prospects come to you rather than you chasing them.** You do this by limiting the supply and increasing the demand. Making it clear that you're charging a lot for the privilege is one way to do that, and it's an up-front way of doing it. You're getting rid of the cheapskates, the complainers, and the people who can't afford what you're offering from the very beginning — and there go most of your future problems. Doing business this way becomes an excellent time-management tool, because **it weeds out the undesirable and the disinterested, so you're not spending any time marketing to the people who aren't serious.**

When you make your price very clear for the outset, and people raise their hands anyway, what they're really saying is, "Sure, I've got ten grand to spend." You can use that against them later, in the closing process. You could go to a prospect and say, "Look now, you came to me. I didn't come to you. We told you very clearly that if you didn't have ten grand to invest, then you shouldn't waste our time or yours." At that point they'll either go away, or write you a check.

Fire Those Suckers!

Take-away selling helps you add a little sanity to the often

maddening marketing world. You can't be all things to all people, and the concept of supply and demand is absolutely key. Your time is what's mostly in demand, and it's incredibly valuable when it starts getting split between everything that you have going on with customers, with your business, with your family and friends, and everything else. As I've already mentioned several times, while take-away selling is a great way to help you build urgency for your goods and services, it's also ideal for helping you rid yourself of your problem customers. It's a sad fact that not all of your customers add value to your company, and in this section, I'll go into more detail on how you can fire those suckers.

Take-away selling demands respect. It also allows for increased margins. **With more money coming in, you're essentially doing less work, so you're able to focus more productively on building a relationship with those customers who bring you the most money.** That means you can fire the worst of your customers, the ones who generate most of your problems. Now, how to you do this? Among other things, you can do it simply by telling them you're going to have to raise prices; or you simply don't offer them the incentives you'd offer someone you want to keep. Most of them will take care of themselves by walking away. Will they be disgusted by what you've done? Probably, but what do you care? **Think about all the money you'll save, not having to deal with that worst segment of your customers.** Meanwhile, your current clients feel privileged. They feel good about being your customer, and feel you're bringing them a great deal of value.

As I've said before, **a lot of business owners are customer whores; they'll go out there and do anything to get customers.** We've all done it, because we want to build our businesses. But this absolutely kills you

▼▼▼▼▼▼▼▼▼▼▼

Rock star or brain surgeon?

Your time is the most precious commodity you have. *So why would you want to sell it for any amount of money?* Don't do this! Find as many ways as you can to make money that have little or even nothing to do with the amount of time you put into it.

MARKETING SECRET

Find as many ways to build believability into every promotion you run.

▼

Mail relentlessly to your best customers!

▼

Most people are walking over the dollars to get to the dimes.

---

when you're dealing with a value-draining customer. At some point you realize, "My God! This customer is draining me — not just financially, but mentally and emotionally — just from trying to keep them happy!" Sometimes they're not worth it, so the cost of serving them is too high. By using take-away selling, you automatically eliminate those people.

Rotten to the Core

One of the best ways I know of to handle customers is by being rotten. I'm not talking about pelting them with old tomatoes or cussing at them: by *rotten*, I really mean ROTten, with a capital "R", a capital "O", and a capital "T." That's Relationship Over Transaction. I want to have a relationship that I control with every one of my customers, one in which I'm continually evaluating them. An easy way to do this is by using surveys so your customers can let you know exactly what they're thinking. That way, you can give your customers what they want, when they want it, at exactly the right time that they want it. Most businesses want to be able to do that. But you can also use these surveys to identify your demon customers — those customers who just gobble up too much of your time, your emotional energy, and your money. You want to get rid of them, and you can do that by developing those relationships and having the mechanisms in place whereby you can grab that the information you need at a moment's notice.

It's not simply technology, though that's part of it; you also have to know how to measure the right things. Look at the information you've gained from your customers; determine which are your best and which are your worst, then go through the process of getting rid of your lowest 20%. If you're ROTten to your customers, then you'll be able to do that. The process that helps you to do that is take-away selling.

Once again, this boils down to time management, and it's simply a by-product that you get with the best take-away selling. **Who do you want to spend your time with: some guy who's spending a few dollars and whining about it, or someone who's spending thousands of dollars with you?** The latter's a better investment, time-wise, and I think that's pretty obvious to anyone. If you have to, put some extra steps in a potential prospect's way to see if they're worth spending time on. Tell them, "Look, you don't qualify unless you do this, this, and this." Once they perform those steps, you can happily take their money. It was a good management of your time, and actually elevated the value, in their mind, of what you had to offer. **If they're not willing to take those steps, fine: they'll go away, and it'll be obvious they weren't worth wasting your time on.** Pretty soon there'll be another person with whom you can try again.

It's important, too, to point out that you don't have to wait until you're booked up to use this technique to your advantage. You don't even have to lie about the numbers. You can simply say, "My time is valuable. So is yours. I want to make absolutely certain we're a good match. Therefore, you must first do this, then do this and this." Act busy, and you'll *be* busy. **Remember the guru on the mountain? If people think you're really successful, and your time is limited, then they'll want you more — and those who would waste your time will generally just melt away.**

Setting the Limits

Everyone should fire customers when they can, if for no other reason than it'll make you feel better, more in control of your business. This is especially important for those of us who have service attitudes. Our hearts are in the right place; we want so much to give, give, and give some more, because giving and receiving are opposite sides of the same coin. We all want to serve customers, and we want to help people. But take-away selling is just like a woman who says: "Look, I'll be with you for the rest of my life and I'll be supportive of you and I'll love you... but if you ever screw around on me or hit me, I'm going to leave you so fast you're not going to know what hit *you*." She sets a precedent, and you need to do that with your customers. In doing so, **you train people on how**

you want them to treat you.

Right away, you let your best customers know that you're not going to be abused. Only do this with the best customers; forget the rest of them. Take it to the point of even firing some of them, if you have to — but then be sure to let the rest of your customers know that you've done it. You should *never* do anything like this unless you make it a part of your marketing, so that all customers know the story. Do it, and you command respect. People know they can't push you around; they become more respectful of your time and end up treating you better, and the business becomes more enjoyable.

Your customers have to understand that, and you have to make that attitude clear. Tell them, **"You've got to qualify to do business with me.** It's not just something you can walk in here and do. There are certain criteria, a certain standard, that I'm looking for in a client." It's important to stress, too, that this can work for anybody; I know I'm mostly using examples Direct-Marketing, but the truth is that take-away selling works in all businesses. Sometimes, exclusivity is nine-tenths of it making a business work; it works for shoe stores, and it works for boutiques (by the way, guys, a boutique is a dress shop that made itself more exclusive and harder to reach — and therefore more expensive).

Rewire Your Thinking

The hardest thing to get over (and you *must* get over this) is to stop thinking the way *you* think about the price of things. This can hamper you severely, just because you're thinking: "Well, I wouldn't pay that much for this! I know how much it cost me." Being the cheapest is *not* the best way to make the most money. I started out in business by being a cheap date. The only thing I had going for me was my low prices, and that's what I made my USP. But since then, I've found out something very, very important: **the best prospects don't want cheap stuff. What they really want is the best stuff for the lowest price.** They want value: as much as they can get for the best price. They want expensive stuff for good prices more than they want cheap stuff. Let's say they're after a nice air purifier. There are some models that can be had for $100 or less, but they're not the best there is; and maybe quality and value are what the customer's really looking for, rather than economy. Money may not be an option. A lot of people equate most expensive with best; sometimes it's true, sometimes it's not. In any case, they may not want to take a chance on their health and the health of their employees, if what they're after is clean air — so it's better to try to sell them the $1000 air purifier first.

What the heck do you want with the customer who only wants the cheapest price, anyway? Those are the best customers in the world to pass on to your competitors! One of the coolest ways of firing your problem customers is to whip out your Rolodex and give them some other numbers to call — preferably those of your competitors! But here's an important caveat: you have to realize that new prospects aren't always looking for the cheapest price, even if that's what they ask about first. Sometimes they don't know what other questions to ask, so don't get defensive right away and give them to your competitors. You want to use scarcity, but you don't want to scare them. Do this in a tactful way; you still want to be compassionate and kind and fair with all your customers.

That said, the best customers are the ones who, when they want something, are willing to pay top dollar for it. Those are the members of your customer base you really want to cultivate. **You need to decide right away what quality of customer you want.** If you're going to be somebody who wants to do massive volume and sell cheap, I don't think you need to be reading this book — though hopefully, I've already changed your mind on that.

Run Away!

Here's an example of the kind of customer from whom you want to run away — though in the end, he was practically begging for what was being offered. Randy Charach tells a story about a client who bought one of his products with resell rights, for a price tag of about $3,000. Not long after that, the client sent Randy this huge five-page fax that Randy describes as "passive-aggressive and kind of nuts." Right then and there, Randy decided he didn't want to have to deal with this guy as a customer, so he just told one of his employees, "Go ahead and refund him and send him a fax." Now, the client wasn't complaining or asking for a refund; he was just weird, or at least that's how Randy perceived him. Of course, the client very quickly sent back another fax, basically saying, "No, I don't want a refund. Please."

That's take-away selling for you. **Randy simply didn't want him as**

MARKETING SECRET

"Advertising tries to bypass the rational side of man and appeal directly to the deep, unconscious forces that lie below the surface." — Aldus Huxley (Mike Wallace interview)

a client, and he could afford to say no. That's quite liberating! It gets into that time management idea I've already brought up: Randy perceived that his customer was going to eat up much more of his time than was warranted, even at the price point they were paying. He wasn't going to be a customer who played nice — so Randy didn't. He took the initiative and got rid of him. It's even smart to get rid of people like this as you're building your business. You have to ask yourself, "Am I better off spending additional hours dealing with this customer, or building my business?" Isn't it worth giving back the $3,000 so that you can go about finding more customers that fit into that profitable 20%?

I'm not suggesting that you should necessarily get rid of your clients if they become needy. It all depends on where they're coming from; do they seem like logical, sound people you can truly help, or are they just plain wacko? If they are, get rid of them; you don't even have to be rude about it. You can be nice as pie and still be firm, like Randy was. Or even better, combine firing your customer with being ruthless with your competitors. At M.O.R.E., Inc. we do that all the time! We put our worst customers on a list, and we seed our list as we put it out on the market for other companies, who use it as part of their new customer acquisition programs. They always get our worst customers — but hey, that's one of the reasons why I call it ruthless marketing!

But honestly, this isn't necessarily as mean as it sounds, either for the customer or for your competitor. It may simply be that **the customer was a bad fit for you, so you're doing them a**

favor by handing them off to someone else. Suppose, if you're performing a service such as coaching, that your client is at a self-imposed roadblock — a boundary they just won't cross over. Instead of spending your time and their money beating them up, trying to get them to move to the next phase when they're not ready, just give up. They may be ready down the road, but at this point, you've done all you can for them. You have to politely say, "This is where we have to end this relationship," and hope the relationship ends on a positive note.

Avoid Power Plays

Here's a theory for you to consider when it comes to your worst customers. I honestly believe that in most cases, their complaining, their nastiness, their five-page faxes — **it's all about power. These people want to dominate you; they don't want an equal partnership, where you both profit.** I realize that there are exceptions to this, but when you're in a relationship with somebody you really care about, someone you've got a bond with, you don't treat them like dirt all the time. Some of these customers are treating us badly, and it's up to us to make sure that doesn't happen — and to then send that signal very strongly by sending the message out to the rest of your customers.

Take-Away Selling in a Nutshell

I could probably write an entire book about take-away selling alone, but I think this chapter covers the basics very well. I realize that some of what I've outlined here is subjective, and that I've used lots of metaphors in trying to explain it. Some people may find the whole concept of take-away selling to be distasteful — but it's one of the most effective tools in the marketer's toolbox. **Yes, I'll admit that it's somewhat manipulative; but before you let that put you off, remember that *all* selling is somewhat manipulative. Don't think about it in a bad way. The advantages are these: you can charge higher prices, work with fewer customers, deliver higher-quality products and services, and have a lot fewer headaches and a lot more time to do the things you love.** With all of those as the advantages, it's worth thinking deeply about how and where you can use the principles of take-away selling in your business. I encourage you to read this chapter several times, take notes, and then ask yourself the tough question: "How can I start using this powerful marketing principle to dominate my competition and gain an unfair advantage in the marketplace?"

SECRET FIVE:

Using Information Products to Build Your Business

No matter how thorough a business education you receive, no matter where you receive it, it's likely to have some significant gaps when it comes to the realities of modern marketing. There are certain methods and ideas that either don't fit the prevailing theories or that most academics find distasteful, so they don't bother teaching them — a practice that can hamstring their students when they get out into the real world. The purpose of this chapter is to redress at least one aspect of that problem. **I'm going to teach you about a specific marketing method that's too often ignored, even by entrepreneurs who should know better.** You're unlikely to hear most of this information from any other source — in fact, I know of only a few people in the world who are teaching this information, because it's totally non-traditional.

What I'm going to teach you in this chapter is how to use informational products to build your business. In particular, **I'm going to outline, in detail, what informational products can do to help to establish your credibility and expertise.** Some of the ideas here are very subjective — that is, different things will strike you at different times — so I recommend that you study this chapter repeatedly to get the maximum benefit.

An Introduction to Information Products

In his book *Future Shock*, Alvin Toffler wrote, "Our society is moving so quickly today that our children have to learn twice as much in half the time just to keep up." The old saying, "Knowledge is power," is as true now as it was a hundred years ago, and it'll be even more true a century from now. Today, it's possible to transfer information freely and easily in a variety of formats, and the number of formats will only increase as our technology advances. Therefore, any business that offers knowledge as one of its products or perks has an advantage. This works for any business at all — offline, online, whatever industry you're in. You couldn't throw an example at me where I wouldn't be able to come up with an informational product that would be useful in attracting customers to that business.

I'm very excited about informational product marketing, because it gives normal business owners the ability to turn themselves into experts and draw in additional business in a very short time. It's not that difficult to accomplish, because it's very easy to self-publish nowadays; in fact, most people can create information products they could never have come up with just five or ten years ago. Self-publishing, especially on the Internet, is also a great tool for getting through that wall of skepticism we, as marketers, constantly face. **People are skeptical because they're not sure what company to go with; they're worried about getting ripped off, and so what they look for is an expert, a respected person in that niche in which they can put their trust.** By creating information products and putting yourself out there as that expert, you're able to take advantage of their skepticism. Plus, there's the added extra benefit of the cult of "celebrity," which I plan to discuss in more detail later. As a rule, celebrities fascinate us; so **if you're a published author, you've got a little hint of celebrity that attaches to you and gives you an extra edge over all your competition.**

> The pain of discipline <u>hurts</u> <u>less</u> than the pain of regret.

Keep this little tidbit in mind when considering informational marketing: no matter what you know, or how little you know about it, somebody's going to know less. In fact, there's a good chance that there are enough people out there who know less than you do that you can make money by sharing your knowledge with them. Let me say that again. *No matter how little you know about something, there are people out there who know less than you, so you can make money by sharing your knowledge with them.* That's what information publishing is all about. Even if you just have an interesting hobby, in many cases your expertise can be turned into an information product that you can share with fellow enthusiasts — whether it's gardening, golf, bird watching, or skeet-shooting. Many

▼▼▼▼▼▼▼▼▼
MARKETING SECRET

How do you become a powerful result-getting copywriter (or anything else you most want to be)? The answer lies in this quote from *Stephen King:*

- "When I talk about my craft, I emphasize one point over and over again: You don't have to be great to do a thing, you just have to not get tired of trying to be good at it."

information products start out in the minds of hobbyists who felt they had some valuable information they could share with other people.

It's easy to go on and on about information marketing. Information marketing should be an important aspect of any business — and why is that? Because **there's a lot of money out there that you'll leave sitting on the table if you don't have at least one information product in your moneymaking arsenal.** An information product is one key to dominate your marketing. If you work it correctly, it's an extension of yourself. It's like a solid salesman who goes around screaming to the world, "Hey, this guy knows what he's doing! His stuff works! Listen to him!" **Like a good Direct-Mail Marketing piece, your information product is working for you 24 hours a day, seven days a week. You pay for it once, and it just keeps right on working. Your business never closes.**

Another thing an information product can do for you as a business owner is this: it can credentialize you. **It can help you dominate the marketplace by making your clientele begin to view you as an expert** — the person who comes to their mind when they think of a problem that needs to be solved, or a desire that needs to be fulfilled. If you think about it — and I've made this point before — marketing is all about separating yourself from your competitors, those people who are after the same customers and the same *money* that you're after. You want to make yourself unique, set yourself apart in the eyes of the public. There's no better way to do that than by publishing your own informational products. **It's a way of gaining credibility in the marketplace by making yourself an expert,** and it's a way for you to let the best prospects and customers raise their hands and say, "Yes, I'm interested in what you have to offer."

Remember my best friend who has a pest control business? She has a report she gives away in her Yellow Page ad titled, "10 Things You Must Know Before You Hire A Pest Control Professional." That's just one of her lead-generation informational products. It helps educate the customers about her company, and lets them know what sets her apart in the marketplace. She needs this, because her prices are more expensive than all the other rip-off artists in her business. She has over a hundred competitors just in a small town like Wichita, Kansas, and she charges more money than they do, and so she has to prove to the customers that spending more money with her company is going to make all the difference in the world. To do that takes an effective presentation, and that's basically what her informational product is. **It's a way of making herself shine brighter than all the others, by telling her full sales story, establishing herself as an expert, and becoming somebody with whom people *want* to do business. When they're in the market for whatever it is that you're selling, they're going to come straight to you.**

Putting Informational Products to Work in Your Business

Before you throw down this book in disgust and say, "I can't *do* informational products in my business," do me a favor: read on for a while, because I'm going to discuss a variety of different types of businesses and give you some ideas about informational products that you can put in place right away. **One of the challenges I see with small businesses is that people don't understand the kinds of informational products they could be providing to their customers.** They haven't seen any in their market, so they don't have a template to follow. In this section, I'm hoping to fix that for you.

The majority of the informational products I'm going to go over are for lead generation purposes. This works just as well for a small business as it does for a large multinational corporation. As I've mentioned previously, my friend Kris Solie-Johnson, of the American Institute of Small Business, works with a lot of hobby stores — knitting stores, bead stores, and like. Now, if you've got a hobby store, it's going to be focused on one niche market — and there are lots of different things you can do to expand your business through informational products.

Let's take a closer look at the knitting store example. Kris recently told me about a meeting she had with the woman who owns her favorite knitting store; that woman had decided to publish a book about knitting scarves and hats. It's full of different patterns that she's modified from other people, and others that she's created on her own. You can do that with any kind of business: beads, model cars, even Boy Scout Pinewood Derby cars. With hobby stores, no matter what the hobby is, you have the opportunity to start with something small. **It doesn't even have to be a huge book — just a useful, informational booklet that makes you into an expert on your subject.**

Let's talk about dry cleaners. If you own a dry-cleaning establishment and can't quite figure out how to get started with an informational product, start with a tips list. Maybe you can include tips on how to get certain stains out, or on how to preserve your clothes. Suppose you include tips on how to treat your furs going into the winter or summer. Where do you store them? How should you store them? How do you get certain types of stains out? How do you preserve a wedding dress? **What are all the different tips lists that you could give to people?** Maybe they're in the form of a little booklet that's only $2.00 per copy. As you start producing more and more of those, you end up with a product line that's profitable. A $2.00 booklet can add to your business — not in a huge way, of course, but if you start doing more and more of these things and get used to information products, you'll start thinking bigger.

Or maybe you own a bookstore. Set up a few Top Ten lists. What are the top ten moneymaking books? Science fiction books? Submarine books? You can publish a variety of different information products about the top books in a particular field, or maybe the best movies ever made from novels. Think about those Top Ten lists as a way to get started in the informational field.

Let's talk about attorneys. **There are many, many topics that we, as consumers, have no desire to learn about — and yet we know we *should* know about them.** For instance: estates, wills, and health directives. There are all these different documents we know we should have. What's a trust? What would it be used for? A lawyer might have a great opportunity to put together a handy information product on this type of thing; maybe it's a "CD of the Month," an information product with audio presentations about the various topics. **For some folks, it's easier to listen than to read the material, so a CD is a good idea.** If an attorney did something like this, he'd separate himself from every other attorney out there just by giving people information in a better format than what's currently available.

Let's move on to clothing stores. Let's say you own a men's-wear store. Maybe you target teens. What are the fashion trends? What related events that are going on in your vicinity? How do you get into fashion merchandising? One of the hottest careers for high school students — especially young women — is getting into the fashion industry. What are some ways that you can get into the fashion industry? They're not going to learn that from the Gap, or Banana Republic, or any of the other big chains. They're going to learn that from you. **If you can continue to feed them information, they're going to keep coming to your store and buying things.**

How about flower shops? You've got "Flowers of the Month." You've got tips on how to cut flowers, and how to create an arrangement. How do you arrange them in a vase? What type of vase should you use? What size of vase? What colors go together? What types of flowers? There are many, many different things that can be done with flowers. How do you care for your flowers? Is a crushed aspirin the best? Does it matter if it's Bufferin? What are the tips that you could offer people?

Accountants have the same issues as attorneys. There are lots of topics that accountants can cover in which they specialize; if the information is currently available at all, it's usually in a hard-to-read format that's difficult to understand. If only you could pop in a CD in your car when you're driving and have someone tell you about tax tips... then you would know to call that accountant to get more information. **You see, all this information you're giving away or selling for next to nothing is really a lead generation tool.** How do you get more of these CDs to people who want to learn more? You could use a Yellow Pages ad, just like my best friend does. **Even when you're sitting next to every other accountant in the Yellow Pages, you can set it up so that your ad is offering something — for free — that actually helps people come back to you.** Here's a good title: "How You Can Cut Your Taxes By 25% And Let The I.R.S. Pay For Your Next Vacation." Everyone will want that report!

SECTION SIX — Ruthless Marketing

MARKETING SECRET

OPERATION MONEY SUCK!

- What makes you the most money?

- How can you spend more time and energy doing only that?

Let's talk about professional organizers. These are the people who come into your small business or your home and help you get organized. If you're an organizer, you could put together a variety of different tips booklets that you could hand out to help folks organize smaller spaces — for instance, your junk drawer. Could you come up with a small book that you could sell or give away on how to organize a junk drawer? Or how about a CD titled "7 Secrets For Turning Your Junk Into Cash?"

Insurance agents have many of the same issues as accountants and attorneys, and they have access to plenty of specialized expertise they can use to create an audio product. Of course, they could produce written products, too, but audio isn't currently something that's consistently being delivered to consumers. **If you buck that trend and hand out an audio product, it's going to set you apart from all the other insurance agents out there, guaranteed.**

Getting It Started

Here's a quick rundown of the typical process for creating an information product. First, start out with a Top Ten list: say, the top ten stains and how to get rid of them; the top ten movies out there and what they mean, or how many people are seeing them in your local area; the top ten western novels of all time. Try Hot Trends lists, too. Lists like these are easy to create. Once you have them, compile them into a booklet. **Booklets can, over time, be formed into a larger book:** for example, the knitting store owner started out with one pattern, and then she had two patterns, and then she had ten patterns, and then twenty... and then she put them together in a book that she could sell to her clients. Audio is another great way to sell or give away information products. There's some inexpensive recording software on the Internet where you can record right into your computer, and then cut audio CDs right there, if you're burning them in low quantities. These are all very easy things that you can do, and how you mix and match them **is only limited by the imagination.**

But here's the danger, once again: everybody thinks their own business is unique. I can imagine the skeptic reading this and thinking to themselves, "Oh yeah, right! That won't work for my business." Well, maybe it won't. The examples given in the last few pages are specific examples for specific businesses. **Here's the real secret: what do *your* customers want? How can you help your customers get more of what they want? I think the more you're focused on why your customers buy the kinds of products and services you sell, the more intimate that knowledge is from an emotional place inside of you. The more you know that intuitively, the more you're going to be able to develop perfectly-matched info products for them.**

Here's something that Levi's jeans did a few years ago: they created an information product, a game, because they wanted to target the teen market. They had teenagers go to a website and play that game. But the code for the game was attached to the label on the Levi's jeans, and *that* drew them into the store. So really, if you use these information products as lead generators in whatever business you are, they're going to bring people into your business, into your store — and that, in turn, is going to make your profits skyrocket.

The Perfect Salesman

Never, never forget this simple but awesome fact: an information product is a perfect salesman in disguise. Here's an example. You put out an ad, and your ad has a little teaser about one of these little information products with a great little title, and it gets people excited about it... and you get them to call an 800-number to request that information. When the information comes, it can deliver exactly those things you've promised, but it can also deliver the perfect sales message, the perfect argument as to why that consumer needs to come in and buy your product in order to fulfill their needs. **This is a situation where you can invest a little time**

into developing one information product that can then make hundreds or even thousands of sales for you — just by using the same information over and over again. The greatest thing about an information product is, it doesn't forget to say this or that about your product, like a flesh-and-blood salesman might, and it doesn't forget the product benefits — what I call "the reasons to believe in your business." It doesn't have "mind-hiccups" and "senior moments," the way a salesman on the phone does, so it's a much more efficient and effective way to communicate with your client base.

Some of the best informational products are designed to do just one thing: and that is, sell more. They're not really designed to educate people *per se,* **as much as they are to educate people on why they should be giving you money. It's sort of the appearance of "how to" without the "how to."** What you're doing is disguising it. But the specific design, of course, has to do with what people do when they get done with it. If you've done it right, after they're done reading or listening to the product, now they *want* to come to you and they *want* to do business with you, **because your disguised sales message that's buried within the product itself is calling them to action.**

Helping Them Help Themselves

Often, people will seek you out hoping you'll be able to do whatever they need done — but they still want to think about doing it themselves. If you're in a business where you can offer people information that shows them how to do something for themselves, then you can do that — but in a way that's complicated, so a lot of people won't want to tackle it. But hey, there you are, and that's why you're there: you're the expert in that field. You're the one who can do it for them, so they don't have to mess with it. Even if they *can* do it, they might still hire it out. **The prospect reads up on the subject (courtesy of you), so they feel like they did their homework — yet it may be more efficient to let you do it for them.** This works with most people, because you're getting your information into the hands of people who then can choose to do business with you.

Now, some people reading this section may be thinking, "But I don't want to tell them what I do, because then they're looking behind the screen and they'll know my secrets. They'll know what I'm doing, and they may think they can do it themselves." Well, sure. But if you write it so that you outline every single step of what you do in excruciating detail, then what you're doing is training them that this is a complicated process indeed. You're telling them that it takes an expert to do it right, and so they need to hire that expert: you.

Once upon a time, a highly respected advertiser literally took all his secrets, and put it into a single book that's hundreds of pages long. My buddy Eric Bechtold talked to him once and I said, "I can't believe you're giving away all your secrets, because normally you'd charge $15,000 or $20,000 to write a sales letter — and with this book you're telling people exactly how you do it, and you're only charging a couple of hundred bucks." The advertiser said, **"Yes, and that's the best marketing tool I have. Because once somebody gets this thick package in the mail, and they realize they have to read through everything to even come *close* to writing a sales letter like me, they'd much rather fork out $20,000 to have me do it." You see how that works? You have the ability to lay out your entire system and all your secrets, and *still* generate a lot of business.**

The plain truth is that people like to feel as if they've made an educated choice rather than having been sold on something. The idea's really to educate them to make you their choice. It's good for both of you, really. They

---

▼▼▼▼▼▼▼▼▼▼▼▼

STOP LOWERING YOUR PRICES!

Low prices are reserved for people who <u>cannot</u> market themselves effectively. If you're competing on price, you haven't established enough value in the minds of your prospective customers. It's up to you to prove — without a doubt — that the best prospective buyers in your market should be giving more of their money to you. Marketing is all about differentiation, but it's up to you to create those perceptions of difference in the minds of the people you most want on your customer list.

SECTION SIX — Ruthless Marketing

MARKETING SECRET

"If marketing could sell anything at a profit — we'd all be selling packaged dirt and living in splendor as a result!"
— Craig S. Rice

▼

Stop selling products or services... And start selling offers!

understand more of the factors they need to consider in making a choice, and luckily, your business is there to provide those things to them. But **they want to feel they came to you — they want to feel they have the power in the relationship.** No one likes to be chased around! Just as dogs can sense fear, some people can sense weakness. No one wants to do business with somebody who's begging them. **Too many businesspeople are selling themselves too cheaply, practically begging for business rather than creating a marketing position where people are beating a path to their door and standing in line to give them money. That's what an information product can do.** It can establish you as an expert, make you the one everybody else is following — the one that all the other competitors look to and are trying to emulate.

Instant Expert, Just Add Words

We're living in the Age of Self-Publishing, and what a great time it is for a marketer to be alive. With the Internet and the various types of software that's available, publishing isn't something at which you have to work hard anymore. In the old days you had to write a book, find a publisher, and then have it published. That was the only way to reach a large audience. **But nowadays, with the freedom of the Internet, you can get a message out there and set yourself up as an expert, and give your clients and prospects the information they need in order to establish that credibility in their minds. This will situate you to do business with them over and over again — because everybody wants to work with experts.** If you do a good job of presenting yourself and a good job of adding value and giving more to your clients, they'll give you more in return, and that's what it's all about.

Self-publishing is flat-out one of the best ways to become an expert. If you think about it, you've probably seen this tactic used numerous times: say there's someone on TV who says, "My name is John Smith, the author of *How To Become The... blah, blah, blah*." A lot of people throw the titles of their books around as a credibility-builder, because it's almost like being a doctor or a scientist. **You instantly get more credibility if you're a published author — and the great thing is, you can publish yourself with ease.** You can sit down, hammer out a book in a couple of days on any given topic, and suddenly be a published author and an expert in that individual field. I think that's really amazing!

One of the things I want to make sure you understand is that it's rewarding to be able to write a book like that — or even a little information pamphlet — because it's going to be doing two things for you. Not only is it going to give you an information product you can use to build rapport with your clientele and prospects, it's going to give you a better understanding of how your business works. This kind of research puts you more in the mindset of your consumer, which is something that's always profitable. And this is a great way to market inexpensively, if you're watching your budget and want to add some flair to your marketing campaign.

One way you can do this effectively is to **create information products for your website, distributing them electronically so you don't have to deal with physically printing brochures or booklets and mailing them out.** One example you'll see on a lot of websites these days (and we've touched on this briefly) is the eZine — a little newsletter you deliver through email. People can subscribe to it on your website. In all the ads and materials you're putting out there to market your company, you drive people to your website and say, "Hey, thanks for visiting my website! Make sure you sign up to get this free informational eZine, which will give you hot tips and tricks on how to save money or solve problems with your business" — or whatever it may be with which you're dealing. If you put enough of these little eZines out there — if you write a few of these every week, or one a week or one a month, even, and you do it for a year or so — then you've got enough material to compile into a book, which can then be sold or given to your customers as a gift or added-value incentive. The key here is that by taking the time to understand your business and put together proven information — information that you know is going to benefit your clients — you're going to be adding value to their experience, and opening up a line of communication that you otherwise would never have had access to.

One of the keys to making money in any business is what's called "branding." You put yourself in front of your consumer so often that when they think about any given product, your name or your product's name is the first thing that pops into their mind. It's also called "top-of-mind awareness." But one of the things you need to understand is that in order to get yourself positioned properly in your consumer's mind, you've got to be in front of them over and over again. By doing an eZine on your website — driving people to your website and getting them to sign up — you can do this. **If you don't feel that a website is a good medium for your business, you can always print up an offline newsletter and send it out in place of an email, and get people interacting with your business that way.** If you give them something that's going to help them, it's not only going to establish credibility in the minds of your consumer, but it's also going to get them interacting with your business on an ongoing basis — which is going to translate into more money in your pockets. That's an easy way to think about information marketing: all you're doing is giving your consumer more of a reason to work with you, and adding value to that process.

Like I said earlier — all the recent technological advances make it easier now to self-publish than ever before. And the neat thing is, **it's actually fun to create informational products! It's enjoyable to share your expertise with people and reach out and try to show them all the ways you can help them. It can become very altruistic.** Then too, when you meet these people face-to-face, you've got a little bit of a celebrity thing going. People value you a great deal; it still shocks me when people come up to me and want me to sign my name in some little booklet that was designed to sell them stuff! It's good for the ego, but it's also good for business.

That's a type of branding in and of itself. My friend Michael Penland recently pointed out to me the example of Lillian Vernon, a leader in the catalog industry. Her catalog became her information product, because it solved problems through the products she offered. Recently a company did an opinion poll nationwide, and according to that poll, more than 39 million Americans now recognize the name *Lillian Vernon*. Think about that. More than 39 million consumers recognize that name, because she's branded herself through her information product — her sales catalog. In that sales catalog she always includes a personal letter and a photo of herself. A small business owner can do that as well, by simply connecting a picture of themselves and information about themselves with every information product they put out into the marketplace.

One of the reasons this works is pretty simple: **there are so few experts in most marketplaces.** Most companies are doing the same thing every other company is doing: they're not separating themselves out from the crowd. **Nobody seems to want to stick their neck out and claim that they're an expert, and I think people are afraid to.** Maybe it's because they've been conditioned all throughout their childhoods not to show off or make themselves out as experts... I don't know. It's hard to say what is it that stops most people from standing up on their soapbox and saying, "Hey, I'm the professional. I'm the one you should call. Forget all my competitors because they don't know jack compared to me!" Maybe it's just insecurity: they haven't been validated. It probably goes back to some Freudian psychology where they think deep down that they're worthless, or were told they were worthless when they were younger. But the fact is — and I can't emphasize this enough — **you only have to know a little bit more than the other people in the room to be the expert.**

So really, most people qualify to stand up and say, "Hey, listen to me. I have something to share." **Once you take that and put it on paper, that's what validates it — in most peoples' minds, anyway! It's like the old joke, "If it's in the newspaper, it must be true." There's a grain of truth in that joke: you gain instant credibility by putting your words in print.** You could be saying the same thing on paper as you have while preaching from your soapbox, but when you put it in print you multiply your credibility by a thousand. So becoming an authority, an expert, a guru, somebody people look up to — it's really like most things in life and in business. It's not that hard to stand out and become great, it's just that so few people are willing to do the things it takes to become the expert, even though it's not that hard. Most people just don't have the confidence to do it.

And here's another thing: **if you tell enough people the same message again and again, it becomes reality, in a sense.** That's what we, as marketers, have to do, within the bounds of both good taste and legality:

MARKETING SECRET

The concept or goal comes first — the details come last.

▼

Go with proven ideas. Why reinvent the wheel?

▼

Strive to develop irresistible offers!

we have to think like a consumer thinks. What do they want to hear? What do they want to know? There's always something a business owner knows that his marketplace doesn't know. If you can tell them consistently again and again, "Look, I'm the expert. Here's how this works; here's what will benefit you." Then, in time, that effort (whether it's in an information product or verbally) is going to etch that fact into their minds. Eventually, when they think about that, they think about you.

Want to know something else? I think a lot of people don't realize how many people actually want to hear what someone else has to say, especially if that someone is selling something or is in a service industry. **People want to know as much as they can about those with whom they're working.** Of course, you can take this full circle. **If you tell them every little detail of what you do, all the little stuff that you take for granted and just do unconsciously, this makes it even more complicated in the consumer's mind.** They're thinking, "Wow! That's just one more thing they do that I didn't understand or that I didn't even realize they were doing for me, and that makes me more excited about working with this person." Do that in your information product without over-killing it, and you'll make money. Obviously, you don't want to write a novel as a sales piece, but you want to make sure that everything is clear and concise. Often, things you never thought would be sales points are the ones that are pushing people over the edge and getting them to work with you. **Don't be scared to go out there and toot your own horn. Tell people what you do for them, and they'll be more willing to let you do it.**

Making Yourself Indispensable

One thing you need to do to succeed is to gain customers for life; this gives you a heckuva competitive advantage. It's like my friend with the pest control business: she charges premium rates for services others offer for less, but people keep coming back, and they're getting good value. Why? Because **my friend has made her business indispensable to the client, which may be the most important thing any business can do. Any business can do this by providing customers with the information they need, in a form they want, and making it easily available to them.** Whether the information is the product itself or a supplement to the business, that's a great way to become indispensable, and that should be your ultimate goal.

A lot of businesspeople never consider this option. It's not just that they don't think about information products; they've never thought of themselves as experts, or believed that they could become indispensable to the customer. What they know is that this is the product they sell, this is the business they're in, and this is how they do it — because this is how everyone else has done it for 50 or 100 years. So they're really focused on being more like an employee of their business than anything else. They have their business; they know the product they sell; they may even sell it extremely well, but this is just the routine, the way they do things. **They've never thought about it from another angle. They've never considered the dynamic of stepping back, putting yourself in the expert position, and then being able to use that expertise to make yourself more money in your business** — and then to also teach other people and become an information marketer who is indispensable to their customers.

My colleague Jeff Gardner recently told me about a lady who runs a website design firm. It has 26 employees, and it's growing by leaps and bounds. She often goes out into the local community and gives seminar speeches; she does a great job, and gets a lot of business from it. When Jeff spoke to her, he said, "Well, that's great! But you're limited in terms of how many people you can reach, both in the amount of time you have to do your seminars, and by the number of people in your local area. What you could do is **take that seminar speech and record it, and you'd have a simple audio CD that's no longer limited to your local area. You can offer it, free of charge, on your website and send it out nationally and** internationally. Or, you can have it transcribed and create a print product."

When you're thinking about information products, I don't want you to think, "I've got to be a big-name author like Stephen King, and it's got to be perfect." That's not true! **An information product that makes you an indispensable expert can be as simple as talking into a tape recorder about what you do in your business — what it is that makes you an expert (which you are). Have somebody transcribe it for you and BOOM!** You've got an instant information product without having to be some English professor who knows all the grammar rules inside and out. People don't really care about that. What they care about is that you come across as an expert who knows what you're talking about — a person has an information product that's going to help them in some way.

It's natural to be a little hesitant, a little afraid, when going into something like this — but don't let it stop you from taking that step. **So what if you're afraid of what your competitors are going to say about you? Who gives a damn about them? You *want* your competitors to talk about you! You want them to be a little bit intimidated by you — or at least to respect you. You shouldn't care less about what any of your competitors say, because you want to be the company they follow!**

I can't help but think about the first seminar my wife Eileen and I ever gave, on September 22, 1990. Russ von Hoelscher hosted it for us. We'd been in the business about two and a half years at that time. The seminar was dirt-cheap — we sold it for something like $195. We had a couple of hundred people there, and we were too afraid to get up in front of the group and just say hello. It's funny, now that I think about it. We were so insecure, so afraid of our own shadows, that we stood in the back and wouldn't even get up to the front of the stage just to wave at people. But all throughout the seminar, people kept coming up to us and talking to us. Finally, by the end of that day we were loose, we were relaxed, we were focused on the customers, we had groups of people around us, and we were animated and passionate and excited. One thing leads to another! **Confidence is something that builds on itself. You don't just come out of your mother's womb with total confidence, do you? I think it's something you have to develop. The more you focus on the customer... that's what really gives you confidence. If your heart's in the right place and you're focused on trying to help people, then you're going** to want to crank out as many informational products as you can. You're going to want to have workshops and seminars and consulting sessions and teleseminars. You're going to want to produce guerilla videos and all kinds of different ways to educate your customers on all the reasons why they should be giving you more and more of their money.

> ▼▼▼▼▼▼▼▼▼▼▼▼
>
> *You can't kill an elephant with a BB gun!*
> — Bill Glazer
>
> People are trying to get HUGE results with a small amount of effort and expense. YOU CAN'T DO IT!

If you don't have the time, patience, or ability to create your own information products, there's no shame in having someone else create them for you. There are plenty of freelancers out there who'll jump at the chance. Randy Charach recently told me that although he likes to do his own writing, he doesn't like to do his own editing anymore. So now he takes all his rough thoughts — whether text or voice recording — and hands them over to a freelancer to transcribe or edit. He's not looking for people to change or correct his grammar, just to take out some of the major problems he makes when putting these things down — the spelling mistakes and such — and to make it easier to read, in a formatting sense. So that's how he does it, and that's how a lot of us do it, because we don't have any problems creating information.

A very popular place I've talked about before is Elance.com. You can go to Elance, hire a ghostwriter, and have somebody write something for you: say, a 30-page eBook about how to sell something. Just remember this: nobody knows your business better than you. If you're going have somebody else put something together for you, let them interview you. If you hire somebody who's going to do all the work putting together a Ten Tips lead generator or an eZine report or whatever, don't be lazy. Don't expect that person to know more than you, because they won't. Provide them with all the information they need: don't make them do all the work, because they won't do as good a job.

Then Again, Good Enough is Good Enough

At M.O.R.E., Inc., we've produced hundreds of informational products. **As long as they're focused on really helping people and giving**

SECTION SIX — Ruthless Marketing 487

MARKETING SECRET

THE HAND: Every offer or promotion must meet these five crucial steps:

1. Is it the right offer?

2. Is it going to the right person?

3. Through the right media?

4. With the right hook? (The thumb)

5. And does it fit together with some kind of long-term plan?

There's only a handful — but they're vital. This lets you focus on the essentials. *(I borrowed this hand concept from Bill Graham, the greatest rock-n-roll promoter who ever lived!)*

them the information we know can help them benefit, then who really cares if it's not done perfectly? Nobody, that's who! We've been doing this since 1988, and it *works*. You know, I only see some of my family members once or twice a year — but every time they see me, they just scratch their heads and say, "How in the world can you charge four or five thousand dollars for people to come listen to you at a seminar?" They think we're ripping people off or something! The blunt truth is, some people charge a whole lot more than four or five thousand dollars: one guy in L.A. charges $25,000. Why charge so much? Because you're offering people information that can do a lot for them, **information that has a super-high perceived value. It doesn't matter what it costs *you*.** In many cases — and I know this is going to sound unbelievable, but it's absolutely true — we've sold products for a couple of thousand dollars that cost us less than $100 to actually produce! When you tell most people that, they'll say, "Oh man, you really *are* doing something illegal." So we don't tell people that. They just don't understand the business.

What matters isn't what it costs you to put the information on the DVD or on the audiocassette tapes or into print. What matters is the perception of its value, and what the information can actually do if it's used properly. Sometimes, just one idea is all it takes to make a few million dollars. If you can clearly express that one idea, so that somebody can really grasp it and use it to make lots of money, who gives a damn if it only cost you a couple of bucks to create and put in that pamphlet or on a CD? If it can make people millions of dollars, then it's worth the thousands of dollars we charge for it.

This brings up another great point, and that's the incredible value of information products in the business sense. You have the ability to create simple products — whether you completely create the product, or just mold it into its finished form — that have an incredible level of mark-up. **You can literally create something that costs $100 to produce and then sell it for a couple thousand dollars, legally — and have people buy it in droves, because they're getting good value from it.** Not only can you sell them the product itself, you can sell them resell rights and make them pay even more money for it. That value is intrinsic; it's built right in.

Now, think about this. First of all, an informational piece doesn't really cost you much to put it together in the first place, because you have the expertise — and if you don't, you can get it cheaply. Experts are willing to submit to interviews with you to get their names out there, and may even provide pre-written articles you can use to boost their branding through viral marketing. It's really a fairly simple thing to do.

Second, you can make a tremendous amount of money on an information product. A jeweler is really happy when he can get double his money on a piece of jewelry. In retail it's called *keystoning* — where you take something and double the price in your mark-up. Our way is *better* than keystoning. We usually multiply by ten — and that's just in selling the information. If you're selling resell rights, you charge even more. **Information is super-valuable whatever form it takes.** Look at it this way: if somebody were to offer you the winning numbers to a lottery, and you knew you'd be the only one with that winning ticket, and it's a million-dollar lottery... are you going to care if they present it to you on a nice plaque or on the back of a napkin? No way! **It's the *information* that's valuable, not the presentation.** That information is worth a million dollars. What are you willing to pay for it? Are you going to look at the value of a napkin that only costs a penny, or is this worth a million dollars to you? The answer is clear.

Consider this very information product you're reading now. It started out as a weekly session in which a total of fourteen people participated over the course of thirteen weeks. Each of us in the session had a minimum of ten years of experience. If you assume each of us made only $100,000 each year (and this is really just to make my math better), you have $100,000 times ten years times the fourteen of us. You get about $14 million of information, which seems extreme! But even half that, or a

SECTION SIX — Ruthless Marketing   489

quarter of that, is a lot of information — and we learned it the hard way. You, the reader, don't have to go through the ten or twenty years of struggle trying to get there. We've run up your experience and told you exactly what you can do to make money; it's up to you to make good use of that information. **How much you paid for this book, and how much I had to pay to have it printed, is irrelevant compared to the information that you're getting.**

Another way to look at it is that if you were to hire any one of us for an hour for consulting, we'd want at least two or three grand, because each of us knows that that's how much we can make in our own businesses when we're working. It's an easy calculation. So sure, the value is there, though some people find that difficult to comprehend. You've got to ensure that they're viewing the situation the right way — that they're not comparing apples to oranges. While it may be true that someone can buy a 250-page book that costs just $20, while you're selling a $1,000 product that costs you $100 to produce, they're not necessarily the same thing. We're in the business of teaching people how to sell dimes for dollars — how to make more money. So when you're selling information on how to make more money, you can charge much more money for that information; the market dictates this. You're not going to buy a book or an informational product on knitting and spend as much money as you are on one that tells you how to make more money in your knitting business, for example. One would be "how to," and one would be "how to make money." It's the same general subject, but the product teaching you how to make more money at it is more valuable. People will desire it more, and they'll pay more for it because they're going to get more money back — as long as the information is good, and they use it right.

Star Power

Earlier I wrote about the value of being recognized as an expert in your field, and **there's one type of expert to which people really pay attention: the celebrity expert. People look up to celebrities.** It's more than just putting yourself out there as an expert who knows everything about a particular business. People want to be close to celebrities, and **this gives you power if you can create your own celebrity by proclaiming yourself an expert and creating an associated information product.** After all, it's printed or recorded — there's the proof of your expertise. If the information is valuable, fame may just follow.

Here's why. When you create any type of an information product, people seem to believe that some magical being has to come down and hit you on the head with a wand and say, "You're an expert," or, "You're an author," before you're special. That's not the way it is! If you've written an information product for your business, then BAM! You're the author of such and such. Let's say you have parents in another state and they respect you, and your aunt and uncle in another state respect you too; hey, you're a nationally respected author! You can actually start using that in your marketing. **People don't actually have to read your book or report for you to be able to benefit from the fact that you have information products out there.** Yes, that can be an additional income stream, and a great way to generate prospects for your business. But just by saying, "I'm a nationally recognized author of this book on carpet cleaning…" — or law or bookselling or whatever — can really help you out in your marketing.

Recently, Jeff Gardner was looking for an attorney to look over some business documents, and he went online and found a lady who was the author of a law book. Jeff thought, "I want her!" Obviously, she's a bit more of a celebrity than everybody else in the field. He didn't have to read the book; he just took her word for it. What I've also discovered is, when you start doing that, you're going to be getting some attention from outside media sources. Jeff did the same thing in acquiring a financial advisor: he looked for someone well known locally — in this case, he chose a guy who was on TV, giving financial advice every Wednesday. Jeff set up a meeting with him, and now he's Jeff's financial advisor. Is he better than everybody else? Probably not; but hey, he's on TV, and his business is growing by leaps and bounds. Not because he gets 200% returns, and not because he's the top expert out there; he probably offers the same financial advice everybody else does. Still, he has that little bit of celebrity that interests people.

How do you get that little bit extra? By putting yourself out there as an expert and letting the media know it. Once you do that, people are going to be pushing your competitors aside to get to you. It's just another way of setting yourself apart from your competition, like I've been telling you over and over throughout this book, so that you're the big winner in whatever business you are. **By creating information products and even going to the next level and becoming a celebrity, you're going**

MARKETING SECRET

Build "Risk Reversal" into every offer.

- Risk Reversal is taking all the pressure away from the prospect or customer...

- It is an irresistible guarantee

- It's a dramatic promise that they must gain a major benefit — or they not only get their money back — but they will also receive something of tremendous value!

- This blows them away — and will get you a lot of attention and interest.

to be the Number One name in a person's mind whenever they're looking for any type of product or service in whatever business you are. That will transfer into a lot of dollars in your pocket.

I know I may seem to be harping on this, but as you read this chapter, I hope you can overcome the notion that your information product has to be perfect — that it has to be a book that looks like all the books in a bookstore. In fact, in most cases the worst thing you can do is to create a product that looks like a book in a bookstore. **Putting it in a format that's too slick may be a turnoff for some people. What you really want to do is create an information product that looks like it was made just for the person you want to attract. It's the quality of the ideas you need to express, not the packaging,** that's important. And then there's the fact that your information products will get better over a period of time. Don't get too bogged down by analysis paralysis: realize that perfection comes with experience, just as confidence is developed over a period of time.

My friend Eric Bechtold produces a lot of information products, just like me. He told me about something that I think all my marketer friends have experienced, and it's something I want you to experience. He talks to people on the telephone fairly often because he's selling these high-dollar packages, and many times, in order to get the largest conversion rate, he actually has to do some phone selling. **People call him and say, "Oh my God! I can't believe I'm talking to you!" That's the kind of thing we want all of our prospects to say.**

If you think about it, most marketers are a

little scared, or even ashamed, about having something to sell. But when you get somebody on the line who's like, "Oh my gosh! I'm so excited to talk to you, and I can't believe you're taking the time to actually tell me more about this!" — well, that's just an open invitation. They're saying, "Hey, sell me what it is you have. I'm already excited about it." **Because you automatically have that star value in their eyes, you can almost walk on water with your prospects if you do it right.** You don't feel intimidated at all when you're talking to somebody who views you as a celebrity. You're up on a pedestal already, so all you have to do is just come down to Earth with them, talk them through whatever it is you want them to do, and it's the easiest sale you'll ever make. **You've basically already won them over, and they're excited about what it is you have to say before you even open your mouth.**

With any other way, I think you're spending too much of your own time selling the person on the fact that they want to be sold. But **if they come to you and they're already excited and ready to buy, all you're doing then is putting your arm around their shoulders and answering their last-minute questions — and closing sales right and left.** I know this sounds amazing if you've never done it before, but Jeff brags about closing ten to twelve sales for more than $5,000 in one day, just sitting on the phone taking phone calls — only talking to the people who are calling him. Few people in any industry can make that claim.

This works because with information products, you establish yourself as an expert. Pretty soon you're no longer a salesman: you're a celebrity who just happens to be selling something on the side. Society really places celebrities on a pedestal, whether they deserve it or not — actors, athletes, even authors. If you can add "author" to your list of credentials — your title — you're right up there with, and maybe even *above*, more commonly-known people like doctors or teachers. All of a sudden you're a celebrity, and why not capitalize on it? Most importantly, do your best to live up to it so it isn't just a nominal title — so there's a good reason for it, because you're sharing great information, you're sharing it generously, and you're sharing it in an ethical and proper manner.

Make That One Simple Change

As I wrap up this chapter, I want to re-emphasize the value of adding at least one information product to your business arsenal. As I mentioned earlier, many business people don't think about this dynamic. They know what they do; they know what they sell. They come into their workplace, their office, their storefront every day, and they know customers will come in and they're going to sell products — and that's all they do. They've never thought about the dynamic of adding an information product to their income stream, but it can work wonders. **In some cases, you can even make more money selling information than you can by selling your everyday products and services.**

I've discussed the formats you can use to accomplish this: on audio you can deliver on cassette or CD, even MP3 and digital audio. You can also deliver your product in printed or electronic book forms, or through live and telephone seminars. **There are all kinds of ways to deliver information to people, and all kinds of angles you can take to do that** — and that's what I'm going to talk about in this section.

One way is to sell information to other people in your industry — other competitors, really. It's a common practice among successful information marketers. If there are other people in your business, they can probably learn something from you; you've probably got some secrets you could teach them, or some specialized information you could share with them. Maybe you've discovered a process that makes it easier to do a certain task, whatever that might be. Your information product could explain that process to them — how you do it, how you've learned to master this problem with which everybody else in your industry deals.

A side note here while I'm talking about dealing with your competitors. If you're a local business, keep in mind that you could sell this kind of information to people outside your immediate selling area without ever worrying about competition — as long as you keep it out of the hands of people in your local market. **You can sell information all day to people who sell the same kinds of products and services, all across the country and even around the world in some cases, and you'll never have to worry about them, because they're not your direct competitors.** They'll be happy to buy information from you if you've got a system to help them succeed in their communities. **As long as your local competitors don't get ahold of it, you're okay.**

If you don't want to sell your expertise to people in your own business, you can also profit from selling information to your customers. I've already talked a lot about this, but here are a few more good examples: if you're a photographer, you could sell a book or a report on how to take professional-looking photographs at home without a studio-quality camera. The product is simple: all it does is show people how to take decent photos at home. Naturally, people will trust a professional more than their Uncle Bob. Along with that information, you could talk about why they should still choose a professional photographer for their more important photographic needs, showing them the things you do specifically and the benefits of employing you.

If you have a lawn and garden business, you could create an information product called, "How to Have the Best Yard in Your Neighborhood Within 30 Days Without Busting Your Budget." This could cover all kinds of tips for creating a nice-looking yard without spending a lot of money. Then, of course, you offer your own service: you'll come out and you'll look at their yard, and for a fee you'll customize something for them specifically.

Like I said earlier, a lot of people just want to feel like they've made a good decision. For them, **getting the information you make available makes them feel they're in control.** They've looked at what you have, they've realized that maybe they could do it themselves, but they still want to hire a professional: they still want to have someone else take care of it all for them.

> You serve yourself best — when you serve others the most.

In giving them that kind of information, you're making them feel like they're making an educated decision. **This helps them choose to make a purchase rather than being sold, so that can put them in the position of power in the business relationship.**

Some businesses actually use information products as a front-end — as something they use to attract new customers, to attract new businesses. Here's an example of how a chiropractor might run an ad in the local paper that offers free information: "Attention back-pain sufferers! Here are five things your doctor won't tell you about your back pain." When a person requests the free information, you send it out and talk about your chiropractic approach to back pain and what makes that better, and all without the use of medicine. **You can use your information product as**

SECTION SIX — Ruthless Marketing

MARKETING SECRET

Marketing is simply a 3-Step process:

1. Attracting qualified leads

2. Converting the highest percentage possible into sales

3. And then re-selling the largest number of these customers

That's it! There are only 3 steps!

- However, each one is distinct. And it must be done right.

"You can learn more from movement than meditation."
— Gary Halbert

a way to get new customers to contact you and then talk about the benefits of doing business with you. The free bonus also approach works wonders: **when someone orders something from you, you can give them that free bonus to helps separate you from your competition.**

So there it is. You can either choose to create information products for your competition, or you can sell or give away information to your customers and let them choose to do business with you. But the main thing is that you add information products to your marketing mix. Use them to create an additional income stream. Some highly successful information marketers have actually dropped their main businesses and gone to a 100% information marketing-based business, because of the success of this approach — so it's definitely something that can take you above and beyond what you've experienced to this point.

Will you make a few mistakes along the way? Of course you will, but they'll be worthwhile mistakes — because that's how you learn. **As a Nobel Prize winner once said, "An expert is someone who knows the worst mistakes that can be made in his field, and who also knows how to avoid them." Sometimes the best expert is someone who's failed, because he not only knows what to do, he also knows what *not* to do. So everybody out there qualifies as an expert.**

Some Final Words

Remember this: *you're an expert the day that you say you are*. People want to follow somebody who knows more than they do.

They don't like to be chased around, either: they like to feel that they're coming to you. I wish I could just grab some business owners and shake them a little bit, because they simply ignore information products. There are so many benefits to publishing these products, and I hope you'll think deeply about some of the things I've shared with you in this chapter. When you get a prospect on the telephone or meet them face-to-face, they'll be grateful for the information they purchased or received from you absolutely free. They *know* you're the expert. You do have a little bit of celebrity status, at least to some degree. They don't have to be sold anymore; they're *already* sold. All you've got to do is finish the paperwork and agree on some terms of the sale. They're ready to buy, and that's the really great benefit.

Look around. There are people doing this right now in your local area, and there are plenty of people doing it in other industries. All this is quite common. So develop your awareness, **get involved with this powerful marketing method, and you'll gain a tremendously unfair advantage over all of your competitors.**

SECTION SEVEN:

RUTHLESS MARKETING SECRETS

VOLUME ONE

Ready to get ruthless? If so, turn the page, and let's get cracking!

Market Domination

An important step in any successful ruthless marketing strategy is planning out how you can dominate your marketplace. You don't have to absolutely crush the competition (though that never hurts), but you do need to find a way to climb to the top of that market and become king of the mountain. In this chapter, I'll outline three aspects of the topic:

1. How to dominate any market... period.

2. How to turn any information into irresistible marketing.

3. How to quickly create stunning information products.

Let's dive right in, shall we?

How to Dominate a Market

To really dominate a market, you need to start with a niche: a specialty market or submarket. Look for something that you enjoy doing already — anything, even adult subjects. Obviously, you can turn sex into money; we've seen the pornography industry do this for years. And there are more non-offensive ways to do, it, too: dating sites, marital advice, counseling, different kinds of couples coaching. You don't even have to be licensed to do that, if that's what you like doing. The point is, be very careful what you wish for, because it's got to be something that you love doing and that you're never going to get too tired of. And let's be honest, we all get tired; as you get older, some things are harder to do 24/7, and you might not be able to maintain your passion for something that you've been doing for a while. **So you've got to be careful that you pick a niche that you're passionate about.**

I deal with clients one-on-one all the time, so I hear the same thing over and over again... and I've got to tell you, it surprises me. Probably 87% of the customers I talk to want to get into the Internet marketing business or sell information about Internet marketing or about marketing in general. While I'm all about information publishing, I have to point out to these people that, first of all, this is a crowded business now. It seems like every three days there are 200 new superstars booming on the Internet,

MARKETING SECRET

QUESTION: What do your customers want the most?

ANSWER: MORE of what they bought from you the first time! Just find new ways to re-package it.

and that may lead a lot of people to believe, "Well, obviously it's easy, and I want to break in." **But, honestly, it's tough.** It's tough to break into any niche, any interest.

You've got to establish yourself as an expert: That's the key to dominating a market. But how do you do that if you're brand-spanking new to marketing? You're not an expert *yet*, are you? Or are you? The fact is, if you find something you're already interested in and know something about, you *are* already an expert. That's something that most people don't realize: if you've been collecting thimbles for six months, you're an expert to someone who just started. You know more than they do. Now, thimble collecting isn't a real profitable hobby. But if you want to get into the Internet marketing business, here's how I see so many newcomers doing it. **This is the magic key: they focus on a niche that they're interested in, applying the stuff they're learning about Internet marketing to that niche, teaching people what they know about Internet marketing.** A lot of people simply don't understand the extent of what you can do with technology these days. In a recent conversation with a fellow marketer, she mentioned that she was talking to a bunch of small business owners who aren't Internet marketing experts, and was telling them about how she's got classes that they can call in and listen to on the phone. And they went, "You mean you can hold seminars on the phone?"

That just blows my mind. In the Internet marketing field, we've been doing that since the early 1990s! **But there are whole segments of businesses that don't know about phone seminars.** Giving away an eBook is new to them, too... and that's certainly not new anymore. It's one of the quickest, easiest things you can learn about and carry over into another area, and most people don't know a thing about it. At that point, if you have some knowledge to it, you've suddenly become the expert.

Here's a great example: a fellow named Joe Polish. This guy specialized in carpet cleaning. He took what he knew and loved about marketing to that arena, and now he's the Mr. Multi-Bajillionaire Super Marketing Expert every carpet cleaner in the world turns to when they want to learn about marketing. In that small circle he's a household name — and he's making tons of money without ever leaving that circle. **Most business people can profit by learning the secrets of marketing:** needlecrafters, bead workers, automotive mechanics, hairdressers, antique dealers. I can't believe how few antique dealers know how to market, for example. All you've got to do is study the things I'll teach you in this book, and in all the other products we produce here at M.O.R.E., Inc., and our Direct-Response Marketing Network (DRN).

But if you were to start looking in the Yellow Pages and newspapers, you'd notice that in every one of those arenas I just mentioned, **hardly anyone is using those techniques.** They go by the standard methods; but if you want to make an impression, you can't just follow the crowd. **You need to establish yourself as an expert in a niche.** A fellow named Brad Fallon is a good example. This guy is the King of Search Engine Optimization among Internet marketers. So how did he get to become king? Well, he started a website selling wedding favors, of all things. That's the stuff you set out for wedding guests; the little gifts you give them for coming, or the gifts you give to your bridesmaids. Sounds like an impossible niche, right?

Well, that's the one thing his wife loved: putting together and catering weddings. So they started selling wedding favors. And they also sell themed stuff; for example, stuff for setting up a beach wedding. Coupled with search engine optimization, this took them to the $10,000,000-a-year mark. Then he took what he learned and turned that into a "How I Did This..." course for his site. That's how he came to the attention of the Internet marketing world — unknown at first, but with solid credentials behind him.

Do you see the carryover there, and how it works? Most people don't.

That's why so many people shake their heads and say, "Why would I waste my time selling 'How To Market Your Business' to beekeepers, just because I love bees?" But why shouldn't you? You understand that market. You understand the customer. You may find that you never have to leave that niche; but if you decide to, **all you need to do is apply many of the same strategies you already know to the new market.**

Perry Marshall is an expert in Pay Per Click strategies. He teaches you to find a niche you can dominate, then after you've achieved that domination — after you've established your foothold there as an expert with customers and great cash flow — you slowly start expanding your niche. **"Expand your universe,"** as he says. That's exactly what he did. He became the King of Pay Per Click. Now he teaches copywriting. He's starting to bring in other elements of marketing and stuff and expand his universe. It just makes sense, since he's made a name for himself and he's got the customers. This is the way that many marketers expand their empires. As the money starts flowing in, and you start developing some customers and you start building your niche, you also gain confidence that you don't have in the very beginning. **With that confidence comes a willingness to try some new things and to expand a little more,** since you're more confident working within your own realm. Now you've got the confidence to march right into a broader arena. That broader arena may be as simple as going from beekeepers to dealing with the larger manufacturing companies as a consultant. It might be adding marketing tools for stores to help them sell more health food products like honey. **But now you're expanding outward; there's still a hook.**

That's one way to dominate any market: **start with a niche that *needs* to be dominated.** There are still hundreds of thousands of them waiting for that expert to come along. Let's say you're into doll collecting. If there's already somebody there or there's quite a bit of information about it, you want to drill downward a little to find a smaller "sub-niche." A sub-niche may involve specializing only in a certain type of doll, or doll clothing, even collectible vintage dolls clothing. Then you might expand to being the expert at preserving collectibles of all types.

And remember, the **Internet has created even more markets, and in fact we're getting smaller niches within niches.** It's happening online because of the cost of setting up that old-fashioned brick-and-mortar store, and the limitations of how far out from the store you can market. Let's say you start out thinking you'd better open a pet store. But already there are three pet stores in town, and now you're competing with all of them in that locality. Online, though, you can open a store that sells nothing but designer leashes for pet geckos and probably find enough customers to make a little money. I'm not going to say it would earn you a living, but I'll bet you could make enough to keep the site open.

I may be getting a little ridiculous here, but that's the difference between the sub-niches and the niches in a nutshell. For example, there are websites that actually sell clothing just for daschunds. Now, that's getting real nichey. Before, the only hope you had of selling anything like that would be manufacturing them yourself and hopefully getting stores to buy them, as one item they'd sell among many. But now you can literally open up a pet store and call it "My Favorite Daschund." It's just incredible.

One thing you want to do when looking to dominate your market is to **look for competition. You do *not* want to drill down to a sub-niche where there's no competition.** That's a warning signal that indicates there's also no money in that niche; it's equivalent to hanging around a place at night where there's light and there are all these moths around. You might say, "Hey, let's go where there aren't any moths." Do that, though, and you can't see — the only place where there aren't any moths is where there's no light. Well, that's great, but you can't see what you're doing. Same thing here. **If there's no competition, it's because no one is buying anything.**

Very rarely will you find an arena where there isn't already somebody there. That's proof that there's money there. But the key is, how big are they? What are they doing to attract the money? **It's still so easy to beat these people; most don't understand real direct marketing principles.** I mentioned earlier that an amazing number of niches are open; you can type the wildest stuff into an Internet search engine and see 10,000 websites supporting it. It just amazes me. But when you start looking at the websites, you'll find that very rarely are there many of them actually selling a lot of stuff. And if they are actually selling, they're doing it wrong! It's so easy to beat five competitors in a little sub-niche than it is one giant established Amazon.com.

On the other hand, maybe you could just be an affiliate and sell books about a topic — drill down into a sub-niche and review those books, really read them and bring them to people's attention, and make them available

MARKETING SECRET

Go where the money leads you:

- Find out what's hot — then channel all your energy there!

▼

Timid salespeople raise skinny kids.

for them to buy. It's a lot easier that way. But in any case, **what you want to do first is study your competition. This is the scary part: you want to become a customer of any competitor.** I see so many people cringe when I mention this. Why? Because they think, "Oh, I'm going to have to buy stuff from my competitor? I don't want to give them my money!" Well, you're giving them money in return for valuable market research. There's no other way to do it. Just look at it this way: **it's legal espionage.** And it's actually moral and ethical, too. A while back I heard about a store that was doing espionage on another store. The guy went into the store and stood there with a notebook writing stuff down, and they started to recognize who he was and kicked him out! They can't do that online.

In his book *Made In America*, the late Sam Walton claimed that he was thrown out of more K-Mart stores than any other person in the whole world. Today, he could just study the K-Mart website. He could buy a few things and see how they follow through. Buy them in his wife's name, so they don't recognize the "Sam" in front of Walton, have them ordered to another post office box somewhere where they don't know it's his, and watch the process. Do they include upsell offers or additional offers in the package when they send it? Does it come quickly? Did they call to verify? Is there email follow-up? You can learn all these things by buying from a competitor. **You study them, and then you start offering ways to improve upon the things you notice that you could do better or differently.** Again, this is the benefit of working in an area you're already excited about, because in a sense you are your own customer!

At M.O.R.E., Inc., we're on a mission to expand what we've been doing since 1988 and reach a much wider audience. **One of the reasons we feel like we *can* do this is because we started within our niche as customers.** Since then we've mastered it; we intimately know everything there is to know about selling business opportunities, and all of the psychographics that go into that particular subject matter, so now we're taking all that we've learned and we're expanding it to a larger market.

That's why I brought up the subject of confidence a little bit ago. A lot of people are hesitant and let fear control them, in what our friend Ken Pederson calls "vapor lock." But that changes when you get out there, work within a niche, and do all these things I've been talking about here. You start the cash register ringing, you get to know your customers, you start looking at other things that they need — and then you develop enough confidence that you can move into a broader market.

Most of our customers are very ambitious people; they want to make millions of dollars. Well, let me tell you, **the niche doesn't have to be that big to make millions.** A second point is that with confidence, knowledge and experience comes the ability to take things to much higher level, a level you can only imagine when you're first getting started. Another advantage of doing it for a while on a smaller scale with a niche is that you also gather resources and suppliers you can count on, people who are now behind you and working with you so that as you expand, you're not looking for the resources and suppliers; you've already got them. All you've got to do is add zeroes to the numbers they're producing. That makes it much easier to expand.

But what are you going to sell people? **Well, I'm a big fan of information marketing, because of the profit margin.** Take Brad Fallon, the fellow selling the wedding favors; he does about $1.2 million a month. Most people reading this are probably thinking, "Wow, a million two a month... I'd be happy as a lark." He doesn't clear that; the markup on that stuff can't be huge, and he's got to battle others who supply the same market. So what if he's number one? That doesn't help if you've got an 8% markup profit when all is said and done. So yes, he makes probably a fine living selling those wedding favors, but then he turned around and started selling his courses on how he did it, and started making millions more with virtually no cost. Then he teamed up with some other people and started this huge thing called Stomper Net that you've got to pay $900 a month to get into, and he just launched a video/audio sharing service that's supposedly competing with YouTube. The guy is going nuts now! **Just like him, you need to keep expanding and expanding and expanding.**

Now, I don't want anybody reading this to think that this is *precisely* how you've got to go. **What's cool is, there's no limit to how far you can go, and there's no one telling you to go beyond where you're comfortable.** So you're making $100,000 and you're happy, stay where you're at! **Look, knowledge really can make all the difference in the world.** It's only when you learn all the fine points of marketing that you can get to the point of looking at things differently. Now you can see all of these competitors and say, "Oh, we can beat him. We can beat that one, too." It gives you the ability to see what people are doing right, but it also lets you see how many people are out there doing it wrong. You've got the experience now. You can spot what's good and what's not, what's working and what isn't. You start knowing in your gut that if you can just find a way to make deliveries arrive at people's doorsteps a day earlier, you've nailed this thing. That's what they want. That's what they'll respond to.

Another thing: just starting out, there are some advantages. And this is another one where people start slapping their foreheads when I mention it — but the truth is, if you're starting out on your kitchen table with a phone and a post office box, **you can compete against major corporations in one area where I *know* they can never beat you at: personal contact.** You're in touch with the customers. If you don't have customer support and a long track record yet, how about this? "If you call my office, you get me." You don't tell them it's because you're so small and new at this, but you can still turn it into a plus. Sure, maybe you can only handle 50, 100, or 200 clients that way... maybe 500 or 1,000, depending on your business. There will be a limit, but man, milk it for all it's worth while that's where you're stuck, because the big guys just can't compete with that. They can't get on the phone with customers themselves every day; they have to have a staff. They've built it too far beyond that. **So right off the bat, you focus on what you can compete with and actually win.** And believe me, there are people who will actually pay you more money than they'd pay a larger competitor because of that.

Another area where a smaller company can compete is the fact that, **because they don't have all the overhead expenses that we have, they can make more money with less percentage of a response than we can.**

We tell this to people who are getting involved in our marketplace all the time. First of all, we like competition. We think it's good for the market-place. We encourage it. Well, starting out, they have all kinds of advantages that we don't have, because our response rates have to be so much higher just to cover our basic overhead expenses, let alone make a profit. We compare it to the ocean, when you have a small boat versus a big huge ship. The small boat can go in circles around that big ship. It's going to take forever to get that big ship turned around. The big ship can carry a lot more, but the small one can make eight trips in the same amount of time. That small has plenty of advantages boat has in certain waters.

> Catch yourself on fire and they will come to watch you burn!
>
> *Winston Churchill said it best: "Before you can inspire with emotion, you must be swamped with it yourself."*

Think about that, and apply it to a cool sub-niche you're excited about. **Information products are a great example, since they have the highest markup.** But it takes a time to put them together. **Here's what you do if you want to start immediately: go to Clickbank.com and become an affiliate marketer.** Start searching for items that fit your sub-niche; these are programs that pay you a percentage on what you sell. They'll get you started and make you some sales. They even give you the sales material to present to the people so that you can study how it's working, and then tweak it. **You don't have to start from scratch. But then, meanwhile, you start working on your own unique information products: eBooks, newsletters, audios, videos.** And when you're working in all those different media, they allow you to do it online. This enables you to sell stuff digitally at no cost to you. You can also take the same product and make them available on CD or DVD or in print, offering multiple versions of just one product. I hope you realize that what I'm handing you here is not only how to get started, but how to get started *quickly*.

Achieving Irresistible Marketing

Start playing with what I've already showed you right now, so you're

MARKETING SECRET

Your intimate understanding of your market and core business is the #1 ingredient for riches.

▼

NEVER compare apples to apples! Always compare what you sell to something else… something much more valuable…

already honing your marketing chops while you're creating your first unique product. There are exceptions to every rule, but in my mind **the basic rule is that you're *really* going to get ahead when you have your own unique products to sell.** That leads us into the next step, because once you've got your product you have complete control over the market. You can control the price. You can control your profit margin. But there's even a better reason, in my mind, for having your own information products — and that's **because you can turn them into irresistible marketing.** That's when it really starts getting interesting.

It's really simple. Let's say you come up with a 140-page eBook you're going to sell, or you record a 60-minute CD. You take snippets out and make points with them and say, "This is on page so-and-so." For example, pull out two paragraphs and say, "The rest of this is on page 13." And take two more paragraphs and say, "For the rest of this tip, look at page 72." You can do the same thing with audio. You can play an audio clip and say, "This is just five minutes into the CD." **The information itself becomes your marketing material;** you almost don't need a sales letter when you use this technique the right way. It's just something to lead in and get people's interest, and then slam them with these hot information tips that don't go all the way, but are still great as they are.

If it's free and it's got valuable information in it, people will read it if it's 10 pages or 100. **Here's the key: Notice that I said to put your very *best* information in there.** So many people think, "Hey, I'm giving this stuff away. I don't want to give away the best material." Don't tell that to the movie industry! I don't think I've ever seen a movie trailer yet that didn't have 90% of the whole movie's production budget poured into the clip. And, as I've often noticed (and I bet you have, too), sometimes those are the only good scenes in the movie! What does that do? It drives people to the theater.

So give them your very best right there in the freebie, right up front. **Always try to over-deliver; you don't want to give them junk.** And if it's repeated in the material itself, that just underscores the fact that they made a wise decision buying from you.

When you give this stuff away on the Web, the cool thing is that you're providing people with the most popular thing sought after on the Internet: **FREE information!** And what you do is say, "Hey, you can download this free eBook." This is really powerful. "Download this free report or this free eBook. All we need is your email address and your name, so we can send it to you." See, a lot of people just put links where you can download it; but I say, send them the link in an email. **That way you have to have their email address and name, so now you're building a list.** What you do next is email the list once a week with updates and additional little nuggets from your information pieces, news about new products you're working on; and in every other email, sometimes every third one, offer something for sale. This is where those Clickbank products can come back into play. While you're working on your next product, offer them one or two. **This is the perfect way to build up a list of people who are interested and already look up to you as an expert, and are now building a relationship with you.**

A while back, Chris Lakey and I were working on a new business plan. We were running some numbers and setting some goals, and our initial goal was to bring in 1,200 people per week, people who are going to raise their hand, initially, to send for a free offer. We figured that at the end of a year, that would be 50,000+ new prospects. And so we started to talk about all the different things we could offer to those people. We could offer them this, we could create this for them, we could do this for them. **People don't realize that that's how millions of dollars are being made.**

The thing that we're talking about here — building a mailing list, finding people who are interested in what you sell, and then trying to find as many other kinds of products and services to offer those people as possible — is part of trying to develop a relationship with them. **It sounds simple, and it *is* simple. It's not always easy to do, though, and sometimes it takes years to really master it.** And yet, this is the basis of making the millions of dollars that I know you want to make.

It's a well-known fact that **it's a lot easier to find more people than it is to create a new product.** A new product is either going to be a hit or a miss. But when you keep bringing new people on board, every product you already have is new to them. **You build a buyer list, so you've got a list of people who trust you and know you, and you keep bringing new ones on.** There's nothing more fun than having a list of 50,000 customers when you've got a new product to announce, especially when they've already bought from you and they trust and know you. You drop a new product on their lap and they go crazy. I've seen Internet marketers pull their servers down because people came crashing to them so quickly wanting a product, just because they had a nice big responsive list. **It's all about the list, your relationship with it, and your understanding of it.**

Remember: **you need to get on the other side of the cash register, be objective and learn how your customers think.** Learn how they think, what they obsess about, what they truly want. You need to buy from all of your competitors so that you get a real feeling for the marketplace, what's out there, who's selling what, and what's working the best. That's what makes success happen.

Creating Information Products

So, how do you create those information products that sell so well? By now, you may be thinking, "Well, that would be great if I knew how to write, or if I *liked* to write." Most people shudder at the thought of writing; it's almost like public speaking. But you don't have to write to create information products. You do need to map out an outline and maybe answer some questions, but I believe everybody has that capability.

In fact, **answering questions is often the very easiest way to create an information product: just ask the people in your market what they want.** There are some systems online you can use to ask your customers to take a survey — or you can just call ten of your clients and say, "Hey, what's the one question you most need answered in your business?" You might be surprised at the results. If you get 10 questions and answer them with three or four paragraphs apiece, you'll end up with a lot of information. Or invite an expert on board, and ask them those questions and record it; viola, you've got an information product! You could also have that transcribed. Now, if you have a 60-90 minute recording transcribed, that translates to a little more than 25-50 single-spaced pages. Ninety minutes can be almost a 75-page eBook. But whatever you do, edit it! A lot of guys crank out these eBooks that are nothing but transcriptions, and nobody likes to read a transcription. That worked for a while, but it's getting old. **All you've got to do is clean it up, get out the uhs, ands, and ahs. You can leave it in Q&A format if you want, but it's really better if you can work it to look more like a paragraph or an actual chapter.**

Now, here's something really cool: **Ask experts to contribute a chapter to a book.** There's a fellow named Willie Crawford who's very well-known in the marketing world. He released an eBook a while back that I thought was really cool. He had 19 experts and himself each write a chapter, detailing their own unique way that someone could easily start generating part-time money at a rate of $100 a day. We're not talking about millions here; we're not talking about getting rich online. Just $100 a day. That's three grand a month. To the average middle- class person looking to start their own business, that's business capital. That's life-changing, a foundation to build on.

Willie ended up with 20 chapters that worked out as a 270-page eBook, and he sold it for $27 a copy. And it's digital! **Other people did all the work; he wrote one chapter.** When people bought the book, they could resell it; **it came with full resale rights.** So he got other people distributing his chapter in that book, and he gave them 100% of the $27. Well, who could refuse to buy the whole thing then? **He collected 52,000 new names for his list in a week.** And here's the other cool thing: when you bought the $27 eBook, up popped an offer before you went to download the book to add $9 to your order and get Willie Crawford's 17-page eBook about how he got those 52,000 names!

This just shows you how that **when you're selling information products, you can create money out of thin air** — sometimes in weeks or days. Another thing is, **finding experts is pretty simple.** They're on websites; some of them are on your competitors' websites. Why not interview a competitor? At least an indirect competitor — someone not

MARKETING SECRET

Break through the walls of skepticism. — Come up with a truly believable reason why you are making them such an irresistible offer.

▼

Look for things that are HOT!

"Whatever is current creates currency."

directly competing, but someone in your niche. Take the doll clothing example; go find some companies that sell Barbie clothes and find out who their CEO or resident expert is, and interview them. You can also look at press releases online. Any time you go to a website, there's always a "Contact Us" page on the site, or a "Press Room." Go into the Press Room online, and you'll find every press release that company has released. Right there on those press releases is the name of the person to contact for interviews. This is a great way to find experts to interview and to create your quickie eBook to build a list.

When all else fails, I tell people, "Go hire a ghostwriter." There's a site called elance.com where you can go post a bid and say something like, "I'm willing to pay $200 for someone to write me an eBook on this subject. Will provide the outline." In fact, you can actually safely say $500 or $1,000 because what will happen is, all these people who write books under contract on elance will come back and say, "I'll do it for $800. I'll do it for $700." They underbid each other. What you do is just check out their references, sample works, feedback, and what have you.

Now, I'm not telling you to take the lowest bid. You might pick the middle bid, because if they've got a fairly decent turn-around time and a good record, the mid-price range is usually the guy that's going to do the best job. The higher-priced ones are going to do a good job, but they're probably going to be out-priced. After all, you want to keep your budget as low as you can. So I like to trim it down. Every time you go below the middle is when you start running into hit-or-miss situations. But the truth is, **I've been shocked at the number of good writers who are more than willing to take on work for dirt-cheap prices,** compared to ghostwriters you find elsewhere. You'll find that some of those people charge exorbitant rates, and yet we've gone on elance and found some very talented people for pennies on the dollar. elance is a great resource for all kinds of things, in fact.

Getting back to ClickBank for a moment, it offers a great way to get started if you don't want to go the elance route. **They've got more than 10,000 products, and you can instantly become an affiliate.** My suggestion is to go pick out some products that you like, ones that are very nichey, and instead of just advertising their affiliate link, go spend ten bucks at Godaddy.com, register a domain name, and make it something unique. And then you can actually give someone the impression they're going to a site that's owned by you, even though all they're doing is going through an affiliate re-direct.

You can make money with all kinds of affiliate programs on ClickBank, and elance is good for finding all kinds of stuff dirt-cheap. I don't know if it's because of all the competition or if people just aren't in tune to what they should be or could be charging, but **you can easily find people to re-write your audio products into text.** If you've recorded an interview, you can find people to re-write that material and make it more like a book, instead of it sounding like it's the spoken word. You can find ghostwriters who will take your topic and write it, charging you by the page. **There are all kinds of things you can do on elance to find any of those kinds of services.** It's a great place to find transcriptionists, too, to take that audio recording of an interview with an expert and turn it into the raw material that you're going to create a book from. This can all be done fairly quickly. When my friend Alan Bechtold was promoting his Franklin Guild, he wanted to do a free report; so he decided, "Let's just hold a teleconference call." They recorded the teleconference call two weeks before they were going to be at an Internet marketing event where they wanted to hand out the printed report.

So they had it transcribed and edited, sent it over to the Kinko's in San Francisco closest to where this conference was, and the printed report was waiting for them when they got there. In two weeks they had a printed book! That's just incredible. **Technology has made it possible for the little guy to do so many things and to make money through all these**

inexpensive high-tech tools. It's such an exciting time to be alive! And I've got to tell you, it just gets more exciting all the time. Consider podcasting: it's *another* way to create content. Podcasting is when you do your recording and put it out on the Internet so people can listen to it on their iPods and play it on the computer. **Podcasting has proven to be very attractive to the search engines.** A lot of people use them for no other reason than to attract tons of people to websites and build an audience, and then the podcast itself becomes your marketing *and* the product. Save the recordings, and what have you got now? A CD. Add PowerPoint, and you've got a DVD. **You've created new versions of the same product.**

You can even make a conference call into an eBook and then make the eBook available for free, digitally. People do this all the time. And then they tell you, "But for just $19.95, we'll send you the original recording of the call on CD *and* a printed book." Even though it's free to get the book, you'll get up to 20% of the people saying, "I'd rather read it on the john," or, "I'd rather have the CD to listen to in the car." And they'll actually order it. **Same event, three different products.**

I mentioned Joe Polish earlier. Twelve years ago I bought one of Joe's products; back then it was a cassette tape. I thought it was so cool! All it consisted of was Joe and a friend who were driving in Joe's car for three hours on their way to seminar, so they decided they were going to create an information product while they were driving! So it's got all the noise in the background from the semis passing them and all the road noise, and it was done on the cheapest little handheld recorder. But they produced this program and sold it by making a big deal of the fact that by listening in, you're like a fly on the wall. You can just see it: this inner-circle conversation between two expert marketers trapped in their vehicle for three hours. What else are they going to do but talk shop? If they were doing it now, they could have done a live call. They could have hooked up via their cell phones into a teleconference system, and had people paying even more for immediate access. "Hey, while we're driving, here's how many hours we're going to be in the car and, hey, no matter what we're talking about, whether it's sports or business or anything, you're going to just be listening in."

I know several marketers now who are starting to do things like that. While driving to a conference they will actually post to their blogs at local coffee shops along the way. Just make a stop, grab some coffee, update my blog. "Well, here's what we were talking about on the way…" It's just amazing! **There are so many tools out there now.** We take for granted today what Joe Polish didn't have access to back then. We've got so many more opportunities to make money now, especially in information publishing and marketing, where the average person can do so much more with so much less equipment or money than it would have taken 10 years ago to do the same — if it was even possible 10 years ago. And that's an important point. People will tell me, "How can you still sell information when there's so much of it free on the Web?" **Well, I want to see *more* of it free on the Web, and I'll tell you why: it overwhelms people.** They're confused and lost, trying to find exactly the information they need, and they'll happily pay you to go get that free information. **There's tons of it out there you can get and re-use legally.** This is another way that you don't have to write a thing; it's all out there. You just want to watch out for copyrights, of course. Just because it's on the web doesn't mean you can use it. But press releases and white papers? This is all stuff that's issued not only for public consumption, but because they hope you'll publish it and redistribute it.

There are a lot of competitors out there, too, and that's a positive thing — never a negative thing. Don't look at it that way. One of the ideas that keeps recurring in this business is that too many people focus on the obstacles to business rather than the outcomes. They look at all of the competition as an obstacle rather than an opportunity. But it's not. **It proves that there's a marketplace that's already established for whatever you want to sell.** Again, we believe that competition is a good thing; it should never be feared. Not only does it make this game fun, it's the best model in the world to study to see what you should or shouldn't be doing with your own business. I order tons of products from what most people would consider my competitors. And most of the time I don't order it because I want the information; **I order it to study the process they use to a) get me to**

▼▼▼▼▼▼▼▼▼▼▼▼

Breakdowns can lead to breakthroughs!

√ Adversity is good for your soul. It builds character. It makes you stronger. It shapes you.

√ Adversity is the great developer of all great entrepreneurs.

▼▼▼▼▼▼▼▼
MARKETING SECRET

Marketing teaches you about the true nature of people.

- People reveal themselves by the items they buy and the actions they take. All selling is emotional. We mess with emotions such as greed — vanity — fear — laziness — lust — pride — EGO — jealousy...

order it and b) deliver it to me and then c) follow it up.

I've got this really sharp marketer right now who's been after me. I know I'm going to eventually respond to her, but I'm holding back until I get that final notice letter, because I'm saving up all of her different sequential mailings. Hey, it's market research! I've bought many an information marketing product where I learned much more from the process than from the product. That's a lesson for everybody reading this. You can learn a lot not just by buying a product, but by receiving the sales material. **There's a lot of research to be had out there by analyzing not only the products and services being offered, but the whole selling process.** Get on people's lead lists, request information, and then study it and think about it like a marketer instead of a consumer, and you'll learn a lot about how to sell your own stuff.

It's all about the marketer's mindset. Again, you've got to get on the other side of the cash register. **You've got to start thinking like a marketer.** A quick warning, though: it can become highly addictive. Some of us can't even go to a restaurant anymore without commenting on the lousy menu, talking about how they didn't present that meal the right way, or how they missed an opportunity to capture their name as they left. Another side effect is that sure does bother your spouse or your significant other. And guests — someone goes out to eat with you, and you're griping about how the waiter didn't even ask you for your email address.

You can get quite an education out of other people's sales material. You see so many bad TV commercials and direct-mail pieces and Internet stuff out there, and that's why we're not afraid of competition: **because 99% of it doesn't know what it's doing!** That's why it's so easy to dominate a niche or sub-niche, especially when you're starting out with a brand new card-table business. Like I said, there are a few niches that are taken, like books. I hate to hand it all to them, but let's assume that between Amazon, Barnes & Noble, Books A Million and a few others, they've pretty much got that sewed up. But there are other book niches. There are rare book collectors; there are First Edition book collectors; there are signed book collectors. You've got to drill down a little more to a smaller sub-niche, and now it's possible to dominate it. Now, exploitable niches may not be as obvious as you might think. For example, many people who think of information marketing only think about books, whereas **I hope I've made it clear that the field also includes teleseminars, seminars, workshops, eBooks, CDs, DVDs, online video, and podcasting — and now there's vodcasting.** That's the video equivalent of podcasting, where it's video for the iPod. There are new iPods that now show video as well as audio.

As technology evolves, there will be all kinds of newer and more powerful ways to sell information. **The market is going to increasingly belong to the smaller company or individual, because the niches will shrink.** The bigger advertisers are definitely suffering right now, and they will continue to suffer. As a matter of fact, here's something that just recently happened: We've got TiVo, where you can digitally record all your TV shows, and whenever you do that you can fast-forward the commercials. And so I told my wife Eileen, "Someday in the future, you're just going to be able to touch one little button and the commercial is going to be zapped out, and it's going to go to your show again." Well, I just read that the new TiVos have that feature in them. That's because they know that sells TiVos, and they're going to sell TiVos like crazy!

But think about how you'll feel if you're an advertiser paying millions of dollars to advertise, as millions of people get these new TiVos. **The market belongs to the small player now, who because of technology has more power than ever before.** And that's exciting for somebody who's just getting into this! I hear this all the time in relation to Internet marketing: "Am I too late?" Holy crap! You're getting on the pony when it's just starting to go! The drink has just arrived! It's far from over! No, in fact, we're just now getting in the area where we've gone through the growing pains of the 2000 dot-com bust. **The survivors are thriving, and now we know what doesn't work.** We've tried a model that failed miserably, so nobody's going there right now; and I'm glad to see that.

I happen to think that every marketer should be selling information products. **It doesn't matter what business you're in, you should be selling information products to niche markets.** I hope this chapter has provided you with a blueprint on how to do it. The thing to do now is to just get out there and start: find the niche markets that interest you the most, see what those people want, what they're looking for, and what their biggest problems are. If you can solve those problems, whether through an eBook, audio programs, CDs, even video podcasts and all the new technology, **then there's a whole lot of money to be made.**

Big Time, Obscene Profits

My colleague Chris Hollinger, a great marketer in his own right, was recently listening to a radio show and he heard a phrase that we marketers absolutely hate to hear: "obscene profits." That's why I've named this chapter "Big Time, Obscene Profits" instead of just "Big Time Profits." When real entrepreneurs hear that phrase, it makes our stomachs turn. We see companies being accused of making obscene profits, but how much is obscene, exactly? When we go to school, we're taught that if we want to be successful we need to study, to learn, to be productive citizens. **But then, if we go out and actually become extremely successful, we may get labeled as making obscene profits.**

I firmly believe that just about everyone of normal intelligence in America can do well monetarily. You don't have to be a genius; **you just have to be smart enough to surround yourself with people who are smarter than you, which is my secret.** But the thing is, with some people it's not a popular to make bold statements that anybody in America can start with little or no money and make however much that they want to make. They frown on that because they don't want to give people unrealistic hopes. They think poor people will always be poor, and they're always going to need help from the government. You see, phrases like "obscene profits" derive from a class warfare mentality that stems from a belief that there are certain people who will always be rich and keep getting richer, and others who will be poor and always keep getting poorer. It's not necessarily true. Lots of people who are rich become poor, and lots of people who are poor become rich. **We live in America, where everybody really *does* have the same opportunity.** You can be what you want to be, with very few restrictions; and most of those are artificial and mental anyway. I think a lot of people have a sort of split mentality where, on the one hand, they want people to make it good... but they don't want other people to make it *too* good.

On MSN.com, they offer an MSN Money site where they post articles about business and finance. You see articles all over that site, and all over the Internet in general, about how to either how to get rich or retire with a healthy nest egg and never worry about money. You see them on the TV news as well. But you also see politicians telling you that we need to hate the super-rich, and that the CEOs of big corporations make too much money. We need to tax the rich more, because they don't need all that money anyway. **So you've got this internal struggle, where many people can't reconcile the fact that they want to make a lot of money with their general dislike of rich people.** They don't want to be seen as obscenely rich.

Well, you know what? There really is no such thing as "obscenely rich," because no matter how much money you make, someone will think you're obscenely rich. Consider the fact that the teeming billions in Africa and Asia who live on less than $1,000 a year probably think the average American salary of $30,000-40,000 is outrageously obscene. But that's an artificial differentiation; there's no line drawn where people say, "Now, it's okay if you make up to $100,000 a year, but no one really needs any more than that. So if you make anything over $100,000, you make too much." **What matters is what you do with the money you have, not so much as how much you make.**

Obscenely rich, I think, is a term that comes from this distrustful mentality of anyone who is wealthier than *you*. It's a popular catchphrase that doesn't really apply to the real world, because you can be as wealthy as you want to be. Some people live very comfortably on $100,000 a year, and other people would starve on $100,000 a year because of their lifestyle is very lavish. So while society says one thing, in reality, you've got the ability to make as little or as much money as you want.

▼▼▼▼▼▼▼▼
MARKETING SECRET

There is a small market for the truth. Most people are searching for the perfect fantasy to chase after!

- They want quick and easy answers…

- Instant solutions!

- Amazing secrets!

- Fast — Easy — Simple relief!

- No-effort riches!

- Zero pain!

- Shortcut strategies!

People may say they don't want these things — but they're lying! Their spending activities say another thing.

In this chapter, I'll let you in on some secrets that will let you do just that.

Lead Generation

One of the keys of business success is learning the secret of lead generation, **which is basically anything you can do to get a prospect to raise their hand and want to know more about what you're selling.** At that point you're a guest, not a pest.

Think about some of the sales calls that you may receive. Let's say you're sitting down at your dinner table, and all of a sudden the phone rings, and it's some guy with a local life insurance or financial planning company wanting to set up an appointment to show you how his planning services can change your life forever. That's what we call a cold calling situation, and most people are annoyed by such calls. **But with a proper system in place, where you can have people calling *you* wanting more information, that reverses the whole table.** That puts you in a better selling position for your business.

But in most businesses that this strategy is directly applicable to, you don't just want people to raise their hands. **You want to qualify that prospect and make them more likely to become a customer.** I'm going to share with you a couple of specific ways that I use to help qualify the people I hope to eventually turn into new customers: specifically, I'm going to share an online method, and I'm going to share a direct-response method.

Online, you can drive people to a website

using any number of basic advertising methods: Pay-Per-Click, banner ads, direct-mail pieces, postcards, or space ads in newspapers or other publications, or opportunity magazines. Once someone is at my website, I'm going to share with them some information that's very bold, that grabs their attention; and I'm also going to have a direct call to action. **At this point, I'm going to make them jump through some hoops, and I'm going to want to start extracting information from them.** For example, one site my colleague Chris Hollinger was using recently has them watch a video. Okay, they've jumped through **Hoop 1.**

Hoop 2 is to gets them to click through to another page. There's another video there with more information. It's very graphic and designed to get their attention. For **Hoop 3,** Chris has that lead jump to a lead capture page, which collects basic contact information. But remember, at this point he wants to qualify them even more; so when that lead ultimately ends up in his email box, he has other information to go on that further qualifies them. And some of the questions that he asks them on this lead page are: How much time do you have to give to a new business venture? How much money are you looking to spend to build this business?

If you look at this situation, here's how it goes. Chris has somehow contacted the leads by various advertising methods, he's driven them to a site, and he's had them jump through a few hoops and ultimately leave him some information. Now, he has their name, their email address, and their contact information all right there; but he also has some key information that qualifies that prospect. That's the time they have to spend, the money they have to spend, and their level of interest. **In essence, they've qualified themselves at this point.** So now, when they get an email back, they're also probably going to get a phone call from Chris. **At that point they're receptive to his message;** in a sense, they're out there waving their hand back and forth, saying, "Chris, I want to know more about this." **By doing it this way he probably ends up with fewer leads, but they're far more highly qualified, which means, ultimately, that he's going to have a better chance of closing each of them.** It's not good enough just to generate a lead. He wants to generate *highly qualified* leads — people who really want the information he has to share.

You can use direct-mail the same way. You should start by looking at the product, the service, or the opportunity that you have to offer, and then spend a lot of time analyzing the people who comprise your target audience. **One of the best ways to start qualifying prospects is to have a good relationship with a list broker,** because you can go them and identify specific traits and demographics of the market you want to hit, and they'll find the right marketing list for you. For example, I can go to my list broker find a big list of people who suffer from heartburn. Then I can write a headline that goes right to their source of pain, something like, "Does thinking about retirement turn your heartburn into a raging inferno?" In other words, I'll craft something I can use to capture that specific market. Having a good relationship with a list broker can help you qualify prospects right from the beginning.

In the direct-mail piece itself, you have to present an offer that really blows their mind. As you're writing, **you need to make some very bold statements and promises in that to get their attention.** If you don't, it's just going to pass by in the heap of mail that people get every day anyway. So create those bold headlines, but back them up with meaningful, passionate, and logical arguments. Be specific enough so they ultimately want to follow your call to action, which is to send off for some more information. But still, you want to go ahead and further qualify these folks, just like you would with the online version. **And nothing qualifies people more than spending their own money.**

Many of us use what we call a five- or ten-dollar hand-raiser. This is basically a call to action, saying, "If you like what you heard here, then go ahead and send me $5, and I'll going to send you the complete packet of information." You've probably seen this format used in the past. **Again, you might not generate a ton of prospects, but those you *do* generate will be highly qualified.** They've sent you that five or ten dollars, and they get a fantastic back-end package that includes a nice, long-form sales letter that sells something much more profitable.

So with every product, service, or opportunity that you have, spend some quality time to generate a qualified lead, and you'll turn a significant percentage of those into big-time profits. **Basically, we're trying to filter and screen.** Think of it as panning for gold, where you're trying to sift through all this rock and mud so you can find those few gold nuggets. **Understanding your market is the most important thing:** the people you're trying to target, what's most important to them, the best possible benefits you can provide, and more. You have to ask yourself some tough questions in the beginning. As Abraham Lincoln was once quoted as saying, "If I had three hours to chop down a tree, I'd spend the first hour sharpening the ax." **So you really think things through in the beginning, and strategize as much as you can.** It's a process of testing and finding out what works best, and really understanding what you're trying to accomplish.

We have a $4,985 package we're trying to sell to business owners. We'll start with the nation first and then, if we're successful, we'll broaden out to the world. There are millions of business owners out there, and not all of them are interested in the coaching programs that we're selling. **But you have to begin with the end in mind;** that's some of the best advice I can give anyone when it comes to lead generation. Our end in mind is this big package that we want to sell to these business owners. So how do we sell the largest amount of these packages? Well, one of the strategies we're using is a radical one. First, we're trying to sell them a $749 package. If that doesn't work, we'll try to sell them a $495 package — and we might even test a $295 package. **The only purpose of that smaller package is to bring us the highest qualified prospects, so we can convert 20-30 % of those people over to the $5,000 package.** And if we're able to pull it off... well, again, there are millions of business owners out there, and all we need to do is make 10,000 sales every year times $5,000 to get $50,000,000 a year. That may not happen, but it's fun to play with numbers like that, and to look at how much money you can make when things go right for you.

> **W**ise men have many doubts.

Most marketers start out realizing that they need to make a lot of sales. **Their fatal flaw is that they think the best way to do it is to go straight for the sale.** The thought process goes something like this: "I've got a $1,000 product. I have a mailing list of people who could be interested in my product. I've targeted the list. So what I'm going to do is mail 1,000 sales letters out to get that $1,000 sale." They feel that their best change to make a sale is to directly mail that $1,000 offer to their thousand-piece mailing list that they rented to buy their $1,000 product.

And that's absolutely the wrong way to think. Instead of trying to get all those people to buy your $1,000 offer, **why not just focus on say, the 5-10% who are going to be the most likely to buy it?** You do that through lead generation. Maybe you ask for five or ten bucks; maybe you ask for

SECTION SEVEN — Ruthless Marketing Secrets, Volume One

MARKETING SECRET

All humans strive for perfection, superiority, and power! — *Alfred Adler*

▼

People perceive specifics as real. They're believable.

- A meaningful specific will out-pull a vague generality 9 out of 10 times.

---

more. We've had offers that ask for $20 as a lead generation amount. And we even do some where it's absolutely free — there's no cost or obligation. You just raise your hand and you'll get the Special Report for free.

The point is that you do something to narrow the field, to get people to raise their hands and express interest in what you have to offer. **By doing that, you end up with a group of people much more likely to buy from you.** That's something a lot of marketers just don't figure out... ever. They never learn the strategy of extracting bigger profits from smaller numbers of people. And, of course, you want the most people to sell to as possible. Common sense tells you the more people that you have to sell to, the more money you can make. So you need the highest possible number of qualified leads.

You can actually lose money by under-qualifying. Here's what I mean. Some people are scared to ask for money to get a lead, because they're afraid they'll get too few. **But in most cases, you can actually earn more money by having a smaller group of better qualified leads.** You figure out exactly where that boiling point is by testing different prices. You should test free leads, you should test a $5 lead, maybe even just a $1 lead. That's been successful for us in the past on certain promotions. Maybe just ask them for $5, $10, or $20. As I've mentioned, we've tested offers where we've asked for $750-$795 as a lead for a $5,000 package. You always want to test, and you always want to do something to get people to raise their hand, take a small step, jump through a small hoop to get themselves qualified before you go on to attempt to make that larger sale. **If you'll qualify your**

leads, **you'll have a much better chance of making more money *and* keeping more of the money you're making,** because you're not wasting it on dead and unresponsive leads.

I know there have been many times early in my career — and I'm sure most marketers can say the same — when I put an offer out there, generated a bunch of leads, and I thought, "Oh man, this is going to be absolutely awesome!" And then I spent so much time, energy, and money going through that whole big pile of leads — and made hardly any sales in the end. That's why *qualified* lead generation is so key here.

Make More Money by Doing Less Work

This tip flows directly from the topic I was discussing previously, lead generation, and it's absurdly simple. **To make more money with less work, you have to keep selling to the people who have purchased from you before.** I see marketers and retailers make the same mistake repeatedly — and I'm sure I did the same at the beginning. They make a new sale, and because they have all this apparatus in place to make a sale, they then move on and make another new sale... forgetting that the real riches are in consistently re-selling to your best customers.

Your existing customers are the best pre-qualified prospects you'll ever get. They're ideal for testing any new offer you have, because if your best customers don't bite, then no one will. This is what the best marketers in the world do, and of course you want to be one of those people, right? **So learn how to consistently make good, solid back-end offers to your existing customer base.** That maximizes your profits, because it's such a highly pre-qualified group. You may have heard the term "the gold is in the list," and that's especially true in our field. **Look at every sal as an opportunity to build a relationship that will lead to another sale down the road.**

Here's a great analogy, courtesy of Chris Hollinger. Every day when Chris drops his daughter off at school, he goes to a little restaurant right down the road and gets a cup of coffee and maybe some breakfast. Now, there are plenty of places he could choose from, but he chooses to go to this restaurant every time. They've built a relationship with Chris. They know what he likes, and he keeps coming back because they take good care of him and have invested time in building that relationship. Your business needs to be the same way. **You need to consistently make good, solid offers to your regulars.**

There are a few key things you should keep in mind when re-selling to your customer list, of course. Obviously, it can get to be a lot of work, because **the first key is that you have to maintain a good list.** And yeah, we've got computers, but still it takes some time to segment that list so you know what lead generation piece a particular customer responded to, what they bought, and how much did they spent. That's how you get to know who your best customers are.

Another key to re-selling customers is this: **absolutely, positively don't prejudge anything unless you know the facts.** What I mean by that is, I've seen marketers go through their list and just arbitrarily delete someone's name because they said, "Oh, they'll never buy." But ask yourself: "Why *won't* they buy?" It's a 100% guarantee that if you don't make this offer to them, they're not going to buy. Now, obviously you do go through your list and decide who you're going to make this offer to, but don't just arbitrarily prejudge anybody. **Make them the offer and let *them* decide.** Ultimately, you may be doing them a big favor by making them the offer; and I can tell you from experience that the flipside is that often it will come back to you if you *don't* make them the offer. They may be offended by you not giving them that opportunity to even see it, particularly if it's gone on and made other people a lot of money and they're missing out. Don't prejudge anybody when it comes to making those offers to your best customers. Get it out there and let *them* decide whether or not it's is right for them.

You need to make your best customers feel special... because they *are* special. You want to give them the first chance to see this opportunity, because it's so hot. **Do that, and you'll make big-time profits easily.** You know, everybody thinks that making money is a numbers game — and at some level they're right. I just told you that if we end making 10,000 sales every year at $4,985 a pop, we'll make about $50,000,000 a year. And here's an example I read about Steve Jobs a while back: When Apple released their iPhones, they sold over a million in the first 10 weeks at $600 each. Well, do the math: that's over $600,000,000 in their first 10 weeks! Talk about your obscene profits! By now they've exceeded the billion-dollar mark.

So yes, at some level it *is* a numbers game. But more importantly, **it's a relationship game.** I think that the restaurant analogy I used earlier is especially apt here, because anyone with half a brain knows that, except for extreme examples, most restaurants could never make it unless they have regular customers who come again and again. **People who buy from you repeatedly have developed a relationship with you;** that's why if they won't go crazy over something, then you'd better just scrap the idea — because if they're not excited by it, first-time buyers won't be either.

When you cultivate those relationships and keep going back to the people who trust you and what you have to offer, you've created your own money machine. Too many people don't realize that they could be selling more stuff to their customers. I used to sit around and worry, "Oh my God, we're making our customers too many offers. They're going to get upset with us and they're going to go away!" But now that I've got some experience under my belt, **the only thing I worry about is not getting *enough* offers out there to our best customers... because they really are insatiable.** Given a good, solid offer that's useful to them, they'll continue to buy. And consider this: **all you need is for a small percentage of your customers to buy from you on any current offer to make the whole thing extremely profitable.** If they don't buy from you this time, then next month, when you make them another offer, some of them might buy. That's the secret we've used to make millions of dollars.

Which brings up another point: **not all of your customers buy from you every single time.** Depending on your marketplace, you might have some people buy everything you offer because they're loyal customers; they like you and trust you, and they know that you're going to provide good value. **But keep in mind that even in a very successful direct-mail campaign, you might have only 5-20% of those you mail to actually buy.** The next time, you again mail to 100% of your customers — and 5-20% of them buy that time, too. Some of the same people might buy each time, but you're likely to attract a different section of your list the second time. Just because you mail to all your customers frequently doesn't mean that all of them are buying every time; **the idea is to get them to buy consistently over time.**

And keep in mind that continuing to do business with your existing clients doesn't mean the situation is exclusive; it's not like a good marriage. Your clients also do business with your competitors, they spend money on

▼▼▼▼▼▼▼▼▼
MARKETING SECRET

Prospect knowledge is much more important than product knowledge. The more you know about your prospect — the easier it is to sell them.

▼

Make your high price seem cheap — by comparing it against something much more expensive!

---

gas, food, and groceries, and they spend money buying jeans at the department store. There's all kinds of money being spent by your clients, and they'll continue spending it. **What you want to do is make sure they're spending as much money as possible on you.** Since they *will* continue spending, no matter what, they might as well be spending money on all the related products and services that you have, or that you can develop or purchase the rights to.

Let me reiterate: **existing clients are a great source of revenue, and most people forget that.** They spend too much time worrying about bringing in new clients, and too little thinking about what they're going to do to enhance the relationship with existing clients. That's a fatal mistake. **You should *always* spend most of your time offering more products and service to your existing clients** and, really, you should see new customer acquisition as something you just have to do for the life of your business, to keep the pool of clients from drying up. It shouldn't be what you focus most of your energy on.

And again, **don't prejudge** who will buy from you or how much they'll buy; I think a lot of people make this mistake. It could be that you've got a group of clients who've already spent a lot of money; if you've got expensive products, maybe this segment has already spent upwards of $10,000-20,000, which puts them above that magic threshold where you think, "Surely they're not going to spend any more money." Wrong; get that out of your head! **The people who have spent the most money with you in the past are the ones who are most likely to spend more money with you in the future.**

Don't prejudge people in the other direction, either. Maybe they've never bought from you before, but they continue to request information. **As long as you're qualifying people properly during your lead-generation process, don't assume someone will never buy just because they haven't so far.** Chris Lakey tried selling cars for a year and hated it. But one of the things they taught in the car business is not to pre-qualify or prejudge the people who come onto the lot looking for a car especially based on appearance. Some of the people he saw wore dirty blue jeans that looked like they hadn't washed them in... well, maybe years. They smelled funny, and they looked like there was no way they could afford to buy a car from you; and you didn't want to bother trying to sell them one, because if you went out there on the lot with them, they'd take hours of your time and you wouldn't have a deal. If you don't have a deal you don't earn commission, and that's not a good thing. **So you start to *want* to prejudge people.** However, some of those people are farmers; they've been busy in the field all day. They didn't have time to take a shower because they've been working, and as soon as they get done buying a car they're going back to the field. That's especially true where I live, because we live in and are surrounded by farming communities.

So you don't prejudge people about anything, because you never know who your customer is going to be. **Some of the most successful people in America are unassuming and look average.** You wouldn't look at them and think that they're worth millions, or that that they could afford to live in all the McMansions you see going up everywhere. They don't look like they could afford a Pinto, let alone a Cadillac. But they can. **These people quietly live very successful lives.** If you prejudge them, you've definitely cut them out of consideration, and there's no way they can become your customer.

There are all kinds of books that have been written about successful people, like *The Millionaire Next Door,* and *The Millionaire Mind*, that caution against prejudging people. Sometimes, the people who walk around wearing fancy suits, eating in fancy restaurants, are drowning in debt up to their eyeballs. But the backbone of America's successful entrepreneurial system isn't necessarily made up of folks you could pick out in a crowd and say, "That person right there is successful." Put them in a lineup and you'd probably pick the wrong people every time. They don't have fancy lifestyles, even though they could. A lot of them are just average people, just as a lot of those guys driving the fancy cars and wearing the nice suits are a paycheck away from being homeless.

A Framework for Success

Next up, I've got a framework for a successful sales organization that I want to share. **These are 10 easy things that you can do *right now* to quadruple your profits, and ruthless marketing takes into account each of these key areas.** Very briefly, they are:

1. Giving people what they want.

2. Developing products/services that appeal to a specific market.

3. Making sure those items have the largest profit margin possible.

4. Developing marketing systems that identify the right prospect and communicate the right message to them.

5. Reaching and selling to those people as fast as possible for the largest profit.

6. Re-selling to them as often as possible to squeeze the largest amount of money out of them.

7. Creating sales messages that build strong bonds with your customers.

8. Positioning yourself so that you can seem unique.

9. Creating offensive marketing strategies that allow you to control the selling process.

10. Making specific offers to your customers on an ongoing basis; that is, taking them by the hand and compelling them to come to you, instead of waiting for them to somehow gravitate to you on their own.

I chose to provide this framework for two reasons: I believe most of the points are self-explanatory, and because I've seen too many new marketers stall out and crumble because they didn't know what to do next. **Business is a never-ending game.** If you return to and address each item on this list regularly, you'll always be improving your business and focusing on it. You're always asking yourself, "Okay, what can I make better? What can I do to position myself so that I seem more unique?" **You can use your answers to create marketing strategies that will allow you to control the selling process.**

Another reason I wanted to share this with you is that **you can use this guide as your business grows.** Maybe someday you'll need to hire employees, or maybe you have them already. If you have this framework, you can bring people into specific areas and say, "Okay, this is the part of this framework that I want you to focus on," and then show them in detail how they can do that. **This allows you to focus on what makes you the most money.**

Basically, these ten items give you a blueprint for a super successful sales organization of any size or complexity. It could just be a mom-and-pop operation or something with lots of infrastructure and employees, but the framework will keep you focused. Here's another quote attributed to Abraham Lincoln: "Good things come to those who wait, but only what's left over from those who hustle." I guarantee you, if you're focusing on these ten aspects of your business, you're always going to have something to do, and you're going to be hustling. It's always there for you to look at and apply to your business.

In the end, the basics of making as much money as you want are so simple. **It all boils down to developing the right kinds of products and services for the market that you're aggressively going after.** You're continuing to look for newer and better kinds of things to offer those people, and trying to get enough people to re-buy from you often enough, at a large enough profit per transaction, to make good

> Never give up! I read somewhere that... *"Success is the ability to hold on, long after others have let go."*
>
> Like many quotes, it sounded good so I committed it to memory. But the longer I am self-employed, the more I know how true this is!

SECTION SEVEN — Ruthless Marketing Secrets, Volume One

▼▼▼▼▼▼▼▼
MARKETING SECRET

The Flea Market Principle — Successful Flea Market dealers have discovered that they sell more from messy tables than from clean tables!

- People love to rummage! They like digging through the pile to find the rare gems!

- This principle is applicable to Direct Response Marketing: Neatness Rejects Involvement.

money. Do that, and the question is not, "Will you get rich?" It's only, "How rich will you get, and when will you get that money?" Because that's really as simple as it is. **Having a checklist like this simplifies things greatly, especially when you're just getting started.** There are so many different variables to consider, so sometimes it can be overwhelming to start thinking about all the things that you *could* do or exactly what you *should* do. Instead, just focus on a system, like this one, that you can put into place and follow religiously, no matter what business you're in or product or service you sell. It really can help take you to the next level, because you've taken things from broad general concepts to a specific ABC process that you can follow. And that's a good place to be.

Speaking of Focus…

One of the points I often make to my clients is this: "You must put as much of your time, attention, energy, passion, and skills into the specific areas that bring your business the largest profits. Focus. Identify these areas and put everything into these activities." **By focusing on those things that make you the most profit, you don't waste time on all the details.** I especially want to drive that message home for those of you that who think they have to do everything.

So how do you develop this focus? **One way is to develop relationships with various business entities that can handle the details that aren't directly related to your marketing.** If you're doing direct-mail, that would include relationships with people like printers. You need a quality printer; someone you can send a job to, and have confidence that it's going to get done to your satisfaction. If you live in any halfway decent market at all, there are business entities out there that can handle complete turnkey mailings. Having someone who can handle those details will free you up to focus on your marketing and those other things that make you the most money. Another type of relationship to develop, of course, would be with people who can handle advertising for you. **One of the cheapest and least expensive ways to start generating leads is by putting nice little space ads in publications around the country.** Identify people you can call who can place those ads quickly, so that task doesn't gobble up a lot of your time. You're developing relationships with these people and setting up systems simultaneously.

Another great relationship to develop is one with a fulfillment house. Many entrepreneurs, like my friend Chris Hollinger and his wife, work from home. Instead of concentrating on having to make sure all these packages are going daily out the way they're supposed to, they can call the guy at their fulfillment house, and boom, it's done. Again, building that kind of relationship helps you to stay focused on what makes you the most money. Even if it's just you and the kitchen table, you have to realize that at some point, you might need to hire (at least temporarily) some help to keep you out of the day-to-day grind. **Do that, delegate everything else, and it will keep that money flowing.** Now, having said that, I'll be the first to admit that I'm guilty of getting bogged down in what I term the day-to-day operations of my business. When this happens I end up working "in" my business and not "on" my business. Subsequently, my profits drop off, because I'm concentrating on the wrong things and not delegating them.

Simply being mindful of this principle will help you avoid the pitfalls of getting stuck in what I call the "minutia" of business. All that stuff that has to be done, but it's not directly connected to your marketing and making money, so it can and should be delegated. **The easiest way to do that is to set up those systems and outsource it.** Ultimately, your overhead is going to be lower than you expect. **Keep that cash flowing,** because again, no business ever went out of business by making too much money… unless of course they got shut down by the government, which can and has happened.

There are so many small businesspeople out there who are working too hard. They come home really tired every night, and the stress and the pressure and the strain are just killing them. It's making them old before their time, and it's robbing them of all of their zest and enthusiasm. And yet their businesses are struggling. Why? Because they're not focusing as they should. They're wearing all the hats in their businesses; they're trying to do everything. If you ask them very specifically what they did today to make bring in more money for their company, they really wouldn't have a good answer for you. Now, I've been one of those people myself, so I don't want to try to pretend for a second that I've got this thing nailed, because I don't. It's something you struggle with. Everybody's got to struggle with it. **But the key, again, is to stay focused on whatever's most important** — and when you can, to narrow that focus even further, to only those things that are of the utmost importance.

There are *so* many ways you can outsource the less profitable parts of your operation. Don't ever fall into the trap of trying to do it all yourself, like many business owners do! They feel like they're the best person to do whatever it is that they're trying to do, that only they can do it the best, that no one else can do it quite like they can, and no one else has as good a system as they have. So they get stuck trying to do everything — whereas there are other people who can do what they need done, and some have developed systems that allow them to do it better than anyone else.

One thing you should always control is your marketing, as long as you *understand* marketing. Now, there are certainly beginning stages when you're just trying to figure things out, when there are good reasons to let someone else help you with marketing. There are benefits to services like the Direct-Response Network when you're just getting started. **Once you have a good understanding of marketing, you shouldn't let other people do that.** But things like fulfilling your products and mailing sales letters should certainly be hired out. I've sat at home in the evening and stuffed envelopes, and it's not fun; it takes a long time, and it's tedious work. Well, there are machines at mailing houses that can do 10,000 envelopes an hour. How many can *you* do an hour when you're sitting in front of the TV? You look up and watch the show for a minute, and you get stuck.

So don't get stuck in this mindset that you have to do it all yourself. Most of it comes from control issues, and some of it comes from money issues — that is, you're worried about spending money, you get shortsighted, and you start thinking that you need to do it all yourself. And yes, it does cost a little money to outsource. **But think about how much faster you could get things done.** Let's say you have 5,000 pieces of direct-mail you want to mail out. A mailing house can get it all out the door in a day, while you might take you a week or two just to get all the envelopes printed. Then you've got to fold the letters, get them in the envelope, hand-address the envelopes, and attach the postage. This is time consuming. **You should be spending your time marketing.**

There are people that can do all kinds of other things for you, too, from designing your letterhead to putting your website online to creating your logo. Again, there are services like elance.com, which we use periodically when we need things like this done. There's all kinds of professionals trolling the site ready to do anything, from data entry work to graphic design, website creation, writing, and more. If you don't want to go the Internet route, you can go to local colleges and companies that can do all those things.

This is a point that's often overlooked. **A lot of marketers have this do-it-all mentality,** where they want to take care of everything themselves... and often that gets them in trouble, because they end up spending too much time doing things that just don't matter in the end, and just don't bring in sales.

Become a Good Storyteller

Stories sell, especially before-and-after stories. Today, many of us have short attention spans, and stories help to grab the prospect's attention. That's why you must create powerful stories that captivate your prospects and your customers. Now, **what I'm talking about here are stories about you, your company, or your products or services.** Choose your stories carefully. Not only must they *be* real, they must *sound* real. **They have to be believable, and they also have to be highly emotional.** There needs to be some drama there, some special secrets, some perceived benefit or a promise to the reader. Stories help you make the sale when nothing else will.

The best stories to use in your sales material are before-and-after testimonials. This is a powerful sales method, because the story tells about the problem, then introduces the solution, and finally shows the great life-changing benefit. **The reader puts himself or herself into the story and**

▼▼▼▼▼▼▼▼
MARKETING SECRET

Create wild and crazy guarantees that blow your market away!

▼

At the heart and soul of every good advertisement is a great promise!

is sold. So when you're writing copy, long-form sales letters in particular, and you need to add something to draw people in, use a story. Stories help you reach the constant barrage of demands for your customer's attention and capture their competition. **They cut through the clutter and help your message get through, enabling you to connect with your prospect.** It engages them and transports their mind to the place where you can weave your message into their reality. Ultimately, they have to experience a moment of clarity where they can see themselves experiencing success.

People tell me I have a great rags-to-riches story, and I certainly use it a lot in my marketing. But stories don't necessarily have to be about you, your company, or your product, specifically. They can be fictional. They can be situational. **They can be written to make a point, or to highlight the pain that you know your prospect is suffering.** Here's an example of a story that my colleague Chris Hollinger recently used in a sales letter:

Always Rising to Meet the Challenge

Today we are faced with a myriad of potential disasters, be it terrorists, natural disasters, recession, inflation, or taxation. We face these things daily. While we must acknowledge that there are dark clouds on the horizon, it is vital that we not lose sight of our most important and endearing national trait — our sense of optimism about the future, and our conviction that we can change it for the better. By taking steps to secure your financial future with me today, we are in essence becoming an agent of social change. Providing prosperity for yourself and the ones you love is more than the American Dream. Today your success makes our country stronger. Join me and see how much success we can spread.

Now, here's some information about me that I wanted to share with you so you'll know who I am and what I'm all about. My wife Kim and I live with our daughter, Milayna, here in Wichita, Kansas. We were both born and raised in small towns here in the rolling hills of Kansas. It's here where we learned the value of shooting straight with folks, and the hardships and rewards of integrity. Five years ago we started our own business, and soon became so busy that I literally was coming home from teaching and coaching and then working until two in the morning. Obviously I could not do both, so I told my fellow teachers and my principal that I was leaving to concentrate on my new business full-time. Many of my colleagues could not believe it, because not only was I giving up a tenured position with benefits, but I had just recently recovered from a very rare form of cancer. They were literally floored when I told them of my plans.

Since then, Kim and I have created a life that allows us the freedom to raise our daughter with all the love and attention to detail that being able to set our own schedule gives. I've been honored to be a speaker at seminars around the country, from Florida to San Diego. Last year I spoke at four very special seminars. All were recorded, and the information my colleagues and I presented is yours free by joining me on my next conference call. If you had attended all four seminars, you would have paid over $19,000. Join me on my next call, and they're yours free.

And that's the end of Chris' story. **You can see how he weaved quite a few themes into one little story.** It's a good example of a story that basically goes back to those key points I discussed earlier, using all parts of his personal story, including one that a lot of people wouldn't have enough courage to use — his struggle with cancer, and his rise above it. That was one of the concerns that many of his colleagues had when he first left teaching, because he had a job with all these benefits and health insurance, and he'd just recovered from that rare form of cancer. Things were honestly up in the air as to whether or not it was going to come back, and I guess you're always in that boat when you've been diagnosed with cancer. That was one of the things that made their jaws drop. **Not only could they not imagine stepping out and starting up a whole new business at that point in Chris' career, they couldn't see him doing it after going through that whole ordeal with cancer.** But that story resonates with people. It takes a lot of courage to do something like telling your story, and talking about some of the struggles that you've gone through.

Stories really do sell. **They help you to connect, and they help put your prospect into that sales vacuum where your message is receptive.** Therefore, if you want to jazz up your sales messages and bring in more money, weave stories into them to make them more compelling.

Earlier, I mentioned my own story. It's an important part of our marketing — telling the story about how for years, my wife Eileen and I struggled for every single penny that we made. We *knew* that there was a way to make millions of dollars. We *knew* that other people had done it. And yet, we kept trying one plan after another, and nothing was working. All of our friends and family told us how absolutely insane we were, and they begged us to quit sending for all of these plans and programs! **And yet, we continued to believe there was a way to do it, and finally we sent away for a couple of good programs. We combined them and made millions.** It sounds good, and yet it's the God's honest truth — that's exactly what happened. Our clients have heard that story for years, and it resonates, because many of them have been sending away for the same types of plans and programs. Many of them have friends and family who have begged for them just to give up on their dreams. And yet, they don't want to do that any more than Eileen and I did. **We finally found a way to make millions of dollars — and so they know that they can do it too!** If we can do it, they can do it. Our story is our connection with the people we want to do business with. It adds all those personal dimensions, it creates the relationships and the bonds with people, and they remember it. Our story is powerful. It's emotional.

So I hope that you will have the courage to take a page out of our playbook and **just be open and be honest with people that you want to do business with.** Tell them things that are very personal about who you are, and help them want to do more business with you. **Try to blend stories around whatever you're selling.** Stories are obviously very powerful when told in the right way and used for the right purpose. In the Bible, Jesus spoke in parables to get his points across; and in fact, people have been using stories all throughout history to do the same. And while I'm not telling you to lie to your customers — never do that — in some cases, the story doesn't have to be true. You can use a fictitious story to illustrate a point, as Aesop did with his fables. It's important to distinguish between the two so that you're not coming across as misrepresenting yourself or a product; **so tell people whether you're telling a real story or a fable.**

> ▼▼▼▼▼▼▼▼▼▼▼▼▼
>
> The 10 most powerful two-letter words in the English language:
>
> If it is to be it is <u>up</u> <u>to</u> <u>me</u>.

I realize that this might be difficult for you. Too many people are afraid to share anything about themselves with their customers; they'd rather not be personal, not put themselves out there. **But people are emotional beings, and we like to hear stories; we identify with stories.** If you're writing to a prospect that you know is like you and would identify with a story about you, you should be unafraid to tell it. Spend some time writing it out, even outside of a sales letter. **Get it on paper, keep it in the file, work on it, perfect it, hone it.** Make additions or subtractions as you go and as you find the time to work on it, and you'll soon have a story that you can weave into your sales material. You can use it, too, when you do personal selling, or if you talk to people on the phone or do presentations from a stage.

People can identify with and appreciate you if you're honest in this fashion (remember the power of honesty?). Oftentimes, people try to *hide* behind their company. They want people to think that they're perfect, that they're not human. And yet, we're all human, and everybody knows that; so why hide it? Why not just tell people a little about who you are and where you came from? This is especially important to the degree that it helps you tell people why they should do business with you; it involves a little more rapport-building, which is always good.

In addition to stories about yourself, **you can tell stories about your product.** Let's say you have a great product you discovered; you can tell the story about how you went to a remote jungle in Africa and came back with this cure for this disease, how all you have to do is eat this special fruit that you discovered and all your worries are gone; those kinds of

MARKETING SECRET

In lead generation, the more you tell — the less you sell!

- Just give them enough information to get them interested and excited! Make them an irresistible promise and get them to send for more information.

things. **You can learn great storytelling by reading catalogs.** Some catalogs, like J. Pederson and Brookstone, have very good copywriters who do a lot of explaining about the thought processes behind the product or a story. That helps draw you in, and shows you why that product is good.

It should go without saying that how you word your story can determine its impact. You could tell the same story multiple ways; one way might be a boring, dry way, while you could say the same thing in another way so that it comes across as emotional, tugging at the heartstrings. **So take your story and learn how to write it in such a way that it draws on people's emotions, and storytelling can be a big sales tool.**

Appealing to the Prospect

In this section, I'm going to re-emphasize a truth that I think too many would-be entrepreneurs miss completely: **it's all about the *prospect*, not the product.** In a larger sense, it's all about the market. **The market is comprised of prospects with similar wants, needs, and desires, with desire being very important.** I've seen marketers fall in love with a product that was indeed needed, but not desired (and I'll be the first to admit that I've done this also). Then the marketer didn't do a very good job of creating desire for the product, and was dismayed when the market rejected their product. To avoid this, you want to really focus on and understand your market and your prospect. **You really need to know what the prospect and the market *really* want.** You need to know exactly who your ideal prospect is; you need to know what they love, what they fear, and what they want most. **And you *absolutely* need to know what in their life is causing them the most pain,** because as I've told you more than once, pain is very important when it comes to this form of marketing. Once you know these things, you need to have the intestinal fortitude to, in essence, jab a red-hot poker into the prospect's heart and twist it as hard as you can so that they can feel the worst imaginable pain (I'm speaking metaphorically here, of course, within the realm of your marketing). **And *then* you can craft a message that's intended to create incredible desire for your product, service, or opportunity.**

Here's a proven way to do that, using your knowledge of the prospect's wants, needs, and desires and what causes them pain: **Start by identifying the biggest selling points of your product. Then find a way to put your prospect in as much pain as possible.** You've got to make them feel it! You really stick that red-hot poker into their deepest fear and twist, and then add some rock salt and grind it in. **Once your prospect is properly painful, you give them the most logical solution to relieve their pain, heavily dosed with your main selling points.** People will do almost anything to avoid pain. This simple tidbit of information has produced billions of dollars in sales, and continues to profit savvy marketers worldwide every day.

So you use these emotional factors to first create pain, and then offer them the solution to that pain. In some ways, it's a terrible, terrible metaphor, this idea of peeling back the scab and pouring salt in there. But it goes back to the last thing we talked about, with the stories. Once you visualize this analogy, you'll never forget it — which is another purpose of telling stories, by the way. People remember stories. **And people will always do more to avoid pain than they will to gain pleasure; that's Psychology 101, and, after all, marketing is just math and psychology.** So *you're* the one that has to put people in pain. *You've* got to make them see that not having what you're offering them will be potentially painful — that they're going to miss out on something very, very special — and you've got to make it real.

Given the number of competitors who are after the prospects you're after, you need to wake up and understand this, and know in your gut why people buy what they buy. That's much more important than the products themselves. When we tell people that products don't matter, **what we're really saying is that the *market* is more important, and that you've got**

to match the products to the marketplace.

Sometimes — again, to illustrate the point you use a story, and in this case it's an analogy — it's salt in a wound. It burns in your mind, because everybody knows how that feels; or if you don't, you can guess. Again, we're coming at this from the premise that you have a solution to their pain. You're not just being mean and rubbing in the pain like a bully on the playground. **You're identifying their pain because you have a solution; and in order to make the solution real, you must first remind them of the degree of their pain.** It's the reminder that brings out the desire for your solution, which is what makes people want your product — because your product cleans the salt away and heals the wound.

Going back to the original point, you have a much better opportunity for profit if you stop focusing so much on the products and start focusing more on the prospects. **It doesn't matter what you sell so much as who you sell to. Your marketplace really determines what you sell.** Too many people go into business thinking otherwise; they have an idea for a product, and from that idea comes the product development. After it's is developed, they sit in their office, admiring their little work of art. Then they start thinking, "Okay, now that I've got this product, who am I going to sell it to?" They struggle, then, with trying to find a marketplace for the product they just created. **Well, you should never have to find a marketplace for your product, because you *start* with the marketplace, and then you find the product the marketplace wants.**

People will always buy what they want, and they'll always buy more of what they're already spending money on. If you can identify a group of people who are spending money on certain kinds of products and services, then you can come along and offer a newer, better, faster, more convenient product or service that fills those same wants in a better way, and you can make a profit. *It starts with the marketplace.* Never get that out of your head. Write it down. Hang in on your wall. Put it next to your bathroom mirror. Stick it someplace in your car, maybe, where you can look at it every day. The marketplace *always* comes before the product. Always, always, always. **If you'll remember that, you'll never struggle for what to sell.** You'll only struggle figuring out what the marketplace wants. Let the product follow the marketplace, and you can create a never-ending stream of products and services to offer to that marketplace once you've identified it. And once you've identified one marketplace, there's nothing to keep you from identifying others that you can tap into with other products and services.

I would look for markets that are very, very rabid. Not long ago, Chris Lakey and I were looking at a rather large market that we wanted to sell our products and services to. It turns out it was a fragmented market and, what's even more, the people in that market weren't really excited about the types of things we wanted to sell anyway. We knew that because there was such an absence of good, strong competitors. That was the one telltale sign, having done a little bit of research. **What you're looking for are places where other people are already making a ton of money!** I know it sounds like common sense, and yet so many people want to be the pioneers. They go out there and fall in love with these products, or they fall in love with a group of people they want to sell something to. They see a lack of competition, and don't even realize that it's because the market they want to sell to isn't crazy about the types of things that they offer. **You always go in the areas where other people are making a lot of money, and design your initial products and services to be very similar to what other people are selling right now.** The time to be creative, the time to be the pioneer, the time to go out there and experiment, is when you already have millions in the bank — or however else you define being financially secure. That's when you can test your other ideas and experiment with markets where there's an absence of competitors.

On TV once, I saw a little special documentary about Simon Cowell, the guy who started American Idol. Obviously, he's a music guy. One of the things they mentioned was the fact that in the mid- to late-1990s, he noticed that people all over the world were going crazy about these humongous professional wrestlers like The Rock and Stone Cold Steve Austin. He saw that people were already making a lot of money with that market, and there was a lot of interest and desire connected with these wrestlers, so he convinced them to cut their own albums. And even though the music was horrible, that was one of his first big breaks. He sold literally millions of recordings of professional wrestlers doing their best to be singers. The market was rabid for these guys; **he just gave them another product and, in turn, made millions of dollars.** And then he kept expanding and expanding, looking for other unique areas to excel in.

Simon Cowell was filling a demand that wrestling fans had; he was able to get on the other side of the cash register and understand his market

> ### MARKETING SECRET
>
> "No man is happy without a delusion of some kind. Delusions are as necessary to our happiness as realities." — Christian Bouse
>
> ▼
>
> Your job is to find the biggest ideas that will captivate the imagination of your market!

at a deep level. That's part of what getting on the other side of the cash register means. Stop thinking like a consumer; start thinking like a marketer. **Start looking at what other people are doing, and ask yourself how you can do things that are similar.**

Now, that anecdote on the previous page is part of Simon Cowell's story. If you don't have your own yet, start working on it; sit down and write a little about who you are, and why people could identify — or would want to identify — with you and your story. And don't write your story as it is, necessarily; maybe you haven't achieved success yet, and at the moment your story is all about struggle. **Go ahead and write your story as if you've gone ahead and found success, because you eventually will if you keep working at it.** When you get there your story can be already written — all you need to do is work in the details.

Dispelling the Marketing Fog

To start off this chapter, I want to take you back about 60 years ago, for just a moment. If you're older than 50ish, you might remember this: London, Friday, December 5, 1952. That date might not mean much to you, but it's well-remembered across the pond, because it's the date of a huge catastrophe. It was a cold winter, and on December 5, everybody was burning coal in their fireplaces to heat their homes. Due to the extreme cold, the smoke from the coal fires was trapped in the city, and it combined with the natural moisture in the air to create this huge fog.

The fog set in thick. At that time, it wasn't that uncommon for there to be a fog over London, so people didn't think too much of it; but by December 7, the fog was so thick that visibility fell to just about a foot. People could literally hold their hand a foot in front of their face and not see it. They couldn't see their shoes.

Hundreds of people died the first day from respiratory distress due to the smog. Within four days, something like 4,000 people had died; the smog had choked the life out of them. They couldn't breathe, and couldn't see to go anywhere. Ambulances stopped running because of the lack of visibility. Business, theaters, concerts, and the like shut down. In the subsequent coming weeks and months, another 8,000 people or so died because of the effects of the December 1952 fog; many survivors of the actual event later developed lung conditions or pneumonia, or had complications from those, so as many 12,000 people died from this unnaturally thick fog.

Of course, that was a tragic event, and a horrible situation; but I think it offers a good analogy to marketing in many instances. **Marketers sometimes sit in this kind of fog; we feel like we have a little information, yet it's indistinct and hard to see.** We can't really see the connections, and we don't know which way is up or down. We're all confused, and without the right help — without someone grabbing us and showing us which way we're going — we're like those people in London in 1952. We just can't see more than a foot in front of our faces and we're destined to fail. **We need some help and we need someone to show us the right way.**

That's what we do with the Direct-Response Network, and that's what I'll present in this chapter. **The idea is to hopefully lift that fog, at least briefly.** If you've been sitting around feeling confused, not really sure where to turn, what to do, or which direction to go, hopefully these strategies will help lift the fog you've been experiencing, help you come out of the haze, and reveal a clear direction to start you down your road to success.

The Minnow and the Whale

Here's a fundamental truth of life: you can't catch a whale by using a minnow as bait. Now, think about that. **If you want something big to happen, as in making big sales and big profits, you've got to do big things!** Bill Glazer, a marketing expert who's a real hero of mine, puts it a bit differently: he says that most businesspeople are trying to shoot an elephant using a BB gun.

Now, here's where the fog analogy comes into play. Most businesspeople are so deluded in their expectations, it's almost as if they're in a fog. **They simply don't realize the high level of forces working against them on a daily basis.** Some of these forces include increased competition, lower profit margins, and consumers who are more and more demanding all of the time. There used to be that phrase that went, "The customer is king." Well, these days, customers are more like dictators than kings. There's a growing skepticism in the marketplace, and that's not going away; it's only going to get worse. **People also have a tremendous amount of apathy towards most marketing messages.** They've learned how to tune them out because of the information overload problem; they feel too overwhelmed to listen to everything, and don't want to learn anything anymore.

There's hostility against advertisers. Everybody hits the "mute" button when a commercial comes on the TV, and there's a strong resistance to all sales messages. **The average consumer today is more educated than ever, and is very cynical, too.** They're on guard constantly; they don't believe a word that you say. And yet, most businesspeople are so "fogged in" that they think that all they have to do is run a few ads or a few TV spots, or drop a few postcards in the mail, and people are going to automatically rush to them. That's a real delusion.

This is one of the big reasons we teach Direct-Mail Marketing (DRM) as the most effective way of doing business, compared with the ad agency methods of advertising. As a small business especially, ad agencies push you to just put your name in the Yellow Pages so that if anybody needs you, they'll find you. Or the businessperson might think, "I'm only going to use word of mouth, and if people want me, they know where I'm at." This all comes back to the quote a mentioned earlier, which is attributed to P.T. Barnum: "You can't catch a whale by using a minnow as bait." Now, I used to fish a lot when I was younger, and I know that you always match your bait to whatever fish you're trying to catch. When you're after little fish, you need a tiny hook and little bit of worm or a

> **Customers go where they are invited — and stay where they are appreciated.**

piece of corn, because otherwise the fishes can't get the hook in their mouth. And there are other times when you want to try to catch huge catfish, so you use larger hooks with bigger bait. Now, maybe you first catch little fish so you can use them to catch the larger fish. Someone who didn't know better might ask you, "Why are you using such a big fish for bait? You're only going to catch a big fish." Well, duh — that's what you want to do! **You're being *selective*.** If the fish is too small you don't want it, so you do your best to arrange things so they can't take the bait. The only way to catch a whale is to use a giant hook and a substantial bait. **The point here is that you have to match the tackle and bait to whatever you're trying to catch.**

In business, you're trying to catch the best possible customers, folks who will spend the largest amount of money for the longest amount of time; so minnows are out. That also means using the right bait — if your target market has no interest in what you're offering, you're probably not going to catch their attention. And if you're using the using the wrong advertising, you're not going to catch them, either. **You have to have to present the right offer (the bait) with the right advertising in the appropriate medium (the tackle).**

The unfortunate reality with most business owners is that when they start a business, all they do is buy themselves a job — and admittedly, they're usually good at what they do. Let's say they're a dry cleaner; well, they're probably really good at cleaning clothes, and can get a stain out like nobody's business. **But it's just as likely that they have no clue how to market their business, and no interest in learning how to do so.** And so all they are is a good dry cleaner. Similarly, someone who has a local clothing store may be really good at measuring you and helping you pick out just the right suit for that special occasion, but they have no clue or interest in learning how to market their business and attract more customers. The two traits often go hand in hand, but what good is a new business that you just start without the ability to advertise and bring in new customers, and continue to resell to the customers you have?

So you have to keep alert to the marketing opportunities, and you have to keep current, because of the problems I've already mentioned:

MARKETING SECRET

Selling and marketing is the ultimate game!

- Show me any game or sport without 10-tons of obstacles and challenges — and I'll show you one boring game! The only game worth playing is the one that lets you test your skills on a daily basis.

- Entrepreneurs thrive on challenges! We welcome the adversity. We need the problems, challenges, and obstacles. Without these things, the game is pretty boring.

the increased competition, the lower profit margins, customer apathy, and consumers who are savvier than they used to be. The Internet has continuously crept more and more into our lives. These days you can buy a refrigerator with an Internet connection built right into them, so it will keep track of your groceries and tell you when you need to go to the store. You can go virtually anywhere the world, and handheld devices keep the Internet at your fingertips. **The Internet is making people smarter consumers because they can research on the world wide web,** find out more about the products, and find out whether they should shop with you or the competition. **They're more educated these days, and demand better service.**

Even 10 years ago, if you were going to buy a new car you had to do a lot of digging to find out what the dealer paid for it. Today it's easy to go on the Internet, pick out the car you want, and know exactly what the dealer bought that car from the factory for. **That means that as a consumer, you have the ability to go in and demand a price.** You can say, "I think that on this particular car, a good profit for you is $150," and they would say, "How do you know how much profit we're making?" You tell them, "I know that you paid this much from the factory, so I'm going to pay you *this* much, and that should leave you a profit of $150." The Internet gives you increased knowledge of the market at a low cost. **As a consumer, that's great; as a marketer, it puts you at a disadvantage.**

Plus, again, there's a lot of doubt in the marketplace in general. **People aren't as trusting *or* as trustworthy as they used to be, so that means there's more questioning.**

Apathy shoots you down; it's so easy to zap forward on your DVR or TiVo and skip the commercials altogether. Many people turn off the radio or change the channel during commercials, if they even listen to a radio anymore. Since people have grown used to just tuning out the sales message, **you've got to do something to stand up and make them pay attention.** People are overloaded with information, and they lead such busy lives these days. If they've got a family, they probably have a kid going this direction one night and a kid going another direction another night. They've got soccer practice, football practice, baseball practice, basketball practice, choir, and school programs in the evening. All these things go on, and they take up people's time. Because people are so overloaded, not only with information but with busy schedules, **you've got to cut through the clutter.**

In general, too, people are resistant to sales messages. **They don't want to be sold — but it's clear that they not only want to buy things, they** *love* **to buy.** If you look at the numbers, even in a bad economy, you'll see that people will still spend their money. People want to buy the things they want to buy. But they don't want to be sold, so you have to break through that reluctance and deliver a sales message that makes them want what you offer. **At the same time, you want them to feel they're making the choice to buy from you, not that they're being pressured into buying something.** They want to feel like they're making the buying decision.

That's where direct-mail comes in; it's part of this whole strategy of using the right bait to catch the right fish. With direct-mail, you can either compile or rent a mailing list of people who are interested in what you have to offer, contact them, and use the method of qualifying leads I talked about earlier to deal specifically with people who you *know* are interested in your offer. **In fact, they asked you to make your pitch.** You can use direct-mail strategies through classified advertising or display advertising; even small businesses can use Yellow Page advertising effectively this way, by getting people to raise their hand and say they're interested in what you have or by getting them to call a phone number, visit a website, or whatever so that you can capture that lead, get them to give you their contact information so that you can present them with your sales message, and give them an opportunity to buy what you're selling. **If you'll do that the right way, you'll cut through that fog.**

The fog analogy is a good one for another reason: Not only are most businesspeople absolutely blind to all the changing market forces that result in more customer cynicism and sales resistance, **they also have a tendency to think people are excited about their product or service just because they are.** Nothing could be further from the truth. It's a mistake that entrepreneurs make all the time, since they love what they're selling. Well, that doesn't necessarily mean other people love it or are even interested in it. And this whole idea that things just sell themselves is one of the biggest lies I've ever heard. It may have been true 200 years ago, but it ain't true today. *Nothing* **sells itself.** Whenever you start hearing somebody try to pitch you on something that sells itself, they're either lying to you or they're deluded themselves — in which case you're still being lied to in an indirect way.

Now, I don't want you to think that any of this is negative, because it's not negative at all. **This is** *reality.* There are certain forces out there that are working against all of us, but that's no reason for you to put your tail between your legs and tell yourself that you can't go out there and make a lot of money. On the contrary, **there's never been a time in history for the average person, someone who has no special knowledge, no special skills, no special abilities, to go out there and make millions!** In fact, with today's technology, including Federal Express and other distribution systems, Internet technologies, modern personal computers and cellular technologies and all of the future technology that will continue to evolve, you have more power than ever before — if you choose to use it. **And you can't delude yourself; you've got to get rid of the fog.**

Here's one quick strategy we're using right now. We have a plan to go out there and dominate a much larger market than the one we've been reaching until now. Well, any fool can have a big goal. Just because you want to go out and make millions of dollars doesn't mean you're going to do it. **But it all starts with a goal, and that leads to a plan.** Here's our plan: we've got a $5,000 package, and we're willing to spend up to $4,000 just to make every $5,000 sale. Now, think about that. We're willing to make a gross profit of only $1,000 on every $5,000 package that we sell. Why? Because **#1,** it has residual income associated with it. And then, **#2,** there's a lifetime customer value that's attached to it too. That lets us be so much more aggressive with all of our marketing. We can do things that most of our competitors would be scared to death to do. We can be aggressive, we can be bold, we can go out there and spend more money.

We can have a bigger presence in the marketplace. In so doing, we'll make sales that our competitors would never have made. We'll get new customers that our competitors would have never been able to reach, because we're going to be able to do so much more. **And that's been our strategy in general: to be as aggressive as possible, to be willing to spend as much money on every new sale as we can — because we realize that the profits are to be made from repeat purchases.** Now, it's not about trying to suck money out of people; you have to get them the first time before you can get them again and again, and every time thereafter you have to give them tremendous value, or they're going to go away. **It's about serving people in the highest way possible, about making them so happy that they're glad to buy from you repeatedly.** Having an aggressive marketing strategy lets you go out there and willingly spend more money in your new customer acquisition, and with the subsequent purchases or offers that you make to your established customer base.

Nine Mistakes to Avoid

Instead of talking about positives as I usually do, this particular strategy illuminates **dangerous errors that entrepreneurs often make.** That's because I think it's helpful, sometimes, to discuss the things that you can do wrong as well as right, so you know what to avoid. Here are the nine mistakes I see all too often, and what you have to do to keep them from grounding you:

1. **No focus.** The list of prospects is of primary importance, and you need to home in on highly qualified prospects and get to know them in the most intimate way possible.

2. **No compelling offer.** You need something to get people to take action now; otherwise, they have no reason to respond to or to buy from you.

3. **No deadline.** You've got to build urgency into your offer. The more urgency you have, the higher your response rate will be.

4. **A lack of testimonials.** You should *always* remember that what other people say about you is much more important than what you

MARKETING SECRET

Spend more money to make more money:

- "In Direct-Marketing it's the cost to get the sale — not to make a mailing (or series of mailings) that counts." — Jon Goldman

- Many times, the secret is to spend more money, not less. This is especially true when you are making offers to your best prospects and customers.

say about yourself. A lack of testimonials is a detriment to your marketing.

5. **No way to measure results**. The only thing that counts in any business is return on investment. Know your numbers. Don't get hung up on response rates, because you can't put them in the bank.

6. **No follow-up**. Most people give up way too soon; 82% of sales happen after the first follow-up. You need a plan to follow-up with your leads to try to convert them to sales.

7. **Trying to be cute and funny using non-direct-response, Madison Avenue advertising**. Don't be cute and funny. Try to make the sale.

8. **Bad copy**. Having a bad sales letter can kill your sales rate. Learn to write.

9. **Too much reliance in one medium**. You need to diversify. Advertise in more than one medium.

As I've indicated above, **what you need to do is the exact opposite of these nine mistakes.** Regarding the first one, which is lack of focus, everybody's heard the little cliché that says, "If everybody is your customer, then nobody is your customer." I think people tend to discount all clichés in general, but they're clichés for a reason, aren't they? Often, there's a lot of truth in them. So ask yourself: **who, exactly, are you trying to reach?** That's the most important thing. **The market comes first,** as we tell people again and again when they come to our marketing workshops. And when we say "market," we're simply talking about a group of people who have some strong commonality that causes them to buy the type of products and services you sell. Who are those people? Where can you reach them?

Next, what must you say to those people in order to get their attention and get their interest? **Most people just don't have a compelling offer;** but to really tear up the sales floor, you've got to do something to get people to take action *now*. **You have to prove to them that what you have is much more valuable than the money you're asking them to give up in return.** If there's not a strong reason to take action right away, most people won't. Think about those TV infomercials where they say, "You'll get this and this and this… But wait, there's more! You'll also get this and this and this and this! And, for the first 50 people who call in now, you'll also get this and this, too!" and they just keep stacking it up. Some of those infomercials have a time clock, and that time clock starts winding down. That's something that creates a sense of urgency.

Which folds into number three on our list: no deadlines. **You have to build a deadline into your offer, and give a good reason why you're not just lying to them about it.** You don't want to lie to people; we're not talking about lying for a living here. But we *are* talking about doing things to dramatize your offer, to give people more reasons to go ahead and do what you want them to do.

Our fourth item is a **lack of testimonials,** which I've already talked about; you've got to have clear, honest testimonials to get other people to buy. Number five — **no measurement of results.** All that matters is how much money you spend versus how much money you make. This goes back to an earlier topic, where I discussed how everybody wants to try to catch a whale by using a minnow as bait; that is, most people are trying to spend as little as they can in order to make each sale. In one sense that's smart, because you don't want to be spendthrift; on the other hand, offering up big bait does give you a competitive advantage. I mentioned the strategy that we're involved with at M.O.R.E., Inc., where we're happy to spend up to $4,000 in order to get that $5,000 sale. We're willing to be aggressive, because it's all about return on investment. **You've got to know what you're numbers are, and you can't get hung up on response rates.** People may say, "Well, I only got a half of a 1% response rate." That doesn't mean anything to us. **The only thing we care about is how much** money you spend versus how much you make — and even then it sometimes takes a while to close the gap.

Not to brag, but there was a time not too long ago when we were bringing in almost $2,000,000 a month. We had a promotion where we were spending huge sums of money just to get the initial sale — I'm talking about *huge* sums of money. **The truth is, we were going negative to get the first sale, but then we had a nice big, fat upgrade attached to the first sale — plus we had continuity revenue, too.** We were just rolling in money while that promotion lasted, and it was great. That's the general type of thinking you need to adhere to.

Number six: **no follow-up. Most marketers give up way too soon.** That would be like asking your girlfriend one time if she wants to marry you. If she says no once, what, are you just going to shut up? Not likely! You're going to keep asking her again and again until, ideally, she finally says yes. The same is true in business. And then number seven — trying to be cute and funny. There was recently a promotion in our market that a bunch of people were involved in, but those people were never likely to make any money, because they were using cartoons as part of their message. **You can't be cute. You can't be funny.**

Number eight: **bad copy. You've got to write great ad copy, or you'll absolutely kill your own ability to make money.** Now, learning to be a great copywriter is a skill that anybody can learn, and it's one of the greatest marketing skills, if not *the* greatest marketing skill, that you can acquire. All it takes is learning how to put words on paper in a way that causes people to send money to you. If you can accomplish that, it's the most amazing feeling that you'll ever experience in your life — and it's within your reach. The importance of writing copy can't be overemphasized, and in fact I've written whole books about it. Of all these items you should avoid, bad sales copy is the worst. **As a marketer, writing good sales copy is one of the most important things you can learn, because it sets the foundation for everything else.** Not only will you learn to write copy that's compelling, you'll learn how to handle follow-ups and other important aspects of the business. If you can write great sales copy, you'll be using DRM, which means #5 will come into play, **where you'll be able to measure your results — because you'll have specific offers that go out, and you'll know the results you got from that particular advertising.** It all starts with great sales copy, and each of the items in this list can be backed with an understanding of writing great sales copy. You should enhance your education on that front at all times. There's always more to learn, always more to study when it comes to being a great sales copywriter. **School is never out for the pro.**

Finally, number nine: **you do have to mix it up.** I love direct-mail, but we're also using space advertising as well as some major Internet marketing. **So you don't want to put all your eggs in one basket.** Think of it like a chair; you need to have at least four different legs before the chair will be really solid.

> The door will <u>always</u> be open to the person who can make money for others.

The Importance of Advertising

Remember P. T. Barnum? He's the man who said that you can't catch a whale by using a minnow as bait. I've got several books about Barnum; in my opinion, he was a great man. Recently, I was going through one of my favorite Barnum biographies and I found this quote. It's great wisdom, and there's a lot to talk about here: "In a typical year (1877), the cost of advertising and publicity for Barnum's circus came to over $100,000." You could do a lot with $100,000 back in 1877; in today's money, that's probably equivalent to about ten million. **But that was almost one-third of his total expenses!** Think about that. Almost *one-third* of his total expenses went into advertising and publicity.

The lesson here is that you have to keep pumping your revenue back into the areas that make you the most money. Discipline yourself to do this on a consistent basis. People often tend to try to get by on the cheap with advertising; and certainly, if you only have a limited budget, you want to do it as little as possible. But even so, the smaller your budget, the bigger the percentage of that budget you want to put towards advertising. And always, **always put aside some portion of your income for advertising.** That's something we've taught for years, basically ever since we got started in the business. **You need to take a percentage of every dollar you bring in and put it into an advertising fund.** Maybe for you, that means opening a bank account called "Advertising" so you

MARKETING SECRET

Marketing secret from *Robert Collier:*

- Showmanship sells! Put yourself out there! Don't be afraid to stand out!

▼

"Good artists create — great artists steal!" — *Picasso*

can stay disciplined. The percentage you put aside for advertising is up to you; maybe it's 10%, 20%, or 50%. The point is, be disciplined about putting that money aside. Then pull that money out once a month (or whatever schedule you determine) and advertise.

This is hard to do, because people are inclined to spend every bit of what they bring in. We live like that as a society; most people are living paycheck to paycheck, with consistent expenses, and often that's what drives people to get into business for themselves. They want a better lifestyle; they want to be able to vacation and do things for themselves. What that means is that when your business starts working and you start bringing in money, you enjoy your spoils by taking a vacation or doing whatever you've been dreaming of doing. **But don't spend it all: keep putting the advertising percentage aside in a separate account and be vigilant about it, or you'll suddenly be right back where you started.**

You've got to feed your business, and the way you do that is with advertising, promotions, marketing, and those kinds of things. **Now again, the key is to keep pumping more of your revenue back into all of the areas that *make you the most money*.** There are all kinds of advertising options you could spend your money on. **Experiment with multiple methods, and keep the ones that work best.** If you find that advertising in a certain magazine does best for you, then you want to keep advertising in that magazine while testing others. If you've found that a certain mailing list has continued to work for you, you want to continue using that mailing list. And you should always test small. Test a lot of things and test consistently, but once you know that something is working and is making you a good profit, continue pumping more and more of your revenue back into that area. **Advertising isn't a cost: it's an investment towards future profits.**

Here's an example of what *not* to do with your profits. When M.O.R.E., Inc. first took off in 1988 and we were rolling in the money, one of my best friends at the time got around our business and fell in love with it. I had a chance to help him get started, and right out of the gate I showed him exactly what to do; and then, lo and behold, he started making thousands of dollars. He was so excited! He was going to build a company just like ours. Well, we had already been in business for a couple years, so we had some infrastructure built. Steve made his thousands, and then took that money and rented a nice fancy office and got all this computer equipment, spending all of the money that he'd made! **He lost his momentum, because then the cash flow dried up.** If he'd just stayed in the game and continued to reinvest his money into more advertising, and had then built it up and started putting some of it into infrastructure, he would have never lost his important momentum. But he did, and it didn't take him long. Within 90 days he had quit. He could have ended up making millions if he'd just practiced what I've talked about.

Every day, you have to discipline yourself to take a percentage of your money and put it back into more of the things that made it for you to begin with. Period. End of story. Ignore that reality, and you're likely to fail.

Doing the Two-Step

Two-step marketing is one of the keystones of modern marketing, and it's the place that you're really going to make your money. I don't think people can hear this enough, because even entrepreneurs tend to under-value the benefits of two-step marketing. They just want to go after the sale, and they feel that asking for it right up front is the best strategy. Instead, they need to remember that two-step marketing is the safest and most profitable way to make money. It's simple. **Step One is to attract a high-qualified prospect first.** Use a great offer. Don't try to sell them too much at first; just get your hooks into them. I talked about using the right bait earlier in the chapter; find that bait, entice them, and then set the hook. Make it easy for them to buy the first time. Sell a low-priced widget.

Educate them. Make them feel that they came to you and not the other way around. Sometimes that's with a low-priced sale; sometimes that's with a free lead, where you're just asking them to raise their hand and request a report. **Step Two is actually making the profitable sale.** Now it's time to bring out the big guns. You have their attention and their interest, and you're in the position to show them how you can give them what they want the most. **It's a great strategy that's responsible for billions of dollars in sales yearly.**

Two-step marketing is nothing less than the best way to make the largest amount of money as safely as possible. Let's say you're in a large, rabid marketplace ours, the opportunity market. Well, there's an estimated 30-50 million people who want to make more money and are willing to do something about it. But how in the world are you ever going to reach such a huge audience if you're not a Fortune 500 company? The short answer is: you're not. **The trick is to narrow it down as much as you can, by finding ways to get to the most serious prospects only.** For instance, we'll advertise in some of the moneymaking magazines, because that's where we'll catch the people who are really serious about making money — or they wouldn't be reading those magazines to begin with. We run small display ads or even small classified ads in those venues, pinpointing our marketing efforts by presenting our offers directly to the people we want to attract the most. We're getting them to come to us by offering them something of value for free or for a low cost. A very small group of people will probably take us up on our offer; they'll go to our website, call our toll-free number, send for the Special Report or program, or even buy whatever we're selling at low cost. **That's Step #1. When they do that, they end up on our mailing list.** Well, that cost us very little, didn't it? **With Step #2, we try to sell them an offer that's related to the one they bit on.** That's all there is to it. There are a lot of different themes you can use here, but they all involve separating the smaller group of qualified prospective buyers from the larger group of people who are less qualified. Once you do that, you can spend more money to reach that smaller group of people who you know are serious because they took the first action.

Two-step marketing is the backbone of what we've been doing here at M.O.R.E., Inc. for many years. It's become almost second nature to us, and yet a lot of businesses struggle with this concept, because it's easy to get caught up in thinking about the total universe size that you could mail or advertise to. And who wouldn't think, "Well, I know that there are 5,000,000 who either want my product or who should, because it's a great product. Everybody in this marketplace should want it." And so you start thinking, "Okay, if there are 5,000,000 people in my market, how do I reach all of them with my sales message?" Of course you could get their names and addresses and mail 5,000,000 pieces of direct-mail, or you could advertise in a magazine those people read and sell your product "off the page."

You get tempted into doing that because you think, "I want to reach everybody." But let's get real; it's true that if I ask for people to just raise their hand, there's no way everybody is going to see my sales message. But that's the wrong way of thinking. The way you want to think is: **"I really only want to focus on selling to the people who are the most interested in and most likely to buy my product."** So you use your lead generation tool, Step One, to attract the right kinds of people. Let's say of those 5,000,000, there really are only about 5,000, or even 500, that are the most likely prospects to buy your end product or service. **Therefore, you focus all your energy on selling to those few.**

It would be astronomically expensive to try to advertise to 5,000,000 people all at once. But let's say, for the sake of this example, that it costs you the exact same amount of money to reach those 5,000,000 as it did to acquire 5,000 qualified leads. You're still better off spending more money to sell to those 5,000 leads than you are spending money to advertise to all 5,000,000, because you're advertising to people who have already gone through one hoop, who have already raised their hand and said they're interested. **Dollar for dollar, you're always better off spending your money advertising to people who've already qualified themselves.**

That's why when you see infomercials on TV, the strategy isn't just to sell you what they're offering on that 30-minute spot. The real strategy is to get you to raise your hand so they can pack on the benefits. They just load them up and make it seem like you'd be the stupidest person on the planet if you didn't pick up the phone right now and order, because they're going to give you all this stuff for only two easy payments of $19.95. And then when you do call, not only do they instantly upsell you on the phone, but you also get a package in the mail. And then you get another offer and, hopefully, you buy from that, and they do some more telemarketing to you.

They've got another package they're trying to sell, but they know that they can't make that sale by just having you look at their 30-minute infomercial — **so they just focus on getting you to take that initial step.**

Relentless, Aggressive Marketing

Previously I talked about how you have to be seriously aggressive when using DRM if you want to make real money, and I want to expand on that concept here. **The concept of aggressive marketing shouldn't be limited to DRM; it should permeate all aspects of your business.** When you own a marketing business (or any business, really), you simply can't afford to be a shrinking violet. Sure, we've all heard about reckless entrepreneurs who ended up burning their company to the ground. But I guarantee, for every entrepreneur like that, there are at least 100,000 others who aren't nearly as aggressive and focused as they should be — and it's costing them a ton of money that could and should be theirs.

I thought this strategy was important to discuss because a lot of people are afraid to take risks in their businesses, and so they end up being timid marketers. These people are costing their companies dearly because they're not nearly as aggressive and focused as they should be. **Instead, they spend their time doing all the things that don't directly bring in money, or they just aren't aggressive marketers.** They haven't learned DRM strategies; they're just floating by. Maybe they've got a Yellow Page ad

▼▼▼▼▼▼▼▼▼
MARKETING SECRET

The easiest sale you'll ever make is to someone who feels bonded to you.

- First win their hearts — then win their pocketbooks!

▼

You need the right bait to catch the right fish!

- You'll never catch a whale by using a minnow as bait!
— P. T. Barnum

running, but they're not aggressive and they're not focused.

I don't want to offend anybody here, but there are people in this world who are Wal-Mart haters. My Dad was; like a lot of folks, he thought that Wal-Mart had destroyed small-town America. I used to tell him, "Dad, nothing is further from the truth. Wal-Mart didn't destroy small-town America. Wal-Mart is a sign of the times." But he hated everything it stood for, and it wasn't until the last years of his life that he would even step into one. And get this: he even had some of his friends go into the local Wal-Mart to buy his prescriptions, because he could get them for lower prices — but he wouldn't step foot inside.

Well, I'm a great fan of the late Sam Walton, Wal-Mart's founder. I told my dad how Walton started out as a small-town Main Street merchant; in fact, he had a Ben Franklin store in a little town in Arkansas. And he was very attentive to his customers' needs; he saw that discounters were coming into the big city and making a fortune by selling products for so much cheaper than the rest of the stores were able to sell them for. So he started buying from some of these discounters, and some of the wholesalers who sold to them, just to stock his small store. Eventually he lost his little Ben Franklin store, so he took the idea that the discounters in the big cities were using and started going into all these smaller towns. **He did a great job giving them what they really wanted — the best prices on as many different items as he could possibly get for them.**

By going where the other discounters failed to go, in less than two decades he was able to build a tremendous foundation. By the mid-1980s, when he took his company public, he had started moving into the same big cities as the other discounters. He finally dominated; **Wal-Mart became the world's largest retail organization, and made Sam a billionaire.** He was the world's richest man by the time he died, and then his fortune got divided between his four children and his wife, and became diluted somewhat.

In Sam's book *Made In America*, the last chapter was specifically devoted to competing against Wal-Mart. You see, nothing made Sam Walton angrier than all the people like my dear, sweet father (God rest his soul), who talked about how Wal-Mart had destroyed Main Street America, so he devoted a whole chapter to responding to that. He was still a Main Street merchant in his heart; **he understood what people really wanted.**

This chapter showed people how they could compete successfully with Wal-Mart. He basically said, "Look, all Wal-Mart can do is give people great prices and great selection. That's all. **But people want so much more than that,"** and he listed a wide range of ways that you can successfully go after Wal-Mart and compete with them.

So many of the people who closed their Main Street shops in the face of Wal-Mart competition were already weak. They had a good thing going for a long time before any real competition came along; but when it did, they almost immediately put out their "For Sale" or "Going Out Of Business" signs. They decided that they just couldn't handle it anymore, and used it as an excuse to quit. Here's a perfect example: Near our headquarters in Goessel, Kansas, there's a little town called Hillsboro. Well, they had a local Ben Franklin store there for a number of years, and then a discount chain called Alco came in. It's like a miniature Wal-Mart — it's about a tenth of the size of a Superstore, and yet it's got pretty good prices and a pretty good selection. Nine months before that Alco store came into Hillsboro, the owner of that Ben Franklin store, who had been there for 30 or 40 years, put a "Going Out Of Business" sign on his storefront. And I said, "Mike, what are you doing? Alco isn't even going to go here for another nine months!" and he just said, "Look, I can't compete with Alco." I tried to argue with him, and I talked till I was blue in the face, but I just couldn't get Mike to see it. He just kept going, "I can't compete with Alco." That's all he would say.

And here's the point. **There are so many small businesspeople who focus far too much on the competition, when instead they should focus on the market itself.** They just won't compete. Are they lazy? Are they fearful? Why, yes, they are. Are they not focused nearly enough on their customers and how to provide more and better services to their customers? Absolutely, positively, yes, they are. **All you have to do is be just a little more aggressive.** But some people are afraid of being aggressive, because they think it's going to lead to bankruptcy. Again, as I mentioned earlier, they've heard the stories about aggressive marketers who have wildly done this, that, and the other thing and have blown up their companies because they've been reckless, they've spent too much money, they've put their companies deeply into debt, and they've used leverage too much — and now they've out of business. But as I said earlier, for every one of those crazy entrepreneurs, there are 100,000 others who are never aggressive enough.

At M.O.R.E., Inc., we offer programs called *Ruthless Marketing* and *Ruthless Marketing Attack*. Now, those names are a little deceptive, because what we mean by "ruthless" is simply "aggressive." Ruthless is a more marketable title; it sounds a little better in print. Really, **it's just about being aggressive, being assertive, focusing on your customers.** How often do we sit around worrying about our competition? Well, we think about our competitors only insomuch as we try to copy their good ideas. We're aware of our competition, but it's not a focus of worry. We're not scared of our competition. **We're not worried about them taking a market share.** There's enough room in our market for our company and a hundred others like us. And the truth is, we feel confident in our game plan. We feel confident in our strategy and our marketing ability. They can bring it all they want, and we'll bring it too!

I've put a lot of thought into what separates the competitors in any given marketplace. What makes one business thrive, whereas others fail? **In most cases, I think, it's attributable to aggressive marketing.** In America, where we've got the freedom to succeed or fail with as little government intervention as possible, you can't get too upset when you see people failing; and you can't be too upset when you see people succeeding, either. If you're jealous of people who succeed... well, just join them, because there's no reason you can't do what they did.

Take Microsoft. Microsoft was founded by a computer nerd. There's no reason *you* couldn't have been that computer nerd. And a lot of young computer nerds are starting other companies that are hugely successful these days, so it's not just Microsoft. And there are people like Jeff Bezos, who started a little book company called Amazon out of his garage. He just decided to have a bookstore, he opened it up, and then he used aggressive marketing to build it. Now, he wasn't necessarily a direct-response marketer, but he was an

> There's an <u>easy</u> way and a <u>hard</u> way to do something.
>
> Only a <u>fool</u> chooses the hard way just for the sake of doing it hard. The smart person strives to keep it as easy — simple — and manageable as possible.

▼▼▼▼▼▼▼▼▼
MARKETING SECRET

A lead-generation secret: Who cares about the cost? The only thing that matters is what you make after the conversion.

▼

Our job as marketers is to attract the right people and repel the wrong ones.

aggressive marketer. He went out there with a plan, and went all out to make sure it succeeded. The founders of Google and eBay have similar stories. In fact, there are countless stories of entrepreneurs who were either small-time tech geeks or even just ordinary, uneducated people who had a dream for a product or knew of a marketplace that needed filling — and they set out to dominate that marketplace. **In most cases, the only thing that separated those who succeeded from those who didn't was aggressive marketing strategies, and the willingness to putting their plans into practice, to work as hard as they could, and to be as determined as possible to see through to success.**

There's no reason that anybody and everybody who wants that success for themselves can't have it. They just have to use the kinds of strategies that we're teaching here, be aggressive, and chase it down. **It's there for anybody who wants it!** If one person can make millions of dollars, then *you* can make millions of dollars, too. Is it going to be easy for you? Probably not, but it does get easier as you go along.

Practice Makes Perfect

Now, let's take a closer look at that last statement in the previous section. As hard as succeeding in marketing may be, **it really *does* get easier as you go along;** all of the hard stuff becomes routine after you do it a thousand times. That's not meant to be cute: it's the absolute truth. And yet so many people never get it. **They give up way too soon, so they never develop the necessary knowledge, skills and experience to succeed.**

There was a great entrepreneur named Joe Karbo died in the early 1980s, and he used to say, **"Everything is difficult until it becomes easy."** I thought he was such a genius for saying that, and then I found that an ancient philosopher had said the same about 2,000 years ago. Ideas are transferable; the same methods that work for one person can work for all, as long as you've put in the time and gained the experience you need. It's like a cake recipe, if you really think about it. I'm a terrible cook; I can cook about seven different things and that's about it, and I don't do a good job cooking any of them. But if I could sit down with a recipe, and if I had the patience to follow it and do the work that's necessary to do exactly what it says to do, I can make something that tastes pretty good. Will it taste as good as the person who invented it or a great chef could make it? No. But if the recipe's written right and I follow it to the letter, I can make something that's tasty.

The same thing is true with making money. When you look at the people out there who are making millions of dollars, the biggest mistake you can make is to think that somehow, someway, those people are better than you. They're not. They've developed certain knowledge and skills, that's all. They've got the experience. Sometimes they have a little bravado. **They have a lot of genuine confidence, because they've actually paid the price: they've learned the things that have to be learned.** Now they've got the skills that allow them to make it look easy — and all of a sudden you start thinking, "My God, I could never do that." And yet, you fail to appreciate the fact that it took them years to develop those skills. They learned just like you have to: they started from the beginning.

Now, of course there are shortcuts. **That's what our Direct-Response Network is supposed to be: a shortcut.** If people use the services we provide in the three business and coaching programs we've put together, they can learn how to apply the same marketing strategies that have made us so much money, except much faster. But it still takes some practice, and the more money you want to make, the more you have to practice.

So again, remember that as hard as something may be, it gets easier. So don't give up before you reach that point. I went to a basketball game recently, and at halftime they carted out some guy they plucked from the stands for a contest. He had three baskets to make. One was from the free throw line, and if he made that basket he'd get a little bit of money.

Then they brought him back to the three-point line and he had to make a three-point basket, and if he did that, he made a little bit more money. And then they backed him all the way up to half court, and if he could make that half court shot, just one throw, he got the big prize — something like $100,000.

Now, obviously it's a little easier to shoot the free throw than the three-point shot, and it's a little easier to shoot the three-point shot than it is to shoot the half-court shot. But if he stood there all day practicing making free throws, whenever it came time for him to shoot the one that was worth the money, he'd have a better ability to do so. The same goes for the three-point shot. And the half-court shot, even though it's a little more luck than skill, if you were to sit there all day long and practice half-court shots, you'd get better, and you might make them. Even though it's rare, your frequency of making that kind of shot would get a lot better, because you practiced over and over again.

By plucking somebody out of the crowd, chances are pretty good they're going to get someone who never practices shooting free throws, so they know there's a much higher chance that person will miss. If they were to grab someone from one of the two basketball teams and put them at the free throw line and say, "All right, you're going to win money if you make a free throw," well, they're a lot more likely to make that free throw. A pretty good player — either at the college level or professional level — should make a free throw about three times out of four without much of a problem.

So there's a big difference between someone who practices and plays the game, and someone who just gets out there once. **Everything in life gets easier when you do it over and over. That's certainly true of marketing, and of DRM specifically.** You don't have to do it a thousand times before it becomes easy, but it *will* become easier the more you do it. So writing that first sales letter can be the hardest thing you do, but by the time you've written ten of them, it gets a little easier. And certainly by the time you've written your thousandth sales letter, it becomes much easier. That doesn't mean it doesn't take a lot of time, and there's not a lot of strategy and planning involved, but you can get all that organized and done with a fraction of the initial worry and difficulty.

Here's a related principle that's attributed to George Washington: "It's wonderful how much we can do if we're always doing." I think that ties in well with this strategy, **because if you're always doing, that means you're getting better.** And we like to say that there's no such thing as making mistakes; there are just certain outcomes with marketing, where maybe things didn't come out as you hoped they would. Well, you learn from that and you move on. **Keep doing, and the more you'll get used to the things you need to do to succeed.** The more you'll get comfortable with them, and the better you'll become at them; because you'll start learning what you didn't do right, what didn't get you the results you were looking for. You'll start learning systems. You'll start developing good habits that can help you get what you're looking for and achieve the results you're looking for. **Eventually, it all becomes second nature for you.**

We're always having people coming to us to see what we're doing. We're an open book. We tell people everything; we don't hold things back. We've always been that way. We share our secrets freely and we hope that other people will share theirs with us, too. So often they say to us, "Man, there's no way I could do that." Or, "That would be way too scary for me." They think we're taking huge risks because we do some pretty aggressive marketing. **Well, sometimes we *do* take big risks, but for the most part all the marketing we do is backed by a series of smaller and less aggressive tests.** We test something over a long period before we really start throwing a lot of money at it.

When they're just starting out, people are scared. And they should be, on some level. Fear can help you; it's a good thing. But it can be a bad thing when it comes to trying a lot of new things, and it can keep you from playing full out. I love this one quote of Dr. Phil's: "You can't play the game with sweaty palms." **But fear holds so many people back, and they never push through those fears.**

One of the things I enjoy doing most is speaking in public. But there was a time when I was so afraid of public speaking that I got physically sick before I had to get up there and speak. That's how fearful I was! And yet, I enjoyed watching people speak in public, and I always wanted to be out in front sharing my ideas. I loved the passion of a good public speaker, and how they put it all out there and influenced people, getting them all excited and fired up. It was something that I wanted to do so badly. But it took many years of getting up in front of a group and being terrified... and I do mean terrified! — before I got used to it. Even while I was up there

▼▼▼▼▼▼▼▼▼
MARKETING SECRET

A formula for success:

1. Make the BIGGEST promises that are centered around the biggest possible benefits.

2. Don't think about how you are going to fulfill these promises... just make them!

3. And make sure they offer very compelling benefits your market badly wants.

4. Put all those promises into your sales material — then scramble like crazy to find the ways and means to deliver what you promised!

speaking, I was shaking in my boots! I lost my voice on more than one occasion. Some of my public speaking early on was just terrible.

And yet, I just kept at it and at it and at it. I'm not going to tell you that I'm a good public speaker now, because I don't think I am. Yet I hold my own, and it's something I really enjoy now. **You see, I really wanted to do it... and yet I was afraid to at first.** And yes, I was afraid for a number of years while I was doing it. And yet I did it over and over and over, year after year... until now, it's one of the things I enjoy most in this world.

The first sales letter that I ever wrote that made our company any substantial amount of money was for a product called "The $2,500 Weekend." **We did over a million dollars with this one sales letter, and I spent three months of my life working on it.** I spent a significant portion of every single day working on it. Today, I could write that same sales letter in a week or less. If Chris Lakey was helping me, I could write it in two days. So things *do* get easier.

A while back I did a call with a friend of ours in Canada, a Direct-Response Network member. He asked me, "How do you come up with all your multi-million dollar ideas?" Well, I didn't have an answer for him, except to say that we've been in the same market since 1988. **We really have a good handle on what our clients want.** We've had a lot of successful promotions. We've learned what they *don't* want, we've got the experience behind us, and it makes it easy for us to do it. Is it always easy? No, it's not. Do we still struggle sometimes? Absolutely. And yet it's easier than it was. I think you've got to make a game out of it; you've got to make it fun. You've got to set your goals high. **You've got to want something so bad that you're willing to go out there and pay the price to get it.** So many people say that they want to make millions of dollars, and yet they won't pay the price! That price, unfortunately, can be very steep, just like I told you with public speaking. It took years for me to get any good at it at all. And yes, it took years for me to learn how to write a sales letter. It took years to learn how to do *anything* that I do now. The same is true for all of the world's richest people. So, whatever it is that you want, you can have it. **If it's making millions of dollars in DRM, then that's exactly what we can do to help you.** *But you have to work hard at it.*

Recently Chris Lakey had a chance to speak at a political rally. There were maybe a couple hundred people in the room as he was getting ready to speak, and one of the other guys who was going to talk came over to Chris and said something like, "Don't be nervous." Chris just replied, "I'm not nervous at all. I'm excited. I'm looking forward to it." Chris didn't know if the guy was telling me him not to be nervous because he was nervous, or thought Chris looked nervous. But Chris has spoken to hundreds of people before, so it was no big deal for him. But had he been in that room with hundreds of people and had never been up in front of people before, he might have been scared to death to do that. **But as with everything else, it because much easier with repetition.**

It's All About the Systems

The theme for this chapter is how to systemize your business. Systems may seem kind of boring, but the fact is that you need to be organized, and you need to have processes in place to help you bring in the money as smoothly and as speedily as possible. In this lesson, we'll look at **three ways to get those systems up and running.** I'm also going to talk about the leverage blueprint; that is, **how you can harness the efforts of others to unlock your dreams.** Finally, I'm going to wrap it up with the **little-known secrets to setting the stage for huge paydays** — why some get a lot, while others get just a little.

Systemize from Day One

First of all, **you need to find something great that you're going to** use as your lure. After all, you can't market something if you don't have something to market! **So again, scrutinize the marketplace carefully, and determine what your market wants.** If you don't want to create your own product, find an existing product that offers something that's very much in demand. For example: if you're with the Direct-Response Network, you know we've got a great product there. Next, look at the timing of the marketplace, and make sure that your product lines up with what's happening there. **You can make some serious money with timing.**

Make sure that your products are supported well, too. I always say, "Look to the field." If you're involved in something or you're thinking about getting involved in something, a good way to determine whether or not that's the right direction is to **look out in the field and see if other people are already making money with it.** If you can find a handful of people who are making $100,000 a month in the program, then it's a workable program and you can make some money. As my colleague Eric Bechtold always says, **"Success leaves clues."** Looking for those clues is a good, cheap way to test whether or not you've got the right product.

Once you've identified your product, **the second step is to generate your message.** How are you going to take that product to market? How are you going to communicate it? Eric uses something he calls the **"Seven Steps to Magnetic Communication,"** and I'd like to share them with you. These are the things you have to do in order to really communicate with people effectively and get them excited. **NUMBER ONE is to look at your product and identify your big promise.** A good way to closely examine your product is to take out a package of note cards, and list, one by one, your product's benefits — that is, everything it has to offer. Don't look at it from a standpoint of physical attributes; write only the benefits on your cards. When you're finished doing that, thumb through those cards, **pick your number one idea,** and move that to the top. **That's what you're going to build your strategy around.** If you're having a hard time figuring out what your big promise is, then you've got the wrong product. **That product *must* have something that makes it stand out.** If it's hard for you to determine what it is, it's going to be hard for those you're trying to sell it to to figure out why they need to be paying attention to it.

NUMBER TWO, once you've identified your big promise, start painting the picture. This is where you **take all those other cards you set aside and use them as an outline for your sales material.** One benefit may serve as a headline in your copy, or as supporting copy that fleshes out those ideas so people understand why they're important.

NUMBER THREE, give them proof. A good way to do this is through social validation: success stories, case studies, or testimonials. In any case, you want to figure out some way of proving you've got the right product that can offer the solutions everybody's looking for. **You want to give them proof to make it real.** If there's no proof, they're not going to buy it.

NUMBER FOUR, you want to build exclusivity. Why is your product unique? Why do they need to buy this from you? Why can't they just go out and find this from somebody else? **Make them feel like this is something that they can't get anywhere else, so they want to buy it from you.** People buy what feels exclusive, what feels exciting and important... so you want to build that into your offer.

> ▼▼▼▼▼▼▼▼▼▼▼
> Step out in faith — and figure it out as you go!

NUMBER FIVE, you want to build urgency, so that people act now. Give them special bonuses. Create limited group sizes. There are a lot of different tricks and strategies in direct-response for building urgency; but here's the reality. You're using the big promise to get people excited, to get them to focus on it. You're using all this other stuff I've just talked about to give them the story and to paint the picture. And then, you're using this sense of urgency to close them on the spot, because **if you can't get them to take quick action, there's a good chance they're not going to take action at all.**

NUMBER SIX, you're going to re-state that big promise and really drive it home. And then, **NUMBER SEVEN, you're going to build in risk reversal.** Risk reversal is very, very important, and you've seen this all over the place. There's one word that will make this all gel for you, and that's **"guarantee." Your goal here is get them to focus on the offer while taking away all the negative aspects they may consider,** like "Oh no, I've got to spend $400 to get this product." You've got to reverse that risk and make them understand that, "Hey, if I try this for 30 days and I'm not happy, I can get my money back!" or whatever the guarantee may be. That will help you in the end.

MARKETING SECRET

It is wrong to lie... Instead, we must put a spin on the truth!

Here's a great quote that sums it up:

- "It is twice as hard to crush a half-truth as a whole lie." — Austin O'Malley

- Use the power of junk science! "If _____ is true, then _____ must also be true!"

Before we move on to the next subject for this chapter, leverage, let's review a bit. **First, you've got to identify that product and then generate your message, using the seven points I've just outlined.** That, I think, is the real the starting point of your entire business. If you've got a product and can't think of a big promise, you're probably barking up the wrong tree altogether. Risk reversal is also a big thing: you've got to make people understand that there's no risk in taking on your product. Now, some companies don't have guarantees at all; they're afraid that by having a guarantee, people will take advantage of them. But we like to say that you can never have too outrageous a guarantee. **The more outrageous the guarantee, the more it stacks the situation in your prospect's favor.** The more you can make it appear that all the risk is on you and none of it's on them, the more likely it is that someone is going to go ahead and place their order.

We've had guarantees that, under certain restrictions, gave our customers double the money back that they spent with us, and that was on a rather expensive offer. We put it on the line, and while we had several stipulations they had to agree to before that happened, it made the offer all the more attractive to them. **And by the way, it's better, in most cases, if you make it as easy as possible for your clients to get their money back if they're not happy.** A standard 30-day guarantee is good, but having a guarantee where you tell them, "Hey, under any circumstances, you can get a full 100% refund, no questions asked," makes people feel more comfortable. **It makes them feel like there's very little chance that they're risking anything at all.**

And again, **the product you're promoting has to be hot.** I've mentioned that in the first four years after we started our company, we brought in more than ten million dollars. And everyone wants to know, what was the secret? In truth, there was no single secret; it was a combination of many different factors, including the fact that we'd struggled for so many years and refused to quit. **Every time we thought we were failing, we were actually learning something.** So by the time we'd failed 50 times, even though we had never made any serious money, we had learned a lot about what *didn't* work. But if there was one thing besides all the experience that made all the difference in the world, **it was the fact that finally we hit on the right idea at the right time. That's so important.**

I see entrepreneurs out there trying to sell what *they* love, not necessarily what the market loves. We've got some good friends who are wasting their time and money selling things that nobody finds exciting but them. There's no market for that; so one of the best things you can do is either partner with someone who already has a hot product or service, or copy something that works for someone else. That may seem a little ruthless, but I'm not telling you to copy it exactly; no, put your own spin on it and make it *better*. **That's basically how we got started.** We took two programs that were already working for others and combined them to create our own very profitable program.

In order to succeed, you've got to get on the other side of the cash register. Stop thinking like a consumer; start thinking like a marketer. All those steps are things that *all* successful marketers are using to various degrees. Some are doing a better job than others, **but you'll never recognize that until and unless you start studying their sales material.** First of all, don't throw it away, and stop calling it junk mail. Get on the right mailing lists, and look at it from a marketer's point of view rather than a consumer's point of view — and you'll start seeing these things used. The untrained eye will never see these things; but if you're aware of them, you can start using them yourself.

The Leverage Blueprint

My second secret for this chapter involves **harnessing the efforts of others to unlock your dreams.** The key here is that you don't get rich by yourself. If you try, you're limited to the money that's in your wallet for marketing, you're limited to your knowledge on how to promote things, and you're limited to how much time you can work every day. Most people who try to get rich on their own fail miserably, and the reason is that they're not leveraging the efforts of others. They're only using their own limited resources. **Finding the right position of leverage is the ultimate solution to the marketing equation.**

Now, how have we used this concept with the previous secret? I just told you how to find an offer and how to develop a good message, because **that lure is how you catch your fish — that is, how you generate your customer base.** Once you get one thing working well and you've got a bunch of people coming in, you're going to start putting all those people in a database, such as an Excel spreadsheet. You're keeping the names of all those people organized, in such a way that you can sort them by various characteristics.

And then here's what you do: Instead of just putting all your people in a program and saying, "Now go out and figure out how to do it for yourself," you tell them, "Hey, I've got it all figured out. I'm going to give you access to the same things I'm doing, and you can do them yourself." **That creates a snowball effect in your business, because you went through the effort of finding the good lure that brought in those people, and then you're giving them access to your methods and secrets.** You're the gatekeeper here. You're not worried about them jeopardizing your copyrights; in fact, you're not worried about your intellectual property at all. Why is that? Because every time they use them, you're leveraging their efforts. They're putting their money into a mailing, or putting up their own websites, or whatever you're giving them. **The easier you can make it for somebody to make you money, the better off you're going to be.** So if you get as many people as you can and make it as easy as possible for others to make you money while they make themselves money, guess what? **Your profits will explode!**

The easiest way to rise to the top is on the shoulders of a bunch of other people who are putting their effort into building their own businesses. We tell people this all the time in network marketing. **The only advantage of network marketing is leverage, the fact they've built a leverage model for you.** If you're not a big fan of network marketing, then go to a Master Distributorship, where you have the rights to sell other people the rights to sell a product. **There are many different ways to build leverage;**

lots of different ways to put more money in your pocket without having to invest more of your time and money to make it happen. The biggest money earners in the world, the Bill Gateses and the Donald Trumps, are leveraging the efforts of other people every single day. Think about the way these guys are making money. Donald Trump isn't building skyscrapers by himself, right? He's got everybody else doing it. He's figured out a way to sit at the top of that big tower and make money by leveraging the efforts of all these other people. If you want to follow in the footsteps of the most successful people, you'll take this leverage blueprint and put it to work for yourself.

That's one of the secrets to our success. If somebody were to put a gun to my head and demand, "Give me your whole secret in less than five minutes!" this is what I'd tell him. It would be that simple. Look, in the opportunity market there are literally millions of people looking for a way to make money. All they really need are three things, and we've made millions of dollars over the years by providing them with a wide variety of different programs and opportunities containing these three basic ingredients, some of which I've already talked about. **Number One, they need some type of product to sell. Number Two, they need some type of sales material to sell that product with, whether that's postcards or direct-mail packages or websites. And Number Three, they need a cohesive marketing system that ties everything all together.** In less than five minutes, that's how our company has generated more than $110,000,000 in direct-marketing revenue over the years. Our goal is to do everything possible to help them make the largest amount of money possible, and that's how we make our money. **So we're helping them, but we're helping ourselves at the same time.** It really doesn't get any more complicated than that. We've been doing that since 1988 in various ways. Everything we do is wrapped up in providing those three things in some form.

When you've built an organized collection of all your prospects, which basically takes the form of a mailing list, you've got the ultimate marketing control. Otherwise, you've got to find a group of people to mail to or to send your offer to. You've got to have a group of leads somehow, so **you've got to do lead generation; you've got to do something to get those leads.** Sometimes that means you can joint-venture with other people if you've got a product. You can leverage your product and find other

▼▼▼▼▼▼▼▼▼
MARKETING SECRET

The way to sell the unfamiliar is to link it with the familiar.

▼

The best salespeople are relentless!

▼

Just one great sales letter can make you millions!

people with a list to sell to. **But once you've got a list, you will have a never-ending revenue stream;** because if you've got a list of responsive buyers, then all of a sudden you've got tremendous leverage. People will come to you saying, "I've got a hot product, and your list would be perfect for it," and all you have to do is take their materials, mail them to your list and you've got orders coming in.

If you've got a mailing list of people that have bought from you, and you've built a relationship with them, **there's almost no question about whether you'll make money every time you mail to that list, because those people know you, like you, and trust you.** That can provide you with a never-ending revenue stream. And it doesn't take a big list, either. Some people we know have made millions of dollars with lists of fewer than 1,000 people. I have friends who've made fortunes with lists of fewer than 300 people. Focusing on building a list is probably one of the most important things you can do.

The Third Secret

There are a lot of people pretending to be marketers who don't really understand how to make a lot of money quickly. And the secret is, **you don't do it overnight.** You don't just come up with an idea, and BOOM, $100,000 comes falling out of the sky (if only!). Nope, it doesn't work like that. **Making money effectively requires systems.** This includes building a list of people to make offers to, as I've discussed previously. Once you reach this point, you're at a stage where your list is basically "stored energy" for you. Your customers are sitting there, and you have to start building rapport with them. A good way to do this to offer newsletters; this lets you communicate with people frequently. You get them on conference calls, too. And again, one of the things that's most important to understand here is that you don't take advantage of your database. **Everything you do has to be sincere, and you have to show them that you have an honest desire and are you're passionate about helping them.** They've got to feel that, because one of the things that will keep the people on your list from buying is if they feel you're not sincere, or not putting your best foot forward.

What you need to understand is that **customers in all markets want somebody to do everything for them.** They're always looking for guidance and direction, and they're always looking for that magic bullet, something or someone that's going to provide them with a neat solution to their problems. The neat thing about having a database is, now you're in a situation where you can communicate with people who are looking to be communicated with, looking for solutions, looking for a leader they can follow to achieve their desires, dreams, and goals. **You've got a leg up because you used that lure, you made that initial sale, and you generated this list.** You need to continue to use that lure until it stops working, and then you find another lure.

The whole goal here is to continue to pile people in. Now, again, I've told you that some marketers don't understand this; they just go out with a sales letter to the unwashed masses and expect to make a bunch of money. But, really, you don't make your money like that. **You make your money on what we call the "back-end."** That is, you take a list of people you've communicated with, that you've established a rapport with, and then come back with other offers that meet their needs. In order to help you determine that, you need to analyze your list based on what people have purchased. What lures have you used? What was the big promise in each case? What are the attributes that sold them in the first place? That's what you're going to use as a determiner when looking for other opportunities, products, or services to plug into. **The more complementary those offers are to their original purchase, the more money you're going to make.**

In a perfect environment, you're going to start with very little, and generate this list by finding a lure to which people are attracted. **You start piling people into your database.** Then you're going to go ahead and start communicating to them with a paper newsletter, an email newsletter, periodic telephone events, or a mix of these and other things. **You're going to just stay in contact, keeping your name in their minds.** As the list gets bigger and bigger, eventually you'll get to critical mass where you've got such a large group of people that you're in the position for big paydays.

Some people brag about things like, "Oh, I was able to do a $100,000 in one sales letter." "I did a million dollars with one big push." Well, that was all stored energy that they tapped into. They "unleashed" all of that. Think about the Hoover Dam; think about all that concrete cracking open and the water rushing out in a huge tidal wave. In a way, that's what they're doing. All that stored energy is being released on that offer, and money comes piling in as a result. **Now, think about the power of being in that situation — continuously having the lure, continuously developing a list, continuously staying in touch with that list.** And then you get into a position where all you're doing is looking out in the marketplace, finding great ideas and opportunities, plugging them in, and those big paydays come on a frequent basis. **Pretty soon you can do one a month or so, and you've got all the money that you've ever wanted.**

Again, it all stems from the system I just told you about. That's pretty much the cycle that you go through, and the power, the *gold*, really is in that list. So start taking those steps I've outlined in this chapter. And no, it won't be perfect the first time out; but as a friend of ours, well-known marketer Dan Kennedy, likes to say: **"It doesn't have to be good, just good enough."** This is especially true when you're tying your first lure on the line and getting ready to throw it out there, trying to attract your first customers. Don't worry about polishing it up until it's the best thing since sliced bread; you're going to fall forward, if you will. You're going to try a few things that are going to work a little... and they may not work to the best of your ability. **But you're going to hone your skills as you move forward, so you'll keep moving down to road. Forward, not backward.**

And here's something I'd like to point out: **Once you have a large, stable group of customers who like you, respect you, and trust you, it's going to be hard to fail.** I think that most marketers don't realize just how insatiable their customers really are. I think a lot of people are afraid to push too hard. When I was younger, I would worry that I was trying to sell too much stuff to my customers. My biggest fear was that they were going to feel I was trying to push too many products and services at them, and they were going to get turned off and not want to do business with me anymore. Now, quite frankly, the only thing I concern myself with is that we're not offering *enough* stuff to them. Because the fact is, if they're not buying from us, they're going to buy from somebody else. **People who are serious about making money are particularly insatiable, and they like looking at new opportunities constantly.** That's one of the reasons we continue to come up with all kinds of new opportunities for them, because that's what they like.

Too many people are afraid of making additional sales to their clients, and I think that's why they focus too much on selling to a customer the first time, and too little on re-selling to them. **Dear Reader,** *do not* **worry about the possibility of offending your clients. The reality is, you can't mail to them too much.** There's an enormous amount of discretionary money being spent in this country every year, on all kinds of products and services. Even though the economy is tight, and people say they're broke all the time, **they** *will* **spend money on things they really want.** It doesn't matter whether we're in a good economy or a bad economy. People are continuing to spend money like they have a never-ending supply, **and if you don't get your share, somebody else will — count on it.**

And when you're talking about discretionary income, remember, you're

---

▼▼▼▼▼▼▼▼▼▼▼▼▼

A good swipe file can make you a ton of money!

> Use it to jump-start your thinking.

> Get new creative ideas that you would have never discovered without it.

> It's a brainstorming tool — <u>if</u> you realize that <u>all</u> great selling ideas can be transferred from one product, service, or business to another.

> In other words, the ideas that are or have brought in a ton of money for one person or company can be worth a fortune to you!

MARKETING SECRET

Your BIGGEST moneymaking ideas never come to you when you're thinking conservatively.

▼

LESS IS MORE!

- Spend more time working on fewer projects that have the potential to make you the largest sum of money.

---

competing with all kinds of entertainment choices: the latest book or movie, dinner at a restaurant, or the purchase of a $30,000 car versus a $15,000 car. In order to get the biggest possible share of that discretionary money, **you need to constantly remind your clients that they should be doing business with you.** And again, it all goes back to the list.

One of the first points I talked about in this chapter was identifying what the big benefit is — that big thing that your prospects are looking for. You've already filled it once by giving them the initial sale; **so now it's just a matter of continuing to find other products and services,** either by developing them yourself, licensing products, or engaging in Joint Venturing with other people. **Then you go back to your list and let them know about new opportunities, products, and services that you have available to them.** If you've done a good job of building your list, then every time you offer something, a portion of that list will decide that they want to spend money on you.

And by the way, **a list has a shelf life.** If you're a timid marketer, if you're afraid of mailing offers, if you're fearful you're going to make your clients upset if you send them another offer... then that list *will* go bad. **If that list isn't cultivated and maintained, if you don't continue with the relationship, the relationship will go cold.** It's just like a friend of yours. If you don't talk to your friend, pretty soon a week goes by and you haven't picked up the phone, and then a month goes by or a couple of months go by; pretty soon it's a few years since you've spoken with them, and you wonder what happened. It's the same thing with a customer list. If you don't continuously work to keep that relationship strong, that relationship will go bad, and the list will become useless to you because they don't treat you any differently than they do anybody else who's mailing them. You're back to square one trying to build your list again.

So you might as well spend your time cultivating that relationship by mailing to them as often as possible. Some people send email offers to their list every single day. For some people, it's several times a week by snail mail. When you're constantly in touch with your customers, that rapport is going to strengthen and they'll be more likely to buy from you. This idea that it's all a numbers game is the wrong thinking. At some level, yes, the numbers do come into play. **But what this is really a *relationship* game, so you have to do things that let people know that you *do* care about them, that you *do* have their best interest in mind.** You have to be honest with them; they all know that you're trying to get something, too, so be very clear about what's in it for you. You have to address their skepticism.

And let me re-emphasize something that I always try to emphasize when I'm discussing this subject: **I feel that a lot of people don't understand the DRM business, because they think that it's somehow different than other businesses.** But it's not. Over and over, I tell people that you should think of your DRM business as restaurant. Everybody has a favorite restaurant, right? You've probably been going there several years. Everybody can understand that no restaurant ever succeeds unless it has regular customers that keep coming back again and again, with some extreme exceptions — like the ones built alongside a busy freeway or inside a mall. But for the most part, if you're not doing something to encourage your customers to return, if you're not trying to treat them right, they're going to start going to the other restaurants in town; and soon you're going to be forced to go out of business, because you just can't make enough money to keep your doors open.

Well, every business is the *same exact way*, the DRM business included. **It's *not* different; it's exactly the same.** You've got to do a good job of serving your customers. You need to be there for them, trying to understand why they buy what they buy, trying to get behind their eyeballs, trying to have a close relationship with them... just the way you understand your friends. **You should consider your customers your friends,** in fact, and really try to understand what it is that they want the most, so that you can serve it up to them in the best possible way.

As I wrap up this chapter, let me steal a comment again from my colleague Eric Bechtold: **success leaves clues, clues that you can follow and learn from.** You don't want to reinvent the wheel, and — I can't say this enough — **you don't get rich by yourself. You don't become a good marketer by yourself, either.** You don't just sit down one day, and a light goes on and you know every single thing you need to know. You do things like you're doing right now. You read, you get on conference calls, you listen to audios, you learn from people who have what you don't have — and you fill in the blanks.

And remember how I was talking about using lures to attract customers? Many times you have multiple lures in the marketing waters. That way, when one lure isn't working, it's not like the presses stop and all the money stops coming in. **When you find a lure that's working, go out and you find another lure, and then another, and try to maintain multiple lines in the water at all times.** If one of your lures doesn't work, offer your list another. In order to do that, you've got to track who came in with what offer in your database, so you can segment out your list by whatever lure you were using at the time. This allows you to know where one lure might work better than another.

Getting your customer in the door is just step one. That's the hardest thing you have to do. **The real money is in selling them over and over; that's the key to success.** It's much easier to sell somebody something or get them to take your desired action if they've already taken an action, because once they've taken that action, they're psychologically bonded to you. They feel comfortable. They were able to justify one purchase, so it's much easier for them now to come back and say, "Okay, this person is a good person. I've already bought a product from them and they did a good job of delivering that product, so I'm going to do it again."

That's why **you need to be constantly on the lookout for other offers, including other Joint Venture partners,** as I've mentioned previously. That means finding people who are doing the same things as you and have similar products and services. **Call them up and tell them you'd like to offer their product to your database.** If you were to call me and say, "I have 10,000 people who bought this product. It's very similar to your product line. Would you mind putting it in front of your audience base for, let's say, 70 percent of the money?" or something like that, I'd probably rise to the bait. **We entrepreneurs always need to have the next**

offer ready to go, and as long as that offer is good and something my audience base would be willing to buy, you just made my life a lot easier.

It really is as simple as having a strategy for bringing in new customers and building new relationships with clients, all the while continuing to do more and more business with the people you already have on your list. **If you do those two things successfully, then not only are you continuing to feed your business with new clients, but you're maintaining the relationship you have with your existing clients.** In a way, it's like a funnel: you're always bringing in new clients, using your front-end lead generation strategy, and then building those relationships you already have with clients who have already purchased from you. If you've got that working like it should be, you'll never run out of people to sell to.

That's our marketing strategy in a nutshell. **We constantly have some new front-end promotions out there that bring us new customers automatically, and then we have as many different systems as we can juggle to re-sell those customers again and again.** We've been doing it since 1988. And yes, there's a lot to it. On one hand, all of this is very basic, very simple. On the other, there are still a lot of unanswered questions, and people get bogged down with the details. The nice thing about having formulas and systems is that it makes it so that any time you get a little confused, you can take a deep breath, relax a bit, and go back to the fundamentals so you don't become overwhelmed and frustrated.

I use the chess analogy as a way of explaining this. There are only six different types of chess pieces; and yet, if you've ever played the game, especially if you've played it with somebody who's really good... oh man, they can smoke you in three or four moves! A good chess player can beat you a hundred different ways, and they're always thinking three or four moves down the road, whereas most of us are just thinking about the next move. Business is like that, too. **There are so many simple and fundamental strategies you can use, and if you put them into play carefully and logically, you'll have a true competitive advantage over everybody else in your market.**

Marketing The Back-End

▼▼▼▼▼▼▼▼
MARKETING SECRET

Keep finding new ways to re-use and combine all of the most successful elements that have worked for you in the past.

▼

Always remember that skeptical eyes are reading every word of your sales copy.

I want to kick this chapter off by talking about why your desire to make easy money is both your worst enemy and your best asset. You see, most of us are kind of lazy when it comes to putting what we know into practice. A lot of people just want to learn the bare bones about marketing, so they can put a sales letter together, send it out, and then sit back and pull millions of dollars out of their mailbox. That's the way a lot of people view DRM.

The truth is, that's just ridiculous. I'm not going to pull any punches here: you're a serious student of marketing and want to really know how this works, or you wouldn't be reading this book, now would you? **You need to realize that almost all the profits in this business of information marketing come from the back-end** — which is literally the tail end of any marketing process, about as far from cobbling together a sales letter as you can get. You can't just sit there and write a letter to people you don't have any affinity with, who don't know who you are, and expect them to start throwing money at you hand over fist. Now, there's a time and a place for that; those big pay days happen, but you need to realize that they happen on the back-end.

Let's break it down. There are two different types of offers: front-end and back-end. **Front-end offers are what you use to develop your customer base.** No matter what industry you're in, that's what you're actually using to pull in your clients to begin with. Those are your new customer acquisition offers, your lead generation. Frankly, **you're going to spend about 20% percent of your time and effort on getting new customers in the front door. Eighty percent of your time is going to be working with existing customers, because again, that's where most of your money is made: on the back-end.**

One way to illustrate this is to think about it as that sales funnel everybody talks about, where you're bringing people in and building rapport. Your offer could be something low-cost or free, just to get them in the door: a loss leader item, as they call it in retail. **Even if you lose money on it, you capture their information, add them to a direct-mail campaign, and start to build a relationship with those people.** This is applicable to a retail environment or anything else, too, but my expertise is in DRM, so that's how I prefer to explain it. Let's say my front-end right now is a $20 offer. We get people to pay us $20, and we really deliver on that. We give them a lot of great stuff so that they're excited about it, and that's part of building that rapport.

But again, most wannabes want to just write a letter, sit back, and have money come pouring in. **That's not going to happen, typically, which is the reason that it's your worst enemy.** The only time it happens is when you've been playing the game long enough, and you've built up the front end and acquired a database of people who are now excited about what it is you have to share with them. **Again, there's that "stored energy"**, a wonderful phrase I stole from my friend Eric Bechtold. Remember when you were a little kid and had one of those little balsa wood airplanes that had a little rubber band engine? You could sit there and wind it and wind it and wind it, and when you let it go, it would fly! But it took effort to get that stored energy in place, right? That's like your database, your list of customers. Once you've developed that list, any time you want to make money, you've got a group of people you can make other offers to. You've already "wound them up."

In addition to being your worst enemy, that desire to make easy money is also your best asset, if you're in the business of providing people with business opportunities and moneymaking solutions. **It really helps you understand what people are excited about; it helps you get into the mind of your consumer, so that you can then position other offers.** This is something to think about when you're trying to develop your front-end offers: **Think about what it is you can sell on the back-end. That**

front-end offer exists primarily to qualify people. It needs to define those people, so that you can use that knowledge to understand what they want to spend money on. This, in turn, tells you what they're truly passionate about. Get in the minds of those people, and you can marry other offers to their desires.

The fact that you like easy-money solutions helps put you in the shoes of your prospects. **You can think about what type of offers would appeal to you, what you would be looking for if you were on the other side of the cash register. This puts you in the position of making huge profits on the back-end,** assuming you're willing to put this knowledge into play. You shouldn't think about jumping into this game and then get frustrated if your front-end is going a little slower than you imagined. That tells you something right there. It's not like you can just send out a little flyer, and all of a sudden all the money in the world is coming in. It takes a little time and mastery to get that database put together so that you can generate those big back-end pay days once you get the ball rolling.

At M.O.R.E., Inc., we call the front-end product the "gateway" product, because it's a good way of thinking about it. That's all it is: a gateway. Part of the secret is that you've got to blow people's minds. **You've got to get them so excited that when they get that front-end gateway package, they're so impressed they can't wait to see what you'll offer them next.** There are so many marketers out there who don't get that and never will — and thank God, because it makes it easier to compete! They'll send somebody something for $20-30, but they'll spend as little as possible on that item, so that when people get it, they're hopelessly disappointed. That leads to very few back-end sales.

We prefer to just pile on the quality; in fact, we'll often spend more on a front-end offer than we could possibly get for it. Remember Christmas when you were a kid? Remember how you couldn't wait, and you opened the packages up and you had such great gifts? It was exciting! So we try to put a lot of stuff into our packages so when people open it up they go, "Holy crap! I can't believe they gave me all of this stuff!" And then we start trying to do things to build that relationship even faster.

One of our current gateway packages is based on a model we're using to create more just like it. Now, I'm not exaggerating when I say that **what we're trying to do, as a rule of thumb, is offer to give people $1,000**

> ▼▼▼▼▼▼▼▼▼▼▼▼▼
> If you don't know it can't be done, you can do it.
>
> An educated person will stay up all night and worry about things that most of us never even think about. We are too damn busy doing the deal to worry about anything.

worth of value for every $10 that they spend. We're doing that by including certificates for some of our high-priced marketing seminars and for certain coaching programs. So we're giving them real value here, blowing their minds in the process. We're making a great impression. Think of it as a first date. If you're a young man and you've found the woman that you want to marry, you're going to make sure that your car is spotless, and you'll shower, wear cologne, and put on the best clothing you own. You're going to be on your best behavior. It's the same thing when you're selling to somebody the first time. You're going to be on your very, very best behavior, because you're trying to make a favorable impression.

So over-deliver; really go overboard. **You need to think about your gateway, your front-end product as putting your best foot forward, because it really is the start of that relationship.** It's the little "seed" that's going to grow, and that's very important to get right. A lot of people think of selling something on the back-end, and want to do something really mediocre on the front-end. Well, that doesn't set the stage for a back-end sale. It just sets the stage for that person to think your next offer is going to be just as cheap as the first one. **So you really don't want to consider your front-end offer as a moneymaking situation for you; there's a time to make money, and it's on the back-end.** You want to think of that front-end as the wooing stage.

Having Affairs with Hot Products

Let's look at that relationship analogy again. I've got another good tip for you: Discover how having affairs with hot products can make you millions. **What I mean by that is this: When you're making a front-end offer, consider involving yourself with other people's offers.** Many of the entrepreneurs I know actually sell other people's products as well as anything they create internally; in fact, **in many cases their primary**

▼▼▼▼▼▼▼▼
MARKETING SECRET

This should be framed and hung on all of our walls: "Business is always a struggle. There are always obstacles and competitors. There is never an open road, except the wide road that leads to failure. Every great success has always been achieved by fight. Every winner has scars... Those who succeed are the efficient few. They are the few who have the ambition and willpower to develop themselves."
— Herbert W. Casson

source of income is other people's products. They like to get involved with other people's offers and promote their offers because, really, you can spend a lot of time and effort falling in love with products and going down the wrong road, developing product lines and putting all your effort and money into projects that nobody's really going to care about other than you. **A lot of people make that horrible mistake of falling in love with a product, when they should be falling in love with the marketplace and *then* figuring out a way to give that market what they want.**

So discover how to have affairs with hot products! You need to get excited about the different markets out there, the different things people are excited about; **keep your finger on the pulse, and always look to what people are buying already.** Again, you don't want to try to predict the future; you want to find out what people are already excited about. That's why I use the word "affair," because it can be hot one day and cool off the next day. If you fall in love, that suggests you're going to have a long-term commitment, whereas if you're having an affair, it can be like a little fling. It can be something you get involved in, you work with it, and as soon as it starts to cool off you can keep your eyes on the horizon for the next fling, the next thing you're going to get involved in.

A lot of people don't understand this; they're always looking for what they call "a home," something they can hang their hat on for 10 or 20 years. **And there *are* certain marketplaces that have that type of longevity, but most marketplaces don't.** They fall into the life-cycle of a bell curve, and of course there are product life cycles. It starts when your product is brand new and just being introduced, and people are just starting to use it. Then it goes through a growth phase where it's starting to increase, and more and more people out there know about it. Then it gets to a maturity stage. It's like the lifecycle of a human: you're born, you're a baby, you grow, and you mature — and then you slowly get older, and you start to decline. It happens in every industry, with every product. You need to realize that you don't want to hang your hat onto something that has a cycle like this for so long that you're married to it — so that when it starts to die off, that's the only thing you can think about. **You need to realize that you want to have affairs with markets while they're hot, because what's current creates currency, and what's hot today might not be hot tomorrow.** You don't want to fall in love with something and become so committed to it that when the next hot thing comes along, you just say, "Oh no, I'm working on this thing. I can't possibly look at something else," because then you find yourself in a situation where that hotter thing, which could have produced a lot more revenue for you because it's more current, passes you by — and you're stuck with something that may be on the decline, so that you're losing out on a lot of big opportunities.

This point interrelates with what we were talking about earlier, **because your front-end offers should always be built around these hot marketplaces.** New things are also like magnets, in that they pull people in and get them engaged because they want to know what's new and what's exciting and what's next. That's exactly what you're providing them by doing that. **And, again, a lot of people make the mistake of sticking with one thing.** I've talked to people who say, "Oh, I've been doing this for five years." I ask, "Well have you made any money?" And the reply is, "Um... I made a little bit in the beginning, and I've really just stuck with it." That's a mistake. If you're not making more and more money as time goes by with a particular product or opportunity, then at the very least you need to be a little "untrue" to it and dabble in a hotter market or better offer.

Fall in love with your market; *don't* **fall in love with your products or services.** We say this to people all the time, and it always seems to shock them, because they just don't understand the game. We tell them that products are a dime a dozen — and really they are. **The product itself is not nearly as important as getting inside the hearts and the minds of**

the people you want to sell to. That's why I have to say this one more time (and I hope I'm not sounding too much like a broken record): **you've got to find a hot market that you have some affinity with.** The business opportunity market is the market I think you they should be focusing on if you're a business opportunity enthusiast, as so many of my clients are. It takes one to know one, as the old cliché goes.

You want to fall in love with the people that you sell to. **The more that you can really fall in love with them, and the more they're your friends, the higher the profits.** You have to think of people that you work with as your friends, and you have to treat them as your friends. **It's all about relationships.** We say that so often, but there are so many people who've just never figured it out. They think it's all just about the money, and that's all they care about. **There are a lot of aggressive, unethical marketers out there, and I try to stay away from them.** Sure, they're playing the game I talked about earlier; but sadly, their game isn't based on trying to treat people with any respect. All they want to do is get as much money as they can as fast as they can, and keep as much of it as they can. They're out there raping and pillaging. And yes, at first some of those guys do make a lot of money. Most of the time, they also end up with serious legal problems — and other problems. They all seem to have problems with other relationships in their lives, too.

I'm not trying to come across like I'm holier than thou, but we've always viewed our customers as friends. **We try to treat people with dignity and respect, show them appreciation, and make them feel important — because they *are*!** These are the people providing you with food, shelter, and riches. We're not playing some manipulative game, trying to trick our customers into feeling important. That's nonsense, because making them feel important shouldn't be hard. They *are* important, and that's why you're treating them that way. Those attitudes rub off, and people can sense that. Now, I'll admit there are some seasoned con men (and women) who do a good job of faking it, but eventually people find them out. It's all about loving people, treating people with respect, trying to give them tremendous value. **When they're not happy you're not happy, and you're trying to do everything possible to right that wrong — even if it's not your fault.** That's just practicing good old-fashioned business, the way it was done 150 years ago, isn't it?

In order to better serve the customer, you have to get their

attention in the first place. If you want to expand the audience base you have to work with, it should make sense that you want to dangle the most powerful product in front of them that you can, because that's what's going to be the "bait," if you will, the lure that gets them in and gets them to pay attention. **This is a world where there's so much "noise" out there in terms of competition.** Imagine yourself in front of a huge auditorium full of thousands of people, and they all have something they want to sell you, and they're all yelling at you. All you hear is the roaring crowd, and you can't possibly pick one out. Well, if somebody has something that really captures your attention, maybe they can hold it up or get your attention, so that you're paying attention to that person. You're focused on them. It's as if they pulled you out of that stadium and put you into a little side room, and now they're communicating with you one-on-one. You're paying attention. That's how you have to handle your customers. **You have to have hot offers, things that will almost literally *force* them to pay attention.** Put yourself on the other side of the cash register. How would they feel in this situation? What are they going to pay attention to? What's in it for them?

If somebody else has a better offer than you, or something more exciting that appeals to them more, they're probably going to be paying attention to that other person. You've got to have something that demands attention, so that you can start forging those relationships; and you have to be introduced to those people before you can build a relationship. **The customer is always the most important thing to us, so we're trying to take care of them and be respectful to them.** Part of this process is searching for hot offers that will continue to attract new customers so that you can build and build.

Developing Great Messages

I've talked about the fact that there's a lifecycle for products, and how to find a front-end offer, and the difference between front-end offers and back-end offers. Now I'd like to talk about developing great sales messages. **Doing so is a process, not an event.** And again, this is the no-punches-pulled bare bones truth here; I'm trying to give you the nuts and bolts you really need. You need to understand that those of us basing our marketing on direct-mail aren't miracle people who just have all the answers handed to us. We weren't just born with all the knowledge we

MARKETING SECRET

Perception is more important than reality.

▼

"EVERYTHING is based on fear." — Mel Brooks as the 2000 Year Old Man

ever need to make money. **This is a process; it takes work, and it takes thinking, and it takes *re*-thinking.** It takes some brainstorming to develop great ideas.

Thomas Edison put it best when he said, "Genius is 99% perspiration and 1% inspiration." That's what I meant when I said that products and offers are a dime a dozen. **It's making them work that's hard.** That's where all the elbow grease and perspiration come in. **Again, I want you to realize that I started exactly where you are at.** We took some ideas and started thinking about our marketplace. We figured out what they wanted, and then went out and we found a hot offer — something that would match up with the desire that already existed in the marketplace — and we wrote out a sales letter and put that into the marketplace to see if we got a good result. If we got a good result, then heck, we went ahead and produced more and put *them* out there. That's something you need to realize; **you test and you re-invest and you continue to build.** You "cheat on" your products with new, hotter products if you need to. It's hard work. None of this stuff happens just by waving a magic wand and saying, "There it is — all the money you ever want is pouring in now." It does take preparation and perspiration and a little bit of inspiration. **But mostly, it's about taking the time to do it.**

The general idea of this book is to hopefully rewire your brain a bit, and make you better understand the reality of the situation. Because this isn't all just about making easy money. If all you want to do is sit in your La-Z-Boy and have money come to the front doorstep, that's not reality. Sure, it *can* happen if you've already done something to put a process into action; maybe you get residual revenue from something you did a long time ago. But even that took effort, desire, careful planning, and thinking and testing to create. **You're never going to make real money without putting effort in first. And then, realize this, too: you're just not going to find something that's going to produce forever.** I wish you could, but I haven't found one yet that I could just hang my hat on and knew that it was going to work as well tomorrow as it does today. So you always need to be thinking about what's next, how you can get positioned for the next big thing, and continue this process.

It's like a roller coaster. You get a good offer out there, and it has its peaks and its valleys; but eventually, it's going to come back into the station, its potential spent. You need to be prepared for that; **you need to always be looking out to the horizon to find another thing you can plug into.** But you're never going to get on that roller coaster in the first place until you start thinking about an offer, putting things on paper, and getting in the front of your audience so you can deliver your sales message, however you want to do that. You've got to get it out there in order to get results. **You've got to take that desire, wrap a system around it, and go out there and make this stuff *work*.**

So again, developing great selling messages is a process, not an event. **And once you do start making money, that's when things really do come together for you.** So many times we find people struggling before they hit it big. I have a friend who spent a good 10-15 years struggling, and now he's making so much money it's not even funny. We're happy for him. He's getting rich. For the longest time he was struggling and now, all of a sudden, the money is flowing in like water from an open fire hydrant. There's no stopping him now. I tell you this to illustrate the fact that what comes in so effortlessly now was once such a struggle for him. **You get better at crafting great sales messages as you go along.** It does get easier, once you're privy to the secrets. For example, **here's one we make a lot of use of: recycling.**

It's so simple. Sure, you do keep coming up with new stuff; but unfortunately the market changes quickly, and the best customers in the market are always limited to some degree. So you have to roll with the changes. **One way to do that is turn to what's worked for you before, and retool it. Add some twists, work in some new material, repackage**

it, and offer it to your customers. For example: we recently had a promotion we called the IAMS-5 promotion, because it's the fifth generation of the promotion. The clients know it as something else. Each generation has looked different from the outside; but at its core it's the same basic premise. It's one way that we continue to find new ways to incorporate the things that worked the very best for us in the past again and again because, you see, **while the market does change to a degree, the people within it really don't change much.** Human nature really hasn't changed significantly in thousands of years. **People are still affected by two primary emotions, fear and greed.** It's been that way since the beginning of recorded history. It's nice to know that the market that you serve doesn't change that much.

When crafting your message to your market, you have to keep in mind what they're really excited about — and that's something usually know as a "magic bullet" or "magic pill." **You need to realize that everybody out there is looking for some sort of cure or solution that fixes their problem yesterday — the miracle cure, the instant solution.** People will throw money at you if they believe that your offer is that one solution to all their ills, real or perceived. Considering all that noise out there in the marketplace, magic bullets or magic pills are very important.

But the only use for a magic bullet is to put it into your gun, okay? You need to realize that a lot of people are out there playing to the fact that they have a solution to whatever ails you. **What they're doing is going out and researching the marketplace, figuring out what the worst pain or the worst problem is within the market, and then just writing their headline:** "We finally have a solution to "X"!" Right? Think about those diet pills on TV you're going to see all over the place around New Year's : "Just take this pill and the fat will magically drip off your body." They're never going to say, "Take this pill, and with a diet and exercise you'll lose weight," now are they? Sure, that's probably what the actual bottle says when it comes. But the magic bullet marketing out there will just say, "Take this and you'll watch the fat melt off your body."

And you need to realize that magic bullets do exist, but just like those miracle drugs on TV, they usually come with that long list of crazy side effects. Magic bullet advertising strategies are effective when you're playing to the pain of the customer base, because it's a good way to overcome all that noise in the marketplace. **But you need to make sure** you tell them about the magic bullet, and then when they make that purchase, you give them *everything* they need in order to overcome that problem. You have to provide what you're claiming to provide. You can't just tell them you've got a solution if you actually don't. **You can make promises, but make sure that your marketing can back that up.** The idea, again, is to create an offer that really plays to people's pain, then that gives them the solution they're looking for, because they're going to throw money at you if you can do that. You want to come at them with something that they feel is the ultimate solution, exactly what they've been looking for.

So when you're out there in the marketplace, take the time to dig in and study those headlines that really capture your attention. Flip through the magazines that are playing to your marketplace. If you're an automotive buff and you want to sell to other automotive buffs, go through the automobile magazines. If you're interested in guns, look to *Guns & Ammo*. If you're interested in business opportunities, go to *Entrepreneur*, *Home Business Connection*, or *Home Business Journal*. **Analyze those headlines that pull you in right off the bat, and normally you'll find a magic bullet — something that stops you dead in your tracks, that plays to your pain.** It makes you want to buy that product, because it's something that's really been agitating you for a long time. "How am I going to solve that? Oh well, I'll just buy that product and I'll feel all better."

> RELATIONSHIP MARKETING:
> Win their hearts — then win their pocketbooks!

We often talk about how "the more things change, the more they remain the same." And yes, we're living in a fast-changing world; but it's always comforting to know that human nature doesn't change. **People want easy answers; and if anything, we're getting lazier than ever.** Most people claim they want to make more money, but they're never going to listen to a moneymaking program. They're not going to take even the slightest bit of action. **They want somebody to do everything for them.** The companies that are providing those kinds of services are making money faster than they can spend it. And you know what? You might as well be one of those people. **Offer to do things for people; let them know**

▼▼▼▼▼▼▼▼
MARKETING SECRET

Do everything possible to change the shift of power, and get them to chase you — rather than you chasing them!

▼

A lead-generation secret: Who cares about the cost? The only thing that matters is what you make after the conversion.

you'll just take care of it for them. That's always been a good tactic, but again, it's getting more and more common in every market. That's the basis of this magic bullet concept. But remember this: **the magic bullet also works for people who *aren't* lazy.** I have some friends in Utah who sell a high-dollar coaching program. Their clients are extremely busy, and extremely successful; and one of their top-selling services is something that handles a very important thing on behalf of the client. And it's not that they're lazy; they're overwhelmed. They've got too much to do already, so they can't handle this particular thing. What they have is a lot of money to spend, so they're more than happy to give it to our friends.

The point is, in every single market you've got people who, for whatever reason, just want you to take care of everything, because you've got a proven track record and they know they can depend on you. **People are looking for somebody else to take the reins.** That's why there are so many people who are providing fast, easy solutions to those kinds of things. **Consumers always want things easier, faster, simpler, and they respond to things that promise them that.** It's an emotional thing. If our competitors are using that method and we're not, then we're losing money by not also having products and services designed to make life much easier for people.

Smart entrepreneurs take things that are extremely complicated, things that they've developed and perfected over the years, and offer to do it all for their clients. That provides them with a lot of value. But there's one little thing I need to talk about that's important in making that process work: **transparency.** One of the ways you can establish yourself as an expert in selling "we do it all for you" processes is to be very transparent with the people you're working with. **You have to go painstakingly through every little detail of how you do something, why you do it, and what the next step is.** You can even build in ways for people to check and balance the system, so they can see it all happening. These are all things that make it easy for people to feel comfortable with that process.

A lot of people try to sell "we do it all for you" programs to people without ever really being transparent, thereby showing people that they know what they're talking about. There are a lot of consultants out there, in various industries, that take you through all these crazy processes and diagrams and say, "Now, you can do this yourself — or you can just hire me. I'll come into your office and put all this stuff into action for you." **They're establishing their credibility by being transparent,** by showing you that what they're talking about isn't just a bunch of fluff and BS, but the real deal, and then offering the "we do it all for you" magic bullet on the back-end. **That's really one of the keys to our success.**

A good way to roll out an offer and attract new clients is to sell them the magic bullet concept on the front-end, where you're a bit vague about what it is you're going to do for them. You tell them how you have all the answers, and get them to request a package of information or attend a tele-seminar, where you can then go into all the details and establish your credibility so that they understand why and how this magic bullet does exist, and how you can actually fulfill the promises you're making. And then at the very end you say, "Of course, I just gave you everything you need to get from Point A to Point B. You can take that information, roll up your sleeves, and go to work. Or use me as the solution to your problem... here's where to sign." **Again, you've got to really take that work and knowledge and roll them together effectively in order to reach the people that you're trying to serve.** The neat thing about this type of offer is that, as I've mentioned, you can put the work, effort, and development in one time and sell that magic bullet a thousand times. **Re-package it, and just continue to roll it out there.** That's one of the things I love more than anything else about this information marketing industry. The pain and effort goes into something once when you create it, and then you continue to benefit from it, sometimes for years to come.

That's very powerful.

So how do you go about doing it all for someone? Here's another analogy that I think works pretty well. Let's assume you're selling trash service, something we all need. I can come to you and say, "Okay, we're a new trash service here and we're replacing your old service. Here's what we offer: We'll pick up your trash at the curb in the fancy little receptacle we provide you. We'll put it into our truck and haul it to the trash station, where we'll weight it in. We'll put it into the trash bin there and we'll pay our ongoing trash fees that we have to pay in order to use the dump. Then we'll hose off our trucks and clean everything out. We'll pay our employees to do the same thing over and over again every Thursday for you, and all you do is you pay a little fee. Or, here's how you get your permits to go get rid of it the dump. You have to take the trash in every Thursday yourself. You don't have any receptacles, so you have to provide those as well as haul your own garbage. Here's the phone number and the address where you need to go. Here's everything you need to do, all the painstaking details. Or hey, just pay us and we'll pick up your trash on Tuesday. It's only $100 a year to do that for you."

So what are you going to do? It's a weird little example, maybe, but these guys know what they're doing. They take your garbage, it magically goes away to where it's supposed to go, and you feel comfortable with that situation. You can think about any business solution the same way. **If it's something they have to get done and they can pay you to do it for them, then that will eliminate the pain, effort, and struggle it would take them to do it.** So by all means, they're going to throw money at you over and over again.

If you're going to do one of these "we do it all for you" services, **try to build it around an ongoing need.** There are plenty of angles you can incorporate into your business if you're open to this type of thinking. The answers will come to you if you take all this stuff, put it in a little mental box, then focus on it; and understand, of course, that a lot of these things are going to take you some time to develop. **But once they're in place, you can just turn on the faucet and money will come pouring out for years to come.**

Along the way, you'll always learn new things. We've been doing this since 1988, and we're still finding new ways to do what we've been doing for years. **You never really run out of ideas. In fact, our goal is twofold:** NUMBER ONE, we want to think new thoughts we've never thought before, so we can come up with new ideas we've never thought of. NUMBER TWO, we look for all the things that have worked for us in the past, and find new ways to re-purpose them. And let me re-emphasize this: it's a process, not an event. People are in a hurry to make millions of dollars, just as I one was. The funny thing is, once you start getting a few of these things in place, the money will come in so fast and so furiously you'll wonder where it was all of those years that you were struggling! Our first five years we generated more than $10,000,000 worth of DRM revenue. **Money can come in very quickly when you pair the right offer to the right market and implement it the right way.** It's just that sometimes there's a struggle; and of course there's a learning curve.

As part of that process, you must realize that you have to earn people's trust. **You have to earn their respect.** You can say that for every relationship. And yet, a lot of marketers, especially those new to the business, aren't even thinking in terms of relationships. They have no plan to build those bonds of trust with people.

The Four Stages of Learning

I want to round out this chapter with an idea in four stages: **the stages of learning something new.** Learning can be distressing and a bit frightening, so let's go through these four stages here so that you can relax a little and come to understand that it's a natural process.

The FIRST STAGE is unconscious incompetence; basically, this is ignorance. You don't know what you don't know, so you really have no idea what's going on; you're a bit scared, and maybe you just don't even think about it. **Then there's STAGE TWO: conscious incompetence, when you begin to realize and discover the things you don't know.** This is the frustration and confusion period. You're still incompetent and ignorant about the whole thing, but at least your eyes are beginning to open, and you realize that there's a bigger world out there — that this is a game, and there are little things that you can do to make it better.

Then you've got STAGE THREE, conscious competence, where you can function in this new area, but it's a major struggle and you're

▼▼▼▼▼▼▼▼▼
MARKETING SECRET

Selling is simply leading the customer to a buying decision and influencing them to take action now!

▼

What do all people want? Someone to do it for them! That's why all of us should be in the "do-it-for-em" business!

---

not very good at it. This is where most marketers are: they're thinking about their business, and they're struggling, and they're really digging in and trying to find the best thing that they can promote and everything. **But at least they're moving forward in the right direction.** You stumble along. This is what I was talking about when I mentioned my friend who struggled for 10-15 years before he started to make lots of money. It's like one of those rock bands that becomes an overnight success, because they've been out touring and in the bar scenes for 20 years. **They just finally hit the point of unconscious competence, where they've mastered it. That's STAGE FOUR here: you get to where you do it naturally, like a duck swims.** People just say, "Oh, you're a natural — you just have this natural ability to make money." No, you've spent a lot of time and effort understanding what you didn't know. You learned how to put it to work for you, and now you can look at something and see it in a different light, and can make it happen a lot faster than most other people. **But the whole process took a long time.**

In that conscious competence stage, you can make a lot of money very quickly, and it can happen very fast. You don't have to master everything in order to play the game and in order to have some victories. But what's going to happen is, **eventually your losses, the things that you try that don't work, will start to get fewer and farther between.** This is especially the case if you treat it like a game because when you really have a true desire to make it work and it's fun, it's the world's best addiction.

So immerse yourself in the field you're

in. Listen to presentations, get new ideas, read books like this one, and try things. Don't just expect to wake up one day and have this unconscious competence, this mastery. **It takes a while.** It's like learning martial arts. Those Buddhist monks up in the Himalayan Mountains go up there as small children and come down as Kung Fu masters. They didn't walk up there one day and just say, "Hand me the pebble, Master, and make me some sort of triple black belt." It took time, commitment, and effort... but it's fun and rewarding, and along the way you get better and better, and then one day you're an overnight success. I think that's something you really need take to heart. **Understand that this can happen for you, and that you can make a whole heck of a lot of money on your road to unconscious competence — but it's a step-by-step process.** Your steps may take a little longer than others, but just keep at it, and eventually you'll get to that point where you're a marketing master.

It's all part of the game.

SECTION EIGHT:

RUTHLESS MARKETING SECRETS VOLUME TWO

Turning small sums of money into a fortune.

Giving Them What They Want

You know, there are certain basics that you have to go through in this business—and sometimes your emotions aren't always your best indicator of where you are in the game. You can put in years, sometimes, just struggling as I did, and then all of the sudden things just magically come together. I call this the "20-year overnight success story." Hopefully, you won't be one of those! **But there *is* something to be said for having to struggle for a while.**

I have a niece who is a great musician and singer; the only problem is, she's young and dumb. She's going through that deluded stage of life where she thinks the world owes her something. She was singing in front of me a couple years ago and she has a beautiful voice, just beautiful. She was talking about her desires to be world famous and have millions of adoring fans and all that, and I told her, "Amanda, here's what you need to do, hon. You need to find a band, get on the road for about five or six years, and practice every single night—**just practice. Keep getting better and better.** After five or six years on the road, maybe you'll be discovered. Then lo and behold you'll be on TV, and you'll have your multimillion-dollar record contracts, concerts, and all these adoring fans. You'll be famous." But of course that advice fell on deaf ears.

Millions of people want to get rich. If you go out on the street and ask a hundred people, "Hey, you want to be a multimillionaire?"…well, most of them would probably think that you're trying to con them or lie to them, so they'd back off real fast. But if they really believed there was some sincerity to your question, I'm sure that most would say, "Absolutely! I would love to be a multimillionaire; who wouldn't?" **And yet, when you ask them to do anything on a regular basis, to pay any kind of price necessary, they're not willing to do it.** True success often requires an investment of money as well as investment in certain actions and the willingness to do certain things—to go through a learning curve, so to speak. Most people, though, will not do *anything*. And if they do, it'll be short-lived.

When you study the lives of the people who have made it in a big way, you'll find that they all paid a price for success. Sure, there may be

MARKETING SECRET

Blow your own horn!

- Nobody's going to blow your own horn for you — you gotta get out there and do it!

▼

Everything becomes clearer as the deadline gets closer.

an exception here and there; but the problem is that everybody wants to be that exception. **The norm is that *you have to pay the price*.** With very rare exceptions—like rich heiresses and lottery winners—**the people who get rich are the people who make a habit of doing difficult things.** Sometimes those difficult things sound easy, when it fact they can be difficult. That's often (but not always!) true of this chapter's theme: *Making Money by Giving the Customers What They Want*. Not what they need, but what they *want*! Sometimes most of the difficulty lies in remembering this. You're not here to give people what you think they need. ***You're here to give them what they want.*** For many of us, it takes a while to crack that part of the code. That's part of the price we pay: that struggle to finally get it, the understanding of which finally opens the floodgate to real wealth.

It was like that for me, and it was like that for my colleague Jeff Gardner. He struggled for years, and it really didn't look like he was ever going to pull it off. Just like me, he had some people in his life who thought he was a little bit crazy to think that he could make millions of dollars. And yet, he's doing it now! **And part of what makes him so great is he really *does* love to help other people.** If you've seen him live at a seminar, you know it!

Jeff's story starts back when he was about 15 years old. Even before then, he knew he wanted financial freedom. He didn't know it was called that, but he knew that he wanted to make money, mainly because he saw his parents struggling all the time. They certainly weren't what you would consider poor, but you certainly didn't want to be around the table on bill night, because there was a lot of stress and a lot of unhappiness there. Well, Jeff just didn't want to live his life that way.

So Jeff tried to figure out a lot of different ways to make money, primarily by going door-to-door and selling this and that. But ultimately, he stumbled onto mail order. In mail order, it didn't matter how young Jeff was; he was able to sell things to people all over the nation—and later, all over the world. He started out selling other people's products, but eventually shifted to his own products that he'd put together. **Over time, he started making some money.** He wasn't a 20-year overnight success, but it did take him a number of years to become successful—nine, I believe.

That's because he took a shortcut by learning from other people. **He found people he could model: that is, he examined their methods, figuring out what they were doing the right way and the wrong way.** You should do the same as Jeff, and in fact you've made a good start! Instead of trying to figure it out yourself through trial and error, you're doing the easy thing by reading this book and hopefully acquiring some workable ideas you can then apply in your own business.

The other thing that really helped Jeff was his persistence—his stubbornness, if you will. He knew other people had made a lot of money working for themselves, and he was going to do it one way or another. Now, you may be thinking, "Heck, I'm very stubborn too, so I'm sure I'm going to make it," and that's great! **But you have to attach taking action to being stubborn.** If you're just stubborn, you're not going to really be super successful; but if you're *persistent*, if you take action and you're constantly getting out there, doing things, marketing, coming up with products, different marketing ideas, seeing what other people are doing and taking the best of what they're doing, putting it in your business, **then I *do* believe that you're going to shortcut your journey to success.**

That's my intention with this chapter, so let's move straight on to the first topic, which we call **How to Create Super-Selling Power That Can Make You the Fastest, Easiest Money Possible.** We all want fast, easy money, don't we? **The way to get it is to become a power-seller.** Now, I know some people think, "Wow, these people who make millions of dollars selling products and services are well-trained, skillful people," and yes, that's one way to do it. If you have to sell products that there's a lot of competition for, or even products that people really don't want, then yes, you've got to have some super-selling skills to get people to buy. But if you want an easy way to get people to buy, if you want to create an almost magical super-selling power in a very short amount of time, **here's the key: You've got to have something that the buyer wants badly, even desperately.** If that's the case, then you, the seller, has all the power. But keep that in mind: **the power isn't really in you. It's in that item that the buyer wants so badly.** That's why you have to look for the hottest possible products and services to sell.

You know, I talk to a lot of people about writing copy. People really get stressed out about writing sales letters. They're worried about things like, "How do I write a headline? How do I write an opening and a close? How do I write a guarantee?" Even starting out, they think they have to be perfect at it. They're so worried about writing the best sales copy that they'll sometimes go out and spend $10,000, $15, 000, $20,000 or more hiring a professional copywriter to write their sales letters for them. **What they fail to realize is that you can sell a ton of a hot product with a poorly-written sales letter, as long as you've enthusiastic and have something that a market desperately wants.**

And conversely, I honestly believe that if you've got a product that nobody wants, it doesn't matter how great your copy is — you're probably not going to sell very many. So the key, in my opinion, isn't having the best killer sales copy. It's great to have it if you can, and you should always work to hone your skills; **but I would much rather have the best, hottest, most in-demand product than the best sales copy.** So when people are looking for products to sell to their market, or they're just getting started and they don't know what to sell, I always tell them, "Find the hottest offer. Find the hottest product, something that people are desperately going to want to buy."

If you do that, and you implement everything right, you've made the whole situation of selling so much easier... because now you're not really selling. **You're giving the buyer the opportunity to buy something they want already, which really does give you amazing super-selling power.** It's like the money just rains out of the sky. We've experienced that a few times over the years — money came faster than we could intelligently spend it. We still knew how to spend it of course, but not intelligently!

To really sell that hot item, you've got to create an irresistible offer.

This starts with matching your offer to the right marketplace. **You have to begin with the end in mind, sometimes, and work backwards in order to create that irresistible offer.** I know that that sounds a little complicated, and sure, it *is* somewhat advanced. But it's necessary, especially if what you have sells for a high ticket amount. With few exceptions, you can't just ask people who have no relationship with you to give you a lot of money, and actually expect that they'll buy in large numbers. One way you can build that sort of relationship, though, is to **work up to it by starting with lower-priced products and stair-stepping your customers to higher-dollar items.** That's one aspect of it. **The second is knowing that it's the back-end products that produce all your real profit,** so you'll want to think some of that out in advance. Because, you see, nobody gets rich by making one sale to one customer one time. **The secret is to resell to your customers over and over again;** so before you sell a single thing, you've go to think that through, in at least a general fashion.

Most businesses just sell people what they need: razor blades, socks, bread. That's one of the reasons they struggle so much. If you want to get rich, **focus on selling people what they *want*.** Now, be careful with this; sometimes what people want really badly is stuff that will put you in jail. In fact, the most profitable things in this world, it seems, are questionable or even downright illegal. Exclude those from your equation, unless you're really into living dangerously; work within the universe of things that are legal. And realize, too, that sometimes people want the craziest things. They can get typical stuff anywhere. **They're really looking for things that are different; things that are *unique*.**

So how do you figure out what people really want? **Market research, of course.** One of the things we tell people in our seminars is to find a marketplace they understand very, very well. We often talk about how to get rich in the opportunity marketplace, for example. So if you're a fan of the opportunity market and want to enter that marketplace, **you need to find the things that excite *you* the most.** You understand the market; so if things get you excited, then you know that they can get other people excited, too. Create an offer like the one that excited you, and make it irresistible. You've got to stack things up, giving people so much value that they just say *holy crap*! and jump at the chance to become a part of it. They just can't help themselves: they all just start giving you their money at once.

SECTION EIGHT — Ruthless Marketing Secrets, Volume Two

MARKETING SECRET

Your most powerful writing comes when you are working with a subject that you know so intimately that you can write without thinking.

- This is such a powerful position to be in! Every day you are writing from your gut. You write from your heart — from your emotional center.

- This is where your most powerful copy will come from.

- This is where the emotional part of you makes the strongest connection with the emotional part of your reader.

Generally speaking, the more someone wants something, the more money you can make selling it to them. **It's not about need; think about it.** If all people needed was transportation, they'd buy a super cheap car that gets great gas mileage. Or maybe they'd just buy a moped. All they really *need* is transportation. But what they *want* is something else again—which is why when you're a car salesman, you can sell people convertible sports cars and SUVs that will get them from Point A to Point B in style. If someone wants to buy a home and they're just filling a basic need, there are plenty of inexpensive homes on the market. You're not going to make a lot on a product like that; the real money's in selling a home that someone really wants—a high-end house that sells for many times the price of basic shelter.

It's the same way in most businesses. If you're selling what people need, you're probably making small profit margins. **If you're selling what people want, you're probably in a high profit margin business.** The greater the want, generally speaking, the more profit is available in that marketplace.

Again, the best way to know what people want is to determine what you're excited about yourself. Chris Lakey likes golf and other sports. Though he's never been in such a business, he could probably get into one fairly easily with a little basic research, since he's a consumer in that marketplace. He knows a lot about golf, he knows what makes him crazy on the golf course, and he knows the parts of the game that he struggles with. He knows the things that tend to frustrate all golfers, no matter their experience level. You may be the same; maybe *you* know your hobby very well. **Any hobby can be turned into a business if the marketplace is right—and if you offer your prospects something they want *really badly*.** The bigger the want, the more money there is to be made.

So you don't look for the biggest needs; look for the biggest, hottest wants. If you know your marketplace well enough, you can easily discern what these are. Those form the foundation for your sales success to that marketplace. They become the basis for your sales material, because you specifically address the wants people have. The bigger the want, the higher in your sales copy it should be placed. **That's why you should take a look at your competitors and determine which ones are making the most money.** Study what they're doing. Get on the other side of the cash register; think like somebody in the business, rather than a consumer, who *doesn't* think. Consumers, especially the most rabid ones, are buying for subconscious reasons; they're not really able to think in a more logical, holistic kind of way.

So many people are beating their heads against the wall because they're trying to sell people things that *they* want to sell, rather than things that the customers want to buy. That's a path to business failure! **You've always got to know where your focus is—and your focus should almost *always* be on your customer, very rarely on yourself.** You're not necessarily your customer; in fact, sometimes you and your customer are two completely different people. But if you know what they want and are willing to deliver just that, you're going to be more successful than if you decide, "Well, I only want to sell this," and try to sell it to people that don't want it. You'd be surprised how many people do that. **Sell people exactly what they *want*,** which you find by studying the hottest products in your marketplace, and you'll be a super-seller in no time.

Let's jump to a related topic: the **Magic Formula for Making Millions Selling Virtually Any Product or Service.** Now, this is a key item, and it definitely connects to my earlier topic. **The concept here is that we must find people who are very hungry for what we sell, and then feed it to them.** Finding an endless supply of hungry prospects is the golden key to becoming wealthy—and there are some markets that really do have an endless supply of new prospects coming in all the time. Here's an example: the matchmaking market. Look at companies like eHarmony.com or Match.com, companies that focus on this market and are making millions of dollars by doing so. This is a market that will always be there; there will *always* be a fresh, new supply of people looking for other people to date and, ultimately, to marry. And once they're ready to get married, they enter what's known as the wedding market. During the short period of time they're engaged, they become prospects for wedding cakes, dresses, invitations, announcements, and wedding bands. That's another market with a constant stream of fresh prospects.

The dieting market is a *great* market. There are always people who want to lose some extra weight, so in that market you're always having new people come in. You're having people drop out and come back, too. They want pills and potions and diet plans. They want to go to Weight Watchers and Jenny Craig, and are always trying new things. The business opportunity and moneymaking market, the one me and most of my colleagues are involved in, is the same way. **There will always be people who want to make more money, who want to know how to ensure their financial freedom.**

Those are both pretty general markets, but there are markets that are as specific as something like back pain. It's a niche market, though; while there are plenty of people in that market, they can be difficult to reach. After all, they don't all read one publication like *Back Pain Monthly*. Nevertheless, it's possible to reach the market—there are plenty of companies that offer pills, potions, and lotions for back pain sufferers. They know, as we do, that there will always to be people who really want relief from back pain.

Focusing on a market with a constant, never-ending stream of prospects is necessary if you want to have a strong, growing business. If you're trying to sell to a group of seven people, and once those seven people are gone that's it, then you aren't going to have a very strong business, are you? It doesn't matter if the number is seven or seven thousand; eventually the pond will dry up. So you need to focus on a market that's fresh and has lots of new prospects, and simply go out and find what they want to buy. Do your research! You might go to their seminars, events, or organizational association meetings; read their magazines; or even conduct surveys or interviews. **Find out what their common problems are, and deliver the solutions.** That's the magic formula here—but it's almost a common sense formula, really. Once you've done all that, it's easy to figure out what to sell.

Let me reiterate: **Making a lot of money in the marketing field is** *not* **about what you want—unless you're able to make yourself want what your market wants.** A lot of people miss this somehow. They say, "Well, I want to sell X," whatever X may be, and that's the end of the argument. They try to shove it down the throats of the people in their particular market—if they even have a market to sell it to. That's the wrong way to do it. You need a vibrant, dynamic market that new people are coming into all the time, one where the buyers are rabid for new products. **Find out the problems they want to solve, and then create or find products that solve their problems.** Deliver what *they* want, and you're going to find it a lot easier to make money than if you're delivering only what you want. And even if you do find a good market, try to home in on that one niche that's more vibrant than the others.

> Always have your next project waiting in the wings!

Let's use the opportunity market as an example. It encompasses many different segments: everything from niches where companies sell dirt-cheap, flimsy reports, to people selling a whole bunch of cheap stuff, mostly to each other, to companies that sell million-dollars franchises. Then there are the big companies like us that are selling what I think is top-notch information, and others that are just doing Internet stuff at one scale or another. Some of the niches are unique. Recently, someone handed me this business card. First he told me that he's involved in this business opportunity where they're making candles—and I had no interest, believe me. But as soon as he handed me his business card, I knew that somebody involved really understood marketing. It was a beautiful three-panel card that did a great job of selling and really got my attention. The next day, he gave me one of his candles, which I later burned as part of my morning quiet time. It's supposed to be a healthy candle, really good for you, and it really is a superior product.

Then I started studying the market niche that he's in. It *is* an opportunity, but it mostly reaches the stay-at-home mom market, a specific segment of the opportunity market. A lot of housewives want to supplement their income and have a little bit of freedom so they don't have to beg their husband for money; that's a big thing. And they want to get away from the kids for a little while, to have something else going on.

▼▼▼▼▼▼▼▼
MARKETING SECRET

Database Marketing in 3 words:

- Segment
- Concentrate
- Dominate!

▼

The way out is through!

They may not want to go into the work force full-time, but they want to do something that feels productive. **Well, when I started investigating, I found that with about 500 hours worth of work, you could make a go of it.** That's always the joke, you know; "Hey, I got a multimillion-dollar idea for you, and it's only going to take 500 hours worth of work!"

But the truth was, with 500 hours of work, somebody could actually put something together that's very similar to this deal. As I've pointed out, you think about the market first; in this case it was the stay-at-home mom type of market. And then you look at all of the companies selling business opportunities to that particular market, and you plan accordingly. It's got to be a large market, and it's got to be reachable. **There should be a lot of competitors already in the market, and they have to be doing well.** By the way, this company out of California doing this candle thing is publicly traded. Usually little rinky-dink companies aren't—so this should make you smell some money there somewhere.

Whatever you come up with, don't copy what the other companies are doing; but do use them as models. **A big part of marketing is differentiation, what separates you from everyone else.** These other companies should serve as your maps into new territories. Take a little from this company, a little from that one, and put them together in a new way to form something that is totally unique that will serve the marketplace.

One of the points I'd like to make here is that too often, people get caught up in worrying more about the product than they should. They focus on creating a product that sounds good to them or, for one reason or another, they come up with a product and then, after it's developed, then they think about who they should sell it to. Or they never really think about who to sell it to at all; they just invented something, and now they want to figure out who might want it. That's a huge mistake! **Find the prospects first.** Find the group of hungry people, and then offer them something to eat. That's the golden formula: Start with the marketplace. **Too many people try to do it all backwards.** Find the group of customers *first*, then make money by filling their wants—not their needs. It all starts with the prospect, not the product. **And be sure the group of people you start with is large—the bigger the better.** Sometimes you can get into a niche that's too small, where there wouldn't be the opportunity for profit because of the number of people in the niche. But you know, ideas are everywhere. There really are too many ideas and too little time, so you have to pick and choose. That's one place where defining your marketplace, your niche, can really help you.

Let's move on to the third item on this chapter's agenda: **How to Create a Never-Ending Stream of Money By Always Doing One Simple Thing.** We're still sticking with this theme of giving customers what they want, and the idea here is to always strive to fill the deepest unfulfilled desires of your customers. How people are, deep down, is very interesting to me—how our egos work, especially. **People constantly** *want things.* We're never at a state of peace where we feel like we have everything. Maybe you want a new car, a new home, more money, better health, better looks—but you want *something*. Usually we want multiple things. What happens is that we take actions to fulfill those wants, and in most cases those actions include buying things. So if we want a new car, we'll buy that new car. If we want a new house, we'll buy a new house. If we want better health we might buy better food, eat at healthier restaurants, get a gym membership, and go to Jenny Craig. We've been conditioned as consumers to know that if we have a want, we can fulfill it by buying something. Which is great—as marketers, as business owners and entrepreneurs, you want to applaud the fact that consumers have been conditioned in that way. **When people decide to fill those wants, they're willing to pay you if you've got a product or service that will fill their wants.**

Now, the great thing about filling people's wants is that **their desire will, in many cases, be satisfied only very briefly by buying something.** This happens a lot in the business opportunity market. Let's say somebody has the desire to make more money. They want to be filthy rich and live in a beautiful mansion, have fancy cars, and purchase everything that catches their fancy. To fulfill that desire, they might buy a course called "How to Make Money in Real Estate." They send away the $500, they get the course, and they feel like they've taken action and fulfilled that want a little—until they start going through the course, and discover they've actually got to take some real action to make their dreams come true. Well, they're busy in their lives, and so what happens is that they set that aside. They put it on their bookshelf, and then—maybe very quickly, maybe very slowly—that little voice in their head starts telling them they still want the money, that house, the trip, the vacation, and the lifestyle that was *not* fulfilled with that first purchase. So what do they do? **They make a second purchase, a third purchase, a fourth purchase and a fifth purchase—and on and on.**

It's the exact same way in the weight-loss industry: someone has that desire to lose weight, so they'll take action to try to fulfill that desire, to fill that want, and they will not get the results that they want. **Most people want instantaneous results, which is unlikely to happen.** If they get that book on "How to Have Super Abs in Eight Minutes a Day or Less" and they read through it, and they've realized, "Yeah, eight minutes a day *for the next twenty years*," but that want hasn't been fulfilled—so now they have to go out and do the next thing: buy the pills or potions, or go to Weight Watchers or to the gym. **They just keep on buying things.** That's how human beings work.

So don't worry too much about over-fulfilling their wants. What do I mean by that? Well, here's what I *don't* mean. Some people say, "Well, I don't want to give them everything, because if I fulfill this desire completely, then they're never going to buy the next thing and the next thing." No, that's absolutely not the right way to think. **Don't hold important information back; make it all available.** Here's a good example: there's a gentleman who sells books and courses on how to have more and better dates. He's got this great eBook that he sells for $20, and it's got all of his best information in it. He's had thousands of people buy that book, and you'd think that would be the last thing that they would buy from him. Well, no, they're unsatisfied. They want still more information. They feel like they've got to have more information, because certainly this simple formula can't be all it takes to get more and better dates. So what they do is buy his DVD courses; they buy his audio CDs; they go to his live events for hundreds and, in some cases, thousands of dollars. They end up having spent thousands of dollars. In fact, some of these people are on continuity programs with the guy.

It's because they have this constant desire that is very rarely completely filled. Don't be afraid to fulfill people's wants, because what's going to happen is they're going to be satisfied very briefly, and then they're going to want some more. **Understanding that at a basic level will help you generate a never-ending stream of money—just knowing that people are constantly wanting, wanting, wanting, and your job is to continue to fill that wanting.** People are insatiable, and thank goodness for that. They just can't get be satisfied. I realize that this causes some real misery in some people, but that's not our purview here. We're marketers, so we take advantage of the fact that people are obsessed with the kinds of things that we sell.

Incidentally, let me repeat something that I'll certainly say again: our consumers don't want the products themselves. They never want the products; **they want *the benefit the product brings.*** If you need a hole in something, you don't really want the drill you have to buy or borrow to make the hole; you just want the hole the drill makes. You're looking for the benefits of the drill. Well, guess what? For many products and services, the associated benefits aren't real in any way; they're just perceived. **In fact, some of the best benefits are perceived benefits. It's the fantasy in people's heads that matters**—and I'll give you an example from my own life. For years, I fantasized about having an RV and traveling all over the country; and I still do, a little, though I realize it's a fantasy. In my fantasy, one day I'll look out my window and there's a big beautiful set of mountains out there. Next week I look out my window, and there's the blue ocean. Then I'm down in the desert the next week, and then I go off to Canada and I'm in the forest. Occasionally in the past, especially when I was having problems in my life, I would, in my mind, jump in my little RV and take off; and in my mind I would be content, and life would be perfect. I wouldn't have any problems.

Then a few years back I went to an RV show. It was my first show ever, and I sat in a bunch of RVs. That's all I did—I just went from RV to RV, and I sat inside each one and I fantasized a little and tried to picture myself driving it. Somewhere along the line, I realized that's not really what I

MARKETING SECRET

"WORDS ARE POWER! The right words can change, shape, and even create reality!"

▼

From the movie *Napoleon Dynamite:* "Tell them their wildest dreams will come true if they vote for you!"

want—not at all. I don't want, for example, to have to dump the toilets and flush out the "brownwater," as they call it. That's part of the reality of an RV; and that's not what I want. It's the fantasy that I want. Now I kind of wish I hadn't gone to that RV show.

People sometimes want the perceived value more than they want the real value. For example: most people who buy into business opportunities don't really want a business. Who wants a business? Some days, I wouldn't wish a business on my worst enemy. People don't really want to have to put up with all the crap you have to deal with to have a business. No, what they want are the *perceived benefits* of the business! They want the dream to be true. They want whatever they envision a business can bring them; and generally it can, if they're willing to work hard and deal with the reality of business life. So if you're selling biz ops, you're not really lying to people; but you're not telling them the whole story, either—that sometimes, owning a business is very stressful.

People want the fantasy, and they want it to be real. They love the benefits and so they focus on those, and they just can't get enough of the dream. Pursuing that fantasy becomes an obsession; they end up buying more and more of whatever it is that promises the benefit of eventually, somehow, fulfilling this insatiability that they have. **The marketing lesson here is that the more people buy, the more they buy. It's a hunger that just can't be satiated.** If someone's in the marketplace for certain types of products, the more they get of those types of products, the more they want those and related products. The buying frenzy continues because they're buying.

And keep this in mind: you have to be right there to offer them more. The longer they go without buying, the more the hunger wanes; and over time, it goes away. Chris Lakey tells me that golf is like that for him. He notices that when he gets busy and can't golf as often, he doesn't miss it as much. That desire wanes because of his lack of participation. He's also an avid technology junkie: he always watches for the latest cell phone, and likes watching the latest high-definition televisions on the marketplace, and reading technology blogs. Now, frankly, he could get by with the old technology if he wasn't out there in the marketplace, always looking for what's new. But he is, so the more he looks, the more he sees other things that he thinks would be cool to own. It's the same thing with any business or product or marketplace: **the more someone is active in the marketplace, the more they want to own things that are related to that marketplace.** And, again, the opposite of that is true. If someone's out of the market and they haven't been active in it, that desire wanes.

So this insatiability is actually a good thing for us. Sometimes entrepreneurs are worried about competition, about prospects buying things from other people in the marketplace. Well, the fact is, people are going to spend their money in that marketplace, and if they're buying something from your competition, it means they're still feeding their hunger for those kinds of products and services, and so it means that they're still hungry. **Therefore, there's still a chance that they'll do business with you.** So don't worry about someone buying something from somebody else, especially if you have consumables or products that people tend to buy a lot.

There are obvious exceptions, of course; for example, if they buy a car, they're probably out of the auto market for a while. But most marketplaces aren't that way, so there should be no fear of them buying from the competition, because that means they're still hungry. Even if they've already bought something very similar to what you have to offer, they may very well buy from you, because **people will continue to want other types of products and services in the broader marketplace you serve.** That hunger keeps them going; the more they buy, the more they feed that hunger, and it's just an endless cycle until someone gets out of the marketplace for some reason.

Remember, too, that some markets are seasonal, so someone who's in a certain marketplace may not always be in that marketplace. **There is a season, a specific period of time, when they are hungry and are buying.** It's the same as any other market in that respect: while they're hungry, while they're in that moment, while they're interested in those types of products and services, the more they buy the more they want to buy. **It can form a continuous cycle, a type of feeding frenzy that can last a long time** and give you plenty of opportunities not only to make sales once, but to continue making those sales, and to continue serving your marketplace by offering them more of what they want and more of what you know they've already bought from you the first time.

This leads to *The Number One Mistake That Costs Inexperienced Marketers Millions in Profit.* It's a simple mistake, and I can certainly understand how people who are just getting involved in marketing would make it. It's in selling logically. **This happens quite often when people are selling something they think people need, and they try to explain why they need it.** They don't realize that people buy based on what they *want*; that is, **purchases are more likely to be based on emotions and desires than on what someone should logically need.** Oh, they may justify that purchase through logic; they may say something like, " I really need that," or "I can use that in the future because it's going to do this, this and this." It doesn't matter; the purchase is almost always based on their emotions and their desires.

Even we marketers, who ought to understand this stuff, are all blinded by our desires. **It's those things that we want that really control us.** I've already mentioned the quote by Edward DeRopp that says, "Man inhabits a world of delusion." If you were to take away the things that we attach to the facts or to products and services, you would have a whole different perception of the world. **But what happens is that people identify products or services with being healthier and happier.** We desire certain products or services because of the results they're going to give us, or how they're going to make us feel, or how they're going to change our lives or our lifestyles. If you realize that most people live in this world of delusion, then that really does give you the opportunity to make more sales.

There are ways to train yourself to see how that delusion works. If you study psychology, you can come to understand, somewhat, how the human mind works. In knowing how it works, you can you create products, marketing campaigns, and sales copy that really does generate an incredible amount of money. I've already mentioned an excellent primer on that: Robert Cialdini's *Influence: the Psychology of Persuasion*. It's a great book about the different types of persuasive methods that you can use to get people to perceive your product as the best in a particular market, especially if you have competition. Now, we're not talking about a product that people don't naturally want; **we're talking about persuading them to go ahead and buy the product they** *do* **want.** Remember, you should already be selling things that people want, just to make the selling process easier. With the information in Cialdini's book, you're going to have them buying it faster, and paying you more, with less hassle.

The second book that I would recommend is *The Science of Influence: How to Get Anyone to Say Yes in Eight Minutes or Less* by Kevin Hogan. Again, it's all about the psychology behind people's emotions, their desires, their thinking, and how to influence them to see you, your company and your products in a certain way, and to get them to take action.

You have to realize that we don't live in a world of reality. **We live in a world of perceptions, and unfortunately, most inexperienced marketers focus their attention and marketing on the features of a product.** Basically, what they're doing is saying, "This book is hardback. It has 237 pages. It's got a blue cover." People aren't out to buy a 237-page document with a pretty blue cover. That's incidental. They want what's between the covers: the information that a non-fiction book provides, or the thrills and excitement they can get from a novel. People don't want a thing to have the thing; **what they want is what that thing will provide, or what they perceive it's going to get them.** They want results!

> Many people are too smart to get rich. Their intelligence is a trap. They use all their mental powers to find and focus on all the obstacles — rather than the outcomes.

Even though people buy because of the results, once they get the product, oftentimes they still don't take action. They don't do whatever additional thing they have to do to get the results they want—so they're soon back in the market again, looking for that next product that they

MARKETING SECRET

Here's some great wisdom from P. T. Barnum, one of the greatest marketers who ever lived:

- "In a typical year, 1877, the cost of advertising and publicity for Barnum's Circus came to over $100,000.00 — almost a third of the total expenses! *(pg. 252, book by the Kunhardt family)*

- THE LESSON: Keep pumping more of your revenue back into all of the areas that make you the most money. Discipline yourself to do this on a consistent basis!

believe is going to get them that result. **Really, this is the foundation for successful marketing — understanding that people buy based on emotions, desires, and wanting, and that they're never going to be truly satisfied.** If you spend even the smallest amount of time learning the basics of psychology, especially by reading these books I've mentioned, you're going to become a powerful marketer who can get large groups of people to give you amazingly large amounts of money.

When I was 25 years old, I had a chance to spend some good, quality time with a man who, at that time, was about 82 years old. He came to visit me and was only going to stay for about a week; but then he got sick, and so he ended up staying seven or eight weeks. It was seven or eight of the best weeks of my life, now that I think about it. We would talk for hours when he felt well enough, and we talked many times into the night, just on and on and on. He was just such a smart guy and he taught me a lot of things. One day I asked him what the perfect business was. He told me, "You know, I've seen all these companies running these small classified ads in national magazines year after year, and I've thought about it a lot. I think that's the business you should be in."

Of course, I didn't do anything with it for a few years. But then, one day, I asked him this question: "Bill, what's the most important thing you ever learned in your whole life?" And he goes, "Well, let me think about it for a few days." I forgot I'd even asked him — and then one day we're driving down the road, three or four days later, and all of the sudden he says, "I got the answer to your question. Everybody in the whole world is crazy." Of course, I thought he was kind of joking with me. But you know what? The more I understand human psychology, especially as it affects marketing, the more I realize what Bill was saying. Emotions bring out the best and the worst in people — the best *and* the worst. **People often buy for unconscious reasons, especially rabid buyers.** They're the ones who buy the most, and most often the ones that are totally obsessed. It's all about the emotions.

Back in the 19th century, there was a woman named Madame Blavatsky who was into the weirdly spiritual, and had thousands and thousands of followers. Basically, she conned a lot of people. On her deathbed, she said that **people believe what they want to believe, and they see what they want to see.** I've thought about that a lot. It's as true now as it ever was. There's a very popular book that sold millions of copies recently, and now they're doing seminars all across the county. The promoters are making a fortune. Basically, the idea behind that book is that if you just sit around and get your mind right, you can command the universe to bring money and riches and all the wealth that you want. You could just sit in your living room on your couch, even in front of the television, and you could command money to come to you. People are buying those books by the millions. I'll admit that I bought the stupid book and the audio CDs myself. *Shame on me!* The crazier the idea, sometimes, the more people gravitate to it — almost likes a child who wants to believe in fairy tales.

I talked about this earlier. **People just don't buy logically.** If we did, we'd all drive Hondas and live in cheap houses, using thrift-store furniture. We'd have no use for televisions, because that's just a waste of money. We wouldn't have two or three cell phones to our names; we might have just a home phone. We'd live very frugal, basic lives — almost like the Amish do.

The reality is that we don't live that way because we don't want to. We don't think through purchases and decide whether they're needed or not; **we buy based on emotion, and a lot of the reasons we buy are subconscious.** We don't even know why we buy, but we do — and we buy often. We spend lots of money doing so. Imagine where our economy would be if we only bought what we needed, how little money would be spent in our marketplace. Of course, that would mean fewer jobs, because most jobs are provided by companies who sell what people want. The truth is, the world economy is driven by emotional spending. We buy what we want, and many times we buy what we want with money we should be spending on things that we *need*. Think about that one. A lot of people will go without health insurance — but they're probably eating out several times a week. They probably have a big screen high definition TV in their house, with cable or satellite dish. They probably have a couple of cell phones — and yet they're among the 47,000,000 Americans living without health insurance.

People *always* spend money on things they want over things that they need, which is why you want to be in the business of selling what people want. That assumes, of course, that you can figure out what they want. Sometimes, they themselves don't know; people don't typically think about it like that. They just know that they're buyers. And sometimes, people don't really know what they want until you sell it to them. Or they know what they want, but really don't know *why* they want it. So it's up to you to determine the psychological angles, and to figure out what they want. **Once you can figure that out, you can sell to people's emotional buying habits — and that's going to make you the big money.**

Getting It Started

I've already mentioned my story more than once in the pages of this book. Many, many years ago, I decided that I wanted to become a multimillionaire. At that time I had nothing, and I do mean *nothing*, that you would think it would take for somebody to make a lot of money. And yet, I was stubborn and persistent; **I wasn't going to quit, and I was willing to do whatever it took.** Well, there's an old saying: when the student is ready, the teacher will appear.

After years of trying, I was certainly ready. Within six months from the time my wife Eileen and really got started, back in 1988, we had the good fortune to meet marketing legend Russ von Hoelscher. Russ simply took us under his wing. He had more than 20 years of experience at the time, so we did everything he told us to, without question — and we made millions and millions of dollars. **Once we got started, our success was based on a combination of us being willing to do whatever it took and then getting expert help.** Because, again, Russ had been in the business for an awfully long time, and he knew exactly what we should do — and more importantly, he knew what we *shouldn't* do. He gave us good advice, and we followed it. It's as simple as that. **Determination, commitment, perseverance, and being willing to do whatever it takes: that's been the secret of our success.** We were *determined!* We had the *dedication*, the *drive*, the *desire*, the *passion* — and that's what you need to succeed. Combine that with really good advice, like Russ gave us, and you really can achieve your dreams.

It takes all that, because **the hardest thing for people to do is get started.** Once you're moving and grooving, once you've built up a mailing list and you've had some experience in making sales and getting customers, then things get easier. But that's not going to happen until you get the ball rolling; and let me tell you, at the beginning, it seems like that ball is glued in place. So if you're one of those people who hasn't started yet, who hasn't really bitten the bullet and started pushing, **just remember that this will be the *hardest* time in your business** — because things go a little slower, and there are so many frustrations, and things just won't work out perfectly every single day.

But that doesn't mean you should give up — or heaven forbid, not even try! Nothing gets accomplished that way. You've got to just keep on pushing, keep on striving, set a goal and believe in it. **Believe in *yourself*.** Try to avoid negative people. If there are negative people in your house, sit down with them and tell them, "Look. This is my passion. This is my desire. Even if you don't agree with me on what I'm trying to do, let me have a little space to do it. I think it's going to turn out well." The whole idea is that *you have to believe in yourself*. You have to have a passion for what you're doing and you have to stay enthusiastic, no matter what happens.

The most practical thing you can do is to build your mailing list, name by name. Run some ads, or send out some mailings to get people to raise their hands. Either they spend a little money or they spend no money — but they raise their hand, and by that I mean they get in touch with you and say, "Yes, send me the information on what you have." This is how you slowly but surely start to build your list. And as the list gets bigger, and people begin to respond more and more, you'll get out of the doldrums of the start and into the mainstream. The river will take you on downstream. You won't have to work as hard; you won't have to pull your hair out and say, "Oh gosh! This is a hassle!" **It'll get easier and easier if you do the hard work up front. It's all about gaining momentum.** One

▼▼▼▼▼▼▼▼
MARKETING SECRET

The power of the right metaphor: Think about your business as if it were a money machine!

- Its only purpose is to crank out lots of cash for you!

- Its purpose is to give you complete and total financial freedom for life!

- Yes, the only intelligent way for you to think about your business is in all of the wealth it can and should be providing to you!

Let this be your #1 focus and your net worth will instantly increase!

---

of the great quotes from the sixteenth century says that **success begets success,** meaning the more you are, the more you tend to be successful. Part of the reason is that you've got momentum working for you.

But most potential entrepreneurs never make it that far — often because so many are confused about what they're going to sell that they just can't get beyond that. But once the momentum is there, and you have a mailing list of people who like you, trust you, and will continue to buy from you in the future, then the idea of what to sell becomes much easier — if only because you know what they bought from you the first time. **Once you recognize that they want more of the things they enjoyed buying from you before, it becomes very simple and obvious.** At M.O.R.E, Inc., we have customers who've been with us 10, 15, even 20 years. Russ von Hoelscher has customers going back 30 years. That's proof positive that it gets easier once you get in the flow and build your list.

And here's something else you should know while you're considering how you're going to get started: **don't stop yourself because you don't know what to sell.** This may shock you, but what you sell isn't that important. What's really important is that you start selling and keep selling. **Once you have a list of people who've brought Products A and B, you can search the market for other variations.** Try to make the best deal in obtaining these products, making deals with suppliers or creators, and create a way to offer those items to your list. Because *people who buy things continue to buy.* If they buy weight loss products, they'll continue to buy weight loss products. If they buy

"How to Get Rich in Your Own Business," they'll buy that again and again from you and from other people.

And it's about more than just selling products and services that people want; you've got to sell things that you, personally, believe in — things that get you excited. Sure, you have to sell people what they like, but you have to sell stuff that *you* like too. **When you really know your market, it means you're like your market.** You know my story. Russ von Hoelscher started out as a teenager loving mail order and sending for stuff by mail, buying and eventually selling comic books. That drove his dear mother crazy — but the point is that he knew the market. Then he got involved in moneymaking and bought all kinds of programs. You see, those of us who become successful as sellers of opportunities were first *buyers* of opportunities. I think that's an important point to realize here. **You first become a buyer. Then you become a learner, and start to implement some of the things you learned. Eventually, you can sit on the other side of the counter and become a seller.**

The idea, as I've said before many times and will certainly say again, is to hook your prospects and resell to them again and again. Remember my restaurant analogy from earlier? We've all got our favorite restaurants, right? How long have you been going to yours? If you like what you get at a restaurant, you go back. **Similarly, if people like what you're selling them, they'll come back and buy similar products and services from you.** The key word here is *similar*. You don't want to start selling business opportunities and then all of a sudden switch to selling insurance. Some of your customers might buy insurance from you, yes, but you'll lose most of them. If you don't sell them what they want, they're going to find some other dealer who will — because the **people in a good market are insatiable.** People who have certain needs or interests, or hobbies, will continue to re-buy for years — especially if they like you, trust you, and believe in you.

It's a personal thing, and that's another point you need to understand. People buy from people they either like or trust, and the best possible world is if they do both, because then they feel secure in giving you money. They know that anything you sell won't help them or make them rich overnight. They know there'll be some programs or products that are better than others — **but they have trust in you.** That's what you need to build, and build on: trust. **Try to personalize your business.** There are so many impersonal companies out there that people are getting sick of it. More and more, they're looking for a name behind the company — a voice, or even a photo. **So don't be afraid to use your photo in your copy; don't be afraid to tell your story; don't be afraid to take phone calls from your customers.**

Some people say, "Look, I'm in the mail order business," or "I'm in the Internet business, and I darn sure don't want to talk to people." That's the *wrong* idea! **You should always be willing to communicate with customers.** Provide prompt, warm customer service. Be willing to write little notes to them. You should be willing to chat with them in person, especially when you're starting your business, so you can personalize your relationship with them. That's what leads them to buy again. That's how Eileen and I became customers of Russ von Hoelscher. He sent us some materials and included a nice personal little note, a few warm words that made him seem real and interested in us. **It was a little bit of humanness that made us want to call him right away.** If he hadn't included that little personal note, I would have probably got around to calling him sooner or later — but maybe I wouldn't have. Then where would we be?

It's good to personalize things when you can, though it's not always possible. If you're mailing out 100,000 pieces a week, you can't write personal notes. But when you're first starting out, or when you're dealing with your best customers or your best potential customers, take out one of those 3M Post-it Notes and use it. Make a little statement about your program in your own handwriting. **Show people there's a real live human being behind the offer, and that they can get in touch with you by email or phone or fax.** Don't hide from your customers. Be accessible, and you'll find out that it'll pay off in more sales.

Now, let me shift gears here and reiterate something I opened this chapter with: **You have to be deeply committed to succeed in any business, to truly believe in yourself and not let the naysayers bring you down.** I started my very first company in December of 1985. It was a little carpet-cleaning business called ABC Carpet Cleaning. I named it that for two reasons: Number One, so I'd be first in the Yellow Pages, and Number Two because I was reading a book at the time that talked about the ABCs of success. "A" stands for attitude, "B" stands for belief, and "C" stands for commitment. **If you have the right attitude, a strong enough belief in what you're doing, you're deeply committed — and**

nothing can stop you. We see people all the time who give up way too soon. They could be losing a fortune because of it.

It's so sad to see, but it happens again and again. In part, this is because we're members of an instant gratification society: we want it *right now*, whether it be food, sex, weight loss, or a million bucks. **Whatever it is, we want a "magic pill."** And, yes, many of us have made a lot of money selling those — but there's one magic pill that will never work for anyone, and that's the one that results in instant success when you start a business. It's *always* hardest at the beginning, before you know the ropes and have everything in place. If things don't go well from Day One to Day Ten, and you give up, there's no magic pill to make that work. You've got to have some determination, some guts and grit. As a nation, we've become too soft; we've been expecting too much too soon. Again, in business — as in most things — the beginning is the hardest part. You've got to tough it out, knowing that it's going to take time for you to build something that's going to be very, very good for you in the future. **Don't expect a miracle overnight. Realize that it's like a ladder, step by step;** and that some of the richest people in the world have had two, three, four, five setbacks in business. But they never gave up, until they found the one vehicle that could take them from where they were to where they want to be. *So don't give up!*

> **Problems contain massive amounts of energy. The same problems that kill some people — cause others to shoot straight to the top!**
>
> **The pressure from the problems should be used to create the solutions!**

A few years back, I saw something on TV about people who survive cancer. The survivors are the people who don't give up. They're the ones who say, "Look, I've got things to do yet in life. I've got my grandkids, or I've got a project that I'm working on, so I'm not giving up." One doctor said that when he hears that from people he thinks, "Hallelujah!" because he knows they have the best chance for survival and remission. We should all learn from that. If these people who are facing terrible medical problems survive because they *fight* to survive, we can do the same in our businesses. **Those of us who are willing to do a little extra work, try new things, and** *just don't*

SECTION EIGHT — Ruthless Marketing Secrets, Volume Two

MARKETING SECRET

People hate to be "sold" — but they love to "choose."

▼

"So long as new ideas are created, sales will continue to reach new highs." — Charles R. Kettering

give up will also be the ones who thrive and survive.

This reminds me of the story of Hernan Cortez. When he and his troops invaded Mexico, Cortez burned the ships in the harbor and let all of the thousands of troops on the shore watch them burn. Cortez told them, "There's no going back from this point forward. There are the ships that got us here; as you can see, they're on fire. We're either going to fight our way out of this thing, or we're all going to die." Sure, that's a little extreme — but we can use some of the same attitude in business. We're not here to fight to live or die, but **we *are* here to go forward and acquire the success that we want — and truly deserve.**

My next topic for this chapter is harvesting customers, another example that often stops new entrepreneurs in their tracks. It's crucial, however, that you learn to do this effectively and correctly. **I generally put potential customers into three categories.** FIRST, there are inquiries or leads, those who raise their hand and say, "Hey, send me the information. I'm willing to take a look at it." CATEGORY TWO consists of those who buy something. CATEGORY THREE is true customers; a person really isn't a customer until they've bought from you at least two or three times.

So there are three steps here. In **Step One, you're trying to harvest people who raise their hands. In Step Two, you want to convert those leads into buyers, which you do by making your most compelling pitch.** In DRM, we don't mail sales letters to them just once; we mail at least three or four times, because people aren't always in the right position for them to take action on your offer. So follow up every 10 days or so with a follow-up mailing. Once you've converted them into a buyer, it's time for **Step Three: go to work on turning that person into a long-term customer.** I don't care what you're selling, you first want to harvest leads, turn them into buyers, and turn buyers into customers.

This is fairly easy after you've done it for a while; and of course in the beginning, just like anything else, **there's a learning curve.** But the funny thing is, although many people say they want to make millions of dollars, they don't want to go through the pain of a learning curve. I've talked about this before; most people want it to be too easy in the beginning. But that's bogus. Let's get real. At the very least, you've got to figure out, first of all, how to produce good sales material; your ads and sales letters have to be first class if you want to make any real money. So learn something about what good copy looks like. Even if you're not going to write it yourself, you should have some idea what great copy looks like so you can evaluate the copy that you purchase or are given. Thousands of excellent products and services have failed due to bad copywriting and advertising. On the other hand, a lot of junk makes people tons of money just because the copywriting is good. Remember the Pet Rock? It was just a chunk of rock in a box — but it made millions back in '75. Copy makes a huge difference in success or failure.

One way you can ensure the quality of your copy is to hire out to a well regarded professional copywriter — or get one to take you under their wing. I'm dating myself here, but 21 years ago, back when I was 29, Russ von Hoelscher reached out and helped us as both a consulting copywriter and a mentor. He still helps people like that — that is, he'll look over their sales letters and ads as a consultant, making suggestions and changes. It's not cheap; if someone wants Russ to write their copy, they're going to pay several thousand dollars if he's looking at blank paper and has to start from the beginning. But if someone has some copy that they wrote, or that someone else supplied to them, something that Russ can look at and make changes to — well, then his price is dirt-cheap, on the order of ten cents on the dollar compared to him writing the copy. So if you have copy you're not sure about, and you've tested it and it hasn't brought in the money you think, get in touch with someone like Russ von Hoelscher — because for a small fee, they can doctor that copy up and make it good. It's much cheaper than writing from scratch.

The winners in the marketing wars are usually the people who captivate the imagination of their marketplace. And by that, I mean they're the ones whose promotional literature jumps off the page and absolutely captivates the reader. **That's the importance of good copy: to really make people get excited.** Now, we've heard a lot of talk about how it has to be believable, how it has to be beneficial; and yes, those things are important to a certain degree. But I'm more convinced than ever that it has to be enthusiastic, and it has to get people excited.

Many people who write copy oversell and overhype. This has always been a problem, but I'll tell you why they do it: because overselling and overhyping often works very well. Now, if we use a little hype (and we do), if we sell hard (and we do), we're nevertheless going to provide you with more than your money's worth. **That's crucial; you can take a little license with the enthusiasm and the hype as long as you deliver the goods.** Sadly, it's often necessary to take that license just to get people's attention. Previously I told you about how skeptical people are; so often, when people are reading your sales material, they start out reading it in an apathetic way. They know you're asking them to give you their money, and they're trying to hold onto it. Without even realizing it, because it's totally unconscious on their part, they're trying to protect themselves. So you *might* think your copy is over the top, and yet often, it has to be to get through to the people sleepwalking through your sales material. **You have to hype it up to make it through sales resistance.** Selling is a transference of emotion; it's one person who believes so strongly in something that they convey that strong sense of belief to another person, who picks up on it and they get excited. **It's all emotional; you've got to be passionate, you've got to be enthusiastic, you've got to truly believe in what you're selling.**

I've got a friend who's really struggling right now, although he's been around our business for a while. I really want to help the guy — but all he really needs is something to believe in. He needs a product or a service to get excited about. If he could just find that, selling would become easy. This is true whether you're selling face-to-face, or writing a sales letter, or recording something. You're excited, you're passionate, you're enthusiastic; and naturally, other people catch that spirit. They catch that energy, they catch that fire, and they get excited — and then they want to buy from you.

So it sounds simple; and for some people, it is. Some people, though, have to really work at it. **There's a helpful acronym for the last four letters of the word enthusiasm: I Am Sold Myself.** Keep that in mind, because it's basic to making sales — and of course the basics cause millions and millions of dollars of business to be done on a daily basis. People tell me that one of the reasons I'm so successful is that I'm really enthusiastic. I believe in what I'm doing; I'm pumped up, I'm excited, and I convey that to the people reading my messages.

Another thing to keep in mind when you're carving out your niche: **sell the cures, not the prevention.** People are only looking for gratification, not prevention. More people will stand in line and pay a fortune for a pound of cure than would ever pay a pittance for an ounce of prevention; it's just human nature. When you're selling burglar alarms, for example, it's difficult to make any sales when there have been no problems in the neighborhood. The easiest time to sell burglar alarms is when someone on the street just got robbed. That's why we have to sell the cure rather than the prevention. People are so busy, so downtrodden about so many things, and their lives are so complicated in so many ways, that they're looking for some relief for their misery. Their worst misery might be not having enough money, or not having good health, or not having good relationships. If you have a cure for their particular misery, they're likely to buy it. **The more completely it cures the problem, the better it will sell.**

It has to be easy, too. Nobody wants to give you their money if they have to do a lot to make your product or service work. **They want that magic pill.** You'll see this strategy used again and again — not just in the moneymaking world, but everywhere. Let's look at the diet ads, for example. When you start exploring the weight loss market, you immediately start seeing commercials that say, "Eat all the food you want and still lose weight!" Or they show you this exercise equipment being used by good-looking, attractive, athletic people who have well-defined bodies and say (or at least imply), "Look! Only 20 minutes three times a week, and you can look like this!" That makes things simple and easy, doesn't it? Of course, some of it's hype, and we all know that; but then again, as I mentioned earlier, we all need a little bit of hype sometimes. I've bought a lot of exercise equipment in the past. I still don't have one of those bodies — and yet, maybe if they hadn't shown me those kinds of commercials, I wouldn't have bought most of what I bought.

▼▼▼▼▼▼▼▼
MARKETING SECRET

Writing great sales copy is an art — skill — and discipline.

▼

Spend more money to get new customers.

There's hype involved in everything. In many states, they have lotteries you can spend your money on — and they run the kinds of TV ads that would get me in trouble with some government agency. They run ads that say, "You can be the next multimillionaire." And it's true. What they don't tell you is you have about one chance in 10 million. So they get away with murder, because they sell the hype; they sell the dream. **And that's another important thing that's even more important than hype: we want to sell the dream.** All of us have latent desires and dreams. Those are different for everyone, but if we get to know our customers well enough, then we get to know what they really care about — what they really want to do with the rest of their lives.

The more we can understand them, by getting inside their minds and to comprehend their emotions and the psychology they live by, the better we can make sales — because we can give them exactly what they want. **That's what good marketing is: it's giving the most people possible exactly what they want.** If you do that you will become rich beyond your wildest desires; it's as simple as that. Give people what they want, and get the most people possible to give you their money for what they want. People don't want to spend money foolishly; times can be tough, as they are right now. **But no matter how bad the economy, people will gladly give you their money if you give them what they want.**

That is, in fact, one of the best definitions of the word selling: you simply find out what people want, and then you let 'em have it. That was what the famous Ray Kroc, the founder of

McDonald's, used to say. He was a master at determining what people wanted. He realized folks wanted cheap hamburgers and they wanted them fast, so he supplied them — and he did it like no one had before him. He implemented other innovations, too. One day, one of his vice presidents was going to the bank to deposit some of the company's money. He went through the drive-through teller and got this idea: "Hey, why don't we do this for fast food? Why don't *we* have a drive-through window?" And of course, that innovation has revolutionized the whole industry. It worked because so often, **ideas are interchangeable: you can take them from one industry and apply them, with few changes, to something else altogether.**

Now, I'd like to return to something I've already discussed, because I want to reinforce the concept. It's simply this: **we don't get rich selling people one time.** As you move forward from your starting point, you have to realize that it's the repeat sales that make a person a customer. You should do everything you can, when you're selling one product or service, to immediately look for a second product or service to sell them. Once you sell your second, you should be looking for the third — etc., etc. Those of us who make a lot of money in this business do so by reselling to the same people over and over.

And again, **the simplest way to do that is to stick to the same things you've already sold to them, or some variation thereof;** in any case, make sure it's in the same category. If you keep up a steady supply of these products the customers want to buy, and treat them right in all things, many will buy from you for years. It doesn't matter whether you develop your own products or sell someone else's. People vote with their checkbook on whether or not you've hit the target.

So how do you know what people want? **You look at what other people are already selling.** In hindsight, this is what I was doing 20+ years ago, back when I first got started: I was doing research, all unknowingly. For years, I had been buying various plans and programs from a multitude of different companies; so when it came time to get into the opportunity market with our own proven plan, it was easier, because we knew what was selling. We were buying those things ourselves, since we were already on the other side of the cash register, doing business with other companies selling to the same kinds of people we wanted sell to. That's one of the reasons I always suggest to our clients that they do get involved in selling to the opportunity market: because so many have been buying one plan after another for years. They've got a bookcase full of these things. **They understand the marketplace as the consumer; now they just need to understand it as a marketer, as a businessperson.** Maybe they don't realize it, but they've already done great research. All they need to do now is go to the bookshelf, pull down some of those programs and books, and start reading them again, learning more about the products.

It's a matter of shifting consciousness, that's all — it's a change of mindset. It's not always easy to do, but it starts with a decision. That's where everything begins: you make a firm decision, a solid commitment, you set some good goals, and then you get into motion and figure things out as you go, trying not to get overwhelmed. Once you get a mailing list put together of people who have bought something from you and like you, it becomes so much simpler, because all you're doing then is looking out for your customers. **You have to look at your customers as if they're friends, or even family — because without them, you are nothing.** You wouldn't even have a business without them. So you have to treat them well, and consistently cater to their needs, because it's in your best interest to do so.

Now, another thing you have to realize is that even when you do get customers, people who have bought more than once, they're not all equal. The smaller part of your customer base will be your most profitable, per the old 80/20 principle. So realize who the superstars are, and treat them with special care. **Treat all your customers well, but treat the best customers a little better than the average customer,** because frankly, they're worth more to you. A-Rod — Alex Rodriguez of the Yankees — is better than the average baseball player. He gets paid that way, too. Now, do you think the Yankees treat him a little better than someone sitting in the bullpen making only a few hundred thousand a year? Yes, of course they do. It's the same with your star customers. You have to treat them better, get more personal with them, talk to them, write to them directly, because these are the people who will make you the most money. **Remember, they're spending that money to show you just how serious they are.**

One of the things that has really amazed me over the years — and I've seen it over and over again — is that **the customers who spend the most money with us are also the ones who cause us the fewest headaches and hassles when it comes to customer service.** Forget the fact that they all spend a lot of money; I'm grateful for that, but that's not my point here. They're just higher-quality customers. I don't even know how to explain it, except to say that they're better people, they're easier to please, and they're nicer than the average customer. It's one of the great mysteries of marketing, but it's a real phenomenon: the people who buy the most, who give you the most money, who are really into what you're selling and become super customers, are so much easier to deal with than those on the fringes. For example, if you ship something a couple days late to those people on the fringes, they're furious. They're very skeptical about anything you ship to them, too. They complain constantly — more than their money is worth, sometimes.

> ▼▼▼▼▼▼▼▼▼▼▼▼▼
> If you always think the way you always thought... **you'll always get what you've always got**!

Personally, I spend a lot of money with just a few companies, and I've been doing so for a long time. I'm a pretty darn good customer for them. I treat them with respect, I'm always very gracious with them, and I feel grateful for them. That's probably why the people who are especially interested in our products are spending a lot of money us: they're grateful that we're there. It all goes back to building a trusting, mutually-beneficial relationship. It's sort of a feedback loop: you treat them better so they treat you better, in an endless cycle. I think one mistake a lot of companies make is that they *don't* treat their best customers any different than their other customers. They treat someone who's spending a thousand bucks the same as someone spending ten.

Here's an example of that mistake: Russ von Hoelscher spends maybe $30,000-40,000 a year at the Office Depot just a few blocks from his office in California. Well, he went and talked to them one day about getting a discount. He said to the manager, "You know, I print a lot of stuff here, tens of thousands of dollars worth a year, and you used to have a program a few years ago where I got a 10-15% discount on most of this printing." The manager said, "Yeah, we hadda get rid of that," so Russ told him, "Look, don't you think it makes business sense to treat your better customers *better*, and give 'em the discount?" He told Russ, "You know something? It does, but headquarters said that whether you come in here to get one copy or a thousand, you'll still pay five cents." And that was

SECTION EIGHT — Ruthless Marketing Secrets, Volume Two   **639**

▼▼▼▼▼▼▼▼
MARKETING SECRET

The million-dollar copywriting formula that never fails:

1. Write 2 to 3 times more copy than you need.

2. Just write fast — and cover every possible benefit and angle...

3. Do this until you're sick and tired and can't do it any more...

4. Then start SLASHING!

5. Tear your copy to pieces! Start chipping away at everything you have worked so hard to write — until only the strongest copy survives!

---

that. Now, Russ likes the folks at Office Depot, but the fact that they're willing to treat someone who spends $0.50 a month the same way that they treat someone who spends $5,000 a month should tell you something. That just doesn't make sense, does it? It doesn't fit with the reality of the market.

Back in the old days, there was an old adage that said "the customer is king." That's just not true anymore; we've got way too much competition for that. **The customers of today are more like dictators — and ironically, the worst dictators are those who spend $50, as opposed to those who spend $5,000.** These are the ones who, if something goes wrong and they don't get their order within a day or two of when they should, get on the phone and talk to your people in the nastiest ways. Now, I'm not saying that people who spend the most money are always better than the people who don't have money; but I *am* saying that they're usually people who realize that there will be mistakes occasionally, and they still treat you with respect. And in return, you not only make their order right, but you give them a nice big bonus on top of it.

The customer is king only when they become a kingly customer. For that reason, you need to segment your customer base, realizing that there will be 10-15% who have spent some decent money with you. **You need to sort those people out, and do very special things for them.** Constantly make special offers and deals, or offer a nice discount to come to a particular seminar. You have to deeply appreciate your good customers, because they really are the lifeblood of your business. **You want to do everything you can for them, treating them**

---

640   How to Make Millions Sitting on Your Ass!

with the greatest respect. **This is what a good business does.** Yes, you should respect all your customers and treat them well, whether they spend $10 or $10,000; but you need to have a few extra perks for your very best customers. This sounds like common sense — but it's not that common, even in the largest corporations.

Let's move on to another thing that will help you keep from spinning your wheels when you're just getting started: **What you should do to learn your business really well.** We've mentioned the basic tactic already: you need to spend some money and time doing your research, not just by buying products or dealerships, but also books and programs that are designed to impart the specialized knowledge required to make you a better businessperson. Go to seminars and workshops. Whether you spend any extra money or not is your business once you're there, but you *should* learn.

Become a devotee of good marketing, because everything in this world depends on it. More and more, even the big Fortune 500 companies are realizing this. **It's marketing that separates the winners from the losers, so learn to love marketing.** Learn to love learning ways to get inside people's minds to understand what they hope for, what they fear, what they trust, what they recoil from — so that you can make the type of offer that will turn them on and make them want to buy. Because people aren't just buying the things they want, and they're certainly not just buying things that they need; **they're buying things that they absolutely feel they must have.**

And the key word here is *feel*. It's all about emotion. **When the emotion is there, they're ready to buy.** They don't always buy the things that are the best for them; they often buy the things they want rather than need, because want is more important than need. **But I've come to the conclusion that even more important than want is *I must have it! I've got to have it! And I've got to have it now!*** When you can convey the message that makes them feel that, you're going to make money hand over fist. They say that marketing is a combination of psychology and math, and I believe that's true. The psychology, of course, is trying to understand what makes people tick — and you should start with understanding what makes *you* tick. **The better you understand yourself, the better you'll understand the people you want to reach.**

I talk a lot about creating powerful offers that get people excited.

Well, you've had times when you've been excited. You've bought things that have made you want to FedEx or wire your money, because you wanted them so quickly. Once again, to comprehend this phenomenon and how it applies to marketing, **you just have to get on the other side of the cash register and start looking at what was it about that offer that really made you excited.** Then, when it comes time to creating your own offers, it's that much easier for you to do so.

And here's a corollary of that. A lot of people get involved with dealerships or distributorships, where they're selling the same thing other people are selling. Now, it's a big country, and there's a huge market out there, so don't worry too much about that; **it's simple enough to make what you're offering a little more attractive than everyone else's version.** There's nothing to prevent you from adding some free bonuses, for example. I've learned over the years that adding two or three bonuses is great; adding four, five, six, or seven is even better. **People love to get something extra for their money, especially if it's vital and relates to the main product.** That turns people on, and ensures that you'll get more orders than your competitors. If you're selling hard products, there are all kinds of things that you can add as a gift; it's easy to find little knick-knacks and gizmos that will go with your main product. In the information field it's usually a free report or some other printed matter. As long as it's relevant it just turns people on, especially if you add multiple bonuses to the package.

Even if you don't have items of your own that you can use as bonuses, there are plenty of them out there that you can obtain; for example, you can buy reprint rights to all kinds of different materials, or establish a joint venture with someone to provide the bonus. The point is, you need to do something exciting to separate yourself from the other people also working their distributorships — whether there are only a few or a thousand. **In fact, in any business you have to differentiate yourself, separate yourself from the crowd, give people more.** Another thing you can do is tell them your personal story, because remember, people want to do business with other people. Never be afraid to tell your prospective buyers and your customers certain things about yourself that help them get to know you a little better. I've always done this, and I know that my mentor Russ is doing it more and more every year.

And you know, when economics are tough, you can do something like take a program that's sold well for $495 and make it available for $395 — not because it needs to be discounted, but because it may help someone buy. You can put a little note with it that says something like, "Look, I realize you didn't buy the first time. I know this is good for you, but you haven't purchased. Maybe the price is a problem; maybe things are a little tight? So here's $100 off." Russ uses little coupons that offer $100 off or more, and it's working like gangbusters. **The more you can separate yourself from the competition by being more personalized, by offering a little extra value, the better your sales will be.**

We've got space for one more secret in this chapter. I've talked about falling in love with good customers, so now **I want to talk about falling in love with your marketing field itself** — whether that's the opportunity field, the weight loss field, or whatever your niche may be. And I don't mean that you should fall in love with your products and services; that's a losing proposition. **First of all,** assuming that you're in it for the long term, **the products and services you sell will change over time. Second, just because you love something doesn't mean everyone will.** It's a big mistake to believe otherwise, because no matter how wonderful you think some things are, people simply aren't going to buy them. At that point, **you have to be able to switch gears and get new products to sell.** That's going to happen from time to time, **so fall in love with the business itself rather that what you're selling.** You really can't get emotionally involved in products and services you sell until they prove they're winners. Then you can hug it, and kiss it, and say, "I'm in love with ya, baby!"

I've seen people fall in love with losing products time and again. I won't mention his name, but one of Russ's clients had this beautiful product, made from a rare Hawaiian wood, that Russ told him from the beginning wasn't going to sell because it was overpriced and cost a lot to manufacture. And the fellow just looked at him and said, "I'm going to find a way to sell it." Well, $100,000 later he had to throw in the towel. It's a shame, because Russ gave him good advice. **But that's why we test things: so if they don't go well, we can shift gears and move on to something else.** If you do this right you can test as many as 10 different things at a time, as long as you're just doing small tests. You take the items that work the best and roll those out. You might actually lose money on nine out of 10 different ideas, or even 19 out of 20 different ideas; but as long as you're testing small and not investing huge sums of money, then all is not lost. **Just roll out big on the things that work, the stuff that**

▼▼▼▼▼▼▼▼▼
MARKETING SECRET

Never, never, never, never delegate your marketing to someone else.

- It's far too important. And nobody is ever going to care as much about it as you do — or be willing to sacrifice as much as you are.

really does take off like a rocket. And by the way — none of us, not me or Russ von Hoelscher or anyone else in the field, really tests enough. But at least we do *some* testing. My advice to you is learn to do these small tests, because they can tell you very quickly whether you have a big winner, a little winner, or *oh my God, let's dump this quick!* **DO NOT fall in love with your products; it's the marketplace, and the business of serving it, that you should be in love with.**

Back when we were first getting started, we went through a rough period, and I'll never forget what Russ told me then: "T.J., just remember that no matter how bad it gets, the real business is inside of you. **It's the knowledge you have, the experience that you've gained.** It's the marketplace, and the people that you can reach, and knowing about what they want — and how to give them more of it." That was wonderful advice, and I never forgot it. I'm passing it on to you because I want you to remember it, and to hold it in your heart for whenever you need it, too. **We *all* need to have to have more belief in ourselves.** Too often, we sell ourselves too short. Too often, when I tell people they can learn to write copy, their response is, "I could never do this." I'll tell them how to define products, and it's, "Oh, I can't do that." There's too much *I can't* there when there should be *I CAN*. We have such a source of power inside us that we do ourselves and the Almighty a disservice when we act like we can't do this and we couldn't even try to do that. No matter how young or how old you are, there's so much more that you can do. **You just have to push yourself a little harder — and reach out for that helping hand when it's offered.**

The End of Your Wealth-Making Journey

In the last chapter, I talked about getting started in your business — so I feel that it's only right that the subject of this chapter is *The End of Your Wealth-Making Journey*. Think about that. By the time you're done with this chapter, **you're going to have a complete road map from here to success.**

It's always easier to find your way if you know where you're going from the very beginning. You may be new to this path; you may have been on this journey for a long time. If that's the case, it may be that you're confused, you're frustrated, and you don't always know exactly what to do. You have to learn all these new things just to get in the door; **there's a painful learning curve, and we all have to go through it.** I see it on the faces of my clients when I meet them in person at our seminars and workshops. Well, my colleagues and I have been there ourselves. We know how confusing some of this can get — which is why I'm hoping that at least some of what I'm going to discuss in this chapter will put an end to your confusion, and help you truly understand what you're trying to accomplish here. That's when you can stop focusing on today, and get an end strategy in place that will serve you well, far into the future.

Most people don't focus much on where they're going or where they're *trying* to get. They focus on today, and sometimes that's out of necessity. We're busier than ever before, so it's hard to get past today. We tend to run around in circles and do the same things repeatedly... and it tires us out, doesn't it? We're stuck in the same routine; we go through another day, and all of a sudden, we look back and we say, "How did we get here?" A year passes, then two; then it's five years; and ten, twenty, thirty years pass, and you really didn't get anywhere. You look back and have regrets, and wonder what happened. How did you get where are today without getting anything done?

Well, now that you've gotten started and there's some momentum there, this chapter's strategies are going to help you get over that hump, so you can take action and chart your course. **You'll be able to plan what you do today based on what your goals are and where you're trying**

to go tomorrow, sort of like a pilot taking off in an airplane. If a pilot took off without planning his destination, he'd get up in the air and fly around aimlessly. Sure, he'd probably end up somewhere — but the somewhere wouldn't necessarily be where he wanted to go. A pilot *has* to chart his course in advance. He has to know exactly where he's going, and he has to point his airplane in the right direction to accomplish that. If he's got to fly from L.A. to Hawaii, he knows exactly how to get there. The cool thing is that during that flight, the plane is slightly off course well over 90% of the time due to wind currents, the jet stream, and other factors. But it's got the automatic computer system that guides it right back — so it constantly readjusts itself. The pilot and autopilot always know exactly where the end goal is.

Life is a lot like that. **You have to know where you're trying to get to in order to figure out what you need to do today and tomorrow, and on into next week, next month, and next year in order to get there.** This is something we don't focus on enough, and a lot of experts don't talk about it at all. They want to talk about what you need to do *today,* and so you get caught up in the today without any real clear objective in mind — and you end up flying around aimlessly.

One of my favorite quotes (and I'll paraphrase it slightly, because it's from the 1800s) says that a person can tolerate any situation if they just keep a strong enough goal in mind. **If there's hope for the future, there's strength for today.** If you've got a really great, powerful goal that's driving you, you don't always know exactly how you're going to figure out how to achieve it; sometimes you don't have a clue, but at least the goal is there. It's a road map, a destination, and if you keep it in mind, you can figure out how to reach that destination. **It's always easier to find your way if you know where you want to wind up.**

Next, let's look at with a series of questions to ask yourself before you start your journey. The idea is to help you define where you want to be, and what will make you happy. This will let you document your goals in writing, so you can focus on them and be motivated to stay the course. Until you know where you want to wind up, it's tough to write that down. **Let's start out with the definition of a destination, first of all.** I think this is a good thing to understand.

One thing I've learned during my years in DRM is that almost all of the profits in your business are going to come from the back end. When I was first getting started in marketing, I didn't understand what the end of my journey would be. Nowadays the end of my journey is very clear, and it's connected with the fact that mostly, **the goal for my business is to make profits — just like everybody's goal for their business should be.** That's one of the end results. I've talked about 80/20 rule before, the fact that you need to spend more of your time and effort doing more business with your existing customers.

> ▼▼▼▼▼▼▼▼▼▼▼▼▼▼
>
> If your customers want to buy rocks... <u>then start digging</u>!
>
> Most marketers are trying too hard to sell people the things that <u>they</u> want to sell... instead of just selling what their market wants to buy.
>
> Seasoned marketers are the <u>most</u> guilty of this. They believe their marketing skills are powerful enough to sell anything to anyone!

A good 80% of your profits are going to come from that back-end business, with no more that 20% being generated on the front end. This information allows you to get more specific, and to define where you want to go in your journey.

For example, my friend and colleague Eric Bechtold's ultimate goal is have ten thousand individuals working directly with him, buying from him in a vacuum. What he means is that he wants their undivided attention, so when he puts something in front of them, they respond right away. He's not competing with a bunch of other people; they're focused on him and his sales materials. Ten thousand is specific number that Eric set as a goal. He figures if he can get to that point — and you always want to set your goals high — his journey will be accomplished. At that point, he can pretty much print money on demand, if you will, by coming up with a new offer and plugging it into his mailing list. At the moment, he's about a quarter of the way there.

I wanted to provide that example right away, so that you would understand the types of specific **cause-and-effect scenarios** involved here. You start out on your journey with nobody even knowing who you are. As

▼▼▼▼▼▼▼▼
MARKETING SECRET

Sell them what they want — and then give them what they need.

▼

JOIN THE 5:00 A.M. CLUB!!!

- Ideas come at 5:30 a.m. (with a pot of strong black coffee) that would have NEVER came to you at any other time of the day.

you roll out your marketing pieces and get out there in the marketplace, people start to understand who you are, and they start to realize that you're a good person to do business with. You put your offers out there, and eventually you've got some brand equity, where people are paying attention to you. **Eventually, you get to the point where you've got people who are buying everything you put out there.** What you're selling is an integral part of the part of the ongoing relationship you have with your customers.

At M.O.R.E., Inc., **we know exactly how much money we want to bring in every single month; that's our destination, at least on a monthly basis.** I've got that number written down in several places around my house, and I'm always thinking about it. I live with that number always. When we don't hit it, I feel it deeply — and it makes me frustrated. I think frustration is a good thing. It doesn't *feel* good, but it's good anyway as long as you're frustrated for the right reasons. **When we're not hitting those numbers that we have to have every single month, I'm spurred to do things better, to tighten things up, to try new things.** Our goal is very real; we have specific things we put into action, processes we put into place to help us achieve that goal, and we're extremely disappointed when we miss it. We analyze our numbers daily, weekly, and of course monthly, and we know at the beginning of the month — after just a couple of days — whether we're on or off target. Are we where we need to be, or are we a little low? Are we a little high? Where are we at? We do this because we want to know where we'll be at the end of every month. **And by the way, that monthly goal also translates** into an annual goal; and of course we know on a monthly basis how we're doing over the course of a year.

The important thing is to have a goal, to have your end in mind. I encourage you to be specific with it, because too many people have generic, broad goals — and there's no penalty in their mind if they don't hit those goals. If your goal is just to make millions of dollars, that's probably not that good a goal for you. **A better one might be to take a million dollars a year and divide it out so you know how much money you need to make every day, every week, and every month.**

We're always looking at those numbers, because that's where it starts with us. **The strategies all evolve out of the numbers.** We determine first how much money we want to make every month; and I won't give that figure here, but it's very high, definitely in the seven figures. Then from that point forward, Chris Lakey and I develop specific marketing strategies to get us where we want to go. The strategies become a little clearer when you start that way. We know the size of our average package; we know how big our market is. That tells us how many packages we need to sell.

Obviously, the end means different things to different people. We work from a specific amount of money, while Eric Bechtold aims for a specific number of customers. Maybe your end goal is making enough money, consistently enough, that you can quit your job. Whatever the case, **when you're off that goal, you need to immediately figure out why so you can get back on point.** That's why you need to start with very specific goals — because **you'll never make the abstract ones.** They're not specific enough, and they're easily avoidable. It's easy to say, "I want to make millions of dollars!" and then, when it doesn't happen, to just pass it off. But if you sincerely have a goal to make, say, $100,000 a week, then if you don't, you know you've missed your goal and you have to adjust your game plan. If your goal is to make $1,000 a week, you can get there. You know how many products you need to sell to reach that goal. You know how many sales letters you need to send, how many ads you need to place.

It all starts with that end in mind, followed by formulating your plan to get there. Sticking to the plan is important, because you can't just have a goal and then randomly go through your week, month, or year and then look back and wonder why you didn't hit it. **You've got to constantly be aiming at that target, and making constant little adjustments** like an airplane does with its course. You've got to adjust every day, every week, every month so that you can hit your goal. Maybe $1,000 seems like a good amount to you... but if your goal is $5,000 a week, then if you make just $1,000 you know you've come up really short. But if you *don't* have the $5,000 weekly goal, then maybe $1,000 a week may seem like enough, and you accept it. **Do that, and you're limiting yourself.**

The times in my life when I've made the most money were when I've had those firm goals in place — and the times when I've suffered financially have been the times when I took my eyes off of the prize. I quit focusing on my goals; and as they say, **wherever your focus goes, that's where your power goes. What you focus on really does expand.** If you don't have some firm goal in mind, whether it's a dollar amount, number of customers, or both, then you're causing yourself a lot of unnecessary misery. Just saying "I want to get rich" is not a goal. **There's a formula to getting rich, and that formula is very simple: get a large enough group of people to consistently give you money, at a large enough profit margin per transaction.** This is the kind of thing you need to start wrapping your mind around. How many customers do you need? How much profit do you need to make per sale in order to make your goal? When you do come up with a number, and then write that down; it makes a big difference.

Here are a few questions I'd like you to ask yourself. **First of all, can you define your destination** — do you know where you want to go? **Next, what will make you happy?** What will satisfy your desires when you get there? You need to think deeply on these subjects — because again, there's no point in running around like a maniac trying to achieve a nebulous goal. **Identifying your goals and internalizing them, making them a part of you so that you feel pain if you don't achieve them, will motivate you.** That's why I keep that specific monthly dollar goal posted all over my house. I can't walk around without that goal staring me in the face. That's good, because it's constantly readjusting me; instead of getting lazy one night and saying, "Okay, tonight I'm just gonna kick my feet up with a bowl of popcorn and veg out for a couple of hours," I might decide to work on a sales letter to help get that goal up to where we need to be. That way, I can experience some bliss and some joy when we attain those goals.

And that's another reason for defining them — so that you can celebrate when you achieve your goals. And once you've celebrated, what do you do? **You set more lofty goals!** You get to the point where you say, "Wow, I was able to achieve that — now what am I capable of doing? Let's set even higher goals." It's kind of like a path to success. **You take each little stone at a time; each goal gets you from one place to another, and if you keep that mentality, you'll be surprised how far it's going to take you.**

Another thing I wanted to point out here is that in addition to thinking about your own goals, you have to realize that you don't get to your destination without also thinking about the destinations of others. This is also a very important thing to think about. **The end of your journey is not going to be accomplished without you wrapping your mind around what's going on in other people's minds to motivate them.** There's the psychology factor again. The reality here is that if you want to get rich, if you want people to part with their money, if you want to make a sale, you have to understand what's in their heads. **That's what selling is: giving people something of value so that they'll part with their hard-earned cash.** Well, if you want to do that, not only do you have to have your own goals in mind, you must be mindful of other people's goals.

It's kind of like when you take your hands and interlace your fingers; **your personal marketing journey is very interlaced with your customer base.** If you want to make money you also have to get to know your customer; again, you have to figure out what their goals are, their desires, their pains, and frustrations. What can you provide them to help them along in their journey so that they can help you along in yours? As Zig Ziglar taught us, **you can get whatever you want, as long as help enough people get what *they* want.** That's something you really need to understand.

So like an airline or ship with its charts, start plotting a way to get from point A to point B. Once you've got your goal in mind, you can sit down and really start pushing towards that goal. The best way to begin that journey is to first decide, "Okay, who am I going to be working with? Who is excited enough out there? Who's got pain and frustration that I can help with?" **One of the key strategies to DRM is to find a frustrated group of individuals and sell to their pain; that's a particularly good motivator.** Most of the best markets out there are like that; the diet industry, for example, where people are frustrated with their weight. It's depressing them. They're jealous of looking out and seeing all these skinny people. They want that, too, so they're angry and they're frustrated. That's

MARKETING SECRET

The more you test — the luckier you get!

▼

People are easy to figure out. Here's the formula:

- The best predictor of future behavior is past behavior!

why the diet industry is a booming industry. So is the home-based business industry. People are frustrated, because they're part of the rat race and they're not making enough money. They're sick of banging their heads on their desk for eight hours and counting down the seconds until when they can leave every single day, so they're looking for a way out. **There's a reason we're tightly focused on business opportunities, because it's a very good marketplace.**

The point is, both your journey and the journey of the people you're working with are very closely related, so you have to keep your mind focused on both in order to achieve your own goals. If you're focused just on what you want, you won't be focused on what your customers want — and ultimately, it all starts with the market. People tend to put the greatest emphasis on the products and services, **but the market is the most important factor in the business equation.** Think like McDonald's or Starbucks. McDonald's used to be just a burger and fry place — but recently they've become this place where you can get healthy food, too, because the people in their marketplace want healthier choices. As for Starbucks, for years it's been known as the place to buy expensive coffee. More recently, they're seeing a lot of competition in the coffee market. So what's Starbucks doing? They now have a $1 cup of plain black coffee, like everyone else. They've adapted to the marketplace in order to try to keep giving customers what they want.

There are endless examples of businesses using this principle to their advantage. They've got their goals; they've got their financial targets they want to reach. But they've got targets that they see through their customers' eyes as well, and so they're trying to give their customers what their customers want. **If you can find someone's biggest wants and deliver them, then your own biggest wants will follow.** You've got to look at your goals through the prism of your customers and *their* goals.

Ultimately, the products and services you want to sell will evolve and revolve around the market that you're serving. **Every great fortune that's ever been earned in the past, and will ever be earned in the future, is built on creating solutions that solve problems.** That's what we're all in business to do, which we accomplish by giving people what they want the most. And let me re-emphasize the fact that what they generally want is an end to a certain pain they have, whether that be emotional or physical. In our case it's emotional. People hate their jobs, they want financial security, and they're worried about the future. They don't trust Social Security to be around when they retire. And even if they think it *will* be around, they know it's never going to be enough. **Plus, people want a business opportunity because they want something to hope for and to dream about.** That's part of what makes life special. People need hope, and that's another great thing we do: we're giving people things they can get excited about. Our opportunities let them move forward and keep active... and of course, it's fun to make money.

Part of the way that you begin with the end in mind is to find companies to emulate, companies that are doing things like you want to do, that are already serving the markets you want to serve. **Look at the business opportunity market.** There are many, many different companies out there, some of them doing some amazing things, and the market has really evolved over the years. We've seen an astonishing amount of change in our market since 1988, and you'd better believe we keep a very close eye on what other people are doing. **We don't copy them — we try to find ways to beat them, to do things even better, with our own unique twist.**

And we actually like competition. It really amazes me how some people think competition is a bad thing. I love competition; bring it on, baby! **I want competition because I want to try to be better.** I want to try to step up my game and improve upon it. Without competition, the business wouldn't be nearly as fun. When you've got competitors, you look closely at other companies to find out what they're doing. **You get on their mailing lists and buy stuff from them.** You don't do it through the eyes of a consumer; you get on the other side of the cash register, and you think about it from the stance of a business person. **You start looking for themes and patterns, to get a clearer idea of what you want to do.**

I've already talked about setting goals as a way to start developing that clear idea of where you want to go, and that's a good start. It's like going to the gym: something you have to do on a regular basis to get better. **You work at it every day;** you look for models, you examine what people both inside and outside of your industry are doing right, and you try to piece it all together with your own style, so you're not just some copycat. Copycats never really last long-term. Oftentimes they'll get started, make money initially, and then crash for lack of initiative and inventiveness. **Until you learn how to blend all your own ideas with what other people are doing, you're never going to make money long-term.** You have to bring to the table as much as you can of your own ideas, creativity, spirit, and talent, and eventually, experience.

So far, I've discussed how to figure out what makes your market tick. You define your market, if you haven't done that yet; do you want to sell to the business opportunity market, to chiropractors, to dentists? Then look for their sources of frustration and pain (whether emotional or physical) and create solutions that address those points. **Immerse yourself in that market so that you can identify those sore spots.** What can you provide to ease that pain or frustration? What can you bring to the table?

This is how you define your front-end offer, the tool you're going to use to capture the minds of your consumers, to get them engaged in purchasing products from you and to get them in your customer database. Think of it, if you will, as a mousetrap — and I don't mean that in a demeaning way. **The goal is to capture your audience base, to pull them in so you can help them.** Once you find an attractive piece of bait, just continue to use it until it stops effectively trapping people.

I like the mousetrap analogy because, first of all, you have to think with the end in mind. Then you have to define your audience base. *Then* you have to come up with the bait — what are you going to do in order to get involved in this game? You can't stand on the sidelines and make all sorts of grandiose gestures and set empty goals and never really get in the game. This is where you start implementing. The key idea here is that once you have people coming in to your sales funnel, they start buying things from you. **And remember, how much pain and frustration exists in your marketplace will determine how long these people are going to need you.** If there's a lot of pain and frustration, buying one little widget from you probably isn't going to satisfy that. But if they continue to see you as the answer, they also continue to see you as somebody they can come back to, again and again. Remember that little three-step process. **Finding a group of individuals, then getting them to make purchases from you, at a high enough profit margin, over and over again, will make you rich.**

What you also need to realize is that we're in the business of buying sales at a discount. **We want to bring people in, and then have other things that we can sell to them once we have them.** And we want to make sure that we're making our numbers, as I outlined earlier. That subject dovetails nicely into this one. You want to be looking at your numbers regularly and saying, "Okay, I'm spending this amount of money. How much am I making? Am I on target? Are we going to hit these numbers?" Now, of course you're going to start with relatively small numbers. You don't want to start out by trying to hit a seven-figure month, like we do at M.O.R.E., Inc., these days. We've been in the business for a long time, and yes, that may be a place you get to in the future. **But for now, you need to start modestly — yet still aggressively.** If you think you might be happy making $1,000 a month, or $1,000 a week, jack that up to $5,000 or $10,000.

Here's an example of that. I remember when my friend and colleague Eric Bechtold first came to me, when he was just getting out of an ad agency and his goals were way, way, low compared to what was possible. When he told me his goal, I said to him, "Well, that's a good goal — but trust me, you'll be able to do that easily, plus a lot more." And I was right! Eric pulls in so much money now that we call him "Young King Midas." I knew how much money he wanted to make, but I also knew how smart and ambitious he was — and I knew the potential of the marketplace, and how many millions of dollars were to be made, because I'd already generated millions of dollars on my own.

> When people pay — they pay attention!

You know, if you tell the average person who's never made any substantial money in their life that you're going to make millions of dollars

MARKETING SECRET

Concepts first — details last.

- The what and why are more important than the how.

▼

"Take the course opposite to custom and you will almost always do well." — Jean Jaques Rousseau

someday, they're going to either think you're crazy or they're going to laugh at you. Some will try to belittle you. But if you go to somebody who started from scratch and has already made millions, they're likely to support you. They may well do whatever they can to help you, because in business we all work together — or at least we do in our market. That's one of the things I just love about direct response in general. **It's fun to be able to befriend your competitors and do business with them.** Everybody makes more money, and your friendships are built around your businesses because your businesses are important to you.

And even if you just want to beat the competition, it's not that hard to differentiate yourself. I've talked about how to do this in other chapters, but one specific way to do this is something called the **unique selling position, or USP.** That's what different about your company that separates it from everyone else. It took us a long time to figure that out, and it took us even longer develop it properly — and we're still kind of developing it after 21 years. The market does change, and you continually have to find ways to improve.

Part of the reason people in this business get so frustrated is that not only do they not have a clear end in mind at first, sometimes when they do start getting that clear idea of where they want to end up at, they become even more frustrated. Now they start to realize, "Holy crap! Look at all the stuff I have to do!" **But rest assured, all these things are the kinds of things where you can earn while you learn.** You don't have to figure it out overnight; and in fact, you'll never figure it all out. It's a game, and the game keeps changing. And besides, success is a moving target — so you constantly have to adjust your aim. The market never stops changing, and you know what? That's a good thing. **That should excite you, because as long as it's a rabid, every-changing market, all those changes spell profits.** The more you're willing to bend and flex with it, the more you'll be able to stay on top of things and cash in on whatever's hot — and there's always something hot. That's part of the joy for me, because there's always something new and exciting. The idea here is that when you start thinking about these things seriously, and you start realizing what's really possible, the whole world opens up to you.

Another question to think about at this point is this: Why should your customer continue to do business with you? **What can you provide on that back end for your customers that will make them stick with you, once they've taken your cheese?** Remember, Eric's goal is to get 10,000 people buying in a vacuum from him. That means they're not only in his trap, but they're happy to be there — because they understand that any time Eric offers them something, it's something good for them, and they want it right away. So ideally, they'll continue to buy.

Hopefully, these questions and concepts are starting to focus your mind on how to take those goals in hand and set out on the journey toward your destination. You plot a course, and figure out what pieces need to be where in order to effectively move you from point A to point B. We talk about the money a lot, and of course the money is important; but remember, the theme of this chapter is "the end of your wealth-making journey." **The real joy has always been the journey; it's never just the destination.** The fact is, sometimes when you reach your goals, they turn out to be anticlimactic. It's like that old Patsy Cline song that says, "Is this all there is?" Once you find that destination, then, you've got to set bigger goals or different goals, and start on a *new* journey. **You always want to be moving forward.** You need a destination just to keep you focused on your journey, to be sure you're not wasting a lot of time. **Get in the game. Enjoy the journey. Have fun.**

Because the truth is, this game of making money *is* fun. It's thrilling; it's like a hunt. When I was a kid, we used to go hunting all the time; and the fun was just in doing the hunting, it wasn't necessarily the killing part. In fact, that's why I quit hunting, because I didn't like to kill — but I always liked to hunt. That's why people go fishing, that's why they go hunting, that's why they go on all kinds of adventures. That's why they take trips down roaring rivers or up to the tops of high mountains.

The worst thing you could do is stagnate, or find yourself facing a stagnant marketplace where there's not a lot of new things happening, not a lot of change. **Part of the fun is the change, and the turnover, and the cycles that businesses go through.** It's very difficult to innovate in an old business or an old marketplace, where things are always done the same way, and the customers expect the same things over and over and buy the same thing over and over, because they're conditioned to act a certain way and to do certain things. That's a difficult place to make money in.

But if you're in a marketplace where there are new trends and shifts in emphasis, or even paradigms, **you can profit from those shifts.** You can ride those waves of success, as long as you're always alert and watching for the next wave, the next trend, the next shift in the marketplace. Since the market is constantly changing, your goals, that end target, have to move to some degree as well. And it's usually a short-term target. In this marketplace, especially in this part of our history, there's so much happening with technology, in the way we do business online and offline. **Just the process of doing business changes so much that you have to constantly be adjusting your strategies and setting new goals.** Take that monthly goal I talked about earlier; that's just for right now. A year or two from now, that goal might be different. I can't see it being any lower, but maybe it'll be a little higher. And maybe we'll have shifted the way we're going about trying to reach that goal. That's because we know that if you're in tune with the fact that things change, you can be in position to benefit from those changes by being nimble, responsive, and innovative — and have a great time doing it.

Even if a marketplace seems a little staid, you might be able to find the excitement if you just do a little digging. We've got a husband-and-wife team who are part of our Direct Response Network; they're out of San Diego, and they're in a business that's anything but exciting to me. It sounds like the most boring business in the world, but as of two years ago they'd done $50 million worth of business in the previous seven years. They're clearing huge sums of money selling, of all things, nuts and bolts. Honestly, they sell nuts and bolts — and doing so excites them. The reason they're excited about their business is because of the lifestyle that it has afforded them. That's really what gets them out of bed in the morning.

They built their company together, and they sell through a worldwide market. I can't imagine a more boring business — but whatever turns your crank, go for it.

This is what I want you to pull out of this whole discussion. **Keeping your goals in mind and understanding where you want to go is just a way to get engaged in the process and to manifest your reality.** Because what you focus on becomes your reality; if you keep thinking about it and keep moving toward it, taking little baby steps every day, eventually you'll wind up there. **Remember, marketing is a three-step process. NUMBER ONE is attracting qualified leads. NUMBER TWO is converting the highest percentage possible into sales. NUMBER THREE is reselling the largest possible number of these customers.** And that's it; only three steps. That's what you need to understand about the marketing side of it.

Once you have the answers to the questions that I've presented here today, you're going to know who you are, where you want to be, who your audience is, what you're going to offer them in order to get there. **Once you know all that, it's just a matter of figuring out what your mousetrap's going to be, and figuring out a way to put it where there's likely to be a mouse.** You might start by running a small little classified ad, or just sending out a few hundred postcards. And that's another thing I'd like to leave you with. Figuring out your destination is one thing, but when you're figuring out the steps that you're going to take to get there — when you come up with ideas and put them into motion — **make sure that you test things in a small way first.** Once you find something that's working, then roll it out big. That'll keep you out of trouble. If you find you're going the wrong direction, those baby steps let you replot and adjust your course a little. You're not going to get into a financial situation where you can't readjust. **You never want to throw all your eggs in one basket;** you want to feel your way along, if you will. Eventually you'll get to the point where you can stride forward in confidence, really roll out big, and get to that first destination you've set before you — so you can pause, take a deep breath, and plan for that next destination.

Starting with your end in mind is the only way to start, because otherwise, how do you ever know if you've accomplished anything? So many small business owners — and I'm talking about a huge percentage — have no destination in mind at all. Every day is the same day lived over and over. They're working hard, they're putting in a lot of hours, and yet

MARKETING SECRET

STORIES SELL!

- Create an emotional story to wrap around your product or service.

▼

"Marketing is simply a combination of math and psychology."
— Dan Kennedy

they're not making enough money. But when you sit down with them and say, "Hey, look, what's your marketing plan? Tell me, I want to see it, I want to help you here," you discover that they don't have one. And if you ask them what their goals are, they really don't have any — or if they do, it's something like "Pay the bills." Or they've got a far off fantasy that someday they're going to sell their business and retire.

The two men that I've loved most in my life, my father and my stepfather, both did a terrible job planning their futures. They were great men, I loved both of them dearly, and I think about them all the time. For the last 20 years of his life, my stepdad was in business. And I tried to help him; I tried to give him some ideas, but he just was so much against them that I might as well not have tried. At first, I thought it was just him, because he was one of the most stubborn people I've known. But over the last 15-20 years, I've run into so many business owners who are exactly like my stepdad. To them, it's not a business; it's just a job. They just go to work every day, and it's not exciting.

To me, **business is an exciting game; it's something you play to win.** Show me any game where you can't keep score, and I'll show you the most boring game on the planet. That may be fine when you're a kid and you're trying to have fun, but when you're older, **you've got to be able to keep score;** otherwise, what's the point? You play to win; and winning isn't the "only thing," by the way, Vince Lombardi notwithstanding. **It's the desire to win that's the only thing.** Because as I've said, many of your goals will seem anticlimactic once you hit them. So you've got a goal to make a million dollars? Well, once you make a million, you'll say, "Hey, wait a minute, I thought this was going to make my life a million times better." Your life probably *is* better, but not by as much as you thought. The real fun is in playing the game. **It's the sport, it's the hunt, it's the chase; it's the thrill of all of that.**

And that's what I hope that you'll learn along the way: **that the journey is the reward. That said, you still have to know where you want to wind up, or you're never going to get there...** and it's no fun being lost. I see so many businesspeople who dream of owning their own businesses but live nothing but a nightmare, because every day they're doing the best they know how to, but they're getting nowhere. They're not focused on hitting any kind of a goal. They're not going for it, because they don't even know what they're going for. They're locked into survival; that's all. They're just trying to survive... and if that's your goal, you don't have a goal. That's just existence. **Real success is grabbing for something outside of your current reach.** It's something to get excited about for the future. It's something that moves you forward, not just going through the same motions that you went through yesterday and the day before. If you're just getting by, if your goal is just to survive in business, then you probably shouldn't be in business. There are a lot of good jobs to be had out there; and if that's your way of looking at the world, that may be a better route for you.

If you're serious about your goals, then I'd encourage you to write them down and think about them. Put them in a place where you can see them every day, so you can be held to that standard. Share those goals with other people who can hold you accountable, so that they can ask you, "Hey, did you mail out 1,000 letters today? Because you said you needed to mail out 1,000 letters today to reach your goal. I'm just checking up on you to see if you really did drop those in the mail." Or "Did you place that ad today?" or "How many sales did you bring in today? Okay, you didn't reach your goal, so tomorrow you've got to bring in an extra "X" number of sales to make up for it." **Go find some people that can hold you to that standard;** and incidentally, don't just get a family member who might ask you for a day or two and then let you go. A fellow businessman or a friend might be a better choice.

And remember that goals can be adjusted, so don't be too hard on yourself if you don't make them. Be disappointed, sure; as I mentioned at the beginning of the chapter, we're upset when we don't make our goals, but it's not the end of the world. We adjust our goals and we keep going at it. **The worst thing you can do is give up and feel defeated.** Goals can be modified as you chart your course, and as you make adjustments along the way. That way, you'll be able to hone them and to keep moving forward.

So that's the main thing: **be a doer, not a talker.** Get out there and be active in your business, doing everything you can to achieve those goals, to set bigger goals, and to accomplish more.

SECTION NINE:

WHAT RUTHLESS REALLY MEANS

How to stock up on your
ruthless ammunition,
how to treat your customers
and competitors both, and how to
become the center of attention
in your marketplace.

What Ruthless Really Means

In this last section, I'm going to tell you what you have to do to become a truly ruthless marketer. I'll teach you how to stock up on your ruthless ammunition, how to treat your customers and competitors both, and how to become the center of attention in your marketplace. Along the way I'm also going to tell you more about what ruthless means — which may not necessarily be what you *think* it means. For example, **when I talk about "ruthless" marketing, what I really mean is** *aggressive* **marketing — it's just that "ruthless" sounds better!** But there's more to it than that, so sit tight, read on, and I'll reveal how you can become the most ruthless marketer you can be.

Positively Ruthless, In Every Way

First of all, "ruthless" isn't necessarily a negative term; a lot of people don't understand that. If you look at the dictionary meaning of the word "ruthless," you'll see that it *can* mean a lot of bad things; for example, somebody who is ruthless can kill a person without a second thought, because they have no conscience. But that's not exactly what I'm talking about here. **Ruthlessness can, in fact, be a positive thing for both you and your customers, though your competitors will never thank you for it.**

In a way, one of the easiest ways for me to describe ruthless marketing to people is by telling them that truly ruthless marketing occurs when we cater to the self-centered emotions of our customers. What I mean by that is this: people buy for emotional reasons. We've covered this before: you've got greed, guilt, fear, pride, and love. Basically, if you think about it, everybody is a self-centered individual living in a mostly self-centered world. From the client-side perspective, ruthless marketing focuses on the emotional reasons people have for purchasing. Yes, you can create a negative situation if you really play to somebody's fear and make them scared to the point where they think they must have your product to safeguard themselves: "Oh my gosh! I've got to run out and buy that because I'm fearful that my house may get broken into next week!" You can almost slap the consumer around and make them pay attention to what you're saying — that's one way to define ruthless marketing.

MARKETING SECRET

What do people want? — The same things they bought as last time — only different.

▼

Strive to be different. Controversy sells!

▼

Overwhelm them with follow-up offers until they buy.

Ruthless marketing also means doing things differently than your competition. A lot of people are timid marketers, or they're "me too" marketers: they're only willing to do what everybody else is doing in terms of their marketing. You can't blame those people, because **whenever you get into a new business, the only thing you know to do is to copy the people who are in that exact same business.** So all the Yellow Page ads look the same, and all the mailers look the same, and so do the door hangers and the business cards; it all looks the same. That's timid "me too" marketing. It's not very exciting, and it really doesn't set you apart from your competition.

That's the root of the issue for me. Ruthless marketing means doing things that set you apart from the competition, that get you a bigger market share, more customers, and more profits. **It's the activities that make your competitors fear you, because you're stealing their customers and the money they want.** And you shouldn't think that's a bad thing, because in doing that, you're building a strong business of your own, thereby serving a lot more customers with the best quality products and services possible. Better yet, you're also building up your income for your own dreams for your family.

Again, in this sense, ruthless marketing is a great thing, not a negative thing. When a lot of people hear the word "ruthless," it conjures images of some kind of ruthless pillager — a Viking who just goes out there and takes whatever he wants. In some ways, that's true: as competitive an environment as the marketing world is, sometimes you've just got to do it that way. You have to tell yourself, "Okay, I'm going to do these things in order to capture my market share, in order to make the profits that I want and need to keep my business afloat." Oftentimes we've got employees to whom we have an obligation; we've also got families who depend on us. The ruthless mindset is just a means to an end, in that we're developing the skills that focus on those human factors that get people to give us their money.

The bottom line is, a ruthless marketer is not paid for his *methods*, but for his *results*. **If you're going to concentrate on manipulating and coercing people's emotional factors and psychological frames of reference in order to get them to spend their money with you, well, yes, that does sound very ruthless. But the reality is that it's just part of capitalism. It's part of being competitive, and part of doing what needs to be done to create a thriving marketing business.** When it comes to marketing in general, you don't want to be timid; you don't want to be shy. Sometimes you don't even want to be nice! So when I hear the term "ruthless marketer," I think it's a good thing that's attached to the end of my name. It's not something of which to be afraid or ashamed. It's actually a point of pride for me that I've invested in the skills necessary to become a ruthless marketer.

That said, **let me tell you a little about what ruthless marketing is** *not*.

1. **It's not taking advantage of people.**

2. **It's not lying, cheating, or stealing.**

3. **It's not ripping people off.**

Ruthless marketing isn't all the things you think of when you think of "ruthless" as it applies to a personal attribute. When you're talking about relationships among friends, the term "ruthless" might conjure up images you find unpleasant. But when it comes to business, especially when it comes to your competition, it's a necessary mindset. **The ruthless marketing mindset is that there's a whole lot of money out that's being spent, and you deserve to make as much of it as you can get. Your goal is to serve customers and make a profit. One of the ways you do that is by charging in there with the overall mindset of "take no prisoners"** — this mindset that you want as big a market share as you can

possibly get, and you want to make as many profits as possible while playing the game *right*. It's not about taking advantage of people or ripping them off. It's about having this mindset that, of all the discretionary income out there, you want the largest market share, the biggest piece of the pie. That's what ruthless marketing is all about.

It's more about being aggressive than anything else. When I was a kid there was a rock-and-roll song called, "No More Mr. Nice Guy." I used to love that song! Plus, I like what Carl Icahn used to say: "If you want a friend, get a dog." You've got to be ruthless! You've got to be aggressive! **You've got to develop the heart of the lion and the mind of the fox. You've got to be bold and audacious, and even a little bit cunning, in order to seize the greatest opportunities for sales and profits.** Like I said, it's not about lying to people or cheating them; it's about mastering the art of getting the largest number of people in *your* market to give *you* the largest amount of *their* disposable income.

When you study the secrets of all great marketers, you'll see that they've all got this ruthless marketing mindset: the mind of the fox and the heart of the lion. Your job is to get as much money out of your marketplace as you possibly can. Your job isn't to be friends with your competitors, and it's not to be worried about what other people are going to think about you. I mentioned earlier that most businesspeople are far too timid. At an early age, we learn that it's not a nice thing to blow your own horn and toot your own whistle. We learn at an early age that we shouldn't be cocky or arrogant or egotistical. Even worse, I think there are too many people in this world who have what I call an "employee mentality." **Even people who've been in business for a number of years... in their hearts, they still think like an employee. I don't mean that as disrespectful to employees, because not all employees are alike; but most employees are waiting for other people to appoint them, to tell them what to do.**

When you look at the people who are the most aggressive and are achieving the largest amount of success in the marketplace, you'll see that they're not waiting around for anybody to appoint them to anything. They're out there tooting their own horns or ringing their own bells. Some of them, in fact, set out to be a little controversial. They're not really concerned about what other people are going to think about them. Their primary focus is doing all kinds of bold and audacious, outside-of-the-box, wild and crazy kinds of things that get the best customers attracted to them, because they know their competitors are all after the best customers too. So you've got to do something to completely separate yourself from everyone else, and get all of the money that could and should be yours, and not your competitor's.

On another note, the ruthless mindset is to **treat business as a something like a sport or game,** as I've mentioned in other chapters. We're in this game to win. It's almost like playing Monopoly. We're not just going to continue to move around the board just for the fun of it. We need to put up our houses, and then put up hotels. That's how we win that game. Ruthless marketing is taking that concept of winning a game like Monopoly into your business. How can you get the houses in the right places? How can you get your marketing in front of the people who need to see it, ahead of all of your other competitors? **We're here to win. Never forget that.**

There's an old fable about a gazelle that gets up in the morning. The gazelle has to run faster than the lion behind it — or, at least, it has to run faster than the slowest gazelle, because if it doesn't, the lion will catch it and eat it, and then it's out of the game. The lion, on the other hand, must run faster than the slowest gazelle, or it'll starve to death. It's the same thing in business. When the lion eats up those weaker competitors, you're next in line. If you're the gazelle, you need to get in front of the herd, and the only way you do that is through ruthless marketing. "Ruthless" is really "aggressive." But I also think that **to be really good at ruthless marketing, you need to have courage. Courage is going to put you at the front of the pack in everything you do.** You can't be timid, because then you're that last gazelle, just waiting to be eaten by the next lion that comes along.

Ruthless Ammunition and the Psychological Edge

My friend and colleague Eric Bechtold talks about something he calls "getting your ruthless ammunition for your business." The definition of "ruthless ammunition" is going to be different for every business, so you really need to internalize this and focus on how it applies to your business in order to understand what it means. Basically, Eric's goal in marketing any program or product or service is to put it into his advertising formula.

▼▼▼▼▼▼▼▼▼
MARKETING SECRET

People don't want the truth. That's why we must constantly look for emotional stories that sound good.

▼

A good plan today (set in motion) is better than a brilliant plan tomorrow!

This is where the ruthless marketing part comes in, because first, in order to perform a good marketing push out there, in order to connect with your customers, you always need to try to figure out what the biggest problem is, or the biggest solution you're providing to your customer. **Think about your product or service from your customer's standpoint, and try to figure out how you make their lives easier.**

Let's say, for example, that you're selling car seats for parents to put their little kids in when they're driving to work or school or wherever. You can broadcast a TV commercial that shows the plain statistics: about how 85% of children who are injured in car accidents are injured because their parents didn't put them into the proper seating. To be most effective, you need to focus in on all these scary statistics, and play to their fear for their kids' safety. This is just one example of how you could get yourself into this ruthless mindset, simply by **figuring out what problems — or worries — drive your consumers. Focus on that, and identify those issues. Obviously, the above example is a very specialized situation, but it illustrates the general method. You want to agitate those issues, bring them to the surface, and really get your consumer feeling the pain.** Make them scared. Make them want to say, "Oh man, I really wish I could do that or have this. My life would be so much better." If you make them feel their pain, you can sell them the solution.

That's one example of ruthless marketing, and that's Eric's advertising formula for handling that situation. But there are also other psychological influences that you can play to, factors that influence how people buy.

These include:

- Scarcity
- Authority
- Social proof
- Consistency
- Liking
- Reciprocity

These are all things on which you can focus when you're searching for those problems that you're going to agitate in order to get people to buy. I've talked about this before in several previous chapters, but it bears repeating as I wrap this book up: you've absolutely got to know your customers better than they know themselves.

There's a book out there called *Non-Manipulative Selling*. I know that sounds like a joke — like it would be a completely blank book, on the order of *Everything Men Know About Women* — but it's not, which I find a little mind-boggling. I can just imagine all these people buying that book who want to be nice people, who don't want to take advantage of others and don't want to manipulate others. But guess what? *All selling and all marketing is manipulation.* **You're trying to get people to spend money with you instead of your competitors. You've got to know all the tricks in the book. You've got to line up your ruthless ammunition and have it ready at all times. Having the best product and service is not enough; the marketplace is unfair in every way. Many times, the people who do a better job of marketing are the ones who are going to make all the money, not the company that delivers the best product and service. That's the reality of the marketplace.** But if you're committed to quality products and services, then you've also got to know all these other little tricks and secrets that other marketers are using to try to get the best prospects in your market to give the money to *them* rather than you.

Take scarcity, for example. I don't think that you must have one of your products for every one of your customers. That may be nice and fair, but life's not fair. Scarcity is something that moves people to make a decision to buy your product. Maybe there's a limited number of free items you're giving away; maybe it's limited access to consultants. **There's got**

to be some sort of scarcity that moves people off the couch to come and give you a call. But it really has to be honest scarcity! You often see those commercials nowadays where they say, "You have to order in the next 30 minutes to get this bonus." You'll see this on an infomercial, and you'll see that infomercial every single night and it says the same thing, every single night. Eventually, no one believes it anymore.

But there *are* some really smart companies that train their customers that the scarcity is real, and if you plan to use this tactic, you have to be like them. Say, for example, you only have seventeen of a particular item and a customer is the eighteenth person, or the twentieth or the fiftieth to contact you. What do you say? Tell them, "I'm sorry, but all those bonuses are gone. We do have these great gifts for you, but all the big bonuses are gone." What you teach them is to respond to scarcity when you put it out there. If you train people to do that, they'll be more responsive whenever you make new scarcity-based marketing offers.

Car dealerships have a big problem with using scarcity tactics; they use them completely the wrong way. A lot of the major manufacturers have special sales, and they're always ending. Then the next week, you see an ad on TV — and the same sale is still going on, or it's been extended, and you find out it's been extended indefinitely — or at least until people stop responding to it. Then they come up with a new deadline or something.

To go ahead and pick on the car industry some more — talk about your ruthless marketers! Car dealers routinely use reciprocity in their message. Have you ever sat there while you're buying a car and the salesman you're dealing with says, "Okay, hold on. Let me go check with my sales manager and we'll see if we can do this for you." He comes back and says something to the effect of, "Well, we were able to do this for *you*." Now, what's that doing in the mind of the consumer who's sitting there thinking about buying a car? It's saying, "Wow, they did this for me; now I should do something for *them*." It's using human nature against that person. "We were able to take $2,000 off this price and give you a better warranty. We were able to do this for you." They're going to be asking for you, the consumer, to do something for them. That's a good example of reciprocity as used in a car dealership. You can use that psychological influence in many different settings with your business, regardless of what it is. All you have to do is identify that it's something you'd want to do in your marketing, and then dream up ways to utilize that psychological influence on people.

Use your ruthless ammunition to declare war against all your direct competitors. There are only two types of competitors: indirect competitors who are selling to the same types of people that you do, but aren't selling the same exact products and services; and direct competitors that are selling the exact same things you are, to the exact same people. **Those people are your enemy!** Start thinking about them that way right now. **Learn how to hate them, if you have to — but just as a psychological tool. You've got to see them as trying to take money away that should and could be yours.** I see a lot of people who don't consider their direct competitors their enemies, and I think in some marketplaces, you can afford to have a better attitude about it. But in other marketplaces there are only so many good prospects and customers to go around, and the pond is not being replenished much. If you're not trying to go after those people, you know your competitors are.

> ▼▼▼▼▼▼▼▼▼▼▼
>
> Great Marketers are Hunters.
>
> *We are happiest when we're on the hunt.* The bigger the hunt — the happier we are.
>
> We must be reaching all the time. All is well as long as our reach exceeds our grasp.

You *cannot* be timid about any of this! You've got to be very aggressive. If you're timid about it, it's only a matter of time until you hang out your "Going Out Of Business Sale" sign, because at some point a competitor will come along and take all your customers. I've seen it happen in the small business world over and over again. A business owner sits and says, "Oh, I've got all this business coming in. I don't have to do any marketing. I'm making so much this year." They never figure out that they need to continue to market. What happens is, either a competitor comes in nearby, or maybe they have to move and can't take their customers with them. They no longer have the right storefront, and they just go down the tubes — and they go down fast.

If you're not a ruthless marketer, you need to change your attitude, even if you're doing well — because success is a temporary state that'll last no longer than it takes for an aggressive competitor to come in and

▼▼▼▼▼▼▼▼
MARKETING SECRET

Always save the details for last!

▼

From the movie Road To Riches — "Hope is the strongest of all human emotions, and not to be ignored!"

---

take your market share. **You can't just sit back and enjoy life, because business is too competitive these days.** It's no longer a situation where you can start a business, hang out a shingle, and people will come. That's a common fallacy. You need to aggressively, ruthlessly go out and grab customers off the street and drag them into your business. It's the only way you're going to stay in business long-term.

Make Audacious Promises

Eric Bechtold told me once that what "really slapped me around and made me change the way I was thinking ruthlessly," as he put it, was something he heard at a Direct-Marketing conference. Someone pointed out that **in every offer you make, you've got to make a bold, audacious promise to your customer — something that you're going to have to struggle like hell to actually produce.** Sure, you're going to have to work really hard in order to fulfill that commitment, but that makes you that much more likely to go out there and over-deliver.

That person also pointed out that, when you make these bold claims, some of your customers aren't going to be 100% happy with what you're offering if it doesn't completely meet their expectations. **You have to make it clear to them that you're going to back your promise with a guarantee:** so you say something like, "If you do such and such, you're going to increase your business by 200%, or I'll guarantee I'll give you every dollar you gave me back." Some people who are going to come back to you and say, "Well, I wasn't happy with what it was you sold me. I want my money back," and you're going to have to give their money back. The philosophy here — and this is what I thought was really ruthless — was that if you're not making enough refunds, you're not selling hard enough. I've always been taught that when you sell anything to your customer, you need to make sure you've got it right there ready to deliver, and that you're managing every expectation, and you want to make sure that *there are no refunds at all*.

But in a ruthless mindset, if you're not making a certain amount of refunds, you're not selling hard enough, and you need to be happy to make those refunds consistently, so you're *still* managing the expectations of your customer and making them happy. That's extremely ruthless, because you actually go into it knowing, "I'm not going to make a lot of my customers happy. I'm going to make a whole lot more money because of it, because a lot of people are going to want my product and will buy it... but I might have as much as 20% refunds on this individual item."

The whole concept of being bold and audacious (and, yes, ruthless) reminds me of the Solo-Flex story. For the first twenty years of his career, the guy who started Solo-Flex was a charter jet pilot who flew people from Los Angeles to Las Vegas and back. He worked for a company that had a rich clientele and he was probably making a good six-figure income, just taking the same small client-base from L.A. to Vegas so they could gamble. They didn't want to spend five or six hours to drive to Las Vegas, and didn't want to take a commercial flight. In any case, he got to know these people, and after a while they were all on a first name basis — but he was still making a six-figure pilot's income. **Many of these people were worth many tens of millions of dollars, and there were probably a couple of billionaires in the mix, too. One morning the pilot asked himself a simple question: "I wonder what it is, really, that separates me from these guys?"**

The answer was that these guys all had a certain level of audacity. They were just a little bit bolder than most people. It was in the way they carried themselves, the way they thought, the way they acted, the way that they took on everything in life and went after their dreams and whatever they wanted. **Once he realized that, his whole life changed. Within a matter of just a few years, he started the Solo-Flex Company and became a multimillionaire himself.** He was bold; he was audacious. You need to be that way, too. There's a famous book out called *Timid Salespeople Raise Skinny Kids*; it was written by Zig Ziglar's brother. I like that title, because it emphasizes part of what we're talking about with this ruthless mindset. **You have to have courage to take that next, audacious step: to advertise in a new, untested way, to reach out to a new segment of the market, to be willing to lose customers by making audacious claims. It's not an absence of fear. It's moving forward in spite of your fear, and that's really a lot of the secret right there.**

Here's something that helps me get in the ruthless mindset, and it may be a good little drill for you, too. **Sit down with a pen and paper and think about your business, and some audacious, bold promises you could make to your consumer. Write those down, and be really outlandish; just write down whatever comes to mind. If you were the consumer, what could I say to you that would make you sit up and take notice?** Regardless of who else is in the field, regardless of the competition, they're going to want to figure out about what it is you're talking and want to pay attention to you. **Write those all down and then go back and weed out the ones that are literally impossible. It will be a good exercise to open up your mind. Focus on picking a couple of those, and then work them into your marketing strategies in some way.** Make sure, if it's audacious and bold, that you offer a guarantee so that any customer who's not happy with the results can definitely get their money back. Or offer some sort of a guarantee to ease the strain, in case it's too much for you to possibly deliver. Try to go out there and do everything morally and ethically, but try to make bold promises that make you stand out.

Pay Your Dues and Open Your Mind

One thing that'll boost your confidence and get you going courageously and boldly is working hard to develop your abilities. When you look at life, you can always tell those people or teams who've put in the time to be confident at what they're doing. Go out there and check the difference in the confidence level. **The people who've paid their dues, who've worked hard at being good at what they're doing, are out there taking on the world and accomplishing everything they want to accomplish, whether they're a courageous entrepreneur or part of a championship team.**

A ruthless marketer has to develop a mindset that continually motivates and encourages them to go out there and take those confident steps, to do those things they need to do to capture that market share. It all starts with study and learning and education: learning from the best, building a library that's filled with all kinds of books, tapes, and programs so you're learning from proven, successful people. There aren't actually a lot of people who go out and buy the books and programs they need to succeed. They'd rather sit down and watch a TV program every night and veg out. A ruthless marketer, on the other hand, goes out and grabs a book, reads it and gets some of these skills, or listens to a tape or studies a program to help him or her develop skills they need to succeed in their business. **It only takes one good idea, sometimes, to impel you into a marketing campaign that's going to return thousands, hundreds of thousands, or millions of dollars — but starting out, you usually can't tell what that idea is, or from where it will come. It all starts with education and study: paying your dues by doing some brain-work, then going out there and trying out some of the ideas you find, and maybe failing a lot more often than you succeed.**

On top of all that, you definitely need to keep an open mind. Nothing will close you down faster than thinking you already know it all, whether it's dealing with colleagues or clients or competitors. The main point I want to make about keeping an open mind is that you have to realize that your peripheral vision isn't as wide as you think it is. Many people go through life with such arrogance that they think they know it all; they know everything, and they don't need to go back to school to learn anything, or get a book or tape or a program, because they think their peripheral vision is so great — when in reality, they're looking through binoculars, and have tunnel vision about a lot of things. I've seen that over and over again — people who use arrogance to cover up their ignorance.

Even though a truly ruthless marketer may appear arrogant, that arrogance is usually backed up by study, research, and a firm understanding of marketing. **So focus on those things that help you become a better marketer, and develop the commitment, the dedication, the discipline, and the desire to learn. That's part of the ruthless mindset: making up your mind that you *don't* know it all, that you need to keep an open mind, that you need to expand your horizons so that next ruthless marketer doesn't catch up to you. If you're not putting in the time to learn and to study, someone else is.**

Bad things happen to a businessperson who's been in business for a

MARKETING SECRET

The safest marketing system that guarantees consistent sales and profits:

1. First generate the highest quality leads you can get from space ads — or small direct mail packages.

2. Get the customer to request more information.

3. Then follow-up and hit them with all kinds of personalized sales material that takes the place of a live sales rep.

while and thinks they know it all. Here's something that many people like that do: they forget how to listen, to really listen, to teach themselves the value and to understand the ideas and the opinions of others before criticizing those ideas and opinions. Because even when you know, deep in your heart, that someone doesn't know about what the hell he or she is talking, you can still learn what *not* to do. It's a good idea to keep your ears open — that's why God gave you two of them — and to teach yourself to value and understand the ideas and opinions of others before you criticize: to learn from them.

If you set things up in your daily life so you're expanding the things you need to expand and you're learning the things you need to learn, you're going to have an overall mindset that allows you to consistently think outside the box and do those things you need to do to succeed. **You'll have the courage to be bold in the marketplace, because your knowledge is grounded in solid, proven marketing strategies, and a mindset that keeps you on the cutting edge.** Now, it's not easy to stay there on the cutting edge. If you're going to be supersuccessful — year in and year out — you have to keep learning and growing.

That, right there, is your basic ammunition for becoming a ruthless marketer. That, and the fact that **you have to be disciplined: you have to know what you want and how to define your goals, and can't just expect great things to happen by chance. You have to put in the effort it takes to develop this kind of mindset, and simply believe you're going to be the best.** Last year, my buddy Chris Lakey's daughter,

Ashleigh, was in a spelling bee. Every night she'd come home and talk about how she did in school that day. They practiced every day: they'd do these mock spelling bees, and she would constantly tell her Mom and Dad how she did, and about how she wanted to win. If she won, she got to go to the next level and participate in a spelling bee against a bunch of kids from other schools. Chris would tell her that if she wanted to win the spelling bee, she had to study better and harder than everybody else, and she had to continuously put in the effort to practice, to study the list of words on which they were going to be quizzed. So she knew the parameters of the spelling bee — but she just wouldn't practice. She wanted it, but not bad enough to put the time in to practice, and so she finished second. Chris told her, after she finished second, that he was proud of her for finishing second — but that she couldn't be too upset when she didn't finish first, because she knew she hadn't put in the time it took to be Number One and to overtake that other person.

Now, that may seem a little harsh when applied to a little kid, but it's the same whether you want to win in kickball or in a spelling bee or in business. **If you don't put in the time and effort it takes to be Number One, then don't get mad when your competitors keep taking your business away from you. You have to put in the time, and you have to do more than say, "I want to be Number One in my marketplace." You have to do what it takes to be there. It's not just a matter of thinking it and writing down your goals; it's about doing what it takes to get to that top position in your marketplace.** You have to have that ruthless mindset that you're going to take as much business out of this marketplace as you can, and that you're going to be Number One. If you'll have that mindset to do that, then you can get there.

Let's use a sports analogy again. My colleague and friend Chris Hollinger used to be a basketball coach. I know for a fact, having spoken to him about it, that he saw players who weren't nearly as talented as others who ultimately performed better and more consistently than the rest. He told me how **he once coached a team that was made up of some extremely talented players; on paper, it looked like no one should have been able to touch them out on the court. But they really had to struggle in some games, simply because there were other teams that worked harder and had more discipline.** They had more dedication to the craft of basketball, and were more serious about coming together as a team than Chris' team was. Because the team Chris coached was so talented, the team members thought they could just walk out on the court and beat everybody with no problem. That's not always the case. As a matter of fact, they got second at State that year with a super-talented team to which no one should have even been close.

This only goes to show that having the right mix of skills and ability can actually be a downfall in some ways, because it makes you complacent sometimes. That's why you have to go back and be true to your craft and put in the time and the effort that it really takes to develop your talent even further. You see that in a lot of sports — and in a lot of businesses as well. You may not realize this, but the great Michael Jordan was *not* the best basketball player in his high school; he was good, but he didn't have all of the talent. By the end of his career, though, he'd trained so much and had worked so hard that he did. Tiger Woods is another example of someone who continued to work at his skills, to hone his craft into something extra special. **It works the same way with businesses, small or large. The people that continue to practice their skills, to work at their craft — whether it's marketing, or running a business as a whole — continue to make their businesses better, bit by little bit. It's an ongoing process increasing their sales and making their profits grow by leaps and bounds.**

One of the things I find interesting about most business owners is that they seem to want to be *out* of their business desperately. Whenever five o'clock rolls around, they all want to leave. Whatever they're doing — whether it's plumbing or maintenance or carpet cleaning — they've started this business because they want a certain type of lifestyle, a certain type of income. They want to be self-employed, but they get buried in the day-to-day minutia of running that business, and so they all want to be out of it desperately. Now, one of the great things about being a ruthless marketer is that there's a lot of creativity involved; you've got a competitive spirit, and so you're always trying to do a little bit better and a little bit better. Instead of getting involved in the minutia of what cleaning products you're going to order this month, all of a sudden you've got your own little game going. **Being a ruthless marketer is like creating your own game, where you're always trying to do better than the competition, or you're always trying to put out better marketing materials, or you're always trying to be a little bit better than everybody else. In doing that, you** get to become more passionate about your business. You get to rekindle the passion about what you're doing.

I think it's very important for you to step outside of that mindset of being the business owner. A lot of people, when they start a business up, fall into that business-owner mindset. You know: "I run a carpet cleaning business." Or, "I run a pet store." Or, "I'm a lawyer... an attorney." Don't fall into the trap. Instead, step into the ruthless marketing mindset where, "I'm a marketer." *That's* where the money is, along with the joy of the chase. **You're a marketer of whatever products or services you're currently promoting; you're not just a carpet cleaner.** As I've said before, that seems like a tiny little difference on the surface, but there's really a big gap between being, say, a carpet cleaner and a marketer of carpet cleaning services. Keep that in mind, and you'll be able to build a much larger, more successful business.

> Remain open, flexible, and curious.

The Case of the Fan Company

I have a little story I wanted to tell about a case study I've been following now for a little while, one about which I've heard marketing coaches and other people talk. **It regards a company that's within one of the most mundane industries you could ever imagine — but they've turned their business around by using ruthless marketing tactics, and by not being scared to try something different. This is a company that sells, of all things, great big fans.** I think it's a good example of a company that wasn't scared to do something different, to go out there and shake up the industry a little bit. The name of the company is actually "Big Ass Fans."

I'm not kidding. That's the reason I wanted to bring this case study to your attention, because... well, think about that name: "Big Ass Fans." This is a company that focuses their attention on developing large fans for cooling down warehouses and other big buildings. The reason I find this to be a great example of ruthless marketing is that somebody really had to be daring, really had to have some *cojones*, to go out there in this quiet little industry and change the company's name to what it is now. It was something really mundane before. But they listened to their customers — and **whenever their customers they saw their product, they tended to**

SECTION NINE — What Ruthless Really Means   681

MARKETING SECRET

Selling money at a discount:

- Always try to offer your customers $1,000.00 in genuine tangible value — for every $100.00 you are asking them to give you!

- It's simple: If you want to sell a $1,000.00 package — Just make sure you can build a believable case — that it is worth at least $10,000.00 in value to them.

- Believability is the key. You must prove it to them — beyond a doubt. Do this — and your closing ratio will be high!

say, "Man, that's a big ass fan!" You see, these fans are six feet or more across, and they have to be, since they sit up in the ceilings of really big buildings and keep the air circulating.

At some point, they took the plunge and changed the name of the company to Big Ass Fans from whatever it was before (I think it was something like Industrial Air Coil Flow Systems). Now, whenever you call the company, they'll answer the phone, "Hello, this is Big Ass Fans. How can we help you?" They're on the Internet; check them out. **At the time they changed their name, it was an action that was completely foreign to this industry. To do something like that that completely shakes up the industry and almost alienates you, because it's so odd. People think, "Man, those guys are weird. The name of their company is Big Ass Fans." But once they embraced the name, they got so much press and so much exposure that their company has since seen phenomenal growth.** They were in an industry where they were just plugging away with a plain name, and then they did something a little bit different and a little bit edgy and fun — and **they captured a huge percentage of the market share, just because they weren't scared to go out there and shake things up a little bit.**

Why Be Timid?

The Big Ass Fans example goes to show that **no matter how mundane your business is, if you're thinking ruthlessly, you can find an edge that'll let you get ahead.** Sometimes this ruthless marketing stuff is actually the *fun* stuff, because you're doing something different and exciting and new, and not necessarily worrying about what your competition is doing. It's all about being controversial. The key can be as simple as just shaking it up and making people question what you're doing. You might get some negative press — but sometimes negative press turns out to be good press anyhow. Be the innovator: I think that's another way to look at being a ruthless marketer as well.

Some people think that timid marketing is also safe marketing. Well, yes, that's true; but sometimes you have to be not so safe. You need to say to yourself, "Okay, I'm doing the same safe stuff everybody else is doing. What could I do, in terms of marketing, that would really push the envelope? **What could I do that would wake people up, slap them in the face and get their attention?"** You might have to get a piece of paper and ask yourself that question, and jot down dozens and dozens of ideas. Go crazy. Just brainstorm. In doing that, you're really training your brain to have that ruthless mindset. Because, really, that's what you're going to have to do: you're going to have to push the envelope, go beyond everybody else, and come up with that one idea that really makes you stand apart from everybody else. No, it's not safe. People are going to say, "I can't believe he's doing that!" But you really don't care what people say. What you care about are those numbers in your bankbook. Believe me, **it's the ruthless marketers, the people who are pushing the envelope, that are making a lot more money than all of the safe, timid marketers in those same industries.**

And here's something else about taking chances: it can be fun. As I've said again and again, most businesspeople are working *in* their business and not *on* their business. They're not having fun. I've got all kinds of friends who get up and go to work and they never have fun at all. But **ruthless marketing is one of the most enjoyable things I've ever done professionally, and I know many of my friends and colleagues feel the same. Done right, marketing is fun stuff! The energy and the ideas that flow out of my office, and the colleagues I talk to all the time, keep me busy enjoying life — and the next thing I know, twelve hours has gone by while I've been working on this marketing campaign, and now I can't wait to get it out there and get it going. Ruthless marketing is such a fun thing to do for a living, and it pays well if you're doing it right.**

That means you've got to get out of the employee mindset, as I've emphasized before. A lot of businesspeople just see their business as a job. You get to talking to them about their business, and you listen to the way they describe what they do, and it doesn't sound much different than most employees. There are plenty of exceptions out there, but with most employees, it's just a job; it's just something they do. It's the same with most business owners. They're involved in the day-to-day aspects of their jobs and they've got no ability to pull back away from it and see the whole thing as if it were more of a war or a sport or a game. I love the example of the Big Ass Fan Company, because you've got to do things that are aggressive and create wild and crazy guarantees and promises. You've got to do things that just blow people away! **Nobody is going to blow your horn for you. You've got to be the one that does it.** Truly ruthless marketers are so dedicated and focused on trying to do things that extract the largest amount of sales and profits out of their marketplace as possible, that they really don't give a damn about what other people think about them, or what other people say about them.

The older I get, the less aggressive I become, and it's really sad. I'm getting close to 50 years old now. I've been in business for twenty years, and I have to fight myself now to be more aggressive. What came natural to me ten or fifteen years ago I now have to do consciously. So I just want to say this: recently, I was scared about something that had to do with the marketing of a certain promotion. What I wanted to do was kind of aggressive and bold, but I was afraid of upsetting the people I was targeting, of turning them off. But then I realized just how unaggressive that was. **The phrase I want to give to all of our listeners now is something that has helped me so much, and here it is: "It doesn't matter who you piss off. It only matters who you *sell*."**

You can't do what I did. I was getting ready to make a bad mistake by playing it too safe, by holding back and being too conservative, by worrying too much about what other people were going to think about me, and how I was going to upset a few customers. **What I should have been focused on, and what I'm focused on now, is extracting the largest number of sales from that certain lead group of people who responded to an initial invitation — and forget about all the people who are going to be upset.** No offense to my good customers who may be reading this, but come on! The tendency is always to hold back more than you should. People are always worried, thinking, "Gosh, am I going to go too far? Am I going to push it too far?" Hey, the truth is, **no matter how hard you push it, you probably aren't pushing it far enough.** Too often, people go for bland vanilla marketing. They think they're trying to sell to everybody, so they try to be everything to everybody.

In doing that, you really don't create a strong basis for your business. In setting yourself apart and in making a stand, and in ticking people off, you're able to create a connection with those people who *do* like what you've got to say — or like whatever controversial thing you've put out there. They like the bold attempts you're making in your marketing. In doing that, you create better customers who are going to do more business with you. You're going to have a stronger business. Those are people who aren't going to run off to your competitors if they offer sales or discounts or things like that. **You have to change your mindset and say, "I'm not going to be everything to everybody. I'm going to be the best I can for this particular section of the market and if other people don't like it, I'm not the best one for them. They need to find somebody else."** If the Big Ass Fan Company hadn't thought that way, they'd still be some boring fan company of which no-one outside the industry had ever heard.

No Doesn't Necessarily Mean No in Marketing

I compare just about everything that has to do with marketing with social situations. **Let's take dating, from a male perspective at least. There are plenty of guys, from the younger teens on up, who are very successful in the dating game. They sure don't let a "no" stop them. Fifteen "no's" just means they keep going at it from a different angle, until finally they get the answer for which they're looking.** You have to be nice but aggressive to get the dates you want, and the same thing is true in marketing. I see so many people out there who are just aren't aggressive enough when it comes to marketing. They're weak. They wait around for business to come to them. They constantly take "no" for an answer way too soon. Whether it's in the dating game or in business, the people who do the best are a little aggressive. They may even keep asking the same person the same thing more than once. If you're a guy and you ask a beautiful woman to marry you, she's probably going to say no right away, especially if you don't know her well. In fact, maybe the first time she's going to slap you in the face, if you ask her too soon. But if you're really in love with her, you don't necessarily take that "no" as a final answer. I'm not talking about stalking her — just not giving up right away.

▼▼▼▼▼▼▼▼▼
MARKETING SECRET

Direct marketing is a personal medium.

- Write and speak to only one person.

- The art is to make the person you are communicating with seem special.

- The more you can make them feel you are only speaking to them — the better.

Here's a great example of something similar from the marketing field. My friend Kris Solie-Johnston once made a pitch to a large billion-dollar bank, and when they came back and said no, you know what? She didn't even hear "no." She heard, in her mind, "Not now." Think of it not as an N-O but as a K-N-O-W. It's not a "no;" it's an "I don't know enough to say yes." Make like you have selective hearing: that one word, "no," you just don't understand. You understand all other English words, except for that word one. "No" is not an option.

There are plenty of people who are very aggressive marketers who really won't accept a "no" as an answer. Because they're so passionately convinced that their product or service is right for their marketplace, nothing in the world is going to stop them. I think that's probably a better way of describing this. It's not about just trying to suck money out of people's bank accounts and trying to get people to hand over their money; it's about being so sure that what you have is so perfect for the people you're trying to reach, that they're just blown away by your total conviction, enthusiasm, and passion.

When you take that type of stance with your prospect or your customer, you're setting yourself up as an authority; you're basically saying, "Here's what you should do and here's why. I'm the expert." I've mentioned this before in other chapters. A lot of people will say "yes" if you just tell them, "Here's what you need. This is what you need to do." You get a lot more yeses that way than if you go out there and say, "I really think it would be good for you if you did this, because this will help your business." You don't want to do that: instead just state bluntly, "I think you should do this because if you don't, here's what going to happen, and you're going to regret it later. Do it now. I'll guarantee your results." That type of authoritative approach works well, as opposed to just going out there and stumbling around. **People respond to authority. It doesn't even have to be hardnosed, highhanded authority, either.**

Consider Oprah Winfrey, for example. Everybody knows Oprah's story and understands a little bit about her past, and how she rose to stardom, and how she comes across as a genuinely nice person who's happy to help people out. But that doesn't mean she's not in charge! She's got this Book Club, and I think it's interesting that **every time she says to read a book, millions of people run out and buy it. She's not some literary expert: she's a woman who has a talk show. But anytime she tells people they need to buy this or that book, they go out and do it, because she has authority and command over her audience base.** It doesn't matter what she tells them to do, either, because she's got so many loyal followers. She can say, "Everybody needs to go down to the store and buy this brand of orange juice," and a large percentage of her audience will go down and buy that brand of orange juice.

That's what you need to strive for with authority, too. If you take that stance and increase your credibility and build yourself into your consumer's mind as the ultimate authority, they'll pretty much do whatever you tell them to do. If you set out to grow that authority and build that rapport in order to use it in that capacity, well, that really is pretty ruthless — but it's very effective. **You want to build emotional bonds with your customers that are so strong that people are not only compelled to buy more of whatever you sell, but they'll feel guilty if they do business with one of your direct competitors.** I have such a relationship with a couple of the people with whom I do business — where it would almost be like cheating on a spouse if I was to do business with any of their competitors. How can you develop those bonds with your customers? That's the question that should keep you up at night.

Ruthless is as Ruthless Does

As I was doing research for this book, I went to my trusty Google to check out the definition of "ruthless." According to Google — which, by the way, I use for everything — "ruthless" means: pitiless, without mercy or pity. I started thinking about that; you know, if it's pit*iless,* that means it would be the opposite of having pity. So, the opposite of ruthless to be full of pity for someone. So I went and looked up the definition of "pity" and Google told me lots of things about pity. But the best definition I could find was, "An emotion, usually resulting from an encounter with an unfortunate, injured, or pathetic person or creature." I thought that was a pretty good definition of the word. But this is usually a term that's reserved for person-to-person encounters, or you and me on the street, or someone about whom you see or hear or read a story.

I drew the conclusion from this that a lot of people get confused about "ruthless," and what we mean by ruthless marketing. Business is different from everyday life. Of course, in business your goal should be to serve your customers and make a profit. If you have pity on your competitors, you'll do all kinds of things to help them out. When someone steps foot in your door, you stop them and show them where your competitors are located, tell them why they should *not* do business with you, and why they should go down the street and do business with your competitors. Right? Well, of course not. That's preposterous — you'd never do that! No business would. Yet, without that ruthless mindset, that's exactly what you're doing. Every time you approach your customers with this lethargic attitude and think, "I'm just going to sit back and let the customers browse. I'm not going to do anything proactively," then you're pitying your competitors. **If you really are in business to make a profit, you've got to maintain the ruthless mindset that says, "Whatever it takes — legally, morally, and ethically — I'm going to get the most profits possible."**

It's the same thing with sports. In sports, your goal is to win. It doesn't mean you don't care about your competition as people; they're fellow humans. If you're watching a football game or playing in a football game, you don't try to kill the other guy. You just try to knock him down and do what you can to win the game within the framework of the rules. Your goal is to win, whether it's an individual competition like tennis or golf or whether it's football or baseball, where you're working within a team. In sports, the second place winner really is just the first loser. You can say, "Well, they still came in second place," if they didn't win — but that just means they were the first losers.

In business, **there really is a lot of money floating around out there** being spent by your prospects and your customers. **They're either going to be spending it with you, or they're going to spend it with your competition.** It's just a fact. Having a ruthless marketing mindset means that you play the game of business to win. You won't get all the money; no business ever does. But you want the largest share of your market's expendable income — the biggest share of the money they're spending — and you've got to have that ruthless mindset to get it.

I once heard someone say, "I don't want all my clients' and prospects' income. I just want all of their *disposable* income." That's the kind of ruthless mindset about which we're talking. It's not about making your customers suffer or sending them to the poorhouse. **It's not about taking the money they should have spent to pay the car bill or the gas bill. It's just about getting the largest share of the money they're already spending on all that extra stuff on which they're going to continue spending money.** You need to think about the term "ruthless" not as it applies to people, but as it applies to other businesses. If you can develop that ruthless mindset about your business competition, then you can succeed, you can be Number One in your market, and you can do the things that produce a winning edge in your business.

This morning I looked up the word "aggressive," and one of the definitions was: "making an all-out effort to win and to boldly and assertively move forward." I like that! It's about being on the offense — not on the defense — by staking your claim, by claiming your greatness. One of the guys **I admire a lot is the General Manager of my best friend's business. They've got over**

▼▼▼▼▼▼▼▼▼▼▼▼▼

Sell yourself first. Bond with them. Then sell your stuff!

√ It's so much easier to sell things to people AFTER you make a strong connection with them.

√ You must break down their sales resistance <u>before</u> you start pitching to them.

√ Honest Abe knew this: "If you would win a man to your cause, first convince him that you are his sincere friend." — Abraham Lincoln

▼▼▼▼▼▼▼▼
MARKETING SECRET

The right marriage between message to market — the closer marriage — the more money Formula

a. Right message/offer

b. To right market

c. Through the right media

a hundred competitors in their local area, and it's not that big an area. He always says, "I have lots of competition, but I have zero competitors." I like that attitude. That's how I see it, too — and I see a lot of other people who have that aggressive kind of mentality. I think business is not for the weak-hearted. You've got to be strong, you've got to be aggressive, and you've got to think of it as if it were a war or a sport or a game.

Nice Guys Really Do Finish Last

Although I perform information marketing now, I often talk to people who run actual physical businesses — for example, veterinarians, or folks who have dry cleaning businesses. One of the things I get from them is they all want to be nice and have a community and not be aggressive or ruthless. Now, everyone advertises, but they all have this mindset of not going after anybody, of not being aggressive, of not competing against everybody else. All the ads in the Yellow Pages are exactly the same size. Everybody's trying to be nice. We're all trying to be friendly. We're all members of the Chamber of Commerce. Yeah, flowers and peace and all sorts of good stuff.

But that's not a way to run a business, and so I think **there has to be a shift in your mindset if you want to succeed.** What you'll find is that's how it is in most marketplaces. **Everybody believes they have competition, but no one is being competitive.** If you think that way, then you really have to develop a different way of thinking. When you understand not only that you have competition, but that you need to be actively competitive yourself, you really change your mindset. In most industries people aren't doing that. Your focus in business (as it's been said before) is to deliver great products and services you honestly believe in, to the most people possible, and to make as much money as possible. It's not to be friendly with your competitors. It's not to send Christmas cards to them and be able to say "Hi" to them in the grocery store. It's to be able to build a large, growing business. In many cases, that means being aggressive, being ruthless, and having that competitive mindset. It doesn't mean you're a mean person; it doesn't mean you're a bastard. Your relatives can still love you; your kids can still love you. But it does mean changing your mindset. And believe me, I've talked to enough business owners who have this friendly-friendly mindset that I do understand it takes some effort to go from not wanting to rock the boat to becoming a truly aggressive marketer.

Let's go back to the sports analogy. One of the things I want to point out is that **you can never defeat an opponent you don't define.** You shouldn't think about your competition as, "I want to go out there and kill my enemy!" It's not like that at all, and that's what really makes it fun for me and for a lot of the marketers I know. We sit around every day thinking, "Okay, if I do this, I wonder what my biggest competitor is going to do? Or, if I do this, I wonder how they're going to react?" Because I'm thinking about their business and what they're doing and I'm thinking, "Man, I can really shake things up if I do this or that." That's what makes it fun! It's ruthless because you're thinking, "This is going to make these people sweat when I do this." You're not out there to say, "Here's the ball. Go run it into your end zone and make a touchdown." You don't want to watch people run by you! If you're in the game, you've identified your competitor. Then you're going head-to-head, and you're formulating plans and strategies that are going to help you get ahead and get into the end zone and make you all the money you want to make. That's how you gain market share.

For example, **here's a strategy. I was recently talking to somebody about this;** they're involved in an industry that's very chummy. They all put their arms around each other and say, "Let's go eat donuts together and get involved in these different community networks." **Even though they're competitors and they're all going after the same dollar, they get involved in these little organizations and network meetings where they all sit around and drink coffee. What's funny is, the smart,**

ruthless marketers are joining those little committees and looking around, and learning what they can, and taking it back to their little laboratories (if you will), and putting it to work against their competitors — who have been lulled into this attitude of, "Oh, everything's happy and I'm sitting here drinking my coffee and eating my donuts and talking about marketing." The ruthless marketers are using those environments as learning environments to figure out what they can do next. My advice is, if you're going to join one of these things, don't do it just to become part of this little community and give away your best ideas. **Join it so that you can get in tighter with your competition and learn their insider secrets, so you can apply them to your business and help you gain market share on those same people.**

My colleague Chris Hollinger recently told me about an interesting experience he had. He went to a convenience store just right around the block, and when he pulled up in the parking lot, there were two plumber vans sitting there out front. One van just had the guy's name on it — something like "Joe's Plumbing." The other van looked a little nicer; it was a little cleaner, and maybe it was newer. The name on the side of this van was, "The Clog Father." The Clog Father van caught Chris' eye; it was a neat name. So he walked into the store, and there was a guy sitting over there sipping coffee out of a Styrofoam cup, in an untucked flannel shirt, playing Keno. The guy in the Clog Father shirt was buying something at the register and talking on his cell phone, conducting business. This guy had a nice shirt on that said "Clog Father" on it. Now, I don't know how successful both plumbers are; but who would you rather have come to your house and open your drains? **The Clog Father guy has done some thinking about how he wants to go about capturing his market share.** There's his competitor over there drinking coffee, playing Keno. That's all that Chris saw, and we don't know any of the details, but obviously the Clog Father has something going on. He's really considered what he's doing in the marketplace, how he's positioned himself, and how he presents himself. So you see, ruthless marketing can be done in every single business there is! You'd be surprised how many people are sitting out there, not really thinking creatively with their marketing. You may be one of them. Ultimately, to me, that's what ruthless marketing boils down to: thinking creatively about how you can go out there and capture that market share.

I think anybody reading this can take comfort in the fact that *most of your competitors are weak marketers.* Most of them are doing what I suggested in the beginning of this chapter: they're following the follower. They're doing exactly the same thing as all their other competitors are doing. Most people are like me. As I've mentioned before, I was a carpet cleaner for another company, and that's how I got into the carpet cleaning business. I started my own business because I was cleaning carpets for another guy, and then I decided I was tired of making him money and I wanted to be self-employed. But, basically, I was still just a carpet cleaner at heart.

Most business people are still employees, even if they're their own boss. I don't mean any disrespect to employees, but as I've shared in other chapters of this book, **the business you're in and the things that your business does — the products and services that you provide to your marketplace — are two entirely different things. Most businesspeople still show up for work every day to punch their clock. They put in as little time as they have to, and then they leave. They're not thinking about this thing strategically.**

Ruthless marketers, on the other hand, are constantly focused on getting as much business as they can. No company — except for an isolated few that got tangled up in personal or legal issues — ever went out of business because their sales and profits were too high. People go out of business because they get tired of working so hard for so little money. So you've got to be aggressive. **You've got to realize that there are a lot of forces working against you. There's the competition, and then there's the overhead. The markets are changing constantly. The solution to all these problems is to increase your sales and profits.** If you think aggressively and practice some of the ideas I've shared with you in this chapter, your business will continue to thrive and grow; your profits will continue to increase year after year.

Now, if you're struggling with the concept of competition and the "ruthless" way of going after someone else — maybe you're having a moral issue with it — then it might be better for you to try competing against yourself. When you're tracking the leads or customers you're bringing in on a weekly basis, ask yourself: how can you get more of them into your business? **Work to continually compete with yourself, instead of everybody else.** Compile your metrics and try to do better every week,

▼▼▼▼▼▼▼▼
MARKETING SECRET

Overview of a successful marketing campaign...

a. Take the best sales points and "schemes" that have worked before...

b. Find new ways to hook them together... new themes, new angles

c. Then smooth it out... So it sounds new and different.

---

and eventually it's going to get to a point where you're bringing in so many clients that the competition will be irrelevant. As you improve your business, one step at a time, the competition will no longer exist for you.

This is the End

Your job as a marketer and businessperson is to do as much business as you can with your customers, to penetrate as much of the marketplace as you can. **Every new customer must be won over, and sometimes you have to do something bold to attract them to you.** Either you get their business or your competitor gets their business; it's your choice. When you study effective marketers, you'll see that they've got this ruthless marketing mindset. They're very aggressive. You need to do the same: **you've got to strike fast, strike hard, and strike often!** Stay in touch with your best customers. Keep trying to do things to do more and more business with them, and they'll be happy to give you more and more of their money.

That Brings Us to the End of This Book

Please keep this book close by and refer to it often. Take notes. Think. Find all the ways you can to use these powerful tips, tricks, and strategies, and in no time at all you will DOUBLE or even TRIPLE your profits!

PLUS, as I also told you at the beginning of this book...

Your FREE business-building gift is waiting for you!

As I told you in the Introduction, I have just finished writing a new eBook, called: *"265 of the Greatest Marketing Secrets You Can Use to Dominate Your Market."* This Electronic Book normally sells for $27.95 — and is worth every penny. But for a limited time it can be yours — absolutely FREE — by simply going to my Web-Site and giving me your contact information. Remember, I am giving you this $27.95 eBook for free because I have other business-building products and services about which I would love to tell you. So I'm more than happy to give you this brand new Electronic Book that gives you 265 of my greatest marketing secrets if you'll give me your contact information (which I will not give out to anyone). Just go to **www.RuthlessMarketing.com/freegift** and immediately download this very special Electronic Marketing book. And don't worry, although I <u>will</u> add your name to my mailing list and send you additional information, there is NEVER any cost or obligation for you to purchase anything else from me, now or in the future. This FREE gift will be my way of thanking you for taking the time to read and study this book.